THE BUILDINGS OF ENGLAND
BE27
LINCOLNSHIRE
NIKOLAUS PEVSNER AND
JOHN HARRIS

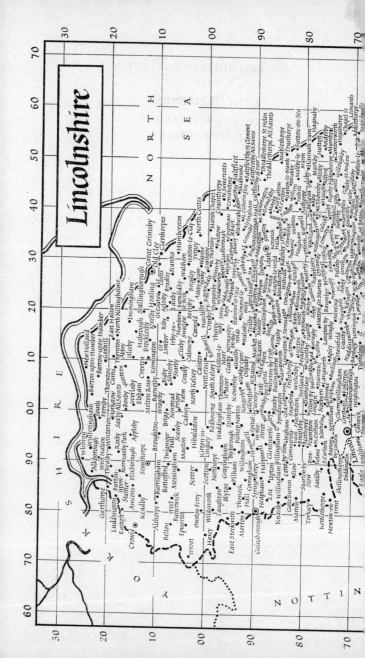

Lincolnshire

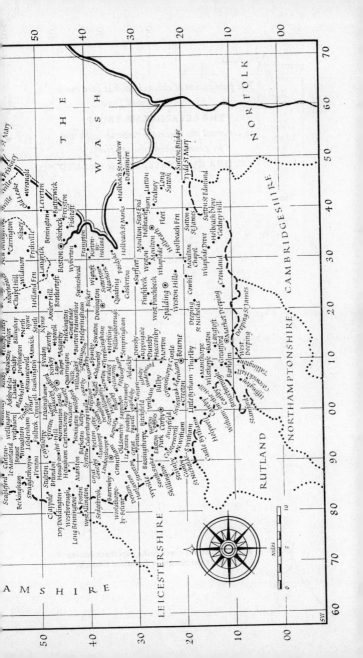

The publication of this volume has been made
possible by a grant from

THE LEVERHULME TRUST

to cover all the necessary research work and
by generous contribution from

ARTHUR GUINNESS, SON & CO. LTD

The roundel on the cover of the paperback edition
represents the piscina in Greatford Church

THE BUILDINGS OF ENGLAND

Lincolnshire

BY

NIKOLAUS PEVSNER
AND JOHN HARRIS

★

PENGUIN BOOKS

Penguin Books Ltd, Harmondsworth, Middlesex
U.S.A.: Penguin Books Inc., 3300 Clipper Mill Road, Baltimore 11, Md
AUSTRALIA: Penguin Books Pty Ltd, 762 Whitehorse Road,
Mitcham, Victoria

—

First published 1964

—

Copyright © Nikolaus Pevsner and John Harris, 1964

—

Made and printed in Great Britain
by William Clowes and Sons, Limited, London and Beccles
Gravure plates by Clarke and Sherwell Limited
Set in Monotype Plantin

TO

MRS KATHLEEN COX

who courageously

and in a masterly way

typed eight volumes of

The Buildings of

England

*

CONTENTS

*

Map References

*

The numbers printed in italic type in the margin against the place names in the gazetteer of the book indicate the position of the place in question on the index map (pages 2–3), which is divided into sections by the 10-kilometre reference lines of the National Grid. The reference given here omits the two initial letters (formerly numbers) which in a full grid reference refer to the 100-kilometre squares into which the country is divided. The first two numbers indicate the *western* boundary, and the last two the *southern* boundary, of the 10-kilometre square in which the place in question is situated. For example Skendleby (reference 4070) will be found in the 10-kilometre square bounded by grid lines 40 and 50 on the *west* and 70 and 80 on the *south*; South Kyme (reference 1050) in the square bounded by grid lines 10 and 20 on the *west* and 50 and 60 on the *south*.

The map contains all those places, whether towns, villages, or isolated buildings, which are the subject of separate entries in the text.

FOREWORD

BY NIKOLAUS PEVSNER

This volume is a new attempt at collaboration in The Buildings of England. *This time Mr John Harris of the Royal Institute of British Architects has done all the preliminary library research and then all the travelling for, and describing of, secular buildings, except a number of medieval ones, and I have visited and described the churches and the medieval domestic buildings just referred to. In addition I have sometimes interfered with his text, and he has in such cases been remarkably patient with me. His parts as against mine incorporate a good deal of first-hand research, as connoisseurs will no doubt notice.*

Lincolnshire made Mr Harris's and my own job particularly hard in some ways. One was weather, worse for Mr Harris on his motor-bike than for my wife and myself in a cosy A40. Thinking back to the various journeys, we now agree that rain might have been rainier, frost might have been frostier, and wind might have been windier – though only just. The other obstacle in the way of producing a good book has been the relative scarcity of printed information, especially on strictly architectural matters. There seems to be little current research, at least finding its way into print. The Ministry of Housing and Local Government (MHLG) is still far from completion of their listing of buildings in the rural districts. At the time of writing, the National Buildings Record (NBR) has for what is after all the second largest county in England a total of 30 boxes plus 16 on Lincoln City compared with the 35 for Leicestershire and 54 for Northamptonshire, both so much smaller in area. Quite often we found Cox's Little Guide (see the bibliography on p. 60) and Kelly the only sources. This means that the following pages may contain more mistakes than other recent volumes of The Buildings of England. If many were in the end avoided, the reader has to thank for such general improvement first and foremost Canon Peter Binnall, Sub-Dean of Lincoln Cathedral, who put his unparalleled knowledge of Lincolnshire churches at our disposal and went, within the limits of the time he could make available, through all I had written. Major alterations made according to his suggestions are marked PB. It was impossible to mark the many minor ones. In addition I want to express my warm thanks to the Rev. Peter C. Hawker, who contributed all that this book contains on church plate, to Derek Simpson and Terence

Miller, who respectively contributed the parts referring to prehistory and Roman antiquities and to geology, to Mr David Etherton, who, at my suggestion, made a special study of flowing tracery in Lincolnshire and as an outcome of this, contributed the drawings and comments on pp. 40–3, to Mr D. J. King, who wrote the entries on motte-and-bailey castles, to Mrs Joan Varley, the County Archivist, who helped, even unasked, on various matters, to Mr F. T. Baker, the City Librarian, for many answers about Lincoln city, to Mrs D. M. Goodman of the Spalding Library, Mr M. Kirkby of the Scunthorpe Museum and Art Gallery, Mr E. H. Roberts of the Skegness Library, and Mr L. Tebbutt of the Stamford Library for answers to questions about their towns; to Canon Cook, Mr Higgins, and Mr Barratt for granting me to an ideal degree the freedom of the cathedral; to the Rev. D. W. Owen for checking my text on Grantham church; to the Vice-Chancellor of Keele University, Dr H. M. Taylor, for allowing me to see the account of Stow in his forthcoming book on Anglo-Saxon churches; and to Rex Wailes for his usual liberal contribution to the entries on windmills. Windmills are here only mentioned if they still have their gear, or for special reasons.

Other limitations of inclusion in this volume are the same as in its predecessors. All churches prior to c.1830 are included, but after that date only selected ones. All houses in town and country are included if they are of more than local architectural interest. Movable furnishings in houses are excluded, and of furnishings in churches (with exceptions), bells, hatchments, chests, chairs, post-Reformation brasses, early decorated coffin-lids, incised slabs, church plate not of silver or gold, church plate after c.1830, and churchyard and village crosses, if no more than base and a minor part of the shaft is preserved.

In compiling this volume I have enjoyed the usual courtesy of the National Buildings Record and of the Ministry of Housing and Local Government, who compile the lists of buildings of architectural and historic interest to which I have already referred. I have also been able to use Mr Peter Ferriday's index of Victorian church restorations (here abridged PF) which he so liberally made accessible to us on a long loan, the Goodhart Rendel index of Victorian churches (GR), Sir Thomas Kendrick's index of Victorian stained glass (TK), and a new survey, still growing, which Mr Geoffrey Spain is making of buildings mentioned in the c19 technical journals (marked GS). I am most grateful to them all for their generosity.

I am also grateful to all those incumbents who answered my, often difficult, questions and checked galley proofs and to the owners and occupiers of houses who showed me round and answered letters. I owe it to them to state here explicitly that inclusion of a house in the following pages does not imply that it is open to the public.

Finally a word on a peculiarity of the introduction which follows. As ecclesiastical and secular architecture were compiled by two different individuals, the introduction had to be divided accordingly. Mine comes first, Mr Harris's second. I have, however, contributed to his the page or pages on medieval secular buildings. Moreover, my introduction is preceded by Mr Simpson's on prehistory and Roman antiquities, and his by Mr Miller's on geology. Mr Simpson, Mr Harris, and myself are of course wholly responsible for our entries in the gazetteer as well, and all three of us would be grateful to readers for writing in about any omissions or errors they may spot.

FOREWORD

BY JOHN HARRIS

As there is a disparate scarcity of published material on post Reformation domestic architecture in Lincolnshire, I had to examine original sources; hence my debt to Mrs Joan Varley, to her efficient Archive Office, and their invaluable Reports. I also found much among the local collection of Lincoln Central Library, and there I must thank Mr F. T. Baker, always courteous and helpful. I owe much to prating long hours with Sir Francis Hill, to Howard Colvin's scholarly observations, and to Rupert Gunnis's unbounded enthusiasm and hospitality in his enormous library. I must acknowledge all those owners who received me in their houses, particularly the Earl of Ancaster, the Earl of Yarborough, and the kindly Trollope-Bellews of Casewick. I want also to thank my friend 'Grimmers', and, of course, Henry Thorold of Marston, and Jack Yeats of Louth. This list would be long if I acknowledged everybody, so I merely say thank you. I should add two other thank-you's, to the local constabulary, who were very patient not to arrest a very suspicious black-hatted character lurking around buildings until twilight; and to my colleague Mr James C. Palmes of the R.I.B.A., without whose genial dispensations my part of the book would not have been written. I began Lincolnshire as a bachelor and ended as a married man. If the perambulation of the City of Lincoln is seen to be better than the rest, then it is due to the percipient observations of my American wife.

INTRODUCTION

GEOLOGY

BY TERENCE MILLER

THE geological structure of Lincolnshire is very simple. Essentially it consists of thin sheets of rock, alternately soft and hard, sloping gently down from W to E. The arrangement is, however, not quite geometrically simple; for the actual outcrop areas converge towards the Humber opposite Hull, so that the geological map, with its variously coloured strips, resembles a partly-opened fan pointing to the SE. The strata form parts of the Triassic, Jurassic, and Cretaceous systems, and thus fall within the upper, or younger, half of the British geological system.

Since the soft rocks – mainly clays, but with thin, harder inter-beds of sandstone and limestone in places – are rather thicker than the others, and are more easily eroded, they form fairly wide bands of low ground, while the major hard units stand out as ridges, with steep westward-facing scarps falling gradually away to the E. To the S and SE all, both soft and hard, pass down gradually under the silts, clays, and muds of the fens that surround the Wash. Apart from these fenlands, there are five distinct regions in Lincolnshire, produced by the soft/hard alternation of rocks – a western lowland running from the Isle of Axholme along the Trent to the Vale of Belvoir; a narrow N-S upland, Lincoln Cliff, carrying Ermine Street; a central clay vale running SE from the Ancholme valley as far as the fens; another, wider upland, the Lincolnshire wolds; and finally the coastal strip, Lincoln Marsh, almost at sea-level from Skegness (L)* to the Humber. This last differs from the other two clay-vales in that it is based on Glacial and post-Glacial boulder-clays, sands, gravels, peats, and salt-marsh silts, rather than 'bedrock', overlying the buried Chalk surfaces of the Wolds.

Although the rocks of these five regions are by no means uniform, they have enough internal similarity to give a general character to the landscapes based on them – the gently undulating, close, heavy country, with high hedges and hedge trees in

* Throughout the Introduction, places in Lindsey, except for Lincoln, are distinguished by a succeeding (L). Places in Kesteven and Holland are those not given any distinguishing mark.

the western and central clay vales; the large open fields of Lincoln Cliff, repeated and expanded in the Wolds, where the land has the aspect of great sea-swells frozen; and finally the fen and marsh country, often only a few feet above sea-level, with the impression of huge skies and the threat of invasion by sea.

Similarly, of course, the materials used for building reflect the underlying geology. Throughout the clay vales, the fenlands, and the marsh, until the end of the C19 almost every village would have its own brick-pit, dug in whatever clay happened to be found there, whether Jurassic, Cretaceous, or Glacial. Often the bricks would be of poorly sifted clay, and the firing somewhat

40b haphazard, as in the case of Doddington Hall, where the effects of using bricks blackened by over-firing can still be seen. However, occasional harder bands occur within the clay formations. In the western clay region brown shelly limestones (the iron ores of Scunthorpe (L) and Grantham) have been used a little for building and, near Swinderby and Thurlby, sw of Lincoln, a 'hydraulic' limestone or 'cement stone', although rather a shaley material, may be seen in use. Similarly in the central clay strip, where the ground begins to slant up towards the Wolds, E of Wragby and Horncastle (both L), brown iron-bearing limestones and pebbly sandstones have been used locally, mainly in farms and the smaller dwelling-houses.

Along the two upland tracts there is rather less variety, for two quite opposite reasons. In the Wolds there are only two rocks capable of being used for building – a four-foot band in the Lower (Grey) Chalk, and the greenish – but brown-weathering – Spilsby Sandstone. The first of these was much used in Louth Abbey (L) and other old buildings near by; the second appears in many of the older churches of East Lincolnshire, having been worked in quarries in the parish of Holbeck and in Harrington Carrs (both L). For the rest, building in the Wolds has been of brick or of imported freestone, and it is this freestone that is prodigiously available in the rock of the other upland, that of Lincoln Cliff, based on the Middle Jurassic Lincolnshire Limestone, one of the most famous building stones of England. Quarries have been opened from time to time along almost the whole outcrop strip of this rock, but the main source area is round Stamford – records of 'Stamford Stone' appear in innumerable account-books from the earliest times – where a group of villages in Northamptonshire and Rutland as well as Lincolnshire give their names to sub-varieties of the stone – Barnack,

Clipsham, Ketton, and many others. Farther N in Lincolnshire the best-known source is Ancaster.

The excellence of this freestone – in geological terms a white, buff, or pinkish fragmental, shelly, often oolitic limestone – and the ease with which, in former times, it could be transported by water, have caused it to be used all over Lincolnshire, and indeed all over eastern England, pre-eminently at Cambridge. An interesting variety is the so-called Collyweston 'Slate', a pale yellow, slightly sandy limestone which can be split by frost-action into thin slabs. This has been much used as a roofing material, blending perfectly with Lincolnshire Limestone walls in architectural-stratigraphical continuity.

ARCHAEOLOGY

BY DEREK SIMPSON

A cursory examination of the archaeological collections of the Lincoln, Grantham, or Scunthorpe (L) museums would convince the visitor of the richness of material from the county. This wealth of finds is not reflected, however, in an equal abundance of surviving antiquities in the field. Intensive agriculture over many centuries has obliterated surface indications of barrows, settlements, roads, and ditches, and it is only in recent years, with the application of aerial photography to the detection of archaeological sites, that some idea of their original density in the county has been obtained. Such discoveries are of interest largely to the specialist, and Lincolnshire will always remain a somewhat disappointing region for the layman in search of the visible remains of early man.

Until the period of the last glaciation there is little evidence of human settlement. One may cite the Acheulean hand axe from Risby Warren (L) which has been assigned to the second of the three major interglacial periods. During the last glaciation, Palaeolithic (Old Stone Age) groups manufacturing small flint blades blunted down one side settled in the N of the county, and, again, their industry is represented among the material from Risby Warren. How far these Palaeolithic groups overlapped with the Mesolithic (Middle Stone Age) peoples of the immediately post-glacial period is uncertain. The latter, whose economy was again based on hunting and fishing, showed a marked preference for sandy areas, particularly in the N around Scunthorpe and the southern Wolds in the vicinity of Spilsby (both L). With the retreat of the ice and increasingly warmer conditions came a steady encroachment of forests which must have presented a formidable natural obstacle to Mesolithic man, who therefore settled on the less thickly wooded, sandy upland, supporting a light forest cover and scrub. Both the Northern Forest Cultures with their characteristic trapezoidal flint arrowheads and flake and core axes – themselves representing a positive reaction to the spread of forests – and the Sauveterrian Culture with its small geometric blades or microliths used individually as arrowheads or collectively as the barbs in a composite spear, appear to be represented in the Mesolithic material from the county.

The first farmers, and incidentally the first people to leave any surviving field monuments, appear to have arrived comparatively late in Lincolnshire, judging by the evidence from the Giant's Hills (L) long barrow where Beaker sherds (see below) suggest a date not earlier than 2000 B.C. and over a thousand years after the initial colonization of southern Britain by Neolithic (New Stone Age) communities. Over a dozen of the earthen long barrows beneath which they buried their dead are known from the county, all with one exception on the chalk. The only excavated example, Giant's Hills, Skendleby (L), gives some indication of the internal features of such structures. Beneath the barrow, which was surrounded by a broad quarry ditch from which the material of the mound was obtained, was a rectangular setting of postholes with the trench for a massive timber façade as the broader, E end, serving either as a revetment for the material of the barrow or representing a mortuary enclosure in which the dead would be stored until a sufficient number had accumulated to warrant the construction of a barrow. Such structures have been recorded from other long barrows in Britain, and the latter interpretation is perhaps to be favoured, in view of the disarticulated condition of three of the eight inhumations found beneath the barrow, suggesting that at least three of the corpses were in a skeletal condition when the barrow was heaped over them. A possible cremation trench may have been encountered under the long barrow at Beacon Plantation, Walmsgate (L). Such a feature would be more at home in the long barrows N of the Humber. Nothing is known concerning the contents of the other Lincolnshire long barrows, although in exterior form all conform to the wedge-shaped plan of Giant's Hills, the broader and higher end normally occurring at the E. From Giant's Hills came smooth profiled bowls with everted rims characteristic of the first Neolithic Cultures, and a similar vessel was recovered from the filter beds of the Grantham waterworks at Great Ponton. The distribution of ground and polished stone and flint axes, which may also be attributed to the culture, although generally occurring in the county as stray finds, agrees well with that of the long barrows. Notable among these axes is that from the Isle of Axholme, found probably at Wroot (L), which is of jadeite imported from Brittany (now in a private collection). The main concentration of leaf-shaped flint arrowheads, on the other hand, is in the sands of the Scunthorpe area (L), not on the chalk.

Shortly after the coming of the first farmers, Lincolnshire was settled by other, more warlike groups termed the Beaker Folk, after the characteristic drinking cups which they placed in graves with the dead. The distribution of the objects attributed to these new invaders suggests penetration by way of the rivers, in particular the Humber, Witham, and Bain. The pottery represents at least two distinct cultural groups – the earlier marked by smooth profiled bell beakers (fragments of this ware came from the mound of the Giant's Hills long barrow), followed by a numerically stronger group manufacturing beakers with long, in some cases vertical, necks, separated from the globular body by a marked constriction. Also to be attributed to this latter group are the beautifully made flint daggers which copy the rarer copper or bronze forms now coming into circulation. An interesting pottery variant, whose decoration suggests an original wooden prototype, is represented by the handled beakers from Grantham and Denton and by several fragments from Risby Warren (L). Unfortunately none of these beakers have been recovered by excavation (except the sherds from Giant's Hills) and nothing is known of their graves or associations. From the evidence of sites elsewhere in England, however, it would be reasonable to infer that some of the round barrows in the county are the work of the Beaker Folk, although this class of monument had a very long life and only excavation can confirm the association. The majority of round barrows lie on the Wolds, where they tend to cluster in small cemeteries, notably at Burgh-on-Bain and E of Tathwell (both L). The surviving barrows must represent only a fraction of the original number on the Wolds, and aerial photography is only now giving some indication of the large number of these sites which have been obliterated by cultivation. A final complication in the cultural pattern in the county in Late Neolithic times is presented by finds of coarse, heavily ornamented Secondary Neolithic pottery

(Risby Warren; L) and flintwork which owes much to Mesolithi[c]
knapping traditions. This material appears to be the product o[f]
fusion between the first Neolithic groups and the aborigina[l]
hunter-fisher communities. It was from this cultural hetero[-]
geneity that the Early and Middle Bronze Age cultures emerged[.]

Two distinct cultural groups may be distinguished in th[e]
Early Bronze Age (*c.*1600 B.C.), but for Lincolnshire one agai[n]
has to rely on material in museums rather than antiquities in th[e]
field. One group is characterized by small, thick-walled, vase-
shaped food vessels, generally decorated with cord impression[s]
or incisions. Rare footed bowls and handled vessels have bee[n]
recorded from Heighington and Caythorpe. Such vessels [N]
of the Humber generally accompany inhumation burials beneath
round barrows, and presumably some of the barrows in the
county are to be attributed to people of this culture. The only
important Early Bronze Age material from a barrow cemetery
comes from a C19 excavation on Broughton Common (L) which
produced a group of collared urns containing cremations.
Associated with the urns were two flint knives and a small bronze
dagger. Like the food vessels, the pottery of this second group
owes much to Late Neolithic ceramic traditions, and even the
rite of cremation can be traced to Neolithic funerary customs.
The urn tradition had a long life and continued into the succeeding Middle Bronze Age, and the same Late Neolithic element can
even be traced in the bucket-shaped vessels from the Grantham
area decorated in some cases with finger-impressed cordons,
which are ascribed to the Late Bronze Age of the region (e.g.
Caythorpe and Belton).

The later stages of the Bronze Age are characterized largely by
the development in bronze tool and weapon types and a growing
abundance of metal objects in general. A reorganization in the
distribution of the bronze smiths' products is suggested by
founders' hoards, over a dozen of which have been found in the
county, containing obsolete and damaged bronzes collected for
melting down and recasting. The distribution of these hoards
again implies riverine settlement. The majority, like those from
West Halton and Winteringham (both L), consist largely of
socketed axes, but of particular interest is the hoard from the
ironstone quarry at Bagmoor in Normanby Park (L), which
contained, in addition to the ubiquitous socketed axes and leaf-
shaped, socketed spearheads, the base of a bronze bucket reinforced with plates set radially. This latter hoard must be a
product of the C6, deposited at a time when Hallstatt influences

re also detectable in the appearance of swords, still of bronze,
but copying a form produced in iron on the continent by Hall-
tatt peoples. Notable among these swords is the antennae-hilted
example from the Witham.

In contrast to most areas in the Midlands, where the settlement of iron-using peoples is paralleled by the appearance of
the first major field monuments, Lincolnshire has few visible
sites which can be attributed to the Iron Age. An early phase of
Hallstatt settlement is suggested by the swords mentioned above,
and by boat-shaped fibulae and pottery from the settlement at
Brigg brickyard (L). Other Iron Age A material has been recovered
from Lincoln and, in developed form, from an open settlement
with grain storage pits in a quarry near Ancaster which is
currently being excavated (1963). At the latter site, the pottery
was associated with querns and an iron involuted brooch characteristic of the culture of the Iron Age B charioteers of Yorkshire.
Without the confirmation of excavation none of the surviving
monuments in the county can be dated closely within the period
of the prehistoric Iron Age. Most significant is the small multivallate fort at Honington guarding the strategically important
approach to the Ancaster gap. The remaining enclosures are
surrounded by extremely slight works which hardly warrant
the title of fort. The site at Careby with its two widely spaced
banks and ditches invites comparison with Iron Age stock
enclosures in South-west England. Other small enclosures exist
at Round Hills Ingoldsby and Yarborough Camp Croxton (L) –
the latter the only presumed Iron Age site on the Wolds.
Attention should also be drawn to the remains of salt-working
sites discovered on the foreshore between Ingoldmells and
Chapel St Leonards (L). Although, therefore, the county has
few major monuments, it has produced some of the finest
examples of Celtic metalwork in the British Isles. In the C3 a
settlement of the region by warriors culturally related to the
better-known group in Yorkshire appears to have taken place.
While there are so far no examples of chariot burials such as
are found to the N, a vessel identical to those found in the Yorkshire chariot graves came from a grave at West Keal (L), and
horse equipment was included in the hoard probably from the
parish of Ulceby (nr Brocklesby; L) found during the construction of the railway from Brigg to Grimsby. In the C2, Lincolnshire appears to have supported a local school of metalworkers
producing parade objects for these Iron Age B warriors. Among
the surviving products of their school, pride of place must go to

the magnificent shield from the Witham below Lincoln. The central boss from a second shield, bronze sword-scabbards with delicate engraved scroll work, and a war trumpet have been dredged from this same river (now British Museum). The large number of finds from the Witham cannot all be interpreted as objects lost while fording the stream, and probably represent votive deposits thrown into the river as offerings to the local deity; such a practice can be paralleled elsewhere in Britain notably in the great deposit from Llyn Cerrig Bach, Anglesey.

How far Lincolnshire can be claimed to have been settled by Belgic (Iron Age C) peoples towards the close of the prehistoric period is a little uncertain. Belgic, wheel-turned pottery has been recovered from a number of sites (e.g. Ancaster), and gold and silver coins of native form (e.g. a hoard from South Ferriby; L), some of which were minted at Sleaford, are evidence of a Belgic element in the regional Iron Age culture. This could be economically explained as cultural borrowings or by a possible Belgic ruling dynasty controlling a population whose culture was still basically an admixture of Iron Age A and B – a people who emerge into history with the Roman occupation as the Coritani.

Lincolnshire was early occupied by Roman arms, and by A.D. 47, with the frontier established at the Severn and Trent, a legionary fortress had been constructed at Lincoln, occupied first by the Ninth and briefly by the Second, *Adiutrix*, Legions. By the end of the C1, in the reign of Domitian, the fortress had given way to a civil establishment, one of the four *coloniae* of Roman Britain established for settlement by retired veterans of the legions. Structural details of the town will be found in the gazetteer, and here it is only necessary to emphasize the quality of the buildings which the fragmentary remains suggest. This is no peasant market town but an outpost of Rome herself – the carefully laid-out town plan, sewage system, elaborate aqueduct, stately colonnaded streets, and lavish use of imported building materials were designed as much to impress the native inhabitants as to provide comfortable quarters for the veterans.

Little is known of the other three Roman townships in the county. The evidence from Ancaster suggests a typical small town, of provincial character when compared with the *colonia*, but which could boast a certain rustic affluence, as attested by the finds of tessellated pavements and sculpture of three Mother Goddesses from the site. The rectangular stone fortifications with massive bastions which are the only surface indication of the site are probably a work of the C4, when increasingly unsettled conitions are reflected in the fortification of many towns in Roman Britain. The defences at Caistor and Horncastle (both L) also appear to date from the beginning of the C4, when Constantius Chlorus was engaged in the reorganization of defences in Britain. Like Lincoln, Caistor may have begun its life as a purely military site, but little is known concerning the early history or internal structures of these two walled settlements, although the arrangement of the road system in the county suggests that neither site supported an important settlement earlier than the C2. Most important of these roads is Ermine Street, which enters the county at Stretton, passing through Ancaster, which must have served as a posting station, and thence due N to Lincoln. On the twenty-eight-mile stretch of the road N of Lincoln to Wintering-ham (L), where a ferry linked it with Brough and a road to York, there are two Romano-British settlements at Owmby Cliff and Hibaldstow (both L) which divide this length of the road into three equal lengths. The other major road is the Fosse Way, which enters the county on the SW and runs straight NE to Lincoln, joining Ermine Street shortly before it enters the town. The only important site adjacent to this road is the villa at Hill Top Farm, Norton Disney, S of the line of the Fosse. E of Lincoln a road runs through the Wolds by Belchford, Tetford, and Ulceby Cross (where there is a small settlement), and thence SE to the settlement of Burgh-le-Marsh (all L). Further improvement in communications was achieved by the cutting of two canals, the Fosse Dyke, which links the Trent at Torksey (L) and the Witham at Lincoln, and the Car Dyke, joining the Witham at Washingborough and the Nene at Peterborough. From the latter canal at Saxilby (L) came the magnificent silver statuette of Mars.

Details of the last years of Roman rule and of the Saxon incursions in the C5 are obscure, but some continuity appears to be represented in the close association of Pagan Saxon cemeteries and Roman roads. At Ancaster, the Anglian cremation cemetery was joined on to the Roman cemetery, an inhumation cemetery of the C5 and C6 existed adjacent to Caistor (L), and two vessels from the neighbourhood of Lincoln appear to share both Roman and Saxon potting traditions. In the absence of reliable documentary evidence, the picture of this early Saxon settlement must be built up from a study of the material from their cremation and inhumation cemeteries. Their distribution would suggest penetration by river valleys and a move on to the Wolds for the first time since the Bronze Age. The majority of burials are

in flat cemeteries, among which one may mention the inhumatio:
cemetery at Sleaford, which has produced over six hundre:
graves and is one of the largest in the country. Such cemeterie:
of course leave no surface indication, and the only field monuments of the period are occasional round barrows, such as thos:
at Cock Hill Burgh-le-Marsh and Caenby (both L), which
covered Saxon interments.

CHURCHES

BY NIKOLAUS PEVSNER

Mr Simpson having surveyed the Anglo-Saxon earthworks, i:
is my first job to do likewise for ANGLO-SAXON STONE
BUILDINGS and Anglo-Saxon sculpture. There is quite a lot
in Lincolnshire, though little of national or more than national
importance. The county had been christianized in the C7. From
the late C8 onwards it was more than most others at the mercy
of the Danes, and when their rulership had been established,
two of their principal *burghs*, Lincoln and Stamford, were in
Lincolnshire. The others were Nottingham, Leicester, and Derby.
Hence the predominance of Danish place names, the Clixby and
Claxby, the Scrivelsby, Scamblesby, and Scremby, the Asgarby
and Aswarby, and also the many -thorpes. The term Anglo-
Saxon, in this introduction as in all current literature, of course
includes Anglo-Danish buildings.

In architecture, the most frequently met evidence is quoins of
a nave which was aisleless, until the present church grew round
it. Such quoins are easily recognizable, if they are of the typical
long-and-short work. The other most frequent evidence of the
Anglo-Saxon period, and always of its last stage, is the tall unbuttressed W towers, usually with a noticeable batter of the
walls and always with twin bell-openings characterized by what
is called mid-wall shafts, i.e. a shaft set half-way into the thickness of the wall and carrying a through-stone at r. angles to the
wall as a lintel. Such towers exist in several Lincoln parish
churches,* and in the county there are about ten in Lindsey
(all along the W border and in the N quarter), and about five in
Kesteven and Holland (four of them again along the W border
and adjoining Lindsey). The wish to build them was enforced
by the insecurity of the times of Danish invasions, but the
Norman Conquest did not terminate their building – which

* Of these St Mary-le-Wigford has its original foundation inscription
preserved.

stands to reason, as Saxon workmen would neither all have
been massacred nor all have disappeared in the wilderness, when
Norman overlords settled down. In fact in some cases (e.g.
Harmston) the capitals of the mid-wall shafts prove a Norman
date. Similarly herringbone masonry seems to have been a
general C11 technique used before as well as after the Conquest.*
Barton-on-Humber (L) tower is different from all others in its 3
decoration, a decoration with lesenes carrying arches or triangles
and these in their turn carrying more lesenes. The result is
reminiscent of timber-framing and looks rather matchsticky.
The nearest parallel is Earls Barton in Northamptonshire. But
Barton-on-Humber is not a W tower. It is in a central position, 5b
apparently with a W and an E extension of about equal length.
So the tower was not a central tower either in the sense in which
such towers in Saxon and later parish churches are set between
a proper nave and a chancel. The W extension at Barton was too
short to be called a nave, and the space under the tower must
have served as the nave. The same arrangement applies at
Waythe and probably Baumber (both L). At Broughton (L) the 4a
W extension did not exist. There is only tower space and chancel.
On the other hand, W of the tower space is a rounded staircase
attachment. This is a motif which is to be found at Brixworth
and Brigstock in Northamptonshire and in Lincolnshire at Hough-
on-the-Hill.

But the most important Anglo-Saxon church from the point
of view of plan, and also the most impressive by far, is Stow (L),
which possesses a complete proper crossing, i.e. one not with 5a
small doorways N and S to lower porticus, i.e. side chambers of
unknown function, as was more usual, but with arches of the
same substantial height and width to all four sides. This became
the Romanesque principle in France and Germany, but only at
about the same time as that when Stow was built, i.e. the first
third of the C11.‡ That this crossing is Anglo-Saxon and not
Norman, as was much remodelling at Stow, needs no proof.
The way the arches are not provided with responds and mouldings in the Romanesque way but have instead elementary
mouldings applied at a certain distance away from the actual
arrises – a decorative surround, not a structural representation –

---

* There is specially much of it at Marton (L).

‡ Though the beginnings of this important motif may have to be dated
back to the late C10 or even earlier (Reichenau). At Stow one detail remained
pre-Romanesque: the fact that externally, in the re-entrant angles between
nave and transepts and transepts and chancel, the angles of the crossing show

is secure Anglo-Saxon evidence. It is a familiar device – see S Bene't Cambridge, Wittering Northamptonshire, and many others such as Lusby (L) in Lincolnshire. It establishes also that the chancel arch at Little Ponton is Anglo-Saxon and not Norman. Other Anglo-Saxon motifs worth watching for are the exceedingly simplified egg-and-dart ornament, again at Stow, 4b arches with double rows of voussoirs (e.g. Scartho, Clee, Holton-le-Clay, all L; cf. Brixworth in Northants), keyhole-shaped windows (Heapham, Barnetby, Greetwell, Brigsley, all L, Coleby, and others), circular windows (more usual in Norfolk), doorways above the tower arch.* At Hough the position of the doorway shows that the nave must have possessed the excessive height in proportion to width which is also typically Anglo-Saxon.

Major Anglo-Saxon SCULPTURE is a rarity anywhere. Lincolnshire has one item to contribute, the dimly recognizable head of Christ high up in the W face of the E wall of the tower space at Barton-on-Humber (L). On the other hand minor sculpture abounds, all of it C10 to C11. Though remains of cross shafts with interlace pattern (or coffin-lids sometimes) are faithfully listed in the gazetteer, they need no comment here. The best with interlace are perhaps those of Creeton (two) and Burton Pedwardine, and with more than interlace those of Conisholme (L) and Harmston with tiny, primitive Crucifixuses, of Crowle (L) with a man on horseback and two figures arguing, and of Edenham with a standing and a seated figure. At Edenham also there is a mysterious large roundel high up in the aisle wall which is filled by four scrolls. Finally, for its function rather than its art, St Guthlac's Cross near Cowbit must find a place here; for it is supposed to be a C10 estate boundary sign of Croyland Abbey. No Anglo-Saxon architectural fragments remain at Croyland, though for Norman architecture we shall soon have to revert to this famous monastic house. With the Norman period indeed evidence becomes so much more frequent, and from the Norman period onwards runs so evenly to the end of the Middle Ages, that a pause may be permitted at this moment to look first at Lincolnshire and her medieval churches in a general way.

Administratively Lincolnshire consists of three parts: the parts of Lindsey, of Kesteven, and of Holland. Roughly, Lindsey is the N, including Lincoln at its SW end, Kesteven is the SW, Holland the SE. The architectural emphasis of the county is,

---

* These, however, continue occasionally right down to the C13.

xcept for Lincoln, Louth, Barton-on-Humber, and a few other places, consistently on Kesteven and Holland. Kesteven is hilly, Holland flat, Lindsey varied. Holland is not named after Holland but for the same reason as Holland, i.e. as a hollow or flat land. For the tourist bent on LANDSCAPE Lincolnshire has really not much to offer, unless he wants seaside entertainment or altogether the bracing air of the sea. The most engaging landscape is perhaps the small, secluded, scarcely visited valleys of the Wold, that range of hills which runs SE through the NE part of the county from the Humber to near Spilsby. A second longer but much narrower chain of hills runs N–S, contributing on its way e.g. the hill on which Lincoln Cathedral rises so majestically and the steep approaches from N as well as S down into Grantham. In places the Wold goes up to 500 ft and then looks quite bare and North English. Otherwise there is the marsh country adjoining Norfolk and in the middle East, and the fen country all along the SE. How this configuration of landscape is the result of geological facts Dr Miller has explained in his Introduction.

He has also referred to BUILDING MATERIALS, but the principal facts so far as they concern the churches ought perhaps to be here reiterated. The first thing to be said is that the county used a quite exceptionally large number of materials. There is of course the splendid oolitic limestone, England's best material, on which Lincolnshire could freely draw. Lincoln Cathedral is built of it. The most famous quarries are Ancaster in the county itself, Barnack just across the border in Northamptonshire, and Ketton just across the border in Rutland. Ancaster is grey as a rule and may be a little dead, but weathers very well. Barnack and Ketton tend to be warmer. In addition, there is the grey stone of the marshland churches of Lincolnshire or Yorkshire origin, the greenstone mostly to be found in a circle round Louth and as far as the coast, though never distant from the greensand band, the beautifully toast-coloured ironstone near the Rutland border and also round Scunthorpe in the north, and more exceptionally chalk round Caistor and round Saltfleet.* With so much good building stone available, brick had only a limited success in Lincolnshire, and first-class timber-framed building is virtually absent. Concerning brick, the material was available early,

---

* To this material, though not as a building material, slate must be added, used for a large number of charming headstones in churchyards, chiefly towards Nottinghamshire and Leicestershire. The source of supply was Charnwood Forest and chiefly Swithland.

Hull being the principal early, i.e. C14, source of supply. The tremendous gatehouse of Thornton Abbey (L) is indeed of brick and was begun in 1382. Theddlethorpe All Saints (L) may be late C14 too. Then come the mid-C15 cases, none more 34 & spectacular than Tattershall Castle (L). In churches, the chancel 35a of Bardney (L) was built shortly after 1434. Other brick or part-brick churches are Cowbit, Freiston (N aisle), Lutton, and Tydd St Mary.

So much for materials. Now a word on TYPES OF CHURCHES, still in the most general way. The architectural glory of the county is the area S of Lincoln, i.e. S to Grantham and SE to Sleaford, Heckington, Boston, and Spalding. Secondly, there is the smaller area bordering on Norfolk, where the spectacular architecture of Walsoken, West Walton, the Walpoles, and the Terringtons carries on to Whaplode, Long Sutton, Holbeach, Gedney, and so on to Deeping St James. Thirdly, the Marshland churches in the NE, places like Theddlethorpe, Addlethorpe, Burgh-le-Marsh (all L). They are remarkably similar to the coastal churches of Suffolk and Norfolk, but not quite as grandiose. Prosperity was great in medieval Lincolnshire, and it decreased later, not as disastrously as in Norfolk with its dozens of ruined churches, but badly enough for aisles and chapels to be lopped off in many places.* On the other hand Lincolnshire was very active in the revival of church life in the second half of the C19, and churches were replaced and new churches built everywhere, especially in Lindsey, the poorer part of the county.

This must be enough by way of a general preamble.‡ We can return to chronology and look round NORMAN ARCHITECTURE in Lincolnshire. The story must of course begin with Remigius's cathedral, begun c.1072–5 and dedicated in 1092. Of this the 14 impressive W front can still be visually reconstructed with its bare, eminently monumental three stepped entrance niches, the middle one very tall, and its blank niches to the l. and r. of the

* I have counted about forty cases in Lindsey, less than ten in Kesteven and Holland. Perhaps another kind of lost architecture should here be appended: parish churches lost to the sea. There are five of them: Mablethorpe St Peter, St Leonard's Chapel, Skegness, Sutton, and Trusthorpe (all L).

‡ Except for a note on rare DEDICATIONS: St Hybald, a local Lincolnshire saint, at Ashby-de-la-Launde, Hibaldstow (L), Manton (L), and Scawby (L); St Radegund of Poitiers at Grayingham (L; one of five in England); St Genewys, i.e. Genesius, a martyr under Diocletian, at Scotton (L; one of two); St Sebastian, a Roman martyr, at Great Gonerby (one of two); St Firmin of Amiens at Thurlby near Bourne (one of two); St Cornelius, a C3 pope, at Linwood (L; one of two); and St Medard of Soissons at Little Bytham (the only one in England).

uter ones and continued round the corners. The two front
owers were recessed behind the mighty block of this hollowed-
ut front. The front we see now, even its Norman parts, is how-
ver only partly Remigius's; for Bishop Alexander in the forties
nlivened it by the fully ornamented three portals and the strip
f sculptured scenes all along. Their style is not uniform, but 6
he principal sources are Northern Italy, St Denis, and Burgundy.
More, and the finest, of the sculpture of Alexander's façade is
now on view inside the cathedral.

For any idea of what major interiors in the Norman style were like
ne has to go to the surviving parts of MONASTIC CHURCHES.
At Croyland, the most important abbey in the county, a
Benedictine house founded first in 699 and again after 966, we
have only the façade of the s aisle and sufficient indications of the 18a
interior system to know that it had a gallery and a clerestory.
In addition there are the naves of Freiston and Deeping St 12a
James, both also Benedictine, and of Bourne, Augustinian; the
piers of an arcade and the Late Norman front of the nave at
St Leonard's Priory just outside Stamford, which was again
Benedictine; and the w end of the s aisle and a little of the nave
of the Augustinian South Kyme. Then, to continue this list
beyond the C12, we still have one chapel *ante portas* in ruins at
East Ravendale (L; Premonstratensian), the refectory and its
pulpit at Tupholme (L; Premonstratensian), fine late C13 fragments of transept and chapter house at Thornton Abbey (L; 18b
Augustinian), an angle of the s transept and an exquisite early C13
chapel *ante portas* at Kirkstead (L; Cistercian), C14 walling at 13
Barlings (L; Premonstratensian), C14 head-stops at Sixhills (L),
and the mysterious tower of the Templars' church at Temple
Bruer, built after it had passed on to the Hospitallers. Of the
important houses of Louth (Cistercian), Revesby (Cistercian),
and Bardney (Benedictine; all L) we know by excavations only.
The same is true of Sempringham, the mother-house of the Gil-
bertines, which, it must be remembered, are the only monastic
order founded in Britain.*

* Lincolnshire had of course far more religious houses than those of
which evidence survives. The lists in Professor Knowles' and Mr Hadcock's
Mediaeval Religious Houses give 14–16 Benedictine plus 2 nunneries, plus
9 alien cells, 7–9 Cistercian plus 7–10 nunneries, 12 houses of Augustinian
Canons plus 1 of Canonesses, 7 of Premonstratensian Canons plus 2 of
Canonesses, 8 mixed Gilbertine houses plus 3 for men only, one Charterhouse, 5 Franciscan, 3 Dominican, and 3 Carmelite houses, and 4 houses
of Austin Friars, 1 of Crutched Friars, and 2 of Friars of the Sack, and
also 5 houses of the Templars and 2 of the Hospitallers. The friars, as was

Of these remains of monastic houses, which have taken us f:
beyond the Norman period, few can be dated with any certaint
and none are of the C12. Nor are we luckier in the case of th
C12 parish churches. We can only establish a system of relativ
dates by comparisons, inside the county but also outside. Wh:
is certain is that the sturdiest work is the earliest, that capita
with few, heavy scallops precede many-scalloped capitals, tha
waterleaf capitals belong to c.1170 and after, and that shor
round piers with square abaci came before other forms of abac
and of piers. Early arcades, i.e. arcades to be assigned to th
second quarter of the C12, are e.g. those of Boothby Pagne
and South Stoke. The other forms of abaci referred to ar
square with nicked corners (e.g. Whaplode; also Peterboroug
Cathedral), and then on the way into the C13 round and octa
gonal.* Arches develop from unmoulded or single-stepped to
step and a slight chamfer (Long Sutton), step, chamfer, and
big half-roll in the soffit (e.g. Whaplode), and finally, again int
the C13, to double-chamfers, the arches still being round
However, one has to be careful not to be dogmatic about sucl
chronological schemes. South Witham e.g. still has the squar
abacus and yet waterleaf, and the pier from Cawkwell now a
Scamblesby (L) even combines the completely E.E. motif of a:
octagonal core with detached shafts (see below) with zigza;
carving on the core – a feature of Durham, the crypt of York
and also of Norwich, to which the only other Lincolnshire paralle
is a fat pier with lozenge decoration at Belton. Another case of th
mixing up of Norman and E.E. motifs is probably Straggle
thorpe.

Arcades or parts of them are among the most frequent thing:
to survive. Occasionally they prove that naves could be of monu
mental length (Long Sutton seven bays, Old Leake six bays)
Clerestorys survive more rarely. At Grantham it is just trace:
of the round-headed windows, but at Long Sutton the windows
are set in long blank arcading, and at Whaplode and Bicker the}
are in a system of a rhythmically varied blank arcading. In this
context perhaps the very minor bit of blank arcading on the

the rule, settled in flourishing towns. Thus Lincoln had 5, Stamford had 5,
Boston had 4, Grimsby (L) had 2, and Grantham and Whaplode 1 each. Of
all these what remains is a gateway of the Whitefriars (Carmelites) at Stamford and a little more of the Blackfriars (Dominicans) at Boston – a shocking
proof of the hatred against the friars during the Reformation years.

* But the N arcade at Ancaster has round piers and octagonal abaci and
yet arches of mid-C12 mouldings.

wer at Branston ought to be mentioned, and certainly the
ʙle, quiet motif of the s wall at Sempringham, where lesenes or
ʟaster-strips and lengths of corbel table, interrupted in appro-
ᴄiate places, divide the wall into panels somewhat similar to the
ᴇrman and Italian system of lesenes and so-called Lombard
iezes. Towers were either in a central position (Horbling,
ᴜtterton) or at the w end. Only two of the latter need comment:
iskerton (ʟ), because it was circular (a type frequent, as is
ᴀmiliar, in Norfolk), and Boothby Pagnell, because it has a
ᴄoin-vault inside, a forerunner of so many Dec and Perp tower
ᴀults. Little need be said on chancels. Fishtoft demonstrates
ᴏw wide they could be, and Horbling provides an example of
ᴊorman sedilia.

Doorways survive in a variety of positions and forms, from the
ɪmplest single-chamfered surround to the richest with several
ʀders of colonnettes, a tympanum, and arch decoration of many
ᴇometrical motifs. The w portals of the cathedral are of course
ᴀmong the most ornately decorated. Others can be seen at
ᴀswarby, Coleby, Crowle (ʟ), Kirton-in-Holland, Middle Rasen
ʟ), Sempringham, South Kyme, and Stow (ʟ). There are no out- 7a
ᴛanding tympana. The most enjoyable one is perhaps that at
ᴇempringham, with a fan or scallop shape filling the available
ᴘace elegantly and in a spirit of classicity. At the other end of
ʜe range are the barbarically jumbled-up motifs on such
ʏmpana as Haltham-on-Bain (ʟ) and Rowston. Bishop Norton
ʟ) has a scene and five roundels with rosettes, South Ferriby
ʟ) St Nicholas(?) and crosses in roundels, Little Bytham two
ᴏundels with birds and a third scooped out and empty. For the
ᴇst quality of Late-Norman foliage carving one or two of the
ᴇarly capitals in Grantham church ought to be looked at. At
ᴛhurlby near Bourne is a mysterious cross, each arm ending in
ʜree loops. It may be a gable cross, and it may be Norman.

Where does the EARLY ENGLISH style start ? In the Canter-
ʙury choir in 1175, in Lincoln Cathedral in 1192 with the begin-
ᴎing of St Hugh's Choir, and where in the parish churches ? St
ʜugh's Choir and the completion of the cathedral up to the w
ʀront must be considered first, and they can in this Introduction
ᴏnly be considered very briefly. It must be enough to put down
ᴀ reminder of the exquisite quality of all this work, its superb
ᴎobility and yet happy airiness and liveliness, and also a reminder
ᴏf all the innovations which thus became available to the county,
ᴛo England, and ultimately to Europe. The strange plan of St
ʜugh's ᴇ end does not survive and apparently had no successors.

It can serve, however, as an introduction to the strangeness of S
Hugh's designer, probably *Geoffrey de Noiers*. The strangest o
10a his feats is the vault of his choir, the first patterned – not straight
forwardly quadripartite or sexpartite – vault, and on top of that
vault with an asymmetrical, lopsided pattern. The same deligh
in the unexpected and the syncopated made St Hugh's architec
10b devise a new kind of blank arcading along the aisle walls, whicl
is in two tiers, one free-standing in front of the other and agaii
placed in a syncopated rhythm. Then there are the piers, ofter
with concave sides, and nearly always with detached shafts so a
to allow us – just as in the wall arcading – to see one thing behind
and detached from, the other. This intention of the separation o
shaft from shaft and shaft from pier is beautifully clarified b
the ample use of Purbeck marble shafts. Even in the buttresse
detached corner shafts are introduced. All this work, i.e. work o
between 1192 and *c*.1210–15, has pointed arches and stiff-lea
capitals of bold and lively crocket forms.

12b   The Second Master at the cathedral was responsible for the
nave. He returned to normality in wall arcading and vaulting
but a Lincoln normality, i.e. still one exceedingly original from
any other point of view. In his nave vault he created a pattern
for many vaults to come and indeed for the first (much later
patterned vaults of Germany and France. The pattern is tha
most simply described as a tierceron star. It consists of diagona
ribs, ridge ribs in both directions, and one tierceron in each cell
This second master seems to have started about 1210–15 and
continued to about 1235–40. We know that in 1233 much timbei
was needed, probably either for the roofing of the nave or for the
centering on which the vault of the nave was being erected. The
Third Master did much less. We see him at work repairing
damage done in 1237 or 1239 close to the crossing tower. We
also see him at the S end of the SE transept, in the galilee porch,
and on the W front, i.e. in the 1240s. His stiff-leaf capitals are
much more disturbed. He used dog-tooth to excess, and he used
a trellis decoration to cover surfaces. The idea of the screen-like
W front of the cathedral as such stretching excessively to l. and
r. and repeating ceaselessly the motif of blank arcading may be
his or his predecessor's. This front marked the completion of the
cathedral. The Angel Choir, begun in 1256, was an enlargement
and involved the demolition of St Hugh's east end. It is a different
story, and we can only come to it after having followed other
architectural events in the county from the late C12 to about
1250.

Pride of place must be given to two major jobs, one small but esthetically uncommonly perfect, the other the largest of this phase in the county – except of course for the cathedral. The first is the chapel *ante portas* of Kirkstead Abbey (L) with its beautiful 13 proportions and its three bays of simple rib-vaulting. Otherwise we have no vaulting to record except for the chancel of Benington, which was built to receive two bays of sexpartite vaulting – this type of vaulting being in evidence in the transepts of the cathedral. The other major work is Great Grimsby church (L) – 11 the parish church of a prosperous port and hence of the size of a collegiate church. It is cruciform, has very plainly moulded capitals – no luxuries – and the interesting and highly unusual motif of a wall-passage inside immediately above the arcade arches and screened by tall arcading which includes the clerestory windows, really a pulling together of the triforium and the clerestory stages into one. The same thing was done more simply, this time in the extreme s of the county, at Deeping St James. 12a But here all that it amounts to is an inner wall-passage in front of the four elementary lancets, a type of thing for which we have already referred to Norman examples. Further E.E. clerestorys with arcading are Whaplode (with round arches), Weston, and, with the narrow–wide–narrow rhythm of the Norman predecessor, Moulton.* E.E. clerestorys are of course not often preserved. As a rule they were rebuilt later in the Middle Ages to allow for more light to come in. In the form of lancets they exist at Long Sutton and Fishtoft, in the form of roundels at Fulbeck, Nettleham (L), and Skirbeck, alternating between the two forms at Bicker, in the odd form of horizontal ovals at Spalding 7b (*c*.1300), and in the form of quatrefoils at Thornton-le-Moor (L).

Now for the other parts of the buildings. E.E. churches, like Norman, were often cruciform. Bottesford (L) is a specially complete example, and Old Clee (L) also has crossing, transepts, and chancel and is moreover specially interesting because the inscription remains according to which it was begun in 1192. That is the same year as the cathedral, yet there is no connexion between the two. E.E. crossing towers, not necessarily with the arches intact on which they stand, are to be recorded at Algarkirk, Caythorpe, Swaton, and Wyberton, the latter only begun but never carried on. At Algarkirk the transept has a w aisle. Spalding has, and Kirton-in-Holland had (before 1804), E and W aisles. At Bicker an E aisle was planned and begun. The same

* West Walton in Norfolk, close to Whaplode, has blank arcading at the clerestory level both internally and externally.

may be true of Uffington and Wyberton. Sutterton has its transept
E aisle properly in operation. After the crossings, transepts, and
crossing towers, towers in other positions. Bourne Priory set out
about 1200 on a scheme of rebuilding its Norman façade with
two E.E. towers. However in the end only one tower was
finished, and that much later. Of E.E. w towers the finest in the
county are no doubt Stamford St Mary and Gedney. The most
ambitious towers make much use of blank arcading, the simpler
ones often use twin bell-openings with a shaft, still in the Anglo-
Saxon tradition. The arches are round for quite a long time,
even if the sub-arches are pointed. Among the most ambitious
towers are two which are or were built detached from the
church, an arrangement paralleled in Norfolk (West Walton,
Terrington St Clement) – and indeed the two are close to
Norfolk. They are Long Sutton and Whaplode.* Long Sutton
has one of the earliest lead spires in England. Otherwise early
17b spires are of stone and of the broach type. Sleaford, Frampton,
17a and North Rauceby must be in the earliest dozen of English
broach spires. Another half-dozen or so are also C13 to the top.‡
North Somercotes and Saltfleetby All Saints (both L) have
quadripartite rib-vaults inside their towers. Occasionally minor
churches, already in the C12 and C13, were satisfied with a
western bellcote or double bellcote instead of the tower. Thornton-le-Moor (L) and South Witham still have round arches.§
Barlings (L), Howell, and West Allington have them pointed.

Next naves. Externally the most impressive sight is the long
blank arcading below ground-floor level all along the s side of All
Saints at Stamford facing down to the centre of the town. The
arcading turns W as well as along the front. À propos blank
arcading, a few internal cases may be appended: the giant blank
arcading in the chancel of Weston and the blank arcading in the
porches of Sutterton and Threekingham. At Osbournby the
arches have gone ogee. One more external motif at All Saints
Stamford, also only as an appendix: slender, chamfered buttresses, taken over direct from the cathedral (St Mary Stamford
has them also), and, à propos buttresses, as an appendix to the
appendix, the priest's doorway at Thornton Curtis (L), set in a
buttress.

So back to naves, and now spatially. Not one aisleless one
needs recording, but Caythorpe is memorable as one of the rare

* And Fleet, as a third, which is however Dec.
‡ Bassingthorpe, Burton Coggles, Creeton, Leasingham, Threekingham.
§ The Thornton bellcote is Norman.

two-naved churches (Hannington in Northamptonshire is another). The usual thing of course is nave and aisle or nave and aisles. Swaton, Westborough, and some a little later churches are particularly impressive because of the wide and high arch openings and slender piers.

On piers a great deal will have to be said. The normal thing in other counties and in Lincolnshire too is that E.E. piers are circular, quite slender, and have circular abaci. There are octagonal piers too, and quatrefoil piers, with the foils more than semicircular, are a favourite too (e.g. Whaplode, Spalding). The foils and equally the shafts of responds or triple responds can be keeled or can carry fillets (both forms at Waddington). There are of course a number of variations on these simple themes. At Swaton for instance there are small hollows set between the foils, a pattern heralding one which was very popular in the Late Middle Ages. At Scotter (L) and Wyberton the foils are thin triple shafts instead. At Alkborough (L) there is a square core with demi-shafts in front instead of normal quatrefoils. At Moulton the core is circular and four thin demi-shafts are attached, and in quite a number of places additional shafts are set in the diagonals between the foils, resulting in an eight-shaft appearance. This is the pattern e.g. at Grimsby, Bottesford, and Horncastle (all L). It comes in plenty of variations of its own: at Navenby the whole thing is set diagonally, at Edenham the diagonal shafts have shaft-rings, at Dunholme (L) the main shafts are keeled, at Old Somerby and Beckingham the subsidiary shafts. At Beckingham also (and at Ruskington too) there is the lively variation of the subsidiary shafts being replaced by vertical chains of dog-tooth. Dog-tooth had been a passion of the cathedral workshop in the 1240s. From there probably it affected the man who designed the bell-openings in the tower of Huttoft (L).

But apart from all these piers of types that can be matched in any part of England, Lincolnshire boasts some richer, more exciting types, and they are the effect on the county of the work in the cathedral during the first half of the century. As we have seen, nothing characterizes it more immediately than the piers with cores of many inventive forms and with four or eight shafts standing detached around them. This was imitated in the parish churches of Lincoln and in churches mostly near Lincoln. The actual form of the piers of St Hugh's Choir (see description p. 92) occurs again at St Mary-le-Wigford and outside the town at Coleby, Fiskerton (L), Ruskington, Skirbeck, and with a slight change, i.e. the diagonals of the core convex instead of straight at Wainfleet St Mary (L). At St Mary Stamford the diagonal have triple shafts instead of being straight. Another form of S Hugh's Choir is copied at St Benedict Lincoln, St Helen Boul tham nr. Lincoln, Scamblesby (L), and Scrivelsby (L; and, with attached not detached shafts, at Ancaster). At Scamblesby, as we have seen, the core still has Norman zigzag decoration. The octagonal core surrounded by eight, not four, shafts on the pattern of St Hugh's transepts occurs at St Mary Barton-on-Humber and Burgh-on-Bain and, in a hexagonal version, at Nettleham (all L).* At Barton this cathedral form is still combined with water-leaf, i.e. Late Norman, capitals. Then there are octagons set diagonally and with detached shafts (St Peter-at-Gowts Lincoln and Weston), circular cores with detached shafts (four at Bracebridge and Weston, and also West Walton and Grimston in Norfolk; eight at St Margaret King's Lynn and again West Walton, both in Norfolk), a keeled quatrefoil with detached shafts (All Saints Stamford), and so on, and finally a quite original form, worthy of the cathedral, at Pinchbeck: a circular central shaft surrounded by four circular and four octagonal ones.‡

Bases of the C13 are not high but very pronounced in their mouldings. The extreme is the so-called water-holding base. Arches are mostly double-chamfered, but the more ambitious masons went in for fine and elaborate mouldings characterized by fine rolls and deep hollows and all parts clearly set off from each other. Capitals are moulded or have stiff-leaf decoration. Stiff-leaf starts almost imperceptibly towards the end of the C12 out of Late Norman leaves. The lobed stiff-leaf comes first in small single rows on stalks (e.g. Moulton). Then the leaves get bolder, but the stalks still remain uncovered, until finally the most disturbed, excited and exciting form is reached in the 1230s and 1240s (e.g. Nettleham; L) and remains the standard of the Angel Choir.

9a, 9b, & 15b

Abaci are usually round on simply-shaped piers, but echo the elements of the more complex shapes. However, there are also occasionally big round abaci over complex piers, which gives a bolder effect (quatrefoil at Bitchfield, Bottesford (L), Deeping St James, Edenham, Great Coates (L), Hatcliffe (L), Langtoft, Lud-

* Horbling has a plain hexagon instead of the usual octagon.
‡ A note to record that shafts at Colsterworth and at Thurlby near Bourne prove the existence of rood stairs, i.e. roods with lofts, as early as the C13. Aymer Vallance calls Colsterworth the earliest such evidence in England.

orough (L), Market Deeping, Navenby, and Skillington, oct-
gonal with detached shafts at Weston).*

The Angel Choir, begun in 1256 and completed in 1280, is the 15a
igh-point of the E.E. style in all England. It is the result of a
ining of Lincoln traditions with the impact of Westminster
Abbey, i.e. two- and four-light openings with Geometrical bar
racery – foils in circles – and even the glorious eight lights in the
window, 59 ft high, double tracery in depth, and the com-
osition and sculptural style of the s portal, some of the wonder-
ul aisle bosses, and indeed some of the angels in the spandrels 16
f the gallery. But the vault and the luscious stiff-leaf capitals 15b
and openwork stiff-leaf friezes in the doorways from crossing
o choir aisles) are typical Lincoln. The remodelling of the façade
f Croyland Abbey is also dependent on Westminster. At Thorn-
on Abbey (L), where a little remains of the s transept, and the
chapter house remains, the latter started in 1282, there is bar 18b
racery of a kind which can be seen as the immediate development
ut of the Angel Choir and going beyond it only in the fact that the
ndividual lights are now pointed-trefoiled,‡ and in the fanciful
eplacement of foils by fleurs-de-lis in the circles. At about the
ame time as work began on the Thornton chapter house, work
vas resumed at Grantham, and a parish church of average size
converted into one of England's grandest. The window tracery
n the new w parts is a primer of development from the late
c13 to the early c14 – fine Geometrical just as at the Angel Choir
N side), then a little freer, with the top circle not only foiled
ut each foil cusped as well (s aisle w), and then with intersecting
racery (s aisle). Just as important is the new width of the aisles
and the new rectangularity of the whole plan, with the w tower
embraced, the former transepts not re-used, and in the end the E
end as flush as the w end. The whole is nearly 200 ft long. At the
same time as Grantham Spalding was built, less revolutionary in
plan, but equally ambitious in scale. The beginning can be dated
c.1284. The way tracery developed from the strict logicality of
the aesthetic perfection of the E window of the Angel Choir to
forms more inventive, freer, and sometimes more wilful can be
watched in various places. Characteristic motifs are unencircled
trefoils (Norton Disney), or circles with pointed trefoils or
pointed quatrefoils inside (Fishtoft), or a middle lancet light of

* Big octagonal abaci over piers with four major and four minor shafts at
Great Grimsby (L).

‡ But on a small scale that had already been done by St Hugh's master in
the double wall arcading.

three or five stabbing up higher than the others right into the zone
of the circles (Barton-on-Humber (L) St Mary), or intersecting
mullions broken into at the top to make space for a circle (e.g.
Carlton Scroop). As for pier forms, the most significant development is that from the quatrefoil of before to a quatrefoil with
deep continuous hollows in the diagonals. At Spalding the earlier
can be seen side by side with the later form, and the later form belongs to the early C14, i.e. the Decorated, no longer the E.E.
style.

For the DECORATED STYLE Lincolnshire is the best county
of all. One need only mention Heckington, Sleaford, Holbeach,
Gedney, Boston (not the stump of course), the s chapel of
Grantham, Claypole, and on a minor scale e.g. Helpringham, to
convince. When did the style start, when did it end? For the
start we have the convenient dates of the beautiful crossing tower
of the cathedral: 1307–11, where ogee arches and ballflower
decoration appear, and of the Wykeham Chapel near Spalding:
1311, where reticulated, i.e. Dec, tracery appears side by side
with intersecting, i.e. pre-Dec.* The cloister of the cathedral,
which was in hand in 1296, and the Easter Sepulchre, which
must be of c.1290–1300, have none of this, though the Easter
Sepulchre has flying ribs, the earliest in England, an unmistakable sign of the growing wish for originality and surprise which
helped to constitute the Dec style. As for its end, it came late,
later than the chronology one learns from the whole of England
would make one expect. The Perp style was present already at
Gloucester in the 1330s and in its full might in the chancel by
the 1350s. Yet these are the dates in Lincolnshire: at Wrangle
some time after 1345 (and before 1371) we still find reticulated
tracery and even still, alongside cusped, intersecting tracery.
About 1350 would also be the date of the reticulated tracery in
the E window of Spilsby (L), if the date of the Willoughby
Chapel, i.e. 1348, can be applied to it. (On this possibility, see
p. 373). The Dec work at Welbourn is connected with John of
Welbourn, treasurer of the cathedral, i.e. a date after c.1350
(and before 1380), at Covenham St Mary (L) the choir was
licensed in 1359, but was not yet complete then. The work at
Old Bolingbroke (L) was probably undertaken for John of
Gaunt, and in this case must date from after 1363. The chancel
at South Ormsby (L) still has flowing tracery yet is of c.1384,
and the door of the great gatehouse of Thornton Abbey (L) has

* At Brigsley (L) intersecting, Geometrical, and reticulated tracery all
appear together.

eticulated tracery, and the gatehouse was begun in 1382. These re very late dates, and one must of course realize that a con-iderable overlap between Dec and Perp can be assumed. One minor proof is the clerestory at Old Leake, where Dec and Perp vindows alternate.

The style is called Decorated, and works of luscious decoration ndeed deserve the top place in a more detailed survey. There s of course nothing in the county (and very little in England) to match the S porch and the choir furnishings of Heckington and 24a especially the Easter Sepulchre – the latter for sculptural as well 24b as ornamental perfection. The Easter Sepulchre forms a group with that of Hawton in Nottinghamshire and that of Navenby in Lincolnshire, and Irnham, though ornamental exclusively, deserves as much praise. It has inside little vaults of flying ribs, a delightful effect noticed by few.

Then windows and their tracery. Reticulation is one familiar and standard motif which has already been mentioned. But the real thrill of Dec is flowing tracery of the most fantastic, un-expected, capricious forms. The diagrams on the following pages are intended to serve the double purpose of showing on the one hand the inexhaustible inventiveness of these designers, on the other the existence of a certain degree of standardization of elements which a close examination proves. The elements are ogee arch, dagger, and mouchette. It would be absurd here to try and list examples. All the Dec buildings so far mentioned have them and many more, mostly in Kesteven and Holland, rarely in Lindsey.* To name just a few individual windows there is of course the Bishop's Eye in the cathedral and there are the E windows of Boothby Pagnell, Haltham-on-Bain (L), St Benedict Lincoln, and Wilsford, the W window of Sutterton, 23b and the S chapel windows of Grantham. Caythorpe has trefoils 23a with long thorny barbs in the tracery, Billingborough quatrefoils 23c equally barbed. At St Peter Barton-on-Humber (L) is a crucifixion carved against the middle mullion of a Dec window. Among less outstanding windows, typical forms in the county are intersecting tracery with ogee arches, straight-headed windows with ogee arches to the individual lights, and the same lights under basket arches, segmental arches or very low-pitched triangular or nearly triangular heads.

Of the interiors of the churches much less is to be said. They often disappoint a little after the external displays. Sumptuous chancels have already been referred to. Leverton, Frampton,

* One of the best in Lindsey is the E window of Haltham-on-Bain.

and Navenby must now be added to them, and the equall
sumptuous chancel, i.e. no doubt chantry, chapels of Langto
and Leverton. Vaulting other than of towers and porches wa
hardly ever undertaken. The s aisle of Kelby, with ridge ribs a
well as diagonal ribs, is the one exception. As for piers, quatre
foils and quatrefoils with additional slimmer diagonal shafts g
on, the quatrefoils now, as we have seen, preferred with foil
connected by deep continuous hollows. The foils are more ofte
than not given fillets (Boston and Sleaford, e.g.). The s chapel a
Grantham has four filleted foils and in the diagonals no mor
than what can be called fillets not applied to foils. Rarer is th
section of four foils and four diagonal hollows, enriched a
26a Holbeach to triple shafts in the main directions and hollows i
the diagonals. There are of course plenty of octagonal piers too
but they need no amplification. Capitals are mostly moulded
and the profiles are more closely moulded than in the c13. Fo
leaf capitals Lincolnshire developed a particularly gorgeous form
a broad leaf band right round all shafts and hollows. Th
earliest examples still have foliage of the naturalistic, i.e. initiall
late c13, kind. Such they are exclusively at Morton, and a
Claypole one can form a chronology on the contrast between th
25b few earlier naturalistic and the later, really Dec, nobbly leaves
All nobbly and mostly very lively are the leaf bands and leaf capi
tals at Alford (L), Barlings Abbey (L), both churches of Barton-
on-Humber (L), Branston, Careby, Castle Bytham, Dunsby

LINCOLNSHIRE TRACERY

Fig. 1. Primary Framework Divisions. (a) Central unit above the mid-
mullion of two arches. (b) Central unit above the mid-arch of three arches
The three arches intersect in two twos. (c, d) Three lights treated as three
distinct compartments, c with normally arched side lights, d with reversed
arches (on this term see 4 below). (e) Two c types intersecting. (f) Two c
types side by side. Of all these c is the most common type, though rigid
subdivision is rather a limitation than an aid to successful design. The details
of the compartments have rarely a sufficient family likeness.

Fig. 2. Examples of centre and (i, j) side-arch details. The basic motifs
can easily be reduced to a very few, and these are shown in 3. The possibilities
of combination on the other hand are beyond counting.

Fig. 3. The basic motifs: a, b. Soufflet (French: bellows). Quatrefoil with
one pair of opposite ends pointed. c, d. Mouchette (Fr. snuffers). A directional
shape with one lobe shorter than the other. Smaller end pointed 3c, or
blunt 3d. Many irregular motifs exist, but these usually occur as a result of
awkward shapes left by the main lines of the tracery.

Fig. 4. The direction of mouchettes as they determine the direction of flow
of flowing tracery: (a) divergent, (b) convergent, (c) reversed, (d) interlocking
divergent and reversed. The most common form is b.

1(a)   1(b)   2(a) Preston   2(b) Frisby-on-   2(c)
(Lancs.)   the-Wreak   Holbeach
(Leics.)

Centre Variations

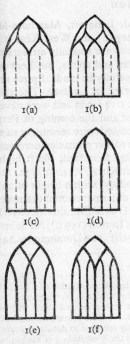

2(d) Grantham   2(e)   2(f) Fleet
Rippingale

Centre Variations

Side Arch Variations

2(g) Soham   2(h)   2(i) Fleet   2(j)
(Cambs.) Algarkirk   Holbeach

1(e)   1(f)

**1. PRIMARY FRAMEWORK
DIVISIONS**

2. CENTRE AND SIDE ARCH DETAILS

3(a)   3(b)   3(c)   3(d)   3(e)

3. PRINCIPAL MOTIFS

4(a) Burton   4(b) Roxby (L)   4(c) Threekingham   4(d) Sleaford
Coggles

Ingoldmells (L), Kirkby Underwood, Langtoft, Mareham-le
Fen (L), North Somercotes (L), Partney (L), and West Keal (L)
At West Keal the figures in the leaves are specially attractive

That leaves some remarks on towers and spires, but here n
division between Dec and Perp can usefully be made. Spires ar
frequent in Kesteven and Holland, rare in Lindsey. The tw
principal types both existed when the C14 set in and were neve
given up, though with the end of Dec and the coming of Perp
21a the broach spire decreases and the recessed spire seemingly sup
ported by flying buttresses down to the corner pinnacles increases
The former type culminates at St Mary Stamford, 162 ft high
and at Grantham (with very small broaches), c.140 ft high, th
21c latter without doubt at Louth (in Lindsey) with a height of 29
ft. The date here is the early C16. The other paramount example
21b of recessed spires are Brant Broughton (198 ft), Moulton (c.165 ft)
Spalding (c.160 ft), Gosberton (160 ft), Lutton (159 ft), All Saint
Stamford (152 ft), Billingborough (c.150 ft), and Donington (c.14

LINCOLNSHIRE TRACERY

Figs. 5–7. Three of the seemingly most fantastical windows in Englis
churches, two in Lincolnshire, one across the border in Nottinghamshire
The great similarity between these and the system behind them will be
patent. All three belong to the type of fig. 1b. All three operate mostly with
soufflets and mouchettes. Differences are really confined to details. A fourth
window of exactly the same type is at Selby in the West Riding of Yorkshire
5 is nearly 36 ft high.

Figs. 8–9. Attempts at applying the seven-light pattern of 5–6 to five lights
The result is a disintegration of the basic motif of intersection. However, the
infilling of the top unit of 8 is for instance identical with that of 7, and that o
9 nearly with that of 5. The side-arch tops of 8 are the same as those of 6.

Fig. 10. Has a central stem and leaves, on the principle of 2(d). The tracery
is perfectly integrated. Energy, tension, and balance.

Fig. 11. Mouchettes and some unstandardized motifs arranged over five
lights so as to leave parallel vertical lines over the second and fourth lights
The result seems at first purely individual. Yet the type is repeated at
Boothby Pagnell and Doddington.

Fig. 12. There are many examples of 4 and 5-petal flowers clumsily
arranged over the window lights. This is an original and exciting exception -
the flower grows from the mullions and the side mouchettes pay homage to it.

Fig. 13. No distinction between principal and subordinate mouldings, but,
looked at from outside, a hint of 1(c). Looked at from inside mouchettes fly
in all directions.

Fig. 14. This defies classification. It is perverse and full of movement.
Suggestions of 1(d) in the oriental-looking centrepiece. Suggestions of
reticulation above the side-arches.

(*The drawings and classification were made by David Etherton, who has
written a thesis on the subject for the Architectural Association*)

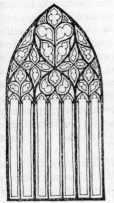

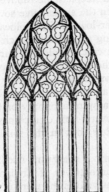

5. Heckington
E Window

6. Hawton (Notts.)
E Window

7. Sleaford
N Transept N

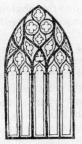

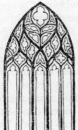

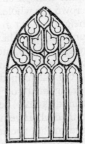

8. Heckington
S Transept S

9. Sleaford
N Aisle W

10. Sleaford
N Aisle N

11. Lincoln, St
Benedict, E Window

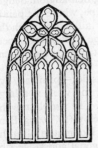

12. Grantham
S Chapel E

13. Grantham
S Chapel S

14. Sutterton
W Window

ft). The Donington steeple stands above the s porch. At Leaden
ham and Welbourn the spires have so marked an entasis as to
remind one of sugar-loaves. The Holbeach spire, *c*.180 ft high, i
exceptional in being a recessed broach spire. A number of re
cessed spires have crockets all up their edges, and that can be
very graceful, if the size of the crockets is not overdone. Lu
carnes, i.e. windows and ventilating openings, in spires are uni
versal. They pose another aesthetic problem. If they project too
far they can give a spire a pimply or even warty appearance
Where there are several tiers of lucarnes, they are usually set in
alternating directions, but in the south-west that is as a rule
not so.

22   The Boston Stump is a law unto itself. With its 292 ft it is the
highest parish church tower of England, and would amaze a
tourist in any country. It is the work of several generations and
the result changed plans. It was begun in 1309 but only completed after 1515. It ends, as everyone knows, in a tall, slender,
quite transparent octagon, and perhaps a spire was intended to
crown the whole. Inside, the tower space is open to the fabulous
height of 137 ft.* At Swineshead they did something equally
uncommon. There they built a spire, but made it start inside an
open octagon, much like John Nash's All Souls Langham Place
with its spire starting inside a rotunda of columns.

On flat-topped towers much less comment is called for. The
arrangement of bell-openings in pairs of very tall two-light
windows had been introduced in the crossing tower of the
cathedral. It remained popular to the end of the Middle Ages,
and in fact specially so in the Perp period. Two varieties were
favoured: one where the pair of bell-openings has an ogee super-
arch over and on this stands a corbel carrying an intermediate
pinnacle on the roof (e.g. Beckingham, Long Bennington, Sedgebrook); the other the so-called Stamford type, where the pair is
treated as one in the sense that the dividing mullion between the
two two-light windows is carried up into the apex of the super-
arch (All Saints, St John, St Martin, all Stamford; also Edenham, Great Ponton, Market Deeping).

Towers are not infrequently vaulted inside – primarily for
structural reasons. As a rule the centre of the vault is a large
ring to allow the bell-ropes to come down. The simplest is the
quadripartite vault (Brant Broughton, Keelby (L), Long Bennington, North Somercotes (L); two bays at Donington). But the
most frequent form is either that with diagonal and ridge ribs

* At Louth (L) the opening is 86 ft, and that is impressive enough.

Coningsby (L), Ewerby, Heckington, Louth (L), Swineshead, etc.*) or the tierceron star (Folkingham, Holbeach, Sleaford, Stamford St Martin, Uffington, and others). Lierne-vaults are under all three towers of the cathedral (late C14 and C15), and a lierne-vault of four stars making up one star is at Boston. Gosberton has another lierne-vault.‡

Much of what has been summarized on the last page or two belonged already to the PERPENDICULAR STYLE. What else has to be reported about it? On its arrival in the county little can be stated. The only relevant date is 1365 for the remodelling of the crossing at Great Grimsby (L), which has panelled piers and Perp arch mouldings. Of whole major buildings the following are outstanding. Louth (L) of course, and Tattershall (L) 26b of course too, both about 185 ft long. Tattershall was begun in 1440 and completed in the 1480s. Louth represents the late medieval ideal of the perfect rectangle, as introduced in the late C13 by Grantham, whereas Tattershall has transepts. But Tattershall represents the other late medieval ideal: the glasshouse. However, the details are gaunt – with a liking for triangles instead of arches and – surprisingly early – for uncusped lights to windows. At Croyland Abbey the nave was remodelled with the arcading all of continuous mouldings, i.e. no break between piers and arches, with a wall-passage, much blank wall over, and the clerestory high up. The nave was vaulted, but the vault is destroyed. But the N aisle (which was parochial) remains complete and this is vaulted, and in addition a big NW tower with a W porch was built.§ In the Marshland of the NE a whole string of churches now appeared in a new, proud Perp form, though none quite up to the Blythburgh or Southwold or Terrington St Clement scale. They are Theddlethorpe All Saints, Addlethorpe, 27a Croft, Wainfleet St Mary, Ingoldmells, the two Somercotes,

* A variation with twelve instead of eight ribs at Grantham, a variation with broad panelled bands instead of the diagonal ribs at All Saints Stamford.

‡ An appendix might here be inserted on the vaulting of porches. Whaplode has a C14 tunnel-vault, Brant Broughton two bays of sexpartite vaulting, Long Sutton, St Martin Stamford, and Folkingham two and one bays of tierceron stars, Spalding (N porch) a fan-vault. A speciality (though more frequent in the northern counties and the adjoining Nottinghamshire and also extant e.g. in the adjoining Northamptonshire) is porches with stone roofs carried on transverse arches. This occurs altogether about ten times. At Honington there are as many as six of these arches. At Sibsey (L) vault and arches are round and the latter look like hoops – but there the date is 1699.

§ W porches occur in several places (Stainton-le-Vale (L), c.1300, Morton), as they do more prominently in Northamptonshire (Peterborough Cathedral, Oundle, Raunds, Rushden).

Burgh-le-Marsh, and so on (all L).* Smaller all-Perp church
are e.g. at Althorpe (L) and Sedgebrook. At Stamford mu
needed doing to all the churches after the violent damage do
to the town by the Lancastrian army in 1461. So we have maj
later C15 work nearly everywhere. A special mention must
to the steeple of All Saints (paid for by the Brownes, Cala
merchants) and to the roofs with angels at St John and
George. On the whole however roofs in Lincolnshire are not
be compared in richness or structural inventiveness with tho
of Norfolk and Suffolk. The usual type is of low pitch and h
tie-beams on arched braces. More interesting is very sturc
timberwork inside some specially broad towers (e.g. Baumbe
Hagworthingham, Haltham-on-Bain, cf. also Great Sturtor
all L).

Tattershall was built by Lord Cromwell, the Treasure
Boston was one of England's busiest ports, the other majo
church enterprises were mostly paid for by wool and clotl
Building could take the form of private generosity (e.g. th
case of the Brownes at Stamford just mentioned) or of the joi
generosity of groups of well-to-do people united in a guild. Guil
built chapels at Boston, at Grantham, at Stamford (the chapel i
27b St Mary with the sumptuous timber ceiling) and in other place:
and at Hogsthorpe (L) the s porch has an inscription recordin
the *fratres et sorores* of the Guild of St Mary.

Little need be said on Perp details. What characterizes pier
(unless they go on being octagonal or of four shafts and fou
hollows) is forms in which the projections to the nave are carrie
on through the arch in continuous mouldings and only th
demi-shafts to the arch openings have capitals, the diagonal
usually being treated in some variety of broad wave moulding
Capitals quite often are castellated. Tattershall (L) has in it
window tracery a penchant for triangular forms instead o
pointed arches, a hard form which suits this somewhat har
building. Another detail most impressive as one looks at th
churches from a distance is clerestorys with windows so closel
set that there are two to each bay inside and they are almos
like a continuous band. Very many churches were heightened
in the C15 and early C16 (as former roof-lines against the towe:
often reveal) and then received such clerestorys. They are not a
Lincolnshire, but an East Anglian speciality, and Lincolnshir

* They were not completely new jobs. Ingoldmells e.g. had its six-bay
arcade already in the C13, and South Somercotes and Wainfleet St Mary
their five-bay arcades.

as nothing as overwhelming as the bands of windows at St Mary Bury St Edmunds, Southwold, Blythburgh, Long Melford, or St Peter Mancroft and St Stephen Norwich. But Boston and Holbeach have fourteen, Holbeach still Dec in style (which is worth recording), Gedney and Kirton-in-Holland have twelve (but Kirton-in-Holland originally had more), and Algarkirk, Burgh-le-Marsh (L), Louth (L), and Pinchbeck ten.

This survey of medieval church architecture has covered the best part of eight centuries. There are not much more than four centuries left between its end with the Reformation and our own day. But before we can set out on that much briefer survey, we must look at the Fine Arts and *Ars Sacra* in the Middle Ages.

In SCULPTURE, other than that still *in situ* on medieval buildings, Lincolnshire happens to be particularly rich – rich in terms of the poor, decimated English heritage, not in terms of France or Germany. The series must be started with the immensely interesting mid or later C13 reliefs at Elsham (L) and Dorrington, fragments of a Last Judgement probably from the tympanum of a French cathedral or an English church inspired by France. C13, and perhaps a little earlier, also is the curious, essentially extremely conservative, cross shaft with a Crucifixion at Minting (L), and C13 too is the small figure of a seated Christ at Swarby. Of *c.*1300 may be the seated Virgin at Bigby (L), and of *c.*1330 the outstandingly fine female figure at Stamford St Mary. Of about the same time is the cruel Crucifixus from Belgium or Cologne in the Catholic church of Deeping St James.* Finally C15 and up to *c.*1500 the good statue of Christ in the N porch at Grantham, the excellent upper half of a female figure at South Stoke, and the French Madonna in the Catholic church of Deeping St James.

Medieval PAINTING requires no more than a sentence or two. Little is preserved, and what is preserved is in a state which makes enjoyment impossible. Pickworth and Corby are the only places worth going to. At Corby e.g. are a fine early C14 St Anne teaching the Virgin to read and, in the clerestory, impressive single figures of the early C15. There are also representations of the Seven Deadly Sins and a Warning to Swearers, and at Pickworth the legend of the Three Quick and the Three Dead can be seen (or hardly seen). Then STAINED GLASS. There is some splendid C13 glass in the cathedral, especially in the Dean's Eye, but otherwise one would not choose Lincolnshire to seek

* The charming figure in a house in the Close at Lincoln, part of a cornice, may of course have a secular origin.

out glass. Croxton (L) has a Crucifixus of the early C14, sti.
with much of the C13 spirit, Gedney has early C14 figures from
a Jesse window, Tattershall (L) has much of the mid C15 an
later, and much more of the mid C15 glass of Tattershall ha
gone to St Martin Stamford. Addlethorpe (L) has some com
plete figures; so has St George Stamford. Many more complet
figures are on the small scale of window tracery.

Now CHURCH FURNISHINGS IN STONE, and first of cours.
FONTS, of which, as usual, more survive than of anything else
C12 fonts are headed spectacularly by the square, black
Tournai-marble pieces in the cathedral and at Thornton Curti
(L), the latter with affronted beasts and birds, and by the lead
font of Barnetby (L), perhaps the most beautiful of that materia
in England. There are plenty of other Norman fonts, but non
outstanding. The motifs are most often intersecting arches, and
19a also elementary foliage. E.E. fonts equally are quite numerous
and not in need of listing here. Stiff-leaf occurs and can be
quite fine. Among Dec fonts the most interesting group is that
in which no division between stem and bowl is made and the
decoration is of blank Dec windows, their tracery nicely if not
specially enterprisingly varied – like pattern books of current
tracery, as it were. Examples are at Claypole, Great Grimsby (L).
and in twelve more places in Lindsey and two more in Kesteven
28a and Holland. At Linwood (L) and St Martin Stamford the blank
windows are cut quite flatly and diagrammatically, a technique
which is more frequent in Norfolk. The tracery usually runs from
intersecting to mildly flowing, but sometimes an odd Perp motif
is also included, pointing to a late C14 date. Lavish Perp fonts
are at South Ormsby (L) and Thurlby near Bassingham. At
Barrowby the stem is transparent and a little devil appears inside. Some fonts belong to the East Anglian type with figures on
bowl and stem (Dunholme; L) or figures on the stem and scenes
on the bowl (Grantham), or just figures on the bowl (Benington,
Holbeach) or just scenes on the bowl (Leasingham). The figures
are conspicuous by hair sticking out like a lion's mane round the
28b head at Huttoft, South Ormsby and in some other places, all
also in Lindsey (Covenham St Bartholomew, Low Toynton,
Maltby-le-Marsh, Saltfleetby St Clement).

Of other stone furnishings the village church of Dembleby
possesses the finest Norman Pillar Piscina in the whole country,
Lincoln Cathedral possesses an exquisite series of stone screens
in the E parts, running from the C13 into the C14 and culminating in the highly Dec Pulpitum. At Tupholme Abbey (L) a

beautiful E.E. Refectory Pulpit is preserved, at Tattershall (L) a substantial Perp Rood Screen, and in the Marshland churches of Saltfleetby All Saints, Theddlethorpe All Saints, and Theddlethorpe St Helen (all L) stone Reredoses, the first of *c.*1300, the other two Early Perp.

CHURCH FURNISHINGS IN WOOD are of course far more copious. Where is one to start ? Perhaps with the Stalls with their canopies and Misericords in Lincoln Cathedral of *c.*1365–70 30a and in Boston parish church of twenty years or so later. Then Screens. The surviving chapel of Kirkstead Abbey (L) has one of the earliest in England: early C13. Ewerby has one which ap- 29 pears to be Dec. But most screens are of the C15 and early C16. The cathedral has quite a number. On the whole Lincolnshire screens are not eventful. Many have just single-light divisions; others, a little more ambitious, have two lights under an ogee arch with small-scale Perp tracery above. To name just a few, there is Sleaford and there are those of some Marshland churches, notably Addlethorpe, Winthorpe, Theddlethorpe All Saints, and Burgh-le-Marsh (all L). In the details much inventiveness is displayed and less standardization allowed than in the much more sumptuous screens of say Devonshire. Some few pleasures may be recorded: the detached buttress shafts at Bratoft and Thorpe St Peter (both L), the openwork strip at the top of the dado at Frampton and Winthorpe (L), the giddy Flamboyant tracery motifs of Kirton-in-Holland, Scrivelsby (L), and Swineshead, the birds instead of crockets on the door gables of Burgh-le-Marsh and Croft (both L). At Cotes-by-Stow (L) and Rippingale the loft coving remains – and at Cotes in fact the loft parapet too.

For Benches and Bench Ends again Lincolnshire is not a bonanza. The best group with a variety of tracery on the ends and poppy-heads is near Grantham and Sleaford. Perp Pulpits exist but require no comment. Of Perp Font Covers the only a little more elaborate ones are at Freiston and Fosdyke. Chests are, as will be remembered, listed in the gazetteer only if they are something special. This applies to Ewerby, Fillingham (L), and Glentham (L) with traceried blank arcading and rosettes on the posts, and to Huttoft (L) with arcading throughout. Unusually good wooden Doors have been preserved at Boston, Swineshead, and Gedney, the latter with a small French ivory of the Crucifixion set in. Ironwork on doors must be recorded at Kirkstead Chapel (L) and Sempringham, iron door-knockers at Boston (C13) and Careby (C14, with St Stephen and lizards).

So on with METALWORK, and in the first place the E.E iron Grilles of the E crossing of Lincoln Cathedral and in the second the Brass Eagle Lecterns of Croft (L) and Long Sutton.* This tradition carried on without essential changes into the later C17 – see the lecterns of Lincoln Cathedral (1667) and of Edenham. Little medieval Church Plate has been preserved: first of all the three C13 chalices and patens from bishops' tombs in the cathedral, then three patens (Scremby, L, 1512, Kirkby Laythorpe and Barnetby, L), a chalice with the remains of a 1522 hall-mark (Lutton), and three patens converted during the Elizabethan Age (Gosberton, Rowston, Wootton, L). That leaves only two more items, the splendid and quite uncommon C13 TILE PAVEMENT of Revesby (L), a bold pattern of broad stripes or bands, and the
30b delightful C15 EMBROIDERY of a Cope at Careby, representing an English type found in many places; and we are ready for funerary MONUMENTS.

There are of course many of before the Reformation, no doubt over a hundred, and a selection on the scale of this Introduction is hard. Before itemizing, the fact must go on record that the county has a number of those storehouses of monuments, of after as well as before the Reformation, the family chapels of lords of manors. Such chapels are those of the Heneages at Hainton (L), the Berties (i.e. Lords Willougby and Earls and Dukes of Ancaster) at Spilsby (L) and later at Edenham, the Brownlows (or Custs) at Belton, the Sherards at North Witham, the Newtons at Heydour. Among individual monuments the earliest is the so-called Remigius at Lincoln Cathedral, a Tournai-marble slab with a much abridged Jesse Tree, dating
p. from about 1140. Then follows the remarkable coped stone at
338 Rand (L), nearly 7 ft long and with decoration apparently of about 1200. Coffin-lids with foliated crosses are listed only very rarely. Two specially rich ones are at Londonthorpe and Carlby.
20a The Knight at Kirkstead Chapel (L) is of stone and must be of before 1250, i.e. he is one of the earliest Knights in England. The Knight at Norton Disney is not much later. Of the mid C13
20b also the Deacon with an open book at Rippingale, again a very early date for this kind of monument. From the late C13 and early C14 there is a whole harvest of stone effigies, mostly of Knights and Ladies together or separate, and also of Civilians – from the 7 ft 6 in. of the Threekingham ones to the less than 2 ft 6 in. of the ones at Newton by Toft (L). The Knights have their legs crossed and either hold sword and shield or pray, the

---

* A wooden Eagle Lectern is at Keddington (L).

Ladies wear the lovely flowing dresses and wimples of the period. The Knight at Old Somerby has his feet against his saddled horse, the Lady at Rand (L) has to the l. and r. of her head angels who are direct descendants of those of the Angel Choir, and the couple at Saleby (L) lie on flowers.

Brasses came in in England in the late C13, and that at Croft (L), only fragmentarily preserved, is one of the earliest four or five in the country, that at Buslingthorpe (L) of the early C14 one of the earliest dozen.* Of the late C14 the clergyman at Grainthorpe (L) is recorded by an exquisite cross on a rock. Late C14 portraits on brasses, about life-size, are the Luttrell at Irnham † 1390 and the Redfords at Broughton (L). The Pescods ^{p.}₂₀₃ † 1398, a merchant and his wife at Boston, are only 4 ft long, but an unknown priest of *c.*1400 also at Boston is again life-size. Of the same date and approximate size a Lady at Gedney, the Massingberds at Gunby (L), and, a little smaller, in the same place, the William Lodynton † 1420. At Linwood (L) one brass († 1419) is distinguished by a lovely, very decorative inscription, on another († 1421) a merchant's mark and a woolpack are introduced. A brass at St Mary Barton-on-Humber (L; † 1433) represents a vintner. Of later brasses, usually less distinguished, the best are William Browne of Stamford (All Saints) † 1489, with two woolpacks, and the four brasses at Tattershall (L) of which one was to Lord Cromwell himself († 1456) and his wife, another to his niece († 1479), and a third, specially fine one, to an early C16 priest. Also of the early C16 is the brass at Great Coates (L; † 1503), and here the figures are no longer cut out but all engraved together on the same oblong brass plate.

Incised slabs are of course worked in the same engraving technique as brasses. There are many in Lincolnshire, but most of them badly preserved. In that case they are not even listed in the gazetteer. Only three must be singled out: Richard of Gainsborough † 1300, master mason to the cathedral, William of Warmington, also a master mason, at Croyland, both with ogee arches, i.e. probably early C14, and Wissel Smalenburg ^{p.}₄₆₉ † 1340, a hanseatic merchant, at Boston. This is a slab of Tournai marble, and so probably was executed in the Netherlands.

A special type of stone slab must now be introduced which was a Lincolnshire favourite particularly in the early C14. They are slabs left untreated except that the bust of the deceased

---

* The indent for the bust of a Knight at Burton Pedwardine was to be filled not by a brass but by some bituminous composition.

appears in sunk relief near the top, often in a recess which may be round (Laughton, Stow, both L) or have a trefoiled arch (Whaplode round trefoil; otherwise pointed) or be a quatrefoil (Heckington, Thurlby, Welby; Utterby (L) pointed quatrefoil and Scotton (L) ogee-quatrefoil). Near the bottom as a rule the feet appear also, as if this were an effigy covered partly by a cloth or a blanket. Sometimes a cross is carved on the untreated part of the slab. There are well over two dozen of them altogether. At South Stoke a couple is under one blanket together. At Welby a babe in swaddling clothes lies on the slab by the leg of his mother. At Howell a little daughter has her own little trefoiled recess.

Alabaster has not yet been mentioned. Though it was introduced into English funerary sculpture early in the c 14, the earliest are in Lincolnshire c.1360 (St Mary Stamford) and c.1375 31 (Broughton, L) and then 1396 (Spilsby, L) and the early c 15 (Harlaxton). There is no major Perp alabaster monument in the county, and there are in fact few major Perp monuments altogether. If one were to be picked out in a parish church, it would 32b have to be the Sir David Phillips † 1506 at St Mary Stamford. In the cathedral there are of course a few more: the Lord Burghersh † 1355 and the Cantelupe chantry chapel founded also in 1355. In addition the cathedral has three chantries actually built out of the c 13 boundaries as projecting chapels: the Fleming, Russell, and Longland Chantries. Bishop Fleming died in 1431, and his monument has a corpse as well as the effigy, the earliest English case of this macabre custom. Bishop Longland died in 1548, and yet there is no sign of the Renaissance. Sir Robert Dymoke (Scrivelsby, L) died in 1545, and the same is true. Even more surprising is the monument to William Thorold at Marston; for this is a current type of Purbeck-marble monuments with a tomb-chest against the wall and a back-panel with a very shallow arch or a lintel on quadrant curves and some finishing cresting on top. It is a type represented in the county at Harrington, at Mablethorpe († 1494), and at Hainton († 1530; all L), and it is repeated at Marston, although William Thorold died in 1569.

So the RENAISSANCE came late to Lincolnshire, and specially late to the churches. But when did it come? It is a curious fact, but what one calls the Early Renaissance, i.e. the kind of decoration which was introduced into London in the second decade of the c 16 and spread, until it was replaced by the Elizabethan style with its mixture of indigenous, Netherlandish, and Italian motifs, is completely lacking in Lincolnshire, except for a few very inor bits of undated decoration in bench ends (North Thoresby, heddlethorpe All Saints, both L, and also at Digby and King-rby (L), and a chest at Heydour). The ELIZABETHAN MONU-MENTS also are all of the second half of the queen's reign. There re good ones among them, none as grand as that of the great William Cecil, Lord Burghley, at St Martin Stamford († 1598). 43)ther specially memorable ones are in order of types: first a omplete exception, the Bertie Monument († 1582) at Spilsby 42 L) in the form of a screen wall, with richly framed panelling only n one side, and with two ill-placed busts between ferocious aryatids on the other. Then, of more usual types, the recumbent ffigies at Bigby († 1581), Glentworth († 1592), and – a free-tanding monument – Hainton († 1595; all L). A favourite of the Elizabethan Age was kneeling figures facing one another, and o that type belong the parents of William Cecil also at St Martin Stamford, probably of c.1587, of the same year monu-ments at Brocklesby (L) and Hainton (L), and of 1600 one at Croft (L). Free-standing monuments with canopies on columns, .e. the six-poster type, are at Snarford (L; † 1582) with very 41 stubby and coarse balusters instead of columns and at Whaplode † 1610 and 1625), where there are ten columns, not six. That s all. We have now entered the decades where, apart from the continuation of the same types, fresh ones come in and establish new traditions for the future. Also names of sculptors now begin to appear, and slowly even signatures. For monuments with recumbent effigies one at Sleaford († 1618) is attributed for good historical reasons to *Colt*, one at South Cockerington (L; † 1623) 45 for good stylistic reasons to *Epiphanius Evesham*, one at Brock-lesby (L; † 1629) is by *William Wright*. The monument at Wrangle († 1626) must for the moment remain anonymous.* Then the kneelers. The two at Uffington (c.1607 and † 1612) are signed by *Green* of Denton. Another is at Croft (L; † 1614), yet another at Tathwell (L; † 1626), with a third kneeling figure above the usual couple, and one at South Stoke was put up as late as 1641. Again of c.1640 must be for stylistic reasons the expensive ten-poster at Ashby-cum-Fenby (L). The Monsons at South Carlton (L) have a six-poster, and this monument of 1625 is by *Nicholas Stone*, the leading English sculptor of the generation after Colt's. A new variation on the motif of the re-cumbent effigy is the semi-reclining effigy, propped up on an

---

* In connexion with recumbent effigies, attention must be drawn to a seem-ingly medieval one at Wilsthorpe. I regard this as a C17 fake (cf. such fakes as those of Chester-le-Street in County Durham of after 1594).

elbow and as a rule treated very stiffly. This occurs at Snarford
(† 1613) and at Stallingborough († 1612; both L), but in the latter
44 case the father is represented frontally, a bust only, and in a niche.
The Earl of Warwick on the other hand and his wife at Snarford
were portrayed in relief in a medallion, he frontally, she in profile. The sculptor probably was again *Evesham*. At Kelstern (L)
we have a lady who died in 1604 and was portrayed seated frontally, and at Spilsby (L) Peregrine Bertie appears upright and in
uniform in a niche above the semi-reclining effigy of his daughter.
He died in 1601, she in 1610.

After this wealth of monuments, the almost total absence of
new CHURCHES may cause surprise, but had of course the good
reason that medieval churches abounded and that the religious
crisis of the C16 did not encourage church building. There is
in fact nothing at all to record except the church at Metheringham, where rebuilding after a fire which occurred in 1599 was
done with Tuscan columns instead of piers, the small chapel
close to the former mansion at Great Humby, which is as late
as 1682 and yet still pre-classical, and the w tower of St George
at Stamford, which has rather primeval classical forms (such as
round arches) and must be of the late C17 too. CHURCH FUR-
NISHINGS are of course not as scarce as churches, but also few
compared with other counties. The only exception to this
scarcity is, as in all other counties, Church Plate. With the
Elizabethan Settlement the necessity suddenly arose for chalices
and patens everywhere. The result is some two hundred pieces
of Elizabethan plate in Lincolnshire. Among them the beaker
from Honington is outstanding. Sixty-five pieces are by the
Lincoln silversmith *John Morley* (1569–71). Wootton (1569)
and Ludford Magna (1571; both L) have the earliest dated
pieces of Hull silver. Of C17 plate the Uffington collection is
outstanding, as it contains work by *Anthony Nelme*, especially
the fine gilt almsdish. The Kirton-in-Lindsey Grace Cup is a
magnificent secular example devoted to church use. As for other
kinds of church furnishings, pre-classical work need only be
recorded as follows: At Edlington (L) is an oddly bleak Font
dated 1599, at Burgh-le-Marsh (L) a Pulpit dated 1623 (and
made on the pattern of that of 1615 at Croft, L), and no doubt
of the same time are the outstanding Font Cover and the
Screen to the N chapel at Burgh-le-Marsh (L). Other dated
pulpits are at Boston, 1612 and quite splendid, at Walesby (L),
1626, Skidbrooke (L), 1628, and at Bassingham, 1674 – 1674,
and yet still entirely Jacobean in style.

The turn to classical forms, i.e. really the forms of Wren's City churches, can be observed in the Reredoses at Goltho, Langton-by-Partney, and Stainfield (all L), the latter dated 1711, in the Pulpit at Lincoln Cathedral of c.1710 which came from the English Church at Rotterdam, and more frequently in Communion Rails. With the Stainfield Reredos we are right on the threshold of the GEORGIAN AGE, and this must now occupy us for a little. A little only, as it has not produced much of more than local interest in Lincolnshire churches, though it has produced quantitatively much in Lincolnshire. The total comes to about forty-five buildings in Lindsey and about fifteen in Kesteven and Holland. Of these nearly half date from between 1790 and 1825, the principal reason being that during these years at last churches were built systematically in the Fens.* Between 1770 and 1790 on the other hand there are very few. On the whole the best or most interesting are among the eight or ten of the first thirty years and the about fifteen of the next forty. The county has produced only two town churches proper, St Peter-at-Arches at Lincoln (partially re-erected at St Giles) of c.1720-4 by *William Smith* of Warwick, and Gainsborough (L) of 1736-44, in the Gibbs succession and designed probably by 52a *Francis Smith* of Warwick, William's brother. About a dozen small churches in the country merit individual attention. First two because they have a Vanbrughian touch: Wilsthorpe of 1715 and Langton-by-Partney (L) of c.1720-30, the latter with a 52b perfectly preserved interior. Then one because of its unusual ground plan: the octagon of Moulton Chapel of 1722 by *William Sands Sen.* of Spalding, influenced no doubt by Dutch churches. Then half a dozen or so because of their medievalism. The first of them is the little church of Holywell, of c.1700, deserving a place in this context only because of the remarkable use made of Norman pillars inside to support the William-and-Mary bell-turret. Then the steeples of Witham-on-the-Hill (by *G. Portwood*), 1737-8, and of Deeping St James of about the same time. Both are medieval in a Vanbrugh rather than a Strawberry Hill sense, and both take the imitation of actual Gothic motifs surprisingly seriously. More in the Strawberry Hill spirit is the rib-vaulting of Boston church, preserved in parts, and are the delightful chancel of Baumber (L; 1758) and the two attachments to Redbourne church (L; c.1775). Remarkably correct again, on the other hand, i.e. Gothic rather than Gothick, is Doddington church of 1771-5 (by *Thomas* and *William Lumby*).

* The Fen Chapel Act dates from 1816.

Finally a few just because they are nice Georgian compositions
or have well preserved Georgian interiors. They are Well (L) of
1733, facing the house at a distance and inspired by Inigo
Jones's St Paul's Covent Garden, i.e. by a building specially
appreciated by the new Palladians, then Cherry Willingham and
53 Gautby of 1753 and 1756, and Saxby of c.1775 (all L). The Fen
type of Late Georgian church is brick, small, with round-
arched or pointed-arched windows, often a pediment, and
usually a bell-turret. Even some of the places where they went
up spell their artificial origin: Frithville, Midville, Eastville
(all L).* Eastville, consecrated in 1840, marks the end of Georgian
church building. As we shall see, Gilbert Scott had already
started then.

There is no need to look at NONCONFORMIST CHAPELS
specially. There is a very early Friends' Meeting House at
Lincoln (1689) – just a cottage – and another only a little later
(1704–5) at Gainsborough (L), and there are specially stately
Methodist chapels in the same two towns, at Gainsborough of
1804, at Lincoln of 1836–7, but church furnishings and church
monuments need a paragraph or two to themselves.

Among CHURCH FURNISHINGS the most interesting set is
the Brass Chandeliers, about ten dated ones, ranging from St
John the Divine at Gainsborough (L; 1678), Uffington (1685),
and Lincoln Cathedral (1698) to Castle Bytham (1810). The
55 most ambitious of them have three tiers of arms, as Frampton
(1722) and Spalding (1766). An C18 Mace Rest of wrought
iron is at Grantham, a splendid Eagle Lectern of c.1700, not
of metal but of wood, at Brocklesby (L), and a Lectern which is
the top of a Corinthian pilaster at Burgh-on-Bain (L). In the
same style the Reredos of c.1730 at Rowston and the Pulpit of
1734 at Old Leake, but in Lincoln Cathedral are a Pulpit,
probably of c.1760–70, and the stone Reredos and Screen of
1769 by *Essex*, and they are Gothick, the pulpit playful, but
the pieces designed by Essex remarkably archaeological. No
more – except the curious two 12-inch Fonts of white earthenware at Asgarby and Biscathorpe (both L), the remarkably
independent and successful way in which *Peckitt* of York set
up the medieval glass in Stamford St Martin with geometrical
patterns all his own, and some uncommonly excellent Church
Plate. The Boston plate with its classical forms and decoration
is perhaps the finest in the country. Harlaxton also has a beautiful

---

* Cf. such names as Pittville at Cheltenham, or indeed Jeffry Wyatt's
name Wyatville, when he was knighted.

ilt set, and the plate of 1824 in the cathedral is by far the best f its date (and indeed the whole C19) in the county.*

FUNERARY MONUMENTS have so far only been surveyed up o about 1630. During the second third of the century recumbent ffigies can still be found (Alford (L) † 1668, attributed to *Edward Strong*) and semi-reclining effigies of course (Gautby L), 1673). Busts in niches are for a while specially popular (in a oundel Thornton Curtis † 1626, in arched recesses Scawby 1640, in an oval with a wreath Cammeringham, 1657; all L). A frontal demi-figure is at Belton († 1638; by *Joshua Marshall*, who also did a minor tablet at North Witham † 1658). The most usual type is tablets with curly pediments, garlands and oliage nicely carved, and perhaps columns l. and r. Examples are in many places. It is the type continued and varied by the Stanton workshop. Monuments by *William Stanton* or his son *Edward Stanton* with or without their partner *Horsnail* are at Belton (William † 1679, and according to Mrs Esdaile another † 1697, Edward † 1721, Edward and Horsnail † 1726), Marston (Stanton and Horsnail † 1719), Nocton (William according to Mrs Esdaile's attribution, † 1680), and North Witham (Edward and Horsnail † 1724, Stanton and Horsnail † 1730). The Grand Manner appears on the stage with the greatest flourish possible, with *Pierre-Étienne Monnot*'s monument to the fifth Earl of Exeter at St Martin Stamford, carved in Rome in 1703. Monnot was a Frenchman, but lived in Rome and was acknowledged enough to be commissioned to do one of the papal tombs in St Peter's (Innocent XI). Here the style of the Georgian monument at its most dramatic is heralded. *Green* of Camberwell's monument at Denton with the standing figure of Richard Welby (1714) is more in the English tradition.‡

Both Stamford and Denton are in Kesteven, and Kesteven was indeed in the C18 the part of Lincolnshire most closely in touch with the artistic events of London.§ Even so the harvest is of course nothing like that e.g. in the home counties. No more than a list is needed. By the men of the early years *Nost* (1727, a dull bust, Revesby; L) and *Carpenter* († 1727, two dull busts, Theddlethorpe All Saints; L). Then by the major men *Henry Scheemakers* and *Sir Henry Cheere* (Edenham, † 1723, a

---

* The chalice with cover at Redbourne (L) on the other hand, though by *Lamerie*, is not among his best. Lincolnshire also has some good Continental plate of the C17 and C18, especially at Appleby (L) and Edenham. To these should be added the Kelby font bowl.

‡ By *Green* also a monument at Stragglethorpe with two busts († 1697).

§ From Lindsey no more than five items will be found listed.

standing figure in Roman costume), *Cheere* on his own (Humberston (L) of the 1730s, an attribution; Grantham † 1747, also an attribution; Belton † 1754, Grantham † 1756, the latter two and Humberston of the same type of composition), *Peter Scheemakers* (Heydour, 1737, † 1746), *Rysbrack* (Heydour, 1734 and 1761, and Tydd St Mary † 1741, an attribution – none of the first order), *Roubiliac* (Edenham † 1741). Of the lesser known names Lincolnshire has a *Thomas Carter* (Branston, c.1730, with busts), a *Palmer* (Caythorpe, c.1730), the *magnum opus* of *Charles Harris* (Edenham, c.1780), an excellent *Fisher* of York (Burton-upon-Stather (L), 1776), and works by *Thomas Tayler* (Denton, before 1755) and *W. Tyler* (Belton, † 1770, seated figure, and St George Stamford † 1772). Local sculptors were also still kept busy, men such as *Bingham* of Peterborough and *Sharpe* of Stamford. One more foreigner appears also, *Bertuccini*, with a Heneage monument at Hainton (L; † 1731). It is chiefly three busts. The sculptor of the monument of 1738 at Edenham with the seven busts is unrecorded. Unrecorded also are nearly always the sculptors of the elegant tablets of the 1750s and 1760s which are often of marbles in various colours. A specially fine example is at Metheringham († 1763).

For the late C18 and early C19 the chief sculptors of the first generation or the earlier style which appear in the county are *Nollekens* (Brocklesby (L), c.1791, Greatford † 1797 and † 1807, Edenham † 1820), *John Bacon Sen.* (Belton, 1793, St George Stamford, 1797, both very good), and *John Bacon Jun.* (Hainton (L) † 1807, beautifully tender). Of the later style Lincolnshire has one example by its leading European representative, *Canova* (Belton † 1814, a Grecian female statue of no special attraction) and three by leading English representatives, *Westmacott* (Belton † 1807, Swinstead † 1809) and *Thomas Campbell* (Aswarby † 1849). The Pelham Monuments in the Brocklesby Mausoleum (L) are by an unknown Italian sculptor and represent Canovian classicism. Mrs *Coade* supplied one tiny monument (St John Baptist Stamford † 1799), two armorial shields (Bloxholm, 1813, West Allington), and a monument in the gardens of Brocklesby Park (L). Messrs *Hardman* supplied two or probably three brasses to *Pugin*'s design (Hacconby † 1841; Horbling † 1849 and † 1848).

But Pugin belongs to the Victorian not the Georgian Age, and so we must now go back to ecclesiastical architecture and sum up VICTORIAN CHURCHES. It is not a big job, though the county has large numbers. Most of them, nearly all those by *James*

Fowler, the Diocesan Architect of the High Victorian decades, are small, particularly those of the Wold villages. Fowler (1828–82) lived at Louth and built churches in the county, and it is interesting that in the C19 successful church architects could still live in small provincial towns. *Charles Kirk* of Sleaford is another example. A specially handsome composition by Kirk is Stroxton, 1874–5, specially large Fowler churches are St Swithun Lincoln of 1869 etc., Binbrook (L) of the same year, St Matthew Skegness (L) of 1879–80, and Spridlington (L) of 1875, and a specially progressive Fowler church is Gedney Hill of 1875. He incidentally did nearly all his work in Lindsey. A group of small churches provided at one go in the late 1860s are in the newly reclaimed country N of Holbeach. Some of them are by *Ewan Christian*.

The first stage of Victorian church building is the pre-archaeological stage, represented by *John Brown*'s St Michael Stamford (1835–6), *Lewin*'s Holy Trinity Horncastle (L; 1847), and by *W. A. Nicholson*'s stock brick imitations of Louth (Raithby 1839, Haugham 1840, Biscathorpe 1847; all L), but his Wragby (L; 1838) is still of the Commissioners' type and his Brigg (L; 1842) is quite archaeological. Sir *G. G. Scott* appeared in Lincolnshire very early. His St Nicholas Lincoln of 1838 is indeed still before his conversion to accuracy and earnestness of reproduction. The change is evident, if one compares St Nicholas e.g. with Saxby All Saints (L) of 1845–9.* Scott did churches also at Boston (Holy Trinity 1846–8) and Spalding (St Peter 1875–6, St Paul 1880), but his outstanding work is Nocton, of 1862, an estate church built and equipped lavishly by the Countess of Ripon. The type of the solidly built Victorian estate church is represented in Lincolnshire also by Manthorpe near Grantham (1847–8 by *Place* of Nottingham), Woolsthorpe near Belvoir Castle (1847 by the same), and Revesby (L; 1891 by *C. Hodgson Fowler*). Little else need be said. Cold Hanworth (L) by an unfamiliar architect, *Croft* (1863), is a High Victorian 64 showpiece. *Teulon* built churches at East Torrington 1848–50, New Bolingbroke 1854, and Burringham 1857 (all L), and they have, as one expects, their minor or major perversities. *Butterfield* altered and built a little (West Pinchbeck 1850 e.g.), *Street*'s Firsby (L) of 1856 has interestingly wilful details, *Pearson*'s Eastoft (L) of 1855 is small but dignified, *Ferrey*'s Riby (L) of 1868 has a vaulted chancel. Finally, to propel us right to

---

* An archaeologically correct church of 1848 is Kirkby Green, but the architect is not recorded.

the end of the Victorian Age the noble chapel of the Bishop
Palace at Lincoln of 1898 by *Bodley & Garner* and the forme
domestic chapel of Walmsgate Hall now re-erected at Langwort
(L). This is of 1901, in the freest Arts and Crafts style, and
attributed for good reasons to *Henry Wilson*.

This chapel was no doubt the finest Late Victorian ensembl
in the county, as Cold Hanworth (L) is the most substanti
High Victorian one. Otherwise only individual items of VIC
TORIAN CHURCH FURNISHINGS: the Font at Boston, elabo
rately Dec, by *Pugin*, given by Beresford Hope in 1853, th
Reredos at Algarkirk by *Crace*, the Organ Case at Denton b
Bentley, 1887, and already with significant Arts and Crafts details
and the Frontal at St Mary Stamford by *Sedding*, 1890, entirel
Arts and Crafts, in a Cinquecento way. This only leaves Staine
Glass, and then this record is complete. Stained Glass remaine
pictorial and glaring in colour up to about 1860. Early cases of
reformed taste are the brothers' *Sutton* excellent imitation of c1
glass in the sixties in Lincoln Cathedral, and the early *Holida*
design at Hackthorn (L; made by *Powell*'s) in the Pre-Raphaelit
taste. This is of *c*.1861 and hence not influenced by Morris
Morris glass is at Ruskington, *c*.1873–4, and at East Ravendale
(L), *c*.1876, nice hieratic *Powell* glass, again in the Pre-Raphaelit
taste, at Saxby (L), 1874, and *Kempe* glass starts as early as 187€
(Saxby All Saints, L) and goes on through the eighties and ninetie
and beyond.

But the beyond hardly concerns us here – not only in Kempe
glass, not only in church furnishings, but indeed in all ecclesiastical architecture. Lincolnshire is a rural county. Population
has not grown much in the C20, and new churches were needed
only to a very limited degree. Not one of them demands inclusion
in this Introduction.

So nothing remains unsaid and unlisted, except the usual
Further Reading. The only general surveys I can refer to are
Murray's *Guide* by G. E. Jeans (first edition 1898) and the *Little
Guide* by J. C. Cox (1916, revised by A. Hamilton Thompson
in 1924). Old surveys still to be used are those of W. J. Monson
(1828–40; new edition by the ninth Lord Monson, 1936) and
H. K. Bonney (1845–8; edited by N. S. Harding, 1937). Also
ancient and more general but of special use in Lincolnshire are
H. Bowman and J. S. Crowther's *The Churches of the Middle
Ages*, 2 vols, 1845–53, F. A. Paley's *Manual of Gothic Mouldings*,
1845 (6th ed. 1902), and E. Sharpe's *Treatise of the Rise and
Progress of Decorated Window Tracery in England*, 2 vols, 1849.

ven more important are the volumes of water-colours of incolnshire churches by Nattes (Banks Collection) in the incoln Library. The Stukeley drawings in the Bodleian Library ght also to be consulted. The archaeological journal of the unty is the *Reports and Papers* of the Associated Architectural ocieties (abbreviated R. & P.). Very recently two small journals ave been started which contain brief but valuable articles. They e the *Lincolnshire Historian* and the journal of the *Lincolnshire ld Churches Trust*. In the latter, to give two examples, Canon innall published a paper on C18 churches in the county and other on medieval stone effigies. As for other books, it goes ithout saying that one would consult Mill Stephenson for rasses, Tristram for wall paintings, Aymer Vallance for screens, d so on. Of special books the *Memorials of Old Lincolnshire* ust be mentioned (ed. E. Mansel Sympson, 1911), which con- ins for instance papers by Hamilton Thompson on Saxon urches, by Jeans on brasses, by Mansel Sympson on screens, d so on.

SECULAR BUILDINGS

BY JOHN HARRIS

he introduction to prehistoric and Roman remains has carried e story as far as the earth defences of the Anglo-Saxons. In e Early Norman decades castles were also still made of earth. hese so-called MOTTE-AND-BAILEY CASTLES are listed in he gazetteer and need no further comment.* Secular NORMAN TONE ARCHITECTURE appears in four forms: the castle, the anor house, the town-house, and the living quarters of monas- ries.

Lincolnshire is singularly poor in remains of CASTLES. Five laces cover not only the Norman age, but also the Middle Ages. incoln Castle must of course come first, with Norman walling, arts of two Norman entries, the Norman shell-keep, and parts f a Norman tower (Observatory Tower). Cobb Hall, another ower, vaulted inside, is of the C13, the exterior of the main ateway of the C14. Of Old Bolingbroke (L), which was once a ubstantial castle, nothing but the mound is preserved. Late 13 are the four angle towers of Grimsthorpe Castle, not identical shape, i.e. not part of a symmetrical plan like those of the

* See Barrow-on-Humber (L), Corby, Fleet, Folkingham, Gainsborough, ough-on-the-Hill, Legsby (L), Moulton, Owston Ferry (L), Redbourne (L), leaford, South Reston (L), Stainby, Tothill (L), Welbourn, Withern (L), Wrangle, and Wyberton.

contemporary Edwardian castles. In one of the towers t‹
rib-vaulted rooms remain. More impressive are the vault‹
rooms in the round angle towers of Somerton Castle, which w‹
licensed in 1281. One of the vaults has a central pier and twel‹
radiating ribs. Add to these the tower-house of South Kym‹
which is a North Country type of fortified dwelling, dates fro‹
the mid C14, and has an octopartite vault in the basement, an‹
what survives of the late C13 and C14 walls, towers, and gat‹
of the precincts of the cathedral, and the list is complete – at lea‹
up to the early C15.

The NORMAN MANOR HOUSE seems a contradiction ‹
terms. Manor houses are supposed not to have developed out ‹
8b castles before the end of the C13. Yet Boothby Pagnell cann‹
be called anything else. Admittedly it has a moat, and the princ‹
pal rooms are on the upper floor. But it is not defended beyon‹
that, and it is late C12. It is the only example of its kind ‹
England. The ground floor is vaulted, the upper floor has tw‹
light windows and one interesting fireplace. NORMAN TOW‹
8a HOUSES are confined to Lincoln. The Jew's House is the mo‹
familiar, and in addition there is Aaron's House, also up on th‹
slope of the cathedral hill, and St Mary's Guild down near th‹
s end of the High Street. The principal rooms are again ‹
the upper floors. In the cathedral close one building (Delorai‹
Court) has a Norman undercroft, with piers with scallope‹
capitals down its centre line.

MONASTIC REMAINS are scarce in Lincolnshire anyway, an‹
of the C12 no more can be recorded than a vaulted room ‹
unknown purpose belonging once to the Gilbertine Newstea‹
Priory (L). The C13 has the remains of the refectory of th‹
Premonstratensian Tupholme (L) with its precious and beautifu‹
18b Reading Pulpit and the chapter house of Thornton Abbey (L‹
late in the century and already referred to on p. 37. For late‹
centuries there is an almost total blank. The exception is th‹
mysterious C14 tower attached to the Templars' Church ‹
Temple Bruer, which was then a house of the Hospitallers, an‹
33b the monumental gatehouse of Thornton Abbey (L), easily th‹
most powerful of all English gatehouses. It was begun in 138‹
It is 68 ft high and faces the approaching friend or foe with ‹
broad front, made to look yet broader by the adjoining parts ‹
the wall being raised. It has a later barbican, i.e. walls l. and ‹
of the bridge and a large archway with lierne-vaulting. Abov‹
are two spacious chambers, one above the other, and a whol‹
system of passages, garderobes, etc. The spaciousness is explaine‹

the gatehouse being referred to as 'the new house over the
e'. It may indeed have been the abbot's house. If this is true,
have made a thrust here already into domestic architecture
the late C14, and we must not anticipate.

So back to the THIRTEENTH CENTURY, and that means for
cular architecture in the county one major and much too
le-known building: the Bishop's Palace s of the cathedral,
ruins but still in a state that makes it possible to recognize
rtain important facts. The hall range was built by the two
shops Hugh, i.e. between before 1200 and before 1234. Yet
e hall is over 100 ft long, had arcades with tall slender piers of
rbeck marble and tall, shafted windows, a richly appointed
rch, and – one of the earliest complete cases – the three door-
ays from the entrance bay to kitchen and offices. The site falls
eeply to the s, and hence the solar was placed in an unusual
ay above buttery and pantry. The kitchen is a separate building
t further s, and to the E lay a range parallel to the hall range
d containing the Lesser Hall above a tunnel-vaulted under-
oft. This is C13 too, and probably earlier than the rest. To the
are buildings of c.1440–5, again on different levels, and in-
uding a three-storeyed gate-tower. Apart from the work of the
ishop's Palace little survives of the C13. Of special interest
e the unexplained enormous C13 respond inside Hougham
lanor House (the Perp windows further E belonged probably
the chapel) and the late C13 s front of the Vicar's Court in the
incoln precinct, with its mighty projections containing garde-
obes (the N front with the gateway is late C14).

The FOURTEENTH CENTURY remains are less coherent:
rst the chapel of the summer house of a prior of Spalding known
Wykeham Chapel and situated outside Spalding. This is a
ery fine building of 1311 and has been introduced on p. 38.
hen at Lincoln the back part of the Chancery in the precinct
f about 1320 etc. which also includes a chapel, part of the
urghersh Chantry House of 1345 etc. again in the precinct
nd again with a chapel, the less eloquent surviving parts of the
antelupe Chantry House begun in 1355, and the rectory at
Market Deeping with the interesting, unique tracery pattern
f its tall two-light windows and a C15 or early C16 hall roof.

Of the FIFTEENTH AND EARLY SIXTEENTH CENTURIES
aturally more has been preserved, and here we must first
eturn once more to castles in order to introduce one of the most
nportant ones of the date in England: Tattershall Castle (L), p. 391
egun in 1434–5 for Lord Cromwell, Treasurer of England.

It was indubitably a castle and still impresses one most forcibl
as such, although the curtain wall and wall-towers have gone
as have also the hall and other domestic structures. Wha
34 remains is the keep; for so it must be called – a tower 110 f
high and spacious enough for a large commodious hall on eac
35b floor (with a fine chimneypiece) and in addition cabinets in th
angle-turrets and passages, lobbies, garderobes, etc., some o
35a them very handsomely, even fancifully, vaulted. It has bee
said that this keep was really not built as a keep at all, that th
windows e.g. are too large for successful defence, but on th
other hand the approach to the tower was made deliberatel
difficult, and there are proper machicolations at the top. Th
most likely answer to the question what was in Lord Cromwell
mind is that the building was intended to be both apotropaei
and defensible. Tattershall Castle is of brick (though the nea
by collegiate church is of stone) and may serve as a reminder i
this Introduction of the important part brick was to play in th
architecture of this part of England. The Thornton Abbe
Gatehouse had preceded Tattershall in the use of brick, an
also in power to impress, and in the peculiar combination of th
domestic and the potentially military. Lord Cromwell also buil
the curious Tower in the Wood outside Woodhall Spa (L
and early in the C16 two defensive brick towers were buil
outside Boston, the Hussey and the Rochford Towers, the latte
at Skirbeck.

There is nothing of C15 secular architecture in Lincolnshir
to emulate Tattershall and Thornton, though there is one majo
36 building: Gainsborough Old Hall (L), large, partly of brick
partly timber-framed, and with stone introduced at least for th
hall bay window. It is an impressive building, impressive als
inside the hall, under its open timber roof, and it would deserv
closer study. It was built in the 1470s, though much of what w
see now is alteration and addition of c.1600. Hardly any furthe
domestic work needs a reference: parts of Ayscoughfee Hall a
Spalding, said to date from 1429, the corbelled-out oriel a
Oasby Manor House, a hall on a vaulted undercroft at Goxhil
(L), wrongly known as Goxhill Priory, Halstead Hall (L) wit
mullioned and transomed windows, the Great Ponton Rector
built for a merchant of the staple of Calais who died in 152c
37a large but much remodelled parts of Irnham Hall dating fron
before 1531, a pretty C15 oriel now in Lincoln Castle, the fron
of the Lincoln Cathedral chancery, and the fine Barn of the
Vicars Choral which was built in 1440.

However, what must be emphasized to conclude this survey
to the C16 is an exceptionally fine group of secular buildings
her than domestic. We may start with the two BRIDGES, both
ique of their kind, the Crowland one of the late C14, because 33a
is three radial bridges in one, originally across two streams and
ow high and dry in the middle of the village, and the High
ridge at Lincoln, because it has preserved its timber-framed 396
C6 shops and houses all along.* Then the pretty CONDUIT
OUSE from the Lincoln Whitefriars now in the churchyard
St Mary-le-Wigford. Lincoln also has its C15 GUILDHALL,
riously placed over a town gate, and, in the cathedral precinct,
ie old cathedral LIBRARY of 1422 with original presses. In
idition to these one inn, one school, and one hospital or alms-
ouse: the INN is the Angel and Royal Hotel at Grantham, late 37b
15, with its fine, quite ornate stone front. The front is nearly,
ut not quite symmetrical, with two canted bay windows and
1 oriel above the central archway. Both bays and oriel are
rettily vaulted inside, and the whole is one of the best of the
uite numerous medieval inns in England. The SCHOOL is the
Vainfleet School of 1484 at Wainfleet All Saints (L), brick, with 38
vo prominent turrets flanking the front, and the HOSPITAL is
rowne's Hospital at Stamford, built at the expense of William 39a
rowne, another merchant of the staple of Calais, who died in
489. It consists of one long and high range of stone with a low
all and high hall over it, and to the E of both a chapel going
irough both floors. It is a model of its kind.

The RENAISSANCE was late in coming to Lincolnshire.
'his has been observed in the case of the churches; it is the
ame in domestic architecture. What remains of Henry Duke
f Brandon's wing at Grimsthorpe, i.e. of c.1540, is still
Late Perp, with no sign of the Renaissance. Life in the mist-
nshrouded Fens and the inaccessible Wolds must still have been
eudal.

After the REFORMATION the rich and extensive monastic
states were parcelled out to courtiers like Edward Fiennes, Lord
Clinton. His share included Sempringham, where, before his
death in 1585, he built a large quadrangular house. Nothing is
known of this, but it was probably built nearly forty years after
he Reformation, a fact that emphasizes the slowness in starting
o utilize Lincolnshire lands.

Now for the ELIZABETHAN AGE. Few fragments remain.
South Kelsey Hall (L) preserves a tower; too little is known of

* A smaller C14 bridge is at Claypole.

3—L

Sir Christopher Wray's house at Glentworth (L; 1560s, rebui
by *Paine*); and this is also true of Sir Robert Jermyn's theatr
40a cally-sited Torksey Castle (L; 1560s?). It would perhaps l
rash to speculate on the date of the porch of the house at Sudbrook
whose elegance bespeaks the London style of the Protecto
Somerset. Perhaps it came from Grimsthorpe. Fortunatel
John Thorpe surveyed several Lincolnshire houses early in th
C17, including the St Pol house at Snarford (L). His survey
comprise a group of Late Elizabethan buildings of the firs
importance. But these are of a later generation than Glentwort
or Torksey, so first a word about the SIXTEENTH CENTUR
VERNACULAR.

There are few dated examples (Barrowby Rectory, 1588), an
undated houses are invariably of simple Early Tudor patterr
An exception is Bassingthorpe (1568), and an uncommonl
interesting one. It was built for a Grantham wool merchant
who employed a mason handling his details in an unconventiona
way; perhaps the mason who worked at Dingley Hall, Northant
(1560). More conventional is Ashby Hall, Ashby-de-la-Launde
dated 1595. It retains a porch set into the projecting stroke o
an E plan.

From the watershed to the JACOBEAN STYLE, nearly every
thing interesting has gone. This is sad; for of no other style unti
after the Restoration did the county possess so many big house
close to the London circuits. Three were surveyed by Thorpe
Horkstow Hall (L), Thornton Abbey House (L), and Dowsby
Hall; and two may have been designed by *Robert Smithson*, the
Midland architect: Doddington Hall (remaining) and Normanby (L) or Butterwick (demolished). Horkstow was built
between 1607 and 1620. It had one of the most ingenious
staircases of the age. Even more remarkable was Thornton of
soon after 1610. It was buttressed (probably revival rather than
survival – i.e. a self-conscious association with the abbey ruins),
the entrance opened directly into a hall via a small oval inner
porch, and the stables were contained right in the centre.
Perhaps the owner loved his horses as much as the later Thomas
Worsley of Hovingham, Yorks, who also built his house round
his stables. In any case they will have been killed when this
gimcrack house 'fell quite down to the bare ground without any
visible cause'. The third house surveyed by Thorpe was Sir
William Rigdon's at Dowsby, built before 1610. Although
truncated, it remains one of the relatively rare cases of a house
surveyed by Thorpe still being in existence, handsome, with tall

gabled elevations.* Fortunately the two *Smithson* houses are better documented. Among the architect's designs in the R.I.B.A. are some for Sir Robert Sheffield, who may have lived either at Butterwick on the Isle of Axholme or at Normanby just across the Trent. They show a quadrangular plan of three storeys. What was built is known from a survey plan to have had distinct Smithson traits: excessive height and verticality, and the use of pergolas or balconies. Smithson was active in the East Midlands (Wollaton, Worksop), and to this region belongs Doddington, the best of its date (1593) in the county and quite abreast 40b of the latest Elizabethan developments: well proportioned relation of window to wall, sparseness of elevation, and clean silhouette. Here the plan is an E, tall and long rather than broad. Two other houses need mention. More should be known about the 'very fine stately building' at Brocklesby (L) built by Sir William Pelham in 1603; and just a little more about the original state of Marston Manor, like Dowsby now truncated, but shown on a survey of 1615 as an ample H-shaped house.

Nor do these houses exhaust the list of what has nearly or entirely gone. Sir John Bolle (of the Spanish Lady's) Francartesque gateway at Scampton (L) stands forlorn in a field; Sir Robert Tyrwhit's house at Stainfield (L) had lots of fussy gabled bays, not unlike the early C17 s front of Grimsthorpe, now the best remaining example of ambitious vernacular in the county; and more ought to be known about Lord Willoughby de Eresby's Eresby (Spilsby; L), once very large indeed. Langton Hall Langton-by-Partney was fortunately engraved. It was not large and had the typical Elizabethan E-plan. Harlaxton was also engraved, the delight of the picturesque topographers. They date it early C16, but John Buckler shows plenty of internal joinery quite distinctly early C17. In other words, Harlaxton may have been a survival of Tudor forms right into the age of Inigo Jones. Two more houses need mention before the county's negative contribution to Jonesian classicism is commented on: the delightful Casewick Hall of the 1620s (once quadrangular and moated), and the evocative Nocton, in plan possibly an H with long wings, extruded towers in the angles (cf. Hainton Hall, L), and bulbous cupolas. Nocton could have been built at any time between 1600 and 1630 and was probably one of the few 'prodigy' houses in the county, in fact its Cobham Hall. It may seem

---

* The association of Rigdon with Dowsby and an otherwise unidentified Thorpe survey was kindly brought to my notice by Sir John Summerson, who suggests that *Thorpe* may have been the designer.

almost incredible that it should be difficult to find any goo
Elizabethan or Jacobean INTERIORS of any consequence – n
sumptuous plaster ceilings, and of major chimneypieces onl
the overmantel at Marston. So the connoisseur of furnishing
will be disappointed.

So indeed will the connoisseur and partisan of CLASSICISM
for the North Italian Palladianism brought to England by Inig
Jones in 1615 had no effect upon Lincolnshire. Here lived non
of Charles's court circle. Heneage and Carre, Pelham an
Willoughby de Eresby were patrons of the indigenous taste, tha
is, the Late Elizabethan, rather than companions to Arunde
or Buckingham.

But how did domestic architecture express itself betwee
1625 and 1649, the first CAROLEAN PERIOD? The representa
tives of this generation are smaller manor houses, of comfortabl
proportions, very often a survival of vernacular forms. Righ
through the century, and even in the following one, Elizabethar
traditions persisted. In the flat fields or the gentle Wolds smal
vernacular houses are a reminder of a comfortable squirearch
or middle class. Their style may often be anonymous, but the
are pleasing discoveries in an age of photographic dissemination
If they are near the borders of the county, their style may partak
of Northamptonshire (West Deeping Manor House, 1634) o
Leicestershire (the texturally attractive Brandon Old Hall
1637). Nearly always they are of stone, of one or two storeys
gabled over canted bays, with from three- to seven-light mul
lioned windows, sometimes with a transom. They are ofter
dated:* e.g. Foston Old Hall, 1616; Moore Farmhouse Little
Humby, 1631. Undated is the slightly larger Red Hall Bourne
of the early C17. Four houses deserve special commendation:
Billingborough, Coleby, Aubourn, and Grimblethorpe Gayton-
le-Wold (L). The first two belong to the 1620s. Both have longish
gabled fronts of stone, and Coleby (1628), commandingly sited
on the Cliff, should perhaps be compared with the similarly-
sized Casewick Hall. They are all enlargements of the usual,
somewhat repetitive, gabled theme, attractive but not distinctive of style. Excessive height was seen to be characteristic of
Dowsby. It is also of Aubourn Hall (brick, late C16). But at
Aubourn the work to examine is the staircase, singular in decoration rather than plan. Instead of the balusters usual at this date,
the balustrade is filled with openwork panels of strapwork (cf. an
advanced example at Ham House, Surrey, 1637), and the strings

* Dates to be accepted with reservations.

entwined with foliage and serpents in a Gothico-Viking
le. It is bizarre and certainly not Late Elizabethan. An
ually good staircase is at Grimblethorpe. This has four flights
und three sides of a narrow oblong space and can be con-
ered the best and most representative of its type in the county.
as is probable, the date is in the 1630s or 1640s, then this sur-
y has reached the Protectorate. But before we leave Grimble-
orpe, one other point of interest must be referred to: the
nt order of pilasters along one front. Giant orders are a
ity at this date (cf. Slyfield, Surrey, 1630s; Rye Grammar
hool, 1636; former houses in Great Queen Street, London,
d Parham House, Suffolk, both 1630s–40s), and, to add to the
ity, the tops of the pilasters at Grimblethorpe are linked by
allow arches. So it is a form of continuous, crazily elongated,
nk arcading.

Dated buildings of the PROTECTORATE (1649–60) are infre-
ent. When they occur they are usually small vernacular
anor houses (Braceby Manor Farm, 1653; Ancient House,
asingham, 1655; The Priory, Brant Broughton, 1658), or
wn houses with similar windows, gables, etc. (No. 44 St
ary's Street, Stamford, 1656). There are two exceptions.
e Welby Almshouses at Denton (1653), with shaped gables 46a
d up by ribbons of stone, may well be called the most delight-
l of any in England. They enchant as much by their naive
tisan style as by the subtle contrast of local stones. Somerby
all near Brigg (L) was built in 1660. Unfortunately it has been
built, but plans show the house to have had links with Holland
Scandinavia, rather than, say, with the City of London.

This is the first time the City has been mentioned in this
rvey. During the Protectorate, and for perhaps about a decade
rlier, the City had been the source of a style of building
ristened by Sir John Summerson Artisan Mannerism. It is
early always a brick style, and it is characterized by a wilful
se of certain motifs. Somerby e.g. had little pediments floating
ee above niches, a disregard for architectural propriety that is
pical also of a local style, here termed the FEN ARTISAN
YLE because it occurs mostly in the Fens.

Artisan Mannerism approached Lincolnshire from the south
Northamptonshire: Thorpe Hall, 1653 by *Peter Mills*; Cam-
ridgeshire: Wisbech Castle, probably also by *Mills*; and Thor-
ey Abbey House, 1660 by *John Lovin*) and is first found in the
unge of the Peacock and Royal Hotel at Boston. There the
himneypiece is close to work at Thorpe and bears the style's

leitmotif of a half pilaster pendant from a shouldered architra
and scrolled at its base. Much later, Bloxholm Hall (1670s)
the best representative, built for Septimus Ciprian Thornto
an off-beat name that went well with an off-beat house. Its m
remarkable feature is a Venetian window, a Palladian motif
ahead of the time of the general Palladian Revival, though
course used by Inigo Jones. Artisan Mannerism probably al
appeared at Culverthorpe, disguised by later additions, and
can be found in a watered-down form at Stamford (No. 19
George's Square), and devoid of mannerisms at Crowland Man
House (1690).

From the Protectorate to the RESTORATION. An examinati
of the Fen Artisan style is in place under this heading becau
it belongs to the second half of the century. It seems to ha
been the preserve of the more muddle-headed builders. T
houses are always of brick and of middling size. Wherev
possible, the builders break every rule in the book: jumped-u
or broken strings, cornices, etc.; discontinued architraves
architraves fading into the wall; knobs, buttons, and studs flu
anywhere regardless of compartition; and lots of strange penda
decorations carved in brick. The style appears at The Mano
Aslackby; Church House, Boston; the Elizabethan House, an
The Hall, Coningsby (L); the stables at Eresby, Spilsby (L); an
bits at White Loaf Hall, Freiston; Old Hall, Hagworthingha
(L); Stukeley Hall, Holbeach (demolished); Blossom Hall and th
King's Head, Kirton-in-Holland (1699); Porch House, Sibse
(L); Walcot Old Hall (L); the Old Hall, Winterton (L); probabl
Worlaby Hospital (L; 1673); and the crazily-decorated Worlab
Hall (long ago demolished). Sometimes there are shaped
46a Dutch gables as well, but few are early (Welby Almshouse
Denton, 1653; Little Cawthorpe (L), 1673, both shaped), an
the only two Dutch gables are on the Old Manor House, We
Allington (1650s) and the porch of Burgh-le-Marsh church (
dated 1702.

As the Restoration brought an increase in building activity
so the traveller will be refreshed by new building types. SCHOOL
are particularly charming. The best are all of the 1670s: Brig
(L), 1674 by *William Catlyn*, is associated with a Hull style jus
across the Humber; Bourne is dated 1678 and is conservative i
46b style; and Corby is dated 1673. The comfortable, reassurin
proportions of Corby School make it one of the most appealin
in the county. Restoration prosperity is seen first and at it
best in the towns. Lincoln, where much has later been rebuilt

as little to offer, Stamford a great deal. There the style is
vernacular and again conservative. Dated houses of the 1660s
(No. 33 St Peter's Street, 1660; Sheepmarket, 1661; No. 15
St Peter's Street, and No. 12 St Paul's Street, both of 1663;
Olive Branch, St Leonard's Street, 1666) are all stone and have
canted gabled bays. They could have been built in 1600. In
fact the type was to go on throughout the C18. In the country-
side the survival of traditional forms follows a similar pattern.
Barholm Hall and Baston are both probably late C17. They
could equally well be a century earlier or later.

With Doddington the county had come close to possessing an
urbane London-style house. It was not, however, as we have
seen, by a London architect, and only after the Restoration does
the sophistication of London make its appearance in Lincolnshire. The centre of Nocton was rebuilt in the 1660s for Sir
William Ellys. It was first-class artisan work, and Ellys's monument in the church is attributed to *Edward Stanton*, again an
artist not quite at the top. It was only when *Wren* was commissioned to design the Honywood Library at Lincoln Cathedral
in 1674 that Lincoln had, as it were, arrived. Occupying the N
side of the cloisters, its light Tuscan arcades and flat planes are
faintly reminiscent of the Quattrocento. On sunny days Italy
at Lincoln is quite a reality. Wren and the Stantons were known to
each other, and it was *William Stanton* who contracted in 1684 to
build Belton House, often erroneously attributed to Wren. The 47a
case for *Captain William Winde* as the architect is a strong one,
and Winde was a London man. Belton is of H-plan, a double pile,
with hipped roof, balustraded parapet, and a lantern. The plan
and silhouette are derived from Sir Roger Pratt's influential
Clarendon House, London (1664). Belton also contains up-to-
date decor: luscious plasterwork by *Edward Goudge*; superlative
naturalistic Gibbons-style wood carving, probably by *Edward
Carpenter*, the 'Watson' of Belton; and *C. G. Cibber* is suggested
as the sculptor of the sundial. So not only was the architect a
London man, but the craftsmen also. Belton has no painted
ceilings. For them one would have had to go to Uffington House,
now destroyed. Here *Verrio* painted the staircase in a house
that had been built in the 1680s. Like Belton it was of stone,
and it also had a hipped roof with balustraded platform. Uffington was the second of three important works in this decade.
The third is the provokingly anonymous N front of Grimsthorpe,
an ambitious and important piece of 1685, rebuilt again by
Vanbrugh thirty years later. There is no evidence that the house

proposed for Scotton (L) in 1684 was ever built. Its prot
Palladian plan of angle blocks or towers was new then (but
Ragley, Warwicks, by Hooke, 1679). If some of the importan
houses of the Charles II and 'good King William cut' a
lost, there are many enchanting smaller ones still with us, a
up and down the county. The most satisfying are Leadenha
Old Hall (1690s?), where a pair of putti in a Marino Mari
style recline among cornucopias on a pediment; and No.
Northgate, Sleaford, a surprisingly unappreciated front by
master-sculptor who must have been inspired by Charmeto
engravings.

So to the C18 and to the Georgian Age: to roads newly turn
piked (better communications), to social gatherings (civi
architecture), and to the influx of new ideas, a feeling for dis
play, and the move away from the vernacular to a more urban
expression in style. Of Lincolnshire houses of about 1700 th
keynote is domesticity, expressed in red brick, stone quoin
47b and hipped roofs. Gunby Hall (L) of 1700 is the only familia
one of them. The others of these appealing QUEEN ANNE typ
houses are unknown to literature: West Ashby House, Littl
Grimsby Hall, Brackenborough Hall, Tupholme Hall, Thorntor
Hall Thornton Curtis; or a town house like the Mansion a
Louth (all L). None are dated, but they must be of c.1690 to
c.1730. They all express some mannerism of local builders
at Tupholme an *œil-de-bœuf* is linked to the keystone of th
door below; at Thornton the chimneystacks are brought up
the side of the house to contribute decisively to the silhouette
and the Mansion at Louth has odd details in its particularly
fine staircase. The elegance of the Mansion's balusters is symp
tomatic of a new appreciation of the joiner's art. Little Grimsby
and Brackenborough both contain masculine joinery exploiting
a Doric theme, which is also to be found elsewhere in the county
(Somersby Manor Farm, 1722; Harrington Hall; both L). Two
houses at the turn of the century strike a grander note: Brocklesby Park (L), a sophisticated London brick house, and the fron
48a of Culverthorpe of 1699 which must be the work of a Londor
artist of considerable calibre. More important still at Culverthorpe is the chapel of 1691; for it has a temple front, and such
are a rarity at this date. Culverthorpe is alien to the current
domestic theme in anticipating the ENGLISH BAROQUE, the
work of Vanbrugh, Talman, and possibly Archer. At Swinstead
there may have been a big house of Kings Weston type by
Vanbrugh. And Vanbrugh must have designed the Summer

ouse, also at Swinstead, which must be regarded as a visual
nk to Grimsthorpe in the adjacent valley. The date of Grims- 49a
orpe is 1722, the year of the plans made for the 1st Duke of & b
ncaster but executed for his son. Vanbrugh died in 1726,
hen the N front only was complete. If Colen Campbell is to be
elieved (*Vitruvius Britannicus*, III, 1725), Vanbrugh's total
cheme was inspired by Campbell's own Houghton, by the new
ovement of Palladianism. There is also some evidence that
awksmoor may have followed Vanbrugh here (doorway to
ate dining room; also Hawksmoor designs for the chapel), so
dgement on this last great work of Vanbrugh's should not be
ade until the facts are clarified.* Elsewhere in the county
anbrugh may be found at Somersby Manor Farm (L; 1722). 48b
t certainly is a toy castle, as they are typical of him; and the
anbrugh succession can be detected at the Blue Anchor Inn
emolished) near Somersby, Grantham, and at No. 3 St Mary's
lace, Stamford.

Panton Hall (L) of *c.*1720 is now recognized as a probable
ork of *William Talman*. The chaste brick elevations are in
alman's late style of Kimberley Park Norfolk and Fetcham
ark Surrey. At Well Hall (L), the wonderfully Baroque, yet
ubdued, gatepiers can be attributed to *Thomas Archer*, who
ad married into the Chaplin family of near-by Tathwell. The
ouse at Well (1725) could perhaps also be Archer, but is closer
o the style of *James Gibbs* as disseminated later in his *Book of
rchitecture* (1728).

PALLADIANISM has been passed by in this survey; for Camp-
ell or Leoni, or the coterie of my Lord Burlington, are unrepre-
ented in the county, unless *Kent* designed the little garden
emple at Belton. Palladianism in Lincolnshire is rather a
uestion of the movement's climax in the 1730s and 1740s. The
plendid interiors of Hainton (L) have been attributed to *James
ibbs* (giant order in the hall, Gibbsian ceilings); Holywell
Iall (?1732) has Palladian stables of London quality, and a
ishing Temple right out of Gibbs's book; and the additions to
ulverthorpe of *c.*1734 are convincingly given to *Robert Morris*,
he self-appointed theorist of the Palladians. For Palladian
NTERIORS (again of the 1730s or 40s), Grimsthorpe has one
f the finest suites of state rooms in the country, tantalizingly
nonymous, but probably by someone like Isaac Ware.

* Important in this context is Vanbrugh's original design for the Grims-
orpe front in the collection of Sir Richard Proby. There the Palladian ele-
ents of the front are notably absent.

Then the EARLY GEORGIAN LOCAL STYLE, apart fro
direct London importations. Two towns are pre-eminen
Stamford and Spalding. The style of Stamford derives from th
pattern books of Batty Langley, William Halfpenny, an
William Salmon. Its motifs are heavy, often blocked architrave
big keystones, 'Gibbsian' doorways, all displayed in a decided
emphatic way. Unless *George Portwood* (Stukeley Hous
design 1741) can be accepted as its chief practitioner, it is a
anonymous style. Dated specimens range from Brazenose Hou
50b (1723) to No. 21 High Street (1732), and to No. 13 Barn H
(1740). So pervading was this local style that it survives
genteel form at the Town Hall (1777), and even as late as 180
at No. 10 Barn Hill. Elsewhere it is found at Leasingham (cop
of the 1740 Barn Hill house), and at Fulbeck (1733). At Spaldin
the style is not anonymous; it is the expression of the work of
father and son, both *William Sands*, from c.1720 to c.177
Whereas Stamford is all stone, Spalding is all brick, provide
with stone dressings. The Sandses love to compress as man
Palladian motifs as possible into a composition. They ador
Venetian windows, smooth stone architraves, and segment
bays. Between them they account for the best houses in th
town (Langton House, Holland House, Westbourne Lodge
and further afield Wyberton Hall of 1761, and the 'Great Room
of Crowland Manor House (c.1775) have been attributed t
50a them. There is no reason why Fydell House Boston of 172
should not be the elder Sands's *chef d'œuvre*.

So much for Baroque, Palladianism, and local imitation
spanning the first half of the century. The years round 175
saw the climax of the ROCOCO, more an interior style of plaster
work than a strictly architectural style. Burwell (L) had it i
profusion (1760), but not of good quality. Elsewhere in th
county it is not worth seeking. The Rococo belongs in date t
the second generation of Palladians, and particularly *James Pain*
Gate Burton Temple (L; 1747) is tentatively attributed to hir
and could be his first work in the county; Ormsby Hall Sout
Ormsby (L) is of 1752, Glentworth (L) of 1753, Burton Ha
Burton-by-Lincoln (L) of 1768. Ormsby and Glentworth hav
smooth brick façades, successors to the style of Panton. Ormsb
has one of the finest Georgian staircases in the county, splendidl
carved by *William Lumby*; and it was *Thomas Lumby* who carve
the notably chaste stair at Doddington Hall (1761). At the sam
time the VERNACULAR still marched ahead oblivious of every
thing. The C17-looking dovecote at Baston Manor House i

ated 1802, a C17-looking barn in the village there is dated
795. The same conservatism is found at Kew Cottage Dorring-
on.

The TOWNS of Lincolnshire are a sheer delight, and few
ounties can offer so many where the attacks of subtopia have
een kept so successfully at bay. Stamford (with some of the 2a
est of English townscape) has been mentioned already, so has
palding (rows of red brick houses along the tree-lined river, quite
Dutch). Equally good are Boston (riverscape, docks, and ships;
varehouses, and houses with elongated doorways), and Louth
L; Market Place and West Street, and the great spire dominating
very vista). Few can deny the charm of parts of Barton-on-
Humber, Spilsby, Brigg, or Alford (all L). And of course there
re the VILLAGES. Attractive ones in the county are legion. As a
ample, Folkingham is Late Georgian, a wide spacious green
oreasted at the top by the Greyhound Inn. Long Bennington
has much to offer; so has Fulbeck, where the delights have to be
iscovered off the main road.

INNS are a speciality, and the county is second to none for the
ange of enchanting unsophisticated hostelries, with real ostlers,
roned newspapers, and an amplitude of fare. WAREHOUSES are
also part of the county scene. There are an uncommon number
of the late C18, nearly always of elementary elevation, just
rows of simple windows in tall or broadly square brick façades
Barton-on-Humber (L), Brigg (L), Boston, Gainsborough,
Louth (L), and Spalding, the last-named with the speciality of
rusticated cement-faced fronts). PUBLIC BUILDINGS have not
been mentioned yet; for there are few before 1770 worth
singling out. Stamford has its Assembly Room (1725), its
Theatre (1768), and its Town Hall (1777); Lincoln's grand
Assembly Room (1744) has unfortunately been mutilated
beyond recognition. TOWN HOUSES also need comment. At
Stamford the severe stone front of Austin House (1760s) in no
way prepares one for the gay Rococo garden façade; at Boston
No. 120 High Street is a sophisticated Late Georgian house
allied to near-by Frampton House at Frampton (1792). Lincoln
has now few good town houses to show. They were probably
all built by the Lincoln builders *Abraham* and *John Hayward*
(Disney Place, 1736, and perhaps the Archdeaconry, etc.).
They are robust rather than sophisticated, always with good
internal joinery details.

From c.1770 Lincolnshire began to reflect the styles of the
emancipators from Palladian canon; of Sir William Chambers,

51 Robert Adam, or James Wyatt. *Chambers* built the fine Coleb
Temple in 1762 and nothing else in the county. Adam is un
represented, but *Wyatt* is, at Belton (1777 with good 'Adamesque
&60 ceilings) and at Brocklesby (L; 1787), where the Mausoleum
must rank among the finest neo-classical monuments in th
country. This NEO-CLASSICAL STYLE is significantly alway
of London importation, and the same applies when one look
at work by the generation succeeding Chambers and Adam
James Lewis at Hackthorn Hall (L; 1792, with slight neo-Greel
details), and *Robert Mitchell* (?) at Willingham House Nortl
Willingham (L; 1790, with splendid *Coade* stone capitals), or
Jeffry Wyatt, later *Sir Jeffry Wyatville*, at Stubton Hall (1813)
When not partaking of the London circuit, the county has stronger
links to the Midlands and the North, particularly through *John
Carr*, who may have first appeared at Somerby Hall (L; 1768)
then at Panton (L; adding wings in 1775), at Norton Place Bishop
Norton (L; his *magnus opus* here, 1776), the County Prison,
Lincoln (1787), etc. Fillingham Castle (L) is a Gothic house
attributed to Carr and is assumed to date from 1760. It is of
characteristically Carr plan, with interiors in the style of the 1770s.

Fillingham introduces the GOTHIC REVIVAL, but there is
in the county only one house worth commendation: Casewick
59b Hall and *Legg*'s front of 1785 there. It is still quite symmetrical,
and has ogee-headed windows. The furthest extension of this
Georgian Gothic, or Rococo Gothic, style is to be found at
Louth (L; *Espin*'s Priory of 1818) and Winterton (L; *Lockwood*'s
Dent's Cottage of 1830), where asymmetry is not yet evident,
although details respect the quasi-scholarship of the age of
Rickman's *An Attempt to Discriminate the Styles of English
Architecture* (1817).

Connoisseurs of Greece will be disappointed in the county.
The GREEK REVIVAL is only represented by the Spilsby Sessions
House (L; *see* below) and the temple in the grounds of the Girls'
High School, Lincoln, a choice and rare imitation of the Choragic
Monument of Thrasyllus. The austerity of the later phase of the
style might, however, be detected at Walmsgate Hall (L; early
C19), and Skellingthorpe Hall is one of the best of the small
Greek villas. The movement towards freer forms is found in
Smirke's Normanby Park (L; 1820), a composition that can only
be described in terms of cubic geometry. Rock House Stamford
(1842) well illustrates the extension of this movement, where the
details, although vigorous, are degenerate.

Now for accessories, for FOLLIES, COTTAGES ORNÉS, and

ARDENS. Brocklesby (L) has a rare root house, and a grotto; enton a grotto. Sir Francis Dashwood's Dunston Pillar was uilt to guide travellers 'o'er the blasted heath', and other folly wers are to be found at Belton (1750), at Saltfleetby St Peter ; Prospect Tower, perhaps by *Wyatville*, 1812), and at aistor (L; *Willson*'s Pelham Column, 1840). Belton has in ddition a Gothic ruin and a cascade; Brackenborough Hall (L) as another ruin. No one should miss *Mr Lovely*'s bizarre gate ers at Branston, or the spidery Jungle at Eagle. Of Victorian llies, the screen at Broadbank House Louth (L; 1859) is erhaps the best, and no folly-lover's visiting list should omit Iajor *Fitzwilliam*'s eccentric but enjoyable display of sculpture Greatford. Lincolnshire has numerous examples of cottages nés. Only the lodges at Langton-by-Partney (L) and Scremby all (L) need here be singled out as representative of them. s the county could only boast a few large parks, famous C18 ondon gardeners were little employed. The ghost of *Stephen witzer* might be detected at Eresby, Spilsby (L; where the eat avenue marches down to a magnificent gatepier and little se),* or *George London* at Grimsthorpe. Succeeding these rmalists, *Capability Brown* is found at Brocklesby (L), Grims-horpe, and Hainton (L); and *William Eames* at Panton (L) and elton. Succeeding them, *Humphry Repton* made designs for rocklesby and Scrivelsby (both L). There are many anonymous ardens, and the enthusiasts of landscape gardening will appreci-e Well Hall (L), Harrington (L), or Holywell.

By the early C19 BUILDING TYPES proliferate. *Bryan rowning*'s ingenious Town Hall at Bourne (1821) should be etter known, and so should his Gaol at Folkingham (1825), a 61a esign which would be more at home in post-Revolutionary rance. With Gaols go Sessions Houses (Spilsby (L) in Greek 61b Doric, 1824 by *Kendall*) and Almshouses, especially in the 1820s nd 1830s (Belton, 1827; no less than three at Stamford: nowden's 1822, and Truesdale's and Fryer's, both 1832 by asevi). Workhouses should not be forgotten (Brigg (L), by licholson, 1837; Boston, also 1837), nor Hospitals (Stamford nd Rutland, 1826 by *J. P. Gandy*). Sleaford sums up the whole ovement to perfection: Sessions House, 1831, Carre's Hospital, 830-46, and the Workhouse, 1838, all by *Kendall*.

So to the VICTORIAN AGE and first COUNTRY HOUSES. he two best are early ones: Harlaxton, begun 1831, and Bayons

* And where, more seriously, the author was struck with lumbago by a Vild Man of the Willoughbys.

62a Manor (L), begun 1836. Bayons is an amateur's house, decided
Late Georgian Picturesque and an immensely successful ess
in the Castle mode. *Charles Tennyson* was probably his ov
architect, although assisted by *Nicholson*. To add a more pr
fessional touch, *Pugin* and *Crace* supplied the wallpapers.

62b Harlaxton, *Salvin* produced designs said to have been inspir
by the ideas of another amateur, the client again, this time Geor
de Ligne Gregory, who was determined to build the bigge
house in the county – and succeeded. Even so early, Harlaxt
would be one of Salvin's greater houses (cf. particularly h
abstract asymmetry of the back front). But what makes Harlaxt
are the interiors, and those that matter are mostly by *Willia
Burn*, who had replaced Salvin in Gregory's affections by 183
Burn out-did and bettered what was being done by *Benjam
Wyatt* in the Neo-Baroque, Neo-Rococo, French style of th
early c18 at near-by Belvoir Castle (*c.*1825). Burn's synthes
of French with Jacobean forms is remarkable. And as if th

63 were not enough, there is the spectacular staircase, theatric
as only German or Austrian ones are. After Harlaxton *Bu*
was busy in the county, at Stoke Rochford South Stoke (1841
Rauceby Hall South Rauceby (1842), and at Revesby Abbe
(L; 1843). Chimneypieces are one of his specialities, but the o
in the Music Room at Stoke must surely be early c17 Flemis
and is one of the best examples of Rubensian sculpture in th
country. After these Burn houses only one more house nee
mention: Northorpe Hall (L; *Goldsmith*, 1875), because of i
belated Neo-Norman style.

The Victorian enthusiast should rather see some examples
BUILDING TYPES other than houses. For RAILWAY STATION
see Firsby (L; 1848) in Cinquecento style, or Stamford Ea
(*Hurst*, 1856), in Gothic. Lincoln is Tudor-asymmetric
(*Joseph Cubitt*, 1848), and Louth (L) is Tudor Gothic (1854
TOWN HALLS have their specialist in *Pearson Bellamy*, wh
delights to build palazzos in streets decidedly not sun-bake
His best are at Louth (L; 1854) and Grimsby (L; 1863). Grimsb
has also another *all'italiana* touch in *Wild*'s Dock Tower of 185
a pastiche of motifs from the Siena Town Hall. VILLAG
SCHOOLS can also evoke pleasure. They are nearly alway
Gothic (Great Gonerby, 1841; Algarkirk, by *Scott*, 1857; etc.
The best TOWN SCHOOLS are at Lincoln (City School, *Georg
Sedger*, 1885; Girls' High School, *William Watkins*, 1893, i
Watkins's terracotta Dutch Renaissance) and Stamford (*Browr
ing*'s sensitive Girls' High School, 1876), or a late example i

ilson's wing of 1904 at Grantham. In the way of MISCELLANEA,
: Temple Gardens Lincoln is a surprisingly good Victorian
:aircase, almost a section from a Pompeian wall painting;
leaford has the Gothic Handley Memorial (*Boyle*, 1850, statue
y *John Thomas*); and Boston the Egyptian Revival Freemasons'
Iall (1860), copied from the portico of the Temple of Dandour
1 Nubia.

As a reflection of the INDUSTRIAL REVOLUTION, Lincoln-
hire workers' housing ranges from the late C18 Lumley's
'errace at Stamford and John Parkinson's crescent at New
Bolingbroke (1824) to the miniature Gothic villa cottages of
Ienry Roberts at Great Gonerby (1848), and to the dreary red-
rick back-to-backs built under the auspices of Richard Horns-
y's ironworks at Grantham. More pleasing, perhaps because
nore rustic, is the ironworkers' terrace at Claxby (L; 1868).
As a postscript to industry, ENGINES. Two good ones are at
palding Pode Hole (1825, *Boulton & Watt* beam engine) and
t Pinchbeck Marsh (1833).

As a result of the Clergy Residences Repair Act (Gilbert's
Act, abbreviated in the text to GA) of 1776, VICARAGES and
ECTORIES are unusually well documented. Most of the
Georgian ones were rebuilt (but cf. the sophisticated Bigby (L),
hortly before 1790, perhaps by *Robinson*), or improved by local
rchitects (*James Fowler* of Louth, *Charles Kirk* of Sleaford) or
ust by local carpenters and builders (*William Barnett*'s box-like
icarage at Heckington). When the benefice or incumbent was
ich enough, London or big provincial architects were called
n for plans (*S. S. Teulon* at Harrington (L), 1854; *Benjamin
Ferrey* at Fleet, 1854; *H. A. Darbyshire* at Navenby, 1859).

Another speciality of Lincolnshire are the numerous ESTATE
VILLAGES, an expression of philanthropy, good estate manage-
ment, or just an unselfconscious growth during the C19. Most
vere probably designed in the estate workshops (Normanby (L),
Aswarby), others keep to a consistent style (Manthorpe near
Belton, 1849–65), while yet others betray the architect's con-
scious composing (Belton, 1828–35; South Stoke, by *Burn*,
1840–5; or Revesby (L), perhaps also by *Burn*, 1850s). Few
villages can equal Denton for continuity of respect for the
genius loci throughout the C19 and up to the present day.

For the TWENTIETH CENTURY Lincolnshire is barren.
Henry Wilson's Pre-Raphaelite, Art Nouveau style was to be
found in the Walmsgate Chapel, now at Langworth (L; 1901).
Both *Sir Arthur Blomfield*'s Denton (1883) and *Sir Reginald*

Blomfield's Caythorpe Court (1899) show a new appreciatic
of local materials and vernacular style. The post-1900 style i
the county is inconclusive. *Brierley*'s wing at Normanby Par
(L; 1906), although Georgian Baroque, has superb quality c
materials as a saving grace, *Stokes*'s Lincoln School (1905) :
sensitively eclectic Dutch-Jacobethan. *Sir Reginald Blomfield*
dixhuitième Gabriel style can be seen at Lincoln Public Librar
(1906) and the Usher Art Gallery (1927). It could not be ex
pected in 1933 that Cranwell College would choose any othe
style than that of between-the-wars Neo-Georgian confidenc
As such it is a failure. And as regards post-war trends, th
situation is still not bright, but getting brighter. SCHOOLS are th
best things. Both Riddings Secondary Modern School at Scun
thorpe (L; 1958, *D. Clarke-Hall, Scorer & Bright*) and the Peel
County Secondary School at Long Sutton (1957, *Architects
Co-partnership* and *L. Barlow*) are admirable; so is the C. o
E. school at Welton-by-Lincoln (L; by *Roy Bright*). *Frederick
Gibberd* is to be found at Scunthorpe (L), and the new Civi
Centre there (Town Hall by *Pearson*) has much to commend it
The most important contribution to the Modern Movement i
Lincoln will unquestionably be *Eldrid Evans* and *Denis Gailey'*
proposed Civic Centre, awarded in competition in 1961. Thi
brilliantly conceived design should give Lincoln some inter
national standing. The site is bounded by the river Witham, N
by Melville Street, E; by Norman Street, S; and by Sincil Stree
w. Sincil Street will be pedestrian – as it ought to be. The Civi
Centre, if it gets built, will provide a focal point for the presen
indeterminate character of lower Lincoln. Whether its quality
of design will be matched by the future development in this are
remains to be seen.

The dearth of C20 architecture is due no doubt to the pre
dominant agricultural interests of the county, reflected by the
muted population increase: 1801, 209, 000; 1861, 412,000; 1901
500,000; 1961, 509,000; for whereas Lincolnshire holds second
place for area in the country, for population it holds the twentieth

For further reading there is little to recommend. There are
half-a-dozen articles in *Country Life* (and more to follow we
hope); Sir Francis Hill's forthcoming history of Georgian Lin
coln will be invaluable. The general background to the county
is found in M. G. Barley's *Lincolnshire and the Fens* (1952),
and for a thorough examination of pre-C18 vernacular, his *The
English Farmhouse and Cottage* (1961) is a necessary reference
work.

LINCOLN

*

THE CATHEDRAL

INTRODUCTION

Apart from Durham, there is no English cathedral so spectacularly placed as Lincoln. The street by which one usually
approaches it is justly called Steep Hill. Another approach is by
the Greestone Steps. The area around Steep Hill is getting
obsolete. Much has already come down. What a responsibility to
rebuild here. It must be done singly and intimately, not compre-
hensively and conspicuously. The hill rises so steeply only from
the s. Once up there, one is on a plateau. The s view from a
distance, e.g. from the railway, is one of singular evenness, the
chancel about as long as the nave, two long horizontals, that of
the nave ridge very slightly higher, and two verticals, the uncommonly slender crossing tower and the two also uncommonly
slender w towers, appearing as one from this vantage point. The
only lines not vertical or horizontal are the diagonals of the spires
of the w turrets and the diagonals of the pinnacles. In the Middle
Ages there were however, in addition, spires on all three towers.

The silhouette is as unforgettable when it is a light grey in th
early morning, or animated by the full mid-day sun, or changin
in colour and seemingly in form when stormy clouds pass over it

The cathedral is essentially of three periods, though two o
them are divided into two phases each: Norman the w front -
Early Norman and High Norman; E.E. the rest, in one campaig
from 1191 to c.1250 and another from 1256 to c.1280; C14 to C1
the towers and some alterations and additions. The cathedral i
482 ft long inside. The crossing tower has a height of 271 ft. Th
chancel vault is 74 ft high, the nave vault 82 ft. The building
stone used is local oolitic limestone.

THE NORMAN CATHEDRAL

A council held at Windsor in 1072 decided that bishops' see
should be in walled towns rather than villages. So Remigius.
first almoner of Fécamp and then bishop of Dorchester, a
town as far away from the former Saxon menace as possible.
moved to Lincoln. There, some time between 1072 and 1075.
he began to build. His cathedral was consecrated in 1092. It
was a cruciform building with an E end of a main apse and
apses to the chancel aisles, flat-ended outside, i.e. the same
arrangement as at Old Sarum in the same years and at Durham
a little later. Its w front remains, though somewhat disguised.
Its forms, however, can easily be disentangled from later ones,
as they have the sturdy directness and the elementary details
typical of the first decades of the Norman style in England.

The centre is a very tall and deep recess, though originally
less tall than it is now. Its round arch must be reconstructed in
one's mind's eye, where the plain Norman masonry is replaced
by the decorated E.E. masonry. The recess steps inward in
slight steps, and they are marked by shafts. To the l. and r. of
this tall recess are two recesses of the same kind, but less tall.
These are fully preserved. The elevation is the same as in the
nave, but still in perfect order. The capitals of the shafts are
of the most primitive volute type. The middle recess represents the nave, the side recesses the aisles. To the l. and r. of the
side recesses are yet much lower niches, again of the same type.
They are continued round what were the corners at the time,
and inside the present building niches of identical form and
detail indeed exist and can be seen. The elevation with these five
stepped, arched recesses is unique – exactly as if it were one
of the most typical Early Norman plans stood on end, that of
the staggered apses (main apse, two apses of the chancel aisles,

two chapel apses reaching out from the transepts – the plan e.g. of Bernay and St Nicholas at Caen, both in Normandy, and Blyth in Nottinghamshire). Tewkesbury has a tall single recess, a motif ultimately derived from Charlemagne's palace chapel at Aachen, but three, let alone five, are a very different matter. What the original portals were like, there is no knowing. Another peculiar feature is the fact that w towers must have been planned from the start and that they are not flush with the front but lie back a little, also from the walls with the N and S niches. It is an odd arrangement to which the only parallels again are in the Empire rather than in Normandy: in buildings such as the collegiate church of St Patroclus at Soest. Inside the building, apart from the two extra niches only one Early Norman feature is visible: windows with roll mouldings looking from the towers into the hall between the towers.

Under Bishop Alexander, nephew of Bishop Roger of Sarum who had much enlarged the late C11 cathedral there, the w front was continued and altered. He ruled the diocese from 1123 to 1148 and was an ambitious and powerful man. Among his buildings the castles of Newark, Banbury, and Sleaford ranked high. He began at the cathedral after a fire of perhaps 1141 and, we are told, vaulted the building – still a rare thing in England in the mid C12. We can see that he replaced the three portals by new, more sumptuous ones. The middle portal is surrounded by an outer frame of large crenellation, up the jambs and round the arch. There follow four shafts on the jambs on each side. They are much renewed, but it is comparatively easy to recognize what is old and what is not. The outer pairs of shafts have geometrical decoration, the inner pairs figured decoration. On the third on the r. are medallions with beasts, affronted beasts, birds, grotesques. On the l., on the other hand, the theme is different: continuous trails instead of medallions and in them, from bottom to top, a naked couple, snakes biting their vitals, then a beautifully composed, dramatic fight between two eagles, then a naked couple like the previous one, and two dressed men. The fourth (inner) pair of shafts has single figures climbing about in trails. One e.g. shoots an arm up against the next. The top figure on both sides is in expressive profile and holds two snakes. The meaning of the figures is not clear, though the naked *versus* the clothed, the biting *versus* the contained snakes indicate a programme. The innermost moulding in jambs and arch has the beakhead motif, i.e. animals biting into a roll moulding. The outer hood-mould ends in large dragons' heads. The side portals have no figures. Their three shafts on each side and their arches are decorated with lozenges, spiral-headed bands, etc., and also again beakhead. The l. and r. sides are not identical. Among the geometrical ornament used is the ubiquitous zigzag, also occurring at r. angles to the wall surface. These latter are all Norman motifs, but when it comes to the shafts of the central doorway, the stylistic sources are quite different. Professor Zarnecki has convincingly pointed to St Denis, and his recent discovery that originally one large figure stood against the flat bare strip outside the outer shafts comfirms this. They must have been 'figures-colonnes', to use Focillon's term, i.e. of the new, Gothic type apparently created at St Denis and then taken over e.g. at Chartres. But the portal at St Denis was only completed in 1140, and so Alexander was quick in adopting it and his master mason in adapting it to Anglo-Norman conventions. However, the stylistic position of the sculpture at Lincoln is much more complex.

Above the low niches and running into the reveals of the side portal recesses is a frieze of sculptured scenes. They are from the Old Testament s of the main doorway, from the New Testament N. The choice is not inconsistent, more consistent in fact than any sequence of scenes in English Norman sculpture up to their date, at least as far as preserved material goes. The scenes on the s side consist of the following: The Expulsion from Paradise, Cain and Abel digging (with a border of foliage above), the Birth of Enoch (again with a foliage border above) and, below it, Lamech killing Cain, then two gaps, then scenes from the Deluge, God speaking to Noah, Noah building the Ark (with hammer and axe), then – evidently not *in situ* – Daniel in the Lions' Den, a scene in a box-frame, i.e. different from all others, and then back to the Deluge, Noah in the Ark, Noah leaving the Ark, and the Covenant, a long piece, and finally, round the corner, i.e. now inside the cathedral, the Deluge itself, badly preserved (and again with a leaf border above).* On the N side starting from the middle first a gap, then Dives and Lazarus, the Death of Lazarus, then a group of six of the Blessed in heaven, then the Harrowing of Hell and, badly restored, the Torments of the Damned.

* Professor Zarnecki convincingly suggests that the Deluge was meant for the gap where now Daniel is, and was found to be too wide and hence shifted.

The motifs and the style of Bishop Alexander's sculptural and decorative work are remarkably mixed. The sculptured scenes arranged in a frieze along a façade are unmistakably North Italian. Modena is the most likely source. Here the sculpture of the w façade dates from some time after 1099, when the façade (the cathedral?) was begun. The short stocky figures also go with Modena. But other figures at Lincoln are quite different, especially the seated apostles. They are long, excessively slim, and wear mantles creased with close, parallel, agitated folds. That seems Burgundian more than anything, of about 1130 (Autun), and had an effect somewhat later at Malmesbury in Wiltshire. Beakhead is an initially West French motif, but by 1145 it had been fully acclimatized in England and in certain parts of the country indeed became very popular. The geometrical ornament used is Anglo-Norman in general, but for the shafts and climbing figures Professor Zarnecki has shown as the closest parallel the w portal of St Denis, and that was only complete in 1140. Moreover, we are told that Abbot Suger of St Denis obtained workmen from many places, and so it is even possible that knowledge of Modena by the one, of Burgundy by the other principal carver had been transmitted through St Denis. Anyway, what is certain is that Bishop Alexander was wholly up-to-date.

Norman also are the frieze of intersected arches above the aisle recesses, the gables exposed to the N and S with more ornate blank arcading and an attractive motif of chains of alternatingly large and small links in the top parts. The towers also were completed, again with blank arcading and again quite ornately. Polygonal angle buttresses with angle shafts.* Inside the cathedral, apart from the niches already mentioned and which were really an external feature, the following can still be examined. Of the sides of the towers facing inward, wide blocked arches, still recognizable with their imposts, must have marked galleries, and above them, no doubt at clerestory height, is a single window on either side, with a continuous roll moulding and shafts with scallop capitals. Also inside the towers are curious small chambers, lit and unlit, especially one on the ground floor, very tall, very narrow, and tunnel-vaulted.

THE WORK OF ST HUGH AND HIS SUCCESSORS TO c.1250

St Hugh of Avalon was born at Avalon, not the one in Burgundy but near Grenoble. He became treasurer of the Grande

* The two statues of bishops in niches on the buttresses to the l. and r. of the main portal seem to be an early C13 addition.

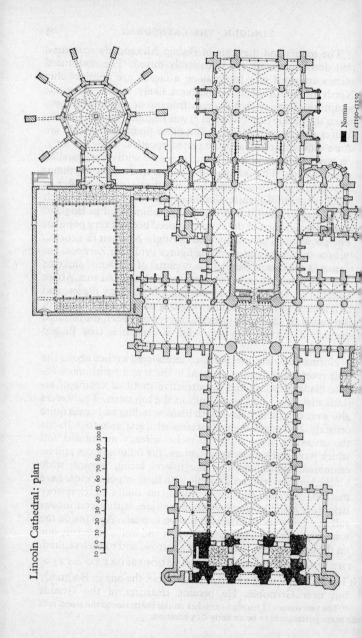

Lincoln Cathedral: plan

10 5 0 10 20 30 40 50 60 70 80 90 100 ft

■ Norman
▨ c1190–c1250

Chartreuse, then *c.*1180 prior to the Carthusian house of Witham in Somerset, and in 1186 bishop of Lincoln. In 1185 a catastrophe befell the Norman cathedral. 'Scissa est', says Roger of Hovenden, 'from top to bottom.' In 1192 St Hugh began the rebuilding. The 'constructor' he commissioned is known to us by name, *Geoffrey de Noiers*, who began the new cathedral 'a fundamentis'. The name sounds French; whether a French architect is probable will be discussed later.

The cathedral has two pairs of transepts, on the pattern of the rebuilding of the E part of Canterbury in 1175–84. When in the Middle Ages churches were built, the start was usually at the E end, for understandable reasons. But of St Hugh's E end, that is the parts E of the eastern transepts, we know only from excavations. His plan, Geoffrey's plan, was the strangest hybrid. It was, one might say, one extremely long polygonal apse, with an ambulatory, i.e. to put it another way, the chancel aisles tapered or converged, and the E wall of the high choir seems only to have been about half the width of the E crossing. Along the curious ambulatory thus formed there were seven radiating chapels, on the pattern which was one of the most usual in Romanesque France and England and in Gothic France: only owing to the odd shape of the high choir, the chapels were also arranged oddly. The E chapel was of three (or five?) sides of a hexagon, the side chapels one pair horseshoe-shaped, the next stilted semicircles, and the pair furthest W much smaller and of unknown shape. The English were great at inventing complicated variations on the simple theme of French radiating chapels. It must have been the strangest experience to wander through these unexpected spaces. But Geoffrey, as we shall see, throve on strangeness and the unexpected. The E end which has replaced St Hugh's is the Angel Choir, and this will be described in due course.*

What remains of St Hugh's work – whether all done before he died in 1200 or whether continued after his death, but still by Geoffrey to his original plan, is irrelevant – is the E transepts.‡ That work must now be examined, and first the interior.

---

* St Hugh's E end is outlined in the floor of the Angel Choir and Remigius's apse in St Hugh's choir.

‡ St Hugh wished to be buried by the altar of St John the Baptist and hurried Geoffrey to complete it. He was duly buried there 'a boreale ipsius aedis regione'. There has been much controversy as to whether this means the N chapel of the NE transept or simply the N part of the building, i.e. presumably the most desirable burial place, just N of the high altar. In favour of the former opinion is the fact that the N chapel was considerably lengthened a

ST HUGH'S INTERIOR. We have to start with one minut
survival of the E end proper. Behind a wooden door on the
side in the angle between the E chapels of the SE transept and
the Perp Longland Chapel added to the Angel Choir is
corbel with elementary stiff-leaf in one row and the springing of a wall arch and another arch. These must once have
been inside the southwesternmost of St Hugh's ambulatory
chapels.

For the rest of St Hugh's work, the start is the EAST TRAN-
SEPTS. The E crossing piers belong to the Angel Choir and do
not concern us yet. The E walls have three more bays, the
first being chancel aisles, the others corresponding to the E
chapels behind. The responds are at once of imaginative and
delightful shapes. The first pair has a semi-octagonal core with
five detached shafts alternatingly of Lincoln stone and Purbeck
marble. The capitals have stiff-leaf, with two tiers of bold individual crockets. Even the shaft-rings have here a little leaf
decoration. The second and third responds are half-cruciform
with curved re-entrant angles and again five alternatingly detached limestone and Purbeck shafts. The passion for Purbeck
shafting and for detached shafts, Geoffrey had caught at
Canterbury. But he played on this theme with much greater
resourcefulness than William of Sens, as we shall see presently.
Inside, the chapels have blank arcading with round shafts, polygonal shafts, and polygonal shafts with concave sides, again a
sign of Geoffrey's sense of play. Lively stiff-leaf capitals, deeply
moulded arches, using fillets here and there. Also stiff-leaf
hood-mould stops. The chapels are vaulted, and it is typical of
Geoffrey that he uses irregular vaulting patterns of five or
six or even seven ribs. Much very small dog-tooth in the ribs.
Stiff-leaf bosses. That the windows were shafted and the
vaults rest on wall-shafts is a matter of course and need not be
repeated. In the outer N chapel three especially fine corbel
heads: a lady wearing a wimple, a man with an open mouth, a
bearded man. From this chapel a doorway with deeply
moulded arch leads to the N. In the S transept S chapel a double

short time after and one might assume that this was done after St Hugh's
canonization in 1220. On the other hand the lengthened chapel was known,
at least in the C17, as the Lady Chapel – and that would correspond to the
form and position of the Ely Lady Chapel. However, the whole question is
not of any importance to us. The E end is gone and the chapel in question
is gone. The only importance which the choice of the transept chapel would
have is to prove that by 1200 this was already complete. But this one would
assume anyway.

piscina and opposite it a double aumbry. This has a Purbeck-marble dividing post with a vertical semicircular projection to push the two bolts into. Above the chapels a gallery, again as at Canterbury, a clerestory, and sexpartite vaults (with small dog-tooth enrichment), except for the outer bays, which differ on the two sides and from the rest and must a little later be examined in detail. The gallery has two twin openings for each bay, much shafted. The sub-arches are low with a little dog-tooth set under higher blank arches. In the tympana of the inner bays trefoils and quatrefoils pierced – a beginning of plate tracery. In the s transept the inner bay has blank trefoils, the outer plain pierced circles. In the N transept first a pierced quatrefoil and a pierced trefoil, then also circles. Single clere-story lancets with narrow wall-passage. At the foot of this passage an extremely odd and never yet explained motif appears: triangular, completely plain openings, evidently not meant to be noticed. The motif carries on right through St Hugh's choir. The vaulting-shafts rise from the ground as part of the composite piers. The shafts for the intermediate ribs start in the gallery spandrels. They are on corbels in their turn supported by busts. The galleries are crossed by heavy pointed arches to help to buttress the high vault. This motif was continued throughout the cathedral.

Now the s transept s wall, or at least its lower parts. Here for the first time an eminently important motif comes in, Geoffrey's most delightful invention: blank arcading in two tiers set in a syncopated rhythm, i.e. pointed blank arcading with detached limestone shafts close to the wall, and another tier of arcading with Purbeck shafts and pointed trefoiled arches set so that the shafts are in front of the apexes behind, and the apexes in front of the shafts. No-one had quite done such a thing before, unless the turrets of the Norman w front of Ely qualify, where shafts run up in front of the arches of blind arcading. The ancestry of the motif is thus English, not French,★ and Geoffrey gloried in it. The system is applied to this particular wall with the most baffling little irregularities. The back arcading ends on the E with a half arch, the front arcading on the w with an embarrassed steep untrefoiled arch. Above the arcading two shafted lancets. The sill tallies with that of the gallery, the capitals tally with nothing.

Here we must abandon the s wall, and first turn to the w walls of both s and N transepts. In the s transept the outer bay

★ But it was imitated in France at Mont St Michel.

has the confusion of the access to the Song School (*see* p. 12 below). Then wall piers with polygonal cores and alternatin Lincoln and Purbeck shafts. The inner bay has as its N pie i.e. the pier where transept and chancel aisle meet, the mo enterprising and surprising of all Geoffrey's piers – octagona core, eight shafts around, alternating Purbeck and Lincoln, th latter concave-sided, but behind the E and N sides, or in the transept the E and S sides, the core sprouts out in monstrousl big crockets forming a vertical row, as was done later up th edges of spires. The closest parallel to this is the crockete cross for the Crucifixus in the Psalter of Robert of Lindseye who was abbot of Peterborough from 1214 to 1222, and this i probably just a little later than the Lincoln piers. Similar to is, however, a Tree of Life in the St Albans Psalter o *c.*1120–40, and so a tradition in illumination existed.

The W chapels, in the N transept the TREASURY, have Geoffrey's syncopated arcading, again with the painful corners The muddle is worse in the S chapel. Six-ribbed vault or shafts which stand in front of the two-tier blank arcading Richly shafted upper blank arcading. What is new now in the syncopated arcading is that busts of angels (and a demo peeping out of stiff-leaf) appear to enrich the spandrels. The NW chapel* underwent a change of purpose before it became the treasury. At some stage, probably in the C18, it was horizontally divided. A floor was put in and, to light what was now the ground floor, oblong windows were put in too. What the upper floor was used for is unknown. Strange openings, oblong and triangular, like *arcosolia* were made for it. On the recent conversion of the N chapel into a Treasury for the display of plate, *see* p. 116. It was done by *Louis Osman* in 1959–60. The gallery on the W side is of course no real gallery but a wall passage, but its front is treated exactly as on the E side, except that a slightly later date – as one would expect, if building went on from E to W – is indicated by the greater variety of pierced motifs in the tympana. They now include diagonally placed quatrefoils.

The N wall of the N transept was treated completely differently and has no exact counterpart anywhere else. Here the whole outer bay was vaulted at ground-floor level. The vault has six

---

* The arches of this chapel to E and S are incidentally braced by wooden beams. This makeshift arrangement existed in other parts of St Hugh's work as well, as the holes show. Even at Westminster Abbey such strengthening was used.

ribs, as Geoffrey liked it; for they do not make a sexpartite vault. Above, a wide first-floor room was gained, for what purpose we do not know. It is the oddest room, extremely high now and decidedly behind the scenes; for from here one looks to the N at the back of the N front, to the S at the back of what one first assumed, standing in the transept, to be the N front. The latter has a gallery front just like the E side, and above two single clerestory lancets with wall passage. But the real N front has nothing representing the gallery, just two tiers of tall lancets. There are plenty of put-holes, but whether a ceiling was put in at once, we cannot say: the small doorway at clerestory level makes one assume it, though it may have led to a wooden balcony. Aesthetically speaking, to make one see the real N front through this stone screen is Geoffrey's boldest experiment in vistas, but not his most successful. Or can there have been a functional reason? Venables thought a tower might have been intended. That is not convincing.

The N wall ground floor, that is under the vault, has Geoffrey's syncopated arcading, stopped however by a somewhat later doorway to the cloister and chapter house. The doorway has a segmental arch on short vertical pieces above the capitals, a motif of the second third rather than the first third of the century (cf. Westminster Abbey).

In the S transept the outer bay also must be taken separately; for on closer investigation this tells a strange story. The wall-arches in the S and W walls prove that here too a vault was planned, and the roughness just S of the SE pier that something of the sort indeed existed, and a screen wall was started above. Then however the plan was abandoned, or perhaps what had been built fell down. In any case the S bay in its upper parts was remodelled or perhaps finally completed. This, it may be anticipated – for reasons of certain motifs – must have been done in the 1230s or a little later. What ought to be noted is this. The gallery bays to E and W have taller-looking arcading, four even arches for Geoffrey's twins. No Purbeck marble is used, but quite excessive amounts of dog-tooth. The stiff-leaf capitals are much more disturbed. The change in the style of the capitals is most patent in the main vaulting-shafts. Here the diagonal ribs of the bay S of the outer one are Hugh's, the capitals of the broad transverse arches those of the later mason completing the bay. The S wall at this level is treated similarly. Above the clerestory

windows decoration with lattice work. The vault is quadripartite with a longitudinal (i.e. N–S) ridge-rib.

To the W of the E crossing ST HUGH'S CHOIR proper continues towards the main crossing. There are three bays, and they
would show Geoffrey's style at its purest, if it were not for
the interference of the choir stalls (see p. 116). They made it
necessary to cut off the projections of Geoffrey's beautiful
piers towards the choir 'nave'. A second even more fatal
interference was caused by the fall of Hugh's main crossing
tower in 1237 or 1239 (see below). Strengthening was undertaken regardless of the aesthetic claims of Geoffrey's design.
The strengthening is recognizable by the use of stubby
Lincolnshire piers, mostly with fillets and an absence of the
brittle Purbeck. So the E crossing NW pier already is not as
Geoffrey had made it. The capital is flatter, more spread out
than Geoffrey's. The SW pier on the other hand is Geoffrey's,
except that the Purbeck shafts flanking the diagonal Lincoln
shafts have been broken out. Their capitals however are there.
They are of Purbeck marble, and this Geoffrey carried on
for the capitals of all the vaulting-shafts in his choir. On the
piers stand the vaulting-shafts with capitals on the S side
Purbeck, on the N side Lincoln stone. Because of the stalls
the vaulting-shafts of the other piers of the choir cannot
stand immediately above the arcade piers. They were instead placed on simple cone-shaped brackets. The arcade
piers which follow are Geoffrey's most elegant: square
cores with chamfered angles and concave main sides, and in
the concavities Purbeck shafts. The capitals are of Lincoln
stone, twice the height for the core as for the shafts. If the
piers now seem to differ from this perfect scheme, this is
due to the haphazard under-propping and the Lincoln stone
thickenings.*

10b   The aisles have syncopated arcading along their outer walls.
The spandrel angels (also a prophet) are continued which had
been missing at the beginning. The stiff-leaf capitals on this
small scale are more abundant. The back arches now start
using dog-tooth and were going to go on with that. The
vaults are quadripartite with an extra fifth rib to the centre of
the outer wall of the bay. The ribs have the small dog-tooth
we have already found in the transepts.

* In the W arch of the N arcade the botching is most patent. An ornamental
ring across the mouldings had to be carved to hide the fact that the voussoirs
would not quite have fitted.

Now the upper regions of the choir. The cut-off vaulting-shafts include Geoffrey's favourite concave-sided octagon section. The gallery remains unchanged, except that yet more forms come in in the tympana. Foils with leaf cusps e.g. appear. The clerestory has a new pattern, a group of three stepped lancets, and to its l. and r. absurdly small arches on absurdly short shafts. Above them, in the spandrels (except for the NE bay) assorted pierced foiled shapes, also upside down. The W bay shows the trouble after the fall of the tower as clearly in the gallery and higher up as on the arcade level below. The separating pier between the two twins is a shapeless bundle of Lincoln stone shafts, a pound of candles, as Venables nicely called it. In the tympana a very small quatrefoil with fleur-de-lis cusps. Between the jamb shafts big dog-tooth. Big dog-tooth also in the clerestory.

And then the VAULT, the vault which Paul Frankl so happily 10a called the Crazy Vault of Lincoln. It is of European importance in that it is the first rib-vault with tiercerons, i.e. the first rib-vault with purely decorative intentions. It is true that subsidiary ribs are also a structural help in that they strengthen the skeleton and in that they reduce the size of cells. But the way it is done here is such that decorative enrichment clearly came first in its inventor's strange mind. To understand the vault one ought to start with an image in one's mind of a normal quadripartite vault. Geoffrey then added a momentous innovation for the English future, a longitudinal ridge-rib. He then proceeded to open and shut one diagonal rib scissor-wise so that it becomes tiercerons and touches the ridge at two points other than the centre. Finally he diverts the other diagonal rib accordingly so that one arm touches the one point of the scissor-tiercerons at its apex, the other the other. The result, as this arrangement is done in the same way throughout, is overwhelmingly lopsided. The vault starts over the E crossing and goes to one bay E of the main crossing. The last bay has a normal sexpartite vault. But the most significant result of the crazy vault is that it invalidates the bay division which to French architecture had been and was going to be for nearly two centuries the basic fact of Gothic composition. The ridge-rib runs all bays into one and stresses continuity. But the tiercerons do more. Geoffrey has no distinction in gauge between his transverse arches and his ribs; so one does not read his vault as bay after bay, but as a bunch of four ribs emanating from one springer and the bunch spreading

palm-frond-wise – not in a way that opposite springers produ
fronds in mirror-image. Instead there is once again the m
convinced syncopation.

Now the MAIN CROSSING. The piers have three Purbe
shafts to the crossing, two to the outside. The capitals ha
stiff-leaf in two rows. But above the capitals the style, i.e. t
plan, changes, and we must stop. If we now turn to the MA
TRANSEPTS we see the same. The E walls of the E aisle sta
to Geoffrey's plan. The front of the three chapels into whic
later low partition walls divide the aisle has syncopated arcac
ing and the five-rib vault of the chancel aisles. But the two
ribs in the S transept, N ribs in the N transept, suddenly cea
using the little dog-tooth enrichment, and in the second chap
of the S transept the syncopated arcading is replaced by norm
arcading. This return to normality marks the break. In the
transept it is even more abrupt. Here the syncopation stop
midway down the second chapel. The last stage of Geoffrey'
work otherwise differs only in small details, though one c
them is significant enough. Geoffrey now decided to replac
his tympana angels by arched holes without figures; for to pee
through them at the apexes of the back arcading was a greate
thrill. In the N transept he altered even more. For the sake c
variety he let the back arcading be trefoiled and the fror
pointed. But the tympanum holes are here not pierced.

So here, where Geoffrey was replaced, we must stop for
few minutes and try to sum up in our minds what manner c
man he was. His initial stimulus had come from Canterbury
that is certain. The detached shafts which he loved so muc
occurred there. But did William of Sens bring them fro
France or adopt them from England? It is not certain; Pro
fessor Bony has not been able to offer a firm answer. They d
occur in the crypt at York and at Iffley just before Canterbur
and in purely English contexts, but they also appear in Par
and Soissons at least in the eighties. However that may b
Geoffrey was the most inventive user of this motif. He loved
because it made for transparency, for letting you see one thin
behind the other, and that is what his syncopated arcading als
does. Syncopation was his other passion. It is the mainsprin
of the design of the crazy vault. Was Geoffrey then a French
man or an Englishman? Here again we shall never be able t
say for certain. But the fact that matters is that the decorativ
vault which he had started became the chief English contribu
tion to C13 and early C14 development. It became a field i

which England kept far in advance of any other country. The same is true of the unexpected vista across a grille. So ought one not to attribute motifs in the event so English to an English designer?

We had left the interior of crossing and main transept in mid execution, and we cannot yet return to them, because we must now first look at St Hugh's exterior architecture.

ST HUGH'S EXTERIOR. Much less need be said here. Again we must take the E transept first, St Hugh's choir second, the transition to the main transept last. The E transept brings in at once Geoffrey's most characteristic and unexpected feature, main buttresses with a section of the front of a strong keeled shaft in the middle, two deep hollows l. and r., and then a chamfered corner in front of which stands another strong shaft, fully detached. Dragons, not always preserved, curl about the top of the base mouldings. The intermediate buttresses are just chamfered. In the N transept front the middle buttress runs right to the third tier of lancet windows. The rhythm of fenestration is $1+1$, then blank–1–blank, then the gable with five steeply stepped lancets, the outer ones blank. In the S transept front the buttress goes up only into the first upper stage, but that is due to the alterations higher up of which we already know, and which express themselves externally by the prominent use of dog-tooth. The pinnacles of the fronts differ. They differ throughout the building. Basically, however, the type remained that stated e.g. in the NE transept, i.e. polygonal, plain, and crowned by a spire, with roll mouldings up the edges of the spire. The pinnacles at the corners of the SE transept add shafts up the octagon corners and eight gables. Also little angels stand on the tops. However, these are of course the pinnacles of the 1230s or 1240s. The E sides of the transepts have the chapels attached. They state the elevational system of most of the rest. Shafted lancet windows with stiff-leaf capitals. Gallery with pairs of small lancets with a shaft between. Shafted lancets in the clerestory. The chapels differ in shape, the most curious being the NE chapel. Can this be original? The elevational forms are perfectly convincing, but the obtusely pointed E wall looks dubious. The chapel is indeed the one which was lengthened fairly shortly after St Hugh's death. This lengthening is still visible in the grass. Then *Essex* in 1772 rebuilt, it is said on the old foundations, and one must assume with the old materials. So the question remains: were they the old foundations?

Essex, considering the time when he worked, was a careful archaeologist. The roof-line of the lengthened chapel can still be recognized. The clerestory had to be altered to accommodate it. The w walls, and indeed the walls of St Hugh's choir follow the same system. In the s transept at the sw corner the system is disturbed by the addition of what is now the Song School (see p. 126). In the N transept it is disturbed by mighty staircase projection N of the w chapel. The clerestory alone has a new motif: a triple group of arches with windows in the outer arches. Flying buttresses, the earliest ones at Lincoln and altogether before 1200 still a motif novel anywhere even in France. The earliest examples there appear to belong to the 1170s, and so do those of William of Sens at Canterbury. In St Hugh's choir the clerestory has a different grouping. Each bay has five arches, four narrow, one wider. The middle three have the windows. The flying buttresses run up to this composition and cut into it. On the pinnacles of the two buttresses in the corner of the SE transept and the s aisle of St Hugh's choir two demi-figures of angels.

The same at the corner of the N aisle and the N main transept i.e. a corner still, we assumed, built under Geoffrey. Indeed the joint between him and his successor which we could demonstrate inside the E aisle appears outside just as clearly. Geoffrey's broad buttresses with the detached angle shafts disappear and are replaced by plain, normal chamfered buttresses, bigger of course still than the intermediate ones. Also the pinnacles all go plain. In the s transept just one has a demon perching on it.

THE SECOND AND THIRD MASTERS. And now back into the INTERIOR of the building and to the second and third masters. We may even know their names; for about 1230 a *Michael* is called *magister operis*, and about 1235 an *Alexander*. The second master continued the main transepts where Geoffrey had left them, the third master rebuilt the crossing tower after it had fallen in 1237 or 1239. The earlier date is recorded in the Chronicle of Peterborough, the later by Matthew Paris and in the Annals of Dunstable. Although chronologically wrong, we take this work first. The CROSSING TOWER starts at once using his typical motif, the typical motif of the 1240s at Lincoln: diagonal lattice decoration of flat surfaces. He uses it inside as well as outside the tower. Inside, in the corners a thin triple Purbeck shaft runs up to support what vaulting was projected. Tall wall arcading in two tiers with wall passages, grouped into threes below, fours above. Still limestone and Purbeck marble, still stiff-leaf capitals. The vault, as we see it now, is C14 work; it will be discussed on p. 111. Outside, the second stage has crockets up the jambs of the arcading between the shafts, a development from St Hugh's crocket piers, and one soon to be taken up in the Angel Choir (p. 106). The lattice in the spandrels has quatrefoils set in. Then the C14 work starts also externally.

In the MAIN TRANSEPTS the second master replaced, as we have seen, the syncopated by plain blank arcading. Otherwise he did not change much. The low partition walls in the aisle could be his design in the s transept. They have blank arcading here with a pendant capital between two arches. In the N transept, where they are roofed like shrines and have Purbeck shafts, they cut across Geoffrey's and the second master's blank arcading. Also they have the big dog-tooth we have so far only found in the completion of the outer bay of the SE transept, that is to say, work to be attributed to the third master. The second master's main piers of the aisle are inspired by Geoffrey's but lack appreciation of his detached shafts. The gallery does not change in essentials. Yet another new motif comes into the tympana: an elongated quatrefoil. In the inner bays the fall of the tower must have caused damage, and repair work is as clearly discernible as in St Hugh's choir. In the innermost single (not twin) arch of the N transept big dog-tooth, as in the repaired bay of St Hugh's choir. Nothing new in the clerestory. Vaults sexpartite, i.e. no craziness. The ribs with small dog-tooth. The intermediate ribs on shafts starting at the sill height of the gallery.

The N and s walls differ. The N wall has a big doorway to the N, leading towards the former Deanery, the s wall a small doorway to a spiral stair. Above on the N follows the glorious composition of the DEAN'S EYE, i.e. a row of seven even lancets, not too high, with five of them pierced as windows, and then a rose of plate tracery. Its date can at least approximately be determined. The *Metrical Life of St Hugh*, written shortly after his canonization in 1220, mentions a s and a N window which he calls *orbiculare*. The pattern of the Dean's Eye is like this. A large quatrefoil in the middle, and its centre a concave-sided lozenge with a quatrefoil. In the outer spandrels a trefoil and two small circles and around the whole a band of sixteen circles. It is an original composition, just a little wilful perhaps, as are the contemporary rose windows of the W front of Laon, the N transept of Chartres, and the transept of Lausanne Cathedrals, but not in the least imitate from any of them or, it seems, any other. The vault springs so low that from a distance it cuts into the rose. On the side is the Bishop's Eye instead, a C14 replacement to which we shall turn in due course (p. 111). The W walls also differ for here, in the S transept, is the doorway to the galilee. (On the galilee *see* p. 127). Otherwise the system is the same. Each sexpartite bay has two plus two steeply pointed blank arches at ground level, then two lancets, then a wall passage of two plus two with dog-tooth, and then two clerestory windows.

Again the EXTERIOR of this part does not need much examination. The N transept front cannot be seen clearly, as it is interfered with by the cloister. It has in the middle a porch with a gable which has some dog-tooth and is flanked by square pinnacles. The porch has a sexpartite vault, but all the details – shafts, vault, portal proper – are Victorian. Only the trumeau is old. In the tympanum an odd and scarcely believable triple blank arching. The date, if one can trust any of all this, must be that of the galilee, on which *see* p. 127, and which was an afterthought, as one can see inside on the upper floor (*see* also p. 127). On the N side follows the row of lancets, and then the Dean's Eye. Of these we have reported. Externally the rose window is surrounded by a kind of stiff-leaf fleurons and dog-tooth. Dog-tooth also in the gable. Three pinnacles, polygonal and shafted. On the S side the buttressing, especially towards the galilee, is more elaborate, and the Bishop's Eye fills a larger area. Of the C14 also the window in the gable, and the bold frill of the gable. Differing C13 pinnacles. That towards the galilee is the most highly decorated up to that date. It has crockets all up its spire. The W sides of the transepts offer nothing essentially new. The buttresses change from the chamfering Lincoln was accustomed to to a square shafted design similar to the S buttresses. The flying buttresses on the E side reach the clerestory in the same place as in St Hugh's choir. The top in the S transept is a C14 frieze of an undulating line cusped. The pinnacles of alternating size are of the C14 too. They are the same in the N transept.

12b THE NAVE. There is no known date for the nave. The date usually given is 1233 for its roofing, and one assumes rightly that roofing means completed walls but not-yet-started vault. However, all that documents tell us is this. Bishop Hugh of Wells made his will in 1233, leaving 100 marks to the fabric and all the felled timber that would be found on his estates at the time of his death. This special mention of much timber, it is argued, implies the need for much timber, and that points to a roofing job. But it can just as well point to the scaffolding and center-ing needed for a vaulting job. The nave is seven bays long plus the odd bay between the towers. The system is not drastically changed, and the second master may have expressed himself like this, where he had more freedom. The piers are still of Lincoln stone and Purbeck marble in various mixtures. And there is still a gallery and a clerestory with wall passage. First the arcades. The arches have no dog-tooth. The piers all have stiff-leaf capitals of Lincoln stone. The arches are wider than St Hugh's and make the piers seem slimmer. The second pair is Purbeck throughout. It has a square core set diagonally and hollow chamfers with shafts in the main directions. The third pier on the N side is octagonal with four Lincoln and four Purbeck shafts, all with fillets. The S pier is quite different. It has short straight projections in the main directions and three hollow chamfers in the diagonals. A total of eight Purbeck shafts and eight very thin Lincoln shafts. The second master certainly did not suffer from any shortage of invention either. The fourth pair is like the second, the fifth like the third S pier, the sixth like the first.

The aisles have pointed-trefoiled arcading. A change in plan is very noticeable here, especially on the N side, where first twin arcading units still continue in the transept way, and then the new design starts. The arches now – we are still on the N side – stand on detached triple Purbeck shafts. Each bay has two lancet windows.* The vault continues the five-rib pattern of Geoffrey but adds a longitudinal ridge-rib and one pair of tiercerons in the longitudinal direction. The vaulting-shafts cross in the best Geoffrey tradition in front of the apex of a wall-arcading unit. The intermediate shafts stand on moulded capitals as corbels. In the S aisle many details are more elaborate than in the N aisle, though the vaulting-shafts do not cross. They divide the wall arcading into groups. The intermediate shafts stand on stiff-leaf, not on moulded, corbels. In the vault the ridge-ribs are interrupted from the tiercerons of one bay to those of the next. Bosses are not only of foliage. Four are figured: three heads, Christ blessing with three heads grouped around, in both cases probably an allusion to the Trinity, a head tortured by beasts, the lamb. Also the

* The first wall-shaft differs from the others by having much dog-tooth.

wall-arcading of the new type does not start after two unit
of the old, but after some blank wall. But all that is minor.

The gallery is richer than that of the transepts. There ar
not two twins but two triplets per bay. In the sub-tympan
are not one quatrefoil or trefoil but three, all cusped. Th
only exception is the first half-bay from the E, N as well as s
and that may be due to the repairs of *c.*1240; for it stands t
reason that the nave must at least have been carried up to th
top for one bay to help support the earlier crossing tower. Th
two W bays are shorter than the others, and here the ol
system of one, not three, motifs in the tympana recurs. The
calculation of units between crossing and Norman towers mus
have gone a little wrong. The shafting is mostly Purbeck
Stiff-leaf capitals. The clerestory wall passage is of thre
arches of even height. The vaulting-shafts start on fine stiff-
leaf corbels of moderate size.

The vault shows this master more conspicuously than anywhere else as the defender of normality. He adopted his predecessor's inventions, both ridge-ribs and tiercerons, but he
made a reasonable, easily-repeating pattern out of them. The
pattern is that which we call the tierceron star. Longitudina
ridge-rib, transverse ridge-rib not of full length, one pair of
tiercerons in each cell leading up to the ridge-rib. It still
reads palm-frond-wise and not bay-wise, indeed even more so
than Geoffrey's, and for that very reason it made an epoch.
It was at once taken over in the retrochoir at Ely, begun in
1234, i.e. perhaps even before the vault of the Lincoln nave
was actually executed.*

Externally the nave brings little that is worth noting. The
elevation after the transept appears two-storeyed. The gallery,
instead of windows, has the smallest of slits. Alternating
buttresses, plain pinnacles, flying buttresses. In the aisles each
bay has one lancet window and one blank arch squeezed
between it and the intermediate buttress. Why? Shafts and
moulded capitals. The clerestory has a rhythm of three arches
with windows and then three narrow blank ones. The flying
buttress runs safely into the middle one of them, not as hap-
hazardly as in St Hugh's choir and, considering their width,
more satisfactorily than in the transepts. Above this on the
s side only a Perp quatrefoiled frieze and highly decorated

---

* The choir at Worcester was started in 1224 and has quadripartite rib-
vaults like Salisbury at the same time, but a longitudinal ridge-rib which may
be derived from St Hugh's choir.

anopied tabernacles for statuary. They alternate in their details. All have little monsters at their foot.

Towards the w end the aisle is covered by the w chapels. Their external architecture does not call for comment, but their existence does, and this cannot be made without first turning to the façade. The only thing about the external architecture that may be worth saying is that the E gable of the s w chapel has lancets with Y-tracery, a motif we have not so far met. There are small figures in the spandrels, a devil (?) and a pilgrim and a beggar.

EST FRONT. The w front was widened into a screen and 14 hereby deprived of the logic of its Norman predecessor, which expressed at least more or less the nave and aisles behind. The English, ever since the Anglo-Norman style had established itself, had had a *faible* for screen façades. St Paul's had one e.g., and the thickness of the outer walls of the Norman w front of Lincoln was excessive too. But the architect who designed the C13 front went the whole hog. He may have been the third master from the start, although it is certain only that the third master was busy on it higher up. Anyway, whoever he was, he spread his façade to the limits, and by decorating it with tier upon tier of blank arcading emphasized the horizontality of the screen yet more. Nor did he care for the discrepancy between his work and the Norman work which he left up. The result is curious rather than beautiful, and such an anticlimax after the nave that that alone may incline one to suppose a change in the lodge from the beginning. A functional justification of the lengthening of the façade, however, was attempted by placing behind it the spacious N W and s W chapels to which we have just referred. The idea may have come to the designer from the longest of all Norman w fronts, that of Bury St Edmunds, which also had such w chapels N and s of the aisles. Even Ely is similar to a certain extent, as it is in the angle turrets. At Lincoln on these turrets – which have spires higher than the middle gable, and thus quite convincingly call a halt to the horizontal spread of the screen – two statuettes are displayed, St Hugh and the Swineherd of Stow, who gave within his means gloriously generously to the fabric fund. The screen on the ground floor has small doorways into the w extensions of the chapels. Above them blank arcading and a small circular window, also flanked by blank lancets. Above the Norman front more blank arcading, exceedingly tall and with gabled

canopies for images. Flat top with a C14 cusped-trian
frieze, except for the nave gable, which has stepped arcadi
Two windows to light the roof, two outer statues, in style w
their stiff, short curves very much like some of those on t
façade screen of Wells which was begun, it can be assume
about 1230–5. But the most interesting thing is what t
architect did with the central Norman recess. The round ar
it had came much too low for him. So he removed it, heighten
the jambs, and put up a new pointed arch at a new level.
this heightening at once his *leitmotif* occurs, the lattice-wor
Shallow sexpartite vault. Cinquefoiled circular window
encrusted with foliage. Small trefoils and quatrefoils open
out of the lattice. As for the dating of this stage, the lattice
equally prominent inside the crossing tower. This was
doubt rebuilt immediately after the catastrophe, say *c*.124
That makes sense for the upper part of the façade – especia
if the roofing or, better still, the vaulting of the nave went
in 1233. So the motif may have come in already about th
time and characterized Lincoln about 1235–45. For the lar
Perp w window *see* p. 112. In the spandrels of the big ar
two more statues, a king and a queen, of the same style a
date as those in the gable.

Behind this façade lie the w chapels and the complicat
and not very satisfactory bay between the towers. T
WEST CHAPELS are both of beautiful, erect yet reposef
proportions. They differ in one essential detail. The N or Mor
ing Chapel has a slim central pier of Purbeck marble wi
eight keeled attached shafts and a Purbeck capital. The chap
thus is of four bays. They have quadripartite vaults with stif
leaf bosses and plain ribs. The pier between N aisle and chap
is also all Purbeck. The screen wall which continues the ais
arcading has arches of a new kind towards the nave. They a
pointed-cinquefoiled. Along the E and N walls blank arcadi
with moulded capitals. Double piscina in the E wall. T
chapel extends to the w only one bay wide, but two bays lor
to the w façade. It is here that one can study the Early Norma
N niche. The w doorway has a depressed two-centred arc
on short vertical pieces – a Westminster Abbey motif, thoug
here no doubt earlier than 1245. Hood-mould with dog-tooth
The round window above is framed inside by shafting wit
stiff-leaf crockets. The tall, oddly shaped double-chamfere
arch must be a remodelling.

The s chapel or Consistory Court is superficially the sam

but it has no central pier – a bold decision to take, a challenge one is inclined to think which the architect made and answered. The vault is thus all one bay, a bay the size of the nave bays. The architect moreover, for the devilry of it, made his vault on paper the same as that of the N chapel – i.e. four quadripartite parts. But now they have to rise to an apex, and thus do not look regular in reality. So perhaps structurally one ought to define the vault as one of four diagonals and two ridge-ribs and four additional diagonals connecting the middles of the sides. Stiff-leaf bosses. Blank arcading as before. Screen wall to the aisle as before. The pier in the middle of that side all Purbeck as before. The other capitals of Lincoln stone and with stiff-leaf, not moulded as in the NW chapel. The W extension here was not open. It is separated by a screen wall with blank arcading like the rest. Only the bay to the W which stands against the tower, i.e. does not belong to the widening which the W chapels meant, is quite different. It has stiff-leaf capitals, one with a fine little head, steep arches, and in the spandrels deeply moulded blank lozenges. It looks as if this was a start of a more lavish system not continued when the provision of the wider chapels was decided on. In the W extension the ribs are not as simple as in the NW chapel. The doorway to the W is the same, but the inner framing of the circular window has a segmental arch instead of the later arch in the NW chapel.

The space under and between the towers is awkward in its details. Between the towers is a full bay but one narrower than that of the nave, as Geoffrey from the beginning did not want his dimensions to be dictated by the Norman ones; but the vault repeats those of the nave. The ground stage is panelled and has side doorways clearly in the style of the early C18. The work was indeed done by *James Gibbs* about 1730. Above to the N and S are blocked C13 arches. To its E a piece of seemingly Perp architecture, but by *James Essex* and of 1761. It is a strainer arch forming a bridge. Something of the kind seems to have been there already in the C13; see the tall blank arches l. and r. of the bridge. The arch hides the rise of C13 shafts. In the side walls the blocked Gothic arches cut into Norman relieving arches and yet higher up the Norman windows already referred to. The broad arch between nave and tower hall is C13 but confused in its details. The W wall, i.e. the back of the façade, again has some of the lattice decoration so prominent outside.

The rooms under the tower have stone panelling and doo ways of *James Gibbs*, but also on two sides Dec blank arcadin very different in mood from any of the C13. The arches a trefoiled and end in ogees. There is plenty of ballflow (in the S, not the N room). The spandrels are filled with bla multi-cusped triangles. C13 and Perp windows. Dec liern vaults of an attractive design: a square in the middle, a st interlocked with it and projecting beyond it – all cusped.

Having now reached the end of this description and analys of the work that went on between 1192 and 1250, it is necessar to sum up and trace the development of certain motifs which might help in the dating of the various parts. What we do n know at all is how far building had proceeded when, aft only eight years, St Hugh died. We must not underestima how much it can have been. At Canterbury the whole r building and extending of the parts E of the main transep took four years. At Salisbury the Lady Chapel and retrocho took five. Building certainly went on steadily after St Hugh death; for in 1205 donors of money for the *novum opus* wen promised acceptance in the *sodalitas* of those for whom praye were said. The motifs which we can hang our tentative datin on to are the capitals, the lattice-work, the large and mo sweepingly displayed dog-tooth, and the lozenges.

Capitals, which seem at first the most promising, prov also the most intractable. What can be said after caref examination is very general. In St Hugh's work there certainl were at once, or almost at once, two designers, one wh liked stiff-leaf more or less of a crocket kind, the other wh preferred smaller, flatter, nobbly leaves, rather more sprea out. What distinguishes St Hugh's capitals from later ones i only this. Even where he uses two tiers of stiff-leaf and eve where the leaves are blown diagonally – a motif which appear remarkably early in Lincoln – there is also a zone below th leaves where the moulded shape of the capitals and the indi vidual stalks are clearly seen. The opposite extreme is th Angel Choir – i.e. just beyond the date limit set for this sum mary – for there the lushest stiff-leaf covers the whole capita In the nave the development from one to the other can b watched. In the galilee (*see* p. 127) the later type is pretty wel reached. But the development is not straight. Repairs intro duce later types into earlier parts and conversely capitals o St Hugh's time could be re-used, where an event such a the fall of the tower had left them unused. Much clearer i the development in leaf corbels for vaulting-shafts. Again the end is the Angel Choir. The nave is half-way on. Now the nave was being roofed, or rather being vaulted, in 1233, and the style of the figures at the top of the W gable is similar to that of Wells in the 1240s. So perhaps one might venture the proposal that Geoffrey went on till say 1210–15, that immediately afterwards the main transepts were completed and the nave built by the second master, and that the nave was ready by c.1230–5, whereupon the third master, starting about 1235, finished the W front and rebuilt the crossing tower.

The lattice motif is a further help. It is, as we have seen, all over the rebuilt crossing tower, i.e. a favourite of c.1240. As it occurs also in the upper parts of the W front and of the rebuilt or very belatedly built S bay of the SE transept, these two parts can be tentatively dated c.1240, or more safely c.1230–50, which is what we have come to accept.

Then the big and demonstrative dog-tooth. It is most conspicuous in the S bay of the SE transept and the galilee. It also comes into the W bay of Hugh's choir rebuilt c.1240, into the N transept inner bay also of c.1240, and into the crossing arches of the same time. That must be remembered when the galilee is being described. It also helps incidentally to date the partition walls in the NE transept E chapels.

THE ANGEL CHOIR. In 1255 the cathedral authorities petitioned 15a Henry III to allow them to take down part of the old town wall – the line was that of the Roman wall – to extend the cathedral. Licence was given. In 1280 the solemn translation of the Shrine of St Hugh took place, in the presence of King Edward and Queen Eleanor, the Archbishop of Canterbury, and eight bishops, including Bishop Quivil, the bishop-elect of Exeter, who must have had a good look at the nave vaults. So 1256–80 is the time it took to build the Angel Choir. The start must have been made almost immediately the nave had been finished. But that was not an exception. More space for the clergy in their part of the church was a universal demand. In length actually the Angel Choir, with its five bays beyond the E transepts, goes beyond St Hugh's apse by only one bay, but in unimpeded space the difference was enormous; for the Angel Choir is an even oblong with a straight end, aisles and 'nave' ending flush.

The Angel Choir still follows the system of elevation laid down by Geoffrey. That means that a wide, not a high room was built. In France and even more in Germany one would

have jumped up to a new height, regardless of what had go
before. The effect would have been sensational, but the ha
mony of the whole would have been destroyed. In that resp
the Angel Choir is a compromise. But how much we owe
However, while the system remained, in detail all is on
again richer, i.e. richer than the nave. The piers alterna
between a square core with strong filleted demi-shafts in t
main directions and two slender detached Purbeck shafts
each diagonal, and all Purbeck squares with filleted den
15b   shafts and no detached shafts. All capitals are of Purbeck. T
arches have big dog-tooth. Spandrels with blank cusped poir
ed trefoils. In the aisles once more the indispensable blank a
cading. But the arches are cusped now, and above them is bla
bar tracery, two twin lights with an encircled quatrefoil. B
tracery is indeed, as we shall see, the principal innovation
the Angel Choir. It came from Westminster Abbey, where
had, in the design of 1245, been taken over from Reims. S
Lincoln took to it after only ten or twelve years. At Salisbu
it took another ten after that. The blank arcading has sha
and a vertical strip of thick leaf crockets. Spandrels wi
trefoils encircled and unencircled. The aisle windows a
spacious, of three lights with bar tracery, two cinquefoil
circles, and a quatrefoiled circle over. Two strips of thi
leaf crockets run up between the shafts. The vault continu
the system laid down by the nave vault, but leaves out th
lateral tiercerons and the transverse ridge-ribs. The BOSS
are superb, the finest probably of their date, i.e. 1260, i
England. The foliage bosses, side by side with the lushest stif
leaf, display naturalistically leaves of the English countrysi
– oak, vine, maple, ranunculus, and (according to Cave) th
yellow water lily. There are also figured bosses, and the
quality also is outstanding. One has a pair of wrestlers – or
good, one evil? – their bodies modelled with supreme realis
and the finest feeling for skin and muscle, and moreover a
equally fine feeling for the *tondo* composition. Others sho
the Coronation of the Virgin, a lady with a page and a pupp
the Tree of Jesse with King David harping in the centre,
Prophet arguing with an Apostle, David and Nathan (?),
man fighting a monster, a monster with wings, two interlace
winged monsters, three interlaced lizard-like monsters, a ma
and a woman kissing and a third smaller head below with
very grim or worried expression, two elegant ladies' head
with wimples, a man battling with a merman. There are tw

types in the figures: some are fleshy and broad-faced, but others – especially the Coronation of the Virgin, the lady with the puppy, the apostles and prophets, and the Tree of Jesse – are extremely slender, their movements supple and their faces of that type which the so-called Joseph Master had established in France about 1240 and which the Westminster angels (in the transepts) took over for England. All the scenes are in the S aisle; the N aisle has only foliage and some grotesques.

The 'nave' of the Angel Choir receives its light from the gorgeous eight-light E window, 59 ft high. The window is the perfectly logical extreme of the bar-tracery started at Reims and in Westminster Abbey for two lights. The system is that each light has its own arch and the super-arch is independent of them. In the tympanum is a foiled circle. This the architect of the nave at Amiens in the 1230s and of the chapter house at Westminster about 1250 had applied to four lights. There were now two super-arches and one super-super-arch, all kept sharply separate from each other. Lincoln has the earliest eight-light window preserved anywhere. The logic of the arches is kept even here. There are seven circles, four quatrefoiled below, two sexfoiled above, and at the top the large top circle filled with a ring of six quatrefoils set alternately upright and diagonally round one sexfoil. The composition combines breadth and generosity with logic, and the sun streaming in in the morning gives a heavenly clarity to all forms. Three strips of thick leaf crockets up the jambs between the shafts.

The gallery openings are again two twins, as in St Hugh's choir. But they have bar tracery too, and that once again adds breadth and richness. Encircled quatrefoils above each two lights. The lights are cusped. The shafts are of Purbeck, many of them, and with strips of crockets between. Foliated hood-moulds on head-stops. And in the spandrels the ANGELS which have given the *novum opus* its name. There are thirty of them, or rather twenty-eight angels plus the Virgin on the S side, at the W end of bay one from the W, and Christ on the N side, at the W end of bay one from the W. Christ is displaying his wound and a censing angel is next to him. The Virgin is giving her breast to the standing child, and there is a censing angel next to her too. Of the angels only a few can here be singled out. One basic stylistic distinction appears at once. Christ and the Virgin belong to the style derived from the

Joseph Master and Westminster. So do King David (E bay
S side) and two angels (with a book and with a scroll – fir
and second bays from W; S side). But most of the angels, an
among them the most famous – Angel with a little Soul, Ange
of the Expulsion, Angel with scales (St Michael), Angels wit
hawk and gauntlet, with two crowns, with a scroll, with a vi
– are heavier, with round faces and stronger limbs. In fac
more than two hands can be distinguished, but only tw
masters. Below the brackets of the angels are exquisite littl
heads. The use of angels in this position was no doub
inspired by the Westminster transepts, where the angel
must have been finished by the mid fifties. But the motif a
such was of course not new. It appeared, as we have seen, on
small scale, in Geoffrey's syncopated arcading. The Salisbur
rood screen also had it before Westminster.

The clerestory carries the most conspicuous innovation
The windows are here of four lights. Each twin has an en
circled trefoil, and the whole an encircled octofoil. But th
wall passage is placed between them and an open repetition
towards the inside of the whole: mullions and tracery. Thi
generous duplication – a waste of money for beauty's sake –
creates the most wonderful sense of transparency, by seeing
one layer through the other. Shades of Geoffrey even here
though it is true that the gallery at Westminster Abbey had
done the same in an inconspicuous context.

The vault is the same as in the aisles, i.e. the nave system
without the lateral tiercerons and transverse ridge-ribs – not
an improvement. The ridge-rib has crockets l. and r. – shades
of Geoffrey again. The vaulting-shafts stand on long, fully
crocketed leaf corbels. One of them at the foot (NE) has the
Imp which has lured more people into Lincoln Cathedral
than anything else.

As for the EXTERIOR, the E view of the cathedral is of course
as much dominated by the great E window as is the interior.
Otherwise the E front is restless. Three parts flanked and
divided by buttresses. Blank trefoiled foliage above the base
moulding. Stiff-leaf capitals. Mouldings with keels and fillets.
Head and leaf stops. The outer reveals of the E window have
two orders of crockets. To the l. and r. just one narrow blank
arch – an unfortunate overdoing-it. The side parts have their
three-light windows also with two orders of crockets. Two
cinquefoils and one quatrefoil over. To the outside, but pain-
fully not to the inside, the windows are connected with the

blank arcading or the buttresses by a normal blank arch. To the inside there is instead an abnormally narrow blank arch with continuous mouldings. It has not even thus enough space, and stands partly on the capital of the window shaft. On the buttresses, apart from blank arcading, places for statues with trefoil canopies coming forward like the head canopies of mid or later C13 funeral monuments. Gablets (also as in monuments) with crockets and head-stops. The main gable of the E wall has a five-light window, with the middle light higher than the others – an end-of-the-century motif – and two trefoils in circles for the side parts, and an encircled cinquefoil for the middle of which each foil is again a trefoil. All mouldings are continuous rolls. To the l. and r. climbing blank arches. At the top of the gable small figure of the Virgin. Crockets on the gable sides. The side gables are of course entirely sham. They are quite small, with a blank window of two plus two lights and a cinquefoiled circle above. Flat continuous mouldings. The twins have above an unencircled trefoil – i.e. we are on the way out of the C13 and towards the style of the cloister (see p. 122). Polygonal pinnacles of the usual type, but more richly appointed than any others. Even the buttresses have steep gables with crockets.

The N and S sides of the Angel Choir have three-light windows like the E walls of the aisles, buttresses with crocketed gables, and flying buttresses, i.e. the system is continued. It is interrupted by the three chantry chapels, two S, one N; but on these see p. 127. The gallery windows – as in the nave – are so tiny that they can hardly be seen. Four-light clerestory windows. They have no shafts; all continuous rolls. The windows alternate with blank arches. The inner shaft of each of these arches is short, because it stands on the capital of the window-shaft. To the l. and r. of each four-light window a tall blank arch. One curious piece of untidiness must be pointed out. On both sides the westernmost aisle window has the tracery left unmoulded. The buttress following borders on, and half hides, that of St Hugh's transept. In fact a fifth window was started, and of this one blocked light, one shaft capital, and the start of unmoulded tracery can be seen. It looks as if there had been a plan to demolish some of St Hugh's work.

That is all, except for the three chantry chapels (p. 127) and two portals, the southern one the more sumptuous. Unfortunately it is over-restored. It is so deep that it has a big

gable over, decorated with blank trefoils, quatrefoils, an
cinquefoil. Two entries with a trumeau dividing them. C
quecusped arches. The trumeau was renewed in the Perp sty
as its section and leaves prove. That the Virgin is not me
eval will be believed without proof. That it is of c.1930 a
not of the Victorian age is less easily believed. Tympan
with seated Christ in a pointed, elongated quatrefoil. Ang
around and indications of the Blessed and the Damned l. a
r. The hairy devils will be noticed at once. The Mouth
Hell curiously enough is below Christ. The jambs of the por
each have three thin shafts with stiff-leaf capitals, or rat
had them. They carry nodding-trefoil canopies with gable
just like mid or later C13 funeral monuments (and just as
have seen them in the E façade), but they are here complet
detached, and behind all this the complete main shafti
goes up to the capitals (shades of Geoffrey once more!). T
voussoirs are of three orders, divided by very fine mouldin
The outer order has sixteen figures in stiff-leaf foliage openi
out to form almond-shaped niches for them. Eight are ma
eight female. The latter represent the wise and foolish Virgi
The middle voussoir is all filigree foliage. The inner has twel
seated figures, six queens and six kings. The origin of all th
the tympanum with the quatrefoil and the composition of t
voussoirs, is the work of c.1250–60 at Westminster Abb
just as the origin of the angels inside was there. In fact t
style of the sculpture of the portal is more like the shar
alabaster-like style of Westminster with its long paral
folds than like that of the angels. The Westminster connexio
come out even more patently in the large figures on the b
tresses by the portal. Facing W and E, i.e. towards the port
Ecclesia and Synagogue, both in very shallow niches. T
brackets stand on three-quarter figures, an angel and Mose
To the outside, facing S two more female figures, al
with the characteristic belts. Against the next buttress
the E the much discussed 'Queen Margaret', against t
broader buttress after that a King and a Queen. They may
original, see their proportions and drapery folds – those brea
ing at the Queen's feet and the baggy ones along the King
side. But the heads and more must be completely re-done.

The N portal is simpler. It also has a trumeau, and this al
is a Perp remodelling. It carries the arms of Richard II. T
C13 details are also all victorianized, except the head-stops
the blank arches to the l. and r. The tympanum has again a b

pointed quatrefoil and a bracket for a figure. But there is no figure. The head beneath the bracket is unscathed.

THE FOURTEENTH AND FIFTEENTH CENTURIES

This at Lincoln is a gleaning operation. Once the Angel Choir was complete, the cathedral was complete. What followed were improvements and replacements. They can be taken in chronological order.

CROSSING TOWER. In 1307-11 the tower was heightened, a daring thing to do. The dates are established by a letter of indulgence for gifts to the *novum opus* in 1307 and a problem connected with the bell ropes in 1311. The master mason was *Richard of Stow*, whose contract for the *novum opus* is of 1306. He had been master mason to the Lincoln Eleanor Cross in 1291-3. Externally the new work starts at the frieze of blank quatrefoils. The C13 buttresses are carried on, but their detail changes of course. The bell-stage has two pairs of exceedingly tall twin openings. Elaborate, far-sticking-out leaf crockets. Each light is ogee-headed and has a pointed trefoil above the ogee. In the tympanum a pointed quatrefoil. Ballflower on the main arches and the gables. The latter match up to the pretty openwork parapet. Later lead pinnacles. The lead spire which had crowned all this was blown down in 1548. Inside, the early C14 is not visible, as a vault is put in to hide it. It is a most ingenious lierne-vault, assigned to the later C14. It is a development from the vault of the SW chapel. On paper it too seems to be a four-bay vault calling for a central support. Only where the four parts had been quadripartite they are now tierceron stars with ridge-ribs in both directions. But owing to the rise of the vault towards the centre this simplicity of design on paper is not noticed. Instead one sees a middle square, set into a diagonally placed square, set into the square walls of the tower, and that is of course one of the ways of setting out proportional systems in the Middle Ages without getting into the arithmetic trouble of square roots.

THE BISHOP'S EYE. Probably in the 1330s the huge circular window of *c.*1220-30 in the main S transept was filled with the most elaborate flowing tracery – two lime-leaves side by side, as it were, and any number of mouchettes taking the place of the veining. To the transept the window is surrounded by a charming double band of filigree quatrefoils etc., one parallel to the wall, the other in the reveals, and all with ogee forms wherever possible. Outside below the window runs a curious

frieze of completely flat, unmoulded interlocked lozenges, an
above is a five-light window also with flowing tracery, bu
this of a more current pattern. It lights – very lavishly indeed
the roof of the transept. The gable at the same time, on
assumes, was given its unique form of crocketing – a band c
pierced double-curved forms.

THE WEST FRONT. Here, probably in the late C14, a larg
window with Perp tracery replaced the C13 windows, which
by the surviving shafting, cannot have been smaller. The aisl
W windows are of the same time. They cut asymmetricall
into the C11 system. Below the W window a Gallery of King
was introduced, as Exeter had received one a little earlier. I
cuts off the top of Bishop Alexander's portal. Nine bearded
seated figures. The carver endeavoured to avoid uniformity
The position of the legs varies and achieves in the midd
figure a high degree of artificiality.

Then, in the C15, at an unknown date, the W towers wer
heightened to take their place beside the crossing tower. Th
buttresses on the W side continue polygonal, as the Norma
ones had been, and on the E side they turn polygonal. The bell
openings in pairs of two lights each were adopted from th
crossing tower. They now have two transoms, but the par
below the lower transom is blank. The details also take th
crossing tower into account; but all is less fancifully decorated
Originally the towers had recessed needle spires, but the
were taken down as unsafe in 1807. Inside, the towers ar
lierne-vaulted, much like the crossing tower. The centre is
square, a star overlaps it and goes beyond it. All is cusped.

FURNISHINGS AND MONUMENTS

They are examined from E to W and always N before S – with
exceptions at the author's discretion.

RETROCHOIR (i.e. Angel Choir behind the Reredos). – PAINT
ING. In the Russell Chantry, see p. 128. – STAINED GLASS
N aisle E. C13 glass, including figures from a Jesse Tree and
medallions with scenes from the lives of St Hugh and S
Thomas Becket(?). Also magnificent borders. The glass i
said to come from the nave aisles. – N aisle NE. Probably
French. Date of death 1859. – Great E window. *Ward &
Hughes*, 1855; not at all bad. – S aisle E. Like its opposit
number, C13 glass, figures from a Jesse Tree and medallion
with scenes. – ORGAN CASE. Small, with some Rococo
decoration.

MONUMENTS. N wall: Bartholomew Lord Burghersh † 1355. Tomb-chest with ogee panels. Effigy, and at his head and feet standing pairs of angels, one holding a shield with his arms, the other his soul in a napkin. Hanging canopy of three stepped ogee arches. Tierceron-star vaulting inside. – Fleming Chantry, see p. 127. – Between N aisle and 'nave' two tomb-chests. Robert Burghersh and Bishop Burghersh † 1340. Against the one pairs of standing figures, against the other pairs of seated figures. On the second, effigy of the bishop. Of the canopies only odd pieces remain. – St Hugh. The special shrine made to contain his head was of course robbed and destroyed. What survives is part of the base – two bays by one – remade apparently in the early C14. Kneeling niches with nodding ogee canopies. Tiny apsidal vaults. Top encrusted with leaf. – In the 'nave' Queen Eleanor. She was, with Edward I, present at the consecration in 1280 and died in 1291 at Harby, not far from Lincoln. The first halting-place of the funeral cortège was Lincoln. The effigy is a copy of that in Westminster Abbey, made by *William Torel* of London. The effigy and the canopy are of 1891. – Between 'nave' and s aisle Cantelupe Chantry, founded in 1355. Tall double canopy, cusped ogee arches and filigree gables. Typically Dec the idea of the buttresses set diagonally. The canopy is thin in depth, but it is vaulted inside all the same. There are now two tomb-chests beneath: Lord Cantelupe, only the trunk of a figure, and Prior Wymbysh † 1461, headless figure. The head lay on a helm. – In the N aisle Bishop Wordsworth † 1885. By *Bodley & Garner*. Recumbent effigy. Big canopy. – In the s aisle William Hilton R.A. † 1839 and Peter de Wint † 1849. 1864 by *William Blore*. Tomb-chest without effigies. But scenes carved by *I. Forsyth* after paintings by Hilton who, in the inscription, is called 'one of the most eminent historical painters this country has produced'. – Dean Butler † 1894. Alabaster, with recumbent effigy. By *Chavalliaud*, working for Farmer & Brindley's. – Russell Chantry, see p. 128.

AISLES OF THE ANGEL CHOIR. STONE SCREENS. The first bays from the E are continuations of the screen at the W side of the retrochoir, and this is the reverse of the screens l. and r. and behind the reredos (see below, p. 114). Their upper parts must be by *James Essex* (see below). But the screen in the next bay of the N aisle is original. It is the back of the Easter Sepulchre (see below, p. 114). – MONUMENTS. A number of brass indents. Evelyn writes in 1654 that 'soldiers lately knocked off most of them'. – Longland Chantry, *see* p. 128. – Katherine Swynford Chantry. She was John of Gaunt's wife. She died in 1410, her daughter, the Countess of Westmorland, also commemorated, in 1440. The monument is not complete. Four-centred arch panelled with cusped lozenges. Two tomb-chests, the western one of Purbeck marble with shields in plain roundels. On both lids with indents for brasses. Iron GRILLE towards the aisle. The aspect towards the chancel has certain peculiar features which will be described presently.

ANGEL CHOIR PROPER. REREDOS. Of stone. Designed by *James Essex*, 1769, and made and signed by *Pink*, a mason. The design is remarkably convincing archaeologically. Essex was indeed one of the first, if not the first, to take the reproduction of genuine motifs or pieces seriously. The reredos is copied from the monument of Bishop de Luda of Ely, i.e. in the style of *c.*1300, a style suitable for the Angel Choir. The tracery of the reredos is by *Pearson* (PB). – SCREEN WALLS, l. and r. of the reredos and one bay on to the W (cf. aisles, above). The parts by the reredos indubitably by Essex, the others may be partly old.*

EASTER SEPULCHRE. This charming piece is worth the closest study. It is of six bays, the three eastern ones being the sepulchre proper. The other three were intended to be a funeral monument and now contain the slab recording Remigius, the builder of the Early Norman cathedral. The canopy stands on arches with pointed cusping. The small capitals of the shafts on which the arches stand have naturalistic foliage. Gables with crockets and finials, buttress shafts with pinnacles. Inside the two threes are divided by a cross wall, and this also and the E end walls have naturalistic leaves all over. Back wall with blank arches, two lights, trefoil-headed, a trefoil over, and an encircled trefoil in the tympanum. The tomb-chest or base of the E part carries three sleeping soldiers in relief. Finally the little vaults inside. They have flying ribs, the earliest on record, i.e. a little earlier than those of the ante-chapel to the Berkeley Chapel at Bristol Cathedral, which must be of *c.*1305. The Easter Sepulchre, judging by its details, tallies with the cloisters, which were in course of erection in 1296. So *c.*1290–1300 might be its most likely date.

SEDILIA(?). This paragraph refers to a curious, not much noted detail to the l. of the Swynford Chantry, which latter has been

* Mr Higgins, Clerk of Works to the cathedral, regards the N bay as old; Canon Cook suggests that the S bay may be *Pink* on his own.

described under s aisle. There are here two bays of a screen with diapers of stylized foliage, flanked by shafts with naturalistic foliage. The tops of the panels are identical with those on the back wall of the Easter Sepulchre. The upper part of the composition is broken off, and here runs a classical cornice said to be of *c*.1670.

NORTH EAST TRANSEPT. PULPIT. A charming piece of mahogany, evidently of *c*.1760–70. The body stands on Gothick ogee arches and carries Gothick quatrefoils. The stairs, however, are simple Georgian (slim turned balusters), except that the tread-ends are carved with tiny ogee arcading. – SCREENS. Two wooden Perp screens to the E chapels, one with two-light divisions, the other including linenfold panels. – DOOR to the Treasury. C13, with long iron branches and scrolls. – SCULPTURE. Statue of a Deacon; C15.* – Also two most valuable and beautiful fragments of Norman relief sculpture. Seated Christ and a Saint. One fragment contains Christ's halo and the dove above it, with scrollwork l. and r. Professor Zarnecki has recently proved that the seated Christ and the Saint fit together, but the halo and the dove with the scrolls do not fit the Christ. He suggests that the former two fragments belong to the s portal of the Norman w front, but the scrollwork with the dove was the top of a Tree of Jesse placed above the middle portal, aptly separating the New from the Old Testament scenes. – PAINTING. Fresco paintings of the ancient bishops. By *Vincenzo Damini*, 1728, a curious intruder. – Annunciation, by the *Rev. W. Peters*, 1799, oil on canvas. Formerly part of the reredos. The picture would deserve a good restorer's treatment.– STAINED GLASS. In the upper room at the N end of the transept a lancet with geometrical patterns, signed by *W. Peckitt* of York, 1762. This was formerly in the great E window (PB).

EAST CROSSING. IRON GRILLES. 1297. A very simple, undated pattern of affronted scrolls and one of the finest pieces of ironwork of the C13 in England. The pattern is much the same as that of the iron railing of the monument to Queen Eleanor in Westminster Abbey. This also dates from the 1290s and was made by *Thomas of Leighton*. – STRAINER BEAMS across from the E to the w crossing piers. They were concealed by Gothic canopy work, made in 1779 by *Essex* (PB).

SOUTH EAST TRANSEPT. SCREENS. Wooden Perp screens to the N chapel and also the w chapel. – In the w chapel

* Found on the site of the Hospital of St Giles (PB).

(Choristers' Vestry) a superb stone SCREEN of the early C14, decorated with big leaf diaper of four-petalled flowers, also to the N, i.e. the choir aisle. In the flowers such unexpected little motifs as a bird's nest and a dog. Beneath a long stone LAVATORIUM, its front decorated with plain Perp panelling. Also, a plain FIREPLACE was at some time put into this chapel. – STAINED GLASS. The three tiers of windows in the s wall and the N chapel windows have excellent imitation C13 glass, probably of c.1850–60, the s ones by *Hedgeland*, the N ones by the *Suttons* (PB; on the Suttons, *see* below, p. 121).

NORTH CHOIR AISLE. First the TREASURY, i.e. the N transept w chapel. This has recently (1960) been converted into a Treasury by *L. Osman*. It is the first in England of a kind handled with much more swagger in Italy. The main feature is a well-designed modern SHOWCASE in the middle. – The STAINED GLASS, abstract, and coloured below, but strangely all in greys above, is by *Geoffrey Clarke*. – The PLATE exhibited from churches in the county is listed with these churches. For plate belonging to the cathedral, *see* p. 122. – SCREENS to the choir. Of stone, with blank arcading. The first late C13, as the leaves of the hood-mould stops turn naturalistic, the other with the big dog-tooth of the 1240s or 1250s, i.e. after the fall of the adjoining tower. Whorls as hood-mould stops. – MONUMENTS. More brass indents.

SOUTH CHOIR AISLE. SCREEN to the transept w chapel, *see* above. – SCREENS to the choir. The first like the first on the N side. The others of c.1310, i.e. with tracery still of pre-ogee type, but ballflower. The capitals with the small naturalistic leaves of Easter Sepulchre and cloisters. – MONUMENTS. More brass indents. – Plain Purbeck base of the Shrine of Little St Hugh, the boy who disappeared in 1255, supposedly the victim of a ritual murder by the Jews of Lincoln. It is a sinister story and ought to be pondered as one enjoys the purity and splendour of nave and Angel Choir.*

ST HUGH'S CHOIR. STALLS. There are three tiers and front desks on the N and s sides, two tiers and front desks in the return stalls, i.e. on the w side. They are for the canons, with below them the vicars choral and below these the choristers. The date of the stalls is fairly well known. John of Welbourn, treasurer of the cathedral from 1350 to his death in 1380, is

---

* In the CANONS' VESTRY a piece of very fine STAINED GLASS. It is a Presentation in the Temple, dated 1544 and considered to be Austrian, so Canon Binnall tells me.

called 'inceptor et consultor inceptionis stallorum novorum'. At the base of a stall close to the Dean's Stall (s31)* are moreover the arms of Dean Stretely, who was dean from 1361 to 1372. So the date must be c.1365–70. Much restoration was done in the C19, and especially of the lowest tier of N and S seats the majority is Victorian. The system of decoration is as follows: The two top tiers have misericords and elbow-rests between the seats. Above the top tier are tall canopies with spires, the earliest enclosing tabernacles with little vaults inside. The statues in the tabernacles are all of 1892–3. The system of the canopies and a good many motifs of the misericords etc. were taken over about 1380 in the stalls at Chester Cathedral. On the N and S sides the third tier has backs with pierced quatrefoils enclosing figural motifs. The front desks have panel tracery with kings and angels in relief. In addition three standing saints on the front desk in the SW corner. The sculptural quality of the carving is not equal. The best work is in the MISERICORDS. Comments on a selection of them and also the SUPPORTERS l. and r. of the misericords and the ELBOW-RESTS between the seats follow. It has, within the space here available, to be a very limited selection. It will, however, be sufficient to prove that there is no system in the subjects chosen or their order. Many misericords and ends of the supporters have foliage, single leaves, flowers, masks, human or animal heads, 'green men' or monsters.

s1 Knight and Griffin, s4 a lion fighting a dragon, s5 an eagle in flight, s6 a King seated, part of an abbreviated Tree of Jesse to which the supporters also belong, s9 Siren, s15 two interlaced peacocks, and pairs of cranes as supporters, a very fine composition, s16 an ape on a unicorn, s18 Sir Percival of Galles (?), s21 Judith and Holofernes, or a more domestic scene, s23 Adoration of the Magi with, as the supporters, angels making music, s25 Alexander the Great raised 30a to the sky by eagles, s26 Tristan and Iseult and a squire and a lady-in-waiting as supporters, s27 a unicorn hiding in a virgin's lap, on the r. supporter the huntsman, on the l. an angel with a harp, s28 the Coronation of the Virgin with

* The stalls are numbered in accordance with the booklet *The Choir Stalls of Lincoln Minster*, published by the Friends of Lincoln Cathedral in 1951. The numbering starts from the E, leaves out the C18 work (*see* in the text), and runs from NI to 31 and SI to 31, ending at the inner ends of the W return stalls, i.e. with the Precentor's and the Dean's Stalls. The second row is numbered also from E to W Na to Nx and sa to sx, the third row NA to NQ and SA to SQ.

angels making music on the supporters, s30 Knight on
stumbling horse (the Fall of Pride) and on the elbow-rest th
Pelican, s31 the Resurrection of Christ with the two figur
of the Noli me tangere on the supporters. In the second ti
the poppy-head by sa has Delilah with Samson's hair an
Samson at her feet. The elbow-rest by sk shows a fine coile
dragon. sl has St George and the Dragon, sq a young ma
fighting a lion.

N1 the Ascension of Christ (only his feet and the hem of h
mantle are visible – which was a current medieval convention
censing angels on the supporters; N2 Assumption of the Virgin
Annunciation in the supporters; N9 lion's head, leaves sprou
ing out of its mouth; a beautiful swan on the elbow-rest; N1
ploughman with two horses and on the supporters a ma
harrowing and a man sowing; N12 a lion and a dragon fighting
N14 a mermaid; N16 St John in the cauldron; N17 on th
elbow-rest a man's head, his tongue sticking out; N20 a boy o
a crane; N24 Sir Yvain trying to enter the castle, the por
cullis falling on his horse*, heads of soldiers on the supporters
N27 a wild man shaking down acorns for the pigs on th
supporters; N28 on the elbow-rest a naked figure crouching
N31 a knight attacked by dragons, on the poppy-head monkey
playing and one monkey hanged. On the next tier note N
with a pelican, NW with a monkey on a bier, and NX (the one i
front of the Dean's Stall) with a naked child rising from
stall to face a dragon (cf. Chester, Manchester, and Nantwi
stalls). The animals in the quatrefoils of the backs of the thir
tier are mostly Victorian. Among the original ones are on the
side crouching lions, a fox carrying off geese, an owl, and, at th
W end, the pelican, on the S side a bear, a squirrel, and, at the v
end, three fables of the fox including his sermon to the geese

PULPIT. 1863–4, designed by *Sir G. G. Scott*. Witl
apostles, scenes in relief, and a tall canopy. – CHANDELIER
Of brass, two tiers of arms. Dated 1698. – LECTERN. Brass, o
the traditional eagle type. Inscribed as the work of *William
Burroughs* of London, 1667. Burroughs also cast the identica
lectern in Canterbury Cathedral.

NORTH TRANSEPT. SCREENS. Two of the wooden screen
to the chapels are Perp. Both have two-light divisions. It i
rewarding to compare their differences. – STONE GATEWAY
to the choir aisle. This, and its companion (*see* below), ar
gorgeous pieces of the early Angel Choir years. Three Purbecl

* Cf. the Boston stalls.

shafts in the jambs, big dog-tooth and a chain of big flowers between. The richest stiff-leaf capitals. Arch with big dog-tooth, then an order of openwork stiff-leaf foliage starting from a dragon at the bottom l. and r., and then again big dog-tooth. Hood-mould with dog-tooth on stiff-leaf stops. In the spandrels blank pointed trefoils with stiff-leaf cusps. – STAINED GLASS. The rose window is the most complete piece of original glass in the cathedral. Its general effect of deep and rich glow and unity in variety needs no comment. What is represented is no easier of recognition than in French glass of the same date. Why then is abstraction – Mr Clarke's e.g. in the Treasury – yet not the same? It is a matter of depth, of layers of significance, which cannot be taken up here. In the centre of the rose God, in the top outer circle Christ. Around God worshipping figures. In one of the foils of the great quatrefoil a contemporary figure from a Tree of Jesse is inserted. Close to Christ the Evangelists and then Saints, Bishops, Angels. Inserted scenes e.g. the Death and Funeral of the Virgin, Jesus among the Doctors, the Foolish Virgins, the body of St Hugh, Joseph chosen as a husband for the Virgin, Adam and Eve. In the lancet windows below original grisaille glass. In the large lancet at ground level to the l. of the doorway five early C14 angels from the great w window. In the lancet to the r. grisaille glass. – MONUMENT. In the S chapel to soldiers killed in the Indian wars. By *E. Richardson* of Melbury Terrace, London, 1851. With the two usual mourning soldiers. They lean on their guns as if these were extinguished torches.

CROSSING. PULPITUM. A gorgeous piece of early C14 decoration, the finest in a county of many Dec splendours. It makes one understand how the Dec style came to be called Dec. The pulpitum consists of four arches l. and r. of the portal. The four arches, really niches, have detached buttress shafts in front – making a depth of about 18 in. But the total depth is of course much more; for the pulpitum contains a vaulted chamber and staircase inside besides the passage through. The passage is vaulted in two bays with moulded diagonal and ridge ribs and bosses. The chamber to the S* is also of two bays (N to S), but the ribs are here plainly single-chamfered. The staircase starts with a small vault too, and even here is a broad leaf frieze for the delectation of the eye. What delectations the front of the pulpitum has to offer can scarcely be

* Known as the Vergers' Arms.

described. The buttress shafts are covered with diapers and
have three tiers of gablets. The back walls are all diaper
divided half-way up by a band of very large leaves. The arches
are of course ogee. They are cusped and subcusped and have
the customary crockets and finials. In the arch mouldings
leaves, flowers, and also tiny animals. At the springing of the
arches grotesques. A little vault inside each niche. Spandrels
with diaper. Flat parapet with another frieze of big leaves.
The portal has two orders of shafts and a big ogee arch. To
the l. and r. of the finial brackets for images. Two more in the
diapered spandrels. – ORGAN CASE. Gothic, by *E. J. Willson*,
1826. Rather spiky and busy to interrupt the calm Gothic of
the C13.

SOUTH TRANSEPT. STONE GATEWAY. Exactly like the N
gateway, except that the band of capitals of the shafts has on the
l. dragons (also owls), on the r. standing little men and
dragons. – SCREENS. To the N chapel, known as the Work's
Chantry, a stone screen, over-restored. In the jambs of the
doorway kneeling pairs of figures, benefactors of the building
as the inscription shows: 'Orate pro benefactoribus istius
ecclesie', in the gable seated bishop, in the finial royal coat of
arms, dateable to some time between 1358 and the early C15.
Inside the chapel a nicely decorated stone BRACKET. – To
the second and third chapels the screens are of wood, Perp,
and similar to those in the N transept. – STAINED GLASS.
In the Bishop's Eye a gorgeous jumble of C12–14 fragments.
He who examines it really closely can make thrilling discoveries. In the lancets below C13 medallions. – In the S
chapel acceptable mid-C19 imitation of C13 medallions. –
MONUMENTS. Bishop King. By *W. B. Richmond*, 1913. An
intruder from Rome, but really a very excellent piece in the
late C19 tradition of bronze modelling, i.e. naturalistic and
very lively. – Dean Fuller † 1699. Tablet with striking head,
not *sympathique*, on a bad, flat bust. – Bishop John Dalderby
† 1320. He was venerated as a saint and received a shrine. Of
this only two brackets have survived, partly fixed to the vaulting-shafts, partly on octagonal shafts. One of them has some
foliage. – In the S chapel Perp tomb-chest to Sir George
Tailboys † 1538 with three big shields in quatrefoils. Back
wall with panelling and five cows. In the spandrels two more.
Cresting, and standing on it a shield.

NAVE AND AISLES. NAVE ALTAR and RAILINGS around. By
Sir Charles Nicholson, C20. – PULPIT. From St Mary, the

English church of Rotterdam, built in 1708 (for other parts see Selwyn College, Cambridge). A fine big piece with a tester, not over-decorated. Curving stair with pierced feathery foliage panels. – FONT. Square, of Tournai marble, one of ten* existing in England. The base has enormous flat leaves on the corners, the bowl palmettes in the top corners. Against the sides of the bowl quadrupeds, mostly monstrous. – STAINED GLASS. Lincoln Cathedral, as we have already seen, has been extremely lucky with its Victorian glass. None is desperately bad, and some of the mid C19 is about the best of that time in England. It is that designed and made – *suis manibus*, they say in one brass inscription – by the Revs. *Augustus* and *Frederick Sutton*, sons of Sir Richard Sutton. The glass is frankly in imitation of the C13. It is successful, and it is never genteel, as so much copying is. By them the last four from the E in the S aisle, two of them dated 1861, the two others also complete by 1862. They also did the great W window, and this is in the C14 style, with large figures under the right canopies and in some of the right colours. They incorporate genuine parts (cf. SE transept, p. 116). No doubt by them also the rose window above. And they must have done more; for *The Builder* in 1862 says that theirs are sixteen windows. Some in the SE transept have already been mentioned as theirs (*see* p. 116). Moreover *Charles Winston* supervised some of the glass of this time. It is not known which. It was done by several artists, and he was not always satisfied with them. One of the artists employed was no doubt *Hedgeland* – S aisle, third bay l. (date of death 1854); for Winston respected him highly. – Its r. neighbour is by *Clayton & Bell* (date of death 1860). – All in the N aisle by *Ward & Hughes* (PB). – MONUMENTS. Probably Bishop Remigius. Black (Tournai ?) slab found in the cloisters. It is in two parts, as Remigius's indeed was. Giraldus Cambrensis reports about 1200 that it was broken by the debris of a fire which occurred *c*.1124. On the slab no effigy – a brief Tree of Jesse instead. The reclining figure of Jesse can only just be recognized. But Moses is above him, and Christ is at the top. More figures in the spaces l. and r. At the head two angels, their wings turned up and of a shape similar to those on the other oldest Tournai slab in England, the monument assigned to a bishop of *c*.1150 at Ely. Dating the so-called Remigius is hard, but if one goes by the angels and by the fact that these two are the only figured coffin-lids with no

* See *The Buildings of England: Suffolk*, p. 35.

effigy but a different kind of representation, then one wou<
have to assign a date *c.*1140 to the Lincoln slab, and it cann<
be the one broken in a fire *c.*1124. The argument is of cour
not conclusive, as Giraldus's date may not be correct.
Bishop Kaye. 1857 by *Richard Westmacott, Jun.* Tomb-che<
and white-marble effigy, recumbent. – Dean Honywoc
† 1681. Tablet of good, restrained character. At the top ope
curly pediment. – In the room under the w tower M
Pownall † 1777. Plain white sarcophagus. The inscription
said to be by Horace Walpcle (PB).

PLATE. Three funeral Chalices and Patens: Bishop Grossetes<
† 1253, the Paten showing the bishop in pontificals; Bishc
Gravesend † 1279, the Paten with the manus Dei; an
Bishop Sutton † 1299, the Paten again with the manus Dei.
Three silver-gilt Cups, the stems copper-gilt: one Germa<
C14; the second Spanish, C15; the third Italian, with Limog<
work, C15. – Two Chalices and Paten Covers, by *John Morl<*
of Lincoln, 1569. – Verger's Staff, *c.*1660. – Wine Cu<
pricked 1686. – Paten on foot, by *Nathaniel Lock,* 1712. – Tw
Chalices, two Patens, two Flagons, and six Alms Plates, b
John Bridge, 1824. Given by Dean Gordon to replace the pla<
stolen in 1805.

ANNEXES

CHAPTER HOUSE AND CLOISTERS. The chapter house mu<
have been begun before 1220, but building must have take
quite some time. The initial date is given by the fact tha
the chapter house is mentioned in the *Metrical Life of St Hug*
which was written between 1220 and 1230. The completin
date is stylistic guesswork. The cloisters, unnecessary reall
in a non-monastic cathedral, were started only about 129c
They are mentioned in a letter of Bishop Sutton, dated 129<
The entry into the passage from the E transept to the passag
into the cloisters is however by a doorway of the time of th
chapter house. Three jamb-shafts with stiff-leaf capitals
Deep arch mouldings. The doorway does not fit the passag
which follows. So, right in front of it, about 1300 another arc<
was placed, typical of its date in capitals and mouldings
Hood-mould with heads of a king and a bishop. The passag<
like the cloister, is extremely characteristic of *c.*1300, i.e. bot<
have four-light openings with Geometrical tracery, alread<
with cusped arches and unencircled pointed quatrefoils, an<
the top circle (which is not yet given up) filled with alternatin<
rounded and pointed trefoils – all of course in bar tracery an<

all, incidentally, on a small, almost miniature scale. Also all nicely and busily shafted inside and outside.* The capitals in the passage are still naturalistic, though just turning bossy, and they are bossy or nobbly or sea-weedy in the cloisters. The passage has a stone vault with longitudinal ridge-ribs and no tiercerons, the cloister wooden vaults. To the E of the passage small rooms with much renewed straight-headed Perp windows on two floors. The best preserved has four cusped lights. Behind this a room with moulded beams. The inner walls of this addition to the passage are timber-framed.

The E range of the cloister is again of the date of the chapter house and also, alas, terribly restored. Blank arcading with stiff-leaf capitals and arches with dog-tooth. The springers of the vault are of stone.

The CHAPTER HOUSE entrance is, like most of the others at Lincoln, double. Quatrefoil trumeau. Arches with openwork foliage, all Victorian. Cusped quatrefoil in the tympanum. The chapter house is a decagon. Polygonal chapter houses became an English speciality. Lincoln has the first. It inspired Westminster. But Worcester has a Norman chapter house which, if not polygonal, is circular and has like Lincoln and most of the others a central pier. Mr Harvey has drawn attention to the fact that the master mason at Lincoln in the years 1239–48 was one *Alexander*, and that an Alexander was master mason at Worcester when the new chancel was started in 1224 (inspired in its vault by the Lincoln nave). It is not easy to reconcile the dates, unless Alexander travelled forward and backward, as later master masons sometimes did; but the suggestion is worth presenting, especially as the work at Worcester was begun when the vault of the Lincoln nave was still on paper.

The Lincoln chapter house has a pyramid roof and each bay has two shafted lancets with a blank lozenge above. Blank arches l. and r. of the lancets and on the buttresses. The lancets have continuous inner mouldings (a keeled roll). All shafts are keeled or filleted and have shaft-rings, all capitals are moulded. The top of the chapter house is Perp. Shallow blank arches with fleurons, quatrefoil frieze. Small corner pinnacles. Eight flying buttresses to enormous outer buttresses far distant. The exterior of the passage towards the cloister has the same system. Impressive w front of the chapter house visible above the E range of the cloister. Bare wall. Big circular

* Only to the w the openings of the passage are left undetailed. This was and is indeed behind the scenes.

window without tracery. Gable with three stepped lancets. Side gables or turrets with saddleback roofs. All the capitals again plainly moulded.

The INTERIOR consists of a passage of access and the chapter house proper. The passage is of two bays with sexpartite vault. Blank arcading with stiff-leaf capitals and dogtooth. Two windows per bay on each side. The vaulting-shafts start at the level of the sill of the windows. Small stiff-leaf corbels, as in the nave. To the W a tier of seven steep arches, all new, and then the circular window which is set inside between two shafts carrying a wide round arch. The chapter house itself has a central pier, decagonal like the building, with ten concave-sided Purbeck shafts. Shaft-rings, crocket capitals. The walls continue the blank arcading, but have dog-tooth only in the E parts. Vaulting-shafts on much bigger stiff-leaf corbels, more like the Angel Choir now. Two windows per bay plus l. and r. narrow blank arches, so narrow that the inner shank stands on a pendant. Vault of twenty ribs emanating from the pier. The ten intermediate ones correspond to transverse ridge-ribs in a longitudinal building. Ridge-rib (as it were longitudinal) around the ridge. Above each bay of the outer walls one pair of tiercerons.

How should we date this chapter house? The *Metrical Life of St Hugh* tells us that he started it and that Hugh of Wells, who died in 1235, completed it. That is surprising. The upper parts certainly look 1235 at the very earliest, namely the lozenges outside which recur at the very W end of the nave (in the SW chapel) and in the tympanum of the galilee, if they can be trusted there, and the galilee is pretty certainly later than 1235. Also the leaf corbels for the vault seem post-nave even if pre-Angel Choir, i.e. after 1230 and before 1260.

The exterior of the CLOISTER is quite bare. There were no rooms needed along it as there were in monastic cathedrals. Inside, wooden tierceron-vaults with many bosses, those of the E range earlier and best. In front of the chapter house e.g. Christ blessing, also the Coronation of the Virgin. In the other ranges much foliage, also monsters, also a lady with a wimple, a man's face with his tongue out, a man's face pulling his mouth open, pulling one side of the mouth, blowing two horns, etc.* Doorway of the C13 in the N wall, one order of

---

* The bosses at the N end of the E range have been interpreted as Occupations of the Months. At the S end of the W range two bosses which seem to be C15 replacements (Cave).

shafts, stiff-leaf. This led to the deanery. Larger archway at the
E end of the N range, perhaps not original. The staircase
behind it certainly is not, and the fine REREDOS architecture
of the early C18 with a segmental pediment below a bigger
triangular one, with garlands down the pilasters and fine
detailing, is not *in situ*. It is not recorded where it came from.
This bay, i.e. the bay projecting E from the N end of the E
range, is incidentally timber-framed, as one can see from the
N outside, where it is gabled. It represents all that is left of the
OLD LIBRARY, built in or about 1422, on top of the E cloister
range. Inside the roof is preserved, low-pitched, with tie-
beams alternating with horizontal demi-figures of angels as
if there were hammerbeams, which there are not. Moulded
beams, purlins with bosses. – Three of the original PRESSES
also still exist, really long double lecterns with poppy-heads
and a dividing rail decorated with pierced quatrefoils. The
library was mostly burnt in 1609, and in 1674 Dean Honywood presented a new one.

The N range of the cloister was in decay and the HONY-
WOOD LIBRARY went up in its stead. Honywood obtained
the services of *Wren* to design it. The builder was called
Evison, and he was to build it 'according to Sir Christopher
Wren's directions and Mr Tompson's model'. *Tompson* was
probably the Thompson who was one of the busiest masons
on Wren's City churches. Arcade with Tuscan columns.
Upper floor of eleven bays. Simple well-set windows with
wooden crosses. The centre window is discreetly emphasized
by a straight entablature and a garland. The main doorway is
from the deanery, i.e. the W. Two Tuscan columns, a pulvinated frieze, and a segmental pediment. The window above
it has volutes at the foot and a straight entablature. Inside one
long room, just like a college library. Book-shelves along both
walls,* originally only low ones between the windows. Cornice
with projections and recessions. Ceiling on coving entirely
plain. The only adornments are the E doorway and the W
window, both large, with a surround of leaf and then vertically
halved composite demi-columns. Segmental pediment.

Adjoining the Honywood Library is an annexe in Tudor style,
the DEAN WICKHAM LIBRARY. It is by *C. Hodgson Fowler*
of Durham and was built in 1909-14.

FURNISHINGS. CLOISTERS. SCULPTURE. In the N walk all
kinds of fragments. The three-quarter figure blowing a horn

* The first in England so arranged, says Canon Binnall.

is the Swineherd of Stow who contributed generously to
building fund and was perpetuated, a companion to St Hu
himself, on top of one of the turrets of the w front (*see* p. 10
– MONUMENTS. Stone coffin-lids with large interlock
circles, Anglo-Saxon rather than Norman. – In the s rar
monument to *Richard of Gainsborough*, 'olim cementarius ist
ecclesie', who died in 1300. Large incised slab. The slab in 1
floor is a copy. The damaged original is on the wall. Trip
canopy with ogee arches and angel pendants. He is shown
his professional dress, praying. By the side of him his L-squa
Greenhill considers the slab foreign – not a likely suggestic
because of the ogee arches which were unknown abroad at 1
time. – To its l. incised slab to Thomas Lovedon, *c.*1400.

CHAPTER HOUSE. CHAIR of *c.*1300, but the lions, the boc
rest, and the canopy are all not original.

THE SONG SCHOOL. This is an annexe to St Hugh's
transept. It is of two storeys, two by two bays, and severe
plain in its details. It was indeed the original muniment roc
and probably treasury. It has a crypt underneath who
windows show outside. Chamfered buttresses. Shafted lance
smaller above than below. All capitals moulded. Flat ro
That the Song School is an addition becomes perfectly cle
from the way in which St Hugh's typical broad buttress
with their detached corner shafts are cut into. Origina
there was only one w chapel, just as there is only one off the
transept. There this is continued to the N by a massive blo
with a staircase. Here there is a staircase too, but there a
also at once three narrow quadripartite rib-vaults, one of the
now divided from the others by a partition wall. Stiff-le
bosses. The capitals are again heavily moulded. The window
have a continuous keeled roll moulding. A puzzle is the fa
that the corbels for the first, i.e. northernmost, bay, t
corbels which adjoin the wall of St Hugh's transept, are pa
of his work. Stiff-leaf on head corbels. Yet it is just here th
St Hugh's buttress is covered by the annexe. So the buildi
must be an afterthought, but it must have been started ve
soon after. The crypt is also rib-vaulted, the ribs being sing
chamfered. There are here two narrow oblong bays wi
quadripartite vaults and then a large bay with a sexparti
vault. The top floor has the same kind of windows as belo
Here even more of the s transept is blocked, including a tw
light window at the gallery level. The finest feature of th
upper floor is a series of large head corbels, including a negr

They must have been meant for an upper vault, or more probably for roof beams.

THE GALILEE. This gratuitously large W porch into the S transept is an anomaly. It takes the place of normal N or S porches into naves. It is two-storeyed and cruciform. Entries from S and W, a tripartite large window-like opening to the N and the short passage to the portal to the E. Externally and internally blank arcading with very steep arches, lush stiff-leaf capitals. Excessive dog-tooth. To the S externally on the upper floor three lancet windows flanked by blank arches taller than they – a perverse motif. Along the top outside a Perp frieze of quatrefoils. Inside all terribly renewed. Rib-vaults, one narrow quadripartite bay to the W, two such bays N and S, two sexpartite bays and one quadripartite from the longer passage to the transepts. The angle-shafts of the cross are concave-sided polygons. Juicy stiff-leaf capitals and bosses. Overmuch dog-tooth. The portal is physically all Victorian. Twin entry with trumeau. At the foot of the trumeau beasts with human heads looking up. In the tympanum a lozenge. The jambs double-shafted with exuberant foliage. The upper floor, now MUNIMENT ROOM, is very light. Three lancets to the W, three to the N, five to the S. Only to the E a blocked two-light window of the transept instead, final proof that the galilee was an afterthought too. But when was it built? The exuberance places it near the Angel Choir, the massing of dog-tooth corresponds to the S bay of the S transept. So the date is most probably c.1240–50.

THE CHANTRY CHAPELS. Three chantry chapels project from the building, two from the S aisle of the Angel Choir, one from the N aisle. They are all Perp and basically all the same, three bays separated by buttresses. Decorated base friezes, decorated battlements; pinnacles.

The FLEMING CHANTRY is the oldest. Bishop Fleming died in 1431. The chapel is also the plainest externally. The forms used are relatively few and big. Inside, the tomb-chest is between aisle and chapel. It has open arcading and behind it appears the corpse of the bishop in the winding sheet. It is the earliest example in England of this representation intended to shock. In France examples go back some thirty years farther. On the tomb-chest recumbent effigy with two angels at the head. Canopy with hanging arches. Angels as pendants. Vault inside the canopy. Top as flat as if it were broken off. Doorway to the W of the monument.

RUSSELL CHANTRY. Bishop Russell died in 1494. T
front of the chapel to the N aisle is tripartite with a doorw
balanced by a sham doorway with panelled back. In the mid
the Purbeck tomb-chest. The arch is so flat that it is really
cambered lintel. It is panelled inside. In the chapel PAIN
INGS round the walls, done recently by *Duncan Grant* (195
9). They are curiously naive and out of touch, with a degree
naturalism, of idealism, and of stylization comparable
Puvis de Chavannes (or Augustus John or Hans Feibusc
rather than to mid-C20 wall painters. – Perp GRILLE to the
of the tomb-chest.

LONGLAND CHANTRY. Bishop Longland died in 154
Externally the chantry is deliberately a companion piece
the Russell Chantry. The two indeed flank the Judgeme
Portal. But Longland wanted to be a little more lavish in
the details – see the decoration of the buttresses and the battl
ments. The tracery also is not quite so rigid. Inside, t
bishop could indulge that wish more freely. The faça
towards the aisle, while also tripartite and also provided with
false, panelled doorway, is extremely elaborate. The most inte
esting fact about this is that, when, at this very end of Goth
design in England, such elaboration was demanded, architec
went to the French Flamboyant for inspiration rather tha
to the native Perp, and as the French Flamboyant is in
spirit, and even in such forms as ogee reticulation, so simil
to the English early C14 Dec, it is almost like a Dec reviv
But there is another equally interesting aspect to this chape
In closely examining the w wall inside, one discovers on t
cornice below the ornate niches unmistakable, though sma
Italian Renaissance details (shell-lunettes). Nothing else
Renaissance. The large punning inscription 'Longa ter
Mensuram eius Dominus dedit' towards the aisle is e.g. still
black letter. – Original panelled ceiling with moulded bean
and bosses. – DOOR original too, with iron handle.

WELL-HOUSE, NE of the E end. Octagonal, shafts with fille
at the corners. Pyramid roof with rolls up the edges. It a
looks perfectly convincing, but it is probably *Essex*'s work
even later; for Dugdale shows a wooden shed instead.

THE PRECINCT

At present Lincoln has no close; for a close must essentially b
closed. As it is, motor traffic, including heavy through traffi
passes all day and all night close to all sides of the cathedra

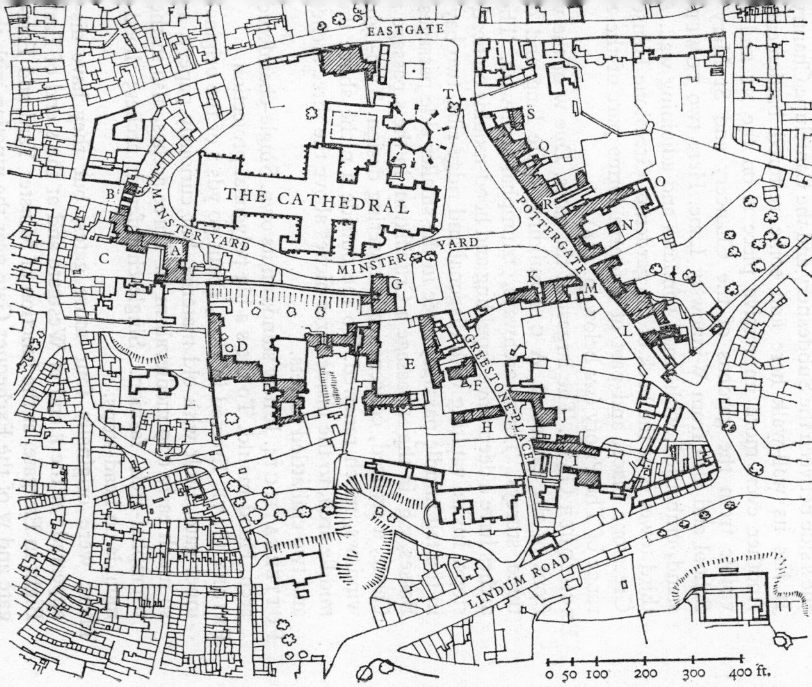

B Exchequer Gate
C Deanery
D Bishop's Palace
E Vicars' Court
F Archdeaconry
G Cantelupe Chantry
H Tithe Barn
I Greestone Terrace
J Greestone House
K Nos 12–14 Minster Yard
L Nos 2, 3, 4 Pottergate
M No. 5 Pottergate (St Mary's School)
N Precentory
O Chancery
P Choristers' House
Q Nos 3, 6, 7, 8, 9 Minster Yard
R Poor Clerks' House
S The Priory
T Priory Gate

Lincoln: The Precinct

0 50 100   200   300   400 ft.

THE CATHEDRAL

MINSTER YARD

EASTGATE

POTTERGATE

GREESTONE PLACE

LINDUM ROAD

N

5—L

the closest along the s, the most obnoxious along the E. Als
there is no open space all round. There is lawn to the w and th
E, a fenced-in piece to the N, and a piece with trees to the s.
But they are not read together. Yet a hundred years ago a sens
of the precinct did exist. It is one of the most urgent plannin
problems of Lincoln to restore dignity to the immediate sur
roundings of the monument which to most people means Lincoln

GATES AND WALLS. The cathedral received a licence t
crenellate, i.e. to fortify its precinct, in 1285. The walls wer
no doubt built soon after. In 1319 a further licence was give
to erect towers. Of the WALLS a substantial part remains o
the s side between the Subdeanery and the Cantelupe Chantry
It has its wall-walk here and some restored battlement
Another even more impressive piece is on the NE and
visible from the gardens of the Chancery and St Mary'
School and also from Winnowsty Lane. Here two TOWER
stand, embattled, with small windows and adjoining wall.
third tower is at the back of the garden of Greestone House
Greestone Place, and part of a fourth forms part of the
range of The Priory (see below, p. 138).

EXCHEQUER GATE. The largest of the gates. Due w of the v
front of the cathedral. A C14 building, quite long and c
three storeys. Three archways, triumphal-arch-wise. Th
arches have a deep wave moulding and hood-moulds on head
stops. Inside vaulting with diagonal and ridge-ribs, two bay
in the tall middle passage, three in the smaller side passages
Bosses, e.g. in the N passage a Crucifixion, in the s passage
Castle, a stylized, concentrically towering design. Two-ligh
windows, much renewed. To the outside a niche above the
middle arch, to the inside three niches above the three arche
and two embattled turrets.

POTTERGATE. C14. It now stands on its own. Single-chamfered
arch. Hood-mould. To the s a big polygonal projection.

PRIORY GATE. Erected in 1816, about 50 yds s of the origina
inner gate. Built with old material, but curiously papery, as
so much early C19 medievalism is. Three arches, also in the
triumphal-arch fashion. Single-chamfered arches; hood-
moulds on head-stops.

There were originally four more gates, but they have disappeared: at the E end of Westgate and at the s end of East
Bight in Eastgate, at the junction of Minster Yard and Eastgate and w of the Exchequer Gate near the junction with the
Bail.

BISHOP'S PALACE. What was until recently the Bishop's Palace is a house in the Tudor style built by *Ewan Christian* in 1886. This was built on to and converted out of a house of 1727 of which the pretty staircase remains (three slim balusters to the step and carved tread-ends). The chapel to this new, i.e. not medieval, house is by *Bodley & Garner*, 1898, in the Dec style, very tall, with windows only high up and two transverse stone arches to separate an ante-room from the nave and the nave from the chancel. In the s wall close to the E end is a lancet window, shafted, and this is the first introduction to the complicated layout and fascinating remains of the medieval bishop's palace. This was started, outside the later close wall, about the middle of the C12. But of whatever was built then nothing can now be seen. The present buildings, or rather ruins, belong to the C13 and the C15. As for the C13 buildings, they were begun by St Hugh and completed by Hugh of Wells, who died in 1234. They are as follows: First the Great Hall, one of the most impressive halls of the date in England, even if the mind must reconstruct much to get the full impression. The hall, which lies due N of Bodley & Garner's chapel, is about 105 ft long inside and consisted of a nave and aisles. There were four bays. The piers were of marble, says the Parliamentary Survey of 1647, i.e. of Purbeck marble no doubt. Only the N and s responds remain. The windows were large, for each bay two twins, shafted outside and inside. The inside shafts were of Purbeck marble; so the effect must have been much like that of St Hugh's choir. The s end had already – the earliest complete case in existence – the English arrangement of a porch leading into a bay, later the screens passage, from which three doorways opened into buttery, kitchen, and pantry. The Porch is spacious and in style, with its excessively steep blank lancet arches, rather after 1235 than before. Stiff-leaf capitals and small dog-tooth enrichment. The arrangement of the blank arches is very odd. Inside the steep arch of the main arcading another small steep arch is set in on paired shafts. The portal into the hall has a lower arch to the porch than to the hall. The three doorways to the s are arranged as one would expect, so that that to the kitchen is wider than the others and in the middle. On the other hand the narrower ones are a little taller, the consequence of using the same arch mouldings on all three.

What were the arrangements to the s? They are very unusual, owing to the steep fall of the land. For the Bishop's

Palace is indeed, as Leland says, 'hanging *in declivio*'. Thi
called for a bold use of different levels. The Bodley & Garne
chapel with its one surviving shafted s window represent
buttery level as well as the solar of the palace, placed at th
office instead of, as usual, the high-table end. Where the high
table end was we know from the addition of a bay windov
to the w in the C15. It was polygonal and only its lowes
courses are preserved. The solar lay above the buttery and
pantry. Between the two a passage led to the kitchen, whicl
is a separate building. Of the buttery and pantry windows
apart from the window inside the Bodley chapel, another
window and a w window, both double-shafted outside, are
extant. Below is an undercroft accessible from a single-
shafted w doorway. Of the solar only the outer wall, the wall
of Bodley's chapel, survives. This has at its s side two polygonal angle turrets, one with a newel staircase. They mark the
s end of the hall range.

We must now descend to the bottom level; for the kitchen itself is there. The distance between the two ranges is at this leve.
taken up by a complex archway-cum-passage. From the E to the
w there is first a tall two-centred arch with a curious ornament
of a kind of billet l. and r. of a roll – almost Transitional-
looking. This is followed by a bay with plain quadripartite
rib-vault, again with almost Norman-looking mouldings
Then two more archways, the outer again with the roll-and-
billet ornament. From the centre of the archway a shafted
doorway to the Kitchen. The kitchen has enormous fireplaces
under double-chamfered arches rising direct from the ground.
Three windows to the s, two small, the middle one tall. The
chimneybreast projections to the w and the buttresses to the
s are later additions. So is the straight staircase on the E side
which leads to a room above the kitchen, i.e. at the level of the
hall.

To the E of this whole range and not in line with it runs
another range, also roughly N–S. It contained the Lesser Hall
and the Dining Room to its s. From the dining room an extension ran E and met the Vicars' Court. This range is also of
the C13. The Lesser Hall is approximately at the level of the
Great Hall, but a little lower. Below the whole range is a
vaulted undercroft, again at a level lower than the kitchen in
the other range. The s part has a plain tunnel-vault, the N
part a tunnel-vault with deep penetrations from the small
single-light windows. The main entrance to the Lesser Hall

is close to its N end. Two orders of shafts with worn-off stiff-leaf capitals. Arch with two slight chamfers. Shafted windows, one with inserted Perp tracery. It looks as if the Lesser Hall might be a little earlier than the Great Hall.

The courtyard between the two ranges was filled by cross-walls and a long wall parallel to the Lesser Hall range as if of a pentice. On the N side both ranges are linked by the buildings of Bishop Alnwick (1436–49). The NE corner of the Great Hall adjoins his three-storeyed Gate Tower with a higher stair-turret, a pretty oriel window to the N and a tierceron-star vault inside. No grand archway runs through. Instead a small doorway to the Great Hall, one to a passage down towards the Lesser Hall, and a third, and more interesting one, to the E into a little passage with two small star-vaulted bays. This led into a spacious room with a newel staircase in its SW corner. The staircase connects with the Lesser Hall, which lies lower than the ground floor of Alnwick's Tower. At the level of that ground floor was Alnwick's Chapel, NE of the Lesser Hall and E of the spacious room just mentioned. The chapel had a large E window of which no details are preserved.

So once more we must descend. The N end of the Lesser Hall, as has been said, has a small doorway to the spiral staircase up to the level of Alnwick's Chapel. It also opens into a dark tunnel-vaulted room. A corresponding doorway leads a few steps down to the level of the undercroft of Alnwick's Chapel. The passage comes out at the S end of the W wall of the undercroft. A corresponding doorway at the N end leads into another dark tunnel-vaulted room. Between the two a wide ogee-headed recess. No indication of any vaulting.

The Bishop's Palace is approached from the Precinct by a thin insignificant archway of c.1500–10 and a second equally thin one which is C19.

PERAMBULATION OF THE PRECINCT

The perambulation starts from the Exchequer Gate, goes along the S side, then the E side, then into Eastgate (for this part see the Town, Perambulation A, pp. 155–6), then takes the Precinct proper again with the 'Number Houses'.

The DEANERY. The front is by *J. L. Pearson*, 1873, the back of white brick, 1827–8 (but on the lowest floor on that side are moulded beams; Canon Cook). A ROMAN HYPOCAUST was discovered in the C18,[*] associated with a simple, white

mosaic pavement. On the Exchequer-Gate-Cottage side, th
is w of this, a cement-covered brick stair-well with C17 cros
windows.

Then the SUBDEANERY. The early part is the wing (includin
PALEY FLATS) on the Precinct from E to W. At its E end
bay window with uncusped lights and battlements. An interi
jamb of one light with the name of *Thomas* the mason and th
probable date of 1491. We must remember that the Clo
suffered from pillage in 1644 and most of the Subdeanery
of after this date. The plan of the rebuilding is fairly clea
two projecting gabled wings in Lincolnshire vernacul
typical of the suggested date in the 1670s. The link betwee
these wings is supposed to have been rebuilt in the 1730s
really the insertion of a big hall in place of one there befor
Forgetting the Victorian addition in one angle,* the proble
posed concerns the two massive moulded and keystoned ma
doorways, one behind the other. Both are *ex situ* and ma
have been paired entrances to a hall. And of what date is th
staircase? It is a double staircase, each arm rising with on
intermediate landing and a return at 180 degrees against on
of the short sides of the hall. The gallery on columns t
connect the two was added only *c.*1780. The balusters ar
strong with a characteristic vase shape near the foot. Yet th
staircase seems to have been re-organized at one time. Di
it serve two separate houses, and was there a cross wall
The fireplace is against that assumption. A pair of entrance
this size to a house this small is ludicrous. Handsome iror
work with overthrows, formerly in the forecourt to the w fron
of the cathedral, where it was put up between 1748 and 175
(PB). In the garden wall following to the E a late C13 or early C1
archway with a pedestrian archway to its r. Single-chamfere
arches; hood mould. The main archway is depressed two
centred.

The CANTELUPE CHANTRY, i.e. the house of the chantr
priests of the chantry founded by Lord Cantelupe in 135
and enlarged in 1366, stands at the corner, where the s sid
of the Precinct widens and forms a kind of turfed square with
trees. To the N two gables, the l. with one oriel windov
on C14 figured corbels but otherwise mostly C19. Above it
niche. To the E, the N part is Georgian in its fenestration, th
s part has two-light C19 Gothic windows but original grotes
ques as hood-mould stops of the doorway. The battlement

* And interiors by *William Fowler, c.*1813.

are old, and to the W are a small ogee-headed window and yet
smaller openings in the gable above.

or the archway to the Bishop's Palace, *see* above.

VICARS' COURT. Founded by Bishop Sutton in the late C13
for the college of Vicars Choral attached to the cathedral.
They were members of the cathedral in orders or minor
orders acting as vicarious or vice-prebendaries, i.e. instead of
absentee prebendaries. Four irregular ranges of buildings
around a spacious, now turfed, court. The entrance range is of
the late C14 (arms of Bishop Buckingham † 1397). Archway
with four-centred arch. Many mouldings. Hood-mould on
head-stops. Inside a pretty lierne-vault, or rather a panelled
pointed tunnel-vault. Each panel has a star of ribs, two diagonal, one vertical, one horizontal. There is a grid of four and
a half such panels in length and two across. But one can also
read the diagonals together and read two by two panels as
one bay with diagonal and ridge-ribs and liernes. It is a pretty
puzzle of interpretation. The arch to the S has two sunk
quadrant mouldings. At the SE corner of the range a hexagonal embattled chimney.

E range running S. Near its N end a doorway with a C14
hood-mould. Inside this house a doorway with an ogee head
and other minor medieval features. Near the S end, where the
dressed stone ends and rubble masonry starts, is a buttress.
The S range is the most interesting one. It has enormous
buttresses or projections to the S, where the ground falls
away. They are large enough to contain rooms. Their tops
have a coping with set-offs, and below the coping are small
trefoil windows. They were monster garderobes. To the N
corbels above the ground floor, probably from some pentice-
roof. Irregular fenestration, all renewed. It includes one
ground-floor window with two pointed trefoiled lights and a
rounded quatrefoil over, i.e. a window of Sutton's time, and
also windows with a large pointed trefoil above such lights, i.e.
a form also possible before 1299. In one of them still some
ornamental coloured and grisaille STAINED GLASS. These
windows have seats inside. To the W is a single-light window
with a very pretty cusped head, really a subcusped pointed
trefoil. The same form occurs in the ruinous W range, but
here for a doorway. Of the upper floor only traces of windows
of one and two lights remain. The N half of the W range is in
good order but Victorian. At the N end was originally the
kitchen, and between this and the gatehouse the hall.

Next to Vicars' Court, No. 15 is on the corner of Greeston
Place. Late C18 front. Nicely proportioned doorcase an
pediment. Upper window to the r. canted out. Around th
corner a medieval moulded stone basement.

To the s down a narrow lane which by steps connects the Precin
with Lindum Road by the Girls' High School. The lane
called GREESTONE PLACE; also, a nice mutilation, Grecia
Place. In fact Greestone is a mutilation too. It was Greese
Place, Greesen being the plural of gree, meaning step. C
the r. the former ARCHDEACONRY. Handsome s-facin
façade. Five bays, two storeys; attic and basement. Brick wit
stone strings and quoins. The showpiece the centre bay –
Palladian builder showing his mettle. Steps with iron railin
to the first-floor level The Doric doorway of the triparti
Venetian or Palladian kind. Thin Ionic Venetian windo
above this. Banded pilasters. Then a semicircular windo
and a broken pediment. The date ought to be the 1760
Inside, staircase with three turned balusters to the step.

Then a splendid TITHE BARN of 1440, once belonging t
Vicars' Court and still accessible from there. Five bays, ston
with buttresses and two small s doorways with symmetric
heads. Nearly opposite is GREESTONE TERRACE, a charmin
cul-de-sac. Four houses forming an irregular terrace, mostl
Late Georgian. The best, GREESTONE HOLME, has
paper-thin stone façade with Venetian windows to the centr
bay. Turning back we come to GREESTONE HOUSE, of
rambling L-shape with predominantly Georgian features. I
its garden a Norman summer house with genuine fragments
e.g. two big dragon's heads as hood-mould stops. About mi
way down a small ARCH in the former close wall. Mostl
new, but one hood-mould stop to the s is original and muc
worn. The garden to Greestone Place with a nice screen o
early C18 ironwork. Gateway with overthrow and grotesqu
mask. This is said to come from St Peter-at-Arches. The
No. 3. Brick, five bays, two floors, with an attic hidden behin
a parapet. Doorway of the Palladian tripartite type.

Back to the Precinct. Nos 12–14 can be treated as a group. No. 1.
Late Georgian with bulgy canted bays to both floors (cf. No.
Eastgate, p. 155). Later porch. Both No. 12 and No. 13 ar
early C19 with asymmetrically-placed porches.

Then another sally down s to Pottergate. In the street POTTER
GATE several stone houses. No. 2 with a brick GAZEBO over
looking Wragby Road. Brick arch and wooden gallery. Bac

towards the Precinct, No. 3 makes an L-courtyard to No. 2. Brick façades, mostly Georgian, with a few balconies remaining to the first-floor windows. No. 4 has a blocked archway with segmental arch and an oriel window of the early C16 (uncusped arched lights). It was one with No. 5 (St Mary's School), which has to the back a large stone chimneybreast with a round chimneystack. The front to the street is C19. Inside, a rich late C17 stucco ceiling.

ow along the E side of the Precinct proper Nos 12 etc. MINSTER YARD. No. 12 is the PRECENTORY or GRAVELEY PLACE. The front has one buttress and remains of a blocked C14 doorway with two-centred arch. Also two grotesque C14 corbels built into the wall. (Inside the stump of a former stone newel staircase.) To its l. the CHANCERY, one of the most interesting buildings in the Precinct. The front part is c.1490, the back c.1320, i.e. the time of Chancellor Bek, later Bishop of Durham. An C18 link of red brick connects the two. The façade is of brick too, with a big stone oriel window in the middle. An archway at the r. end with a hood mould on lozenge stops. The rest is symmetrical, three bays and three gables. The oriel is canted, two plus two plus two uncusped arched lights. Boldly moulded bracket. Again a hood mould on lozenge stops. It runs right along the oriel below the battlements. Inside the front part the Drawing Room on the first floor has moulded beams with bosses with the arms of the see and of Bishop Russell (1480–94). They recur in the fine lintel of a fireplace in another first-floor room. Also tracery, an eagle, and a bird-headed quadruped with wings. This room has moulded beams too. It lies in a timber-framed back part of the N range which has a bargeboarded gable to the S. Beneath it the present Kitchen, with a pretty, small original doorway and door to the E. The Drawing Room otherwise is of c.1750, see the panelling and monumental and over-decorated chimneypiece with open pediment. To the S of the drawing room and connecting down with the archway a stone newel staircase. In the C18 link Dining Room with panelling and a small chimneypiece re-set from another room in the same house. The back range is a remarkable survival. To the S, now protected by a loggia, three doorways of the early C14, two small and low, the other one wider and taller. Single-chamfered. Hood moulds on head-stops. They were originally the entries to kitchen, buttery, and pantry of a house whose hall extended to the S and was pulled

down in 1714. The offices behind have gone too. There
now a staircase with timber-framed walls. It leads up to th
C14 CHAPEL of the house, complete with a piscina (oge
headed) and the SCREEN, a Perp, not a C14 screen. Ceilin
with moulded beams. The N and S windows too, if medieva
are of c.1490 or later. Three uncusped arched lights. Fro
the room to the W of the chapel two tiny two-light squints i
the timber-framed wall allowed a view of the altar.

No. 10 is the CHORISTERS' HOUSE. It dates from 1616. Fou
bays, gabled two and two. The gables of stone but repaire
and edged with brick – a pretty effect. No. 9 Late Georgia
brick. Competently carpentered doorway and interiors, i.
front room with Ionic pilasters. Then Nos 7 and 8, a seve
bay, three-storey brick pair. Probably Later Georgian bu
on an earlier stone basement. No. 6 is Early Victorian bu
still in the Georgian style. Iron balconies. Nos 4, 5, and 5
were known as the POOR CLERKS' HOUSE. Georgia
cement-rendered face. (Inside a medieval spiral stair.) No.
stands slightly higher above the road. Probably Early Victoria
but with early bits, i.e. the N wall.

Then, by the Priory Gate to No. 2, wrongly called TH
PRIORY. It lies back in a garden and has features similar t
those of the back part of the Chancery. Externally the house i
all Victorian, except for a doorway with a slight chamfer an
a hood mould which looks late C13 rather than early C14
Very archaic imposts. To its l. inside is a newel staircase
then to the E of that and at r. angles to the doorway anothe
such doorway, and yet further E a third with a hollow chamfer
25a Between the two, re-set, an early C14 cornice with lovely flowing
tracery studded with tiny ballflowers. On the l. and r. side
little caryatid busts. Above, again re-set, a frieze of fin
quatrefoils also studded with ballflowers. The N range of th
house has on its W gable a short, polygonal embattled chimney
stack of medieval date. Adjoining the W gable are the remain
of one of the towers of the Precinct walls (see p. 130).

Finally, an almost detached wing making an L at the S
angle, dated 1695. Opposite, on the lawn, the TENNYSON
MONUMENT, 1905 by G. F. Watts, the painter. He wears
wide mantle and holds a wide-brimmed hat. His dog is by hi
side.

We are now at Eastgate again, and but for the main traffi
artery the Precinct proper should continue l., opposite James
Street, past Atherstone Place. But this part is so much town

as well, more town in fact than Precinct, that it is dealt with in the Town Perambulation (A) (pp. 155–6). Where the Precinct proper takes up again, we have reached, with the cathedral, Exchequer Gate, and the 'Number Houses', the most picturesque group. The 'NUMBER HOUSES' are on our r. and all joined in a single composition. All are brick and date from various stages of the Georgian era. No. 23 has four bays, two storeys, parapet, and brick pilasters at the angles. Later porch and bay window etc. Nos 22 and 21 must have been one house. Again two storeys, but seven bays in four–one–two. Bay five is a two-storey porch. Stone door surround and open scrolled pediment. Probably a refronting of a C17 house. Then No. 20, late C18 with bow windows through two storeys. Single-bay annex to one side. Finally, adjacent to the Exchequer Gate, No. 19, also Later Georgian.

THE TOWN

ROMAN LINCOLN

The choice of Lincoln, first as the site of a legionary fortress and later as that of a town, must have been dictated both by geographical and strategic considerations – accessibility to the sea and the narrowing of the Witham and its marshes at this point, coupled with the need to provide a watchful garrison over the Brigantes to the N and their allies the Iceni of Norfolk and the Coritani of Lincolnshire and Leicester. There is little evidence for previous settlement on the site, but the Roman name, Lindum, is derived from the British *lindos* – marsh. *See p. 767*

The legionary FORTRESS appears to have been constructed within a few years of the invasion (A.D. 47–8), when the frontier was established on the Trent. It was first garrisoned by the Ninth Legion. Excavations in the grounds of WESTGATE SCHOOL and in the NORTH ROW have thrown light on the defences of this military work, but nothing of it is now visible above ground, as the fort defences are overlain by those of the later town. The fort was surrounded by at least one ditch (and probably more) behind which was a timber revetted rampart of stone and clay. The defences were later altered, and a sloping dump rampart with timber fighting platform was constructed.

In the last quarter of the C1 the TOWN or *colonia* was established for the settlement of retired veterans of the Ninth Legion. The town was of rectangular plan and enclosed 40 acres on top of the hill. It was defended by a broad, rock-cut ditch, the best preserved stretch being in the gardens of Fosse House in

CHURCH LANE, where it is 100 ft wide and 25 ft deep. Behin
the ditch was a massive stone wall, portions of the N side
which are visible in EAST BIGHT, E of the Newport Arch. A
the facing stones have been removed. The surviving cor
consisting of mortar and small limestone slabs, is some 10
thick. Another stretch of the N wall, still bearing its ashl
facing, is visible W of the Newport Arch. Portions of the W wa
again only the core, are preserved at the NE corner of DRUR
LANE and UNION ROAD. The wall supported corner towe
and bastions along its length, but none of these are now visibl

The town was entered by four GATES, one in the middle
2b each wall. The NEWPORT ARCH is a portion of the N gate of th
colonia. It now consists of a central arch for a 16-ft carriagewa
and a smaller E arch for a 7-ft footway, with the footings of
corresponding arch on the W. This W archway was blocked i
Late Roman times with alternate courses of masonry and tile
Only the inner portion of the gateway survives, the front havin
been removed during the construction of the medieval gateway
The remaining inner face is badly weathered, the present ur
happy proportions being the result of the raising of the roa
surface by some 8 ft. There is evidence to suggest that the gat
originally supported an upper storey.

Of the E and W gates nothing can now be seen, although the
position is known and they were visible in the C18 and C19. A
that survives of the S gate above ground is a portion of the v
walling of the carriageway on STEEP HILL on the site of a
antique shop (once the Leopard Tavern). The gate appears t
have been similar in structure to the Newport Arch.

There appear to have been four principal streets which crosse
at the centre of the town. BAILGATE now more or less follow
the line of the N–S street. On the W side of this street, near th
centre, was a monumental COLONNADE, the N limit of whic
is bounded by the MINT WALL, which still exists, althoug
obscured by the North District School. The wall is 70 ft long
3 ft thick, and 18 ft high. A number of TESSELLATED PAVE
MENTS belonging to the large buildings which fronted on thi
colonnade have been found. Others came from the cathedra
precinct and near the castle. In 1957 excavations in Cottesfor
Place, JAMES STREET, revealed the site of the public BATI
BUILDING.

The *colonia* was enlarged in the late C2 by extending the
and W walls and constructing a new S wall, enclosing 56 acres
S of the original town. A portion of the EAST DEFENCES of thi

tension can be seen S of the BISHOP'S PALACE where the
rviving wall section is 10 ft thick and 14 ft high. A further
ction of the ditch can be traced in the grounds of the Usher
rt Gallery, LINDUM STREET. Buildings have been recorded
the area of this extension, but no traces are preserved above
ound.

MEDIEVAL AND AFTER

etween the time of the Roman occupation and the establish-
ent of the medieval town the extent of Lincoln is not clear.
his was the period of the Danish five 'burhs', of which
incoln was one. When the see was transferred to Lincoln in
72, it was transferred to a place close to the northern extremity
the diocese, which was the Humber. The diocese was the
rgest in England; for it went as far S as Dorchester in Oxford-
ire, where the see had been transferred at the time of the Viking
vages. For the medieval town we are closer to reality today –
rprisingly close. By c.1100 the straight Roman lines were
eing ironed out. The Roman wall then enclosed sixteen churches
here are now three of medieval foundation left in that area).
ut we now find a significant ribbon development on the line
f the present High Street. Throughout the street's incredible
ngth of just over one and a quarter miles from the Strait to
anwick Road, thirteen churches were strung out (there are
ow four remaining). By c.1300 the Roman grid had been prac-
cally obliterated and the town above Stonebow was spreading
ut mostly to the E and W, especially along the area of the
itham's banks. But we are now in the Middle Ages, and the
ver was navigable for the shipping of wool direct to Flanders.
xcept for bulges N and S and a slight fattening, this is the plan
f Lincoln until as late as 1840: a narrow waist with long feelers
and S. Then suddenly Lincoln exploded, and by 1880 it had
ecome (on the map) a corpulent mass. The reasons were the
ndustrial Revolution and, of course, the railways. The situation
ow, in 1963, shows the bulge taking two directions: NE, that
, housing estates laid out in the first half of the century between
he prongs of the A15 and the Wragby road; and SW with the
ew housing estates of Hartsholme and the concentration of
ght industry in this area. The population figures also reflect
incoln's growth: 7,000 in 1801; 21,000 in 1861; 77,000 today.

CHURCHES

ALL SAINTS, Monks Road. 1903 by *Hodgson Fowler*. Brick,
with a flèche but no tower. Tall and large, Dec in style. The

w front with three slender windows divided by buttresse
Five-light E window. Nothing spectacular or personal, b
dignified.

ST ANDREW, Canwick Road. 1876–7 by *James Fowler*. The
arcade is that of the former church of St Martin, which w
built in 1739. S chancel chapel 1890. The chancel decorati
is by *Bodley*, 1882–3.

ST BENEDICT. Short Late Anglo-Saxon W tower with tw
bell-openings with mid-wall shaft. The tower stands mi
way between the present nave and N aisle W gables, and tl
W gable of the nave has an Anglo-Saxon square-headed ope
ing, now blocked. Where did it lead from? Where did it le
to? The present church is C13 and early C14. Of the C13, i
the cathedral style, one window, in the S wall close to its
end. It is a double-chamfered lancet with one order of shaft
Simple stiff-leaf capitals. Of the same date the N arcade. It
of two bays but was intended to go on. The two bays hav
semi-octagonal responds and a pier with an octagonal core an
four detached shafts. Stiff-leaf capitals. Arches to the nav
deeply moulded with two keeled rolls, to the aisle simp
double-chamfered. Nave as well as aisle end to the W in lar
blocked arches. The nave arch is deeply moulded, the ais
arch double-chamfered. There is also between the tw
facing W, a tripartite respond, the middle shaft filleted. Wh
does all that indicate? The answer is probably that a ne
chancel was built where the Saxon church had been and th
the intention was to pull down the Saxon tower and build
nave. The aisle was probably completed later, but the inten
tion remained. The aisle windows are Dec, with simpl
tracery (much renewed). The nave received new windows a
the same time. The E window is of five lights with flowin
tracery. The S windows have three lights and more elementar
flowing tracery. Dec sedilia, tripartite with pendant heads c
lions and a joint ogee top. The simple double piscina wit
a chamfered shaft however is, it seems, C13 and belongs t
the window above it. – FONT. C18; basin-shaped bowl wit
swags. – BOX PEWS in the N aisle. – SCULPTURE. A cruc
form leaf capital (N chapel E end) comes from the churchyar
and probably belonged to the nave. – Also a good ston
statuette of the Magdalen, *c*.1530, in the Antwerp style. – F
addition, as the support of the pulpit, Perp panels. – PLATI
Chalice and Paten Cover, London, 1569. – MONUMENT. S
Thomas Grantham † 1651. From old St Martin's church, sti

dissembled. Two recumbent effigies. The tomb-chest looks entirely Perp, with shields in quatrefoiled niches.

ſ BOTOLPH, High Street. w tower as built in 1721 by *Henry Grix*. His church replaced a grand cruciform medieval church, 123 ft long. The rest, as it is today, all of 1878 etc., by *Watkins* (GS). – Inside some C13 bits, including a pretty head-stop of a lady wearing a wimple. Also C15 Pietà, probably from a cross-head. – PLATE. Paten, by *William Darkaratt*, 1723.

ſ FAITH, Charles Street West. 1895 by *C. Hodgson Fowler*. Brick, in a brick suburb. Quite big, Perp, without a tower. – PLATE. Paten, by *John Leach* (?), London, 1706; Flagon, by *Ed. Barrett*, 1717; Plate, by *Thomas Moore*, 1722.

ſ GILES, Lamb Gardens. 1936 by *W. G. Watkins*, largely from the remains of St Peter-at-Arches, which had been built c.1720–4 by *William Smith*. The original church had been of stone, the new church is of brick, but the trim is stone, and much of this is the original work. Substantial W tower.* The sides as they had been except that the church was lengthened by one bay, and, as in the first bay from the W there had been a circular window, above the N and S entrance the motif of the circular window was repeated. The apsidal E end is again as it was. (One reconstructed C12 doorway and the arch to a side chapel taken from the old St Giles's Hospital.) – In the vestry PAINTING by *Damini* (*see* p. 115). It is an oil sketch for the apse of St Peter-at-Arches.

ſ HELEN, Hall Drive, Boultham. Nave and chancel and shingled bell-turret. Externally nothing old (restoration by *C. Hodgson Fowler*, 1887). The chancel was rebuilt in 1864 by *Michael Drury* (GS). Its details point to c.1300. Internally blocked E.E. two-bay S arcade. Octagonal pier with four detached shafts, stiff-leaf capitals. Responds chamfered and with a strong demi-shaft. Double-chamfered arches. Hood moulds on primitive heads. The chancel arch has semi-octagonal responds. – PLATE. Chalice, by *John Morley* of Lincoln, c.1569.

ſ HUGH (R.C.), Monks Road. 1893. By *Albert Vicars* (GR). Rock-faced, Gothic, with a tall 'NW' steeple. The interior must be earlier. Wide, and inexpensively done. Narrow aisles, wide polygonal apse. See p. 767

ſ MARK, High Street. 1871–2 by *Watkins*. Large, C13 in style, with lancets and plate tracery. N tower slender, with spire, rather over-moulded. Polygonal apse. Lower W apse for the font. Aisleless nave. – FONT. Octagonal, Perp, simple

* Ritually W; in fact E.

decoration. – SCULPTURE. Behind the organ and not com
pletely visible a number of Norman and perhaps Saxon frag
ments, from the original church. They include a roll-moulde
arch on shafts with scalloped capitals, some zigzag, and als
two panels with interlace. – PLATE. Chalice and Paten Cover
by *G.R.*, Lincoln(?), 1569.

ST MARTIN, West Parade. 1873 by *A. S. Beckett*. Geometrica
style, rock-faced, with a SE tower with pyramid roof. Polygona
apse. Aisles with round piers carrying naturalistic lea
capitals. – (In the Lady Chapel, ceiling and REREDOS b
Temple Moore, 1912.) – STAINED GLASS. All by *Henr*
Hughes, 1878 (TK). – PLATE. Chalice and Paten Cover, b
A., London, 1569; Chalice and Paten Cover, *c.*1620; Chalic
and Cover, by *Edward Conen*, 1724; two Flagons and
Font, by *Gurney & Cook*, 1758; Spoon, by *Peter & An*
Bateman, 1795.

ST MARY-LE-WIGFORD. Tall Anglo-Saxon tower. Narrow
over-restored W doorway. The imposts with chequer orna
ment. To its r. the triangular foundation inscription: Eirtig
me let pirce a n 7 fios godian Criste te Lofe 7 Sce. Marie.*
Recessed bell-stage with twin openings and mid-wall shafts
The shafts carry heavy volute capitals of Early Norman type
Tower arch towards the nave tall and wide. The imposts als
with chequer ornament. The rest of the church is essentially
E.E. Fine chancel with flat buttresses, two widely spaced
lancets, shafted inside, and above a pointed quatrefoil with
cusps. Inside, the chancel arch has semicircular responds with
the earlier type of stiff-leaf and leaf crocket capitals. All the
E.E. capitals in the church are of the earlier type. Double
chamfered arch. The N chapel of two bays has a pier of cathedral type. Octagonal, with concave sides and four detached
shafts. The responds are like those of the chancel arch
Stiff-leaf capitals; double-chamfered arches. Low tomb
recess in the N wall. The N arcade also of the same time
Three bays. Tall piers, octagonal, with the main sides concave
and again four shafts set in. Stiff-leaf capitals. Hood mould on
stiff-leaf stops, double-chamfered arches. The s doorway again
E.E. Two orders of shafts, pointed arch with dog-tooth and
many mouldings. The N doorway was E.E. too, see the shafts
to the interior of the aisle. Outside the doorway a badly
weathered statue. The windows of the aisle are Dec (reticulated E and W) and Perp (N). s aisle built in 1877. – FONT.

* Eirtig had me built and endowed to the glory of Christ and St Mary.

Octagonal, Perp, with flowers, leaves, and one shield. – CHANDELIER. 1720, two tiers of arms. – SCULPTURE. On the s side of the tower arch a length of Anglo-Saxon interlace. – MONUMENT. Effigy of a Civilian, *c.*1300, praying. Badly preserved. – In the churchyard CONDUIT, brought from the Whitefriars in 1540. Stone, oblong, with pitched roof. To the N and S some blank arcading with ogee arches. Also many fragments built into the walls.

т MARY MAGDALENE, Bailgate, close to the Exchequer Gate. Built between 1280 and 1299 as a parish church just outside the cathedral precinct to get parish services out of the w parts of the cathedral. Of that building however nothing now exists. The church was rebuilt in 1695 and again by *Bodley* in 1882. One blocked straight-headed window of 1695. The others, tall, of two lights and with minimum flowing tracery, no doubt by Bodley. Short NW tower. Narrow N aisle. The arcade has quatrefoil piers with continuous hollows between the foils and with fillets. Are they Bodley's? Nice Bodleian ceiled wagon-roof, decorated with crosses in the chancel. – Nice Bodleian ORGAN PROSPECT. – PLATE. Chalice and Paten Cover, by *James Carlill*, Hull, *c.*1580; Alms Basin, by *John Penfold*, 1723; Alms Basin, by *William Hunter*, 1746.

Sт MICHAEL, Christ's Hospital Terrace, just below the cathedral. By *Teulon*, 1853, in the Geometrical style. Not large, aisleless, with a polygonal apse, each side gabled. Tricky bellcote on its w end. No tower; quite elaborate s porch. Inside half the N wall has no windows but a detached blank arcading halfway up. – PLATE. Chalice, by *Samuel Courtauld*, 1757. – (In the Vestry MONUMENT to William Wilkinson and wife † 1837 and 1838. Two Christ's Hospital boys l. and r., one crying, the other kneeling and pointing to the inscription. NBR)

MONKS' ABBEY, *see* p. 147.

Sт NICHOLAS, Newport. By *Sir G. G. Scott*, i.e. *Scott & Moffatt*. Won in competition in 1838 and according to Scott's *Recollections* his earliest church. It was still without a proper chancel, which Scott would not have done later. His first chancel came at St Giles Camberwell in 1841. The chancel of St Nicholas was added by *C. Hodgson Fowler* in 1909. So was the N aisle. Scott's church is E.E., with a SW tower with broach spire. Two tiers of lucarnes. The windows mostly lancets, and all the details blunt.

Sт PAUL, Westgate. 1877–8 by *Sir A. Blomfield*. Stone (perhaps

from the Georgian predecessor) with red brick dressings
Lancet style. No tower; only a flèche.

ST PETER AT GOWTS, High Street, ¼ m. s of the railway
Anglo-Saxon nave, *see* the long-and-short w quoins. Late
Anglo-Saxon w tower, not bonded in. Tall, with an incongru
ous neo-Norman w doorway. Above the single-light w window
worn-off relief of Christ (cf. e.g. Monkwearmouth). Recesse
bell-stage with twin bell-openings with the familiar mid-wall
shafts. Uncommonly tall arch to the nave with the plaines
imposts and no mouldings. Doorway above, as so often. A
s aisle of two bays was added in the C13. A plain Norman
doorway was re-set in it. The arcade has a pier and respond
with an octagonal core set diagonally. In the diagonals fou
keeled shafts in front of it. Leaf-crocket capitals. The aisle
windows are Dec and restored. The s chapel was founded as a
chantry in 1347. Arch to the w with demi-shafts, round capi
tals, and double-chamfered arch. The windows still have
cusped intersecting tracery, i.e. a form of c.1300. This
chapel was added to a Norman chancel, witness a window
now still w of the chancel arch and another yet further w
of which only the horizontal moulding that once rose to go
round it is evidence (visible inside the s chapel). The present
chancel is of 1888, the N aisle of 1853. – FONT. Norman,
circular, with arches on short elementary shafts. – STAINED
GLASS. N aisle w by *Kempe*, c.1891. – PLATE. Chalice and
Paten Cover, Elizabethan. – MONUMENT. To Radulfus Jolyr
and wife, who founded the chantry. Canopy on short triple
shafts. Arch once cusped. On the arch inscription which
has been deciphered as:

> Radulphus Iolif, sua conjux ac Amisia,
> Hic capella paratur; Virgine mater
> theos qui sibi salvet eos. Pro
> quibus oretis opus hoc quicunq' videtis.

ST PETER IN EASTGATE. 1870 by *Sir A. Blomfield*. Nave,
chancel, and bellcote. The s aisle 1914 by *Temple Moore*.
Chancel decoration by *Bodley*, 1884. – STAINED GLASS. E
window by *Ward & Hughes* (TK). – PLATE. Chalice, by *G.R.*,
Lincoln(?), c.1569.

ST SWITHUN, Free School Lane. 1869–87 by *James Fowler*.
A large church, its spire, seen at some angles, competing
with the cathedral. The style also is that of the cathedral.
The bell-stage of the tower e.g. has the trellis decoration of
the cathedral work of c.1240. Spire with flying buttresses (with

tracery) supporting it from the pinnacles – the motif of e.g. Louth. The windows with tracery of *c*.1300, except for the clerestory, which has a long, even row of blank arcading with small pointed windows set in in groups of three. This system comes out more clearly inside. Arcades of alternating round and octagonal piers. Stiff-leaf capitals. Nave roof with collarbeams on arched braces and tiers of wind braces – a curiously domestic motif. – ROMAN ALTAR. This was discovered 13 ft below the surface while digging foundations for the tower. It bears a dedication by C. Antistius Frontinus to the Parcae. – PLATE. Chalice, Elizabethan.

MONKS' ABBEY, Monks Road. A cell of St Mary's Abbey, York. In ruins. The unbuttressed chancel still stands fairly complete. Perp window tracery, but in chamfered surrounds which are probably older. The surviving SE respond of the arcade certainly is older. It is exactly like those of the E.E. arcade of St Helen. Remains also of a building to the W with a S window with a four-centred arch, and of another building further E.

CEMETERY, Canwick Road. Laid out by *H. Goddard*, 1856. Chapels by *Michael Drury*. A pair, Gothic, usual linking arch. The best monument, a sombre OBELISK, to the Thornbury family.

NONCONFORMIST CHAPELS

One group of three can be seen together and makes up a kind of development, especially if supplemented by chapels in other parts of the town. These three are all in the High Street, S of the railway.

UNITARIAN, 1819. Plain cemented box with arched windows and a front pediment across. – METHODIST, 1874 by *Bellamy & Hardy*. Grand; with Corinthian giant columns, but plain stock brick walls behind. – PRIMITIVE METHODIST, 1905. Brick and much stone. Baroque, with a 'NW' tower (ritually NW), and as its companion-piece a pretty little turret, typically Arts and Crafts.

An equally instructive group the following four, not situated close to each other.

WESLEYAN METHODIST CHAPEL, Clasketgate. 1836–7 by *W. A. Nicholson*. A pastiche of Smirke's 'Cubist' style, that is, an essay in intersecting cubes. Front with Ionic portico *in antis*. The material brick, stuccoed.*

* Demolition pending at the time of writing.

BAPTIST CHURCH, Mint Street. By *Drury & Mortimer*, 1870
but still in the style of 1850, i.e. grey brick front with arched
windows and some plate tracery; however, on the whole
rather Italian Romanesque or Norman. Very plain, with
'sw' tower. Pavilion roof on it. Round the corner the former
SUNDAY SCHOOL, 1897, in an Arts and Crafts version of
Latest Flanders Gothic.

NEWLAND CONGREGATIONAL CHURCH, Newland. 1876.
Gothic, with 'sw' tower with broach spire. The details in
the style of *c.*1300. Next door the earlier building, erected in
1840. Also Gothic, but grey brick not stone, lancets not
tracery, and a general Late Georgian plainness. Three-bay
entrance loggia.

But the most impressive of the Nonconformist places of worship
is the FRIENDS' MEETING HOUSE, Park Street. This is
dated 1689. It is just a cottage with Georgian fenestration.
Inside, the meeting room has its original balustrade on the dais.
A gallery on three arches was added at the back in the C18.

BAILGATE METHODIST CHURCH, Bailgate. *See* Perambulation
A, p. 157.

THOMAS COOPER MEMORIAL BAPTIST CHURCH, St
Benedict's Square. *See* Perambulation E, p. 162.

METHODIST FREE CHURCH, Silver Street. *See* Perambulation
D, p. 160.

PUBLIC BUILDINGS

GUILDHALL and STONEBOW, High Street. C15, but much
restored. The Stonebow, i.e. archway, is quite simple. Four-
centred arch. But around it is a three-storeyed building. The
ground-floor and first-floor windows have basket arches with
hood moulds on grotesque heads. To the l. and r. of the archway two tall niches with stiff, elongated figures of the Annunciation, really in the C13 tradition. The side towards the N is
plainer. Inside, on the upper floor, the Guildhall itself, i.e. a
long room with an open timber roof. Tie-beams with three
bosses. On the middle boss kingpost with two-way struts,
on the outer ones longitudinal arched braces to the purlins.
Behind the Mayor's Chair a 'reredos' with the arms of
George II. Segmental pediment on Corinthian columns. –
REGALIA. Sword, probably presented by Richard II in 1387.
Double-edged blade, grip covered with silver wire. Pommel
with the royal arms. The scabbard is of 1902 (designed by
St John Hope). – Sword of the C15, perhaps given by Henry
VII. Original blade. Pear-shaped, polygonal pommel. Dama-

scened quillons. – Sword Blade of the C17, made at Solingen. – Sword Handle of 1734, silver-gilt. – Large Mace, c.1650(?), silver-gilt. Head with rose, thistle, harp, and fleur-de-lis, surmounted by a crown and orb. – Small Mace, c.1650(?). The arms of Charles II on both maces are a later addition. – Mayor's Ring, bequeathed in 1578. – Mayor's Staff of Brazil wood, first mentioned in 1581. – Wait's Chain, 1710. – Two Caps of Maintenance, 1734 and 1814. Of velvet.

CIVIC CENTRE. A competition held in 1961 was won by *Eldred Evans* and *Denis Gailey*, both very young. Work is to start in 1965. The Civic Centre will occupy the site bounded N by the river Witham; E by Melville Street; S by Norman Street; and W by Sincil Street. Here will be grouped the hitherto scattered civic offices of Lincoln: Civic Halls, Police, Council Chamber, Administrative Offices, and Courts. For the first time in Lincoln's history the 'indeterminate character of the lower town will be provided with a focal point to guide future development in this otherwise mediocre area. The visual relationship of the centre to the old town and cathedral on the hill should be a particularly happy one. The cathedral crowns a summit from which Steep Hill is seen from afar as a series of shadowed shelves. This slightly Cézannesque effect Evans and Gailey have appropriately caught in their design, an essay in cubic relationships, where the curve has no place. Main groupings will occur at interconnected deck levels. From the pedestrian Sincil Street the spectator will find the main accent to the N: the Civic Halls raised on a platform above the covered market area. To the S a series of nine low access towers will bring the pedestrian up to the different levels. In Melville Street the accents are reversed; now the predominant one is to the S with the Administrative Offices, and a low line of piazza-covered car parks is to the N. Centred within this spatially fluid arrangement of cubes the Council Chambers will rise above the other parts as the appropriate major visual accent. This will be square with square towers projecting above. The materials are intended to be *in-situ*-reinforced concrete faced with glazing tiles.

COUNTY OFFICES, Newland. By *H. G. Gamble*, 1932. Brick and stone dressings. Insignificant. C18 bits at the back.

CASTLE. First built by William the Conqueror in 1068 inside the SW quarter of the upper Roman enclosure. A hundred and sixty-six houses had to make way for it. The area of the castle, as it now is, comes to 6¼ acres inside the walls, 13¾ including

the ditches. These are prominent on the E, N, and W side
The banks are 20–30 ft high and 150–250 ft wide. The wal
have some herringbone masonry, a sign of Early Norman dat
On the W side a plain Norman GATEWAY with two Norma
slit-windows above.* Projecting W from the Norman gatewa
was a barbican of which the N wall and part of the S wall can st
be seen. Access to the top of the S wall was by a small Norma
doorway with a relieving arch. But the main entry to the cast
was from the E, i.e. the cathedral. The mighty EASTER
GATEWAY here still has its Norman tunnel-vault insid
though the outside is of the C14. Wide arch, double-chamfere
on big corbels. Above, angle tourelles and an aggressivel
pointed wall between. Passing through this gateway one ha
on the r. a very pretty oriel window. This comes from the s
called House of John of Gaunt, a house of the Sutton famil
which stood opposite St Mary's Guild in the S part of the Hig
Street. The inner gateway, thin, with round towers, is a piec
of early C19 romanticism.

Inside the castle the GAOL (now the Lincolnshire Recor
Office), of brick, built in 1787 by *Carr* of York and *Willia*
Lumby (cf. the motif of the blank arcade at his Blue Coa
School, p. 158) and enlarged in 1845–6. The CHAPE
probably dates from the time of the enlargement. It is
unique and terrifying space. Tiers of cubicles, head high
ensured that the convicts could see the preacher but no
each other. The side walls of each cubicle hinge to form th
doorway into the next, so that the system is self-locking
once in place, the row of felons could only be extracted on
at a time, and in order. The detailed design is truly brillian
and truly devilish, a fair reflection of the age which devise
philosophical theories to whitewash sending six-year-old
down the mines.‡ Also inside the castle the ASSIZE COURTS
Tudor, with turrets and cloister, built in 1823–6 by *Sir Rober*
Smirke, and, close to the N wall, a Gothic SUMMER HOUSE

But the chief medieval interest of the castle lies in its wall
and the towers along the walls. First the OBSERVATOR
TOWER in the SE corner. This is square, 40 ft by 40 ft in size
and consists of a Norman part, rectangular, 40 ft by 25 ft
and a C14 part added on the E side. In the Norman part th
difference between original masonry and C14 masonry high

---

* A little to the N of this gateway was the ROMAN WEST GATE. Remain
of it were found in 1836, buried beneath the castle mound.

‡ This account of the chapel was kindly contributed by Mr Ian Nairn.

er up can clearly be seen. The main doorway of the tower is C14. Its arch stands on head corbels. Single-chamfered lancet windows to the S and E. Battlements on big corbels. The round tower covering this keep so picturesquely is, needless to say, early C19. The whole keep stands on a mound. Then the LUCY TOWER, a shell-keep standing on another mound, a most unusual arrangement (but cf. Lewes). The keep belongs to the late C12, as is indicated by its doorway. Round arch, outer hood-mould with a billet and a scallop motif, inner arch segmental. Remains of shafting to the l. and r. of the doorway inside. The back exit has also a segmental arch. Where the keep joins the wall carrying on to the W a GARDEROBE in the wall at rampart level. Inside the keep a big tree and C19 graves of prisoners kept in the gaol.

Finally COBB HALL, the NE tower, quite small and rounded to the outside. It dates from the C13 and has slit windows in deep recesses. It has two rib-vaulted storeys. Single-chamfered ribs, small bosses. The vaults consist of two quadripartite bays in the centre of the tower, and one bay with nine radial ribs in the rounded part.

But the real keep of the castle – at least visually speaking – is, in spite of the existence of two medieval keeps, the WATER TOWER, just outside the N wall, a massive, solid, stone-built erection, designed by *Sir Reginald Blomfield* in 1910.

POLICE STATION, Monks Road and Lindum Road. The old gaol and sessions house. By *William Hayward*, 1805. Plain brick Georgian. Appropriately massive rusticated entrance to the gaol.

POST OFFICE, Guildhall Street. 1906 by *W. T. Oldrieve*. Arts and Crafts Tudor, of stone, three-storeyed, including the dormers.

CITY AND COUNTY MUSEUM, Greyfriars Pathway. The museum is housed in what remains of the GREYFRIARS', that is Franciscans', establishment. They had settled in Lincoln before 1230, and the remaining range may well have been built soon after. It is 101 ft long and almost certainly represents the church, or rather the undercroft of the church. Of the upper part no significant features remain, and externally indeed, apart from the masonry including the buttresses, nothing significant remains at all, except the E window with intersecting tracery and the small almond-shaped window over. The latter could be of *c*.1230 etc., the former must be late C13. The undercroft is vaulted and well preserved, but not

part of the scheme of *c*.1230. This is certain, because duri
restoration the sills of N lancets and E lancets were four
below the present upper floor level. However, the deta
of the undercroft make a date fairly soon after probable, ar
the late C13 is quite an acceptable one. The undercroft is tw
naved, nine bays long, and has octagonal piers and singl
chamfered ribs. Small, elementary bosses.

USHER ART GALLERY, Temple Gardens. By *Sir Regina*
Blomfield, 1927. Like his Library (*see* below) of twenty yea
earlier, still mostly French *dixhuitième*. He thought himse
the successor to Gabriel. All stone except for brick betwee
giant pilasters. Lots of swagged bucrania in a pseudo-friez
(For the ROMAN DITCH, *see* p. 141)

PUBLIC LIBRARY, Free School Lane. By *Sir Reginald Blon*
field, 1906. Of stone, one-storeyed, but with a two-storeye
domed centre. The style is Blomfield's usual mixture o
French *dixhuitième* with William and Mary motifs.

BISHOP GROSSETESTE COLLEGE, Newport. A nucleus wa
formed in 1841, then more added in 1862, then *Sir Arthu*
Blomfield's simple Gothic CHAPEL in 1873. The Constanc
Stewart Hall is by *R. E. M. Coombes*, 1950. Finally, th
Assembly Hall and Music Block, also by *Coombes*, 1961–2
Characterless.

CITY SCHOOL, Monks Road. 1885–6 by *George Sedger* c
London. Symmetrical, brick, Dutch Renaissance, with tw
gables and a clock-turret.

LINCOLN SCHOOL, Wragby Road. 1905 by *L. Stokes*. Re
strained and well-detailed Vernacular Jacobean style. Fifteen
bay cloister on the S front. Long ranges of mullions an
transoms over C17 'artisan'-style pedimented centrepiece and
cupola above.

GIRLS' HIGH SHOOL, Lindum Road. 1893 by *William Watkins*
Brick and red terracotta. Symmetrical, mostly round-arched
but also with Gothic bits. Pretty Greek-style TEMPLE
copied from the Choragic Monument of Thrasyllus. Early
C19. Figure of Niobe on the parapet.

COUNTY HOSPITAL, Sewell Road. Main nucleus by *Alexande*
Graham, 1878, in the Hatfield-House style. Low ancillary wing
by *W. Watkins*, 1891. These with a figure of Charity in a niche

BISHOP'S HOSTEL, Wordsworth Street. Formerly the In
firmary, and this part by *John Carr*, 1776 – although *William*
Lumby superintended the works. The S front is all that matters
Nine-bay centre and wings projecting three bays forward. Al

brick; three-storeyed. Three-bay pediment to the centre and stone Venetian windows to the ground and first floors of the wings. Odd square tripartite window above these. The wings, however, have been brought forward two bays; so this window is probably not original. Porch with Doric columns and pediment. Attached to one side, the CHAPEL, 1906 by *Temple Moore*. Brick, in the Dec style. Inside, ORGAN CASE, also by *Moore*, and in the Sacristy the C18 REREDOS.

ROMHEAD MATERNITY HOME, Nettleham Road. By *Scorer & Gamble*. Red-brick gabled style. Dutch-flavoured. 1926.

AWN ASYLUM, Union Road. What matters is the s front, and this is 1819–20 by *Richard Ingleman*. High centre block, five bays, three-storeyed, with a giant Ionic portico (not part of Ingleman's designs). On the portico wall a mounting range of Vitruvian openings. Low wings to r. and l. with two-bay wings slightly forwarded. At the old entrance a LODGE with Greek Doric order *in antis*, and *Thomas Milnes*'s statue of the benefactor, Dr Charlsworth, now boskily enshrined with roses etc.

T ANNE'S BEDEHOUSES, Sewell Road. For Richard Waldo Sibthorp, 1847, probably not completed until the 1860s. Sibthorp employed *A. W. N. Pugin*, but the patron's frequent changes of religious coat may have affected the character of the design. In plan this is remarkably loose: like a P open at the back of the head, open that is to the E. All single-storey with overhanging eaves. Red brick, hard stone details. The well-head in the court is probably closest to Pugin. Facing the court, the CHAPEL – and this is by *Butterfield*. Also brick. Four bays, steep roof with flèche, porch at the SW bay. Windows only in two bays. These are oddly placed: four-light and three-light adjacent, both in blank pointed arches. Four-light E window. The interior simple with wagon roof. The WARDEN'S HOUSE may also be by *Pugin*, but again it is 1860s in execution.

WEST VIEW (the former WORKHOUSE), Upper Long Leys Road. The stock brick parts by *W. A. Nicholson*, 1837, the red brick parts by *Watkins*, 1879. Both grim and messy.

BARRACKS, Burton Road. By *Goddard*, 1857. Castellated of course. Also barracks on the angle of Upper Long Leys Road and on Broadgate. Again castellated.

PRISON, Greetwell Road. By *F. Peck*, 1872. Open grid plan. Castellated Gothic with Romanesque touches. All red brick with stone details.

STATION, St Mary's Street. Completed in 1848. *Joseph Cubitt*,

the engineer to the Great Northern system, was probably h
own designer. The building is Tudor, grey brick. The ma
part seems at first symmetrical, but is made picturesque t
the deviations, culminating in the tower on the l., the lon
low extension on the r.

ST MARK'S STATION, High Street. Grey brick, symmetrica
Grecian, centre with giant Ionic portico, fluted columns, si
pavilions with giant Doric pilasters. The date is 184
Architect?

GRANDSTAND, Saxilby Road. 1826; stock brick. Altered, b
still with iron verandas on Doric columns. From this poir
one has a view of the cathedral w front dead-on.

ARBORETUM, Monks Road. Opened 1872. A successful terrac
layout between Lindum Terrace above and Monks Roa
below. Gay Victorian cast-iron bandstand and pavilions.
very sheepish-looking LION, signed by *Austin & Seeley*. Als
a Gaudí-esque, rocky FOUNTAIN in the pond.

PERAMBULATIONS

A) Exchequer Gate to Greetwell Gate, Newport Arch, and Bail-
ate; (B) Castle Hill and Steep Hill area; (C) Stonebow to Salter-
ate and Monks Road, Arboretum to Lindum Terrace and
Lindum Road; (D) Stonebow to Silver Street; upper end of
ne High Street to West Parade, and to Brayford and New-
and; (E) from the Stonebow s along the High Street and into
ne Markets area.

A) *Exchequer Gate to Greetwell Gate, Newport Arch, and Bail-*
gate.

Not the Castle Hill to start with (cf. p. 157), but first to the N
into BAILGATE, with at once a nice brick, three-bay, early
C18 façade over a garage (cf. Nos 6–7 Castle Hill, p. 157).*
Nearly opposite, the WHITE HART, its original façade of the
1840s. Bold pedimented first-floor windows. Many additions –
the latest by *Watkins, Coombes & Partners*, 1962. Now turn r.
into EASTGATE with not much to mention until on the r.
the plain front of No. 32, C19 but added to an earlier house.
At the back, really in the minster yard, two projecting wings
of unequal length. We now impinge on the PRECINCT proper,
but Eastgate continues as a through road, and so we must
continue. But first a little sally up JAMES STREET on our l.
No. 3 is unassuming early C19, then DELORAINE COURT, an
L-shaped building externally Georgian. In fact, however, it is
as old as anything around the Precinct. The W range in
its N part contains a Norman undercroft, at least five bays
long and probably longer. Round piers divide it along the
middle. The surviving capitals are still scalloped. The hall
of the house was presumably at r. angles to this range in the
N wing. In the W wing above the undercroft a fine panelled
room dated in the stucco frieze 1602. Panelling with pilasters.
Wooden overmantel. To the w a three-light transomed window and a canted oriel window of altogether seven lights.‡
Then James Street winds on, narrow between high walls, to
No. 7, the BURGHERSH CHANTRY, founded in 1345 for five
priests. The house is now mostly of the mid C18. The front
has an attractive squat Doric porch, but at the back is a wing
facing E and probably containing the original domestic chapel.§
We retrace our steps to Eastgate again, noticing on the corner
No. 8 (the Cathedral School), brick, late C18, with two canted

* The house next door has a vaulted E.E. undercroft.
‡ In the wall of the pantry a C15 sculptured slab. Subjects: St Catherine
tortured; St Catherine beheaded; Crucifixion.
§ This wing has recently been gutted by fire.

bays the height of the front. Later hooded porch. Then, nex
door, ATHERSTONE PLACE, a façade of the C17 with thre
semicircular pediments in the parapet. In the façade, at
characteristically low level, a Norman doorway. Two order
of shafts. Capitals with small decorated scallops. Arch an
hood mould with zigzag. The two tall C19 Gothic window
on the ground floor have genuine hood-mould stops of the C1
or C15. At the back, at the same low level, the remains of a doc
with chamfered jambs, probably C13. Atherstone Place is reall
one of a pair of houses which was once one. It adjoins what
now the BISHOP'S HOUSE. This presents an amorphou
grouping somewhat difficult to disentangle. Three gables on th
s front and 3–2–2 bays with the centre recessed. It might b
early C18. The E front has a later C18 canted bay and furthe
N two smaller gabled parts. This, on the other hand, might b
early C17. Inside, Drawing Room with screens of Dori
columns, and upstairs (in a bedroom, behind C18 panelling
linenfold panelling. Then on the s side – i.e. opposite – th
CATHEDRAL SCHOOL. This occupies the DEANERY, buil
in 1847 to designs of *William Burn*. It was placed to the E o
the site of the medieval Deanery. Of this no more is preserve
than the N wall, now the wall separating the garden from
Eastgate. In it to the s a fireplace of the Deanery, to the N
blocked C13 window with dog-tooth enrichment and a niche(?
with an ogee head. To the s a large number of architectural an
sculptural fragments from the cathedral, including a whole lat
C13 statuette of a King, about 5 ft tall. Also a Dec window head
a piscina, a length of quatrefoil frieze. Opposite, the EASTGAT
HOTEL, on the site of Sir Cecil Wray's splendid late C17
mansion. Nothing needs comment about the present architecture, but in front of it the foundations of the EAST GATE-
WAY of the Roman *colonia* were discovered in 1946.

We now pass Northgate on our l. and continue in Eastgate
No. 17 is probably Georgian, and next door, No. 18 is a front
of three bays and two storeys with Venetian windows and a
later Greek Doric porch. Basically the house is older, but no
so old as the plain brick addition. Past St Peter's church
(cf. p. 146) the best houses are on the s side. Nos 25–27, a
long, low, irregular eleven bays and two storeys in rough
stone, C18. Then DISNEY PLACE of 1736 by *Abraham*
Hayward, squashed between later C19 wings. The main front
brick, five bays, three storeys, segment-headed windows, stone
trimmings, cornice and parapet. The earlier doorway now

attached to a later porch. The back elevation repeats the front with inset balustrade to the parapet. Inside, the staircase has simple balusters and a plain plaster ceiling. A characteristic contemporary chimneypiece in one room. If we go on along GREETWELL GATE as far as ST LEONARD'S LANE, turning l. here, we pass a Tudoresque, 'villagey' SCHOOL of 1851. No. 2 St Leonard's Lane has a late C17 façade incorporating a mass-dial from the demolished St Leonard's church. Then into LANGWORTH GATE with our eyes on the cathedral towers again, and retracing our steps to the Eastgate Hotel, where EAST BIGHT, a walled, picturesque narrow lane, strikes N. Then W, passing a group of undistinguished buildings on the l. with medieval fragments, and on the r. a portion of the ROMAN WALL, see p. 140; for we are now just within the N boundary of the Roman town and East Bight debouches on to Bailgate at the point of the NEWPORT ARCH (cf. p. 140). Then, taking a S direction now, the BAILGATE METHODIST CHURCH, 1879, in *Bellamy & Hardy*'s Gothic, Nos 39–40 with medieval masonry bits, No. 34 early C19, and Nos 24–27 above the N end of a ROMAN COLONNADE, which continues for 275 ft under Bailgate. On the l. No. 76 is the ASSEMBLY ROOMS.* The front in dry classical style is of 1914, but some yards behind this can be seen the bold quoins and fine entablature of the front of 1744. The interior is certainly the finest Georgian room in Lincoln. Ionic pilasters, and each bay with a small square window near the cornice. WESTGATE on our r. provides a splendid view of the CASTLE walls and *Blomfield*'s WATER TOWER (cf. pp. 149–51). Continuing Bailgate there is not much (except No. 8 with a medieval undercroft), and we find ourselves back at the Exchequer Gate.

The Castle Hill and Steep Hill Area

From Exchequer Gate into CASTLE HILL, a misnomer, for this part is not a hill at all, but an irregular space in front of the castle gate. On the corner of Bailgate, No. 9 is timber-framed with two overhangs and three gables. A king carved against the angle bracket. This side, that is the N side of Castle Hill, has the best houses: Nos 6–7 a pretty pair, early C18, of brick. Five bays and three storeys, a part-balustraded parapet, segment-headed windows, and stone details. Stone doors with segmental pediments. Everything inside is paired. Notice the pine-panelled walls with arcaded treatment and a

* At the time of writing its future as such is uncertain.

fluted Doric order to the chimney wall. Might they be
Hayward? Then the finest house of its date in Lincoln,
JUDGES LODGING of *c*.1810, which is by *William Haywa*
Smooth, cold stock brick. Nine bays, three – three – thr
two storeys, the centre pedimented. Above the stone doorw
with Tuscan columns *in antis*, a window with flanking nich
DRURY LANE leads s from Castle Hill and passes the Bisho
Hostel in Wordsworth Street (cf. p. 152). CASTLE VIL
has a concoction of medieval bits said to come from
Catherine's Priory: some Norman and Transitional capita
some C13 arch stones, and a later C14 foliated boss. If t
perambulator walks further, to the junction with UNIC
ROAD, on the corner can be seen the so-called DE WIN
HOUSE, of the early C19. On the opposite corner is the lod
to THE LAWN and Dr Charlsworth's STATUE (cf. p. 153).
Then back until we reach the top of STEEP HILL, a cobble
narrow passage with bright glimpses to the distant gre
slopes of Canwick. The first houses to notice are Nos 25–2
No. 25 late C18 and Nos 26–27 incorporating a fragment
the Roman SOUTH GATE about 12 ft high (*see* p. 140). Then
our l. AARON THE JEW'S HOUSE on the E side at the ang
with Christ's Hospital Terrace. The house is called after the ri
Jew Aaron who died in 1186, but without any evidence of
connexion. The doorway was once similar to that of the Jew
House (*see* below). One order of thin shafts. Crocket capita
(which makes pre-1186 an early date). In the arch an orname
like a Norman ballflower. Hood mould heavy, with a slig
chamfer. It rests on a head and a caryatid bust. Above
probably was a chimneybreast like that in the Jew's Hous
The twin window which is still visible is re-set and most
re-done. (Tunnel-vaulted basement.)
The intersection with MICHAELGATE at this point creates t
most picturesque vista in the Steep Hill area. On its corne
a timber-framed house with two overhangs and curved brace
Now a diversion into CHRIST'S HOSPITAL TERRACE wi
on the s St Michael-on-the-Mount. On the N, nicely placed,
the old BLUE COAT SCHOOL (now Lincoln School of Art
designed in 1784 by *William Lumby*. Five bays, three storey
brick with stone details. The ground-floor windows are od
square, set in a blank arcade with a stone head – the same mo
as on the Carr–Lumby prison (cf. p. 150). Also stone is t
doorway with a Doric pediment. To the r. a slightly lat
extension, with similar arcading. Venetian window lighting

Great Room'. Nice details inside, particularly the staircase. Back to Steep Hill, pausing for Nos 3–4 in Christ's Hospital Terrace. Odd giant pilasters on the upper floors and no proper basement. It looks early C19. We now continue down Steep Hill – still cobbled – to Nos 21–22, picturesquely placed on a corner and half sunk into the road. Overhang to the N and E. Perhaps late C15, but certainly much restored. Nos 49–50 is a shadow of a rebuilt medieval house, stone below, timber-framing above. Past the junction with Danes Gate, Steep Hill continues still cobbled but now for pedestrians only (as all Steep Hills should be, a lesson Lincoln has not learned). At the junction with Danes Terrace it becomes the STRAIT with the JEW'S HOUSE on the r., a two-storeyed stone house 8a of the later C12. The hall was on the upper floor, but quite an ornate entrance is at ground level. One order of shafts. Arch with interlaced chain-links, broken round the angle of the order of voussoirs. Shallow chimneybreast above it. Two twin upper windows remain, though in the r. one the middle division has gone. The l. window has the two sub-arches, but no shaft either. The mouldings of the main arches are quite elaborate. Immediately to its r. is JEWS COURT, a front without any medieval features.* There is not much to notice in the rest of the Strait, so we return to Exchequer Gate, but we should notice on the way, opposite the Jew's House, DANES TERRACE with a nice early C19 range of dwellings.

) *Stonebow to Saltergate and Monks Road, Arboretum to Lindum Terrace and Lindum Road*

In SALTERGATE the FALCON HOTEL on the l. 1937 by *T. Cecil Howitt*, chunky Metroland style. Then a small verdant breathing space, an old graveyard, with early C19 houses on the N side. Passing St Swithin's church to BROADGATE with the Greyfriars (cf. p. 151) on the l. and to MONKS ROAD with *Hayward*'s Police Station (cf. p. 151) on the corner and St Hugh's R.C. church (cf. p. 143) on the r. Also on this side is ROSEMARY LANE, where we can see the pretty WESLEYAN DAY SCHOOLS in patterned red and white brick. Tall thin tower and gay cupola. By *Bellamy & Hardy*, 1859. These are the parts towards the river Witham, bordering the in-dustrial area. In the C19 the workers were kept near their

* The house is believed to have been the Synagogue. Inside in the front wall a shallow niche attributed to the purpose of holding the Torah rolls. The evidence is inadequate. Can the niche not be the remains of a fireplace like that of the Jew's House and Aaron's House?

factories, and so their housing spread in a grid of twenty-fo
N-S roads in just over three quarters of a mile off Mon
Road. Neglecting these dull roads, however, we pass to bet
things, that is, to the ABORETUM (cf. p. 154), on Monks Ro
again. We leave the Arboretum by the NE corner for t
COUNTY HOSPITAL (cf. p. 152), for ST ANNE'S BED
HOUSES (cf. p. 153), and for the Early Victorian developme
of LINDUM TERRACE – houses mostly in long thin garde
with long views S. On the r. in UPPER LINDUM ROAD
the old Lincoln Grammar School (now St Joseph's Conven
by *W. Watkins*, 1884. A hall like a small C17 City of Lond
Hall, with a cupola. Then, just before Lindum Road is reache
LINDUM HOLME, terraced above the road and most
Georgian. All that is worth noticing is on the r., and especial
the USHER ART GALLERY (cf. p. 152), the pretty TEMPL
on the hill (cf. p. 152), and the Early Victorian houses at a
angle to TEMPLE GARDENS. One has a columned veran
over a low arcade. Between the two a linking Ionic corrid
and to its r. the prettiest piece of Victorian confectionery
Lincoln: an ingeniously devised staircase, almost like
baldacchino from a Pompeian painting transposed into th
superimposed iron columns. Glass dome and frills of acanth
and acroteria.

(D) *Stonebow to Silver Street; upper end of High Street to We
Parade, and to Brayford and Newland*

Adjoining the Stonebow on the l. is the NATIONAL PRO
VINCIAL BANK, in a sombre Renaissance palazzo style, 188
by *John Gibson*. Just NE of this is the area where St Peter a
Arches stood. What has been substituted is far less good, an
nothing deserves mention. SILVER STREET is a good ex
ample of Victorian refulgence. Lots of eclecticism here: th
ROYAL INSURANCE CO. of 1857 by *Pearson Bellamy* –
much underrated architect. Again in the palazzo style (cf. h
town hall at Louth). Enrichments of vermiculation, rustication
grotesque masks and swags. Then on the N side a Venetia
Revival building and an example of *Watkins*'s familiar loca
Dutch Renaissance with Dutch gables. Further along, on th
S side the former METHODIST FREE CHURCH, 1864 b
Bellamy & Hardy (GS), white brick, in a debased Renais
sance style. An odd and lively arrangement. Coupled column
flanking a big niche with a pediment 'floating' out of th
parapet above. Adjacent is the CONSTITUTIONAL CLUB o

the corner of Broadgate, 1895 and presumably by *Watkins*.
Lots of terracotta reliefs. A domed circular vestibule at the
angle. Now we turn into CLASKETGATE with DANESGATE
on the r. and the decent modern NATIONAL ASSISTANCE
BOARD OFFICES, and, further along, a very plain Perp
gateway. Four-centred arch. We can then by-pass *Nicholson*'s
Methodist Chapel (cf. p. 147) by taking GRANTHAM STREET
(Victorian terraces) and turning l. by a cobbled lane into
Clasketgate again. There is nothing more to see until the
High Street. Turn r. here towards the Strait. The old GRAND
CINEMA boasts stumpy Venetian windows of the mid C18.*
On the corner of Grantham Street, No. 268 (Halifax Building
Society) has a recent brick ground floor, but round the angle
part of a masonry ground floor. The rest late C15, timber-framed
with two overhangs. Moulded angle shafts. ST DUNSTAN'S
LOCK faces along the High Street. Really the corruption of
Dernestall Lock, that is, gate to a medieval grotto. Now the
upper parts of undistinguished C18 houses. Turn l. into ST
MARTIN'S LANE (for a view of the cathedral) and cross
Hunt Gate to Motherby Lane and West Parade. On the r. is
MOTHERBY HILL, cobbled, narrow, and steep, with stepped
Victorian terraces on both sides. For those who take this hill,
an alley on the l. leads via VICTORIA STREET back to WEST
PARADE. Here Nos 30–54 are brick terraces, still with pedimented doorways, i.e. in the Georgian tradition, but dateable
to the 1840s or 50s. Passing St Martin's church on the l. (*see*
p. 144), into THE AVENUE, and into NEWLAND, with the
County Offices (p. 149) on the l. Opposite are Nos 78–88, an
early C19 group of two – two – three – two – two bays, a
pedimented centre and porches tucked into the angles. On
the r. LUCY TOWER STREET with *D. Clarke-Hall, Scorer &*
Bright's LINCOLNSHIRE MOTOR COMPANY SHOWROOMS,
1959, facing Brayford Wharf. This is the best point to see in
one picture the old warehouses on the wharves and the anima-
tion of road, rail, and water transport. All the best WARE-
HOUSES are on the E side, from three to seven storeys and
from Later Georgian to Early Victorian. WATER LANE should
not be missed for its view of the back of High Bridge and the 39b
characteristic top-heavy jettied effect which as a rule can only
be seen on drawings of medieval bridges. From here, l. to Newland again, and we shall find that we have missed only the
Newland Congregational church (cf. p. 148) and a nice early

* Demolition is pending in this area.

6—L

C19 terrace with iron balconies. Then in GUILDFOR
STREET, past the Post Office (cf. p. 151), we are back at th
Stonebow.

(E) *From the Stonebow s along the High Street and into th
Market area*

To the r. on the corner of Guildford Street, the MIDLAN
BANK (former Lincoln and Lindsey Bank), 1848. Lower par
with fat Dietterlinesque pilasters. Upper parts with Earl
Georgian details. As we are taking the w side of the Hig
Street, nothing more here until HIGH BRIDGE, mediev
but much restored. On its E side a projection carried a chap
of St Thomas Becket. The w side – and this is unique i
England –still carries a row of C16 shops and houses, timbe
framed. Two overhangs. All windows project like oriels. The
are much re-done. Original angle-brackets with demi-figure
39b of angels. At the back, visible from along the footpaths l. an
r. of the Witham, stone base and bridge-arch. The timberwor
is here rough-cast. Two symmetrical plain oriels on bracket
Only the top floor has the timberwork exposed. Then th
punctuation of St Benedict's church and ST BENEDICT'
SQUARE. At the w end the THOMAS COOPER MEMORIA
BAPTIST CHURCH, 1885 by *J. Wallis Chapman*. On the angl
LLOYDS BANK, 1890. Dehydrated Georgian Baroque wit
Baroque cupola. Did *Blomfield* design the WAR MEMORIA
looking like a Gothic dovecot? The first stone was laid i
1922 by John Harris. Then nothing more to notice until th
upper parts of Nos 190–191. François Premier terracott
façade, by *Watkins*.

We can now make a sally along BRAYFORD STREET to se
• BRAYFORD WHARF, but then back again to Nos 184–186
Mutilated mid-Georgian front built by *William Lumby* fo
Alderman Gibbeson. Across the railway lines to the GREA
NORTHERN HOTEL, thirteen bays on the railway side. I
was built by *H. Goddard* in 1847, but has ceilings and chimney
pieces still 1770 in style. Behind, WIGFORD HOUSE, earl
C19 with Ionic door surround. Still the High Street continues
past the OMNIBUS STATION (1958) to St Mark's Statio
(cf. p. 154). W of this, ST MARKS HOUSE, the most elegan
expression so far of the 1960s in Lincoln. Note particularl
the handsome staircase boldly exposed behind glass walling
Otherwise white glass and wooden slat infillings. Black met
framework. We now cross the second set of railway lines, pa

the Methodist Chapel of 1905 (*see* p. 147) to No. 117, where, at the back, bits of John of Gaunt's Palace (a late C15 traceried window with cusped lights. MHLG). A medieval corbel on No. 113. In ALFRED STREET C19 industrial terraces. Then GOWT'S BRIDGE, rebuilt after the bridge of 1813 which was by *William Hayward*. Returning from this long N–S perambulation, for a S–N one, still along the High Street. First St Peter at Gowts (cf. p. 146), then at once ST MARY'S GUILD, an interesting Late Norman or Transitional stone building, originally three ranges round a long courtyard. But only one has architectural features of interest still *in situ*. It is the range towards the street. The façade has flat buttresses. Big round-headed archway. At the top of the jambs chamfer with two heads. Arch with several orders, including one studded with flowers, another with small individual dog-tooth forms. Above runs a frieze of stylized leaves still entirely Norman. Above this two heads, perhaps re-set. To the l. one small window. Evidence of upper windows. Inside, more evidence of the upper hall, namely two large blank arches to the N, on a shaft. There were no doubt two major windows here. In the S gable outside re-set Norman bits and also a head under a canopy; C13. The archway opens towards the courtyard with a segmental arch. In the N range towards its E end what seems a separate house. It has twin openings, one still with its octagonal shaft.

Back across two pairs of railway lines, past St Mary-le-Wigford and the Conduit (cf. p. 144), and turn r. into ST MARY'S STREET. Here we notice the CENTRAL STATION (cf. p. 153) and the Victorian ALBION HOTEL. The adjacent assembly room is a Georgian hangover, complete with Venetian window. From here a detour to PELHAM BRIDGE, a thirteen-hundred-foot curving span. Opened in 1958. It provides the best view of the cathedral: the whole of the S front with the medieval buildings hanging on the hillside. From St Mary, SINCIL STREET opens to the Market area, that is, first the CORNHILL opening on to the High Street. On the corner is BARCLAYS BANK by *H. G. Gamble*, 1873. Three-storeyed, a mixture of Italian Gothic type and English Transitional motifs. Then the old CORN EXCHANGE by *W. A. Nicholson*, 1847. Classical with a projecting Corinthian portico at *piano nobile* level. The back parts are of 1878–80, by *Bellamy & Hardy*, who did the newer EXCHANGE adjacent. The predominant feature is the emphatic arcading of the S flank. To the N is

the old front of the BUTTER MARKET (near where St Peter
at-Arches was), built into a modern, sympathetically-designed
front. It is dated 1737. Two bays of rusticated arches on the
ground floor, a balustraded Venetian window above, and
pediment with Rococo cartouche. We are now in the area of
WATERSIDE SOUTH and WATERSIDE NORTH. In the
former first No. 21, probably early C16 beneath the stucco
skin, then the GREEN DRAGON INN, timber-framed with
two overhangs and four gables. Much of it is recent restoration
but what could be preserved, was preserved. Then across
THORN BRIDGE to the mills which flank the banks of the
river Witham. The best is DOUGHTY'S MILL of 1863. Grey
brick. Towering Flemish-style centrepiece. Further along is
RUSHTON AND HORNSBY. This is in contrast red brick. It is
also still C19. Returning to the High Street by the N bank and
High Bridge, on the l. we have only missed another terracotta
Watkins façade. All there is to note before we are back at the
Stonebow is the old SARACEN'S HEAD HOTEL. Late
Georgian with a particularly fine array of sixteen panels of
wrought iron to the balcony. The patterns come from one of
Taylor's pattern books.

LINDSEY

*

ABY

½ m. E of Belleau

ALL SAINTS. 1888. – PLATE. Chalice(?), C17.

ADDLETHORPE

NICHOLAS. An ashlar-faced Perp Marshland church. W tower with two tiny niches and a shield above the W window and three-light bell-openings. The arch towards the nave has concave-sided semi-octagonal responds. Embattled clerestory with a crocketed E gable. Embattled aisles with pinnacles and, on the N side, gargoyle-like figures at the top of the buttresses, some with inscription scrolls. Sumptuous S porch similar to that at Winthorpe. It was built at the expense of John Godard (see the inscription on the E wall of the porch inside). Fleurons in a moulding and the hood-mould of the entrance. Niche over, leaf trail of nobbly leaves in the parapet (but quatrefoils in that over the W and E walls). Fine cross at the top with the Crucifixus and at the back the Virgin. The porch has its original roof with bosses and a stone niche in the NE corner. Five-bay arcades inside with octagonal piers and double-hollow-chamfered arches. Chancel arch in the same style. Roof of low pitch with tie-beams and queenposts, and 27a angels against the principals between those connected by the tie beams. Angels also in the S aisle roof. It is unfortunate that the church was deprived of its chancel, in 1706, the same year in which this was done at Ingoldmells. – FONT. Octagonal, the stem patterned, the bowl with rough tracery patterns. – SCREENS. Tall and noble rood screen, now at the E end. Two-light divisions with Y-tracery and cusped ogee arches under this. Also panel tracery. Varieties of single-light divisions with ogee arches and panel tracery now in the E bays of the two aisles, at the W ends of the two aisles, and also under the arch. The latter has an inscription recording the donors John Dudeck and his wife. The inventiveness in the details of this

screenwork is a constant source of delight. – SOUTH DO‹
Perp, with tracery. – BENCHES. Many and with good pop›
heads. – STAINED GLASS. In the NE windows compl‹
figures in the tracery heads and also canopies; C15. – PLA‹
Chalice and Paten, by *T. G.*, London, 1686.

AISTHORPE

9080

ST PETER. 1867 by *T. C. Hine*. W tower with short broach-sp›
Nave and chancel windows with plate tracery and other c›
looking details.

ALFORD

4070

ST WILFRID. A large, greenstone town-church, larger now th‹
it was in the Middle Ages; for *Sir G. G. Scott*, in 1865–‹
added the outer N aisle in the style of the rest. This rest‹
mostly Dec, and decidedly over-restored. The four-stage
tower, however, is Perp. Wills contributing to its cost d‹
from 1529 and 1530. The doorway moulding is typica‹
Perp. On top eight pinnacles.* The spacious S porch is proba‹
also Perp. Some windows of the church are Perp too, and the ‹
window of the S aisle, four lights with a transom, must ‹
Elizabethan or a little later. But Dec the chancel (reticula‹
tracery N, S, and – of five lights – E, sedilia with crocket‹
gables), Dec the N chapel (reticulated tracery and the E wind‹
with a curious kind of reticulation of ogee-headed trefoils), a‹
Dec the S aisle (see the mouldings of the S doorway) and t‹
four-bay arcades. They have octagonal piers, quite spectacu‹
big-leaf capitals and double-chamfered arches. – SCREEN. ‹
wide, ogee-arched divisions, with panel tracery above t‹
arches. – PULPIT. A splendid Jacobean piece, especially t‹
one side with quite undecorated panelling but in an u‹
common pattern. Otherwise the familiar low blank arches a‹
also odd, barbaric figures. – SOUTH DOOR. With trace‹
– STAINED GLASS. Good C14 glass in the chancel N, and t›
N chapel N window. – PLATE. Chalice, London, 156‹
Chalice, Paten, Flagon, and Almsdish, by *Wm. Darkara‹*
1722; Font Bowl, by *John Fossey*, 1736(?); Spoon, by *W›*
Homer(?), 1761. – MONUMENTS. In the S aisle scrolly tab‹
with a small bust right at the top, the inscription quite illegib‹
the date probably the second third of the C17. The lady‹

* The open-cage tower staircase of wood, C19 probably, is fun to see a‹
use.

supposed to have been of the Tiptoft family and married to a Neville. – Sir Robert Christopher † 1668 and wife. Large standing alabaster monument surrounded by its original iron railing. Recumbent effigies, he in armour, his hand on his breast. Back wall with open segmental pediment and garlands l. and r. The monument is attributed to *Edward Strong*, who, however, was born only in 1652.

PERAMBULATION. Start in the MARKET PLACE, which pleases by its irregular shape. On the w side the WINDMILL HOTEL with Doric porch. Turn s from the Market Place and then at once w to the end of CARR LANE to sample the WINDMILL with ogee cap, not Alford's best. Then from the NW end of the Market Square along WEST STREET, and here first on the r. the MANOR HOUSE, said to have been built in 1661. Brick, H-shaped and gabled. Then the METHODIST CHAPEL of 1864, by *W. Botterill* of Hull (GS), big, of stock brick, Gothic, with Geometrical tracery, a high doorway, and two-storeyed fenestration along the sides. To its l. a nice semi-detached stock-brick pair with steep two-bay pediment, probably of about 1840, then thatched cottages and opposite, on the l., MERTON LODGE, Late Georgian, of five bays and two storeys, with a thin Doric porch.

From the start of West Street E, first along HIGH STREET to the church along its s side. The houses to note are No. 6, white, of three widely spaced bays, window and doorway with fanlights, mostly segmental; No. 15, a good early C18 five-bay house with fluted pilasters and a metope frieze surrounding the doorway and with dormers with alternatingly triangular and segmental pediments; No. 12, a C17 house (see the brickwork and the line of the former gable) with C18 fenestration and a nice doorway. On to EAST END, where, on the l., a Georgian house at r. angles to the street, six bays, pediment with lunette window, doorway with thin Doric porch, and so, past some early C19 villas, to the other WINDMILL, one of Lincolnshire's finest, a six-storey brick tower of 1837 with ogee cap and sails and fan-tail in working order.

ALKBOROUGH

ST JOHN BAPTIST. Anglo-Saxon w tower, see the w window and the unmistakable twin bell-openings.* The church was

* Roman masonry bearing mouldings has been used as imposts and bases of the arch between tower and nave.

given to Spalding Priory in 1052. The upper part of the towe
is E.E. The s doorway also E.E. and quite sumptuous, wit
three orders of shafts, capitals with upright leaves, and
richly moulded arch with some dog-tooth and some bille
Of the same time the arcades inside. They are of three bay
with quatrefoil piers, or rather square piers with four broa
demi-shafts. Stiff-leaf capitals on the s, moulded capitals o
the N side. Circular abaci. Double-chamfered arches. Dec :
aisle windows, straight-headed with reticulation motifs. Per
s aisle windows. Chancel by *John Oldrid Scott*, 1887. – In th
base of the N respond of the tower arch, below floor level, a
Anglo-Saxon STONE with interlace. – In the floor of the s porc
MAZE, a small copy of that mentioned below. – In the church
yard gloriously weathered shaft of a Churchyard CROSS, lik
a successful piece of recent sculpture. – PLATE. Chalice an
Paten Cover, by *John Morley* of Lincoln, 1569; Chalice, Paten
and Flagon, by *Charles Fox*, 1830.

WESLEYAN CHAPEL. 1840. Yellow brick. A two-bay front wit
three stone Ionic pilasters and a pediment. In this a segmenta
panel.

COUNTESS CLOSE. On a hill top overlooking the Trent valley
lies a roughly square EARTHWORK with sides 300 ft long
broken by an entrance on the N. The site is undated, and i
may represent the remains of a fortified medieval steading.

MAZE, to the SW of the church, against the cliff-side overlookin
the confluence of Trent and Humber. Circular, 40 ft across
Cut roughly out of the grass. Its traditional name is Julian's
Bower, from Julus, son of Aeneas. The Troy Saga is traditionally connected with mazes.*

WALCOT HALL, ½ m. SW. Mid-Georgian, and ambitious in a
plain way. E front of five bays, two storeys, and slightly
projecting centre, once pedimented. The big Doric porch
with an iron balustrade looks C19. N and S fronts each
with pairs of three-window canted bays and a three-bay
three-floor centre between. STABLES with three pedimented
projections.

See
p.
767 WALCOT OLD HALL. L-shaped, brick, in a mid-C17 Artisan
style. Three-bay w front of two storeys. The windows on
ground floor and upper floor are vertically bound together
by placing them in a flat projection. The same applies to doorway and window above it. The windows are all mullioned with
a transom. Those on the ground floor and the doorway have

* See W. H. Matthews: *Mazes and Labyrinths*, London 1922.

orick pediments. A pediment also at the top of the centre bay.
Plenty of wilful details, all in cut brick.

ALTHORPE 8000

OSWALD. Built by Sir John Neville in 1483 – see his arms
below a helm up on the w side of the tower. The whole church
is in fact of a piece, except for the chancel arch, whose responds
are clearly Dec. The funds provided by the donor were chiefly
lavished over the tower and the chancel. The tower is ashlar-
faced and has in one moulding of the doorway coarse faces,
square leaves, etc. Buttress shafts with pinnacles l. and r.
Fleuron-frieze below the w window. Hood-mould with stops
over the w window. Two-light bell-openings with transom.
The nave clerestory and the N aisle embattled. Two-storeyed
NE vestry. Plain C18 brick s porch. Chancel of three bays,
embattled and with gargoyles. Three-light windows with
figural hood-mould stops. The windows have an embattled
transom above the middle light just below the small panel
tracery. Five-light E window. The interior is somewhat disappointing after this display. Four-bay N arcade with octagonal piers and double-chamfered arches. Two-bay N chapel
arcade. The pier also octagonal, but the arch of two sunk
chamfers with a three-quarter hollow between. Good sedilia
in the chancel with turret-like projecting, solid, embattled
canopies. In the N aisle a prettily carved bracket for an image,
also with the Neville arms. – SCREEN. Some original work in
the dado. – PLATE. Chalice, by *John Morley* of Lincoln,
c.1569; Paten Cover, early C17. – BRASS to William de
Lound, rector, c.1360; demi-figure (chancel s wall).
LD HALL. L-shaped, with a later C17 doorway, all of brick.
Broad pilasters and a heavy pediment.

ALVINGHAM 3090

r ADELWOLD. In the same churchyard at Alvingham in which
also, a little further w, lies the parish church of North
Cockerington. Both churches can only be reached through a
farmyard. Late C13 w tower (w window with intersecting
tracery; bell-openings with Y-tracery; many-moulded tower
arch). Perp nave windows. Brick chancel of 1806. Beneath it,
during restoration in 1933, foundations of two distinct chancels were found. – FONT. The font is a reversed octagonal

capital of the C13. – PLATE. Chalice and Paten Cover,
John Morley of Lincoln, 1569; Chalice and Paten Cover
c.1600.

There was a priory of Gilbertine Canons and nuns at Alvingham
founded c.1150. But no remains other than odd blocks
carved stone are visible, and no plan has been found by excava
tion.

8010 AMCOTTS

CHURCH. 1853. Nave and chancel and w steeple. Rock-faced
even the spire. Lancet windows. A thin hammerbeam roo
inside.

(RECTORY. By *James Fowler*, 1862 and 1880. GA)

5070 ANDERBY

ST ANDREW. 1759. Of brick, with short w tower and arche
keyed-in windows. The chancel and the polygonal apse are
1887. – PLATE. Chalice, by *John Newton*, 1747. – CROSS
the churchyard; base and part of the shaft.

RECTORY. 1852 by a builder, *George Abbott*. Nice stock-brick
box with pilasters (GA).

1070 APLEY

1⅜ m. NNE of Stainfield

ST ANDREW. – PLATE. Chalice and Cover, c.1568.

9010 APPLEBY

ST BARTHOLOMEW. The arcades of three bays are both Dec
with piers partly octagonal, partly quatrefoil with fillets an
deeply hollowed out diagonals. A little nailhead in the abac
Double-chamfered arches. Perp chancel arch with a charmin
single leaf in the deep hollow of the respond moulding on eac
side. The tower below perhaps older than above.* The bel
openings are Victorian. The ornate nave and aisles with flow
ing tracery in the windows and with battlements, fleuron
friezes under, and pinnacles all of 1883. – FONT. Norman
drum-shaped, with intersecting arches. – PULPIT. With man
small Flemish C16 reliefs. The tester looks c.1820–30.
COMMUNION RAIL. A Flemish C18 piece with luxurian
* Hamilton Thompson noted herringbone masonry in the w wall.

foliage, the chalice and host, a can, etc. – STAINED GLASS.
E window by *Capronnier* of Brussels, 1862, and so different
from English High Victorian glass – more pictorial and less
Gothic. – In the s aisle w window by *Kempe*, 1901. – PLATE.
Chalice and Paten Cover, by *John Morley* of Lincoln, 1569;
Chalice, German, C17; silver-gilt Tazza with the story of
Esther, by *Christoph Leneker*, Augsburg, *c.*1610; two Patens,
Dutch (Amsterdam?), 1712. – MONUMENT. Dec tomb-chest
with panels of big blank tracery to the s and E, two blank three-
light windows with more intricate tracery to the w. – In the
vestry a square panel with a rose-window, its centre a quatrefoil, probably from THORNHOLME PRIORY, a house of Augustinian Canons, founded in the mid C12 and situated 2 m. SE.
APPLEBY HALL.* Only outbuildings remain, perhaps those
built by *Joseph Fowler* for Mr Winn, 1821–3 (Colvin).

ASGARBY
3060

¾ m. SW of Lusby

ST SWITHIN. Brick on a greenstone base. Early C19. Round-
arched windows with Y-tracery or three stepped lancet lights.
Are the latter of the restoration of 1882? – FONT. A one-foot-
high earthenware vessel with Gothic decoration. Another of
them is at Biscathorpe. – PLATE. Chalice, mid-C17. – MONU-
MENT. A tablet with a draped urn is signed *Rayson*, Horncastle. So even in so small a town there was a statuary for this
kind of work. It is indeed still entirely Georgian, though the
date of death is 1846.

ASHBY *see* SCUNTHORPE, pp. 356, 358, 359

ASHBY-BY-PARTNEY
4060

ST HELEN. 1841. Red brick,‡ modest and in outline still
Georgian. Pointed windows; re-detailed in 1892. L. and r. of
the altar shields in quatrefoils. They may come from a tomb-
chest. – PLATE. Paten, by *William Lukin*, 1700; two-handled
Cup, by *Thos. Ewesdin*, 1721; Beaker, London, 1737. –
MONUMENT. George Gilbi † 1580. Small tablet, clearly by the
sculptor who did the Bertie Monument of 1582 at Spilsby.
Arms in a scroll surround and inscription.

* The house was drawn by Nattes in 1794.
‡ Still in English bond, *incredibile dictu*.

2000

ASHBY-CUM-FENBY

St Peter. Unbuttressed E. E. w tower with high bell-opening
Y-tracery on a shaft; dog-tooth decoration. The tower arch o
head corbels. The rest of the church low and modest. The
aisle with late, poor, domestic windows, the s side with De
tracery and traces of what may have been a s arcade. Th
interior does not reveal anything. But there is a N arcade, als
E. E. Four bays, quatrefoil piers, keeled. The capitals (excep
for one) and the arches are no doubt as late as the aisle wall
The chancel also post-medieval, of brick, but with re-use
tall and good Dec windows. Reticulated tracery. – FONT
Octagonal, Perp, with quatrefoils or mouchette wheels i
circles. – PILLAR PISCINA. Norman, on four shafts, with
scalloped capital, now at the w end. – SCREEN. Under th
tower part of a C14 screen. The arches, ogee-headed an
cusped, two deep (which is a charming conceit), stand o
polygonal shafts. – STAINED GLASS. Bits in the chancel
windows. – PLATE. Chalice, by *John Morley* of Lincoln
c.1569. – MONUMENTS. Effigy of a Knight, cross-legged
early C14. – Suzanna Drury † 1606. Standing wall-monument
The surround with big fluted pilasters, a flat arch, and putti i
the spandrels is Jacobean all right, but the semi-reclinin
effigy, one hand lying on scattered flowers, and also the tw
hounds supporting the sarcophagus lid and the wreath
against the back wall, must be a replacement of c.1700 (in th
style of Bird). – Sir Anthony Irby † 1623 and Lady Frances
Wray, his wife, † before 1647. The monument evidently o
c.1640 (see the foundation date of the almshouses, below). Ten-
poster (four by two). Reclining effigies, the children leanin
against the base, except for one recumbent baby by the
parents' feet. The angels' draperies are typical of the date.

Wray Almshouses. Facing the w end of the church. Built of
brick in 1641. For six persons and very humble.

Rectory, sw of the church. Just a brick box. Built in 1844 by
John Carr, a builder (GA).

Hall Farm, N of the church. Georgian with Venetian windows.
The later outbuildings enlivened with blank semicircular
lights.

3070

ASHBY PUERORUM

St Andrew. *Puerorum*, because the living was appropriated to
the support of the choir boys of Lincoln Cathedral. Green-

stone; mostly E.E., except for the Perp w tower (semi-octagonal, concave-sided responds) and the Perp, ashlar-faced N aisle. N and S doorways. – COMMUNION RAIL. C17, with massive balusters. – PLATE. Two-handled Cup, by *I.C.*, London, 1676; Paten, by *John Wetherall* (?), London, 1787. – MONUMENTS. Brasses of a husband and wife, and of a man in armour; *c.*1560, though the inscription displayed with them refers to Lytleburys who died in 1521 and 1523. – Incised slab to a priest, early C14, figure under a canopy (beneath the altar). OLBECK MANOR, 1¼ m. NW. A house of 1823, now much added to. The landscape of 1834 in the best Salvator Rosa taste, craggy, planted with firs and bracken, with a romantic lake. Its origin is a sandstone quarry said to have been worked as early as Roman times. Lots of architectural fragments about the gardens collected by the owner. They include parts of Denton Hall near Grantham (bay window) and bits of quatrefoil friezes, also a pedimented archway with Ionic pilasters from Eastgate House Lincoln and an Italian fountain from Sudbrook House Lincoln.

ASTERBY 2070

ST PETER. Of greenstone. W tower with pyramid roof. The S side much repaired. One small Norman head should be noted. Of the N aisle the two W bays have been demolished. The others remain. Circular piers, double-chamfered arches. – PULPIT and LECTERN. Carved very naively. The pulpit is of 1890, the lectern of 1899. – PLATE. Chalice, probably 1629; Paten, by *Hugh Saunders*, 1730.

DUTCH HOUSE, 1½ m. S. A three-bay front beneath one big shaped gable. That far it is a C17 house. But the gable is topped by an urn and the windows of ground floor and first floor are vertically joined under blank arches. That gives it the look of a Palladian farmhouse. The house now has a large date 1829, but old photographs show the date 1..8. Sited in trees on a plateau, the ensemble is most attractive.

ASWARDBY 3070

ST HELEN. Dated 1747. Stone, but with a brick-faced S wall. Victorian bell-turret. The S windows segment-headed and curiously Dutch-looking. The E end has an arched window and an oval one in the gable. But the chancel was rebuilt in

1840. – PLATE. Paten on foot, before 1697; Chalice and Paten
by *Humphrey Payne*, 1736.

ASWARDBY HALL. Built on the side of a small valley. The
front, wings and three-bay centre, belongs to a C17 house.
This was completely remodelled by *H. M. Fletcher* in 191.
and all the details are his.

AUTHORPE
4080

ST MARGARET. 1848. Of greenstone, nave with bellcote and
chancel. The windows have Y-tracery. Medieval parts were
also re-used in the church. Late Perp N and S windows, Perp
doorway, and a N doorway which seems still to be Dec. –
FONT. Octagonal, of the pattern-book type, i.e. seven patterns
of windows, all Dec; the eighth a large tracery motif. – PULPIT
Simple, Georgian, with fluted pilasters at the angles. – PLATE
Chalice, Paten, and Flagon, by *A.M.*, London, 1667.

AYLESBY
2000

ST LAWRENCE. Of ironstone. Perp W tower. The details
most of the rest Victorian. But the W window of the S aisle
may be correct (intersecting tracery), and the S doorway is
Hood-mould on heads, dateable to the later C14. The arcade
of the three bays inside both E.E., both with round piers and
round abaci and double-chamfered arches, but the S side a
little earlier – see the 'water-holding' bases. The S side also
has seats round the piers. The chancel E.E. too – see the two
E lancets. In the N wall a recess whose sunk quadrant moulding
however, indicates an early C14 date. – FONT. Of tun shape
with four angle-shafts; C13 and primitive. – BOX PEWS
1759. – PLATE. Chalice, *c.*1570. – MONUMENT. Early C1.
effigy of a lady.

BAG ENDERBY
3070

ST MARGARET. Greenstone. All Perp: W tower, nave and chan
cel. The building can be dated by an inscription to Albinus
de Enderby † 1407, whose donations built 'istam ecclesiam
cum campanile'. The windows with segmental arches are
worth noting. – FONT. Octagonal, Perp, with representation
of the Pietà, a seated figure with a lute, a fox biting its tail (?)
a shield with the Instruments of the Passion, etc. – SCREEN
One-light divisions with ogee arches. Only parts are ancient.

STAINED GLASS. Original bits in the nave window and a chancel s window. – PLATE. Chalice and Paten Cover, by *John Morley* of Lincoln, 1569. – MONUMENTS. Tablet with kneeling figures in flat relief facing each other across a prayer desk. Short Ionic pilasters l. and r. The monument commemorates the family of Andrew Gedney, whose wife died in 1591. AG ENDERBY HALL, s of the church. Once C17 with later bits, but now, after a fire, truncated.

BARDNEY

ARDNEY ABBEY. All that is visible of the venerable abbey is a ditch, remains of one compound nave pier, bumps where others had been, something of the w wall of the nave with traces of the middle doorway, and many hillocks of no precise message. Yet the whole site was excavated in 1909–14, much was found to stand at least in its lower masonry courses, and an admirable account was given by Sir Harold Brakspear (*Arch. J.*, 79, 1922). He described that, when operations started, there were only 'various mounds and depressions' and pointed out warningly that owing to the eight and more years of unprotected exposure of the finds, they were 'gradually crumbling away'. It is exceedingly sad to see how radically all has been obliterated that had been recovered of this famous house of Benedictines, founded probably late in the C7, ravaged by the Danes, left desolated, and refounded by Gilbert of Ghent c.1087. It was then a cell of Charroux, but was made an independent abbey in 1115. Building seems to have begun then. The church was started at its E end and not completed till c.1160/70. It was about 236 ft long. The original E end had probably a main apse and two aisle apses, but that is not certain. In the mid C12 they were all given straight E walls. Chancel 'nave' and chancel aisles were divided by arcades with piers consisting of a sturdy round core and projections to nave and aisle, rather as at Ely and Norwich. At the time when the E walls were straightened, the transepts were built and received pairs of straight-ended E chapels, so that the whole composition assumed a Cistercian character. The piers between the chapel W openings and also the W crossing piers were compound, with twelve and sixteen shafts respectively. In the s transept waterleaf capitals were used. The nave was nine bays long and not at all uniform in detail. The second s pier from the E had a circular base, presumably

still Norman and made for some variety of round pier (th
s.aisle s wall is Norman). The opposite N pier had twelv
shafts, the principal four keeled. This system was the
continued W, but further W replaced by the simpler scheme o
four keeled and four subsidiary unkeeled shafts. The
respond however had its shafts not meeting in sharp groove
but connected by deep hollows without any sharp break,
sign of the coming Dec style. Also some of the shafts ha
fillets. The W front had dog-tooth enrichment of the doorway
and much blank arcading.

The Norman CLOISTER had open arcading with couple
shafts set at r. angles to the wall and given scalloped capitals
The CHAPTER HOUSE was of about 1130/40 at the latest an
rectangular in shape. The DORMITORY was rebuilt in the late
C13. The undercroft was two-naved, of nine bays with piers
of four main and four subsidiary shafts and single-chamfered
ribs. It was subdivided by cross walls. Of the REREDORTER
or lavatories also sufficient was found to determine its mid C12
date and the stone-paved drains. The REFECTORY along the
s walk of the cloister, of the same time as the chapter house, was
82 ft long. Seats and tables stood on stone supports, those of
the tables having towards the centre of the room carved heads.
The W range was of the mid C12. To its W stretched an
irregular group of rooms of different dates used by the cellarer
and also the abbot. The ABBOT'S HOUSE stretched to the
W, from the SW corner of the church and the NW corner of
the cloister. The GREAT GATEHOUSE of the abbey was 260 ft
W of the church and dated from the C14. The s end of the W
range of the cloister was a large square C15 KITCHEN, and
s of this lay the detached GUEST HOUSE, early C13 to C14.
The INFIRMARY, also early C13 to C14, was some distance E
of the cloister E range. – MONUMENTS. Sixty-five funerary
slabs were found during the excavations, with foliated C13
crosses, incised figures, indents for brasses, etc.

ST LAWRENCE. Built after 1434, when the old parish church
by the abbey collapsed. Ashlar-faced, except for the brick
chancel. The chancel is contemporary with the rest all the
same, i.e. the brickwork is as old as that of Tattershall.
Diaper patterns. To the N a small doorway all of brick, and a
low-side window all of brick. The other chancel windows of
stone. Broad, low W tower with eight pinnacles. The windows
of the church mostly of three cusped lancet lights under a
four-centred arch, i.e. without Perp tracery. The arcades are

of five bays, the piers octagonal with concave sides, and the responds of the chancel arch too. – PLATE. Chalice and Paten Cover, by *F.R.*, London, 1569; Paten, by *John Payne*, 1751. – MONUMENT. A large incised slab to Abbot Richard Horncastle † 1508, from the abbey. Inscription scroll round his head and shoulders. – Also from the abbey a large number of ARCHITECTURAL FRAGMENTS (S aisle W and N aisle E), Norman, E.E., and after, e.g. voussoirs of ribs, a part of a big scalloped capital, small C12 leaf capitals, a waterleaf capital, filleted capitals, and also the little vault inside a Perp canopy, probably of a sedile, and the lower half of a late medieval figure.

METHODIST CHAPEL. The front rebuilt, but the rear of 1837. A box with pointed windows. Inside, gallery on four sides supported on cast-iron columns.

PETER HANCOCK'S HOSPITAL, E of the church. Dated 1712. Facing the Green and grand in a portly way. Brick. Eleven-bay front, two storeys and a pediment. Stone angle quoins and stone strings.

THE MANOR. A long Georgian front. Otherwise Victorian. In the garden a pair of good stone GATEPIERS with brick ball-finials.

BARLINGS

2 m. ENE of Reepham

ST EDWARD. Norman the plain S doorway, the N doorway, as its traces indicate, and the re-set doorway into the chancel. E.E. the shafted bellcote with a hood-mould on whorls. Dec one three-light S window. Then, in 1876, *Charles Kirk* began to rebuild the church. The chancel and the E part of the nave by him. It looks odd enough, outside with its higher roof than the medieval church, and inside with its greater width.

BARLINGS ABBEY, 1 m. SE. Of the Premonstratensian abbey founded in 1154 all that remains is a wall with attached responds and springers of vaulting. The wall stood between nave and N aisle just W of the NW corner of the crossing. Why it should have been a solid wall, without an arch of the arcade from nave to aisle, remains unexplained. What can be seen is the shafts of the NW crossing pier, the respond of the last bay of the N arcade, and the springers of the aisle vault and the high vault of the nave. All the details are Dec, the capitals with big, quite sumptuous leaves. In the adjoining ruined cottage a boss of the vault with ridge-rib as well as diagonal ribs, in the intact cottage a finial and bits of an arch. So this part of the abbey was apparently completely rebuilt early in the C14.

BARNETBY

ST MARY. Desolate at the time of writing. Big, square, short Norman W tower and SW quoins of the nave. But in the s wall un unmistakably Saxon keyhole window. Low E.E. chancel, see also the chancel arch responds. Demolished N arcade of three bays, with brick infilling. Also one nice segment-headed Perp window set in. Small and pretty panel tracery.

ST BARNABAS. 1926–7 by *W. Bond*. Brick, with Perp details, quite large, but still unfinished. – FONT. The lead font from St Mary is now here. It is a piece of classical perfection, rare in English Norman work. It is circular, drum-shaped, and was cast in one flat strip. It has three bands of leaf or free palmette ornament. One motif repeats thirteen times along the top band, the other twenty-six times along the other two bands. The leaves are upright in the low bands, upside down in the top band. Each motif is perfectly composed and rounded off in itself. Professor Zarnecki dates the font *c*.1150–60 and refers to illuminated manuscripts for comparisons. – PLATE. Paten with vernicle, *c*.1475–1500; Chalice, *c*.1570.

BARNOLDBY-LE-BECK

ST HELEN. The oldest piece in the church, visible outside, is the modest, single-chamfered S doorway, probably of *c*.1200. Of the late C13 the S windows of the chancel (rebuilt in 1860) with Y-tracery and the S aisle windows with Geometrical and intersecting tracery. Then, still outside only, the N aisle, minor Dec work. After that the w tower Late Dec or Early Perp (rebuilt in 1901), see the bell-openings on the one hand, the arch inside with its moulding and head stops on the other. Finally the Perp clerestory. The three-light windows have depressed straight-sided arches. Now the interior. The four-bay arcades consist of three bays of the late C13 and an easterly lengthening, not much later. Both sides have quatrefoil piers and double-chamfered arches, but the piers on the N side with keeled foils and circular abaci, those on the s side with filleted foils and in one case a little nailhead in the abacus. Perp probably the roof of the N aisle with rustic bosses. Some bosses are re-used on the PULPIT. – FONT. Intersected arches, but not Norman. With its flat cutting and absence of capitals probably late C13. – STAINED GLASS. In the S aisle E window C14 glass, including a Crucifixus. – PLATE. Chalice and Cover, by *Edward Mangy* of Hull, *c.*1676; Paten, by *James Morrison*, 1753.

OBELISK, NE of the church, just outside the churchyard. To the memory of William Smith, huntsman, who fell from his horse, 11 April 1845.

BECKLANDS. Surrounded by firs. Said to have been built in 1870. Cast-iron entrance lamps and a highly polished, lavish interior such as one would expect in the orbit of Grimsby fish.

BARROW-ON-HUMBER

HOLY TRINITY. The W tower, ashlar-faced, is Dec below – see the arch towards the nave and the doorway – but Perp above. The straight-headed aisle windows all renewed. The W window of the N aisle 'debased', i.e. C16 or perhaps C17, and set in repair brickwork. E.E. chancel, see the simple priest's doorway, the N lancets, and the plate tracery details on the S side. The interior of the church has earlier evidence. The N arcade of five bays is a Late Norman piece of work. Circular piers, many-scalloped capitals, round arches with a single step. The fifth bay is a late C13 lengthening for which the Norman E respond was re-set. The rest of this bay corresponds to the S arcade. Four bays, late C13. Keeled responds, an octagonal pier, a circular pier, a quatrefoil pier with fillets. Double-chamfered arches. The inserted pier on the N side is also quatrefoil with fillets, but in the details a little later. – SCREEN. Odd Perp parts, but not much. – RAILINGS. Of wrought iron, by the font. C18, and probably secular. – PLATE. Chalice, by *Christopher Watson* of Hull, 1622; Paten, by *Richard Green*, 1709; Flagon, by *Phillips Garden*, 1751.

The character of Barrow is similar to that of Barton (*see* p. 183), close by. The MARKET PLACE is surrounded by small, low C19 houses. It retains the base and shaft of a BUTTER CROSS.

VICARAGE. 1805. By *R. Johnson* (GA), a builder of Barrow. His plain style suggests that he was the author of much of the local vernacular at this time.

BARROW HALL. Said to have been built for George Uppleby in 1777, but a view by Nattes shows a house of different

proportions. Now an oblong block, six by two bays and two
storeys. A little severe, trimmed up with a pedimented porch
inset balustrades to the parapet, and a stone tripartite central
window.

See
p.
767

DOWN HALL. A Late Victorian towering block in red, yellow
and patterned brick. It has a turret for a view of the Humber

THE CASTLES, at Barrow Haven, about ¾ m. NW. This earthwork is a MOTTE-AND-BAILEY CASTLE, with a large, low
motte and two very large baileys. There seem to have been
outer dependencies, and the whole must have covered a very
large area which derived most of its strength from its moats.
These were originally no doubt wet.

BARTON-UPON-HUMBER

Barton was once a considerable port. So it is not as surprising
to the historian to find two major churches here as it must be
to the tourist passing through the uneventful little town.

ST PETER. St Peter is really two churches, one small and Anglo-
Saxon of which two-thirds stand, the other to its E fully
grown and of the C13 and later. The Saxon building first. It
consisted of three parts, the central and most prominent one

3 being a tower serving as the nave. This is approximately
22 by 22 ft outside and about 70 ft high. To its W is a forebuilding, to its E was a chancel 15 ft long. This church must
be assigned to three periods, the mid C10 for the forebuilding
and perhaps the chancel, the later C10 for the tower, the C11
and perhaps even a date after 1066 for the bell-stage of the
tower. Below the tower heavy earlier foundations have been
traced, but they do not seem to belong to any of the existing
parts. The forebuilding has long-and-short W quoins. This
is the reason why it cannot be earlier. It is, however, earlier
than the tower part, as it is not bonded with it. The W wall
is disturbed below so that one cannot be certain whether it
originally had a W doorway or not. Above are two circular
windows, one above the other. The tower part has the strange
tall blank arcading in two tiers with matchstick-thin lesenes and
arches as well as triangle-heads which is familiar from Earls
Barton in Northamptonshire. There are a blocked N doorway
with a triangular head and a more elaborate S doorway with the
flat surround band at a distance from the actual jamb and
arch opening which is familiar from Anglo-Saxon work,
e.g. at Stow. The lesenes have plain blocks serving as capital

and abacus together. The upper order stands utterly un-
structurally on the apexes of the lower orders. There are
twin windows with mid-wall shafts and with arches both
round- and triangle-headed. The top stage, i.e. the C11 stage,
is of different masonry and has the tall twin bell-openings
with mid-wall shafts which occur so often in Lincolnshire.
To the w the bell-opening is a Dec replacement.

Inside, from the tower to the E is an arch with again un- 5b
moulded blocks as capitals and abaci and again a surrounding
flat band. A similar arch to the w. Above both are doorways
or openings which must originally have led into the roofs of
the w and E attachments. On the w face of the E wall is a head
of Christ in relief, continued originally no doubt in painting.
A relief in a similar position occurs at Bradford-on-Avon
(angels), and a whole figure of Christ outside the upper storey
of the w porch at Monkwearmouth. In other countries external
sculpture is rare at so early a time. This earliest part of the
church was lit by the lower tier of upper windows. One of
them is now cut into by the roof-line of the Gothic church
which replaced the Anglo-Saxon chancel.

On this we must now concentrate. It is a whole new nave
with aisles and a new chancel, wide and airy. The exterior
should first be looked at, and especially the s side with its
fine late C13 three-light windows. The lights are pointed-
trefoiled and above are two unencircled trefoils and a pointed
trefoil upside down. Only the E window is a Perp replacement,
set in a wall repaired in brick. This window can be dated
from its former stained glass, as the glass was given by Robert
Barnetby, who, according to a brass inscription on the floor,
died in 1440. The Perp clerestory with nine closely-set windows
is also of brick, and so is the chancel arch, behind its stone
facing. The s doorway goes with the windows (one order of
thin shafts with fillets, finely moulded arch), and the s arcade
goes with them too. This is of five bays, or was, as the E
end of the E bays is cut into by the Perp chancel. The piers
are octagonal with a little dog-tooth in the abaci. Double-
chamfered arches. The N arcade is an odd mixture. Dec, but
with re-used C13 capitals. The Dec work is distinguished by
the broad, animated nobbly leaf capitals of the responds and
the E pier. The sw respond also received such foliage. This
Dec work corresponds to the N aisle windows. They have
reticulated tracery, but alternate between two-centred arch-
heads and segmental heads, an unusual rhythm. The E

window, now inside the church, is a beauty, of four lights ar
flowing tracery and against the three mullions small figures
Christ crucified, the Virgin, and St John. The N doorwa
also has a typical Dec moulding. Perp chancel with elementar
windows. There is no date for the chancel, nor for the N aisl
but the S aisle and both arcades have been connected with th
grant of the manor to Philip Davey in 1307, a date which seem
too late for the S aisle and too early for the N arcade. – SCREEN
Much of the C15 work remains. The loft is of 1898. – STAINE
GLASS. Two panels of the early C14 with figures in the
window. – HELMS and other ARMOUR; C17. – PLAT
Chalice and Cover, by *Edward Mangy* of Hull, *c.*1670; Pate
on foot, by *Benjamin Pyne*, 1706; Flagon, by *Thos. Wrigh*
1754.

ST MARY. A majestic church, only 150 yds away from S
Peter and originally no more than a chapel of ease of it. I
contains much that is architecturally rewarding. One ought t
enter at once to examine the arcades. The N arcade must hav
been made late in the C12. Five bays plus a taller, later E arcl
Sturdy circular piers, multi-scalloped capitals, round abac
but pointed arches with much zigzag, lozenges, and also othe
motifs. Opposite, the S arcade is quite different, yet can hardl
be later. It is more spacious in its setting-out, four bays in
stead of five for the same length, and has E.E. octagonal pier
with eight detached shafts, a motif of St Hugh's choir in th
cathedral, but the capitals have waterleaf, not stiff-leaf,
motif more of *c.*1170 than of *c.*1200. Round seats surroun
the piers. The arches are double-chamfered. The aisle fenes
tration does not help. Here the N wall seems earliest, as i
has lancet windows only. Could the building on the N hav
taken long enough to bridge say twenty years between 118
and 1200? The N doorway with its slight chamfers fits a dat
*c.*1200. Some Perp window replacements. On the W side th
original lancets can still be traced. The S aisle windows on th
other hand are a good deal later than the S arcade and separate
from it in time by the W tower. This has an excellent doorwa
with four orders of shafts and a broad, finely moulded arch
tall shafted windows with shaft-rings, a good arch toward
the nave, with five-shafted responds, the middle one filleted
stiff-leaf capitals (now all Victorian) and a triple-chamfered
arch, twin bell-openings also shafted, and as its final Per
finish very elaborately decorated battlements and eigh
pinnacles. So to the beautiful S aisle windows and the mighty

s porch, work presumably of the masons who worked on the
s side of St Peter's as well. The windows are of three lights,
the middle one taller, and have three niches above. The
lights are cusped, the circles mostly unfoiled. This must be of
c.1275 or so. The s porch is two-storeyed. It has a big entrance
and three orders of lively stiff-leaf capitals and some dog-
tooth in the arch, details probably earlier than the aisle
windows. Niches l. and r. of the entrance. The chancel follows the s aisle immediately, see its ornate E window of five
lights. The middle one shoots up much higher and carries a
large cinquefoiled circle. Above the other lights big pointed
trefoils. In the N wall of the chancel windows with Y-tracery
and plate tracery. The s chapel has Y-tracery in two windows
too, but reticulated, i.e. Dec, tracery in the third. The E
window is curious: five lights, the middle one slightly taller,
and all under one depressed arch. No tracery at all. The three-
bay arcade towards the chancel is unmistakably Dec. Quatrefoil piers with fillets. Shallow diagonal shafts between. The
broad nobbly leaf capitals are obviously by the hands that
worked at St Peter's. In the chapel surprisingly elementary
sedilia. The main Perp contribution, as at St Peter's, is the
clerestory with its closely-set windows, eight here on each
side. The wall is mixed stone and brick. – MONUMENTS.
Bust of a Lady, c.1380, brass, 15 in. long (nave w). – Brass to
Simon Seman, vintner, † 1433, an inscription scroll round his
head. The figure is 5 ft long (chancel floor). – Monument to
Jane Shipsea † 1626. Inscription tablet standing on a black
marble column. At the top bracket probably for an allegorical
figure (chancel N). – Will Long † 1729. Pretty convex inscription tablet surrounded by garlands, scrolls, putto heads.
OUR LADY AND ST AUGUSTINE (R.C.), Whitecross Street.
1938 by *J. H. Beart-Foss*. Cubic, brick, not yet completed.
Round arches, in a kind of Norman, inside.
The village presents a surprising homogeneity of early C19
housing in the Georgian tradition. Waterscape and WARE-
HOUSES at WATERSIDE. Both FLEETGATE and HIGH
STREET are visually delightful, and BARGATE has three-
storey terrace fronts with fluted columns to the doorcases.
BECK HILL debouches on to lots of trees, the village pond,
and the churches. E of this is TYRWHITT HALL, C17 and
partially a courtyard house. Inside a Georgian ceiling with
musical trophies. In PRIESTGATE the grandest house is No.
24, a Georgian house of four bays, two floors, and parapet.

CHAPEL LANE has its big CONGREGATIONAL CHAPEL (1816). Near by the PROVINCIAL HOUSE SCHOOL, in a heavy ill-managed staccato style of the 1840s.* There are only two more houses worth individual mention: BARDNEY HALL, with a later C18 front in rubbed brick, an earlier N wing, and a plainer back elevation; and BAYSGARTH PARK, the big house of Barton. Georgian, and approached by gatepiers supporting unicorns and baskets of fruit. A longish seven-bay front sparsely decorated.

WINDMILLS. Remains of two tower mills, one with an ogee cap.

2070   BAUMBER

ST SWITHIN. An absorbingly interesting and on top of that visually very appealing church. The latter is due to its appearing at first entirely the Georgian brick church of 1758 that it is, one of the best in a county poor in good ones. The former has more complex reasons. The Georgian church is surprisingly big, considering the fact that it stands in a field. It has W tower, nave and chancel. The windows are pointed and have intersecting tracery, but this was renewed and cusped in W. Scorer's restoration of 1892. The aisles have at their W and E ends blank quatrefoils, typical of the earliest Georgian Gothic Revival. The W tower has a W porch and battlements. It is quite astonishingly broad, and that leads to the problems of the church. For this is a W tower much earlier than it seems. It has a Late Norman W doorway with one order of colonnettes and an arch with zigzag. One of the capitals has a small crouching figure, the other waterleaf. To the inside the arch is perfectly plain, and so is a second arch from the tower to the nave, no wider than a doorway. Now, do not these two narrow arches in conjunction with the large space inside the tower suggest an Anglo-Saxon origin and a building of the type of Barton-on-Humber and Hough? Inside the tower there stand two impressive timber trusses on strong posts to support the bell-chamber. They must have been regarded as a technical necessity in a tower of such dimensions. The medieval church also had aisles. We can see that inside the Georgian church. They are of three bays and E.E. On the s side is one round pier and one octagonal, on the N side both are octagonal. Double-chamfered arches. The N pier has a round seat. The medieval chancel arch has gone, but the responds of E.E.

* Unless this is the house designed by R. Mays of Hull for B. Hyll in 1829 (Colvin).

chancel chapels have been exposed. They had one detached shaft (cf. e.g. Hameringham) with a shaft-ring. The chancel is now delightfully Gothick, with a pretty coving with quatre-foils, and divided from the nave by two posts carrying three ogee arches. Their crockets have an unmistakably Georgian featheriness. – PULPIT. The former tester or sounding-board is Gothick too. – PLATE. Chalice, 1816, and Paten, Flagon, and two Alms Basins, 1817, all by *Robert Hennell*.

BAYONS MANOR
E of Tealby

1090

The house is the expression of the lineal aspirations of its 62a builder *Charles Tennyson* (d'Eyncourt), uncle of the Poet Laureate. Tennyson, the politician, could never acquire a peerage, so he invented a quasi-Gothic lineage for himself, dis-covered a dim d'Eyncourt connexion, and surrounded himself with a panoply of baronial objects. Before 1835 Bayons was a plain bay-fronted Regency 'cottage'. Around this Tennyson first built a modest gabled house, calling in *W. A. Nicholson* as the executant architect. The foundations of the GREAT HALL were laid in 1836, and a little later the LIBRARY wing was built to the N. The hall faces S and has its proper porch, louvre, and wide bay, on the pattern of say Eltham. On the W front two of the Tudorized Regency bays remain. Then, over the centre of the N front, the massive tower was built. This is the first hint of Tennyson's inclination towards the picturesque, romantic castle style. The date is about 1839. At this stage Bayons was still only a medium-sized manor house. Then the mood changed – perhaps in ratio to Tenny-son's increasing frustration over his peerage – and the works began to get operatic. Inner and outer defensive works were erected, a moat dug, and an embattled barbican with a mock drawbridge provided. In 1842 the huge KEEP was built by the E inner wall. The character of these later works is remarkable. Debouching from beneath the barbican to the inner bailey is one of the most convincing of post-medieval experiences. The KITCHEN front to the W is an essay in cubism a century before its time. The considerable Tennyson correspondence reveals Charles's constant preoccupation with the progress of the building. Yet the professional touch is only too apparent. But whose? *Salvin* seems to have been consulted about the LIBRARY, where the wallpapers were all supplied by *Pugin* and *Crace*, the sophisticated chimneypieces carved by Mr

Tomline. Yet Bayons is a pre-Victorian house. Its mood
painterly, the mingling of scholarship and amateurism
Georgian Romantic rather than Early Victorian pedantry. Th
picturesque principles are succinctly stated by the way
approach. From the s, instead of entering directly to the hal
the visitor is guided around the outer bailey on a wide detou
to the barbican on the N. Then through the barbican to th
inner wall, and through the splendid N gate tower, and into
stable court. After that through two more gates by the kee
and by an arch to the s front, ending up but fifty yards fro
where one started a quarter of a mile away. The Duke
Northumberland sums it all up, if he really said on visiti
Bayons: 'At Alnwick I have only three gateways, *you* have six
Bayons is now in total decay and never looked better. I
incorporated fragments from the destroyed Palace of Wes
minster. Two STATUES of Kings from Westminster Hall hav
recently gone back to where they came from.

BAYSGARTH PARK *see* BARTON-UPON-HUMBER

2000
BEELSBY

ST ANDREW. By *R. H. Fowler*, 1889–90. All Dec. Nave an
chancel and Hodgson Fowler's bit of fun, a spirelet on th
bellcote. The lower courses of the walling are medieval. I
addition, in the w wall, the former tower arch, in the N wa
built-in bits of original Dec tracery, the C13 three-bay
arcade complete inside with octagonal piers and double
chamfered arches, and the three-bay s arcade also complete
also C13 but a little later. One pier circular, one quatrefo
with fillets. Double-chamfered arches. Another arch into
former N chapel, now vestry. – PULPIT. Is this C17? It i
quite simple in its decoration, and this includes fluted panel
almost like a renewed and modernized linenfold. – PLATE
Chalice, by *John Morley* of Lincoln, *c.*1569.

OLD RECTORY. By *T. C. Hine*, 1868 (GA). Big and spreading
in red brick, just as Victorian rectories ought to be.

BEELSBY HOUSE, ¼ m. s. Mid-Georgian. On one front
Roman Doric porch, a semicircular rusticated window, and
canted bay.

2090
BEESBY

ST ANDREW. The two big corbel heads of the chancel arch, C1
evidently, are unexpected. One opens his mouth with on

hand and supports the corbel with the other, the other gnashes his teeth. The chancel could indeed be C13, though it is much renewed. The nave is of 1841, with a fiery red s front of brick, but a stone front to the N, and with a wooden octagonal bell-turret. The windows are pointed and have Y-tracery but are heavily keyed-in. Flat white ceiling inside. – PLATE. Chalice, Paten, and Flagon, by *John Schofield*, 1787.

BELCHFORD

T PETER AND ST PAUL. Of the church built in 1781 only the w window survives. The chancel was rebuilt in 1859–60, the nave in 1909, at which time the upper parts of the w tower were taken down. – FONT. Octagonal, Perp. Panelled stem. – PULPIT. The small reliefs seem to be amateur work. – PLATE. Chalice, by *John Morley* of Lincoln, c.1569.

BELLEAU

T JOHN BAPTIST. By *C. E. Giles*, 1862 (PF). Greenstone and white limestone. W tower with pyramid roof behind a kind of token machicolations. Lancet windows and plate tracery. From the old church Giles took over the three-bay E.E. arcades (octagonal piers, double-chamfered arches), parts of the E.E. s doorway and the E.E. priest's doorway, a fine big Dec leaf corbel in the chancel, and the Dec piscina with ogee arch and buttress shafts. – FONT. Octagonal, the panels just with a roll border. Is that C17? – BENCH ENDS. Two poppy-heads only, in the chancel. – PLATE. Chalice with modern Paten Cover, London, 1568. – MONUMENT. Late C13 effigy of a cross-legged Knight wearing a surcoat and holding the hilt of his sword with his r. hand, the scabbard with his l. Angels by his pillow. At the foot end of his tomb-chest, probably not *in situ*, big ogee motifs. – CROSS in the church-yard. Base with shields in quatrefoils; part of the shaft.

MANOR HOUSE. The farmhouse and a barn at r. angles to it are built of Tudor brick. The farmhouse has no features of that date, the barn must once have been part of the mansion of the Lords Willoughby. A big three-light window with transom and straight top and two smaller windows all blocked are recognizable, and to the l. of the transomed window the jamb of a doorway with a Perp moulding. So all this may be of c.1500 or indeed earlier. But the most interesting survival, built into a C20 building, is the mighty bearded head and bust

which once stood at the top of one of the two entry arches of
gatehouse of about the same date. Old illustrations of th
context exist. The arch is four-centred and also characterist
cally Perp. The figure is a Wild Man or Wodewose, the symb
of the Willoughbys.

About ½ m. s, by the brook, a nice HOUSE of three widel
spaced bays, with tripartite windows and the date 1822.

BELTOFT HALL *see* BELTON

BELTON
Isle of Axholme

ALL SAINTS. Except for the Dec windows of the N aisle wit
reticulated tracery, the outside of the church is all Perp. It
also all ashlar-faced. Short W tower. Short embattled aisle:
clerestory with an E window, long chancel, S porch with
handsome entrance with angel-busts l. and r. A heavy vestr
or treasury at the SE, the windows barred. The aisles wer
originally continued or intended to be continued further t
the W. The arches separating these bays from the rest of th
aisles have the same sunk wave mouldings as the tall towe
arch. The interior also is Perp. Tall three-bay arcade:
Octagonal piers with castellated capitals, but re-used E.E
arches of fine roll mouldings, four of them keeled. Three-ba:
N chapel arcade, also with castellated capitals. The W arc
into the chapel has continuous mouldings. In the chance
good sedilia. Three niches with cusped ogee tops. Straigh
castellated cornice. – PLATE. Chalice and Paten Cover, b:
R. Robinson, Hull, c.1635; Tankard, by *W.S.*, London, 1680
Tankard, by *Robert Timbrall*, 1715; two-handled Cup, b:
James Young, 1785(?). – MONUMENTS. Between chancel and
chapel tomb-chest with much-cusped panels. – In the chape
C14 effigy of a Knight. It is made from a coped stone, perhap
of Anglo-Saxon origin. As it is, only the head and bust and th
feet are brought out. But the whole is too badly preserved to b
reliable for details. – Katherine Johnson † 1786. Nice bi
tablet of various marbles. At the top urn in front of an obelisk

BELWOOD. The Early Georgian house stands in ruins, and th
Early Georgian style does not make for suggestive ruins. Tc
the N a C17 FARMHOUSE with mullioned and mullioned and
transomed windows. At the S entrance to the estate a castellated
Georgian LODGE. Also S of the house a 50-ft-tall brick
OBELISK in memory of the squire's favourite dog and horse.

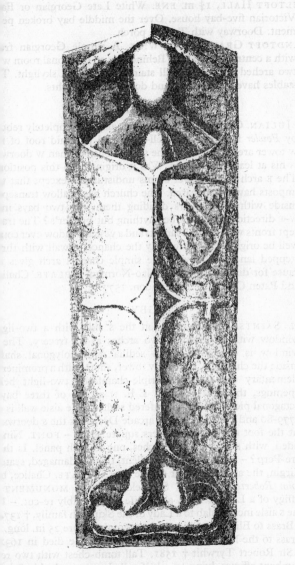

elton, effigy of a Knight made from a coped stone, fourteenth century

BELTOFT HALL, 1¾ m. ENE. White Late Georgian or Ea
  Victorian five-bay house. Over the middle bay broken pe
  ment. Doorway with Tuscan porch.
SANDTOFT GRANGE, 3 m. WNW. A simple Georgian fr
  with a central canted bay. Behind this an octagonal room w
  two arched recesses. Small staircase with oval skylight. T
  stables have all windows and doors with fanlights.

BENNIWORTH
2080

ST JULIAN. Of greenstone, E.E., but almost completely rebu
  by *Fowler* in 1875. The bell-stage and pyramid roof of t
  W tower are his entirely. The sumptuous Norman W doorw
  is his at least nine-tenths. Was it originally in this positio
  The E arch of the tower seems undisturbed, except that t
  imposts have disappeared. The church has shallow transep
  inside with round piers dividing them into two bays in
  W–E direction. Can they be anything but Fowler's ? The tra
  sept fronts with two tall lancets and a vesica window over cou
  well be original, as is probably the chancel E wall with thr
  stepped lancet windows. The simple chancel arch gives
  cause for distrust. – FONT. Neo-Norman. – PLATE. Chali
  and Paten Cover, by *A.*, London, 1577.

BIGBY
0000

ALL SAINTS. E.E. chancel, on the S side with a two-lig
  window with an arch on two arches as its tracery. The
  window is of *c.*1872. Plain sedilia with polygonal sha
  inside the chancel. Late C13 W tower, short, with a prominer
  elementary corbel table. Triple-chamfered two-light be
  openings, the lights cusped. E.E. N arcade of three bay
  octagonal piers, double-chamfered arches. The aisle wall is
  1779–80 and built of brick. S arcade Dec, as is the S doorwa
  At the foot of the arcade piers square seats. – FONT. Nin
  sided, with simple cusped arches, one to each panel. Is th
  pre-Perp ? – SCULPTURE. Excellent, though damaged, seate
  Virgin, the style *c.*1300 or a little later. – PLATE. Chalice, b
  John Roberts & Co.(?), Sheffield, 1803. – MONUMENT
  Effigy of a Lady, *c.*1300, above life-size, terribly re-cut. – I
  the S aisle incised slab to a Lady of the Skipwith family, † 137
  – Brass to Elizabeth Skipwith, *c.*1520, the figure 25 in. long.
  Brass to the Neyler family, a small panel. He died in 163
  – Sir Robert Tyrwhit † 1581. Tall tomb-chest with two re
  cumbent effigies, lying on a half-rolled-up mat. At his feet

hairy wild-man is busy with the mat. At her feet, curiously (ominously?), a lion. The twenty-two children kneel along the tomb-chest. Tall back decoration with two columns, a strap-work cartouche, and bald intersecting circles. – Sir Robert Tyrwhit † 1617 and Lady Bridget Manners † 1604. Erected by him to her memory. The two figures kneel and face one another. Columns l. and r. Top obelisks and achievement. Long Latin epitaphium, but no inscription.

ᴇCTORY. On the side of a hill. Built according to the *Gentleman's Magazine* shortly before 1790. Five by three bays and two storeys. Pediment to one front. It looks a typical pattern-book house* and surprisingly urbane.

BILSBY
4070

ᴏLY TRINITY. C18 W tower and nave with arched, keyed-in windows. The tower and part of the nave are of regular blocks of greenstone. But the tower top is of brick and has pointed windows. Medieval the following parts: the Perp chancel, the N arcade also Perp (three bays, octagonal piers, and double-chamfered arches), and some re-used E.E. dog-tooth mould-ing in the porch entrance. – PLATE. Chalice, by *Emes & Barnard*, 1817. – (WEATHER-COCK. C18; good. PB)

ɪLSBY HOUSE. Mid-Georgian,‡ five bays and two floors, Doric porch. Additions of 1906.

ᴍOAT HOUSE. Late C17, brick and two-storey porch.

BINBROOK
2090

т MARY AND ST GABRIEL. 1869 by *James Fowler*. Of iron-stone, a large church, surprisingly formal for a village. High tower with broach spire, aisles of five bays and a polygonal apse. The details in the late C13 style. – PLATE. Chalice and Paten Cover, inscribed 1569.

ᴀ spreading village, the Green on the side of the hill.

ᴍANOR HOUSE. A Late Georgian essay in brick with stone trim. The centre bay in the best local builder's Palladian: door with broken pediment, Venetian window above, and above this a semicircular window. Nice urns on rusticated GATEPIERS.

BISCATHORPE
2080

т HELEN. Bonney in 1847 says the church was built by *Willough-by* of Louth and *W. A. Nicholson* of Lincoln. Considering the

* If the drawing in the Spalding Gentlemen's Society is a design, then the ᴦchitect was *T. Robinson*.
‡ White's *Guide* says 1740.

close affinities to Haugham and Raithby, the latter name
convincing. The tower here has a wide open octagonal be
stage below the spire. The openwork parapets, the pinnacle
and the choice of brick cemented as a building material
link Biscathorpe with the other two. – PULPIT, PEWS, et
are original. – FONT. A white earthenware piece, 12 in. hi
on a bracket. It is in the Perp style and signed St Mary Mag
Oxford. – PLATE. Chalice and Paten Cover, by *John Morl*
of Lincoln, 1569.

The church lies in the grounds of BISCATHORPE HOUS
tucked away by the river Bain, really quite a small strea
The house, its subsidiaries and lodges are of yellow bri
and clearly also of the 1840s, see for instance the windows
three or two arched lights, but in an Italianate and a Goth
style. They were a favourite with Loudon. The pediment
gables – no longer pediments, not yet real gables – are equal
typical. One of the subsidiary houses is cruciform.

9090
BISHOP NORTON

ST PETER. Georgian (faculty dated 1737). W tower, nave an
chancel. In the W wall of the tower small Norman tympanun
a defaced scene with a recumbent figure and the *signur
triciput*. On the arch roundels. The date seems to be *c.*115(
The scene is surrounded by five beaded roundels with rosette
– PLATE. Chalice and Paten Cover, by *John Morley* of Lincoln
1569; Paten by *George Smith*(?), London, 1729.

NORTON PLACE. Set on the edge of plantations in forme
parkland. The house for John Harrison M.P. by *John Car*
1776, and one of his best small designs. Stone S front of seve
bays and two storeys, the three centre bays more widely space
beneath a pediment. Triangular pediments to the ground-floo
windows, flat entablatures to the upper ones. The entrance
Doric porch against a tripartite motif. Above it an Ionic Ven
etian window, and above that in the pediment a circular ligh
garlanded with foliage and tied up with a bow. The side front
have deep canted bays, topped with urns. The one on the V
side is the taller. The porch on this front is later, probably b
L. Vulliamy, 1836 (Colvin). All the rooms have good chimney
pieces and ceilings. The staircase in an oval top-lit well an
with curved steps. S-scroll balustrade of iron and gallerie
upper landing. The STABLES make a courtyard to the rear
Three-bay arcaded centre and wings. – BRIDGE. Across th

lake. Three arches and balustrade. – LODGES. With screen
walls, urns, and rusticated piers.

BLYBOROUGH

ᴛ ALKMUND. Very thin and not high C18 W tower, but with
medieval gargoyles (re-used). The rest by *James Fowler*,
1877–8. Inside, much more is preserved of the ancient
building. Tall E.E. three-bay N arcade with circular piers,
keeled responds, stiff-leaf capitals, and double-chamfered
arches. The chancel arch has keeled responds too. Arch to the
N chapel a little later. Nailhead in the abaci of the filleted
responds. Bold ogee-arched tomb recesses between chancel and
N chapel and in the N chapel N wall. – FONT. Disused octagonal Perp font in the N chapel. Foot with leaf motifs. –
SCULPTURE. Part of a Saxon funerary slab with interlace. –
(ROOD. From Thornton Abbey. Part of it was dug up in the
rectory garden. PB) – PLATE. Paten, by *W.P.*, London, 1722;
Chalice, by *Matthew Lofthouse*, 1725. – MONUMENT. Effigy of
Robert Conyng † 1434, priest (N chapel).

LYBOROUGH HALL. Early C18 house of L-shape, two-storeyed,
and with a hipped roof. The entrance front has seven irregular
bays. A pre-1794 wing has gone.* This was on the N side,
where there are puzzling pseudo-medieval columns built as a
small cloister.

BLYTON

ᴛ MARTIN. Plain, wide, unmoulded Norman tower arch. The
rest of the tower Perp. Chancel E.E., but much restored in
1866. Part of the three-light E window with three foiled circles
is original. So is the double-chamfered chancel arch on keeled
responds. The arcades of three bays, N one keeled quatrefoil
pier and one octagonal pier, s all octagonal. N arcade probably
Dec, s Perp. Perp also the embattled clerestory and the
embattled s aisle with its straight-headed windows. – FONT.
Perp, octagonal, with tracery motifs. – PLATE. Chalice,
*c.*1570; Chalice by *Samuel Wheat* or *Samuel Wood*, 1765. –
(MONUMENT. An incised C15 stone from the demolished
church at Southorpe is used as the mensa of the s aisle
altar. PB)

ᴄlose to the church and competing with the tower a derelict
TOWER MILL, the brick tower and cap only.

* The house was drawn by Nattes in 1794.

BOLINGBROKE HOUSE *see* OLD BOLINGBROKE

0010

BONBY

ST ANDREW. Small C18 brick tower with pyramid roof. Featureless brick chancel. Norman nave, see the doorway visible inside and the masonry on the S side, white with brown quoins. On the N side a puzzle. There was a N arcade. It had four bays, octagonal and circular piers and double-chamfered arches, clearly C13. But the C13 chancel arch is continued to the N by the start of an arch running N and in its respond also C13. Yet it runs right into the incomplete E bay of the arcade. The solution is probably that the arcade had indeed four bays, that an organ chamber was added in the C19 cutting into the fourth bay, that its S arch into the chancel received one genuine C13 capital coming from the arcade E respond, and that the seemingly incomplete cross arch was made for the organ chamber and given as its respond the N respond of the chancel arch which is now missing. – PLATE Chalice and Paten, by *Thos. Whipham*, 1742.

BONBY LODGE. Late Georgian. Typifies the prevalence in the county of the canted-bay motif – in this case on big protruding wings.

BOOTHBY HALL *see* WELTON-LE-MARSH

8000

BOTTESFORD

ST PETER'S CHAINS. Externally all E.E. and very complete, cruciform, with a W tower. The only exceptions are the re-set N porch entrance of c.1200, with dog-tooth, but still with a round arch, the simple also Transitional N doorway, the two renewed S aisle windows of c.1300 with intersecting tracery and the Perp tower top with eight pinnacles (and once a spire that made it 210 ft tall). Now the E.E. work in detail. The tower has tall lancets below (and a very tall arch to the nave inside), and tall two-light bell-openings with a middle shaft, pointed trefoiled lights and a quatrefoil over (i.e. late C13 forms). The S aisle has a small W lancet, the nave clerestory alternatingly lancets and circular windows, the transepts lancets, and the N transept to the N an arrangement of three with two circles over.* Dog-tooth is used freely, and whorls occur as hood-mould stops. The chancel is of the same forms,

* The S front of the S transept is Victorian.

but partly the work of the restorer, as it is known that it was almost rebuilt about 1630. The very tall N and S windows have moulded surrounds inside. In the E wall three lancets with dog-tooth in the hood-moulds and two lancets with a circular window over.* The arcades inside do not differ in date from the exterior. They are of three bays, with seats round the bases of the piers and with double-chamfered arches. The piers are quatrefoil with thinner shafts in the diagonals. On the S side they have shaft-rings and round abaci, on the N side no shaft-rings and abaci following the lines of the shafts. The chancel arch (in fact, oddly placed W, not E, of the crossing), the arches into the transepts, and, as we have seen, the tower arch all go with this same date. In the transepts stone altars, in the N transept a pillar piscina, in the chancel sedilia and double piscina and opposite an aumbry with dog-tooth decoration of the hood-mould. – SANCTUS BELL. Of bronze; C15. – PLATE. Chalice, with lion passant, c.1670.

he TEMPLARS' BATH recalls a manor of the Templars of Willoughton. They would not approve of the crude C19 Tudor-Gothic additions in two-colour bricks.

MANOR HOUSE. Built in a romantic baronial style by Edward Peacock, the antiquary. In the elaborate turret he had his library. PB)

BOULTHAM see LINCOLN, p. 143

BRACKENBOROUGH HALL

½ m. SE of Little Grimsby

3090

Georgian house of five bays and two storeys, with hipped roof and dormers. Pretty, contrasty stone details and a rusticated Gibbsian doorway. The Doric joinery of the hall compares with that at Harrington Hall and Little Grimsby Hall (*see* pp. 268, 299). On a mound by the moat is a felicitous FOLLY concocted from the remains of Fotherby church (*see* p. 238). Part of a C13 arch, a Dec window, and a three-light Perp one, all built into a rugged ruin.

2000

BRADLEY

T GEORGE. Of ironstone. Unbuttressed C13 W tower. Bell-openings as pairs of lancets with a lozenge over in plate tracery. In the nave on the S side a small lancet. The N arcade, three bays, two pointed arches and one round arch between, has been pulled down. – FONT. Dec. With the inscription:

* It is said that the wall was rebuilt accurately early in the C19.

'Pater noster ave maria and criede leren ye chylde y^t es ned
(Cox). – PLATE. Chalice, c.1580. – In the churchyard CROS
the whole shaft and part of the crenellated top.

MANOR HOUSE. L-shaped and dated 1689. The much restore
exterior preserves a stepped gable.

(The former METHODIST CHAPEL, dating from the late C1
is at the time of writing a hen-house.)

4060

BRATOFT

ST PETER AND ST PAUL. W tower of 1747, brick, with arche
W window and very elementary segment-headed bell-opening
The rest is of greenstone, nave with clerestory and aisles, an
a chancel rebuilt rather than restored. The style is Per
throughout – note the three-light clerestory windows unde
almost straight-sided depressed arches – except for the simpl
S doorway of the early C14, the tiny low-side light below th
W light of the SW chancel window, and certain minor feature
of the interior. Here the tower arch remained in a pre-Per
state, and the C18 tower arch was set in it, the chancel arc
is on an earlier base, the mouldings of the Easter Sepulchr
in the chancel are Dec, and one N pier stands on an earlie
base. Otherwise the three-bay arcades are Perp, S earlier, $\aleph$
later. – FONT. Octagonal, Perp, with leaves and heads agains
the underside and simple tracery and the Instruments of th
Passion against the bowl. – SCREENS. The rood screen i
largely reconstruction, but the openwork buttress shafts ar
said to be original. One-light divisions of round under oge
arches. – One tracery top of another screen re-fixed on th
pulpit. The same *parti*, but different details. – BENCH ENDS
With extremely good poppy-heads, including profile heads
pairs of birds, angels, and at the top of one a little preacher i
a pulpit. On two ends coats of arms in lozenge fields. – PAINT
ING. Allegory of the Armada. Signed absurdly prominentl
Richard Stephenson. The picture shows a red dragon and, i
the four corners, England, Scotland, Ireland, and France. Th
inscription reads:

> Spaine's proud Armado with great strength and power
> Great Britain's state came gapeing to devour,
> This Dragon's guts, like Pharaos scattered hoast,
> Lay splitt and drowned upon the Irish coast.
> For of eight score save too ships sent from Spaine
> But twenty-five scarce sound return'd again.

– PLATE. Chalice and Paten, by *Edward Vincent*, 1727.

; moated site of the Massingberd house demolished in 1698 when the family moved to Gunby (*see* p. 259). Remains of a brick bridge.

BRATTLEBY

9080

CUTHBERT. Unbuttressed w tower, CII – see the small arch into the nave. Also parts of the C14 w doorway. N arcade of two bays, E.E. Round pier, keeled responds. Big stiff-leaf capitals. Double-chamfered arches with broaches at their start. C14 arch to the N chapel, dying into the imposts. The exterior of the church mostly by *Fowler*, 1858. Tower with recessed lead spire. C13-style fenestration in nave, aisle, and chancel. – In the churchyard s of the church Late Saxon shaft of a CROSS with interlace, hardly recognizable now.

RATTLEBY HALL. Early Victorian. Three by three bays and three storeys, cement-faced. On the w side the ground floor projects slightly. Doorway with unfluted Ionic columns *in antis*. Stables dated 1813.

BRIGG

0000

r JOHN EVANGELIST, Bigby Street. 1842–3 by *W. A. Nicholson*. Neo-E.E., with a SE porch tower. The material is small stones almost as if they were grey bricks. Inside, arcades of octagonal piers with double-chamfered arches. The w windows unusually high up. The chancel of one bay has a sexpartite vault, presumably of plaster.

walk of Brigg is short and uneventful. It can start at the MARKET PLACE with the TOWN HALL of 1817 at the acute corner of Bigby and Wrawby Streets. Yellow brick. Canted angle projection with square lantern. Arcaded sides. First down BIGBY STREET. On the r. the DYING GLADIATOR INN, with lots of gory realism in the figure. It is full-size, white with a red, bloody wound in the side. Then the church, awkwardly squeezed in, and the METHODIST CHURCH, a brick horror of 1865 (by *W. Watkins*). After that No. 11, quite a large Late Georgian town house. A tall central canted bay with, to the l. and r., side pieces, their roofs rising in steps towards the highest bay. A side entrance has Doric columns with bands of stalactite rustication. Back to the Market Place and w to the BRIDGE. Single rusticated arch and niches above the piers. The foundation stone was inscribed: '*J. S. Padley* of Lincoln, county surveyor. *Geo. Willoughby* of York, mason and contractor. W. T. Leake of Louth, clerk of the

Works'. Beyond is BRIDGE STREET with many inns, nota
the WHITE HART, low and vernacular-looking, and
BROCKLESBY OX with an unusually high pitched roof a
massive central stack. It may be Georgian. The WESLEY
CHAPEL strikes a grimmer note. Grey brick, giant pilaste
tapered windows and door. Top parapet. It must be of t
1840s. Back to the Market Place, noticing now from the brid
the early C19 WAREHOUSES on the wharfs to the l. The b
façade is Nos 26–28 of ten bays with a balcony over the cent
arch. Once more in the Market Place,* and now turning
WRAWBY STREET one may look at the NATIONAL PR
VINCIAL BANK, just N of the town hall, a well-hand
Queen Anne Revival building of 1923, by *F. C. R. Palmer* a
W. Holden. In Wrawby Street the CONGREGATION
CHURCH of 1813. Details anticipatory of the Victorian A
At the end of the street is the former WORKHOUSE. By *W.
Nicholson*, 1837, in forbidding stock brick. Near by, t
GRAMMAR SCHOOL, founded by Sir John Nelthorpe,
whom a contract was drawn up 4 July 1674 with *Willi*
Catlyn of Hull. This refers to the schoolroom. A tall, singl
storey front of seven bays, stone quoins, the centre emphasiz
by Ionic pilasters and a pediment above roof level. Hi
bases to the pilasters and stone capitals. The original ar
entrance is now blocked. On the street side the original tv
bays have been extended, by *F. H. Goddard & Sons* in 187

²⁰⁰⁰ ## BRIGSLEY

ST HELEN. Small, with an unbuttressed C11 W tower (see t
arch to the nave with two orders of voussoirs on the plaine
imposts) but Perp bell-openings. Perp also the clerestory. T
chancel is of chalk (on ironstone lower courses). The chanc
windows are memorable – Geometrical, intersecting, and re
culated tracery all belonging together, though forms typical
1270, 1300, and 1330. Both sides of the nave had aisles origi
ally. The S side is recognizable to a certain extent. The pie
seem to have had four shafts and four hollows. – PULPI
Late Georgian, the tester oddly but attractively on two flute
pilasters. – COMMUNION RAIL. Also Late Georgian, as
presumably the PANELLING of the E wall too. – PLAT
Chalice and Paten Cover, Elizabethan; Paten by *Charl*
Perrier, 1731; Flagon, by *William Williams*, 1745. – CROSS

* (No. 7 has a staircase with 'Chippendale' fret balustrade. MHLG)

the churchyard, s of the church. Base and ivy-hung stump of the shaft.

BRINKHILL 3070

ST PHILIP. 1857 by *Maughan & Fowler*. Nave with bellcote; chancel. Brick and greenstone striped. Lancet windows. – PLATE. Chalice, by *John Morley* of Lincoln, 1569. – CROSS, in the churchyard. The whole shaft and the castellated knob are preserved.

BROCKLESBY 1010

ALL SAINTS. Heavily weathered ironstone. The chancel is all Dec. Thin w tower, the front with a deep giant arch dying into its imposts and, set in it, but lower down, the w window. The E half of the tower projects into the nave. Two-light bell-openings. The lead broach spire was rebuilt in 1784, but* a lead spire had already been repaired in 1621, i.e. may well have been erected before the Reformation. The nave and chancel windows all have chamfered surrounds, some double, some triple, though the tracery is Victorian. The doorway with the typical Dec sunk wave mouldings. Chancel arch of two continuous chamfers. Two C18 brick porches. – FONT. 1948, in excessive forms derived from the Georgian. Pretty, small Wren-style cover. – LECTERN. A splendid piece of the late C17. Of wood. Eagle top, generous baluster stem, and volutes with putto heads. – ORGAN. Of beautiful, elegant design and excellent craftsmanship. Late C18. From Brocklesby Park. – PROCESSIONAL CROSS. Bought recently in the South of France. – PLATE. Chalice, Paten, and Plate, by *John Richardson*, 1761; Lid of glass box, by *George Richards*(?), London, 1837. – STAINED GLASS. Fragments in the chancel windows. – MONUMENTS. Sir William Pelham † 1587. Alabaster. Standing monument. He and his wife and children kneeling, the male facing the female members of the family. – Sir William † 1629. Alabaster. By *William Wright* of Charing Cross, who asked £100 for it. Two recumbent effigies, he behind and a little above her. A King's head at her feet. Sixteen children kneel against the tomb-chest in two rows in depth, girls to the w, men and boys to the E. – Marcia Countess of Yarborough, 1928 by *Sir W. Reid Dick*, designed by *Sir R. Blomfield*. Standing figure with two children, white marble, in a neo-Flaxman spirit. A very pleasing group.

* According to an inscription found recently by the Earl of Yarborough.

BROCKLESBY PARK. We ought to know more about S
William's Pelham's 'very fine stately building' of 1603. Trad
tion says it was rebuilt in 1730, but c.1710 is a date accordi
much better with the style of the present house and with t
old tongue-say that Buckingham House was its mode
Brocklesby is a refined brick block, oblong, nine by six bay
three storeys, with a parapet. The bay-division of the mai
E, front is two–five-projecting–two, whereas the garden fro
of Buckingham House was four–three–four. Brocklesby h
contrasting (restored) stone details to window surround
aprons, cornice, and urns. The post-C18 architectural histo
is complicated, and nearly all was swept away by Clau
Phillimore's recent successful restoration. It is worth, howeve
relating. Charles H. Tatham – a Lincolnshire man as well as
London architect in the school of Henry Holland – added
picture gallery of one storey to the W in 1807. In 1827 anoth
block was added to the W again. Then in 1858 William Bur
added two storeys above the gallery. There was a fire in 189
when Sir Reginald Blomfield meticulously reconstructed th
main block. The formal S terrace with piers and balustrades
his doing. Phillimore reduced this incredibly complex group t
the block of 1710, and Tatham's gallery bit on one end, whic
got a new exterior. The inside of the house is mostly Blom
field's, with rich stucco in the late C17 style. But the EAS
HALL of two storeys with a coved ceiling is C18. This wa
inserted by Capability Brown in 1772 and cost him 'a grea
deal of trouble'. Tatham's gallery was also gutted by Blomfiel

The STABLES lie to the E of the house. They are L-shape
and built of brick with dormers and a hipped roof. W of th
gallery is the CONSERVATORY, a little essay in recesse
planes with the front plane pedimented. This is perhaps b
James Wyatt, working here in the 1780s (see below). NW o
the conservatory is the ORANGERY, in heavy Roman Doric
This looks like Tatham. It contains a collection of antiqu
sculpture, the remains of the famous Museum Worsleyanum
removed from Appledurcombe House on the Isle of Wight
Near by is the HOLGATE MONUMENT, an urn on a triangula
pedestal supported on three tortoises. Similar ones are a
Mount Edgecumbe Devon, at Stanmer Park Sussex, and a
Lucan House Co. Kildare. They are all in Coade stone, and i
is tempting to ascribe their design to Wyatt. The Brocklesby
inscription is worth quoting. It was erected by the first Baror
Yarborough 'to the memory of George Holgate of Melton

a tenant and a friend, who as a mark of gratitude and regard bequeathed to him a small estate at Cadney and who deserves to be remembered in the class of farmers as a most excellent character, entirely free from affectation of anything above that respectable station in life to which he was so great a credit. He died in 1785'.

The NORTH GATES are by *W. D. Legg*, a big Tudor-Gothic affair of 1801 with an asymmetrically placed tower – a proto-Victorian composition to be compared with his neo-Elizabethan entrance at Burghley House, Northants. The upper park was landscaped by *Brown*, to whom may be attributed the remarkable BRIDGE. It has seven arches with neo-Norman details, and Gothic aedicules containing figures of saints. The lake here is mentioned in *Humphry Repton*'s *Sketches* (1794) but it is not known what he did. Spanning one of the drives to the w of the house is the MEMORIAL ARCH, inscribed 'To Charles Anderson Worsley 2nd Earl of Yarborough by his Tenants and Friends 1864'. The architect is not known. Other entrances are simpler, the SOUTH LODGE with a modest Tuscan portico, the SOUTH EAST LODGE bargeboarded with pointed windows. Similar the lodge by the Memorial Arch. A curvaceous ride was formed to the s of the house, eventually leading up to the Mausoleum. First, to the l. comes *Wyatt*'s DOG KENNELS, then via plantation walks to ARABELLA AUFRÈRE'S TEMPLE, which could be by *Brown*. Behind this to the l. is a path leading to the ROOT HOUSE, a rare survival nowadays. It is an octagon of tree branches housing rustic seats and tables. Behind it is the GROTTO, like a dank London tube, curved, with a U-shaped room in the centre. Returning to Arabella's Temple and continuing s, the ride opens out to a plateau commanded by the majestic MAUSOLEUM, undoubtedly *Wyatt*'s masterpiece. It [59a] commemorates the beloved Sophia Aufrère, who died as a young wife in 1787. Wyatt may by this time have been working at Brocklesby. In any case he began the Mausoleum almost immediately, and it was complete by 1792.

The Mausoleum stands upon a low mound (traditionally a Roman burial place) encircled by bold iron railings punctuated in twelve places by wonderfully crisp neo-classical sarcophagi, each with pediments, swags, and ram's heads. Within the railings is a deep fosse with the mausoleum rising from the central area. This is Wyatt's interpretation of the Temples of Vesta at Tivoli and Rome. Rusticated basement

having arched openings with grilles and sarcophagi carved
shallow relief. Upon this podium stands the main cell
surrounded by twelve fluted Roman Doric columns. The wa
of the cella is articulated with big niches containing mo
sarcophagi. It is a lesson in vibrant neo-classicality, and nothir
more so than the frieze of swags and bucrania. Above th
frieze is the balustrade, the flattish dome, and a circula
S-fluted lantern. From the N side an intricate arrangement
stairs leads down into the fosse and up to the gigantic doo
of the Mausoleum. These open to reveal the lavish spectac

60   of the interior. The plan is a chamfered Greek cross wit
pairs of imitation porphyry Corinthian columns at th
angles supporting a richly coffered dome. The lantern
glazed with glass painted by *Francis Eginton*. A cool diffuse
light illuminates the *raison d'être* of the Mausoleum: the figur
of Sophia carved by *Joseph Nollekens* about 1791. It is a ver
poignant and moving figure. Sophia's pedestal reflects th
twist of the outside lantern, is set in a pavement with a radia
ing pattern of inlaid marbles and brass, and is surrounde
by a splendid brass rail. In three recesses are family monu
ments of members of the Pelham family. All are of a slightl
frigid Canova-classicality and are said to have been importe
from Italy. There is William Pelham, the one who died i
1587, with a more than demi-nude female allegorical figure,
peacock, and putti; Charles Pelham with a semi-reclinin
female figure on a sarcophagus holding his portrait; an
Francis Anderson with putti and a shield. Below the oute
stairs is the discreet inscription, 'James Wyatt Esq Archt'.

9000

BROUGHTON

4a ST MARY. Very spacious Anglo-Saxon W tower. Herringbon
masonry. Heavy S doorway with thick columns and plainl
chamfered capitals. Strong roll moulding in the arch. To th
W a staircase attachment, more than semicircular, and no
bonded in, i.e. later than the tower. The arrangement i
familiar from Brixworth, Brigstock, and Hough-on-the-Hill
To the E into the church a wider arch, again with thic
columns, two in the reveals, two in stepped splays to the E
The usual oblong opening, a doorway or window, above it
The doorway to the staircase is perfectly plain. But was th
whole a W tower and not rather the towering body of a churc
to which only a chancel belonged? The problem is the sam
as at Barton-on-Humber. The tower top is Perp with eigh

Broughton, brasses of members of the Redford family, late
fourteenth century

pinnacles. It was the C12 that disposed of the Saxon chancel
and made the remaining Saxon structure into a W tower.
For there are two bases preserved in the N arcade which are
Norman and have spurs, and in the chancel S wall is a Norman
window with deep inner splay. The arcades (three bays) themselves are of the C14, first the S arcade with octagonal piers
and double-chamfered arches, then the N arcade, similar but
with ballflower in the abaci. The chancel is E.E., see the
window of three lights with three foiled circles. Much else is
the restorers' work, but the N chapel was built about 1660–70
as a family mausoleum – *see* below. – Former PULPIT.
Jacobean parts of a former pulpit, or domestic parts fitted
together. The angle figures rather worldly for a pulpit. –
SCULPTURE. Late Anglo-Saxon slab with interlace (N chapel).
– PLATE. Chalice, *c.*1635; two Chalices, *c.*1640; Paten,
London, 1681; Paten, by *Edward Barrett*, 1719. – MONU-
MENTS. To members of the Redford family the sumptuous
monument between chancel and N chapel and the sumptuous
brasses in the chancel. The monument has two alabaster
effigies of *c.*1375 on a tomb-chest with shields in cusped fields,
a coarsely panelled arch with big head-stops, and a similar
small doorway to the l. – The brasses are 5 ft 10 in. long, of
excellent quality and must be of the late C14. – Sir Edmund
Anderson † 1661. Erected in 1671. Alabaster. Tomb-chest
with semi-reclining life-size figure, propped up on one elbow
and holding a book. – Sir Edmund Anderson † 1676. With a
bust at the top.

De la Pryme in 1699 saw a spring that turned moss to stone. It is
still there towards Far Wood.

GOKEWELL PRIORY FARM is 1½ m. NE, a Georgian house on
See
p.
767
the site of a Cistercian nunnery founded probably before
1143. Slight remains of C13 work in the farm buildings.

9070

BROXHOLME

ALL SAINTS. 1857 by *T. C. Hine* (GR). In the Dec style, rock-
faced. Perky little turret S of the W gable. – PLATE. Chalice
by *A.F.*, London, 1664; Paten and Flagon, by *E.G.*, London,
1676.

BRUMBY *see* SCUNTHORPE, pp. 356, 358

1060

BUCKNALL

ST MARGARET. Of greenstone, the external features almost
entirely Victorian. Timber S porch (by *James Fowler*, 1884).

But inside arcades of *c*.1300. Both are of four bays and both have low double-chamfered arches. Quatrefoil piers on the N side with deep continuous hollows between the foils, octagonal piers on the S. Both aisles are still as narrow as they were when built. Both have their original W lancets, the N side also an E lancet. No chancel arch. – PULPIT. A fine piece, given in 1646 (price £100). At the angles the typical motifs like exclamation marks. In the panels several motifs including an arch in perspective with a pavement in perspective too. – PLATE. Chalice, Paten, and Flagon, by *John Wakelin & Wm. Taylor*, 1787.

OLD RECTORY. Early C18, with shaped gables and blank oval lights.

BULLINGTON

0070

On the Stainfield road a PILLAR of stone, about 8 ft high, said to have been built from fragments of Bolington Priory, a Gilbertine house founded *c*.1150.)

BULLY HILL *see* TATHWELL

BURGH-LE-MARSH

1060

ST PETER AND ST PAUL. A proud Marshland church, Perp except for a few details such as the S doorway with hoodmould on big heads and the N chapel N window, if this can be trusted. It has three round-headed lights with four ogee arches standing on them and carrying reticulation units. Straight top. The W tower is 'an ornament and landmark for many a tedious mile' (*Gent. Mag.*, 1857), with a four-light W window, a niche with a canopy over it, a small window over that, an immensely tall arch towards the nave (concave-sided semi-octagonal responds), and tall, paired, two-light bell-openings with castellated transoms. Parapet with blank quatrefoils and battlements of fancy shapes. Clerestory of ten (N side nine) closely-set windows of three lights. E gable with pinnacles and a frieze of quatrefoils. The tower is of grey stone, the clerestory of greenstone. The S porch of brick, though dated 1702, has still got a Dutch gable. The E end is all rebuilt. Five-bay arcades to the aisles, octagonal piers, double-hollow-chamfered arches. Nave roof of low pitch with tie-beams and bosses. The chancel arch is Perp too. – SCREENS. With crocketed ogee gables and panelled tracery over, but of different patterns, all enjoyable. The screen now serving as a reredos

is mostly reconstruction, but the screen now under the tow
is in a good state. Here the usual wider arch over the entran
has a variety of birds instead of crockets. – Other woodwork b
an outstanding Jacobean carver who dated the PULPIT 162
He also did the FONT COVER and the N chapel SCREEN. Th
pulpit has back panel and tester, all elaborately ornamente
Even the door to the pulpit is preserved. The usual stubb
blank arches have big leaf motifs inside. At the corners of th
pulpit pairs of Ionic colonnettes. In the parclose screen ther
are also colonnettes, exceedingly elongated and of baluster
like shapes. The arches are replaced by scrolls meeting arch
wise. At the top are openwork obelisks, a motif also used in th
font cover. This opens with doors for baptisms instead c
having to be pulled up. At the top of the font cover the emi
nently curious device of a bird standing on a book and holdin
in his beak a cylindrical and a smaller bottle-like containe
What is their meaning? Inkhorn and sandbox will hardly dc
– LECTERN with a surprisingly large eagle. Carved by *Jabe
Good*, a hairdresser and sign-painter, 1874. – PAINTINC
Saint, whole figure. He is reading a book. North Italian
early C16. – PLATE. Paten Cover, by *R.C.*, London, 1625
Paten, by *Richard Gurney & Thomas Cook*, 1737; Chalice, b
S.H., 1801. – MONUMENTS. Two tablets to two Willian
Cookes † 1831 and 1844, both with an urn and branches o
weeping willow, the first signed *E. Gaffin*, the second *Gaffin*.

W of the church the MOTTE of an early castle, and further w
first a TOWER MILL with caps and derelict fan-tail and the
ST PAUL'S SCHOOL. Brick buildings. The main building is o
the 1860s. The chapel by *Sir Ninian Comper*, 1890; n
jarring details, in fact quite insignificant. Inside the impressior
is of a thin Gothic Revival with a panelled roof and ribbec
cove to the ceiling.*

E of the church the MARKET PLACE forms a pedestrian space of
the main road and the roaring traffic to Skegness. At the E exi
of the village another, specially impressive TOWER MILL; fo
this one, dated 1833, has its five sails and its fan-tail complete
ROUND BARROW, on COCK HILL. This large barrow covere
a Pagan Saxon inhumation burial lying on the old lanc
surface, at the centre, accompanied by a bronze buckle. A
large quantity of Romano-British pottery was recovered from
the body of the mound. The site was later used as a cockpit
from which it took its name.

* The STAINED GLASS is by *Comper* too.

BURGH-ON-BAIN

ᴛ HELEN. Norman tower arch, tall, narrow, unmoulded, on the simplest imposts. Of the same type the re-set doorway into the N aisle. This aisle with its arcade dates from 1870–4. The arcade copies the S arcade. This is of two bays, E.E., and clearly inspired by Lincoln Cathedral and Lincoln parish churches. Piers with an octagonal core and four detached shafts in the main directions. The shafts have rings. Keeled W and E responds. In the church on the walls are many Victorian inscriptions on scrolls. If they are of 1874, they are very progressive. – LECTERN. The top of a fluted pilaster with Corinthian capital, of wood, so beautifully done that it could come from a Wren church. – PLATE. Chalice, by *W. S.*, London, 1635; Flagon, by *Thos. Whipham*, 1749; Paten, by *Robert Jones*, 1780. – MONUMENTS, Thomas Pindar † 1741. Two profiles in oval medallions in front of an obelisk. Black sarcophagus with acanthus decoration. Signed by *Peter Scheemakers*. – Lister family, last death recorded 1796, marble, Grecian, arched top with an urn in relief (cf. Burwell).

ɢɪRSBY MANOR. Demolished. At the time of writing only a neo-Baroque gateway of 1909 and the entrance gate and screen of 1840 remain.

ʟONG BARROW, on BURGH TOP, 350 yds s of Burgh Farm. Only 90 ft long, this is one of the smallest long barrows in the county and, unlike the others, which are on chalk, lies on greensand. The barrow supports a clump of beech trees and has in the past been considerably damaged by rabbit burrows. Other evidence of Neolithic occupation in the parish is provided by a number of leaf shaped flint arrowheads from the near-by Baxter Square Farm.

BURRINGHAM

ꜱᴛ JOHN BAPTIST. 1857 by *S. S. Teulon*. Red brick with some black brick. Aggressively short, stumpy W tower with spire or steep pyramid roof, short nave and apse in one. The tower acts as a porch, and above the entrance to this is a big blank trefoil, set out with three small trefoils of rubbed brick. The windows are C13-type, lancets or with bald plate-tracery. At the NW angle a sudden polygonal turret. Interior without structural division. Yellow brick with some red and a little black brick. The tower is open to the nave, its E wall propped on three-times-projecting corbels. Open timber roof. – FONT.

Of the Teulon time. Octagonal, with blue and yellow encaustic
tile panels. – STAINED GLASS. One window of *c*.1870 is
signed by *Gibbs*.

BURTON-BY-LINCOLN

ST VINCENT. According to an inscription inside, the short W
tower was built in 1678 or a little later. The bell-openings are
cross-windows, but the W doorway has a late C12 arch
slightly pointed. Hood-mould with a frieze of small lobes.
The church otherwise dates from 1795–6, but the windows
were gothicized later. In the N vestry two windows with
embattled transoms. They look original Perp work. – PAINT-
ING. On the W gallery small copy on copper of *Bronzino*'s
Christ in Limbo. – PLATE. Flagon, by *G.G.*, London, 1636;
Paten, by *I.M.*, London, 1638; Chalice, by *I.W.*, London,
1649. – MONUMENT. Christopher Randes † 1639 and wife.
Tablet with kneeling figures.

BURTON HALL. Unfortunately this has been demolished. The
noble S front of 1768 was by *James Paine*. The remaining
STABLES are probably by *Paine* and the mason *Hayward*,
and one range of the early C19 is likely to be *Thomas Cundy*'s
work of 1808. – Very elaborate mid-Victorian GATEPIERS.

MEXBOROUGH HOUSE. Plain but visually attractive. Just three
bays, two storeys, and a Doric porch.

BURTON-UPON-STATHER

ST ANDREW. The earliest feature of the church is the amazing
N arcade of three bays. Round piers with octagonal abaci.
Multi-scalloped capitals. Pellets and a kind of coffer-shaped
but chamfered billets in the abaci. Much-moulded arches with
rolls, keels, pellets, the same billet, and also chains of V-
shapes instead of zigzag. All this suggests the late C12. The
S aisle is E.E. It has a four-bay arcade with octagonal piers
and double-chamfered arches, an original W lancet, and a fine
doorway with three orders of shafts, small upright leaf capitals,
and a richly moulded arch with keeling and fillets. The N
arcade received a fourth bay too. The pier is quatrefoiled with
keeled foils, the arch double-chamfered. E.E. also the clerestory of five single lancets, and E.E. as well the W tower,
broad and unbuttressed. Tall W lancet. One-light shafted
bell-openings. Low broad stair-turret on the N side of the
tower, rectangular with chamfered angles. E.E. tower arch,

quite plain. The Dec windows with flowing tracery are all Victorian, certainly on the s side, as they are not there in the Nattes drawing. The chancel arch and the angels supporting the chancel roof are eminently Victorian (1865 by *Edward Browning*). – STAINED GLASS. Christ, early C19 figure, pictorially treated (s aisle w). – E window by *Ward & Hughes*. – W window 'by *Pearson*' (Kelly). Patterned glass with one good roundel in the C13 style. – PLATE. Silver-gilt Chalice, Paten, and Flagon, by *Emes & Barnard*, 1809 or 1811; Alms Basin, by *John Bridge*, 1825. – MONUMENTS. Under an arch with ballflower in the chancel on the N side a cross-legged Knight; early C14.* – Sir Charles Sheffield, 1776, signed *Fishers* sculp. York. Over-lifesize draped woman standing mourning over an urn. Obelisk behind. The draperies are ample and with close folds. On the base of the urn relief of a stork, on the urn itself of a pair of doves. The high plinth of the monument beautifully detailed. – Sir John Sheffield † 1813. By *Bacon Jun.* Kneeling woman praying over an altar. Grecian and dull. – Lady Sheffield † 1858. Small tablet with corn sheaves l. and r. By *T. Gaffin*.

The village stands above the Trent with a small hamlet of a riverside nature at the base of the CLIFF called THE FERRY. There are vernacular cottages at Burton, of clunch dressed with brick. The SHEFFIELD ARMS is dated 1687 and was re-built in 1830. Near by an early C18 L-shaped house.

BURWELL

3070

ST MICHAEL. The church lies a little elevated above the Wold village. It is of greenstone and possesses a Norman chancel arch of the early C12. One order of columns, one of the capitals with two affronted horses (stags ?), the other with volutes. The arch is decorated busily but flatly (cf. Muckton near by). The W tower is Perp but has a brick top probably Late Georgian. The s windows of the church all straight-headed. The N side is too exposed to do much about windows. There was a s aisle, see the four-bay pointed arcade with two narrower and lower w arches, but no details are recognizable. – FONT. Octagonal, Perp, with shields in quatrefoils and a panelled stem. The inscription says that Thomas Fitzwilliam gave it in 1460. – PULPIT. Jacobean, with the usual blank arches and panelling on other sides. – Attached to it an HOURGLASS

* Canon Binnall tells me that this monument comes from the Sheffield Chapel at Owston.

STAND. – LECTERN. Also with a Jacobean blank arch; but
this is perhaps re-used. – SCULPTURE. Under the tower three
long, stiff angels from the roof. – To the N of the altar
pretty Perp bracket. – PAINTING. N of the chancel arch
fresco fragment, a crowned head looking C12, and an M for
Maria. – PLATE. Chalice, by *John Emes*, 1805; Paten, by
Wm. Bennett(?), London, 1810. – MONUMENTS. Hugh
Alington † 1674. Good tablet of alabaster, without figures.
Black columns l. and r., garlands at the foot. – Lister family,
the last death recorded 1786. Draped urn before an obelisk.
By *Whitelaw* of New Road, London.

BUTTER CROSS. A nice essay in moulded and cut brick. Octagonal with a blank arch on each face and a pediment separated
from the arch by the string course. Conical roof with a small
open cupola. It all looks early C18 or even late C17. A market
had been granted to Burwell in the late C13.

BURWELL HALL, 1½ m. ENE. The house built for Matthew
Lister in 1760 and containing splendid Rococo plasterwork
was ruthlessly demolished in 1958. Only the brick STABLES
remain.

BUSLINGTHORPE

ST MICHAEL. 1835 by *E. J. Willson*. Yellow brick, but with a
short medieval W tower. One W lancet and a small single-
chamfered doorway to the nave. The chancel arch responds
are partly old too. – STAINED GLASS. Small fragments in the
E window. – PLATE. Flagon, London, 1578; Chalice, by
Wm. Howlett(?), London, 1642. – MONUMENTS. Effigy of a
Knight, cross-legged, late C13. Two angels kneel by his pillow.
– Brass to Sir Richard de Boselyngthorpe; demi-figure on a
coffin-lid of stone with a Lombardic inscription. Early C14
and thus one of the earliest dozen or so military brasses in the
country. The pillow on which his head lies is placed diagonally
and has ogee corners.

CABOURNE

ST NICHOLAS. Of ironstone. Unbuttressed, much renewed C11
W tower. The bell-openings with their block or cushion capitals
are entirely *Blomfield*'s of 1872. Original W doorway (cf
Rothwell) with chamfered imposts, plain tympanum, and hood-
mould. One W window. Tall tower arch, with chamfered imposts too. The blocked N doorway to the nave is of the same
type. The E.E. style is represented by one small S lancet in

the chancel and one re-set in a Victorian N addition to the chancel. Most of the windows, however, are of 1872. – FONT. Norman, of drum-shape. A rope moulding, a band of inter-sected arches, a double rope moulding. The font was found fairly recently under the floor. – PLATE. Chalice and Paten Cover, by *Peter Carlill*, Hull, c.1570.

CADEBY HALL   2090
1½ m. WNW of Ludborough

An early C18 stone front of seven bays and two and a half storeys. Moulded window surrounds and keystones. Open segmental pediment on brackets to the door. Inside a good staircase with alternate twisted and straight balusters. At the time of writing derelict.

Both the villages of NORTH CADEBY and SOUTH CADEBY have disappeared, the former probably at the Black Death, the latter in the C15, when the rectory was joined to CALCE-THORPE of which in its turn also nothing is visible except an earthwork around Manor Farm known as Priest's Close (*see* Beresford: *Lost Villages*).

CADNEY   0000

ALL SAINTS. W tower of ironstone, E.E.; see the W lancet and the twin bell-openings. The chancel is also E.E. Two N, two S lancets, a low-side window. The E window is Perp. Early C14 S aisle. The doorway has continuous mouldings, the win-dows are of three ogee-headed lights, straight-topped. The E window has intersecting tracery. The nave N side is the result of *Sir Charles Nicholson*'s restoration of 1912–14. The win-dow details with their round arches as at his St Augustine at Grimsby. The interior, pleasantly unrestored, unfolds quite a different story. The S arcade is Norman, of three bays, with square abaci on round piers and capitals with unusual highly stylized flat leaves on simple canted projections, smaller and larger. The added chapel arch is C13, as is the chancel arch, tall, on corbels of which one is supported by a Green Man's head. – FONT. Norman, of tub-shape, with blank arches. – SCREENS to the S chapel, not *in situ* (from Newstead Priory?). To the N tall, slender, one-light divisions with busy little panel tracery. Illegible carved inscription. To the W three-light divisions with cusped intersecting arches, but also Perp. – SCULPTURE. In the S aisle an image bracket on a head and

two uplifted arms. Also a modest canopy. C14. – PLATE.
Chalice, late C17.

CAENBY

ST NICHOLAS. Mostly of 1869, though the masonry is medieval.
A small church. – PLATE. Chalice, by *Robert Lucas*, c.1735;
Paten, by *John Stewart*(?), London, 1741.

CAENBY HALL. Late Georgian. Six bays, two storeys, parapet
and hipped roof.*

MANOR FARM. Early Georgian, on a medieval moated site.

MANOR HOUSE. L-shaped, and once the seat of the de Tourney.
Now mostly late C18.

CAISTOR

ST PETER AND ST PAUL. Anglo-Saxon w tower of ironstone.
N and S doorways blocked, but to the w a C12 doorway with
zigzag. The triangle-headed windows again Saxon. The
Saxon tower arch re-done, but with the typical Saxon impost
blocks.‡ The next stage of the tower is E.E., the (heightened)
top stage Dec. The w quoins of the nave are enormous and
may be Saxon or Norman. E.E. S doorway with a cluster of
shafts, many rolls, much dog-tooth, and some small nailhead.
The doorway is reported not to be *in situ*. E.E. also the
transept, see one blocked w lancet. Perp clerestory. N aisle
windows all of *Butterfield*'s restoration of 1862. He also provided the coarse roof of the nave with tie-beams, kingposts,
and struts forming big bold arches. The interior of the church
is somewhat dull. S arcade of four bays, E.E., octagonal piers,
bits of nailhead, double-chamfered arches, square seats at the
base. Head label-stops. The N arcade of the same period, but
slightly different. No nailhead, and whorls instead of heads as
label-stops. Also E.E. the tall chancel arch. The respond capitals have small upright leaves and crockets. Again of the same
period the entries to N and S chapels. The N entry with keeled
responds, the S entry with broad, pointed upright leaves and
nailhead. But the real mystery is the responds further E
with a tall shaft and hollows running up straight to as high
as the apex of the chancel arch. Why can they have been
built? Do they indicate the intention of a crossing (cf.

* A billiard room is said to have been built by *William Fowler* in 1829
(Colvin).

‡ Hamilton Thompson calls the tower Norman and the arch a survival of
Saxon technique.

Spalding), perhaps with a tower to replace the Saxon tower? –
STAINED GLASS. In the E, the N aisle E, and some more
windows glass of c.1860, not a usual hand and quite a strong
one. – By *Kempe* a N window of c.1880, the chancel N and
S windows of c.1895, another N window after 1915 (*Kempe &
Tower*). – PLATE. Chalice, Elizabethan; Chalice and Cover,
by *John Bathe*, 1706. – MONUMENTS. Effigy of a Knight, slim
and cross-legged, and effigy of his Lady, early C14. – Also
effigy of Sir John de Hundon, c.1380, with moustache. Two
angels by his pillow. – CURIOSUM. The Gad Whip to be
cracked on Palm Sunday by a man from Raventhorpe, on
entering the church, and then to be held over the vicar's head;
an unexplained custom.

of the church the small SCHOOL, a building of ironstone,
dated 1631 but with new windows, and to its r. the CON-
GREGATIONAL CHURCH of 1842, yellow brick, with giant
Doric pilasters and a pediment. The window and door surrounds taper so determinedly that they look more Egyptian
than Grecian.

ROMAN TOWN. Few structural remains survive above ground,
largely because there has been subsidence caused by springs.
The general plan, however, appears to be that of a square
with sides 500 ft long. A short stretch of the original town wall
survives on the S side of the churchyard, associated with a
massive circular bastion. Building operations have revealed
further buried lengths of this same defensive wall. Most of
the Roman finds from the interior are of the C3 and C4.

What Caistor now is, is an agreeable early C19 red brick
development, notably around the SQUARE. Here the grandest
house has a centre bay with Ionic porch, an arched window
above, and a circular window and small pediment above that.
The whole affirmed by giant Ionic pilasters. An ungainly
composition of the late C18. A garden in MILL LANE has a
gay castellated wall and a circular tower. To its l. a house
dated 1701 (WHITE HOUSE) with a staircase of strong,
turned balusters. A little above the Square, by the George
Inn, a more urban brick house with a doorway displaying
Tuscan columns and an open pediment.

PELHAM'S PILLAR, 2 m. NE and 5 m. S of Brocklesby Park.
128 ft high, but now dwarfed by pylons. It was built by Charles
Anderson Pelham in commemoration of the great Yarborough
plantings. The architect is *E. J. Willson*, the date 1849. A
square tower tapering to a square lantern with an ogee roof.

3070

CALCEBY

1¼ m. s w of South Thoresby

ST ANDREW. In ruins, i.e. some quite substantial chalk mason:
representing the W tower and the N wall of the nave. The tow
arch is still intact, Norman, of greenstone with an unmould
arch.

CALCETHORPE *see* CADEBY HALL

9080

CAMMERINGHAM

ST MICHAEL. The church is now no more than a nave wi
bellcote and a chancel, but there was originally a strong No
man N arcade of two bays. Circular pier, square abacu
capital with leaf crockets (much colour preserved), roun
arch with a slight chamfer. The N chapel, now also no long
up, has a blocked entrance arch probably of the C14. – FON
Small marble bowl of 1755. – SCULPTURE. Big, good La
Anglo-Saxon slab with interlace decoration. – PLATE. Chalic
by *John Morley*(?), *c.*1571; Paten and Flagon, by *T.*
London, 1668. – MONUMENT. Mrs Jane Tyrwhitt † 16
(*posuit* 1657). Large tablet. The inscription on a lozenge
shaped slab. Above bust in a lush oval wreath. Below anoth
inscription as follows:

> Loe here she sleeps in sacred dust
> Untill the rising of the just
> Untill the bridegrom call and say
> A wake my love and come a way.

MANOR HOUSE. Looks mid-C18. The side elevations with tw
pitched roofs in profile, the main front formal with mould
window surrounds. Blocked rusticated entrance on the
front. This used to be a Tyrwhitt seat and was bought by th
Chaplin family early in the C18 for the unusually large su
of £20,000. What else can this large sum have purchased?

4060

CANDLESBY

ST BENEDICT. 1838. By *E. D. Rainey* of Spilsby (GR). O
brick, and – as against the neighbouring Ashby – definitel
post-Georgian; see e.g. the long pointed windows. W towe
nave and chancel. Nave and chancel were originally divide
by a tripartite screen. – PLATE. Wine Cup used as Chalic
by *I.I.*, London, 1591.

CANDLESBY HALL. A Massingberd house of the late C18

w front of three bays, two storeys, parapet, urns, and balconied porch. The s front has a big two-storey bow and a stepped and shaped gable-end.

CARRINGTON

1¾ m. s of New Bolingbroke

ST PAUL. 1816. Perhaps by *Jeptha Pacey*. Brick, with deep white roof-eaves. Pointed windows, but a Georgian octagonal cupola. The short polygonal chancel of yellow brick with the depressing chancel arch is of 1872. – Against the w gallery small ROYAL ARMS of cast iron.

CASTLE CARLTON see SOUTH RESTON

CASTLE HILLS WOOD see THONOCK HALL

CHAPEL FARM see HORKSTOW

CHAPEL ST LEONARDS

ST LEONARD. 1794, but in the nave old masonry was re-used. The nave windows are arched and of brick. The tower with tiled pyramid roof is of 1891–1901 (by *W. Scorer*), the chancel of 1924–5.

CHERRY WILLINGHAM

ST PETER AND ST PAUL. Built in 1753, and one of the most dignified Georgian churches in Lincolnshire. Of stone entirely, with a doorway surrounded by Tuscan columns and pediment, and an octagonal lantern above a pediment. The lantern has an ogee cap. The pediment appears rather unfortunately half-sunk into the zone of the parapet around the rest of the church. The church has quoins, arched windows keyed-in, and an apse with two windows. The reason for this anomaly is the fine Georgian REREDOS inside. The interior has a white ceiling, of the same height for both nave and apse. – The FONT is a shallow carved stone bowl on a square baluster stem. – PLATE. Chalice and Paten Cover, by *John Morley* of Lincoln, Elizabethan, but the Cover now bearing the date 1662. – MONUMENTS. Large purely architectural monument to Thomas Becke † 1757, who built the church. – Also tablets † 1795 and † 1809 by *Stead & Son* of York and † 1836 by *George Earle* of Hull.

CHURCH END FARM see KEELBY

1090

CLAXBY

ST MARY. Of ironstone. W tower E.E. to the bell-openings and a later Perp top with bell-openings and eight pinnacles. Nave and aisles and clerestory. Much of the external details Victorian except for the N doorway, pointed and single-chamfered, and the S doorway with a characteristic Perp moulding. Of the two arcades the S one is of 1871, the N E.E. Two bays, octagonal pier, double-chamfered arches. The E.E. chancel arch has two very big and very rude corbel-heads. One sticks his tongue out, while his raised arms hold the arch, the other opens his mouth with both hands (the wrongly so-called tooth-ache gesture). In the chancel N wall a plain chamfered recess and a plain tomb-chest in it. – PLATE. Chalice, by *F. S.*, London, 1678. – MONUMENT. John Witherwick † 1605. Two kneeling figures facing one another across a prayer-desk. Big standing wall-monument with crude decoration.

In the village, ½ m. to the NW, two plain, townish brick terraces of cottages, built for iron workers in 1868.

3060

CLAXBY PLUCKACRE
1½ m. S of Hameringham

THE GRANGE. A Georgian three-by-three-bay cube of two storeys with a central chimneystack. Attractive silhouette and simple, convincing proportions.

4070

CLAXBY ST ANDREW
1⅜ m. WSW of Willoughby

ST ANDREW. 1846, of stock brick, in a starved Norman style. Norman details inside too. The church lies prettily with trees to the W in a little valley of the Wolds. – PLATE. Chalice, London, C17.

CLAXBY HALL. The history of this house is confused – so much so that stylistic comments only can be made. There is the tradition that it was built for Samuel Dashwood about 1768. Externally, however, it looks plain, dull early C19 and has in fact a lowered roof of this date. Within this shell there is an enchanting suite of rooms with wood carving, panelling, and good ceilings in a London style that could be of the 1730s. In one overmantel is a portrait of Lord Bateman, and over the stairs are the arms of Chaplin. This might have been a dower house to Well Hall (*see* p. 416).

ONG BARROWS, ½ m. NW, on the slope of a ridge overlooking
a dry valley. The w barrow is the better preserved. It is 160
ft long and 6 ft high at the E end. The second barrow, 150 yds
to the SE, although larger, has been considerably damaged by
a chalk pit at its centre and now 'stands little more than 1 ft
high. Both sites support stands of beech trees and are
surrounded by arable land.

CLEATHAM HALL see MANTON

CLEE see OLD CLEE

CLEETHORPES   *3000*

T PETER. 1866–7 by *J. Fowler*. Stone outside and genteel and
rather advanced-looking, but inside with arcades of brick, the
arches alternately exposed and painted white as if of ashlar
blocks of two colours. Moreover, the arrises studded with big
nailhead to make them spiky.

T JOHN, New Clee. 1879 by *J. Fowler*.

T AIDAN, New Cleethorpes. 1906 by *C. Hodgson Fowler*.

COUNCIL HOUSE. 1904 by *Herbert C. Scaping*. Brick and stone
dressings. A small Baroque façade with a lantern.

The date of the Council House marks the time when Cleethorpes'
principal development into a popular seaside resort took place.*
There is nothing in connexion with this that needs comment.
On the Promenade a sham RUIN of 1885, and also on the
Promenade – with that typically English slant on holiday
festiveness – the RAILWAY STATION, 1863, with a thin
tower ending to the accompaniment of openwork iron volutes.
As for the domestic architecture, only the varieties of certain
verandas on the front may please. The front is built up along
a good mile and a half. Lord Torrington, who wrote in 1791,
would not recognize what he called 'three miles of boggy turf
to Grimsby'.

ESKIMO FOODS, Pelham Road. A new curtain-walled office
building by *Manning & Clamp* was completed in 1962.

CLIXBY   *1000*

ALL HALLOWS. This is only the chancel of a medieval church,
restored in 1889. The chancel arch and the E responds of

---

* But the *Gent. Mag.* says Cleethorpes was frequented for sea-bathing in
1829.

aisles show in the w front. Their details, including nailhea[d]
friezes, tell of the C13. The re-set w doorway is of the sam[e]
time. It has dog-tooth in the arch and up the jambs. Tw[o]
pieces of C13 arches re-set inside as well. In the chancel itsel[f]
some Dec windows, an ogee-headed priest's doorway, an[d]
an ogee-headed sedile.

COATES see COTES-BY-STOW

COCK HILL see BURGH-LE-MARSH

0080

COLD HANWORTH

ALL SAINTS. 1863 by *J. Croft* of Islington. All on its own in [a]
field, small, but a showpiece of High Victorian self-confidenc[e]
at its most horrible. With Teulon and Basset Keeling, [J.]
Croft must share the laureateship of what Goodhart-Rend[el]
called rogue architecture. The lychgate is a perfect introduc[-]
tion. Then the church itself, rock-faced of course, and with [a]
thin w tower, octagonal top and spire with tiny spikily tre[-]
foiled lucarnes and three tiers of separate warts. Spiky also i[s]
all the tracery, a pattern of ill-applied inventiveness, flowing
i.e. Dec, in its derivation, but undeniably original. The minut[e]
vestry on the N side is polygonal with a sharp pyramid roof[.]
One had almost been waiting for it in walking round th[e]
64   church. Inside, the effect is determined by the contrast of ex[-]
posed brick and lavishly carved stone. The windows fo[r]
instance are quite small, but flanked relentlessly by leafage[.]
The w tower has a rib-vaulted baptistery below, the FON[T]
has thick dock-leaf, the REREDOS carved angels, and th[e]
arched braces of the roof stand on detached little column[s]
which stand on brackets. The church was built at the expens[e]
of Commodore Peter Cracroft, who died in 1863. – PLATE[.]
Chalice and Paten Cover, 1569.

2050

CONINGSBY

ST MICHAEL. Tall, ashlar-faced w tower, the ground floo[r]
open to N and s for processions to pass, but closed to the w[,]
except for a sexfoiled circular window with openwork cusps[.]
This and the arches have mouldings of sunk waves. Vaul[t]
inside with ribs and ridge-ribs and a big ring. The w doorway
inside has the same mouldings and a rose window with radia[l]

ogee arches over. The windows outside the tower are ogee-headed too. So all this can be regarded as Dec, whereas the three-light bell-openings are Perp. Dec the N aisle windows with reticulation units under four-centred arches, Perp the s aisle windows and the two-storeyed s porch. Of 1870 (by *T. C. Hine & Son*) the polygonal apse and the over-assertive clerestory. Low arcades of five bays, with octagonal piers and double-chamfered arches. They are E.E. with a Dec E lengthening. The earlier parts have typical E.E. bases and stiff-leaf capitals. The early N capitals are more sumptuous than those on the s, and their label stops include one with two dogs biting the ears of a man's face. The aisles were of course widened and not only lengthened, Dec N, Perp S. – FONT. The step is half a circular late C12 capital with broad leaves, the oldest piece in the church. – SCREEN. With Perp dado tracery. – PULPIT. Georgian; plain.

BAPTIST CHAPEL. 1862, and without any question terrible. The only buildings in the village worth individual mention are examples of the Fen Artisan-Mannerism: the ELIZABETHAN HOUSE, ½ m. NE of the church, on the main road, with a two-bay, two-storey gabled front decorated with erratic carved brick motifs, the gable divided by crude pilasters; and the HALL, with similar decoration and a Dutch gable.

Across the river, NW of the church, a house of Tudor brick with Georgian fenestration and re-used bits of medieval sculpture: a shield in a cusped field in a blocked window and little figures as gable copings.

¼ m. NE the LEA GATE INN, with, in a gable, a big wooden head boss from a church.

WINDMILL. Tower type with ogee cap. Dated 1826.

TUMBY LAWN, 3 m. NE. Early C19, in thinly detailed Gothic.

CONISHOLME

4090

ST PETER. Nave and chancel, with a brick bellcote of *c*.1860, and now poorly to look at. But in the Middle Ages it was a sizeable church. One after another its parts were lopped off. On the s side to the r. of the doorway scant remains of the scalloped arch of a Norman doorway. The w wall shows that a w tower has stood in front of it. The N wall inside has the marks of a four-bay arcade, E.E., with circular piers and double-chamfered arches. The E bay was lower than the others. Then, past the chancel arch, there was a two-bay N chapel,

also E.E. and of the same type. But what do the blocked
arch and blocked E arch signify? There can hardly have bee⟨n⟩
a crossing here, abolished already in the C13, when the ⟨N⟩
chapel was built. – SCULPTURE. A very interesting head of a⟨n⟩
Anglo-Saxon wheel-cross, with a tiny, very primitive Cruci⟨-⟩
fixus, interlace above his head, three disks by his feet. ⟨–⟩
PLATE. Chalice, Kings Lynn(?); Chalice and Paten, c.1610
– BRASS to John Langholme † 1515 and wife, 2 ft figures, th⟨e⟩
children small below.

8090

CORRINGHAM

ST LAURENCE. Anglo-Saxon W tower with the customary twi⟨n⟩
bell-openings with mid-wall shafts.* On the ground stage t⟨o⟩
the W a tall E.E. lancet. The tower arch is very strange. It i⟨s⟩
wide and tall and probably Saxon, but the arch with its fou⟨r⟩
roll mouldings must be Transitional or even later. Above, ⟨a⟩
typical Anglo-Saxon blocked door opening. Norman two-ba⟨y⟩
N arcade. Circular pier, square abacus, round arches with ⟨a⟩
slight chamfer. The capitals are flat and uncommonly fine, o⟨f⟩
the leaf-crocket kind, but with many pretty details. The ⟨S⟩
arcade is taller and belongs to the early C13. Octagonal pier⟨s,⟩
simple single stiff-leaves. Double-chamfered pointed arches⟨.⟩
Small lancet in the aisle W wall, as also in that of the N aisle⟨.⟩
The arcades were soon lengthened to the E. The new bay⟨s⟩
were perhaps a transept. The details of the responds diffe⟨r⟩
(S side keeled). A new chancel was also built. It has lance⟨t⟩
windows. In its N wall is a pretty small doorway and to its E a⟨n⟩
Easter Sepulchre with segmental arch. Deep E.E. mouldings⟨.⟩
After that came a new N transept, late C13, see the naturalisti⟨c⟩
leaves of the arch from the S, and incidentally the way it cut⟨s⟩
into a N lancet of the chancel. The arch from the W int⟨o⟩
the transept has chamfers dying into the imposts. The N
window is large, of three lights with pointed trefoiled head⟨s⟩
and a big pointed trefoil over, i.e. c.1300. But the transept ⟨E⟩
window is of a very nice Perp variety, generously cusped and
with an embattled transom above the middle light. Perp als⟨o⟩
the aisle windows and the clerestory. In 1883–4 *Bodley* re-
decorated much of the church, and his work is pleasant to
behold, especially the painted ceilings, but also the amply
decorated ORGAN CASE and the SCREEN with coving and
rood, of which only a few lower parts (and the CHOIR

* But the Nattes drawing shows a plain, quite different bell-opening.

SEATS against its back) were original. – COMMUNION RAIL. C17. – STAINED GLASS. In the N transept E window († 1862) by *Wailes*, pictorial and terrible. – In the s aisle E window († 1878) by *Kempe*, Tree of Jesse, typical early Kempe. – In the E window by *Powell* (designed by *Wooldridge*) 1873, close to Kempe in style. – PLATE. Two Chalices, by *L.G.*, London, 1661. – MONUMENTS. Several tablets to Becketts of Leeds and Somerby Park, e.g. Sir John † 1826 by *Walsh & Dunbar* of Leeds, the Rev. George † 1843 by *William Behnes*, Grecian with a lunette with books, and Sir John † 1847, also Grecian, with profile in roundel and two nicely elongated urns. Is it also by *Behnes*?

COTES-BY-STOW   9080

ST EDITH. Low and small, of nave with bellcote and chancel. Norman windows in the chancel, opened up and restored by *Pearson*, 1883–4. Transitional s and N nave doorways, the latter plain and straight-headed,* the former with a round arch and big dog-tooth. A w tower was projected. The arch between it and the nave survives and looks early C13. In the chancel N wall Easter Sepulchre, a segmental arch and above it, in incongruous panels, small figures in relief, Christ risen and one angel (the others have been destroyed). – In the nave N wall a cusped funerary recess. – SCREEN. Good Perp piece with two-light openings under ogee arches. The coving is preserved and above it – the only remaining parochial case in the county – the loft with parapet and a canted middle projection on which probably stood the rood. A tiny twin window in the s wall lights the loft. – PULPIT. Perp, of wood, with blank cusped arches. – BENCHES. A nice, plain, rustic set. – FAMILY PEW. At the w end; Jacobean. – PLATE. Chalice and Paten, by *T.K.*, London, 1670. – MONUMENTS. Brasses to William Butler † 1590 and wife; small figures. – Brian Cooke † 1653. Demi-figure of alabaster in an arched niche. Open scrolly pediment and garlands.

COUNTESS CLOSE *see* ALKBOROUGH

COVENHAM ST BARTHOLOMEW   3090
¼ m. NW of Covenham St Mary

ST BARTHOLOMEW. Of chalk. Nave, chancel, and s transept. Slate-hung turret over the nave E end. – FONT. Octagonal,

* Traces of a painted rood remain (PB).

Perp. With the twelve apostles, the Virgin, and the Trinit
The apostles stand in pairs. Their hair stands round the
heads grotesquely so that the coiffure is as wide as the
shoulders. A stray East Anglian piece.

COVENHAM ST MARY

3090

ST MARY. w tower of chalk and ironstone. Are the bell-openings
early C14? Very large, but simple Dec three-light E window
The tracery pattern a usual one. In the chancel N wall cuspe
and subcusped recess; ogee-topped. The chancel was license
in 1359, though not quite complete yet. Most windows Perp.
FONT. Octagonal, Perp, an unusual pattern (but cf. Ea
Barkwith). A frieze of little round arches upside down an
with finials on every second. In the space between the finia
shields with the Instruments of the Passion. – PLATE. Chalic
and Cover, by G.D.(?), York(?), 1653.

COXWOLD

1000

ST NICHOLAS. Short unbuttressed w tower with lancet bel
openings, perhaps lowered. The tower arch is Norman,
not earlier. Simple imposts with one chamfer.* A former
aisle arcade is visible outside. A former N chapel has left th
springing of the arch with continuous mouldings. The double
chamfered chancel arch dies into the imposts. Most of th
fenestration of 1860, Geometrical style, by Fowler. – FONT
Norman, of trough-shape, with a band of flat scallops at th
top. – PLATE. Chalice and Paten Cover, inscribed 1569.
COXWOLD HALL. Tudor-Gothic, by James K. Colling, 186
(GS).

CRAISELOUND see HAXEY

CROFT

5050

ALL SAINTS. One of the major Lincolnshire marsh churches
but still Dec in its salient features. Built of greenstone, but th
tower top of grey stone. Dec the moulding of the w doorway
the ogee-headed staircase doorway, and also the bell-openings
Dec also the s doorway, though the s and N aisle windows an
the windows of the embattled clerestory are Late rather blun
Perp and the chancel fenestration is Perp altogether. Th

* Hamilton Thompson considers the tower to be Saxon and not too late

clerestory windows are of two tracery patterns used in alternation. Then, however, the arcades inside are Dec again, of
five bays with octagonal piers and double-chamfered arches.
The tower arch and also the chancel arch go with them. Nice
Perp decoration round the doorway to the rood-loft stairs.
The nave roof has cusped arched braces. – FONT. Octagonal,
big, with shields in simple panels, the bowl supported by
busts. – PULPIT. The pattern for that at Burgh. Coupled angle
colonnettes, panelled panels. The door, the back panel, and
the tester are all preserved. The date inscribed is 1615. –
SCREENS. Several, all on the principle of the ogee-headed
crocketed arch with panel tracery over, but all different,
namely the rood screen (the crockets over the entrance are
birds just as at Burgh-le-Marsh, and in the spandrels of the
dado panels are beasts and birds and human faces), the s
parclose screen, and the N parclose screen. – BENCHES. With
simple tracery and doors, and no poppy-heads. – LECTERN.
Brass eagle on a mighty support. They were a medieval East
Anglian speciality and were sent out freely. Similar lecterns
are at Woolpit and Cavendish Suffolk, Chipping Campden,
Corpus Christi Oxford, Upwell Norfolk, and Wrexham.
– SOUTH DOOR. Dated 1633, panelled. – PLATE. Chalice and
Paten, by *T.R.*, London, 1660; Paten and Flagon, by *Edward
Holaday*, 1713. – MONUMENTS. Brass, late C13 or early C14,
Knight wearing chain-mail. Only head, shoulders, and arms
are preserved. He is praying (s chapel). This is one of the four
or five earliest brasses in England. – William Bonde † 1559.
Standing monument of stone. Two columns, achievement at
the top, and no figurework (chancel arch). – Sir Valentine
Browne † 1600 and John Brown † 1614, both with wives, both
monuments of alabaster, and both identical in decoration.
Kneeling figures facing each other, achievements at the top.

CROMWELL'S GRAVE *see* SWINHOPE

CROSBY *see* SCUNTHORPE, pp. 356, 357

CROWLE

7010

ᴛ OSWALD. Of the Norman church the whole s wall of the
nave is extant, and the w wall too – showing that the nave
was remarkably wide. In the latter a plain tall doorway, now

into the tower. It has a tympanum with an incised trellis pa
tern. The s wall has outside the complete frieze of eaves corbe
with faces etc. In addition a sumptuous doorway with tv
orders of colonnettes, decorated capitals, and an arch
several orders, two of them with zigzag. The Norman na
was about as high as the present E.E. chancel with its lanc
windows. This, however, was rebuilt in 1850. Was this do
correctly? The chancel arch responds certainly look qui
trustworthy. Also E.E. the s porch entrance and the N arcad
of four bays, or at least its responds; for the rest was rebui
in 1792 (and again, it seems, in 1884). The responds hav
triple shafts, the middle one keeled. Again E.E., but perhaps
little later, the lower parts of the unbuttressed w tower – s
the charming small w window with dog-tooth. The continua
tion of the tower Perp. Perp also the clerestory and the
aisle and N chapel details. – SCULPTURE. In the church a
important fragment of an Anglo-Saxon cross-shaft of Vikin
inspiration. It is coarsely done and probably dates from th
C11. To the (present) N and E heavy interlace, but to the s
man on horseback, two figures in profile above addressing on
another, and two symmetrical dragons above them. Also pa
of a Runic inscription. – PLATE. Paten Cover, Elizabethan
Chalice, London, 1651.

ST NORBERT (R.C.). By *M. E. Hadfield & Son*, 1872. Small, c
brick. Nave and chancel and bell-turret on the E end of th
nave.

HIRST PRIORY, 1¾ m. s. Georgian, of brick, five bays, tw
storeys, hipped roof. But the details Victorian, and a larg
addition of the 1850s to the w.

CROXBY

A hamlet in one of the diminutive valleys of the Wolds.

ALL SAINTS. Externally over-restored. Nave with a wee bell
cote and chancel. But the chancel arch is early C12 (plainl
chamfered imposts, single-stepped arch), the s side has th
Late Norman arcade to a former aisle (two bays, circular pier
octagonal abacus, multi-scalloped capitals, but upright lea
crockets on the respond capitals, double-chamfered round
arches with broaches), the re-set s doorway seems of *c.*120
(round arch, one order of shafts, one slight chamfer, one ro
moulding), and the N arcade to another former aisle of *c.*130
(two bays, quatrefoil piers, double-chamfered arches). Ther

vere also arches into a N chapel. So the medieval church was
very different from the building 30 by 16 feet, as we see it
now. – FONT. Norman, drum-shaped, with intersected
arches. – BENCH ENDS. Some, straight-headed, with busy
tracery. – PLATE. Chalice, by *A.K.*, London, 1571.

CROXBY HALL. With a nice mid-C18 silhouette, wide wooden
eaves-cornice, pitched roof, dormers, and a pair of chimneystacks.

CROXTON

0010

JOHN. Unbuttressed w tower, Dec. Triple-chamfered tower
arch dying into the imposts. Twin bell-openings with a
polygonal shaft and ogee-headed openings. Perp top with eight
pinnacles. The s doorway was re-set and is Dec too. Earlier
the N arcade. Three bays, quatrefoil piers with four thinner
diagonal shafts as well, all filleted. Plain capitals. Also a w
lancet in the N aisle. – STAINED GLASS. An exquisite panel
of the Crucifixion in a s window, assigned to the early C14. –
PLATE. Chalice, by *Henry Chauner*, 1794; Paten, by *Robert
Cattle & J. Barber*, York, 1810.

ARBOROUGH CAMP. A small rectangular earthwork, enclosing
approximately $2\frac{3}{4}$ acres. The site lies in a densely overgrown
plantation and access is difficult. A Roman coin hoard of the
C4 was found in the interior.

CUMBERWORTH

5070

HELEN. 1838. Nave and chancel and a polygonal leaded bell-
turret. But the priest's doorway is apparently of *c.*1200, the
s doorway is Perp, one N window has Dec reticulated tracery
which seems original, and the reticulated s windows have at
least original label-stops. – FONT. Octagonal, Perp, with four
flower or leaf motifs, and four shields with the Instruments
of the Passion. – PLATE. Chalice, by *Peter Carlill*, Hull,
*c.*1570.

CUXWOLD *see* COXWOLD

DALBY

4070

CHURCH. 1862 by *James Fowler*. Nave and chancel, bell-turret
with spirelet on a w buttress. Early Dec style. Brick-faced
inside with some enrichment in yellow and vitrified black
brick, i.e. all typical Fowler. – FONT. Octagonal, with quatrefoil panels. – PLATE. Chalice, Paten, and Flagon, by *Charles*

Wright, 1772. – MONUMENTS. William Llanden † 1621 an
wife. Small alabaster tablet with the usual kneelers. – Muc
less usual Julyan Llandon, dated 1631, a small alabaster pan
with inscription, a little strapwork, and her kneeling figure
the top, all incised or in low relief.

DALBY HALL. A fire burnt down the C18 house, and the presen
one was built in 1856 for J. W. Preston by *Fowler*. Stock bric
It is certainly a surprise to find him as the architect of s
conventional, Latest Classical a house. Probably he on
adjusted and enlarged an older house; for while the front wit
its two bows seems at first symmetrical, the r. bow is of tw
storeys, the l. bow of three. Additions at the back and insid
by *Temple Moore*.

2060   DALDERBY

MANOR FARM. L-shaped Georgian house with a gabled fron
Ranks high for the picture-postcard cottage of the county.

2080   DONINGTON-ON-BAIN

St ANDREW. Broad unbuttressed Norman w tower. The ta
narrow tower arch suggests the C11. No details survive. De
bell-openings. Nave and chancel. In the nave one s lancet, i
the chancel two low-side lancets. The N aisle is gone, and onl
traces of the three-bay arcade remain. They go well with th
lancets. There were round piers with round abaci and doubl
chamfered arches. One capital has very crude, large, il
detailed tripartite stiff-leaf repeated twice. The next capital ha
a small head sticking out, not even in the middle. The chanc
arch also E.E. – FONT. Circular, Norman, with incised inter
sected arches and a rope moulding. The font stands on
circular E.E. capital reversed. – BRASS, early C17, with a
inscription whose first lines run as follows:

> Both Chrysostome and Polycarpe in one
> United lye intered beneath this stone
> This one a Phoenix was all eminent
> The learned prudent pious Thomas Kent.

3070   DRIBY

St MICHAEL. 1849–50. Nave and chancel and an open poly
gonal bell-turret. E.E. style. – FONT. Octagonal, Perp. Nicel
panelled stem, on the bowl angel busts with shields, on th
underside four more, larger, angel busts with shields. – Th

STAINED GLASS of c.1850. – PLATE. Chalice, by *J. Denzilow*, 1783. – BRASS. James Prescott † 1583 and family. Kneeling figures.

DUNHOLME

0070

ST CHAD. A completely E.E. church, except for the N aisle wall with a Dec ogee-headed doorway and some Dec windows and the other windows of the church, which are all Victorian and represent Dec and Perp forms. The W tower is un-buttressed and has lancet windows and pairs of smaller lancets as bell-openings. The arch to the nave has a hood-mould on two whorl stops. The eight pinnacles look Perp but do not seem to belong. The S doorway is single-chamfered with a hood-mould on a head and a whorl stop. The arcades are of three bays. Keeled responds (as are the responds of the chancel arch), quatrefoiled keeled piers with thinner shafts in the diagonals. On the S side some nailhead enrichment. To the l. and r. of the altar two brackets on heads. – FONT. Alas defaced. It is of an East Anglian type, with fleurons on the base, seated Saints (and the Annunciation) against the stem, and more seated figures against the bowl. – BENCHES. Mid-C19 Gothic (of the restoration of 1853?). – LEATHER CASE for the sacramentary vessels, round, with stamped branches. Probably early C16. – PLATE. Chalice and Cover, Elizabethan. – MONUMENT. Robert Grantham † 1616. Of stone, with columns flanking the kneeling figure. Inscription and some bald strapwork above.

RECTORY. Of before 1864. Symmetrical with crazily steep gables, the highest, middle one scissor-braced in front of a stone bay window which is supported on a buttress and runs right up against the gable.

DUTCH HOUSE *see* ASTERBY

EAST BARKWITH

1080

ST MARY. Chancel 1846 by *J. B. Atkinson*, N aisle and arcade, nave roof, and windows by *Withers*. The masonry of the predecessor well re-used. Perp W tower (see the tower arch) and probably C17 bell-openings, Perp S doorway, Perp porch entrance with, above, a poor statuette of the Virgin, in a niche. Original also the S arcade of four bays with octagonal piers and double-chamfered arches. (Interesting lancet window

at the w end of the s aisle. PB) – FONT. Octagonal, Perp, qui
ornate. Heads and fleurons at the foot of the bowl. On tl
bowl itself shields above upside-down shallow arches wi
trefoil leaves where they meet. Cf. the font of Covenham
Mary. – PULPIT. Metal, gilt, in the Arts and Crafts tast
By *Christopher Turnor*, the squire of Panton. – STAINE
GLASS. Small fragments in the chancel N. – PLATE. Chali
and Cover, inscribed 1706.

1010   EAST HALTON

ST PETER. E.E. chancel, the E lancets with round heads, b
in the s wall a window with plate tracery. In the N wall
blocked doorway and to its E a double-chamfered wall rece
(Easter Sepulchre?). Dec s and N aisles with their doorway
Heavy w tower, probably Dec too, and Dec the aisle arcad
with octagonal piers and triple-chamfered arches. – BENC
ENDS. Straight-headed, castellated, and with simple blar
two-light arches. – PLATE. Chalice, by *William Atkinso*
1725.

3060   EAST KEAL

ST HELEN. E.E. arcades of four bays. The s side with quatrefc
piers with fillets and thin shafts in the diagonals, some nailhea
and double-chamfered arches, the N side with octagonal pier
The w tower of 1853–4 (by *Stephen Lewin*) consequently E.
too, quite a domineering piece, partly inspired by Friskne
but with a naughty sw corner at ground level where the bu
tresses develop crocketed gables. The tower arch is Perp an
allows for the view of the ground stage and the next stage of tl
c19 work, that is the stage with the plate-traceried window
The rest of the exterior all 1853–4 too, with plate tracer
except for the s doorway, whose jambs are quite a charmin
Perp job, sweet, with fleurons, busts, and one little figure l., o
r. Is the heavy, impressive chancel roof of the 1850s too? – FON
Octagonal, with fig leaf motif and small faces against the unde
side. – PLATE. Chalice, Elizabethan; Paten, by *Wimans*, 171
Flagon, by *Ben Cartwright* (?), London, 1754; Plate, by *Jame*
Young, 1775; Chalice, by *Crespin Fuller*, 1806. – MONU
MENTS. Susanna Kirkman. Small Elizabethan stone table
very rustic. Frontally seated figure, her elbow on a skull, i
her other hand an extinguished torch. Short fluted pilasters

and r. – Peter Short † 1681, good bust, no doubt from a monument.*

ETHODIST CHAPEL, ¾ m. sw. Red brick, 1863, yet still essentially classical.

LD RECTORY, ½ m. sw. The prettily managed brick front looks late c18. A middle three-storey bay recessed in an arcade, next, l. and r., a lower bay, then a blank recession and pilasters at the angles. The movement is continued by screen walls curving slightly forward.

ANOR HOUSE, N of the church. Late c18 incorporating earlier work.

EAST KIRKBY

NICHOLAS. Of greenstone, with a s porch tower. The church is mainly Dec. The tower has a quadripartite rib-vault (single-chamfered ribs and a big head boss) and walls with simple blank arcading. The mouldings are typically Dec, and the staircase doorway is ogee-headed. The w wall has a tall Dec window (perhaps not original) and the s aisle an ogee-headed piscina. The aisle windows are Victorian. The chancel E wall and clerestory date from 1906, but the old parts are Dec also, especially the N and s low-side windows with their simple tracery, still E.E. in spirit, but with ogee details. Inside the chancel on the N side an odd assembly of sculptured FRAGMENTS, especially one strip with three women holding objects (Cox suggests the three Maries and a connexion with an Easter Sepulchre) and one with naturalistic foliage. At the E end of the N aisle a chapel was added later than the straight-headed windows with ogee lights. Interior of four-bay arcades. Very tall octagonal piers. Double-chamfered arches. The date is c14, but whether Dec or Perp it is hard to decide. – FONT. Octagonal, Perp, of white stone and re-cut. Leaves and heads in odd cusped fields (cf. the chimneypieces at Tattershall Castle). – SCREENS. Parts of five screens, the rood screen (tall, with cusped ogee arches), s aisle E chapel, two different ones, W end, N aisle E end. Even where only the dados remain the patterns are every time different. – BENCH ENDS. Simple, with poppy-heads. – PLATE. Chalice, by *John Neville*, 1745; Paten Cover, unmarked. – MONUMENT. In the s aisle at the E end slab with a good cross to Sir Robert Sylkestone † 1347. Could this give a hint about the rebuilding of the church?

* Information on the two monuments was kindly given me by Mrs olman Sutcliffe.

8010   EASTOFT

ST BARTHOLOMEW.* 1855 by *J. L. Pearson*. Nave and chan‹
with a tall bellcote at the E end of the nave. Yet, in all t‹
modesty, a dignified church, quite out of the common ru
It is stone-built and has lancet windows, well grouped at t
W and E ends and inside shafted and provided with dog-too
in appropriate places. Also the roofs and the gable of t
bellcote are exceptionally steep. Narrow aisles with quatref‹
arcade piers. – FONT and PULPIT seem to belong to the sa‹
years. – Also STAINED GLASS is in all windows, but it
consistently patterned only, save one small panel of the Cru‹
fixion in the middle E lancet – a remarkable refinement. – T‹
GATEWAY to the churchyard is probably *Pearson*'s too.

2090   EAST RAVENDALE

ST MARTIN. By *James Fowler*, 1857. Nave with bellcote a‹
chancel. Lancet windows, shafted inside, but at the W e‹
some tricky details. – STAINED GLASS. One two-light wind‹
evidently by *Morris & Co.* (*Burne-Jones*), chastely and beau
fully drawn, in pure colours, quite light, not yet as sentiment
as Burne-Jones could be later, and with Morris's delightf‹
ornamental details. The window commemorates a death
1875. – The E window is by *Kempe*, 1882, and is really ‹
comparison with Morris. – PLATE. Cup, gilt inside, Londo‹
1745.

SCHOOL, N of the church. Also by *Fowler* and of the same tin
as the church. Red brick, Gothic, asymmetrical, with a tow‹
Beyond this on the l. side a later addition.

CHAPEL RUINS, at West Ravendale, 1 m. w. Of the Pr‹
monstratensian Priory, founded *c.*1202, nothing exists no
but an eloquent but not instructive ruin of a chapel on a hi‹
formerly perhaps *ante portas* of the priory itself. The chap‹
is 23 by 12 ft, built of chalk and greenstone. Climbers hide t‹
upper parts, and no feature can be recognized.

7090   EAST STOCKWITH

ST PETER. 1846 by *T. Johnson* (GR). Stone outside, brick insid‹
Nave and chancel and a thin turret at the SE end of the nav‹
Lancet windows. – STAINED GLASS. In the E window, sign‹
by *W. Wailes* and dated 1846.

        * The church is really just across the West Riding border.

he proximity of the river Trent gives the village its character. On the partially pedestrian quay the OLD VICARAGE in early C19 Builder's Gothic. Pointed windows, Greek-key strings, acroteria, and scallop shell ornaments.

EAST TORRINGTON 1080

t MICHAEL. 1848–50 by *Teulon*. Nave and chancel. Dec tracery. The thickly crocketed, diagonally placed buttresses for the gable of the bellcote are the one place where Teulon decided he might have a go. – PLATE. Chalice, by *I.P.*, London, 1569.

EASTVILLE 4050

t PAUL. On its own, 2 m. N of the station. Not orientated; the W tower is in fact a N tower. Consecrated in 1840, but built probably earlier. The architect was *John C. Carter*, but the style is much like *Jeptha Pacey*'s. Yellow mixed with red brick. Tower, nave, transepts, and short polygonal chancel. The tower with brick windows, battlements, and even pinnacles. Inside, the centre on four sturdy, plain wooden posts, yet the composition with this centre and the transept is that of Dutch C17 churches and some of Wren's City churches (St Anne and St Agnes).

VICARAGE. It lies to the N of the church and is of yellow brick. Its doorway with Gothic detail is in axis with that of the church tower. Otherwise some more Tudor details, but essentially Latest Classical with deep eaves.

t JUDE, New Leake. Probably of the 1860s. Red brick, nave and chancel and a small wooden bell-turret. Lancet windows.

EAST WYKEHAM 2080
1¼ m. N of Burgh-on-Bain

WYKEHAM HALL. Close to the house a pretty FOLLY, made up about 1800 from fragments of the old church.

EDLINGTON 2070

St HELEN. Quite a big church; of greenstone. The earliest part is the tower arch, perhaps about 1100, see the mouldings of the imposts and the one-step arch. The rest of the tower is Perp. Then the three-bay arcades, which are C13. The N aisle has gone, but the arcade can be seen. Octagonal piers.

Double-chamfered arches. On the s side most of the arcade is Victorian (1859–60 by *J. Fowler*). The clerestory is Victorian too. In the N wall windows formerly in the s aisle. One has Geometrical tracery (trefoil-headed lights and a plain circle over), one intersecting tracery. They allow the arcades to be dated Late E.E. – FONT. Square, chamfered at the corners, with blank arcading, shafts, and round arches. Dated 1599.

EDLINGTON HOUSE, of which there is a view by Nattes of 1792, has gone.

0010

ELSHAM

ALL SAINTS. In the w tower a Saxon opening above the Norman arch into the nave. The latter is shafted at the angles. Norman also the N wall. The chancel N doorway, very simple slightly chamfered, seems Transitional. Other medieval bits, e.g. two nice head-stops of *c.*1300 in a chancel N window, probably one of the Dec s windows of the nave, and apparently also the really delightful w doorway with many filleted shafts and nobbly leaves on the capitals forming a continuous undulating band. But essentially the church is that built by *Scott Champion* in 1874. – SCULPTURE. On the w buttresses of the tower two exceedingly interesting reliefs, 45 in. long and 23 in. high. They are part of a frieze of the Last Judgement and look as though they might come from a French late C12 tympanum or an English imitation of such a piece. On the r. panel angel and five of the doomed, marching to the r. in a row. The l. panel is almost entirely obliterated. Yet one small figure climbing out of a grave can still be distinguished, and another in typical late C13 drapery. The two reliefs were already in their present position when Nattes drew them in 1796. – PLATE. Silver-gilt Paten, by *Thos. Tearle*, 1722. – In the churchyard a gravestone signed: *Scun. Co-op*.

Near the church is a brick house dated 1696. It has moulded string-courses.

ELSHAM HALL. When the estate came to the Corbett family in 1788 there was an early C17 house here with a N wing rebuilt in the 1740s. The architect of this wing ought to be known. Three storeys with three bays each side of a narrow, slightly projecting pedimented centrepiece. The base of this is stone channelled and there are quoins above. The darkly shadowed deep entrance arch is singular. Above it a Venetian window with a rusticated head, and above this a small oblong window. Round the corner on the E front the two-storey bow may be post-1788. The attic storey above was rebuilt by *Guy Elwes* in 1933, who also duplicated the bow at the S end. The centre part had been rebuilt after 1796. Elwes's work included the whole of the S front. This has an incongruous Gothic oriel corbelled out above the entrance. The interior also by Elwes.

ORANGERY. Three arched windows in a rusticated wall divided by Roman Doric columns. The entablature breaks, and there is a pediment over the middle bay. It is said to have been built in 1760.

STABLES. Victorian. Three pedimented pavilions with lower links.

EPWORTH   *7000*

small clustered town rather than a village.

ANDREW, N of the village. The exterior is all Perp, except for the tall chancel, whose three-light S windows have reticulated tracery, i.e. are Dec, and except for the re-set, cusped and subcusped entrance arch to the N porch, which looks *c.*1300. Perp ashlar-faced W tower, Perp S and N aisles. The W chapels embrace the tower and are embattled. Perp clerestory. Perp embattled N chapel. And Perp also the interior of the N porch with its pointed tunnel-vault and transverse arches. But inside the arcades are of the C13. Three and a half visible bays – the half-bay because the tower was built complete with its mighty E buttresses into the nave. The arcade has octagonal piers and double-chamfered arches. Its W continuation is in fact not of one bay, as it seems, but of two bays, but the bays are narrower and lower than the others. Was this then the site of the small original church, and was it substantially lengthened in the C13 and the old arcading at the same time rebuilt in the new style? Another puzzle is the arch at the E end of the S aisle, an indication perhaps of the plan to build further E, before the Dec chancel was built. And what has happened to the fifty stone figures of angels, saints, martyrs, and bishops which a Mr Fox dug up in the King's Head yard in 1844 (*Gent. Mag.*)? – PLATE. Chalice, by *John Fawdery*, 1705.

ESLEY MEMORIAL CHAPEL. 1888–91. 'Churchy', with a (ritually) SW tower and spire. School, manse, and other premises around as one group.

LD RECTORY, Rectory Street. Rebuilt after a fire of 1709. Brown brick. Of seven bays, not quite regular. One-bay middle projection. Brick quoins. The roof is half-hipped. The Wesley brothers spent their childhood here.

OLD WINDMILL, to the NW of the church. Brick with cap ar remains of sails and fan-struts. Another WINDMILL near with the fan-struts only.

FALDINGWORTH

0080

ALL SAINTS. 1890, by *Hodgson Fowler*, with a shingled broa spire. In the tower some original Dec details. Medieval al the capitals of the chancel arch responds. – PLATE. Chalic by *T. S.*, 1617; Paten and Flagon, by *Wassell & Marrio* 1825.

RECTORY. By *Pearson Bellamy*, 1858 (GA).

FARFORTH

3070

ST PETER. 1861. Nave with bellcote and chancel; land windows. Inside two large panels of Victorian EMBROIDER with passages from the 119th Psalm. – PLATE. Chalice, Pate and Flagon, by *Thos. Moore*, 1722.

FARLESTHORPE

4070

1¼ m. N of Willoughby

ST ANDREW. Built in 1800 (White). Nave largely of stone, b brick-faced, two bays, the chancel rebuilt in 1912. One E. corbel r. of the chancel arch. This was found in the vicara garden at Bilsby. – PLATE. Chalice, London, 1726(?).

FILLINGHAM

9080

ST ANDREW. The architectural evidence is puzzling. The dat we have are 1768 for the rebuilding of the chancel, 1777 f the tower, 1866 for a restoration. The visible facts are thes The W doorway is of the late C12, with round arch and o order of colonnettes. One of the capitals has waterleaf. Th tower of 1777 stands in front of this and is nicely and un expectedly open to the W, N, and S. Large two-light be openings. The N and S windows of the nave look late C1 But two on the N side, originally groups of three stepped lanc lights, have one of them cut off, the easternmost its E ligh the westernmost its W light. This begins to make sense whe one steps inside. For there were aisles, and their arcades three bays (with octagonal piers and double-chamfered arche have indeed been cut short at both ends and deprived of the responds. Why this was done cannot now be said. The tower arch of the same date and the chancel arch, possibly of the same date too, are also shifted. – CHEST. Splendid early C14 piece. The angle posts with rosettes, the front panel with intricately intersected arches, rosettes, whorls, etc. in the interstices. – PLATE. Chalice and Paten, by *Robert Cooper*, 1698; Plate, by *S. W.*, London, 1785.

FILLINGHAM CASTLE. Sir Cecil Wray is said to have built his Gothic castle in 1760. But according to style and plan it is a decade later, and *John Carr* may have been employed to design it. The house is felicitously placed astride the ridge. To the E an avenue to Gothic lodges and an arch, to the W an escarpment dropping steeply down to the gothicized tower of the church, worked deliberately into the composition. To the NW is the MIDDLE STREET GATEWAY, with niches and cross-shaped openings above them. The E or ERMINE LODGE is similar to the later one at Redbourne Hall (*see* p. 340), where *Carr*'s participation is also probable. The castle is raised upon a podium. Rectangular with circular towers at the · angles and crenellated parapets. Arched W windows of moulded stone recessed into the wall. Between the towers, the long front has four bays, the short front three, an ogee-headed doorway, and an oddly jumped-up drip mould. The offices _{See} make a long courtyard from the N front (cf. Carr's Grimston _{p.} Garth) in two odd sets of four bays each. The interior is ₇₆₇ competently classical, i.e. 1770s, with good chimneypieces, except for the fan-vaulted entrance hall and some Gothic work in upstairs rooms. This is executed in plaster and *papier-mâché*

MANOR HOUSE. A C17 cottage done up with pointed lights as an agreeable object in the parkscape.

RECTORY. It retains a Georgian room with Doric pilasters. Additions by *Thomas Calvert* in 1853 (GA).

FIRSBY   4060

ST ANDREW. 1856 by *G. E. Street*. Nave with a double bellcote, chancel, and apse. Tiled. Rose in heavy plate tracery at the W end. But the E end is much odder. Street lets a tall E gable grow out of his apse, or rather imposes the gable on it. It rises like a dormer into the apse roof and has a three-light window with plate tracery. There are plenty of other wilful details, especially in the bellcote and the S porch. The windows of the church are paired cusped lancets. The chancel arch is in the E.E. style too. No doubt also by Street the stone PULPIT and the attached LECTERN on a detached Purbeck shaft. – PLATE. Chalice, Elizabethan. – MONUMENT. Mary Alice Walls † 1877. An uncommonly excellent tablet of inlay of various colours and gold. A young woman in white robes against a background of an all-over pattern of two stylized flowers in square fields. Flower borders l. and r.

STATION. 1848. The line was constructed by Sir William Cubitt. A three-part composition. The centre stone-faced with three arches and four pilasters, in a free Cinquecento style. The links and pavilions brick with stone dressings, rather Georgian. Very similar to Gainsborough Station (which is by *Weightman & Hadfield*).

Opposite the Railway Hotel on a wall a C13 label-stop and two late C14 heads.

0070

FISKERTON

ST CLEMENT. A church full of problems and puzzles. The first is straightaway – on arrival – connected with the W tower. This is Perp and has the most unusual buttresses. They are of the clasping type, but four sides of a hexagon set diagonally. This curious arrangement is probably due to the fact that the body of the tower itself is round. So it seems that the Perp work went on round the only round tower of Lincolnshire. The tower is ashlar-faced, as is the clerestory with its Perp three-light windows under four-centred arches. The head corbels supporting the nave roof inside are of course of the same date. The other puzzles of the church concern the interior. Externally the following further features deserve recording. E.E. N and S doorways, both with one order of shafts carrying stiff-leaf capitals, but the N doorway also having a tympanum with a curved underside, a Norman motif, and the S doorway being a good deal higher. In the W wall of the N aisle a small lancet, in the W wall of the S aisle a cinquefoiled window. The aisle windows are simple Dec and may not be original.* The chancel has a five-light E window with reticulation units under a segmental arch, and this also is not certain to be original. As for the interior, the best thing is to describe first what is there. The arcades differ entirely from each other. The N arcade is Norman, the S arcade E.E. They are of two bays. The N arcade has a strong round pier with scalloped

* The S aisle is certainly different in Nattes's drawing of 1797.

capital and square abacus and arches with a strong half-roll
and slenderer accompanying rolls. Hood-mould with billets.
The s arcade is a Lincoln Cathedral conceit. Square slightly
chamfered pier with concave sides and fitted into these four
detached shafts. The s arcade starts further w and ends
further E than the N arcade, i.e. it marks the wish to extend
the church in both directions. But the chancel has a N chapel
which, though referring to a chancel starting further E than
the Norman arcade would make one expect, is Norman too
and indeed with its unmoulded arches older-looking than the
aisle arcade. The pier is like the aisle pier. The responds are
obviously not in their original state. And here the puzzles
begin. The chancel arch is clearly also not in its original
state. Nor is the single arch to the s chapel, nor is the tomb
recess in the s chapel. The anomalies must be enumerated.
First: along the E wall of the s chapel runs a frieze of charmingly decorated Norman scallops. This is in two different
patterns, and may not be *in situ*. Second: the responds of the
s chapel are not in order. They are of rich stiff-leaf, but one
waterleaf capital seems to be awkwardly fitted into them.
The former part may be original, the latter cannot be *in situ*.
Moreover the E respond has a semicircular base which does not
suit it. Third: the chancel arch has its arch of a late C12 or
early C13 form with a big keeled roll, but it stands on big,
clumsy, later capitals, and these stand on head-stops (one
over-restored) which, however, do not carry the capitals but
decorated springers of a rib. Fourth: above the Norman pier
of the N chapel arcade towards the chapel is another springing
of ribs, and this is quite evidently not *in situ*. Fifth: of the
responds of this N chapel arcade one has dog-tooth, which
contradicts the Norman pier. Sixth: the tomb recess in the
s chapel is Dec with its big ogee arch, but the colonnettes
carrying the arch are E.E. What does all this in the end
amount to? The only answer seems to be an extensive use of
fragments brought from somewhere else. The suggestion is
made more probable by the fact that FRAGMENTS are built
in in the N aisle at its E end: a beautiful big Norman capital, a
small Norman capital, a small E.E. capital, a late C12(?)
capital with grapes and much of the original colour left. Could
it not all come from one of the monastic houses in the neighbourhood, Bardney or Tupholme? The idea has much to
recommend it. But when would it all have been put to use?
– FONT. Square, on five supports, thin band of nailhead

at the angles. Probably C13. – BENCH ENDS. In the N aisl
Square-topped; blank arches with simple tracery. – PLAT
Chalice, late C17(?). – BRASS. Priest, 35 in. long, in the
chapel.

FLIXBOROUGH

8010

ALL SAINTS. 1886 by *C. H. Fowler*. Small. Nave, chancel, ar
wooden bell-turret. Dec detail. – FONT. Norman, of roug
trough shape and absolutely plain, but 3 ft across. – PLAT
Chalice, by *W. S.*, London, 1636; Chalice, by *Charles Wrigh*
1774; two Patens, by *Joseph & Albert Savory*, 1834; Flago
by *W. Bellchambers*, 1835.

FOTHERBY

3090

ST MARY. 1863 by *Fowler* of Louth. Largish, with a broad
spire. E.E. forms. No aisles. Brick facing inside. Mediev
the double-chamfered tower arch with its keeled responds
i.e. genuinely E.E.

FRIESTHORPE

0080

1 m. SE of Faldingworth

ST PETER. 1841 by *Young* of Lincoln (GR). Lancet windows an
windows with Geometrical tracery. Medieval the unbuttresse
W tower with E.E. bell-openings and a Perp W window, an
the E.E. chancel arch with keeled responds. – PLATE. Chalic
by *R.H.*, London, 1671.

FRISKNEY

4050

ALL SAINTS. One of the most rewarding of the Marshlan
churches. It is essentially Perp, and only the following feature
are earlier. First, some fragments of a Norman arch, re-use
as a base in the churchyard, S of the S porch. Then the door
way to the tower staircase, i.e. the lowest part of the towe
which seems Norman, and the N doorway, which is late C12
It has one order of colonnettes, one waterleaf capital, and
slight chamfer. Then the next stages of the tower, which ar
of the second half of the C13. They have lancets, Y-tracery
and, on the upper stage, large, rather bleak, two-light window
with a circle in the bar tracery above. The top stages are Perp
but the tall, triple-chamfered tower arch inside seems to b
Dec and yet opens impressively on both the E.E. stage
which became possible only by taking out the floor of th

upper. Perp aisles (rebuilt by *Butterfield* 1879), Perp clerestory of five two-light windows, big Perp chancel with a large five-light E window* and large four-light side windows, gargoyles, battlements, and pinnacles. Pretty niches in the buttresses standing on animals. Inside, l. and r. of the E window, two funny little men holding tapers. The sedilia are Perp too, but the back panel with tracery is rather too big for its setting, and the whole does not seem to be in its original state. Only the chancel arch (two continuous chamfers dying into the imposts) is Dec. That it is earlier than the Perp windows is proved by the remaining roof-line of the former chancel. The aisle arcades are of five bays with tall octagonal piers and double-chamfered arches, again Perp. Rough roof with tie-beams on cusped arched braces and collar-beams on cusped arched braces. In the spandrels of the tie-beams at the E end PAINT-INGS of the Annunciation and of two censing angels. – FONT. Octagonal, Perp, rather crude. Quatrefoils on the bowl. – SCREENS. Four are preserved in a more or less repaired state. First the rood screen, tall, of two-light divisions with round-arched lights, the round arches being made use of for a cusped ogee super-arch. Panel tracery over. – Also, N aisle E, S aisle E, and S aisle W, all on the same principle, yet all different. It pays to compare e.g. how far the S aisle W details match those of the others. – PULPIT. Entirely Jacobean in style, with the familiar squat blank arches, also with back panel and tester. Yet the piece is dated 1659. – BENCH ENDS. In the chancel; with poppy-heads. – PAINTINGS. On the clerestory walls, early C14, much faded. N side W to E: King David and the Prophets, Annunciation, Nativity, Resurrection, Ascension, Assumption. – S side W to E: Pope and Doctors of the Church, Gathering of the Manna, Last Supper, King doing homage to the Host, the Irreverent Woman, the Jews stabbing the Host. – STAINED GLASS. E window 1850 by *W. Wailes* (see his monogram). – PLATE. Chalice and Paten, by *R.A.*, London, *c.* 1660; two Chalices, London, 1774; Flagon, by *John Jackson*, 1813; Paten, by *William Kingdom*, 1835. – MONUMENTS. Effigy of a Knight, later C14, defaced (nave W end). – Tomb-chest with four shields in cusped fields (chancel N). – CURIOSUM. A Hudd, i.e. a kind of sentry box in which the parson could stand dry at funerals while it rained. Georgian. – In the churchyard CROSS. On the base four impressive animals. The shaft survives also,

* The tracery is said to date from 1570.

and at the top the Crucifixion, repeated on the other side re-done, it looks, in the C17.

FRITHVILLE

St Peter. Dated 1821. The architect was perhaps *Jeptha Pacey*. Red brick with a pedimental gable. Nave and chancel in one. Hexagonal cupola. Three pointed side windows, their areas defined by pilaster strips. – WEST GALLERY.

FRODINGHAM *see* SCUNTHORPE, p. 356

FROG HALL *see* WILDMORE

FULLETBY

St Andrew. 1857 by *Maughan & Fowler*. Nave with bellcote and chancel. Greenstone. Lancet windows. The sedilia at least in their upper parts genuine and quite sumptuous Dec work, with buttress-shafts and crocketed gables. – PLATE. Chalice and Paten, by *I. S.*, London, 1688.

FULNETBY

½ m. NW of Rand

Fulnetby Hall. Rebuilt in the C18. Brick, with an irregular five-bay front, porch, and, beneath later cement facing, stone quoins.

FULSTOW

St Lawrence. 1868, in the lancet style, with a big bellcote, but remains of the arcade of a demolished E.E. s aisle (three bays, circular piers and abaci) and N aisle (two bays, probably quatrefoiled, keeled piers and cruciform abaci) and also a nice E.E. s doorway with a cluster of fine triple nook-shafts. The oddly thin tower has also been demolished. – FONT. E.E. Circular with four attached shafts. – PLATE. Chalice and Paten Cover, by *John Morley* of Lincoln, 1569. – MONUMENTS. Early C14 effigies of a cross-legged Knight and a Lady. There were angels originally to hold her pillow. The effigies are in the porch, standing upright to receive you.

GAINSBOROUGH

Gainsborough is one of the dreariest of the Midland red brick towns. The factories are all red brick, and those in the centre

nnot for a long time have been proud of the appearance of their
uildings. Neither the manufacturers nor the council seem
apable of thinking of their town in post-Victorian terms.
ainsborough was an important wool town in the Middle Ages,
id the steeple and the size of the parish church tell of this. It lay
the N end of the town, with the Old Hall to its W and the river
eyond. The town itself extended S, very much as it is today. Pros-
erity may have declined between the C16 and the C18; yet the
own was still affluent enough to rebuild its church in the classical
yle. And then, about 1850, prosperity rose again with the estab-
shment of engineering works. But population remained more
: less stationary. Gainsborough had 4,500 inhabitants in 1801,
,600 in 1871, 12,300 in 1881, 19,200 in 1901, but only 17,000
1961.

CHURCHES

LL SAINTS. Of the medieval church the strong W tower 52a
survives, 90 ft tall, Perp, with angle buttresses, a four-light
W window with a transom, four-light bell-openings, divided
into two plus two and also with a transom, and eight pinnacles.
The two vestries to S and N are of 1903 (architect *Bodley*), the
NE chapel was rebuilt in 1933 (*L. Bond*). The Perp church
extended beyond the present one to the E, as marked out in the
ground, and was thus just under 150 ft long. Rebuilding of
nave and chancel began in 1736 and was completed in 1744.
The architect is not known. *Francis Smith* of Warwick gave a
plan and estimate. In any case the source of the style is the
Gibbs of St Martin's in the Fields and of All Saints Derby,
begun in 1722 and 1723, and also Holy Trinity Leeds by
Halfpenny, begun in 1721. Six bays, giant pilasters, windows
below with basket arches, above with round arches, all with
Gibbs surrounds. Apse with a Venetian window. The entrances are in the first bays from the W and have circular
windows over. Inside, unfluted Corinthian columns carry a
straight entablature and a coved nave ceiling. Wooden
galleries. – PULPIT. By *Pearson*; 1869. Circular, on a thick
shaft with a Corinthian capital. Iron stair rail and parapet. –
BOX PEWS. – (ORGAN CASE. 1793.) – CHANDELIER. Of
brass, 1723, with three tiers of arms, uncommonly ornate. –
PLATE. Paten, by *I.S.*, London, 1688; Flagon, by *I.S.*,
London, 1688; Flagon, London, 1692; Paten, London,
c.1697–1718; Almsbasin, London, 1721; Almsbasin, by *Richard
Hutchinson*, 1728; two Paten Covers, by *John Eckfourd*, 1732;
Paten, by *William Bateman*, 1821.

ST JOHN THE DIVINE, Ashcroft Street. 1881–2 by *Micklethwaite & Somers Clarke*, enlarged 1902; and further enlargements, very different in character, are under contemplation.
The original building is of red brick, very simple, without
tower, but apparently intended to have one; tall, earnest, and
restrained. The windows are all lancets, mostly in stepped
groups of three. The front has a buttress up the middle and
two small round-headed entrances. Inside a long spacious
nave, eight bays of very tall arcades. Octagonal piers. The
aisles partly not yet built. – REREDOS. White and gold
Flemish(?), *c.*1700, with two figures and lush acanthus, oddly
in opposition to the architecture. The reredos comes from S
Peter Barnsley. – CHANDELIER. Brass, of two tiers, inscribed
1678. – CANDLESTICKS. Tall, C18(?), Italian(?), of wood.
They are said to come from Egypt. – SCULPTURE. Large
statue of St John, very Baroque-looking, but by *Harry Hems*
1893. Made as part of a rood for the Chicago Exhibition. The
Crucifixus is as Buckfast Abbey, the Virgin as Stow.

ST THOMAS OF CANTERBURY, Cross Street. By *M. E
Hadfield & Son*, 1865–8. Small, of red brick, with a few
lancet windows and no tower or turret.

HOLY TRINITY, Trinity Street. 1841–3 by *T. Johnson o
Lichfield*. Still entirely pre-archaeological. Stone-faced
Meagre proportions and meagre lancet windows, but very
spacious inside. Thin W tower with spire. The nave is fou
bays long, the transepts have three bays. The chancel was
enlarged in 1864. – PLATE. Silver-gilt Chalice, perhap
Estonian, with date 1653.

JOHN ROBINSON MEMORIAL CONGREGATIONAL CHURCH
Church Street, S of All Saints. 1896 by *R. C. & E. Sutton*
Brick, in a free Tudor style with a fancy doorway.

FRIENDS' MEETING HOUSE, Market Street. 1704–5. A
modest brick cottage with a pitched roof. Inside the origina
furnishings, with a dais for the elders and a women's gallery
opposite. Alterations and additions 1876.

PRIMITIVE METHODIST CHAPEL, Beaumont Street. Brick
of 1877.* Debased Frenchy-Italian with two stunted tower
carrying French pavilion roofs.

WESLEY CHAPEL, Beaumont Street and Roseway. Brick, o
1804. Placed diagonally at a corner. Broad two-storeyed fron
of five bays. One-bay pediment. Doorway with Tuscan columns

* Is this the Wesleyan Chapel referred to in *The Builder* of 30 December
1882 as by *Parry & Walker* (GS)?

and a broken pediment. The ground-floor windows have basket arches, the upper ones round arches, just like those of the parish church.

PUBLIC BUILDINGS

OLD HALL. Sir Thomas Burgh's mansion was burnt by the Lancastrian army in 1470 and rebuilt shortly after. In 1484 he could entertain Richard III; so the new building must have been ready then. Of this building much is preserved. The rest of what we see today dates from the ownership of William Hickman, a London merchant, and the years 1597–1600. The Hall deteriorated in the late C17 to C19. In 1760 it became a linen manufactory. It is now gradually being restored and re-instated. The Hall consists of three ranges round a court-yard. The fourth, to the S, has disappeared. It probably contained the Burgh gatehouse; for the chief survival of the Burgh period, the N range, has the hall. In the same range and also of the Burgh time are the NE tower and the NW kitchen block, projecting W beyond the W range. This and essentially the E range are of Hickman's time. The NE tower is a tall, polygonal, irregular structure of brick with polygonal projections and a higher stair-turret. Pointed-trefoiled friezes, windows mostly of brick, but the bigger ones of stone. There follows on the N side to the W the hall front, all timber-framed and mostly of uprights with only a few diagonal struts. Only the bay window is of stone. It has tall two-light windows with simple Perp tracery and nice bits of tracery below the transoms. The hall front has three-light windows high up with cusped lights and three irregularly placed gables. The kitchen wing is again of brick.* It has buttresses, small brick windows, and a louvre. To the W an oven projection. Then the wing turns E, and there has a big chimneybreast with a steep stepped gable.

The W side of the W range has four mighty projections with steep stepped gables. They contain cabinets and lavatories. The wing was no doubt individual lodgings (cf. Chenies, Buckinghamshire, c.1530). All this is Hickman's work, as are also the brick S gables of this and the E wing. One of them originally had the date 1600. The courtyard side of the W wing is, above a brick base, all timber-framing with narrowly-placed uprights. Two wooden five-light windows with cusped lights. Several staff doorways lead into this wing. The hall

* The bricks are 10 in. long, a size unusual after the early C15.

range to the s is also mainly timber-framed. The brick ground
stage of the boldly projecting main staircase is Victorian, as is
the brickwork following to the E. The timber-framing here has
diagonal ogee struts of *c.*1600. Of *c.*1600 also all the details of the
E wing. The courtyard front of this is like the courtyard front of
the w wing, but behind runs a corridor. The E wing E front is
a proper Late Elizabethan front with mullioned and transomed
windows and, at the centre, an irregular arrangement of a
canted bay, a chimneybreast, and a shallow straight-sided bay.

The hall has a noble roof with arched braces nearly up to
the ridge and two tiers of wind-braces. The bay window has
a four-centred entrance arch and a vault with ribs connected
at the tops of the cells by uncusped arches. Pendant in the
middle. At the start of the r. jamb of the r. window in the bay
a lion. Below this window a mysterious little doorway out
of the hall, apparently original. At the w end, where the
screens passage must have been, remain the three doorways
to buttery, kitchen, and pantry. The kitchen has enormous
fireplaces to the N and s. Its timber roof continues that of the
hall. Most of the upper floor of the E wing was made into a
ballroom when the building was restored in 1849.

The history of the building and its transformations would
deserve renewed research.

TOWN HALL, Market Place. 1891–2, enlarged 1908, but the
s and E fronts 1956: unenterprisingly Neo-Georgian. Brick,
two storeys, the main façade seven bays, hipped roof, lantern.

COUNTY COURT, Market Street. 1870, yet still quite Georgian
looking, with careful detailing. Brick and stone dressings, three
storeys.

LIBRARY, Cobden Street. 1905 by *Scorer & Gamble*. Brick
Early Tudor, with a symmetrical front and a lantern.

STATION. 1849 by *Weightman & Hadfield*.* Long front. The
centre is stone-faced, with four unfluted Ionic columns and
arches between. The rest is brick, with angle pavilions.

OAKDENE, Lea Road. 1837. Built as the WORKHOUSE. Stock
brick.

POWER STATION, West Burton, 3 m. ssw. By the *Architects
Design Group* (*G. Godham, R. Savidge, R. Cullen, J. Pike*).
Begun in 1961. The chief interest of the design lies in the
visually well considered grouping of the remarkably many
cooling towers. They are also intended to be coloured, some
dark, some light.

* So Professor Welsh kindly tells me.

PERAMBULATION

perambulation is not necessary nor advocated. Gainsborough is a decayed town with great slum clearance problems. For the perambulator it is a town of gaps and empty sites. If we start from the Old Hall passing s to LORD STREET, which runs E–W through this older part of the town, we find several pleasant Georgian houses on the s side. The most picturesque area is CLASK GATE STREET, cobbled, winding through a mixture of warehouses and small Georgian fronts. ELSWITHA HALL is rather grand: early C18, five bays, three storeys, all brick except for the stone door surround which carries a broken, scrolled segmental pediment. The MARKET PLACE opens from Lord Street, and here we can only notice the robust Neo-Georgian NATIONAL PROVINCIAL BANK, 1926 by *F. C. R. Palmer*, quite lively in contrast to the dreary, enervated façade of the town hall. Then BRIDGE STREET hugs the Trent-side and here are the better warehouses. Shipping was the source of income of early Gainsborough. GLEADELL & CO's WAREHOUSES are probably the earliest; No. 54 late C18 but still with C17-style gables, No. 90 probably early to mid C19. For those interested, everything on the l., around the area of POPPLEWELL ROW and WILLOUGBY STREET, is slum terraces. The *petite* NOTTINGHAM PLACE is dated 1821, and Nos 134–136 on the r. are a pair of Late Georgian pattern-book houses. Finally we come to the TRENT BRIDGE, designed in 1787 by a local builder and architect, *William Weston*. Handsome. Three arches, niched bulwarks, balustrade. On the Nottinghamshire side a good view of Gainsborough's warehouses strung along the river. From the bridge, turning into the town again, we find BEAUMONT STREET taking the E part of the town – overpowered by the long façade of MARSHALL SONS & CO. The oldest part is of 1850, two-storeyed, of brick, Italianate, with a frontally seated Britannia above the entrance. From Beaumont Street back into BRIDGE STREET on our l. where the COUNTY COURT OFFICES occupy an early C18, five-bay, three-storey house. A fine wood modillion cornice.

CASTLE. Near the NE end of the town, in a thick wood, is a strong earthwork castle, consisting of a ringwork, double-banked on one side, between two baileys. It was built a little before 1142, when it was retrospectively licensed by King Stephen.

GARTHORPE

8010

ST MARY. 1913 by *Wilfrid Bond*.

THE HALL, at the S end of the village. Not quite regular la⟩ C17 façade, cement-rendered. Inside good small staircas⟩ The string has a laurel-garland, the balusters are sturdi⟩ turned.

COTTAGE, a little to the NE, in the main street. Now dated 192⟩ but called 1726 by the MHLG. The door and window su⟩ rounds are so weird as to deserve the recording.

GATE BURTON

8080

ST HELEN. 1866. Nave and chancel, Geometrical tracery. FONT. Norman, drum-shaped. Arcading with segment⟩ arches. In it flowers or faces.

GATE BURTON HALL. William Hutton set about rebuildin⟩ his house between 1774 and 1780. It is a plain five-by-four⟩ bay block of three floors in brown brick. Pediment over th⟩ centre three bays of the S front, otherwise no adornmen⟩ Along came *Detmar Blow* in 1913 blowing his fanfare of Nec⟩ Georgian, and his is the N front or wing, giant stone pilaster⟩ etc. – entirely unsympathetic to the earlier house or to th⟩ place. Additional wings were added in the 1920s or 30s. Th⟩ interior preserves work by *Joseph Fowler* of 1824–7. The de⟩ light of Gate Burton is the landscaping of the park, across th⟩ Gainsborough road, to the Trent-side. Here on a kno⟩ beside a coronet of trees was erected in 1747 the delightfu⟩ prospect TEMPLE, a staccato composition in *James Paine*⟩ style. Built of stone. The plan is a rectangle with narrowe⟩ square projections at each end, and then square projection⟩ again as balconies supported at first-floor level on alternatel⟩ blocked columns. The centre part three bays and two storey⟩ with Ionic pilasters and a pediment. Urns to the parapet an⟩ lower wings. Behind the temple is an overgrown MAZE.

GAUTBY

1070

ALL SAINTS. Built in 1756. Of brick. w tower with recesse⟩ spirelet and four medieval pinnacles. Nave with two keyed-i⟩ windows along the side. Low chancel with a Venetian window⟩ of brick, blank oblong recesses to the l. and r. of the arch⟩ Surprisingly ambitious chancel arch with fluted, strongl⟩ tapered Ionic pilasters. – WEST GALLERY with balustrade⟩

parapet. – Two-decker PULPIT and VICAR'S PEW, both from the predecessor of the present church of Skelton in the West Riding of Yorkshire. – FONT. Octagonal, Perp, with pointed quatrefoils. From Laughton near Gainsborough. – PLATE. Paten Cover, engraved date 1569; Chalice and Paten Cover, by *Charles Wright*, 1771. – MONUMENTS to Sir Thomas Vyner and to Thomas Vyner, erected in 1673 and brought here from St Mary Woolnoth in London. Two semi-reclining figures, the details of the dress brought out with much gusto.

GAUTBY GREAT PARK. Few places have such an air of deserted splendour. The Vyners' house, probably by *Matthew Brettingham*, has gone. The park has returned to arable. There are brick STABLES and the kitchen garden, and still the remains of the lake. On an island here stood for many years the equestrian Charles II by *Jasper Latham*. It is now at Newby in the West Riding of Yorkshire.

GAYTON-LE-MARSH 4080

ST GEORGE. Perp w tower of greenstone with a high arch towards the nave. The body of the church rebuilt in 1847. Red brick and rather depressing. Inside the very badly treated E.E. arcade of the N aisle and N chapel. The piers seem to have been circular, the abaci octagonal. The whole thing is distasteful to look at. – BOX PEWS. – Handsome mahogany PULPIT and more inventively decorated LECTERN. They could be of *c.*1850.

GAYTON-LE-WOLD 2080
1 m. ESE of Burgh-on-Bain

ST PETER. 1889. Small, of brick, nave and chancel only. – PLATE. Chalice, by *Mathew West*(?), London, 1699.

GRIMBLETHORPE HALL, ½ m. N. From a distance it could be mistaken for a C19 warehouse. It may be for this reason that it has been ignored by architectural historians. Upon closer inspection it is seen to be early to mid C17, though the roof is later. E front of eight bays and two storeys divided by giant pilasters banded across their centres. They are joined at the top – and this is unique – by flat arches. That is, the front is conceived as a shallow blank arcade. The end fronts are marked by pairs of widely spaced and projecting chimney flanks, rising from the ground to above the gable. The w side has a strongly recessed centre with three ascending windows marking the staircase. The fenestration can be ignored, as it is early C19 and on the E front even later. Here the windows spoil much of the effect. The interior at once surprises. An elaborate staircase rises for four flights around three sides of a narrow oblong space. Rusticated newels and obelisks with ball finials. In one room a crude pilaster treatment and strapwork cartouches, in another room Ionic pilasters and an elaborate chimneypiece with details of a type unmistakably related to the Artisan Mannerism of the woodwork in such houses as Thorpe Hall near Peterborough. The giant order points in the same direction. Its relations are those of Slyfield (Surrey) and Parham (Suffolk).

GIANT'S HILLS see SKENDLEBY

GIRSBY MANOR see BURGH-ON-BAIN

0090

GLENTHAM

St PETER AND St PAUL. The W tower is of 1756. In the W walls of the aisles C13 lancet windows. The rest mostly Perp, e.g. the S and N windows of the aisles, the big and impressive entrance to the S porch (a window above holds an image of the Pietà), the S doorway, and also probably the tall three-bay arcades with octagonal piers and double-chamfered arches. The details differ between N and S. The chancel arch goes with the S arcade. In the N aisle E wall a recess for a reredos. The former N chapel was of two bays at least, i.e. the chancel has been shortened. – FONT. The underside a sumptuous circular stiff-leaf capital. – CHEST. A fine C14 chest in the S aisle. The posts with rosettes, the front panel with intersected arches and rosettes etc. in the interstices. – BOX PEWS. – STAINED GLASS. Fragments in the N aisle. – Also a window of c.1915 by *Christopher Whall*. – PLATE. Chalice and Paten Cover, by *John Morley* of Lincoln(?), c.1571; Chalice, by *John Edwards*(?), London, 1811. – MONUMENTS. C14 effigy of a Lady; defaced. – Brass demi-figure of Elizabeth Tourney † 1452; utterly defaced.

9080

GLENTWORTH

St MICHAEL. W tower of the C11, with the typical twin bell-openings with mid-wall shaft (much repaired – *see* the Nattes drawing). The arch to the nave contemporary. Nave and chancel in one. The nave is of 1782. The chancel arch however must be of the late C12. Double-chamfered, depressed-pointed arch on semicircular responds with elementary stiff-leaf capitals. Also late C12 the priest's doorway. Semicircular hood-mould; one waterleaf capital. The chancel E window looks Elizabethan or even later: five lights, straight top, one transom, lights with depressed-arched heads. – COMMUNION RAIL. With dumb-bell balusters; later C17. – STAINED GLASS. W window by *Kempe*, 1882. – PLATE. Chalice and Paten Cover, by *T.E.*, London, 1695; Paten and Flagon, by *William Gamble*, 1697. – MONUMENTS. Sir Christopher Wray † 1592 and wife. Alabaster. Standing wall-monument. Two recumbent effigies, he behind and a little above her. Coffered arch, back plate with inscription and strapwork. Columns l. and r., carrying obelisks. At the very top kneeling figure of Sir Christopher's son in profile. Against the tomb-chest kneeling daughters. – Elizabeth Saunderson † 1714. By *Edward Hurst*. White marble. In the centre three cherubs' heads under a baldacchino. Columns l. and r., and l. and r. of these standing wailing putti.

GLENTWORTH HALL. Derelict at the time of writing. Soon after 1566 Sir Christopher Wray built here a large courtyard house with turrets to the inner angles.* Of this, part of one stone-built range with mullioned and transomed windows and an archway survives behind the present house and facing N. This present house is but one wing (its upper storey removed) of a grandiosely conceived design of 1753, by *James Paine* for the Earl of Scarbrough. Only the E front was completed. Brick, of eleven bays with the ends slightly advanced and the middle three bays pedimented. Simple pedimented doorway. Large staircase in axis with the doorway. It projects to the W and has a large Venetian window. The STABLES were built first, and are in a finely dressed brick with the typically Palladian angle erections carrying pyramid roofs.

GOKEWELL PRIORY FARM *see* BROUGHTON

GOLTHO

1¼ m. WSW of Wragby

ST GEORGE. In the fields and at the time of writing disgracefully neglected. Built *c*.1640 of brick with moulded brick

* As shown by Nattes in 1793.

windows. The chancel C18, also brick, formerly with an ov
E window. The broad bellcote Victorian. Inside a statel
REREDOS of *c*.1700 with a big segmental pediment, two halve
of Perp BENCH ENDS with poppy-heads, a COMMUNION
RAIL with dumb-bell balusters, a Georgian two-decke
PULPIT, and BOX PEWS. – PLATE. Chalice and Cover, b
P.B., London, 1653; Paten, by *R.C.*, London, 1678; Flagor
by *Thomas Parr*, 1716.

GOLTHO HALL, ½ m. S. The tall red brick doll's house of th
Grantham family has gone. Only a GAZEBO and STABLE
remain of *c*.1700.

2070   GOULCEBY

ALL SAINTS. 1908 by *G. H. Allison* of Louth, but with ol
materials. Low, of nave and chancel in one, the nave wit
bellcote. The window heads on the S side are old and interest
ing in design, with an uncusped circle above the two arche
under a four-centred arch, i.e. Perp plate tracery. – FONT
Large, octagonal, the panels with the simplest patterns o
incised saltire crosses. Is this Perp too?

0020   GOXHILL

ALL SAINTS. E.E. chancel, over-restored. But one original N
lancet, and one blocked S lancet. Also the double piscina wit
pointed-trefoiled arches. In the spandrel quatrefoil, the point
made into fleurs-de-lis (cf. Thornton Abbey). The rest of th
church Perp and ashlar-faced. Tall four-stage W tower
Buttresses with many set-offs. W doorway with head-stop
to the hood-mould. W window of four lights also with head
stops. Top with eight pinnacles. Aisles embattled and wit
angle pinnacles. The N doorway has in the hollow of it
mouldings heads, fleurons, grotesques, etc. The clerestory
with eight closely set three-light windows (cf. Barton-on
Humber). Tall four-bay arcades. Octagonal piers, double
chamfered arches. Corresponding tower arch and chance
arch. – PULPIT. 1634. With the usual blank arches, but her
depressed. – PAINTING. Mural painting of the Crucifixio
in the S porch; mid C15. – PLATE. Two Chalices, by *Kath
Mangy*, Hull, 1694 and 1699; Paten, by *Robert Abercromby*
1737. – MONUMENT. Effigy of a Knight, cross-legged, wit
surcoat and chain-mail. It must have been a good piece o
carving. Second half of the C13.

GOXHILL PRIORY seems to be a misnomer. There is no evidence of the existence of such an establishment, and the tall late C14 building is probably of a secular nature. It consists of a high hall on a vaulted undercroft and is extremely impressive. Octagonal piers, single-chamfered ribs. The hall has to the w a three-light Perp window and an asymmetrically placed main doorway with shields in spandrels. There is a spiral stair in the sw corner. The N and S sides have three very spacious blank arches, the blank wall ashlar-faced. To the E this arcading is of two bays and the arches are segment-headed. What was this building? The most likely explanation is a domestic hall.

To the w is the present house, a delightful piece of c.1700. Five bays and two storeys, of brick with stone dressings, with a one-bay projection, a quite ambitious doorway with a moulded frame and a segmental pediment on brackets, rooms with Queen Anne panelling, and a staircase with strongly twisted balusters.

Like New Holland (see p. 321), Goxhill owes much of its character to the Hull Ferry. BRIDLINGTON HOUSE is late C18, and CHURCH FARM is in a brick C17 vernacular style with a massive central chimneystack.

GRAINSBY

2000

ST NICHOLAS. Tall Norman S doorway. One order of big shafts with scallop capitals. E.E. w tower of grey stone. w lancet, triple-chamfered E arch, original bell-openings. Much repaired S side. The N side of brick, 1834, yet even at this late date not laid in Flemish bond. – SCREEN. Parts of the tracery Perp. – FAMILY PEW. – PLATE. Chalice, by *John Morley* of Lincoln, c.1569.

GRAINSBY HALL. Of about 1850–60. In an indescribable style. Asymmetrical, with a square tower over the porch, and upper windows with the typical, weak rounded upper corners. What is it by origin? Italian, French, Elizabethan? It is just Victorian. The semicircular porch is of course later. At the back the remains of an C18 house.

GRAINTHORPE

3090

ST CLEMENT. Tall, four-stage, ashlar-faced Perp w tower. Doorway with traceried spandrels. High three-light w window. Then small windows with two-light reticulation (i.e.

still Dec) motifs, but definitely Perp bell-openings and eight pinnacles. In fact the church is part Dec, part Perp. The chancel Dec, see the tall three-light windows with reticulated tracery. Also Dec the N aisle. Again reticulated tracery, of an elongated form, in the E and W windows. Doorway with ogee gable. The N chapel to the N has a five-light reticulated window. Both aisles are embattled and have pinnacles. So has the clerestory with its three-light windows. Good roof of low pitch with bosses. Oddly long S porch. Wide, light, not high, typical Marshland interior. Brick flooring, which is always attractive. Four-bay arcades, rebuilt Perp, but only rebuilt for all the bases have spurs, i.e. a C12 to C13 motif, and the responds on the N side are clearly E.E. The piers then octagonal, the arches double-chamfered. – WEST GALLERY C18. – Also C18 BOX PEWS re-used widely as wall panelling. – PLATE. Chalice, by *Hester Bateman*, 1790. – MONUMENT. Brass, perhaps to Stephen de See, rector about 1380–90. Exquisitely detailed cross on a rock of Golgotha. The cross head is 2 ft 7 in. in size and has concave sides with cusped foliated or finial-like ends, and a quatrefoil in the centre containing a small cross.

GRAINTHORPE HALL. Five bays, three storeys, brick. Late Georgian doorcase.

1¾ m. SW on the LOUTH NAVIGATION, by the bridge, a canal warehouse.

GRASBY

ALL SAINTS. Against the hillside. Late C13 W tower. To the S the bell-opening is Victorian. The Victorian spire has been demolished recently. C13 also the S doorway with dog-tooth in the hood-mould, the N aisle E window (three stepped pointed trefoiled lights under one arch), and the N arcade. This is of three bays, with quatrefoil piers with fillets (or rather a square core and four broad demi-columns). Heavy capitals. Double-chamfered arches. The N aisle said to have been rebuilt in 1850. Much rebuilding by *Hakewill* in 1869 (PB).

GRAYINGHAM

ST RADEGUNDA. Very broad W tower of the C13 to C14. W doorway C13, with two orders of shafts. Dog-tooth in the arch. Capitals with simple upright leaves. But the broad, low, triple-chamfered arch towards the nave with triple-shafted responds, the middle one with a fillet, rather early C14 than

C13. Under the tower fragments of Dec responds or piers, the pattern quatrefoil with deep hollows. The rest of the church was rebuilt in 1773 but victorianized by *Fowler* c.1870. Nave and chancel in one. – (REREDOS. By *A. B. Skipwith*, with a copper-gilt relief of the Crucifixion by *Conrad Dressler*.) – PLATE. Chalice and Paten Cover, by *John Morley* of Lincoln, 1569; Flagon, by *Thos. Whipham*, 1753.

OLD RECTORY. Largely derelict. With a London-type façade of c.1820. PB)

MANOR HOUSE. Mid C18. The four-bay s wing is later. The chimneystack straddles, in an unusual way, the whole width of the N side of the house.

GREAT CARLTON 4080

T JOHN BAPTIST. Perp w tower, the rest 1860 by *Fowler*, and quite a large church. The style is that of c.1300. The N aisle has its own pitched roof; to its E is a polygonal vestry. Interior of brick with stone and lozenge-shaped panels of encaustic tiles. The octagonal piers and double-chamfered arches of the arcades are medieval, but not the details. Medieval also the corbels of the tower arch, big bearded heads, and the capitals on them. Reredos with mosaic.

CARLTON LODGE. This was by *Lewis Vulliamy*, 1833, and has been demolished. Near by, a tall, narrow, three-bay three-storey house of the C18. On the N side wing with Venetian windows. Early C19.

GREAT COATES 2000

ST NICHOLAS. W tower of ironstone, Perp. Frieze with shields in quatrefoils over the doorway. The top part ashlar-faced with pairs of two-light bell-openings and eight pinnacles. In the N aisle a nice Early Dec doorway with five continuous mouldings and an E window with intersecting tracery. Dec also the s aisle and chancel windows. The arcades inside are more complex. They are of four bays, the first pointed and narrower, the rest round-arched and wider on the N side, slightly pointed and wider on the s side. The arches are single-stepped on the N side, slightly chamfered on the s. This looks as if s came a little after N. But there is another story as well, told by the piers. There were three bays originally, and to this belong two piers and the responds. They are quatre-foil and have round abaci. The fourth, number one from the w, is of different stone and has a round seat at the base and a

quatrefoil abacus. That means that the arcades were of *c*.120
and were lengthened a little later. – FONT. Octagonal, Per
With shields in cusped panels. – PLATE. Paten, by *I.C*
1669(?); Chalice, London, 1790. – BRASSES. Isabella Kell
(Barnardiston), *c*.1420. The figure is 32 in. long (chanc
floor. – Sir Thomas Barnardiston † 1503 with wife and childre
An oblong panel with kneeling figures, inscription scro
coming out of the mouths of the parents.

2010   GREAT GRIMSBY

Grimsby with nearly 100,000 inhabitants is by far the large
town in Lincolnshire. Its vocation is fishing, its modern develo
ment the outcome of the building of the Royal Dock in 1849–5
The railway had reached the town just a little earlier. The pop
lation in 1841 had been 3,700. It rose to 9,000 in 1851, to 15,0
in 1861, to 63,000 in 1901. But Grimsby is not a recent town a
the same. The port flourished in the Middle Ages, and its paris
church is spectacular proof of that. Norwegian ships are mentione
as early as the late C11, and the fish trade occupied the town ful
in the C13. The first civic charters date from 1201 and 1227.

ST JAMES. A large, cruciform church, externally all C20-lookin
with its ashlar-facing and its neat detailing. In fact the churc
was built in the early C13, but the S transept was rebuilt i
1858–9 and the chancel in 1882–4. The Lady Chapel wa
added E of the N transept by *Bodley* in 1906 (Perp and nothin
special), the Chapel of the Resurrection E of the S transept b
Sir Charles Nicholson in 1920 (freer Perp), and the one-storeye
vestries etc. by the same, also in 1920. What remains intac
even if much restored, is first of all the nave, and the N transep
the latter with a tall, monumental lancet front and both wit
polygonal angle-turrets like those of a cathedral. The nave ha
single small lancets also along the clerestory. The Dec aisl
windows are of 1910–12. The nave W doorway, with shaft
and many roll and hollow mouldings, still has a round arc
the S transept S doorway a pointed arch, a full eight orders o
thin shafts, many fine mouldings too, and dog-tooth in th
11   hood-mould. Now the interior. The nave is of six bays, th
piers of four main and four subsidiary shafts, all with fillet
the abaci large octagonal slabs, the arches with many roll
What is however most remarkable is the upper part of th
nave. In major churches in England this upper part is usuall
a gallery and above this a clerestory with a wall-passage i

front inside, the wall-passage being screened towards the nave by its own arcading. At Grimsby the gallery is left out, and the wall-passage, its screen, and the clerestory windows already referred to follow immediately above the apexes of the arcade arches. The wall-passage screen alternates between tall and low arches and triplets of low–tall–low without any system and without reference to the arcade below. The wall-passage has triple shafts, the middle one filleted. In the N transept there is a similar system, applicable because of the existence of an E aisle or E chapels – replaced by the Lady Chapel. The pier has its major shafts keeled, which the nave piers have not, and the triforium arcade has no stepping. The shafts here are alternatingly round and triple in the rhythm keeled–round–keeled. The crossing was remodelled in 1365, as an inscription on one of the piers (orate pro anima of John Ingson) tells us. Yet it is entirely Perp. Piers with blank panelling ending in small ogee arches, the mouldings of piers and arches complex but not fine. The arch from the N aisle into the transept dies into the imposts. The exterior of the tower has pairs of three-light bell-openings set in wide blank arches. Parapet with small blank arches. – FONT. C13 base of nine supports. C14 bowl with simple arched panels. – SCREEN. Fragments, probably from the rood screen, in the S porch. – PLATE. Chalice and Paten Cover, by *Marmaduke Best*, York, 1667. – MONUMENT. Sir Thomas Haslerton, later C14 Knight (Lady Chapel). – In the churchyard base (with simple pointed-trefoiled arches) and weathered shaft of a CROSS. It is said to be the former market cross.

T AUGUSTINE, Legsby Avenue. 1910–11 by *Nicholson & Corlette*. Brick, low, and very pleasingly modest. Nave and wide s aisle with very tall, straight parapet. Simple interior, whitewashed, and green seats. Square, chamfered piers, only slightly pointed arches, and all tracery lights and motifs based on the semicircle.

T LUKE, Heneage Road. 1912 by *Sir Charles Nicholson*. Long, of brick, with a SE turret, with free Dec ornament. Interior with low aisle passages. Nave and aisles almost in one. The arches die into the piers.

T MARK, Laceby Road. 1959–61 by *E. Vernon Royle*. W porch or concourse. The church is of light brick with red-brick panels for the aisles. Separate NE tower with a terracotta grid wall.

T MARY (R.C.), Heneage Road. 1879–83 by *Hadfield & Son*. Brick, with Geometrical tracery. Very tall interior, the aisles so high that the effect is almost that of a hall-church. T▮ chancel very tall too. The walls are painted with figures und▮ canopies, said to be by *Hardman*'s and of *c.*1900.

ST PAUL, Corporation Road. 1886–1908 by *Withers*. Brick, wi▮ lancet windows. The N (i.e. ritually W) front a lively compos▮ tion of lancets.

ST STEPHEN, Roberts Street. 1911–14 by *Sir Walter Tappe▮* Tall, of brick, with low aisles (that of the S side not yet buil▮ and windows high up. The nave piers are really intern▮ buttresses connected high up by longitudinal arches. The ro▮ supported by transverse arches. Asymmetrically placed bellcote.

WELHOLME CONGREGATIONAL CHURCH, Hainton Avenu▮ 1907 by *Bell, Withers & Meredith*. In a free Arts and Craf▮ Gothic style, very capricious – see especially the heav▮ pinnacles and parapet round the recessed spire.

TOWN HALL. 1863 by *Bellamy & Hardy*, and hence both op▮ lent and restrained. Grey bricks and grey stone. Italian detail▮ No tower or other vertical accent. And just two blocks fro▮ the docks. – INSIGNIA. Large Mace, silver-gilt, 1645; sma▮ Mace, C17; Mayor's Chain, 1849; Badge of Office, 1854. Also a Flagon of 1707, an C18 Salver, and two Candlestick▮ and two Coasters *temp.* George III.

PERAMBULATION. The DOCKS make Grimsby what it is. U▮ to 1850 there was the little town E of the church, with i▮ market place and some few streets running W–E and inter▮ connected. Then the railway came, the station was built clos▮ to this centre, and the principal street, VICTORIA STREET▮ runs first W–E, then S–N with a total absence of noteworth▮ buildings on one side, the warehouses of the docks on th▮ other. Among them the most spectacular is the VICTORIA▮ FLOUR MILLS of 1906, towering, and in a Flemish style▮ To the E of the top of Victoria Street, in CLEETHORPE ROA▮ the group of Docks Station, the brick-Gothic ROYAL HOTE▮ (1863–5 by *M. E. Hadfield* of Sheffield), the DOCK OFFICE▮ with their debased turret (1885), and the MONUMENT t▮ Prince Albert (by *William Theed*) in a car park. At the corne▮ of this a sweet cast-iron FOUNTAIN of 1869.

Other buildings can only be named individually.

DOCK TOWER of 1852, by *J. W. Wild*, brother of the tower o▮ Siena Town Hall and hence an elder brother of Birmingham University.

ʀᴇᴀᴛ Gʀɪᴍsʙʏ Eʟᴇᴍᴇɴᴛᴀʀʏ Sᴄʜᴏᴏʟ Bᴏᴀʀᴅ Sᴄʜᴏᴏʟ, Heneage Road. By *Charles Bell*, 1876, and displaying a tall tower above its single-storeyed premises.

ᴏʟʟᴇɢᴇ ᴏꜰ Fᴜʀᴛʜᴇʀ Eᴅᴜᴄᴀᴛɪᴏɴ, Laceby Road. 1951–4 and later additions. By the office of *J. V. Oldfield*, the borough engineer. Brick.

ᴡɪᴍᴍɪɴɢ Pᴏᴏʟ, Scartho Road. 1961–2 by the same.

See p. 767

1000

GREAT LIMBER

ᴛ Pᴇᴛᴇʀ. Of ironstone. Short and broad w tower, the doorway triple-chamfered, the bell-openings of two lights with reticulated tracery, i.e. *c.*1300–30. Long nave and long aisles. Dec s doorway, blocked Dec N doorway. The s windows Dec, the N windows Perp. The chancel mostly Victorian, but the arch c13. Wide aisles. Five-bay arcades with octagonal piers and double-chamfered arches. Plain capitals, those on the s side certainly c13. – FONT. Bowl with dog-tooth frieze, i.e. c13, and standing on a splendid stiff-leaf capital reversed. It was made for a pier with octagonal core and eight shafts such as those at St Mary, Barton-on-Humber. – STAINED GLASS. In the s aisle old bits, in the N aisle a *Kempe* window of 1890. – PLATE. Chalice, by *R. Robinson*, Hull, *c.*1630. – MONUMENT. William Richardson † 1850, yet still entirely Georgian.

ᴇᴡ Iɴɴ. 1840s, but still Georgian; ambitious in a nicely restrained way. Local brown brick.

GREAT STEEPING

4060

ʟᴅ Cʜᴜʀᴄʜ, ½ m. sw of the new. Built in 1748, but on a medieval base. Brick. Nave of two bays with arched windows. Later weatherboarded bell-turret. The w doorway has a moulded surround. A keyed-in oval window over. – PLATE. Chalice, by *John Morley* of Lincoln, *c.*1569; Paten, by *William Darkeratt*, 1719.

ʟʟ Sᴀɪɴᴛs. 1891 by *Bassett Smith*. Fiery brick. Nave and chancel and wee bell-turret a little E of the w gable. Lancet windows.

ʙᴀᴘᴛɪsᴛ Cʜᴀᴘᴇʟ, Monksthorpe, 1 m. ɴᴇ. Early c18. A plain oblong with plain oblong windows.

GREAT STURTON

2070

ʟʟ Sᴀɪɴᴛs. Of greenstone, with a modern turret. The s doorway is Norman – see the enormous lintel stone and also

the voussoirs appearing l. and r. of the porch roof. Dec chancel
renewed. The chancel arch anyway is in order, and with it
filleted responds suits the period. The cusped tomb recess in
the N wall also fits. It is cut off by a shortening of the chancel.
A N aisle has been pulled down at some time. The arcade
arches are still visible, but no details. A W tower was also
removed. Is the wooden turret then so recent, and were the
timbers carrying it brought in from a barn? They are old
timbers without doubt, and the whole construction is very
impressive. Nice nave ceiling of the time of *Micklethwaite's*
restoration (1904). – PAINTING. Time and Death; early C17.
– PLATE. Chalice and Cover, by *I.B.*, London, 1641.

STOURTON HALL, ¾ m. SW. Of 1873, in a vigorous Italianate
style, but now in ruins.

GREBBY HALL *see* SCREMBY

3070
GREETHAM

ALL SAINTS. Small, of greenstone, nave with bellcote and
chancel. The church had a W tower. Traces of the walls and
the arch towards the nave are unmistakable. The imposts of
the latter are Norman. In the nave also old masonry, but the
whole mostly, and the chancel entirely, of 1903. S doorway
simple, of *c.*1200, re-set, as traces of the arcade of a former S
aisle are also unmistakable. – SCREEN. Only the muntins are
original. – PLATE. Chalice, inscribed 'Gretham Cuppe',
Elizabethan.

0070
GREETWELL

ALL SAINTS. Essentially C11 – see the long keyhole window on
the S side, a Saxon rather than Norman motif, the completely
plain chancel arch on chamfered imposts, and the tower arch,
equally plain, though probably widened when the E.E. W
tower was built. The rest Dec or Perp, including the S doorway
with continuous mouldings, one of them carrying a fillet. The
apse is supposed to be structurally Norman too, though it
looks all very recent now. – PLATE. Chalice, Elizabethan;
Paten Cover, London, 1571. – MONUMENT. An early C13
inscription in the apse records Adam de London *quondam rector
ipsius ecclesie.*

GREETWELL HALL. Probably Jacobean, see the remains of
mullioned windows. L-shaped, with a C19 addition to one end.

Of this latter date the windows replacing the mullioned ones. LODGE dated 1856. Plans for rebuilding the house were made by *John M. Hooker* in 1881.

GRIMBLETHORPE HALL *see* GAYTON-LE-WOLD

GRIMOLDBY

3080

T EDITH. An impressive greenstone church, typical of the Marsh in that it is all built as one enterprise. The style is Early Perp, except for the aisle E windows, which still have reticulated tracery. However, that may have been carried on to *c.*1380. Tall W tower, the arch to the nave triple-chamfered and dying into the imposts. Aisles and clerestory embattled and with big gargoyles. The nave E gable and the aisle E walls have crockets. All this is very similar to Theddlethorpe All Saints. The chancel (rebuilt in 1876, but apparently correctly) is remarkably wide and has a five-light E window. The arcades of the nave are of four bays and have octagonal piers and double-hollow-chamfered arches. Roof with tie-beams with bosses alternating with stiff angel-figures carrying thin arched braces. Another angel in the aisle. – SCREEN. The dado is original; Perp.* – BENCH ENDS. Bench ends of unusual design with rosettes and tracery are re-used in the pulpit and a shelf in the chancel. – NORTH DOOR with tracery. – PLATE. Chalice, Elizabethan. – CROSS. In the churchyard to the N. Base and nearly the whole shaft.

GRIMSBY *see* GREAT GRIMSBY

GUNBY

4060

T PETER. By *Fowler*, 1868–70. In a field SE of the Hall. Of medium size, but aisleless. In the E.E. style. – PLATE. Chalice, Paten Cover, Plate, and Flagon, by *Edward Vincent*, 1727. – Two important BRASSES are in the church, a Massing-berd of *c.*1400 and wife, 5 ft 6 in. figures under ogee canopies on buttress shafts, and William Lodynton † 1420, a 4 ft 8 in. figure in a similar surround.

GUNBY HALL. Built in 1700 (according to a dated keystone on *47b* the W doorway) for Sir William Massingberd. The house is

* Cox in the *Little Guide* tells much of the pulley holes for raising the lights of the rood. Others survive at Addlethorpe and Winthorpe.

supposed to be Tennyson's 'haunt of ancient peace'. A maso
bricklayer's rather than an architect's design, and similar
the better-quality Brocklesby (*see* p. 200). Seven by four ba
three full storeys, a basement, and a panelled parapet. Pair
end bays break forward on the E and W fronts. Stone strin$
quoins, and moulded window surrounds. The W doorw
with a broken, scrolled, segmental pediment enclosing
cartouche is of course also of stone. It is the only orname
of an austere, puritanical house. The two-storey five-b
extension to the N is a sympathetic addition of 1873. Coac
houses dated 1735 may fix a period of alterations by Willia
Meux-Massingberd, including the insertion of the prese
main staircase with twisted balusters and Early Georgi
panelling, cornice, and ceiling. At this time its Venetian st.
window was put in the S front. *Mrs Peregrine Massingberd,* :
amateur artist, was probably responsible for the Regen
carpenters' doorcases and details of the interior. She may al
have designed the little domed ROTUNDA in the garder
The clock-cote over the STABLES came from Hook Pla(
Hampshire (1778), and was erected here in 1917.

1010   HABROUGH

ST MARGARET. 1869 by *R. J. Withers* (or *James Fowler*
Small, but with aisles. The W tower with octagonal bell-sta$
and a small spire. Plate tracery. – STAINED GLASS. W windo
by *Kempe*, 1891. – PLATE. Chalice and Paten Cover, Londo
1560.

9080   HACKTHORN

House and church lie in beautifully landscaped grounds with
lake to the S of both.

ST MICHAEL. 1850 (PB). An ambitious building, erecte
by the Amcotts of the Hall. Nave, N aisle, and chancel, :
with much enrichment, e.g. a large number of funny litt
heads for the eaves-corbels. W tower with ornate battleme
and eight pinnacles. This top looks Perp, so do nave and aisle
but there is also an elaborate neo-Norman N doorway.*
Much WOODWORK of the same date as the church, e.g. th
ORGAN GALLERY. – STAINED GLASS. E window by *Waile*
one chancel S window by *Holiday*, made by *Powell's*, *c*.186

* In the Nattes drawing the church had a Norman W doorway. Was
re-used and re-modelled?

This has the large figures of Faith and Hope and much coarse foliage above – influenced by the Pre-Raphaelites, and a parallel to Morris's endeavours. – PLATE. Secular Plate, by *Y.T.*, London, 1692. – MONUMENT. Large slab in *pietra dura* by *J. Darmanin & Sons* of Malta. It commemorates Mrs Amcottes † 1857 and represents a standing angel in a modest architectural surround.

HACKTHORN HALL. A square Yorkshire stone villa of restrained details. Designed by the neo-classicist *James Lewis* in 1792. N entrance with a semicircular Ionic porch and windows in arched recesses. The S front is of five bays. Alternating straight hoods and triangular pediments to the ground-floor windows. The rooms are grouped around an oval, top-lit staircase. The W front is longer than the S front. The STABLES, E of the church, make a nice, modest C18 composition.

HAGNABY

3060

1 m. WSW of East Kirkby

ST ANDREW. Late Georgian, but much altered in 1881 (W end) and 1903 (transept). The original church is mainly recognizable in the arched W doorway and the pilasters inside the apse. – PLATE. Chalice, Paten, and Flagon, by *Chas. Plumley*(?), London, 1826.

HAGNABY PRIORY. A fragment of *Charles Kirk*'s big neo-Tudor-Gothic house of 1835. It formed part of the office wing.

HAGNABY ABBEY see HANNAH-CUM-HAGNABY

HAGWORTHINGHAM

3060

HOLY TRINITY. Of greenstone. The building must basically be of the C11, see the herringbone laying of the stones in the two middle bays of the nave N wall. The W tower is so broad that here also an early origin is likely. Inside, a timber construction of strong beams and posts and some bracing to support the upper floor. The upper part of the tower is of brick, and the bell-openings are Victorian. Low E.E. S arcade of four bays with circular piers and abaci; elementary capitals and double-chamfered arches. All windows Victorian. The drastic restoration took place in 1859 (*Fowler*). – STAINED GLASS. E window by *Wailes*. – PLATE. Alms Basin, London, 1661; Flagon, by *John Read & Daniel Sleamaker*, 1701; Chalice, by *T. B. Pratt & Arthur Humphreys*, 1782.

OLD HALL, on the main road. 'Fen Artisan-Mannerism' wi
the leitmotifs of brick-rusticated window surrounds a
jumped-up strings to form pediments. The C19 additions a
a successful imitation of the same style. To the W of Old H₂
a Georgian HOUSE of five bays with a one-bay pediment.

1080   HAINTON

ST MARY. The W tower of ironstone carries a recessed spire
grey stone.* The rest by *Willson*, 1848, with full use of o
masonry and already in an archaeologically correct styl
Even of the three-bay arcades (octagonal piers, doubl
chamfered arches) little is old. Nice re-set head corbe
from the roof, probably of the late C13. Also a small re-s
stiff-leaf capital (nave W). Off the chancel the N chapel w
converted into a family chapel, and here most of the Heneag
MONUMENTS are to be found. They make the church memo
able. Both entries, from the W and S, have C17 iron RAILING
Into the entry from the S a stone archway (with continuo
mouldings) was built in 1694. – Now for the monument
First John Heneage † 1530 and wife (chancel N wall). Tom
chest (of Purbeck marble ?) with unusual, restless decoratio
This is continued on the back wall, against which the kneelin
brass effigies are placed. Above, an almost straight-sided lo
arch and a cresting. – Also in the chancel Mrs Franc
Heneage † 1807, aged 25. By *Bacon Jun.* and unusually tende
Five children playing by an urn, the eldest garlanding i
Above, Mrs Heneage and angel-heads in the clouds. – G. I
Heneage † 1833. By *S. Manning*. Much more conventiona
with a draped urn. – Then in the Heneage Chapel Brasses
John H. † 1435 and wife, good, the figures 2 ft 6 in. long.
John † 1559 and his wife † 1587, the latter no doubt the da
of the monument. Stone; standing against the wall and bi
The kneeling figures face one another across a prayer-des
Columns l. and r. and on the prayer-desk. – Sir George † 159
Alabaster; free-standing. Recumbent effigy. On the tomb
chest nice strapwork round the shields. – Sir William † 161
and his two wives. Alabaster; standing against the wal
Kneeling figures facing each other. The children below
usual; on the top relief of the Fall and the Resurrection, a
not at all usual. – Three Sir Georges, the last † 1692. Table

* Canon Binnall suggests that the spire may have been added by *Capabilit*
Brown (see below) as an eye-catcher.

with open scrolly, garlanded pediment. L. and r. strips with
skulls, bones, and an hourglass. – George † 1731. By *Bertuccini* See p. 767
(*Berruccini*?, not in Thieme-Becker). Big tablet of marble,
his bust standing against grey drapery. Pilasters l. and r., a
segmental pediment on top. Below his bust, to the l. and r.,
are the busts of his two wives. All three faces are alas expression-
less. – Mrs Frances H. † 1842. By *Manning*. Two 'addorsed'
putti in front of the pedestal of an urn. – George Fieschi H.
† 1864. By *Haderwood* of Camden Town. In spite of the date
entirely, deceptively Georgian. Mourning woman kneeling by
the pedestal of an urn. – PLATE. Chalice and Paten Cover,
by *H.N.*, London, 1660.

AINTON HALL. The house where the Heneages have lived
and live. The earliest visible part is on the s front. A centre,
one projecting wing, and an extruded octagonal turret, ogee-
cupolaed, in the angle. The corresponding half has been
demolished, but the escutcheon of 1638 may provide the date
of erection. The fenestration is now sashes with moulded
surrounds, and the centre is of five bays, two storeys, with an
attic above the cornice. About 1807 *Peter Atkinson* rebuilt
and heightened the W wing so that it now presents a face of
seven bays and three storeys. To him must also be due the
facing of the whole house in stucco, probably Atkinson's
Cement. The porch is by *William Burn*, 1875. Behind the s
front are Georgian rooms of some splendour. First a two-
storey HALL with a giant fluted Ionic order, a good ceiling,
and a chimneypiece with caryatids in profile. Behind this the
STAIRCASE, with an Ionic screen, a big Venetian window, and
a tripartite Ionic arcade to the upper landing. Plasterwork in a
competent Rococo style. The MORNING ROOM is particularly
rich. Broken voluted pediments to the doorways and carved
friezes. The style of the work, especially the ceiling patterns,
suggests *James Gibbs*. The STABLES are perhaps by *Atkinson*,
stuccoed and impressively bare. The CHAPEL in the grounds,
in thin Gothic, yellow brick, Perp, by *E. J. Willson*, 1836.
Several estate cottages are by *William Danby*, also 1836.
Capability Brown landscaped the park about 1763.

HALSTEAD HALL

1060

1 m. NNE of Stixwould

What remains may be a N–S wing of an L-shaped brick range.
The date is probably early C16 rather than the suggested late

c15. There have been considerable restorations, one in 18
and another, by *Sir Reginald Blomfield*, in 1922. W front
four bays and two storeys. Reading from the N end, a doorw
with flattish head and square drip mould, then a bay of wi
dows paired three and three, each with two mullions and
transom, then a doorway, and then another bay of similar
paired windows. Extending s still further is one bay and o
of a pair of three-light windows, belonging to the origin
front. The basement is stone-edged and there are stone quoin
In the N face small single windows light the stairs, and in t
gable-end is a three-light window with mullions and transor
The interior seems always to have consisted of two compar
ments on this floor, opening out of each other by sto
arches with flattish heads and two orders of moulding. In t
NE angle is the staircase. One chimneypiece remains wi
foliage in the spandrels.

BARN. To the NE. Later c16. Brick with black-brick diamon
pattern and small moulded brick lights.

2060   HALTHAM-ON-BAIN

ST BENEDICT. Of greenstone. Nave and chancel and very lo
bell-turret. The s doorway has a Norman tympanum an
roll-moulded arch. The tympanum is a barbaric jumble
motifs. The cross in a roundel in the middle, a figure (deface
to the l., leaf to the l. of this, a kind of knot to the r. of th
cross, a cut-off rosette to the r. of this, and some patternin
with little triangles above. But the glory of the church is i
Dec chancel and especially the E window, of five lights, wit
flowing tracery good enough for the s of the county and quit
an exception in Lindsey. The N and s windows are straight
headed but also have a little more than the usual ogee-heade
lights. Angle piscina with polygonal shaft and ogee arche
The chancel arch has unfortunately been demolished. Lat
Perp w front and N aisle windows. The interior of the churc
is nicely crowded. First the N arcade, which is Early E.E
Three bays, double-chamfered arches still round. Stiff-lea
capitals; respond on heads. One pier has an octagonal sea
around. The bell-turret stands on a timber structure insid
the nave, of sturdy posts, sturdy beams, and diagonal cross
wise bracing, just as in the Essex towers. – FONT. Hexagonal
with square leaves as used in the diapering of backgrounds
– SCREENS. Of the rood screen the ogee tops of the single-ligh

divisions only survive, with panel tracery. – The parclose
screens have hanging arches and a cresting. – BENCH ENDS.
With minimum, lozenge-shaped poppy-heads. – Also plain
three-decker PULPIT and FAMILY PEWS. – PLATE. Chalice
and Flagon, by *Francis Crump*, 1765.

MARMION ARMS. Timber-framed with overhang and thatched
roof. Looks C16, but much restored.

HALTON HOLEGATE

4060

ST ANDREW. A Marsh church, though of greenstone; nearly
entirely Perp. The exceptions are the tower and the E end,
which are by *J. Fowler* under the supervision of *Street* (1866),
and the C13 to C14 S doorway (two continuous chamfers).
Clerestory of eight closely-set three-light windows. S porch of
grey Ancaster stone with a parapet of two tiers of quatrefoils
and pinnacles. Entrance with traceried spandrels. A small
vaulted niche over, and shield above that. The aisles rather
dull (rebuilt 1846), but two windows (NE, S aisle E) with
basket arches. Priest's doorway in the chancel with flat juicy
leaves in the spandrels. Tall arcades of four bays. Octagonal
piers, double-chamfered arches. Roof with tie-beams, arched
braces with traceried spandrels and raking queenposts
forming arches. Angels against the principals not trussed by
tie-beams. The chancel arch goes with the arcades. Two-bay S
chapel, the arches with two wave mouldings. In Nattes's drawing the arcade is blocked, i.e. no S chapel exists. – CHOIR
STALLS and BENCH ENDS. With rich tracery and sumptuous
poppy-heads, including little profiles 'addorsed', a coat of
arms with a crest, two bearded men, etc. Many are Perp, but
many also are of 1846 and were made by a local carpenter. –
STAINED GLASS. S aisle by *Powell*. – PLATE. Chalice and
Cover, London, 1567; Paten, by *John Read*, 1704. – MONU-
MENT. Knight, cross-legged, praying. He wears a helmet.
The arms on his shield are carved.

HALTON MANOR, 300 yds w. C18, but a pilastered C19 face.
OLD HALL, ¼ m. N. Brick and brick quoins, C18 and later.
WINDMILL, ¼ m. SW. Tower mill with an ogee cap, complete
with its four sails.

HAMERINGHAM

3060

ALL SAINTS. Mostly by *Hodgson Fowler*, 1893. Small, greenstone, the old stones used. Wooden bell-turret. Poor Victorian

brick chancel, of course of before Fowler, though the
window is presumably his. Inside a genuine E.E. S arcade o
three bays. Octagonal piers, one moulded, one stiff-lea
capital. The E respond is a detached shaft with stiff-lea
capital. – FONT. Octagonal, Perp. The stem partly wit
seated figures, partly with panelling. On the bowl pointer
quatrefoils and three shields. – PLATE. Chalice and Pater
Cover, Elizabethan; Chalice and Cover, by *I. I.*, London, 1690

HANBY HALL see WELTON-LE-MARSH

4070
HANNAH-CUM-HAGNABY

ST ANDREW, Hannah. Of greenstone; tiny. The church was
built in 1753 and has keyed-in arched windows and a Venetian
E window with very wide pillars between the three parts (cf.
South Thoresby, 1738). The only re-used medieval piece is
the Perp W doorway. – Inside BOX PEWS. – Even the marble
FONT, with a wooden cover the size of a dish cover for the
dinner table, is boxed in in a corner of a pew. – The COM-
MUNION RAIL is not only three-sided but in the middle
comes forward in a curve ending in a point. – PLATE. Chalice,
by *Thomas Wright*, 1755.

HAGNABY ABBEY FARM, 1¼ m. WNW. The Premonstratensian
priory founded in 1175 stood ½ m. N. Much fragmentary
material remains near the farmhouse, including window
tracery and octagonal shafts.

HARDWICK HILL see LAUGHTON

3060
HAREBY

ST PETER AND ST PAUL. Nave and chancel. Greenstone base,
but the upper parts brick. Victorian windows and bellcote
(1858). A small genuine Dec niche above the W doorway.
– PLATE. Chalice, by *Wm. Howlett*, King's Lynn, c.1630. – A
TABLET commemorating the Wingate family and dated 1920
has remarkably good lettering for its date.

HAREBY MANOR. Of no architectural merit, but there may
have been a Gothic house here of c.1785 (date on a rainwater
head attached to the modern stables). In the garden are two
fine octagonal turrets surmounted by ogee crown-like domes.
These were obtained about 1918 from a demolished manor
house near Grantham.

HARPSWELL   9080

St CHAD. Anglo-Saxon w tower, not tall. Twin bell-openings with mid-wall shaft (much restored – *see* the Nattes drawing). An inscription on the tower commemorates the presenting of a clock (not this clock) in 1746 in honour of 'the victory over the rebels'. The arch towards the nave is probably C14. Late C13 s arcade of three bays. One circular, one octagonal pier; double-chamfered arches. Fine w window in the aisle with late C13 plate tracery: trefoiled lights, three trefoils over. The s windows of the aisle with flowing tracery and straight heads. One has two diagonally-placed pointed quatrefoils (or interlocked pointed figures of eight) as its tracery, an interesting pattern. – FONT. Norman, drum-shaped, with blank arcading, the arches straight-sided. – BENCH END(?). One panel with a shield displaying the Wounds of Christ. – STAINED GLASS. Small bits in the w window. – PLATE. Chalice and Cover, by *Thomas Morse*, 1723; Flagon, by *Whipham & Wright*, 1763. – MONUMENTS. Incised slab to John Gere, rector, *c.*1300. – Immediately E of it (s aisle) effigy of William Harrington, rector, *c.*1350. At his feet corbel with green man's face. – Brasses to Knight and Lady, *c.*1480, the figures 2 ft long.
HARPSWELL HOUSE, where the Whichcotes lived, has gone.

HARRINGTON   3070

St MARY. 1854–5 by *S. S. Teulon.* Of greenstone. Nave and chancel; slated. Of the medieval church the tower arch survives and a few other very small details. – FONT. Octagonal, Perp, with panelled stem and a bowl on whose panels angels hold shields with coats of arms. – BENCH ENDS. Two, with poppy-heads. – PLATE. Paten Cover, inscribed 1570; Chalice, by *T.P.*, *c.*1660. – MONUMENTS. Effigy of a cross-legged Knight, praying. – Brass of Margaret Copuldyk, *c.*1480. She stands slightly turned to the l. – no doubt towards the brass of her husband, which is lost – and has her hands raised as if in imprecation, rather like a Virgin under the cross than like an effigy. The figure is 3 ft long. – Tomb-chest of black stone with three shields in roundels. The back panel held brasses. They are lost too, but the inscription (Sir John Copledike † 1552) exists. – The paradigm on which this tomb-chest was made is in the chancel. It is surmounted by detached shafts carrying a flat-topped arch, a quatrefoil frieze,

and a cresting. All this is of Purbeck marble. The soffit o
the arch is panelled. Against the back wall now brasses of S₁
John Copledike † 1582 and wife, but the architectural pa₁
must be pre-Reformation. – Francis Copeldyck † 159₉
Alabaster, with the kneeling husband and one son facin₉
across a prayer desk the wife and one daughter. Obelisks l. an₆
r. – Thomas Copledike † 1658. Plain but good tablet. – Charle₁
Amcotts † 1777. A very unadorned white sarcophagus on
black base.

HARRINGTON HALL. A part of the long W front of the house i₁
clearly Elizabethan. This is what remains of the seat of th₆
Copledykes. There is said to be a beam dated 1575. Vincen₁
Amcotts rebuilt the house in 1673 etc. (the weather-vane i₁
dated 1678, the sundial 1681). Of the front the stone plintl
is Elizabethan and marks the extent of the Elizabethan build
ing. At the N end can be seen the base of an octagonal angl
buttress, once 26 ft high.* The lower part of the porch retain
its early brickwork, and also such thin octagonal angle but
tresses. When it came to the rebuilding of 1673 etc., the lengtl
of a front 125 ft long perhaps presented a problem to a loca
builder. So instead of making his façade a monotonou
expanse of thirteen bays, he retained the old porch as a vertica
accent. The porch projects almost alarmingly and is dresse₆
up with an Artisan-Mannerist show face of exceedingl₁
elongated Ionic brick pilasters running all up l. and r. of th₆
porch window on the first and on the second floor. To th₆
N and S of the porch the façade is of six bays each, two storeys
a projecting wooden modillion cornice, hipped roof, and dormers. The windows have plain wooden frames and, according
to their proportions and glazing, must be an C18 alteration
At the N end a lower extension looks Early Georgian an₆
follows the hipped-roof theme. The E front shows a confuse₆
pattern. Of the Elizabethan period there is only some brickwork near the S end. The double gable and the gable furthe₁
N mark the 1678 rebuilding. Between the two gables the two-
storey front with a parapet is an C18 infilling of a small courtyard. N of the single gable and S of the double one are C2₀
parts. The ground floor of the porch is panelled with an early
C18 Doric order, which is also the architectonic theme o₁
the Hall. A wide elliptical arch (cf. Somersby Hall) replace₁
the Elizabethan screen, but behind the S wall are said to be the
blocked-up screen entrances. The ceiling is divided into square

* The present front is 27 ft high.

compartments with Greek key pattern ornament. E of the hall is a room panelled c.1678, and to the SE the Early Georgian staircase hall has superimposed Doric pilasters and arched openings, the staircase itself three balusters to the tread, one fluted and two twisted, and carved tread-ends. Of arched openings and arched built-in cupboards, a standard early C18 motif, there are in fact plenty. Upstairs a C17 oak stair to the attics.

The present lay-out of the GARDEN is C18. On the w front a wide court with brick walls and piers. The s wall is the boundary of an elevated garden terraced on the w to the fields and ornamented with rusticated piers and urns.

RECTORY. 1854 by *S. S. Teulon*.

HATCLIFFE

2000

ST MARY. Ironstone. w tower with a s window of c.1300 (Y-tracery) and odd, small, single-light, almost Norman-looking bell-openings. Nave s doorway late C12, round, single-chamfered arch. The chancel of 1861–2 by *Rogers & Marsden* of Louth. On the N side a nice *mélange*. From E to W, a blocked arch and, set in it, a window with intersecting tracery. Then a two-light window of two arches under one, with the spandrel open, i.e. a late C13 form, as is Y- and intersecting tracery. This also stands in a blocked arch, but one not visible from outside. The third blocked arch has below a re-set small lancet, and below that a blocked doorway. What it all amounts to becomes clear inside the church. The blocked arches belonged to a N arcade with quatrefoil piers with round abaci. So all these remaining medieval forms fit a late C13 date. – FONT. In the vestry a strangely shallow font bowl with a floral motif in the middle of the bottom. – PLATE. Chalice(?), London, 1729; Paten, by *James Morrison*, 1753.

HATTON

1070

ST STEPHEN. 1870–4 by *Fowler*. Red brick, with an apse and a SE turret with spirelet. Geometrical tracery; naturalistic foliage. – PLATE. Chalice, by *I.C.*, early C17(?).

HAUGH

4070

ST LEONARD. Small, of nave and chancel. Partly greenstone, partly chalk. The church has an C11 chancel arch (chamfered imposts, unmoulded arch), a N doorway (blocked), probably of *c.*1200, and a Dec s doorway with ogee arch. – FONT▸ Octagonal, Perp, like a pattern book of window types, si of them, Dec and Perp, and two larger tracery motifs. ◂ CORONA. Of iron, attractive, perhaps of the time of th restoration (1873). – PLATE. Chalice, by *I.B.*, London, 1682 – MONUMENTS. Charles Bolle † 1591, small alabaster table without figures. – Sir John Bolle † 1606.* Larger alabaste tablet with kneeling figures facing each other.

HAUGH MANOR FARM. This seat of the Bolle family was neve very grand. It is low and T-shaped, of brick with stone dress ings. Basically it is C16, post-Reformation, and to this date belong the big stepped chimneystack, the line of crenellation running along the E front above the ground floor and i▪ front of the slightly recessed upper floor, and a moulded blocked brick doorway at the s end of the same E front with ▪ two-centred arch and a square surround.

₃₀₈₀   HAUGHAM

ALL SAINTS. By *W. A. Nicholson*, 1840. Paid for by the vicar, who was a member of the Chaplin family. A miniature Louth, of brick, cemented, but with the same steeple, the same crocketed spire, the same openwork flying buttresses, and the same polygonal turret pinnacles. Also with openwork parapeting and battlements and pinnacles. The churches of Raithby and Biscathorpe ought to be compared. The roof and the FURNITURE, including Gothic FAMILY PEWS, are all of the 1840s. – Also the E window still has nearly complete STAINED GLASS of the same date, still pictorial and quite ignorant. – FONT. Octagonal, Perp, with shields in cusped fields.

₂₀₉₀   HAWERBY
                3 m. SW of North Thoresby

ST MARGARET. Chalk and ironstone. Nave and chancel, and a strange gabled double-bellcote the width of the nave. The arches are round-headed. Were they originally pointed and the bellcote E.E. like the rest of the church, i.e. the doorway and one lancet formerly no doubt belonging to the demolished s arcade, and the chancel with the low-side lancet, also in all probability not originally round-arched? Cox mentions a restoration in 1846. Of the s arcade one capital still appears now in the wall, and this is E.E. too. – FONT. Norman,

* The carver made it MDEVI.

drum-shaped, with a band of saltire crosses. – STAINED
GLASS. In the E window Crucifixus, early 1930s, in a pleasant
wood-engraving style. – PLATE. Paten, London, late C17. –
MONUMENT. Mrs Marneis † 1848. White bust, as if it stood
in the entrance hall of a Victorian mansion.

HAWERBY HALL. Hall and church at a distance from one another, but both in the grounds. The house was built c.1781.
Three by three bays, generously proportioned. Plain, except
for the pediment to the S front windows and for a balcony with
cast-iron railing, on the E side, where the centre is recessed.
To the N is a range of notable Georgian FARM BUILDINGS in
brick, with blank arcading.

HAXEY   7090

ST NICHOLAS. The church exhibits a complicated history. It
starts with the Norman four-bay N arcade. This has round
piers, scallop capitals and one with flat leaves, and square
abaci. But the pointed double-chamfered arches are later.
Originally there must have been round ones, and the piers
must have stood more closely together. The E respond also is
later. It corresponds to the S arcade, but this also has its problems. It has two round piers with square abaci, though their
backs were made semi-octagonal to match the third, which is
octagonal with an octagonal abacus. The double-chamfered
pointed arches fit this well. However, the W respond is still
clearly late C12, see the nook-shaft and its capital by the side
of the keeled respond. And, to make matters more puzzling,
a W bay was added to the arcades, leaving the space of the
former W wall visible, and this on the S side has again just
such a respond as the E side. So, at the moment when a S
arcade was built, its lengthening was already decided. Was
it to embrace a projected W tower? To the final form of the S
arcade and its arches correspond the chancel arch, the arch
from the W into the E bay of the N arcade, and the N chapel
arcade of three bays. The elaborate chancel decoration is
Victorian.* Externally nothing of all these problems can be
expected. All is Perp. W tower, ashlar-faced, with three-light
bell-openings and eight pinnacles. Tall tower arch to the nave
with castellated capitals. Ashlar-faced aisles and embattled
clerestory. Low-pitched nave roof with bosses. Tall S porch
with battlements and pinnacles. Embattled N chapel. The E

* The chancel S window with intersecting tracery is not in Nattes's
drawing either.

vista of ashlar-faced embattled chapel and ashlar-faced embattled chancel under one low-pitched roof is excellent. Both have four-light windows, and both are entirely a Victorian rebuilding. – PLATE. Chalice, by *John Morley* of Lincoln *c*.1569; Chalice, with puzzling marks, one of York, 1636; Plate, *c*.1680; Flagon, by *Benjamin Watts*, 1698; Flagon, by *Nathaniel Lock*, 1711; Alms Basin, by *F.A.*, London, 1717 – MONUMENT. Priest, C15 (N chapel).

METHODIST CHAPEL, E of the church. 1856. Brick, façade with two long thin arched windows and a segmental pediment

LOUND HOUSE, Craiselound, 1 m. SE. Georgian, of five bays and two storeys with quoins. Wooden porch with thin Tuscan columns.

2010

HEALING

ST PETER AND ST PAUL. W tower with C13 responds to the E arch, the upper parts Dec and ashlar-faced. Four tall pinnacles probably of 1840, the date when the doorway with its crocketed ogee gable and buttress shafts was provided. Nave and chancel in all its features of the restoration of 1874–6 – PLATE. Chalice, by *W.R.*, London, 1608.

8080

HEAPHAM

ALL SAINTS. Anglo-Saxon W tower. Of the W doorway only the arch. Keyhole W window. Twin bell-openings with mid-wall shafts (much restored). Plain arch to the nave. The big embracing buttresses are of course later. In the S wall of the nave also a plain Saxon doorway. The porch entrance seems C18. C13 chancel and lancets, also a group of three stepped lancets under one arch. Inside chancel arch, double-chamfered on corbels, and piscina with pointed-trefoiled head and concave jambs. A little nailhead decoration. Of the C13 also, but earlier, the N arcade. Two bays, octagonal pier, double-chamfered arches. Keeled responds. Simple crocket-leaf capitals. – FONT. Plain, of drum or trough shape; Norman. The embattled foot is Perp. – PLATE. Chalice and Paten Cover, by *John Morley* of Lincoln, 1569; Chalice, Paten, and Alms Basin, by *Emes & Barnard*, 1815.

2070

HEMINGBY

ST MARGARET. Built in 1764 (*John Clark*) and rebuilt in 1895 (*W. Scorer*). Of the former period the arched windows of the nave (of course minus the tracery). Of 1895 the whole W tower and all the rest, minus a few odd bits such as a piece of quatrefoil frieze in the E wall and bits of tracery in the S chapel wall. – PLATE. Paten, by *Francis Spilsbury*, 1737; Chalice, by *W. & J. Deane*, 1764; Paten, by *Timothy Renou*, 1800.

ALMSHOUSES. A plain brick terrace of five cottages, two storeys high. The inscription reads: 'This Hospital and School were erected in the year 1727 by Jane Dymoke'.

HEMSWELL

9090

ALL SAINTS. Externally a W tower of 1764 and the rest of 1858. Internally an E.E. three-bay N arcade. Octagonal piers, double-chamfered arches, only slightly pointed. The E respond has angle shafts and a stiff-leaf capital. In the church Dec sedilia, the pointed trefoiling in the arches in openwork. Crocketed gables.

In CHURCH STREET stands the MAYPOLE – a rare survivor nowadays.

HIBALDSTOW

9000

ST HIBALD. W tower by *Lawrence Bond*, 1958–60. Simple shape with pyramid roof, but still Perp details. The tower arch E.E., but almost entirely redone in 1866. The nave was rebuilt by *Fowler* in 1875. The style is E.E. – FONT. Perp, octagonal, of unusual design. Along the bowl a carved kind of cresting, on the underside fleurons. – PLATE. Chalice Cover, Paten, and Flagon, by *John Jackson*, 1698.

HIGH TOYNTON

2060

ST JOHN BAPTIST. 1872 by *Ewan Christian*. Greenstone, nave and chancel, lancet windows and windows with Geometrical tracery. S W porch tower of awkward outlines, e.g. with broaches to the octagonal upper storey. Short spire. In the porch, against the N and the S walls, lengths of Norman zigzag from an arch, probably the chancel arch. – STAINED GLASS. In the N windows glass of the first half of the C19. – Also a German C16 roundel. – PLATE. Chalice, by *Peter & William Bateman*, 1806.

HIRST PRIORY see CROWLE

HOE HILL see SWINHOPE

HOGSBECK HOUSE see WILLOUGHBY

HOGSTHORPE

St Mary. Greenstone. E.E. w tower with much brick repair. Characteristically flat E.E. buttresses. Two w lancets and traces of the nook-shafted bell-openings. The tower was heightened later and has three-light Perp bell-openings. The arch to the nave is triple-chamfered on responds with fillets. E.E. also the five-bay arcades. They have circular piers with circular abaci and double-chamfered arches. Two capitals on the s side have stiff-leaf, all the others are moulded. Dec doorway with ogee arch. The s aisle wall mostly C17 brick. The s porch Perp. It carries an inscription that it was built by the *fratres* and *sorores* of the Guild of St Mary. The chancel is of 1870, but has at its SE corner two Perp shields. – FONT. Octagonal, Perp. Against the bowl shields in cusped blank arches, except for one panel which is of the blank window type so popular in this neighbourhood. Panelled stem. – TOWER STAIRS or Ladder. Jacobean with flat balusters. – In the s aisle some typical early C19 coloured GLASS. – PLATE. Chalice, London, 1775.

HOLBECK MANOR *see* ASHBY PUERORUM

HOLME *see* p. 767

HOLTON BECKERING

All Saints. The chancel by *Nicholson*, 1851, the rest over-restored by *Sir G. G. Scott* in 1859–60 and 1870–4. The medieval features which remain are C13 to C14. C13 are the simple, single-chamfered doorway, the plate-tracery window in the w wall of the s aisle, the w tower with w lancet and E arch of three chamfers, and the s arcade of three bays with octagonal piers and double-chamfered arches. The N arcade was rebuilt by Scott. Dec bell-openings, Dec s doorway with fleurons up the jambs and round the arch, fleurons on the hood-mould, and an ogee top. Finally Perp s windows, their hood-moulds with good head-stops original. Original also the two big shields at the SW and SE corners. – REREDOS, all glittering mosaic, no doubt from the Scott, not the Nicholson, period. (Made, according to Canon Binnall, by a Catholic Italian who insisted on smoking his pipe while doing it.) – PLATE. Chalice and Paten Cover, inscribed 1569.

HOLTON-LE-CLAY

ST PETER. A rough and, at the time of writing, neglected church. CII W tower, see the narrow, tall arch to the nave with two orders of voussoirs. One CII W window; Dec bell-openings. – FONT. Norman, drum-shaped. The incised rope moulding probably original, the incised intersected arches no doubt re-cut or altogether apocryphal. – PLATE. Paten Cover, London, 1636.

HOLTON-LE-MOOR

ST LUKE. Partly of 1854 (by *George Place*), partly of 1926 (by *H. G. Gamble*). The early part of ironstone and small with billets and lancet and Geometrical windows, the new part unfinished. But the S doorway is Norman, plain, with chamfered imposts and a tympanum, and the stoup inside is a C13 octagonal capital. – FONT. Norman, with cable-moulding, but little of it original.

SCHOOL, to the W of the church. 1913 by *Gamble*. Nice, friendly, symmetrical, with large windows, and a steep pediment, decorated with rose branches.

HOLTON HALL. The S front of brick, five bays, three floors, a porch with fluted Doric columns and open pediment. White, nicely contrasted, wooden window frames. It may have been built by *J. Warmer*, a builder, about 1785 for Thomas Dixon.

HORKSTOW

ST MAURICE. Short, unbuttressed W tower. It is E.E., see the pairs of small lancets which serve as bell-openings. Ashlar-faced aisles (by *R. H. Fowler*, 1895). Brick chancel, but with an E.E. E wall of stone with two lancets. The interior is more rewarding. Arcades of three bays, N C13, S probably early C14. The former with round, the latter with octagonal piers. Both with double-chamfered arches. Keeled responds N, semicircular S. E.E. also the chancel. It is raised by two steps on account of a family vault underneath, and it is very strange otherwise too. The chancel arch is clearly in order. But the two further transverse arches can hardly be in order too. They were in existence in 1846 though. The responds are entirely Victorian. Anyway it makes an impressive sight. – FONT. Ornate Victorian E.E., dated 1877. – PLATE. Chalice and Paten Cover, by *Edward Mangy*, Hull, c.1670; Paten, by *T. Hebden*, Hull, c.1680; Paten, by *Gabriel Sleath*, 1708.

HORKSTOW HALL. Between 1607 and 1620 Sir Thom
Darrell built a house here surveyed by *John Thorpe*. It po
sessed a remarkably ingenious staircase. This has all gon
and the present house is a mid-Georgian builder's job wi
some pattern-book pretensions. Pedimented E front, massi
doorway with rusticated frame and Doric columns with squa
rusticated blocks partly hiding them, and Venetian window
in the link walls to pavilions. Only one of them remains. Th
staircase has a delicate Rococo ceiling. The important Roma
mosaic PAVEMENT discovered in the park in 1796 is now o
permanent loan to the British Museum. Near by is a farm
house where *George Stubbs* is said to have dissected his horse
SUSPENSION BRIDGE. Over the NEW RIVER ANCHOLM
and dated 1844. Across the entry are rusticated stone arche
CHAPEL FARM, 2 m. E. A gothicizing Later Georgian job.

2060

HORNCASTLE

ST MARY. A proper town church, built of greenstone. The
tower is so broad and square that one suspects an early origi
at once. Its lower parts are indeed E.E., and only its uppe
part is Dec, the spike at the top probably being later stil
The E.E. origin is documented by the two w lancets and th
responds of the arch towards the nave. Their lower par
cannot be later. Then, however, they are cut short and d
into a triple-chamfered arch which forms the transition to th
Dec style. E.E. also the four-bay arcades. Quatrefoil pier
with fillets and thin shafts in the diagonals. Of the four bay
three were built first, the fourth, the E, bay later. The earlie
parts have stiff-leaf capitals, the capital of the last pier is i
its mouldings already Dec. The Victorian chancel arch cu
into it. The N and S chapels on the other hand are Per
(octagonal piers, double-chamfered arches). Externally th
impression is predominantly Perp and Victorian (*Ewa
Christian*, 1860). The best Perp piece is the N chapel, wit
large four-light windows and very ornate battlements wit
pinnacles. The S chapel also has four-light windows, but i
built of brick. The aisle windows are Victorian; so is th
chancel E window, a copy of that at Haltham. Perp clerestory
faced in grey stone. Of later internal details the best is th
corbel at the E end of the N aisle with lions' heads and boss
leafage, Perp rather than Dec. – SCREENS, to the chance
chapels, each division of two ogee-headed subdivisions, th

arches crocketed. – CANDLESTICKS. The sanctuary candlesticks, presumably of *c.*1860, are very good Victorian Gothic work. – PLATE. Chalice (modern gilding), London, 1569; Pair of Bowls, one *c.*1670, the other a copy by *Benjamin Smith*, *c.*1825; Paten, by *William Gamble*, 1717; Flagon, by *Gabriel Sleath*, 1740; Paten, by *William Bell*, 1818. – MONUMENTS. Brass to Lionel Dymoke † 1519 (N aisle wall). Kneeling figure and some fragments of the other parts of the brass. In the floor near by effigy bundled up in a shroud, said to represent the same; very defaced. – Sir Ingram Hopton † at the Battle of Winceby 1643. Hatchment-shaped painting of most probably the 1660s, as the 'Arch-rebel' would hardly be mentioned before. Painted tablet with black painted columns l. and r. and painted cherubs at the top. Big trophies l. and r., appearing to be behind the tablet. – George Heald † 1834. Standing monument of white marble; very Grecian, but with black drapes of polished marble falling over the sides. At the foot a sarcophagus in a niche. To the l. and r. piers with, in shallow relief, very elongated urns. No signature. – CURIOSUM. In the w wall of the s chapel thirteen Scythe Blades, connected traditionally with the Battle of Winceby or the Lincolnshire Rising of 1536, but without evidence.

HOLY TRINITY. 1847 by *Stephen Lewin*. Tall nave, chancel, bellcote, lancet windows. In the chancel long, slender lancets.

PERAMBULATION. The MARKET PLACE is just NE of the church, an irregular space with lopped trees and the STANHOPE MEMORIAL, a Gothic and crocketed affair designed by *E. H. Lingen Barker* and put up in 1894. From here w along BRIDGE STREET with nice bowed early C19 shop-fronts (Nos 11, 13, 14). Across the bridge, and then ROLLESTONE HOUSE is a Late Georgian five-bay house with a heavy Tuscan porch. Then in WEST STREET at once No. 2, of eight bays with a doorway whose pediment stands on Corinthian columns. Nos 20–26 has nice bow windows on the ground floor. WATSON'S INFANT SCHOOL is of stock brick, with gabled dormers and a courtyard at the back. Then back to the Market Place and along HIGH STREET with a nine-bay block on the l. It is of two and a half storeys and has a three-bay pediment (and was Sir Joseph Banks's Horncastle house; PB). At the end of the short High Street the BULL RING, and now first s, then N. Going s one reaches straightaway the most attractive spot of Horncastle, the basin of the HORNCASTLE NAVIGATION CANAL, completed in 1802 by *William*

Jesson and now disused. Trees on both sides of the basin and
WAREHOUSE of four storeys and nine bays. From here furthe
s in the gardens of HAMERSTON HOUSE are (at the time
writing) pieces of German Rococo garden sculpture, apa
from a group of putti by *Matthias Shee*. Further E in EAS
STREET No. 28, a builder's attempt at grandeur, a La
Georgian composition of a three-bay centre block and wing
The centre has a pedimented doorway and heavily detaile
arched windows l. and r. At the corner of QUEEN STREE
the plain former INDEPENDENT CHAPEL, with nice letterin
It is of 1821–2. In Queen Street, nearly opposite, a charmin
semi-detached house dated 1827 on an urn in a roundel. Mor
pretty doorways further down Queen Street. Parallel to Ea
Street a little further N, i.e. off Bull Ring, runs Banks Stree
In its continuation BANKS ROAD, along the canal, a timbe
warehouse in the form of a three-pavilion composition. Finall
for a moment N from the Market Place, where at the end c
NORTH STREET, in the vista, the Italianate COURT HOUS
of stock brick (by *C. Reeves*, 1865).

ROMAN HORNCASTLE. The Roman town is of rhomboid plan
the form being dictated by the rivers Bain and Waring, whic
enclose it on three sides. The NW corner of the town wall ca
still be seen in DOG KENNEL YARD, associated with the con
crete core of a projecting circular bastion. In this same NE are
twelve handled jars were found in the C19. Other portions c
the wall can be seen on the SW (near the school), where i
still stands to a height of about 10 ft. The facing stones hav
disappeared, and all that remains is the core of large block
of local sandstone.

1060   HORSINGTON

ALL SAINTS. 1858–60 by *David Brandon*. Lancets and cuspe
lancets and a s tower with broach spire, all this in brick with
ample stone dressings, even the spire. The whole is thoroughl
unsympathetic to its surroundings, and the interior is col
and unsympathetic altogether.

Brandon also built the RECTORY and the SCHOOL, to the N
They are of no interest.

3000   HUMBERSTON

ST PETER. Perp W tower, ironstone below, ashlar above. Th
church was rebuilt in 1720–2. Brick, not yet in Flemish bond

Nave and chancel in one. Arched windows, only the first
from the w circular. – PLATE. Chalice, by *Thomas Parr*,
1755(?). – MONUMENTS. Matthew Humberston † 1709, but
no doubt of the 1730s at the earliest. It is a Rysbrack conceit,
but the style is not his. Mr Gunnis believes it to be *Sir Henry
Cheere*'s work. White, brown, and purplish marbles. Seated
allegorical lady resting her elbow on a medallion with Mr
Humberston's portrait. Columns l. and r., broken pediment.
The inscription tells us that Mr Humberston reached 'places
of Trust and profit in the Custom house whereby he acquired
an ample Fortune with great honour and reputation' and that
he left £1,000 to rebuild the church, £500 to build a school
and almshouses, £600 to endow them with, an unspecified
addition to the Vicar's Stipend, and £300 to pay for his
monument. – Edward Humberston and others, the last
date of death being 1755. But the monument seems too
neo-classical even for that. White, grey, and pink marbles.
An urn before an obelisk, and a finely carved relief on the
urn.*

ALMSHOUSES. *Robert Adam* made designs which were not
executed.

MANOR HOUSE. Probably c17. Now L-shaped, with a long, low
line of outbuildings to the w.

Round the church altogether there is quite some part of the village
left – unswamped by Grimsby and Cleethorpes.

HUNDLEBY   3060

ST MARY. 1854–5. Of greenstone, with w tower and clerestory.
Medieval only the label-stops, the Perp tower arch, and the
Perp three-bay arcade (octagonal piers, double-chamfered
arches). – PLATE. Chalice and Paten Cover, inscribed 1569.

Hundleby runs into Spilsby. Along the street from the church
to Spilsby church some nice Georgian doorways, and especially
a semicircular Greek Doric porch. GABLES HOSPITAL was
built as a workhouse in 1838. It was designed by *G. G. Scott*
after seventeen architects, among them Donthorne, W. A.
Nicholson of Lincoln, and Wilkinson of Oxford, had been
invited to send plans.‡ Then a formidable former UNITARIAN
(or Methodist?) CHAPEL, of 1865, stock brick, with a mighty
Venetian window in the middle of the front.

* The seeming tumulus in the churchyard hides an ICE-HOUSE.
‡ Information kindly given me by Mrs Joan Varley.

HUTTOFT

ST MARGARET. Of greenstone. Unbuttressed later C13 tower with lancet windows and twin bell-openings with pla[ ] tracery, crazily studded with dog-tooth all up jambs and sha[ ] and even the arches. The arch towards the nave has respon[ ] with fillets and a little nailhead. C13 also the chancel arch wi[ ] two fine corbel heads, one with the so-called tooth-ach[ ] gesture, the other with a dog on his r., a big leaf on his [ ] Are the five-bay arcades (octagonal piers, double-chamfer[ ] arches) later? They look Dec rather than E.E. Perp s ais[ ] with gargoyles, the windows renewed but their hood-moul[ ] with fleurons original. Perp also the s doorway and s porc[ ] both with big leaves up and around one moulding. Perp th[ ] N aisle too, except for the simple N doorway, which seems t[ ] be a little earlier than the earliest parts so far discussed. Th[ ] clerestory, though at first E.E.-looking, is later; see the ol[ ] roof-line against the E.E. tower. Is it Victorian? C18 bric[ ]
28b   chancel with Victorian windows. – FONT. On the bowl th[ ] twelve apostles in pairs of two plus the Virgin and the Trinity[ ] The apostles have famously sprouting hair standing out fro[ ] their heads and are the brothers of those of the font a[ ] Covenham St Bartholomew. Against the underside of th[ ] bowl angel busts with spread wings, against the stem Saint[ ] against the foot, placed in the diagonals, the Signs of the fou[ ] Evangelists. – CHEST. A remarkable C14 piece, the front wit[ ] fine crocketed blank arches with Dec tracery (ogee arches o[ ] ogee arches). The ends and back also have blank arches, bu[ ] a simpler pattern. – MONUMENTS. Two incised slabs[ ] Batholomew Note † 1473, defaced (E of the font), and Mau[ ] Note of about the same time.

WINDMILL. Tall tower-mill with a nice ogee cap. Close to it GRAIN STORE, presumably Early Victorian, four storeys an[ ] only two bays wide.

IMMINGHAM

ST ANDREW. Norman the SE nave quoin and the W and [ ] responds of the N arcade. Then follows the s arcade, early C13[ ] four bays, with round piers, octagonal abaci, and round arche[ ] with one step and one slight chamfer. In the s wall a simpl[ ] doorway and one pair of original small lancets. C13 also th[ ] keeled responds of the chancel arch and one N lancet. Late[ ] C13 N arcade. Four bays, octagonal piers, double-chamfere[ ]

arches. The aisle windows are Perp. Perp also the ashlar-
faced W tower with eight pinnacles (but the responds of the
tower arch are partly C13), the clerestory, ashlar-faced too,
and the nave roof with tie-beams and kingposts. – FONT.
Perp, octagonal, with shields and, on the underside, fleurons.
– PAINTINGS. Six of the Apostles, large, between the clerestory windows; C18. – PLATE. Chalice and Paten Cover,
Elizabethan.

DOCKS. Begun in 1904 and opened in 1912. A further dock was
completed in 1960.

½ m. W of the docks is the VILLAGE, built also shortly before the
First World War and since enlarged. The most prominent
buildings are the COUNTY HOTEL of 1910 (by *G. H. Mumby*)
and the polygonal and bepinnacled WATER TOWER of 1909.

BLUE STONE. An upright blue stone, probably a glacial erratic
(T. Miller), stands at the bend of the A road, ½ m. S.

INGHAM

2 m. N of Brattleby

ALL SAINTS. Nave and chancel, the nave of 1792 (see the
characteristic wide pointed windows), the chancel windows
probably of 1896. W porch 1931. – PLATE. Chalice(?),
c.1610.

INGOLDMELLS

ST PETER AND ST PAUL. A large church, large already in the
C13; for the arcades are E.E. and of six bays, admittedly not
built all at once, but the E bays very shortly after the others.
They all have round piers and double-chamfered arches, but
the older part has stiff-leaf capitals, the younger has not. The
old part has spurs to the bases, the younger has not. In fact at
the joint it can be seen that the bases to the W were originally
responds. There are other minor differences cutting across
those caused by date. On the S the abaci are round except
for the younger, which is octagonal; on the N all are cruciform
with chamfered sides to the cross arms. Then the early C14,
i.e. the lower parts of the W tower. Only its bell-stage is Perp.
On the buttress set-offs pretty little gablets. The tower arch
has for its capitals a sumptuous big band of nobbly leaf.
Dec also the S porch entrance, the S doorway with a hood-
mould on big heads, and the aisle windows with simple
flowing tracery. The chancel was alas pulled down in 1706
and an arched brick window set in the closing wall. – FONT.

Octagonal, Perp. Stem with panelling and beasts' heads, bow on such heads and leaf motifs, against the bowl barbed quatrefoils with leaf motifs. – BENCH ENDS. With primitive poppyheads and also panelled backs. Or are they the re-used dado of a SCREEN? – BRASS to William Palmer † 1520, a 20 in figure, and next to him his crutch. William Palmer gave the porch of Winthorpe church. – CROSS. s of the church. On the base an inscription of 1600 and numerals connected with its use as a sundial. Only part of the shaft remains.

BUTLIN'S HOLIDAY CAMP. This is of course the chief attraction of Ingoldmells and the coast all along, but it is social not an architectural attraction. The buildings that line the main road are partly frankly utilitarian, partly frankly show business, and the paraphernalia can only be described as in the Las Vegas style. The buildings are of 1936–9. The top population at any one moment is in the neighbourhood of 8,500.

Besides, and chiefly further N, there is a sea of caravans which makes the real sea twice a day retire far out in shame.

SALT PANNING SITES. On the coast between Ingoldmells and Chapel St Leonards are a number of briquetage sites. They produced coarse pottery used in the process of salt boiling and can be attributed to the Early Iron Age. Timber structures have been found in association with these salt workings and the former are still visible in suitable tidal conditions.

4060

IRBY-IN-THE-MARSH

ALL SAINTS. Greenstone. Broad w tower with the top repaired in brick and the lower parts re-detailed Georgian in 1770. Of the same date the nave of two bays. Greenstone with brick bands. Arched windows. But this is also only a remodelling. For the stone base is medieval, and there was in fact a two-bay N aisle arcade. The chancel is of 1886. Yet the niche inside to the r. of the E window, is genuine Perp, and the arch with the hollow chamfers towards the vestry is said to be Perp too. – PLATE. Chalice and Paten Cover, by R.C., London, 1608.

1000

IRBY-ON-HUMBER

ST ANDREW. Unbuttressed w tower with Perp bell-openings. Plain s doorway of about 1200. Most of the exterior renewed or new. The N arcade inside is of the first half of the C12 and impressive. Two bays, fat circular pier, square abacus, scalloped capitals, unmoulded round arches with hood-moulds. The s arcade is a little later. The pier slimmer, the capitals moulded, but the abacus still square and the arches still unmoulded. To the s arcade belong the remains of the chancel arch. The remains of blocked lancets at the E ends of the aisles must be somewhat later. – MONUMENT. Incised slabs of a Civilian and wife, later C14.

OAKLANDS. Dated 1875. In the Elizabethan style.

KEADBY

POWER STATION. 1948–52. The architects were *Farmer & Dark*. In the cubic brick style established before the Second World War by Sir Giles Scott at Battersea and still going strong. The only BRIDGE* to the Isle of Axholme is at Keadby, and so industry is spilling over here from the Scunthorpe side. (The bridge was completed in 1916 and has a lifting span of 165 ft. PB)

KEDDINGTON

ST MARGARET. Nave and chancel. A brick bellcote on a brick w wall. The E wall also brick. In the nave s wall a small Norman window. The headstone has two mouldings, the inner in the form of an elongated cat-like beast. The s doorway must be of the late C12, see the shafts, one still with waterleaf, the other with leaf-crockets, and see also the round arch with separate dog-tooth, but also more Norman motifs. In the chancel a straight-headed Dec window. Inside parts of a glorious E.E. arch re-used for the organ chamber. It has rolls, hollows, and dog-tooth and was found on farmland about 1850. It probably comes from Louth Abbey near by. – FONT. Octagonal, with three little pointed trefoiled arches to each bay. – LECTERN. A splendid wooden eagle on a shaft and four feet; C15. – WHEEL CROSS. C12 or C13. Perhaps a gable-cross. It has rosettes but also a central cross of small leaf reminiscent of stiff-leaf. – PLATE. Chalice, Elizabethan.

KEELBY

ST BARTHOLOMEW. W tower of ironstone, Perp. Inside a quadripartite rib-vault. The top parapet with blank quatre-foils. The rest all over-restored, but the chancel masonry may be early, and inside the low s arcade is original early C13

* By *Sir James B. Ball.*

work. Three bays. Circular piers with octagonal abaci an
double-chamfered arches. – FONT. Octagonal, Perp, with
four-petal motif formed of intersecting semicircles. – PLAT*
Chalice and Paten Cover, by *John Morley* of Lincoln, 156*
– MONUMENTS. John Smith † 1591. Small and pretty al*
baster tablet. – Alice Smith † 1605. Frontal demi-figure in
circular recess.

PRIMITIVE CHAPEL. 1850. This is what the inscription says
Yellow brick with the usual arched windows, but a buildin*
unusually tall for a village.

CHURCH END FARM. Attached to its W end are the remains *
the C14 house of the South family. A rectangle of two storeys
The room below with a piscina (chapel ?), that above with
hooded fireplace on corbelled brackets, and blocked pointe*
entrances in the E wall. In the W front are two windows, on*
of three lights with cusped ogee tracery and a drip mould o*
head corbels. This is Dec.

KELFIELD *see* OWSTON FERRY

KELSTERN

2090

ST FAITH. W tower with Perp arch to the nave. In the nave o*
the N side Dec windows (reticulated tracery), on the S Perp
Perp also the chancel arch, but the chancel of 1886–7. – FONT
The base with eight demi-shafts; E.E. – BENCH ENDS. I*
the shape of pointed arches. Tracery, also a fox, and on anothe*
end two hounds. – (STAINED GLASS. Three windows by S*
Ninian Comper, 1954–8.) – PLATE. Chalice and Paten Cover, b*
John Morley of Lincoln, 1569. – MONUMENTS. Elizabet*
Smith † 1604. Standing monument of alabaster. She is seate*
frontally; on her left putto with a spade and Nil sine labore
on her r. putto with skull and extinguished torch and In alt*
requies. Flat arch above, and in one of the spandrels a clock
face. – Also a tablet by *Earle* of Hull († 1837).

KELSTERN HALL. Virtually all of 1860, but preserving Geor*
gian work on the W front. The E front betrays the rebuildin*
of an earlier one, i.e. with two projecting gabled wings an*
gabled extruded angles.

3080

KENWICK HALL
2 m. SE of Louth

The house has been pulled down, but the STABLES remain
three sides of a courtyard, with a lantern, and the SE LODGE

They are in the so-called Queen Anne style and interesting in so far as they were designed by *Temple Moore* in 1888.

KETTLETHORPE

8070

ᴛ Peter and St Paul. Small unbuttressed w tower, the w doorway with Perp parts. Nave basically medieval, but mostly of 1809, yellow brick with windows of 1896. Chancel of stone, also with victorianized windows (ᴇ 1874, the others 1896). Bare interior, a ɴ aisle formed by two iron rods. - PULPIT. From Brittany, late c 17, of tulip shape with acanthus foliage and rustically carved scenes from the Passion. - PLATE. Almsdish, by *Thomas Mangy*, York, 1677; Chalice and Paten, by *John Penfold*, 1725. - MONUMENT. Charles Hall † 1743. Pink and white marble with an urn in front of an obelisk; no effigy.

ᴋETTLETHORPE HALL. Of the c14 house of the Swynford family only the GATEWAY remains. Of stone with battlements and typically c14 sunk mouldings. The back later strengthened by brickwork. Even from the c18 rebuildings little remains except for the present Dining Room with its chimneypiece.* The panelling and the niches are Queen Anne, the chimney-piece is of *c*.1771. In the adjoining room a delightful stucco ceiling with very thin decoration, trails, cornucopias, etc. The original staircase is now said to be at Ripley Castle in Yorkshire. In 1863 everything was pulled down and a new house built on the site. There are moats to the s and ᴇ.

KINGERBY

0090

ᶴᴛ Peter. What is the date of the w tower, of ironstone, with extremely tapering sides ? Does the small circular window to the ᴇ (now inside the church) indicate a Saxon date ? Are the bell-openings E.E. ? Or is the date that given by the small ogee-headed doorway into the nave ? Norman doorway into the s aisle. Plain chamfered imposts. Re-set E.E. entrance to the s porch, with dog-tooth. E.E. s arcade of two bays. Octagonal pier, double-chamfered arches, small nailhead. The arcade of the demolished ɴ aisle looks as if it were E.E. too, as is the chancel arch (nailhead again) and as are the chancel windows to the s, including one low-side window. The ᴇ window is Dec, and Dec also the window with the reticulated tracery set in

* The design for this is in the Victoria and Albert Museum, inscribed for ᴄharles Amcotts.

the N aisle. Jacobean nave roof with decorated corner piec
between principals and purlins. – BENCH ENDS. Tracerie
boards re-used in the chancel seats. – ALMSBOX. A pla
chunk inscribed: This is God's treasury. Cast one mite in
it. 1639. – STAINED GLASS. In the S aisle E window a c
figure of St Catherine. – PLATE. Silver-gilt Chalice, Pate
and Cover, by *G.G.*, London, 1639; Paten by *J. E. Terry*
Co., 1819. – MONUMENTS. In the w corner of the S aisle
cross-legged early C14 Knight, puppies by his pillow, and
late C14 Knight praying. They are placed on parts of a tomb
chest with shields in quatrefoils. The latter are barbed. – I
the chancel bearded later C14 Knight in low relief under an og
gable. Only the upper part of the figure is visible and the pointe
shoes. The shoes come out in an ogee-headed recess whic
forms the base of a cross decorating that part of the slab when
no figure appears.

Opposite the church gates is the base and shaft of a CROSS
inscribed and dated 1451. It refers to the PONS EPISCOP
i.e. Bishop Bridge across the river Ancholme E of Glentham
The RECTORY is to the E, early C19 brick of three bays an
two floors to the S and the entrance in a side front with th
gable made into a pediment.

KINGERBY HALL. The moat and earthworks surrounding th
house are large, but nothing remains of the house they pro
tected. The present one was built in 1812 for James Young.

KIRKBY-CUM-OSGODBY

ST ANDREW. E.E. w tower with twin bell-openings, sti
managed on the Anglo-Saxon principle. Nave with arche
windows of *c.*1790 (*see* the Nattes drawing). Chancel of *c.*130c
see the Y- and intersecting tracery. Double aumbry or reces
with polygonal shafts. – FONT. C18. Hemispherical bowl o
baluster shaft. – PLATE. Chalice, Elizabethan. – MONU
MENTS. Two members of the Wildbore family (*see* the coa
of arms), both later C14. The tomb-chests are nearly the same
A curious ornamental motif is a star of spokes ending i
fleurs-de-lis. One effigy, a Knight, is in the usual high relie
the other, a Lady, in sunk relief. She is placed under an oge
arch, with two angel busts by her pillow and much foliatio
up her sides, below the angels, and above the arch.

BLESSED LADY AND ST JOSEPH CHAPEL (R.C.). Built fo
the Youngs of Kingerby (*see* above) in 1793, it occupies th

upper floor of one wing of an L-shaped farmhouse. The simple interior is pleasing, just with a tripartite screen of fluted Doric columns at one end.

KIRKBY-ON-BAIN
2060

ſ MARY. 1802. Of greenstone. Nave and chancel and Victorian bellcote. The windows with intersecting tracery. The surrounds of 1802, the tracery of 1879–82, when the white brick w porch and the polygonal chancel were also built. The chancel arch of the restoration too. The church formerly had a completely wooden steeple. – FONT. Square baluster stem and small hemispherical bowl. – PLATE. Chalice and Paten, by *M. Lofthouse*, 1725.

KIRKSTEAD ABBEY
1060
1 m. sw of Woodhall Spa

he Cistercian abbey was founded in 1139 and moved to its final site in 1187. The tall crag remaining is the SE angle of the s transept. On its s side there is the low string course and one vaulting springer of the passage or sacristy adjoining the transept and opening to the former cloister. Above this the line of the former dormitory roof. To the N, i.e. inside, bare wall except for a window high up above the dormitory roof. The angle-shaft in the SE corner has a Norman capital and the start of the wall-rib is preserved. Then running on E a chunk of the s wall of the s transept E chapel with an indication of vaulting. Above this a mysterious start of a large, unmoulded arch on an unsplayed jamb, and above that the upper windows, shafted and with scallop capitals.

That is all of the strictly cloistral part of the abbey. But some distance s a gem of a chapel is preserved which must have been the chapel *ante portas* of which other examples exist (e.g. Little Coggeshall in Essex). This chapel, of *c*.1230–40, now the church of ST LEONARD, belongs to the finest pieces of C13 architecture in Lincolnshire and is up to the Cathedral standard. It is quite small, about 44 by 20 ft, and has a w doorway shafted, with lively stiff-leaf capitals and dog-tooth, and above it a blind arcade of three bays with lively stiff-leaf capitals and dog-tooth and a vesica window in the middle one. The sides are of three bays and have a corbel table and lancet windows, two for each bay. Buttresses without set-offs. Small blocked N doorway also with dog-tooth.

The E wall has three stepped lancets. The chapel was w
restored by *Weir* in 1913-14. The gables e.g. are treated
that they should at once appear as recent and yet not jar. T'

13   interior is delightful. It is vaulted and the arches and ri
and shafts are of a biscuit-coloured stone of an almost Pente
colour. The vaulting-shafts again have splendidly agitat
stiff-leaf capitals. Just as splendid are the stiff-leaf boss
The vaults are quadripartite except for the chancel ba
which is sexpartite and has in the middle of its boss the lan
and cross. The windows are shafted, and the E windows aga
distinguished by stiff-leaf capitals and dog-tooth. The tran
verse arches are given some dog-tooth enrichment too.
FONT. Circular, Norman, with lugs. – SCREEN. With
polygonal shafts and simple pointed trefoiled arches th
could well be coeval with the chapel and would thus be or
of the earliest wooden screens in existence (but cf. Compto
Surrey; late C12). – DOOR with scrolly ironwork, also coev
with the chapel. – PLATE. Dish, by *R.F.*, London, 165
Beaker, by *N.S.*, London, 1658. – MONUMENT. Effigy of

20a   Knight. Forest marble. The effigy must be of 1250 at tl
latest and is thus one of the earliest military ones in Englan
Broad slab, face hidden by the visor of the cylindrical helm
flat stiff-leaf l. and r. of the head. Surcoat with broad shoulde
and stiff arm-holes. The shield is held low, the hand is at tl
sword. The legs unfortunately are lost. They were probab
not crossed.

ABBEY LODGE INN. Reputedly a lodge or gatehouse. The
were extensive vaulted medieval cellars, now filled in.

OLD HALL. Built from old Abbey stone and not much late
than the C16. L-shaped with a N–S wing, brick-faced on thre
sides in the C18.

1010   KIRMINGTON

ST HELEN. W tower of very weathered ironstone, E.E. Th
bell-openings of two lancets under one arch. Copper spire
1838. All the rest of the exterior by *Teulon*, 1859. Inside
arcade of four bays, early C14. Quatrefoil piers with dee
continuous hollows in the diagonals and with fillets. Double
chamfered arches. The capitals are moulded but blossom ov
in the most remarkable heads and busts, e.g. the *signu*
triciput, a Bishop with hand raised for a blessing, and Syn
gogue, blindfold with a broken staff. S arcade with octagon

piers and double-chamfered arches. The arcade without the aisle, i.e. blocked, is represented in Nattes's drawing. – PLATE. Two-handled Cup, by *Peter and Ann Bateman*(?), London, 1807.

KIRMOND-LE-MIRE 1090

ST MARTIN. 1847 by *W. A. Nicholson*. E.E., with shafted windows, shafted porch entrance, shafted doorway, and even shafted bellcote. – PLATE. Chalice, by *John Morley* of Lincoln, *c.*1569.

KIRTON-IN-LINDSEY 9090

ST ANDREW. Quite a large church, with a mighty w tower and a clerestory. Chronologically the priest's doorway (chancel s, but re-set) comes first. It is Norman. The tympanum has close beaded interlace and also tongue-like leaves. In the arch zigzag. Next the N arcade, late C12 evidently. Four bays, circular and octagonal piers, capitals with broad upright leaves curling into crockets. Double-chamfered pointed arches. Then the w tower, an impressive piece of the C13, so broad that the w front has four original buttresses, shallow with sparse set-offs. Splendid w doorway with three orders of shafts, stiff-leaf capitals, and dog-tooth in the arch. Tall pairs of bell-openings, amply shafted, with shaft-rings. On two of the lancets a grotesque figure and grotesque heads as stops. The arch towards the nave is very impressive too. It is divided in two and has a strong circular pier and in the spandrel a trefoiled circle, a Butterfield or Street motif.* The chancel is E.E. too; see the side lancets. The wall plate stands on grotesque heads, perhaps re-used eaves-corbels. The chancel arch is of 1861 (by *Ewan Christian*). The s arcade cannot so easily be dated. Octagonal piers, double-chamfered arches. Very coarse capitals. Finally the aisle windows, including the s aisle E window of five lights and the clerestory windows. All this is Perp. – STAINED GLASS. E window by *Clayton & Bell*, 1868. – PLATE. Chalice and Paten Cover, by *I.P.*, London, 1565; Wine Cup, by *R.S.*, London, 1610; Flagon, by *Richard Gosling*, 1743. – MONUMENT. In the s aisle defaced effigy of a Knight, his legs crossed; late C13.

* The nave was restored in 1861 by *J. H. Hakewill*, and it is reported that the tower was then opened to the nave. The w doorway and the tower together are three steps below the nave and yet the bases of the arcades are set on plinths 2 ft high.

The village is spread out across the side of a hill in a picturesqu
honeycomb of narrow, criss-crossing streets. The housin

See
p.
767
development on the periphery is an example of how not to d
housing.

(TOWN HALL. 1887, by a local builder. PB).

The Kirton BRIDEWELL has gone, but *Thomas Berry* (
Gainsborough supplied designs in 1789. In his tend
Thomas Post of Willoughton presumptuously said: 'for
think I have Settup Stone Bulding rounde this neiberhou
more than aney man that canbye all Most found, wha
Housies and churchies and Steepels and Repairing are t
teadeous for to mention'. The authors are sceptical!

8080   KNAITH

ST MARY. Close to the river Trent. A curious building of whic
one does not know at first how it may be orientated. It is s
short, because the chancel has been demolished. C II W wa
with herringbone masonry. Short nave. To the S two ta
windows of the early C14; reticulated tracery. Also one larg
domestic-looking window probably of 1630. Inside three bi
early C18 arches on the plainest piers are set right across th
short nave to divide it into nave and chancel. – FONT. A goo
Dec piece with typical panels with cusped ogee curve:
Friezes of heads below and above them. The ogee pane
also on the stem. – PULPIT. Jacobean; with a small tester.
CHOIR SEATS. In the same style. – BENCH ENDS. Heavy
rustic work with simple poppy-heads. Is it C17? – PLAT!
Almsdish engraved with head and shoulders of Charles I
by *A.F.*, London, 1659–60; Chalice and Paten, by *W.S*
London, 1671; two Flagons, by *T.L.*, London, 1671.
MONUMENTS. Incised slabs to William, son of Lord Darcy
† 1408, and to a nun (a widow?), c.1440. The lower part c
the latter is missing.

KNAITH HALL. The Cistercian nunnery of Heynings wa
dissolved c.1539. There seems to be no domestic work o
before that date.* It is obscure when the present house wa
built, and both the owners in the late C16, Lord Willoughb
of Parham and Thomas Sutton of the Charterhouse, have bee
named in this connexion. There is just one long wing wit)
four chimneystacks on the E front. There seems to have been
Late Georgian re-fenestration, and the addition of a cante

* The MHLG refers to some C15 brickwork.

bay is also Late Georgian. Then the Victorians added the pleasing black and white half-timbering – oddly alien to the county but inspired perhaps from nearby Gainsborough Old Hall (*see* p. 243). With the proximity of the chapel and the lawns sloping down to the Trent-side, it is still as Lord Torrington wrote in 1791, 'in a great rurality of taste'.

LACEBY 2000

St Margaret. Rough C13 w tower. The w window a lancet, the arch to the nave double-chamfered and dying into the imposts. The top part is ashlar-faced and has bell-openings with Y-tracery and eight pinnacles. Most of the exterior of nave, chancel, and N aisle is Victorian. The Perp chancel windows are correctly renewed, and the plain Norman s doorway is original. To its l. and r. are Norman windows, the E one supposed to be Victorian, but looking old. The interior continues the Norman theme, but confusingly. The N arcade is of five bays, only the middle arch being Norman. It has zig-zag and crenellation as ornamental motifs.* The arch stands on a Norman round pier with a square abacus a little chamfered at the corner and another round pier consisting of a Norman half and an E.E. half with water-holding base and a primitive capital. The remaining piers are octagonal and the arches double-chamfered, except that the E respond has another water-holding base. What happened then? Where did the Norman w wall run? The chancel interior was E.E., see the remains of blank arcading round the walls with short triple shafts. – Plate. Paten, by *F. S.*, London, 1676; Chalice, by *John le Sage*, 1724.

LANGRICK 2040

St Margaret. 1828. In all probability by *Jeptha Pacey*. Red brick, still – it is amazing – laid in English bond. Nave and short chancel, w porch, bellcote with stepped gable. The windows pointed in the Late Georgian way but with wooden Perp tracery. Big, flat brick modillion frieze under the eaves.

Witham Lodge. Visually satisfying owing to its position on the river, its attractive colour, and its maritime character.

LANGTON-BY-HORNCASTLE 2060

St Margaret. A miniature greenstone church, just of nave and chancel and not even a bellcote. Mostly by *W. Scorer*,

---

* A few of the zigzag stones of the porch entrance are said to be Norman too.

1890, in the Dec style. But the N wall is medieval and show
the existence of a N arcade of two bays. Octagonal pier ar
double-chamfered arches; probably Dec. – FONT. Put to
gether from several pieces. The foot is a keystone of a Norma
rib-vault. It comes from Kirkstead Abbey. The bowl is
stoup and comes from the former church of St Laurenc
Horncastle. – PULPIT and LECTERN. Very finely carved i
the Elizabethan style, with arabesque patterns, by *J. Conwo
Walter*, Rector, in 1891. – CHRISMATORY. Found in th
moat of Poolham Hall and called medieval. It is of terracott
Its purpose was to sprinkle the child (the Chrisom chil
with salt and oil before the baptism. – BAPTISMAL SHELI
Silver, circular, with eight sunk medallions with scene
from the Life of Christ. C19. Brought back from Bethlehem
in 1860.

³⁰⁷⁰
LANGTON-BY-PARTNEY

52b ST PETER AND ST PAUL. The date is not known, but *c*.1720–3
is likely. Red brick, five bays long, with arched windows an
a high parapet with blank smaller windows or sunk panel
The front with a classical little stone doorway and a gabl
and, rising behind it, a strange, heavy octagonal bell-turre
with circular openings in two tiers, and an abrupt flat ending
in short somewhat Vanbrughian. (It dates from 1825. PE
Overhanging white eaves. The E wall has only blank window
and above them the sunk panels. The interior is perfectl
preserved, with BOX PEWS facing inwards, college-wise,
three-decker PULPIT with tester in the middle of the S side
a shallow altar niche from whose upper angles big whit
volutes help to support the flat white ceiling. The REREDO
has fluted Corinthian columns and a segmental pediment
The COMMUNION RAIL is three-sided with curves instead
of corners, and the WEST GALLERY stands on thin flute
columns. Cox in his *Little Guide* says of all this: 'a compara
tively modern brick church'. This blindness to the C18 is hi
one shortcoming. – FONT. Octagonal, Perp, of the pattern
book type. The window patterns all Dec except for one Per
one. One panel has no window pattern but simply a tracer
motif. – SCULPTURE. In the porch a very primitive Crucifixus
Yet the foliation of the cross makes an early C13 date probable
– PLATE. Chalice and Paten Cover, by *John Fawdery*, 1719
Paten, by *John White*, 1738.
OLD HALL, ¼ m. NW. Once a poignantly romantic house, the

home of Dr Johnson's friend Bennet Langton. Rebuilt in 1822, but now demolished except for the stables.

ANGTON HALL, ⅝ m. NE. In the Elizabethan style, by *James Fowler*, 1866–7. The grounds were laid out by *Veitch & Son*. At the time of writing all is in decay.

ECTORY. 1839, by *William Pickering*. N of the church. Red brick.

OTTAGE ORNÉ, E of the church. Eminently picturesque. Circular with a conical, thatched, overhanging roof.

ONG BARROW, on the S slope of a valley ½ m. S of Langton Grange. The barrow, which has a total length of 182 ft, has been badly damaged by stone robbing and now presents the aspect of three isolated mounds. A large number of bones are reported to have been found beneath the barrow, but the nature and circumstances of the find have not been recorded.

LANGTON-BY-WRAGBY   *1070*

T GILES. Early Perp W tower. The rest of 1866 (by *Atkinson* of York). Nave and chancel; Geometrical tracery. – PLATE. The Chalice, of 1677, 'vanished into Nigeria'. – MONUMENTS. Two nice tablets, to William Saltmarsh † 1657, and Ann Marwood † 1660.

ANGTON COURT, NW of the church. By *William Pickering* of Wragby, 1841. Red brick; nothing special.

LANGWORTH   *0070*

T HUGH. 1960–2 by *Haynes & Johnson* of Brigg, but mostly a rebuilding of the chapel of Walmsgate Hall, built in 1901 as a memorial to the son of Thomas Yorke Dallas-Yorke. The architect is unrecorded. Mr John Harris suggests *Henry Wilson*. The original bricks could not be re-used, but the plan was retained, though it was lengthened by one bay to the W. The original roof construction with its tunnel-vault was also retained, and the little W lantern rebuilt. The window surrounds are of 1901 too, and so are the large sliding DOORS at the W end with their lovely bronze handles, the FONT, the ORGAN, the MEMORIAL PLAQUE with a relief of the young man as a soldier* and the sumptuous gilt ALTAR CANOPY, the bronze hanging LAMPS, the carved BEAM at the entrance to the chancel, the marble floor, and the skirting of the chancel.

* In the RIBA is a design by Wilson for a soldier on a tomb-chest. This may well relate to Walmsgate Chapel.

The plaster decoration – half Art-Nouveau-, half Pr
Raphaelite-looking – could unfortunately not be saved. Wi
it the chapel was one of the outstanding ensembles in Engla
of the style of 1900.

LAUGHTON

ALL SAINTS. A church of much interest. The history star
with the N arcade of three bays, which must be of the la
C12. Round piers, the abaci square but with recessed round
corners, or round but with square projections, a significa
stage of transition between square and round. The capita
have waterleaf and also certain finely detailed leaves, un
commonly pretty. The arches are round but double-chamfere
also a stage of transition. The W bay is an addition, but clo
in style to the other bays. Cox in fact regarded it as earlie
The arch is the same, the E respond replaced by an odd she
on three brackets. Then the C13. To this belongs the S arcad
four bays built at one go. Octagonal piers, double-chamfere
of course pointed arches. Also the graceful S doorway. Sti
C13 but later the N chancel window of three lights with
Geometrical tracery – three quatrefoiled circles at the top
and its roll-moulded mullions and tracery. Dec the low
parts of the W tower, see its doorway. Higher up, the tower
Perp. It has eight pinnacles on the top and a tall arch to t
nave with big hollow chamfers dying into the imposts. Th
is more probably a Dec than a Perp moulding. Perp also th
S aisle with an exceptionally charming little E window of thr
lights. It has a straight top, tracery of mouchettes in alter
nating directions, and head-stops to the hood-mould. The
Bodley & Garner entered the scene in 1894. They rebuilt, i
1894–6, the chancel, most impressively tall with Dec
windows and a windowless E wall. They also designed the
porch with its pretty niche above the entrance. Inside, their
is the roof with tie-beams, kingposts, and struts, the SCREEN
the tall wooden REREDOS with the stone panelling round it,
and the ORGAN CASE. All this was done for Mrs Meynel
Ingram, for whom Bodley had already done the famous churc
of Hoar Cross in 1872–6. Her husband's MONUMENT wit
white marble effigy, asleep, is by *Thomas Woolner*, 1874, an
was made for Hoar Cross. – Other MONUMENTS: In the
aisle upper part of a monument of *c.*1300, with a completel
re-tooled head of a lady, sunk in a roundel. – Brass of

* The painted triptych is by *G. Jackson*, 1903, to Bodley's design.

member of the Dalison family, c.1400. A splendid piece, the
figure 5 ft 8 in. long, placed below a triple canopy. – The
brass is on a tomb-chest to William († 1546) and George
(† 1549) Dalison. This has two large lozenge panels on each
of the long sides, crossed by a wide scroll which is, on the
l. and r., held by hands. The inscription records the making of
the tomb in 1556, in the reign of King Philip and Queen
Mary. – The STAINED GLASS of the Bodley remodelling is
by *Grylls* and disappointing.

ALL FARM. Late C18. Brick; five bays and two storeys.
Plain stone angle pilasters, stone string and door surround.

OMAN SETTLEMENT, on HARDWICK HILL, near the SW
end of Scotton Common. Numerous finds of Romano-
British pottery, ornaments, and coins indicate the presence
of a settlement in this area. Quantities of iron slag may imply
the existence of a foundry on the site.

LEA   8080

T HELEN. Perp W tower, E.E. chancel drastically renewed, a
nave also looking all Victorian, but a splendid Dec N aisle,
big and wide. The windows have flowing tracery, the N
windows under straight heads. The arcade of two bays again
all renewed. It must have been E.E. Octagonal pier, double-
chamfered arches. In addition S chancel chapel of one bay
(re-erected in the C19, as the Nattes drawing shows only the
blocked arch to the chancel) and N chancel chapel of one bay,
the arch of the latter on corbels with big faces. In the church
a chantry was established about 1330. Does this refer to the
N aisle or the S chapel? – STAINED GLASS. Two fine figures of
c.1330 in the N aisle E window. – Also a C15 Crucifixus.
– PLATE. Chalice and Cover, by *John Morley* of Lincoln,
c.1569 (gilt in 1876); Paten, Exeter, 1738; Dutch Snuff Box
(for Hosts), Middelburg, 1796; Chalice and Flagon, by *Charles
Fox*, 1828. – MONUMENT. Effigy of stone, a Knight, cross-
legged; c.1300.

EA HALL. Early C17 but much altered in 1857. The N and
S fronts still have their Jacobean gables, but the S front centre
of four bays is C18. The entrance, in the traditional way,
leads into the hall at one end, where the screen once stood.

Nice elongated village GREEN with a few old trees. One cottage
has a shaped gable.

LEA GATE INN *see* CONINGSBY

LEGBOURNE

ALL SAINTS. Chalk walling shows itself here at its most friab.
The chancel is essentially Early Perp, i.e. probably of *c.*13
or so. In the N aisle one Dec window, probably old. The
doorway with shields in the spandrels has mouldings st
close to Dec, and the masonry is typically Early Perp. Tl
W tower fits the dating too. The chancel however is by *Roge*
& Marsden, 1865–8. The tower arch inside, the four-bay
arcade (octagonal piers), and the chancel arch are all the sam
so the church was probably built quickly and consistentl
like so many of the Marsh churches not far away. – FON
Octagonal, Perp, with shields in quatrefoils. – SCREEN. Wi
ogee-arched single-light divisions and panel tracery over.
STAINED GLASS. In the chancel S windows old fragment
not too small; their centre an eagle with the device Die
merci. In the N aisle E window also parts of a canopy. – PLAT
Chalice and Cover, by *John Morley* of Lincoln, *c.*1569.
(WINDMILL. 1814. Wailes)

LEGSBY

ST THOMAS. A medieval church, see the masonry of the
tower, its arch to the nave, the chancel arch, and the Per
chancel E windows. But the church must have been change
in the C18, as is shown by the bell-openings, the (conservativ
obelisk pinnacles ending in knobs, the proportions of tl
nave, and the shortening of the chancel. Also by the PULPI
with back panel and tester, and the COMMUNION RAIL.
FONT. Norman, drum-shaped, with a double band of rope.
READER'S DESK. The panels with Flamboyant tracery an
coats of arms. – PLATE. Chalice and Paten Cover, inscribe
1569.

THE MOUNT, *c.*1 m. S, at a road junction. A surprisingly sma
but quite unmistakable MOTTE.

LINWOOD

ST CORNELIUS. W tower of ironstone with a recessed spire
grey stone. The arch towards the nave has a double-wav
moulding. The S aisle has a Transitional doorway and
window, the N aisle a nice Perp E window with a segment.
arch. The clerestory windows also with segmental arches. Th
chancel was once E.E., see the handsome piscina with sho
shafts and a pointed-trefoiled arch, but was rebuilt in 185.

Linwood, brasses to John Lyndewode † 1419 and wife

Three-bay arcades with octagonal piers and double-chamfered arches, somewhat different N from S. One-bay S chapel with arches from N and W. – FONT. Octagonal, with blank window in flat carving, all motifs of *c.*1300, as if taken from a pattern book. – STAINED GLASS. One C15 figure (chancel S), and some bits in the S chapel windows. – PLATE. Chalice and Paten Cover, by *I.S.*, London, 1591. – BRASSES. Two of outstanding quality, both under canopies on buttress-shafts, though differing in details: John Lyndewode † 1419 and wife, and John Lyndewode † 1421. The latter has his feet on a woolpack with his merchant's mark engraved on. The couple are 3 ft 6 in. long, the single figure 4 ft. The inscription below the couple is quite delightfully engraved, with little bits of foliage decoration, as if in an illuminated manuscript.

1080

LISSINGTON

ST JOHN BAPTIST. Built *c.*1796. Of ironstone. Nave and chancel with arched windows, the arches of red brick. Original glazing bars. Even the bellcote has a brick arch. Interior with panelled dado, but otherwise no attraction. – The COMMUNION RAIL, worked into the screen, looks older than the late C18. – PLATE. Chalice and Paten Cover, by *A.T.*, early C17.

3080

LITTLE CARLTON
⅜ m. SW of Great Carlton

ST EDITH. 1837; cemented. With a W tower with spire. The tower arch to the nave with a crocketed ogee gable. The windows, as suits the date, wide lancets or provided with Y- or intersecting tracery. Nice chancel roof. Panes of coloured GLASS in the E window. – FONT. Perp, octagonal, each panel with three cusped arches and a little panel tracery. – PLATE. *See* p. 767 Chalice, London, 1569; Paten, Dublin, 1709.

3080

LITTLE CAWTHORPE

ST HELEN. 1860 by *R. J. Withers*. Red brick and slate roof. Nave and chancel. Bell-turret with spire. Black brick bands. *The Ecclesiologist* called it 'a truly excellent design . . . the arrangements thoroughly correct'.* This is interesting, as today it would strike one as really very dreary.

* So Mr Ferriday tells me.

MANOR HOUSE. A T-shaped brick house of 1673. The E front has a shaped gable and blank arcading on the ground floor. The latter continues round the angle and along the N side of the wing. The S and W gables are also shaped, and both have chimneybreasts attached. The S wing, the E porch, and the offices to the N are a modern imitation of the style.

LITTLE COATES
2010

ST MICHAEL. The church testifies to its nearness to Grimsby by consisting of a small old part, formerly nave and S aisle and chancel, of ironstone, and a large new part of 1913–14, added by *Sir Walter Tapper*. It is a broad W tower, a new nave, and an exceptionally impressive new chancel. The chancel is rib-vaulted in four bays, in a late C13 style, with an E vestry behind the reredos. This, accessible by the doors l. and r. of the reredos, is a Norfolk motif (but cf. also Donington and, in the West of England, All Saints Hereford). The old arcade is of two bays, with octagonal pier and double-chamfered arches; Dec probably. Small Perp windows. – STAINED GLASS. In the old E window, by *Kempe*, c.1908. – PLATE. Chalice by *R. Robinson*, Hull, c.1620.

LITTLE GRIMSBY
3090

ST EDITH. Near the hall and hiding in trees. Minute (20 ft long) and all whitewashed. Nave and chancel. Above the Perp W doorway a date-stone 1500 in C18 script and in an C18-Gothic quatrefoil. The E window also probably of c.1800. – The piscina seems to be a Georgian FONT bowl; fluted. – STAINED GLASS. Bits in the chancel (s). – PLATE. Chalice and Paten, by *Thos. Farrer*, 1726. – MONUMENTS. W of the church urn to John Nelthorpe † 1784. – White marble bust of Lady Beau-clerk † 1875, carved, according to Mee, by her son.

LITTLE GRIMSBY HALL. One of the most visually satisfying of Lincolnshire houses. Built for the Nelthorpe family; according to a tradition c.1700. Brick with stone quoins. Seven by four bays and two storeys, wooden eaves cornice, hipped roof, and dormers with alternately triangular and segmental pediments. The windows tall and slightly segment-headed. A stone bolection surround to the doorway and also an open scrolled pediment. Inside is excellent joinery: fluted Roman Doric pilasters to the hall (cf. Brackenborough Hall, p. 195)

and equally excellent stairs with alternating twisted, straigh
fluted balusters. 1720 or even 1730 is perhaps a better date.

LITTLE STEEPING
4060

ST ANDREW. Greenstone with much brick repair. Perp w towe
with three-light bell-openings. Nave and chancel in one. Per
windows, except for the Dec s aisle w window, an ogee-cuspe
lancet. The s doorway is also Dec. The hood-mould stands o
grotesque faces. Dec indeed the s arcade too. Three bays
octagonal piers and double-chamfered arches. The N arcade i
a little later. In the chancel on the N side a single-chamfere
tomb recess. To this belonged the MONUMENT to Thomas c
Reading, rector from 1318 to 1353. Hieratically draped figure
hands folded, the pillow placed diagonally. This and the in
scription in Norman-French all still in the C13 tradition.
FONT. Octagonal, late C14, with figures standing small unde
little twin ogee canopies. – PLATE. Paten, by *William William
son*(?), Dublin, *c.*1740; Chalice, by *William Holmes*(?)
London, 1770.

LOCKSLEY HALL *see* NORTH SOMERCOTES

LOUTH
3080

An uncommonly compact town with an intricate pattern o
streets. No large open spaces and no obviously principa
thoroughfare. The town is of course dominated by the church
steeple, and how anyone could have decided to give the marke
hall a relatively high tower too, remains a mystery.

CHURCHES

ST JAMES. That Louth parish church is one of the most majestic
of English parish churches need hardly be said. It is what it is
210   thanks to its steeple, which has good claims to be considere
the most perfect of Perp steeples. With its spire it is 295 ft
high, and the spire belongs to the Late Perp years. The date o
the tower is not known, though it is in all probability the second
half of the C15, but the accounts for the spire survive. It was
built in 1501–15 and cost £305 7s. 5d. The first master was
John Cole. He was replaced in 1505 by *Christopher Scune*, who,
however, was too busy at Ripon Minster and at Durham
Cathedral to pay many visits. The resident mason seems to

have been *Lawrence Lemyng* and, moreover, at the very end, *John Tempas* of Boston was called in. The tower is slender and places consistent emphasis on the verticals, and the way in which the extremely slim recessed spire is supported by lacy flying buttresses resting against solid turret pinnacles is perfect, whether seen from close by, as one sees it all the time in the town, or from a distance of a mile or two. The height of the tower is almost exactly equal to the height of the spire.

The tower is now embraced by the aisles, but was built with evenly developed buttresses on all sides, into the aisles and into the nave. It has a doorway with cusped and subcusped arch set very charmingly in front of the outer mouldings. The W window is of five lights and very high. On the N and S more moderate windows appear above the aisle roofs. Then follow twin two-light windows to all sides, again remarkably slender, and then the bell-openings, once more erect and tall, once more two twins, but without transoms. They have high crocketed ogee gables. The buttresses are gabled at every set-off, and at the bell-stage replaced by buttress shafts. The battlements are of course decorated too. The spire has crockets up its edges, the motif used discreetly, and the pinnacles have their own crocketed spires.

The church that follows is long (total length with tower 182 ft). The clerestory has six windows for the nave, four for the chancel. The plan is a plain rectangle. All parts are ashlar-faced, as is the tower, and have battlements and pinnacles. The W windows of the aisles are of five lights, the E windows of the chapels have two, and the N and S windows three. But the chancel E window is a seven-light affair with embattled transom, four plus four intersected. The E end is crowned by an open-work quatrefoil parapet and crockets curving up to a point with the gable cross. Angle buttresses with niches. On the N and S sides the chancel and the chancel chapels are distinguished by fleuron friezes below the battlements. In the nave and aisles these are missing. The tracery patterns are all conventionally Perp, except for the nave clerestory, where the panel motifs are unusually broad and have curved sides as if still inspired by Dec reticulation. Additions to the rectangle are the porches, the S porch much the bigger. In height it reaches the top of the aisle. Fleuron friezes in the entrance wall, a niche with a nodding ogee arch above the entrance. The inner doorway (and that of the N porch) has five shafts with broad fillets. At the NE end a one-storeyed vestry, also with pinnacles.

The interior is spacious, but exorbitant neither in appearance of length nor of height. The nave is of six bays, the piers
of an odd shape, octagons with the diagonals given a hollow
down their middles. It has been suggested that they are really
the piers of the preceding church remodelled. That would
explain the simplicity of the plain double-chamfered arches.
Another puzzle is the way in which the w bay is divided from
the others by a piece of plain wall. The solution is probably
that here the former w wall ran, or the E wall of a former tower.
The new tower was then built completely outside the old
building. Good head-stops for the hood-moulds, good angel
figures for the nave roof. In the aisles, leaf paterae are placed
where the sill-course connecting the windows ends.

The chancel is divided from the chapels by piers with the
familiar Perp four-shafts-four-hollows section. The arches are
much moulded and have little ogee tips. Shafts lead up to the
roof principals. The s chapel has very pretty sedilia with little
lierne-vaults, the N chapel a crocketed ogee top to the small
doorway into the vestry.

The tower arch is of prodigious height. The mouldings of
the responds are again on the principle of the shafts and
hollows. To the N and s arches of the same type but of course
lower. But then the climax of the interior, the fact that the
whole next stage of the tower with its twin two-light windows
to all sides is open to the interior like the lantern of a cathedral
crossing. High above, 86 ft high, a lierne-vault making in plan
four stars of eight rays or four squares with a cross and a
saltire cross. Wide ring in the centre. Bosses with shields.

FURNISHINGS. FONT (N aisle w). Octagonal, Perp, with a
panelled stem and a leaf frieze on the bowl. The font was
found in a garden. – SCREENS. To the N chapel with one-light
ogee-headed divisions, to the s chapel with narrower openings
neither anything special. – STALLS. Six plain stalls in the N
chapel. – CHEST. In the vestry. With busts of a King and
Queen on panels, said to be Henry VII and Elizabeth of York.
The chest was given by Thomas Sudbury, i.e. before 1504. –
SCULPTURE. In the N chapel two good, rather stiff, but finely
stylized angels from a roof. – In the N aisle at the w end some
roof bosses on show. – DOOR. Small traceried door to the staircase in the w wall. – PAINTINGS. Virgin and Saints, Italian
Mannerist, late C16. – Moses and Aaron from the former
reredos. – Descent from the Cross by *William Williams*, bought
in 1775. – PLATE. Flagon, by *I.D.*, London, 1585; Alms Bowl

London, 1635; Paten, by *G.G.*, London, 1688; Almsdish, by *Benjamin Pyne*, 1724; pair of Candlesticks, by *William Colson* of Lincoln, *c.*1725.

MONUMENTS. From E to W. Against the E wall John Emeris † 1819. By *Earle* of Hull. The inscription flanked by scrolly supports still placed diagonally in the Baroque and Rococo way. Urn on top and on its base a relief of Faith. – Thomas Orme † 1814. Sarcophagus in front of an obelisk. On the sarcophagus dove in rays. – In the nave high up two tablets with columns l. and r. and nicely detailed open pediments; no doubt of *c.*1725. – In the N aisle at the W end William Allison, 1845. Big sumptuous Gothic memorial with a diapered background and at the top an ogee cupola in relief. – At the W end of the S aisle Wolley Jolland, 1835 by *T. Waudsby* of Hull. – In front of it indent of a large double brass, the figures under concave canopies.

ST MICHAEL, Church Street. 1863 by *James Fowler* of Louth. W front with a naughty polygonal NW turret and attached to it an open two-bay W porch. Geometrical tracery. Inside brick-faced, red with some yellow and black. Much in the way of naturalistically carved stone foliage. The S chapel has an apse and to the N and W effective stone screening.

HOLY TRINITY, Eastgate. 1866 by *Rogers & Marsden*. Big and rock-faced, with a massive, crude tower. Octagonal top and higher stair-turret. Geometrical tracery. Five-bay interior with yellow-brick arches, the arrises all spiky.

WESLEY CHAPEL. *See* Perambulation, p. 306.

LOUTH ABBEY, 1½ m. E. The ruins are picturesque in a certain light, but that is all that can be said visually about them. What stands up is no more than two lumps of wall belonging to the S chapels. The abbey was Cistercian. It was founded in 1137 and moved to Louth in 1139. It had, as ascertained by excavations, a nave and aisles of ten bays, a crossing and transept, and E of them in the Cistercian way six chapels, all straight-headed, three to each transept and in the middle the farther-projecting chancel. Of the W range of the cloister a certain amount has also been found. The excavations took place in 1873, but little has been left uncovered.

PUBLIC BUILDINGS *see* PERAMBULATION

PERAMBULATION

The MARKET PLACE and CORNMARKET are linked, the latter almost a pedestrian space, the façades in a bucolic 1840s style.

In the far corner the wonderfully decayed former CORN
EXCHANGE by *Pearson Bellamy*, 1853, its façade* like a rotting
cadaver. Three storeys, Italianate, with a statue in the middle.
Next door is the vernacular MASON'S ARMS in the best town
pub tradition. Good florid lettering and lantern over the
entrance. Opposite a nice Georgian brick house with five
widely spaced arched windows on the upper floor. Then the
MARKET HALL in the Market Place. The style is Byzantine
Gothic, the material red brick. By *Rogers & Marsden*, 1866.
A tall thin tower is pushed back between narrow projecting
wings. A seven-bay hall divided by giant-arched iron girders.
On the Square proper, the Early Victorian PRINTING
OFFICE, still Grecian of a sort, and two late C17 houses with
altered fronts (Nos 20–21). In MERCER ROW more of the
1840s and especially one quite grand house with giant com-
posite pilasters, doubled for the central bay, and GOULDING'S
BOOKSHOP with its nice bulgy Regency shop-windows. Next
some Georgian upper parts of façades, especially Nos 17–23, a
mid-C18 eleven-bay front, and then the C17 KING'S ARMS
HOTEL, dressed-up in Early Victorian Gothic. At this point
UPGATE crosses Mercer Row. To the N are mostly early C19
terrace groups, at the corner to the S CROMWELL HOUSE, a
C16 timber-framed house with overhangs but Georgian details,
then on the other side of Upgate and nearer the E end of the
church (which has now begun to appear) the MANSION
HOUSE, probably late C18. A quoined rendered three-bay
front with slightly ill-proportioned Corinthian pilasters at the
first-floor angles and windows carrying triangular pediments.
Inside one large room with Ionic pilasters and a tripartite
screen dividing it from a lower room with Adamesque details.
No. 8 is the best house in the street. Brick. Ground-floor bay
windows and five windows on the first floor. It boasts the two
leitmotifs of the country Palladian builder: the central Venetian
window and the arched window above it. Then comes the
church precinct and, taking up its S side, the VICARAGE. This
is Victorian Tudor-Gothic, by *C. J. Carter*, of 1832 and
replaces a thatched building called the Hermitage. The rustic
jollities in the garden have disappeared, except for the most
unexpected of them, the top of Louth spire.

From here into WESTGATE, the best street of Louth. There are
plenty of nice doorways, more than can be individually commented on. Worth special notice are No. 47, mid-C18, and the

* At the time of writing.

somewhat grander No. 45, which is detached and lies back. Five bays, two and a half storeys, an advanced centre, and segment-headed windows. Then comes the complex of KING EDWARD VI GRAMMAR SCHOOL, consisting mostly of once private houses. THE LIMES is mid-C18, five windows to the drive and six to the garden. LINDSEY HOUSE, which once belonged to the Pahod family, is of the same date: grey brick, three-bay centre, single-storey attached wings, and the ground-floor windows set in blank arches. Porch with fluted Doric order, paired at the angles. The entrance hall with a circular flattish dome on Soanian pendentives. Opposite No. 56, Early Victorian, red brick, with a big tripartite window on the ground floor and thick cast-iron railings. Back to the other side and to WESTGATE HOUSE, early C19, with bows through three storeys, each cut away at ground level and supported on Tuscan columns. In the middle a horseshoe stair. There are also later school buildings by *James Fowler* (1866). Continuing Westgate, THORNTON HOUSE with a plain pedimented front to the street and to the rear, bows and a big recessed blank arch between. Then THE SYCAMORES, in later C19 red brick, Tudoresque, and next to this the grand house of Louth, THE MANSION, on a terrace above the pavement. A two-storey front of seven bays of segment-headed windows and a narrow centre bay slightly advanced. The cornice concave in section and over the centre a deep segmental pediment. In plan the house is an L. The side elevations are notably bare. There was a date 1704, although at Louth one would have guessed *c*.1720. The interior is very complete in a plain joinery manner. Bolection panelling and chimneypieces and a spaciously planned stair. Twisted balusters and oddly planned risers. The KITCHEN GARDEN opposite with a hooded alcove seat.

Returning towards town one can enjoy the steeple right in front as the focal point. Passing the church on the r., proceed w and then N, along BRIDGE STREET. Mostly early C19, including one ambitious terrace group. By the bridge is a MILL with a plaque inscribed '*Fran Julien* Engineer 1755'. Back to the church and E from its N side into CHEQUERGATE, noting No. 13 of the early C19, and then into NORTHGATE, with picturesque small terrace houses. ENGINE GATE opens on the l., and here BROADBANK HOUSE has the most enchanting of follies. A screen with octagonal towers at each end, in between a row of big Gothic windows filled with coloured glass. The

edgings brick, the infillings black coke, and the cornices an
mouldings picked out with white snails, and conch shells a
corbels. Castellated parapets and turrets topped by iron fleurs
de-lis. Inscribed in white shells the date 1859. At the end c
Engine Gate, in High Holme Road, is the COUNTY HOS
PITAL, the former workhouse, 1837, on the typical radial plan
Back to Chequergate, up Nichol Hill and to EASTGATE. The
first notable building is the large WESLEY CHAPEL of 1835
still dignified Georgian. A front of six bays, brick, with arche
windows and two entrances. Swags below the upper windows
Then comes the *tour de force* of Louth, *Pearson Bellamy*'
TOWN HALL of 1854, his best work. A massive, highly articu
lated affair, it looms by the street like a great Italian *palazzo*
Seven by three bays. The order of each bay is a rusticate
ground floor with an arched window, then a balconied window
then another balconied window carrying a deeply projectin
segmental pediment. The entrance with paired Ionic columns
a tripartite opening, and balcony. The pattern for the side
elevations is the same except for closer spacing and a pilaste:
treatment to the ground floor. Above all this heavy cornice:
and a heavy finialled balustrade. The opulence of the exterior
is reflected inside. Galleried upper room with a highly en
riched ceiling. The front of the town hall faces the back o
the Market Hall. Continuing along Eastgate, No. 124 has an
early C19 stock brick treatment, then the late C18 MANOR
and then Nos 140, 142, 146, all with vigorous door surrounds
Past *James Fowler*'s ORME ALMSHOUSES of 1885 to TH
PRIORY, a picturesque Gothic villa built by the local artist
and amateur architect *Thomas Espin* in 1818. The plan a little
essay in intersecting cubes dressed up with gables, openwork
cresting, octagonal turrets, cusping, and quatrefoils. The
interior beautifully preserved, all in Gothic, notably the library
and stairs. In the grounds is Espin's MAUSOLEUM on one side
of the lake and a folly concocted from bits of Louth Abbey on
the other side. Still further out of town is the RAILWAY
STATION in Tudor Gothic; 1854. Quite large and with a big
arcaded *porte-cochère*. Beyond Eastgate is RIVERSIDE ROAD
and the disused head of the LOUTH NAVIGATION. The canal
was opened in 1770 and the head is surrounded by late C18
and early C19 WAREHOUSES.

THORPE HALL, at the w exit from the town. Of the house built
by the romantic Sir John Bolle (Ballad of the Spanish Lady's
Love), allegedly in 1584, only the w front shows any remains.

An L shape and part of a gable. The windows and massive stacks are C18, as is the E front. Red brick, stone quoins, hipped roof. The grounds descend to the river by a series of (Elizabethan?) terraces.*

LOW MELWOOD see OWSTON FERRY

LOW TOYNTON
1¼ m. NE of Horncastle

2070

ST PETER. Built in 1811. Stone, with arched windows. The chancel arch is called Late Norman, but it has semi-octagonal responds, and the arch is completely unrevealing. – FONT. Octagonal, Perp. Against the stem eight figures, against the bowl a flower, another flower, an angel, a seated figure, a standing figure, another angel, a branch, and two panels with two figures each. What characterizes the figures is the way their long hair stands on and around their heads (cf. Covenham St Bartholomew, Huttoft, etc.). – PLATE. Chalice, by *W. S.*, London, 1641; Paten, London, 1802.

LUDBOROUGH
2090

ST MARY. Partly of chalk. E.E. chancel. To the E two lancets and a pointed quatrefoil above. To the N three tall lancets. The priest's doorway has whorls on the outer ends of the abaci and paterae as hood-mould stops. E.E. also the sedile and piscina, a somewhat lopsided composition. On the S side of the chancel otherwise Dec re-modelling. The arcades are E.E. again. Three bays, keeled quatrefoil piers, double-chamfered arches of chalk. On the N side the abaci are cruciform, and there are stiff-leaf label-stops, on the S side the abaci are round. Of the same date, it seems, the small arched clerestory windows. Can they really have been round-arched? They were only discovered at the time of *Fowler*'s reconstruction of 1858–60. He also found the S base of the E.E. tower-arch respond. The high tower arch now is Perp, as is the whole strong ironstone tower. – PAINTING. On the sill of one of the N lancets a large painted scroll dated *c*.1300 by Cox. – PLATE. Chalice, by *John Morley* of Lincoln, *c*.1569.

THE MANOR. Long, low brick house. On the S side porch with a four-centred arch to the doorway and a pediment above it.

* The garden was laid out by *Mrs Jekyll* in 1906. In it stonework from *Sir Christopher Wren*'s church of St Mildred, Poultry. It was intended for use in building a private chapel, but none was built.

Also a pediment to one of the adjoining windows. It must ▮
Elizabethan, or Jacobean at the latest.

LUDDINGTON
8010

ST OSWALD. 1855, the architect unknown. Entirely on its ow▮
and quite ambitiously done. W tower with broach spire. Lanc▮
windows. Aisles. – STAINED GLASS. That in the E, SE, S ais▮
E windows is by *Gibbs*, 1855 (TK). – PLATE. Chalice, give▮
1725; peg Tankard, Norwegian, *c.*1723–66. – MONUMEN▮
Richard Worsop † 1723 and his wife † 1739. Nice surroun▮
with carved flowers and scrolls.
(ST JOSEPH and ST DYMPHNA (R.C.). By *M. E. Hadfield ▮
Son*, 1877.)

LUDFORD MAGNA
2080

ST MARY AND ST PETER. 1864 by *James Fowler*. Biggish, in th▮
style of 1300. Nave with high bellcote, transepts and chance▮
Inside, the arches to transepts and chancel are brought ov▮
perversely by being of brick, red with some black, and havin▮
the arrises as nailhead to make them look spiky (cf. Clee▮
thorpes). Also typically High Victorian leaf-carving inside.
FONT. The stem is E.E., six-lobed with two fillets. – PLAT▮
Chalice and Cover, by *Peter Carlill*, Hull, 1571; Paten, b▮
John Taylor(?), Dublin, 1731; Chalice, by *Thomas Dexter*(?▮
London, 1819.

LUSBY
3060

ST PETER. Greenstone, nave and chancel. The open Victoria▮
bell-turret replaces a W tower whose traces are visible. Th▮
church is of great interest. To the l. and r. of the chancel arc▮
with its plain chamfered imposts the stumps of pairs of semi▮
circular shafts have been exposed, and they are quite evidentl▮
Anglo-Saxon (cf. in Lincolnshire e.g. Stow). The triangle▮
headed niche in the reveal of the chancel arch is anothe▮
matter. It is certainly not in order. Above the two l. shafts tw▮
blocks probably representing the familiar combined capita▮
and abacus chunks. Above these two mysterious blocks with ▮
kind of sunk keyhole top. In fact there is in the chancel N wal▮
a surviving keyhole window. So all this is probably pre▮
Norman, i.e. earlier than the Norman N and S doorways, the▮
former with zigzag, the latter with a small cross over. In the

nave N wall an exposed recess, and this at its foot on the r. has a small Norman volute capital. In the chancel S wall a C13 lancet window and an oblong low-side window. – SCREEN. With wide ogee arches and panel tracery over. – SCULPTURE. A fine small C13 King's head (S window reveal).

ome mid-C19 estate housing. The SCHOOL is indeed dated 1847.

MABLETHORPE
4080

T MARY. There were once two churches at Mablethorpe; but St Peter was swallowed by the sea in the time of Queen Elizabeth I. St Mary has an odd camel-back appearance, with a low W tower and chancel whose no doubt Victorian roof is just a little higher. The tower is in its upper part of C17 brick. The nave is of brick too, and the date 1714 on a preserved piece of timber with the names of churchwardens would suit it. Domestic straight-headed windows on the S side, much of the medieval stone-walling left on the N side. The chancel is in layers of boulders and bricks. It is recorded that Sir Roger de Montalt gave the site for the church in 1300. But the simple round-headed N doorway must be about a hundred years earlier, and the arcades also – four bays, octagonal piers, double-chamfered arches – might only just be 1300. The tower cuts into the arcades; so must be later. – FONT. Panelled stem, bowl of the pattern-book type. Six blank windows, Perp as well as Dec, with two blank tracery motifs in addition. – COMMUNION RAIL. Also dated 1714; yet in appearance entirely C17, and not late C17 either. – PLATE. Chalice, by *Wassell & Marriott*, 1825. – MONUMENTS. Tomb and Easter Sepulchre supposed to be of Thomas Fitzwilliam † 1494. The tomb-chest has three shields in quatrefoils. There were brasses against the back wall of an arched recess whose reveals and soffits are panelled. The arch is so shallow that it looks almost a horizontal line. Cresting with a quatrefoil frieze. – A HELM above. – BRASS to Elizabeth Fitzwilliam † 1522; an 18-in. figure.

MALTBY-LE-MARSH
4080

LL SAINTS. Of greenstone. The wide nave is of *c*.1300, see its windows with Y- and intersecting tracery. Such a window also occupied the centre of the W wall before the W tower was built. The mouldings of the surround and even the slot for the glazing are clearly visible. The tower, though unbuttressed, seems

to be Perp. Its arch, standing against the older w wall, ha
responds of concave-sided half-octagons. The chancel is tru
cated. A foundation is exposed to its E. The chancel arch di
into the imposts. – FONT. Octagonal; Perp. Against the ster
at the angles, four men with excessively standing-out hair (c
the four at Covenham St Bartholomew). Against the bowl fo
angels with spread wings. – COMMUNION RAIL. C18.
PLATE. Chalice, by *W.C.*, London, 1632; Paten, by *Emes &*
Barnard, 1816. – MONUMENT. Slender cross-legged Knigh
wearing chain-mail and a surcoat. His legs are convincingl
placed. Two angels by his pillow and l. and r. of his head tw
shapes like the arms of a stone seat. They are the part of th
armour called ailettes. At his feet two lions biting each othe
one with a prodigiously long tail. The date is *c.*1300.

BAPTIST CHAPEL, s of the Manor House. Founded in 169c
Simple brick box with hipped roof. The fenestration
evidently later, though the building might be as early as 169c

MANOR HOUSE. Georgian, of five bays and two and a ha
storeys.

A HOUSE close to the Crown Inn is dated 1720 and yet still has
C17 look, e.g. a straight-sided gable.

WINDMILL, ¾ m. NE. Tower-mill with cap and fan-tail.

MANBY

ST MARK. Of greenstone. Tall Perp w tower, the arch to th
nave with concave-sided semi-octagonal responds. Perp nav
windows. The chancel by *Sir A. Blomfield*, 1889. In the chance
however some re-used parts of the Perp roof, with two angel
and a boss. – FONT. Octagonal, with medieval faces against th
underside, but the decoration of the bowl with types of rosette
emphatically post-medieval. Is it C17? – SCULPTURE. A
impressive Late Anglo-Saxon slab, 26 by 19 in., with rop
moulding along the edges and a symmetrical pattern of inter
lace in figures of eight. Remarkably well preserved.

MANBY HALL. Of the Tudor house of the Welfitt family only a
few fragments remain. Also parts of C18 wings.

AIRFIELD. 1936–7 by *Q. Bullock*. Neo-Georgian. Extensive
buildings. Barracks; married quarters in terraces of cottages
The water-tower looks curiously like Terza Roma, or as if i
were taken out of a painting by De Chirico.

UPP HALL, ⅝ m. SW. Partly rebuilt in 1840. Five-bay, three-
storey front plus a porch and a pedimented window above.

MANTON

Γ HYBALD. 1861 by *Hooker & Wheeler*, small but done at some expense. Nave and chancel and thin s w porch tower with spire. Geometrical tracery, e.g. the fanciful w window. Inside the chancel twin s windows with a detached dividing shaft of polished marble.

OLD RECTORY, N of the church. A good c16 house. PB)

CLEATHAM HALL, ½ m. S. The surroundings now disparked. When Mr Maw lived here in 1802, his house was a plain Georgian box. Then the present STABLES were built by *William Fowler*, and in 1855 the house was rebuilt, perhaps by *J. M. Hooker*, with cement-faced façades broken up in a staccato way by heavy bracketed pediments and paired banded pilasters at the angles. The garden is of rich Victorian lushness.

CLEATHAM HOUSE, ½ m. S of Cleatham Hall. Georgian and later. An early c19 storehouse of five bays, three floors high, adjoins. A LODGE to the s w is dated 1813. It is of three by three bays with a pyramid roof and pointed windows. Stone with brick dressings.

RECTORY. By *J. M. Hooker* of Tunbridge Wells, 1854.

MAREHAM-LE-FEN   2060

ST HELEN. Of greenstone, quite big. The exterior is Victorian, of 1879. The w tower late c13 below (tower arch triple-chamfered and with some nailhead, according to Cox), Perp above. The s aisle Late Perp with pinnacles. Against the w pinnacle the small figure of a Knight, the costume late c14. Nice s doorway, one hollow with fleurons and heads. The N aisle also with pinnacles. The chancel early c14; also the chancel arch, but all victorianized (the E window e.g. is Victorian). c14 four-bay arcades, probably late c14 (see the bases of the piers) with octagonal piers, big nobbly leaves in the capitals, and double-chamfered arches. – FONT. Octagonal, Dec. Simple panels with low flat ogee arches, big finials, and heads at the top corners. – PLATE. Beaker, by *I.G.*, *c*.1665.

MAREHAM MANOR. The house is c19 and the gardens a ghost of what had been done for their embellishment early in the century by James Roberts. He erected huts resembling those of Tierra del Fuego, a country he had seen when he had accompanied Sir Joseph Banks, of near-by Revesby (*see* p. 341), on Cook's voyage. But these huts have unfortunately disappeared.

MAREHAM-ON-THE-HILL

ALL SAINTS. Of stone, painted white. Nave and chancel in one.
Tiny open bell-turret of wood. The church was restored in
1804: hence the arched windows, the pointed E window, the
two-decker PULPIT, and the BOX PEWS. – PLATE. Chalice
inscribed MAY·RINGE ON YE HEIL, Elizabethan.

MARKBY

ST PETER. Nave and chancel, no longer even a bellcote. The
church is thatched, that is the most interesting thing about it.
The windows all probably C17. Only the N doorway medieval,
round-arched and very modest. Inside, among ARCHITEC-
TURAL FRAGMENTS, there are some of the C13; especially the
chancel arch with dog-tooth, obviously not *in situ*. It comes
presumably from Markby Priory, a house of Augustinian
Canons founded probably in the C12. The little church is
fitted with BOX PEWS. – There is also a two-decker PULPIT.
The COMMUNION RAIL is three-sided. – PLATE. Chalice and
Paten, by *Wm. Shaw & Wm. Priest*(?), London, 1750.

CHRIST CHURCH, NE of St Peter. 1885, of corrugated iron, but
bravely Gothic, even with a sort of NW tower. The colour
scheme is battleship grey with pitch-pine. (Inside SEAT
designed by *Ewan Christian* for a church in Surrey. Kelly)

MARKET RASEN

ST THOMAS. Just N of the Market Place but separated from it
(at the time of writing) by a disgraceful shed with any old wood
– a sign how visually callous the citizens of English towns are.
The church has an ironstone W tower, very similar to that of
Yarburgh, which is of the early C15. The arch to the nave
(three continuous chamfers) looks c.1300, but there is documentary probability that the tower was built c.1405. Anyway
the W doorway and W window are Perp. The rest is externally
all of 1862, except for the interesting deep gable sheltering the
priest's doorway and the Late Norman S doorway with thin
shafts and three rolls in the round arch. Inside, the arcade
partly original (octagonal piers, double-chamfered arches), but
mostly 1862, as is the rest of the interior. – On the W wall of
the S aisle an INSCRIPTION (not *in situ*): Who so loces yis
work upon Pray for all yat yt bygon a patir nos(ter). – PLATE.
Silver-gilt Chalice and Paten Cover, by *D.G.*, London, 1630.

Flagon, by *Gurney & Co.*, 1740; Communion Set for the sick, by *Geo. Smith*(?), London, 1835.

HOLY ROOD (R.C.). In 1824 (GR) a simple church was built of white brick. It had arched windows, and its W front remains. The Presbytery to the E with its bargeboarded gable must be a later addition, perhaps of 1869, when *M. E. Hadfield & Son* added to the modest church a new S aisle with a dominant porch tower and a new N aisle. All this is of red brick, and the tower has a saddleback roof. The interior with its Early Christian allusions looks yet later.

Little is to be reported about the town. The most prominent building is the CENTENARY METHODIST CHAPEL of 1863, stone and red brick, with a tetrastyle Ionic portico and pediment. It looks up UNION STREET. By the river is an early C19 WAREHOUSE. In QUEEN STREET the CORN EXCHANGE by *Goddard* of 1854. Further E *James Fowler*'s GRAMMAR SCHOOL of 1862. No domestic building of any note.*

LYNWODE MANOR, ¼ m. W. 1883 by *C. G. Wray*. GS)

MARKET STAINTON

2080

ST MICHAEL. Greenstone. Old masonry but Victorian windows. They are in the Dec style, as the church was supposed to have been before restoration. The W tower was and is Perp, see e.g. the arch to the nave. The only noteworthy feature is the quadripartite rib-vault of the chancel, apparently of 1848, when the chancel was rebuilt. – PLATE. Chalice, by *James Sutton*, 1781.

MARSH CHAPEL

ST MARY. A large, unified, ashlar-faced, embattled, wealthy and unmysterious Perp church, clearly built all at one go, a type characteristic of the Marshland. The bells are called newly hung in 1420. The prosperity of the place is connected with salt workings mentioned throughout the Middle Ages. High, four-stage W tower. A big band above the doorway. High, four-light W window. Eight pinnacles. The aisles with three-light windows, the chancel four lights and to the E even five. Two-light clerestory windows. Handsome N doorway with ogee gable on head-stops and an inscription scroll round the little niche above it. The S doorway has alternating heads and fleurons, and also an inscription scroll up one hollow of its

* The TOWN HALL has recently been replaced by a modern-looking Co-op shop.

mouldings. Again an ogee gable on two head-stops. Again
niche, but this one supported by an angel. Four-bay arcade
inside. The octagonal piers have concave sides, high bases, an
embattled capitals. Double-chamfered, four-centred arches
The chancel arch is four-centred too. Tall tower arch with tw
continuous hollow chamfers. – SCREEN. Now in the towe
arch. A good piece, with cusped ogee arches and small pane
tracery. – PLATE. Chalice and Paten Cover, by *John Morle*
of Lincoln, 1569. – MONUMENT. Small alabaster tablet t
Walter Harpham † 1607. Tiny kneeling figures facing on
another; elaborate surround.

MARTIN-BY-HORNCASTLE
2060

ST MICHAEL. Norman s doorway, much repaired. One order c
shafts, arch with lozenge decoration and palmettes as part c
the lozenge pattern. Very narrow chancel arch, the respond
Norman. They have two orders of shafts, one with volute, th
other with scalloped capitals. The arch is steep and in it
mouldings E.E. It does not fit the responds, and the chance
arch must originally have been wider. Perhaps it was narrowe
to house the segmental REREDOS niche to the l. The E windov
probably also Norman, see the inner splays. To its l. a bracke
which is a late C12 waterleaf capital. Of the windows part of
s lancet seems in order. One N window has a surround mos
probably C17. – PLATE. Chalice, by *C.P.*, London, 1661.
MANOR HOUSE. The stables have an arcaded front and curve
screen walls to the E.

MARTON
8080

ST MARGARET. Essentially an C11 church, and rarely will on
see so consistent a use of herringbone coursing as in the towe
of Marton. But whether this is pre-1066 or post-1066, no-on
can say. The tower arch is too plain to help, the twin bell
openings sit above a set-off, and have Norman-looking capital
on their Saxon-looking mid-wall shafts. The C11 roof-line i
still visible against the tower, and there was a door high up
into the roof, in the Saxon way. The nave NW and SW quoin
do not tell anything either, and the chancel arch is, with it
strong roll mouldings and its nook-shafts and their old capitals
characterized by spoon-like depressions, Early Norman rathe
than Late Saxon. The chancel masonry is C11 too, thoug
exclusive of the E bay. Late Perp windows. Perp windows i

the aisles, the best in the s wall. Battlements everywhere, also
on the Perp s porch. Late C12 N arcade of two bays. Circular
pier, semicircular responds. Round arches with one slight
chamfer. Low capitals with leaf-crockets. The N chapel was
of two bays but has now only one. Simple E.E. details. The s
arcade also E.E., but different. Octagonal pier, keeled responds. Double-chamfered pointed arches. In the chancel s
wall a big niche with a pedestal for an image. – SCULPTURE.
Small Crucifixus (chancel N wall). With long, thin arms and
legs, the feet not yet nailed with one nail. That is a sign of a
pre-C13 date, but the proportions do not look so early. –
Fragments of a Saxon cross shaft with interlace (s aisle, w wall,
outside). – In the churchyard base and a considerable part of
the shaft of a CROSS. – PLATE. Fragments of a funeral Chalice
and Paten, C13; Chalice and Paten Cover, c.1569 (restored
1888).

The RECTORY HOUSE has a canted s bow and balcony probably
added in 1835 by *G. H. Rollett*, a builder.

THORNLEIGH. Georgian. Brick with stone quoins and stone-
faced basement.

MAVIS ENDERBY ₃₀₆₀

ST MICHAEL. The w tower mostly 1894. Nave and aisles over-
restored by *Fowler* in 1875, who then also contributed the
dormer windows. Chancel rebuilt in 1870. The N windows and
N doorway Dec, the s windows Dec and Perp. Pretty Perp s
doorway with fleurons in one of the continuous mouldings.
Low s arcade of four bays. Octagonal piers, arches with one
greenstone chamfer and one grey hollow chamfer. – In the s
porch a Norman PILLAR PISCINA on a quatrefoil shaft. –
FONT. Octagonal, with elementary ogee-arched panels. –
BENCH END. One; with poppy-head. – SCULPTURE. Three
angels from the roof. – Also a small German(?) relief of Christ
before Caiaphas. – PLATE. Paten, by *Thomas Langford*, 1785.

MELTON ROSS ₀₀₁₀

HOLY ASCENSION. 1867 by *Ewan Christian*. Nave and bellcote
and low broad apse with small windows, i.e. very dark inside.

MESSINGHAM ₈₀₀₀

HOLY TRINITY. E.E. N arcade of four bays. The piers round
or octagonal, the responds semicircular or keeled. Double-
chamfered arches. Dec s arcade of four bays. Quatrefoil piers

with fillets. Double-chamfered arches with broaches. D‹
straight-headed s aisle windows, that to the E with one reticul‹
tion unit and two half-units. The rest Perp, except for the lo
Georgian w tower. – STAINED GLASS. Many fragments co
lected in the early C19. They come from various places, e.‚
Laughton, Scotton, Kettlethorpe, Snarford, Scampto›
Malvern, Manchester. The finest piece is a C14 figure in the
window. Most of the other glass is C15 and early C16.
PLATE. Chalice and Paten Cover, by *John Morley* of Lincol›
1569; Paten, by *Emes & Barnard*, 1825.

0080

MIDDLE RASEN

ST PETER. Of ironstone. The s doorway and the chancel arc
are both Norman, and among the most impressive Norma‹
work in the county. The doorway is heavy going, but all th
more powerful. It has continuous mouldings only, an inne
zigzag, then a band of crenellation, the band itself being nearl
5 in. wide and 3 in. deep, and an outer band of beakhead. Th
chancel arch is improbably tall and flanked by large patera‹
an outer circle of beads, an inner of scallops, and a roun‹
recess as the hub. The arch itself is pointed and later. The ›
arcade is of about 1200. Three bays, semicircular respond
with nook-shafts, circular piers, octagonal abaci, arches wit›
divers rolls, one keeled. The N aisle externally by *Bellam›
& Hardy*, 1861. Tall Perp w tower, but the arch to the nav‹
proves an earlier beginning. Tall Perp s windows of three an‹
four lights. The arches straightened so that the windows reall›
have triangular heads. This s side of nave and chancel is embattled and has pinnacles. The priest's doorway is older, an‹
the Dec chancel N window and reticulated tracery comes fron
the demolished church of St Paul at Middle Rasen. – SCREEN
Tall, of three-light divisions, with cusped intersected arche‹
and panel tracery. – STAINED GLASS. Some fragments in the
chancel low-side window. – PLATE. Two Chalices and Pate›
Cover, by *John Morley* of Lincoln, 1569. – MONUMENT. Early
C14 effigy of a Priest on a low tomb-chest with plain quatrefoils. It was originally at St Paul. The priest lies under a
nodding gable, supported by little busts, holds a chalice, and
wears very ample, beautifully draped vestments.

3050

MIDVILLE

ST PETER. Dated 1819. Probably by *Jeptha Pacey*. w front with
pedimented gable and deep eaves. Pointed doorway, but an

octagonal, purely Georgian cupola. The side windows also pointed, their tracery Victorian. Short chancel. West gallery. – FONT. The base with its odd fluted corner motifs is dated 1663.

MININGSBY 3060

T ANDREW. Mostly by *James Fowler*, 1878 (greenstone, nave and chancel and double bellcote; lancet windows), but the S doorway Transitional, i.e. with a hood-mould still round, but a doorway with one slight chamfer and pointed, the window to its W Norman though entirely reconstructed, and the chancel, though called rebuilt by Fowler, original E.E. and apparently well preserved. Two lancets and an almond-shaped opening in the E wall, lancets and a pair of lancets in the side walls. This is taken down inside to form a sedile. The r. arm is simply marked by a chamfer of the corner. An arch to a chapel in the nave on the N side. – FONT. C14. The base has shafts with fleurons; against the underside grotesques. – SCREEN. Of two-light divisions, the lights round-arched with a super ogee arch over and panel tracery. – BENCH ENDS with poppy-heads in the chancel. – SCULPTURE. A slab with close Anglo-Saxon interlace, also in the chancel. – PLATE. Chalice and Paten Cover, inscribed 1569.

MINTING 1070

T ANDREW. 1863 by *Ewan Christian*. With a small bell-turret and spirelet on a W buttress. In the chancel medieval masonry. The style of fenestration Dec. The N arcade of three bays may make use of E.E. fragments. – SCULPTURE. A most rare and interesting cross shaft of the Anglo-Saxon type, but of *c.*1200. Two pieces both tapering from about $14\frac{1}{2}$ in. to about 12 in. Both with a border of nailhead. On one long, coarse, still Norman-looking trails, on the other finer, also still Norman foliage, but above it a Crucifixion in small figures, and Christ's feet nailed with one nail, which is Gothic and a feature unknown before the early C13. – PLATE. Chalice and Paten Cover, inscribed 1569.

MONKSTHORPE *see* GREAT STEEPING

MOORBY 2060

ALL SAINTS. By *Fowler*, 1866. Stone with brick bands. Lancet windows. Small NW turret with slated spire. Interior brick-faced. To the vestry a three-bay opening, the arches supported

on marble shafts, two deep. – FONT. Square, chamfere
Against the sides a Virgin with Sun and Moon l. and r., s
kneeling figures, a seated figure, and a cadaver and two figu
(one an angel) attending to it. – SCULPTURE. In the vestry
small stone panel with a man playing the bagpipes and tw
women and a man dancing; first half of the C16. – PLAT
Paten, by *John Stocker*, 1712.

MOORHOUSES
2050

1¾ m. WSW of New Bolingbroke

ST LAWRENCE. 1875 by *James Fowler* (GR). Small, red bric
nave and chancel in one, lancet windows, wooden bell-turr
with spirelet.

MOORTOWN HOUSE *see* SOUTH KELSEY

MORTON
8090

1 m. N of Gainsborough

ST PAUL. By *Micklethwaite*, 1891, but dull externally. Insid
prettily painted ceilings in nave and transept. – STAINE
GLASS. By *Morris & Co.* (*Burne-Jones*), much, from 1891 in
the C20.

MORTON HOUSE, E of the church. Late Georgian; rendere
Centre of five bays and two storeys with top balustrade and
porch of unfluted Ionic columns. To the l. and r. one mo
bay, flush on the ground floor but recessed above. On th
ground floor a tripartite arrangement of two unfluted Ion
columns and the rest all glazed.

MORTON HALL. Georgian, of brick, five bays with the fir
floor middle window minimum-Venetian, a lunette windo
over, and a pedimental gable. Neglected at the time of writing
– The STABLES behind the Hall are of brick also and have
pediment and the usual lantern.*

A nice bit of village close to the river Trent by the corner o
TRENTSIDE.

MUCKTON
3080

HOLY TRINITY. The church has an impressive Norman chance
arch of blackish greenstone. The arch has zigzag, varied abac

---

* According to E. J. Willson, the antiquary *William Weston* 'built tw
elegant small villas' here (Colvin).

and untidy shallow motifs (cf. Burwell nearby). From this arch *Fowler* took his cue when he had to rebuild the church in 1878–9. So it is a Norman Revival church, at a time when that style was not popular. Nave with bellcote and chancel. The E end has a rose window, but at the W end the Norman breaks down, see especially the shape of the buttress. – FONT. Octagonal, Perp, with simple arched panels, but though all are simple, all are different. – PLATE. Chalice, Paten, and Flagon, by *T.L.*, 1637.

MUMBY

5070

ST THOMAS. The earliest parts of the church are the arcades, first N, then S, both C13 and both with double-chamfered arches. The NW respond is still purely Norman (scalloped capital), and the N piers are circular with elementary upright stiff-leaf capitals and circular abaci. The S capitals are much freer stiff-leaf varieties, the abaci are octagonal and the E respond is keeled. On the N side the hood-mould stops still include one of the long-snouted Norman monsters. Another is a beast devouring a man's head. The S side has leaf stops and dog-tooth on the hood-moulds themselves. These two arcades are three bays long, but a fourth was added on both sides shortly after, and the chancel arch goes with this. The chancel itself is of 1874. The S doorway on the other hand belongs to the earlier parts of the S arcade. It is nice, with its two orders of shafts, the dog-tooth band between them, the stiff-leaf capitals, and the dog-tooth in the arch. Dec N aisle windows (reticulation in the E window). Perp W tower, quite stately. This is of ashlar, the E.E. clerestory with pairs of small lancets of greenstone. – FONT. Dec, octagonal. Tall bowl, and in each panel a different motif of flowing tracery, set between thin buttress shafts. Most of the motifs are familiar from windows, but one or two are pure fancy. – SCREEN. With fine two-light divisions consisting of a Y and cusped ogees in either half of the Y. Coving and loft are not original. – BENCH ENDS. Some tracery now used in the chancel seats. – PLATE. Chalice and Paten Cover, by *John Morley* of Lincoln, 1569.

NETTLEHAM

0070

ALL SAINTS. The three-bay arcades differ in a telling way between bay one and bays two and three. The latter are sumptuous E.E., in the Lincoln Cathedral style. Responds of three detached shafts, pier hexagonal with six detached shafts.

Fine, mature, lively stiff-leaf capitals. Double-chamfer
arches. The w bay, separated by an indication of the former
wall, is an addition made shortly after. The responds are sem:
circular, the capitals rather elementarily moulded. This is t'
same in the arch of the w tower towards the nave, though t'
arch here has a roll as well as two chamfers. The w tower
embraced by the aisles, and the arches towards these a
simpler. The w bay of the s aisle has been pulled down. Tl
tower has externally flat clasping buttresses, a w lancet,
lancet over, and tall twin bell-openings, amply shafted, i.e.
c13. The clerestory is Perp, but on the N side it is clear
recognizable that there was an E.E. clerestory of circul:
(probably foiled) windows above the spandrels, not the apexe
below (cf. Spalding). E.E. also the doorway into the s aisl
with two orders of shafts, stiff-leaf on long stalks on tl
capitals, and a steep triple-chamfered arch. The doorway mu
be re-set, as the original width of the aisle can be seen in the
wall. The aisle windows and chancel windows are all Victoria
As for the chancel, it was restored and lengthened in 1882 l
Bodley & Garner and then received its large Dec window
with flowing tracery. But the chancel arch, though also muc
restored, is original and E.E. Like the arcade responds, it ha
three detached shafts, but on semicircular bases. The decor:
tion of the nave roof can perhaps be attributed to Bodley.
COMMUNION RAIL. C17. – PAINTING. On the nave wal
scrolls, chequer, and powdered flowers. Is this c13?
STAINED GLASS. In the N aisle w window an unusually goo
single light by *Kempe*: St Francis and the Birds. It dates fro:
1883. – In the NW window also *Kempe* glass, *c*.1898. – PLATI
Chalice, London, 1568; Processional Cross of brass, by *I*
Wynants, 1721. – MONUMENT. Dorothy Nethercootes † 160:
Simple stone tablet with bald strapwork; quite big.

BISHOP'S PALACE. The palace was demolished in 1630, an
only grassy mounds remain.

The village is bisected by a stream with the Green NE of th
church. Only the WHITE HART, w of the church, deserve
notice, mid-Georgian, with moulded stone surrounds to th
windows, brick quoins, and a Venetian window with octagona
glazing bars.

NETTLEHAM HALL, 1½ m. NW. Gutted by fire, and only three
quarters of the Georgian stone shell remains. The ENTRANCI
GATES with C19 piers come from the demolished church o
St Peter-at-Arches, Lincoln. This was designed by *Francis* o

William Smith, c.1720–4, who presumably also designed this ironwork. The gates were given to the church at Lincoln by Lord Scarbrough. *James Gibbs* made a design for gates for Lord Scarbrough.* Could they have been these?

ETTLEHAM FIELDS. Late Georgian, with six flattish Venetian windows.

NETTLETON

1000

t JOHN BAPTIST. Of ironstone. The w tower Saxon, but with a Norman w doorway and s window with deep inner splay, hidden behind a buttress, cut out at its back to allow light to get into the tower. Tall Norman tower arch, the arch moulding one half-roll and one hollow. The rest of the church by *Fowler*, 1874, after a rebuilding had already taken place in 1805. – PLATE. Chalice, by *I. E.*, London, 1630.

NEW BOLINGBROKE

3050

t PETER. 1854 by *S. S. Teulon* (who also designed the VICARAGE behind). Brick and stone and some black brick. Late C13 to early C14 style. Nave and chancel. In the corner between chancel and vestry a savagely busy tower with spire. Inside the building it is corbelled out and out.

RESCENT. In 1824 John Parkinson built a factory at New Bolingbroke, 120 ft long. It was to weave crepes and bombazines. For his workmen he built this crescent, a six-bay centre of two and a half storeys and wings continuing it on the curve of six bays either side. The date is confirmed by the small METHODIST CHAPEL, 1825. Straight terraces of cottages also further N and S.

NEW HOLLAND

0020

HRIST CHURCH. 1901 by *C. Hodgson Fowler*. Decidedly Methodist-looking. Red brick with brick windows and a short NE tower.

he later C19 development around the ferry to Hull caused speculative building. An example just N of the church is the YARBOROUGH ARMS and the houses between this and the church, laid out round three sides of a grassed square. Eight–eighteen–eight bays.

NEW LEAKE see EASTVILLE

* Ashmolean Museum, Oxford.

0000
NEWSTEAD PRIORY FARM
1¾ m. s of Brigg

One room in the farmhouse is a vaulted room of the Gilbertin
priory founded in 1171. It is two-naved with groin-vault
Corbels on the N, S, and W walls. Two octagonal piers wit
simple capitals. The room originally continued to the E. It
most probably part of the refectory. The SW quoins ar
original too. Above it, in the W wall, a three-light Perp window

0080
NEWTON BY TOFT
1 m. SE of Toft next Newton

ST MICHAEL. Mostly 1860 by *James Fowler*. Nave and chance
and bellcote. Early Norman chancel arch. Plainly chamfered
imposts, unmoulded arch. Of a former N aisle the E.E. arcad
of three bays is still recognizable. – PLATE. Chalice, by *Joh*
Morley of Lincoln, *c*.1569. – MONUMENTS. Two miniatur
effigies of stone, late C13, a Civilian and a Lady, he 29 in., sh
24 in. long. On his slab the name William, on hers Helaine

8070
NEWTON-ON-TRENT

ST PETER. Norman S wall much interfered with. One window
the big quoin stones, and the masonry with thick morta
joints remains. E.E. the W tower and the N arcade. The towe
has a W doorway with stiff-leaf capitals and deep moulding
in the arch, also an E.E. W window (the top is later) and
double-chamfered arch to the nave. The arcade (of three bays
has beautiful piers, quatrefoil with keeled foils and slendere
round shafts in the diagonals, stiff-leaf capitals of severa
varieties, and double-chamfered arches. The leaves are up
right, or diagonal, in a narrower or a broader band, or diagona
with much interweaving of the stalks.* The chancel looks Lat
Georgian inside (probably 1828), Victorian outside. The r
aisle was rebuilt in 1876. – BENCH ENDS. Traceried straight
topped ends now under the tower. – PLATE. Chalice an
Paten Cover, by *John Morley*(?), *c*.1571; Paten, by *Wn*
*Paradise, c.*1718.

In the HIGH STREET just two houses of note: No. 30, red brick
stone dressings, and dated 1724, and Nos 38–40, L-shaped
with shaped gables to the longer wing. There is a steep
pediment on the N side with a date 1695.

* Canon Binnall points out the easternmost capitals as outstandingly fin
and suggests that all this may be the work of a cathedral mason.

ECTORY. Red brick, Gothic, 1864, by *Michael Drury*.

UNHAM TOLL BRIDGE. Built in 1837. Three cast-iron arches on stone piers.

NORMANBY-BY-SPITAL

0080

T PETER. Externally some indication of a Norman original: the E arch of the unbuttressed W tower (plain chamfered imposts, unmoulded arch; but the bell-openings with bar tracery are late C13), and also the blocked N doorway, the N aisle W window, and the NW quoins starting with one enormous upright stone. The N arcade is indeed Norman. Three bays, circular piers, square abaci, beautiful capitals with big crockets, their borders all frilly. Bases with spurs, arches round with a slight chamfer. The S arcade was built later, say *c*.1230. Circular piers and circular abaci, good stiff-leaf capitals. The chancel arch was made at the same time, though the leaves of the capitals are a little thinner. In the S wall of the chancel a two-light window with bar tracery like the bell-openings of the tower. In the N wall of the chancel blocked opening with a segmental arch. Perp clerestory of two bays. To the E of the chancel the foundations of an apse. Are they Norman?

NORMANBY-ON-THE-WOLDS

1090

ST PETER. On the bare top of the wolds, about 500 ft up, not in what one thinks of as a Lincolnshire landscape. E.E. W tower with twin bell-openings, heightened Perp and given new bell-openings. Low tower arch, really just a doorway. S doorway E.E. and one S window with plate tracery. The rest outside 1868 by *James Fowler*. The interior is surprising. There are N and S arcades, the latter mostly by Fowler, but with old parts and anyway identical with the former. There is first an octagonal pier, but the double-chamfered arches stand only partly on it. The outer arch is supported by a corbel with a trumpet curve. The second arch dies against a square pier only slightly chamfered, i.e. a piece of wall left standing. Then follows a third arch, also dying, and there is in addition an arch across the aisle as if leading to a transept or chapel, and this dies into the pier but stands on a big rude head corbel on the S side. It represents a man holding his mouth open with one hand, while the other touches his forehead, or perhaps supports the corbel (cf. Claxby next door). – FONT. Perp (Dec?) drum, with a wavy band, a band of saltire crosses, and between them a wide band of quatrefoils. – STAINED GLASS. In a chancel S

window by *Kempe*, 1897 (from Claxby). – PLATE. Parcel-g
Chalice, by *T.B.*, London, 1636; Flagon, by *Langlands*
Robertson, 1785.

LONG BARROW, in the w corner of the former Swinho
Park. The barrow, which is in a fine state of preservation,
orientated NE–SW, with a length of 128 ft and a breadth a
height of 53 ft and 7 ft respectively at the NE end.

8010 ## NORMANBY PARK
1¼ m. NE of Flixborough

The house of the Sheffields near here, or at East Butterwick (s
p. 67), may have been designed by *Robert Smithson*.* On tl
present site was a plain mid-Georgian house, and here tl
family lived until 1820, when *Sir Robert Smirke* built the hou:
as it now stands. The design typifies Smirke's 'cubic' styl
It is an essay in intersecting cubes. The w front with slight
projecting two-storey wings, each with a tripartite window an
a balustraded parapet. Between them a higher three-bay, thre
storey centre with tapered windows to the lower floors and
porch of paired unfluted Ionic columns. On the s front tl
single outer bays are the returns from the w and s sides respe
tively, and a three-storey pavilion composition rises out of tl
body of the house with two of its bays slightly projecting. Thr
the bay order around the house is 1–3–1, and 1–1–2–1–
Smirke's treatment of the attic is masterly, and his use c
decorative detail remarkably restrained. *Walter H. Brierley*
wing of 1906 (part of which has recently been demolished) :
assertive in a Neo-Georgian Baroque, yet of superb qualit
and craftsmanship. In the hall are Brierley's fluted Ionic scree
and Smirke's stairs, one flight up and two back. Fine cast-iro
balustrade with capitals. To Smirke also can be attributed tl
design of the splendid series of marble chimneypieces, execute
perhaps by one of the *Westmacott*s.
In the village of Normanby a number of identical ESTAT
COTTAGES, four bays and one storey. One of them is date
1805. Recent estate cottages are in the Garden Suburb styl

9070 ## NORTH CARLTON

CHURCH. Perp w tower. The rest of 1771–3. With arche
windows, a high parapet, and an apse. Coved ceiling inside. ·

* There are plans for Sir John Sheffield in the Smithson Collection at tl
RIBA, and a sketch, perhaps of this early house, shows a towering façade i
Smithson's style.

Polygonal baluster FONT. – COMMUNION RAIL with slim turned balusters, the centre part curving forward. – PLATE. Chalice and Paten Cover, *c.*1580; Paten, by *E. G.*, London, 1676; Flagon, London, 1676.

ORTH CARLTON HALL. Elizabethan, L-shaped, with the main front on the s. Gabled, with mullioned and transomed windows and a two-storey porch set asymmetrically.

NORTH COATES   *3000*

r NICHOLAS. 1865 by *James Fowler*. The w tower in a coarse E. E., with octagonal parapet and pyramid roof. In the rebuilding of the rest of the church old masonry was used. The surviving medieval parts are all E. E., namely the small s doorway, the three-bay N arcade with quatrefoil piers and cruciform abaci, the s arcade with keeled quatrefoiled piers, and the chancel arch. The original arches are all double-chamfered, and the chancel arch responds and the SE respond have headcorbels. – FONT. Upper half of a C13 bowl, mostly with flatly carved intersected arches but also two foliated crosses.

m. WSW of North Coates, at Thoresby Lodge, by the LOUTH NAVIGATION a brick warehouse.

NORTH COCKERINGTON   *3090*

r MARY. The church lies in the same churchyard with St Adelwold Alvingham, and in fact a little nearer the village of Alvingham. Both are approached the homely way through a farmyard. Nave and chancel and a SW tower. In the nave windows with intersecting tracery, i.e. *c.*1300. In the chancel on the N side a small Saxon window with a little moulding in the headstone. The s arcade of two bays is late C12. Circular pier, square abacus, double-chamfered arches. The chancel arch seems E. E. – A complete set of BOX PEWS. – MONUMENT. Alabaster effigy of a Knight, later C14, sadly mutilated. No head, no legs, but the lion with a wondrous long tail survives.

NORTH ELKINGTON   *2090*

r HELEN. 1851–2 by *S. S. Teulon*. Very short; nave and chancel in one. Was an additional chancel intended? Steep roof; bellcote. The windows mostly lancets. None of Teulon's perversities. The charming idea of copying the refectory pulpit at Tupholme for his PULPIT cannot be called a perversity.

What it amounts to is that the incumbent ascends the pulp
by a twin-arched passage in the wall. – LECTERN. Iron, tran
parent, with big leaves; a fine piece. Made in 1854. – PLA
(also of South Elkington). Paten, London, 1704; Pla
London, 1748.

NORTH KELSEY

oooo

ST NICHOLAS. Short W tower with small bell-openings of pai
of lancets. The W doorway seems earlier but is interfere
with.* In the nave S wall quite a large Norman slab wi
closely set horizontal zigzag. What can it have been? It is to
big to be part of a tympanum. Can there have been zigzag wa
decoration (cf. e.g. the Bristol Chapter House)? Most of th
church is of c.1860, notably the N arcade with its ill-chose
marble shafts. – MONUMENT. In the chancel a coffin-lid wit
a foliated cross, but foliations also richly branching out of th
cross shaft. The cross stands on two dragons. The most like
date is the mid C13.

W of the church a nice whitewashed HOUSE with black trin
symmetrical, bargeboarded, hood-moulded Neo-Tudor.

NORTH KILLINGHOLME

1010

ST DENIS. We must start with the bafflingly sumptuous towe
arch. Norman, with many-scalloped capitals and roll mould
ings. The lower masonry of the tower may in fact well b
Norman. The top is Perp and ashlar-faced. In the chance
chamfered, round-headed priest's doorway and two lancets i
the E wall, i.e. c.1200. But the chancel S windows are of c.130
(intersecting tracery, and an arch upon two arches). Dec the
aisle exterior with intersecting tracery in the W, reticulate
tracery (almost entirely unrestored) in the E window. But th
S and N arcades are Perp. Four bays, octagonal piers, double
chamfered arches. And what can be the date of the clerestor
windows? C17? C18? – BENCH END. Just one, identical wit
those at East Halton. Simple tracery, castellated top.

MANOR HOUSE. Probably Tudor and still partly moated. Th
N–S wing is relatively intact. In the S front of the W–E win
three shields set in panels separated by little brick shafts. Eac
panel has a trefoil-cusped brick top – like the trefoil-cuspin
of the late C15 brick friezes in East Anglia. The motif i

* And in the Nattes drawing the W bell-opening looks Saxon or Norman
but damaged.

repeated in the same front a little further E, and a single panel
is set in the Victorian porch. Some windows have brick drip
moulds.

NORTH ORMSBY   2090

ST HELEN. By *Teulon*, 1848. Nave and chancel; bellcote on the
W gable. Late C13 details. Entry by a W porch perversely
squeezed between the buttresses. – FONT. Octagonal, Perp,
with quatrefoils and one shield. – MONUMENT. Urn on
pedestal, E of the church, to John Ansell † 1797 and his wife
† 1808. Soanian details and a sans-serif inscription on the urn.
An exceptional piece.

ORMSBY ABBEY. The house is Victorian. Against the hill, just
S of the house under some trees, stands the WHITE LADY, a
Late Roman figure with an aura of mystery. She has become
the patroness of the valley.

NORTHORPE   8090

ST JOHN BAPTIST. Impressive Norman three-bay arcades, S
and N. Round piers, the bases with spurs, the flat capitals with
varieties of scallop and also one with leaf. Unmoulded round
arches. The blocked chancel N doorway apparently also
Norman. The arcade was lengthened to the W, at some time
probably late in the C12. The bay is wider and higher and has
an arch with a slight chamfer. Fine late C13 chancel N and S
windows of three lights with three circles over, two cinquefoiled, the third quatrefoiled. The chancel E window is Late
Perp. Nice minor doorway into the S aisle, Dec. Hood-mould
with ballflower and fleurons. Perp W tower, Perp clerestory
and nave roof with bosses. – SOUTH DOOR. C14. With tracery
and a border of leaf trail. – COMMUNION RAIL. Flat balusters,
Jacobean. – BELL. – PLATE. Chalice, Elizabethan.

NORTHORPE HALL. Near by stand the ruins, in eminently
picturesque decay, of the earlier house. They are mostly C16
and undistinguished. In 1875 *G. H. Goldsmith* designed the
new house in a Norman Revival style. But his is not the powerful Revival style of, say, Hopper. Northorpe is really just a
case of applied Romanesque gimmicks. Splayed-out NE angle,
doorway on colonnettes, etc. The inside is a better interpretation of the Revival. Corridor ceiling with a pattern of squares
and bosses, and arcaded stair hall.

VICARAGE. Also by *Goldsmith*, and also of 1875.

NORTH OWERSBY

ST MARTIN. Built in 1762–3 of medieval masonry. Very plai[n]
Tall nave, thin w tower with flat pyramid roof, apse. Of iro[n]
stone. The flat Venetian tracery in the windows is of 1888 an[d]
was no doubt intended as an improvement. – Baluster FONT. –
PLATE. Paten and Flagon, London, 1676; Chalice, by C.C[,]
London, 1702.

NORTH RESTON

ST EDITH. Nave and chancel and bell-turret. By *Wither[s]*
1868–9, but with medieval parts. The masonry of greensto[ne]
is Early Norman – see the renewed windows in the nave N an[d]
s and the chancel arch, unmoulded on single-chamfered im[-]
posts. Before Withers the church went through a period whe[n]
it had a Venetian window at the E end and a cupola at the [w]
end. – FONT. Octagonal, Perp, with on each side three cuspe[d]
niches and above them, as tracery, six tiny ones. – PLAT[E]
Chalice and Paten Cover, by *I.P.*, London, 1569; Paten, b[y]
Sarah Holaday, 1741.

NORTH RESTON HALL. Partly Georgian, partly Victoria[n.]
Quite informal, except for a nice porch with fluted Ioni[c]
columns.

NORTH SOMERCOTES

ST MARY. A large Marshland church, much rebuilt in the lat[e]
C17. Unbuttressed w tower, E.E. (see the bell-openings) bu[t]
with a tall C14 tower arch (two chamfers, dying into the im[-]
posts) and a former quadripartite rib-vault inside. E.E. als[o]
the two chancel doorways. Their position shows that th[e]
chancel is shorter now than it originally was. And E.E. clearl[y]
the three w bays of the six-bay arcades. They have roun[d]
piers and round abaci, but their plinths show a heightenin[g]
when – in the C14? – the other three bays were made. Th[e]
piers of these are octagonal, the arches are all double-cham[-]
fered. Is the handsome s doorway with its capitals as a ban[d]
of nobbly foliage also C14? Dec in any case the N aisle window[s]
even if they are very renewed. The w window is a quatrefo[il]
in a circle. In the chancel a pretty shelf with fleurons and tw[o]
minute heads. – FONT. Octagonal, Perp, big. Shields i[n]
cusped fields, but in one the Christ of the Resurrection. –
SCREEN. Dado of the screen at the E end of the s aisle. Th[e]
panels are painted alternately green and red. – BENCH ENDS
Plain; with poppy-heads.

OCKSLEY HALL, ½ m. s. A much restored house, perhaps basically c16. Notable for its collection of STAINED GLASS. This includes two c14 panels from St Peter Mancroft at Norwich, an archangel of *c.*1425 from the bishop of Lincoln's palace at Buckden, an early c14 roundel, an English c15 saint, some c15 armorial panels, and much c16 to c17 glass.

NORTH THORESBY   *2090*

ST HELEN. Mostly E.E. The W tower has a W lancet and bell-openings with a lozenge above the two lights. Low tower arch with a little nailhead and whorls as hood-mould stops. Eight Perp pinnacles. Chancel s window, all smallish lancets, first a pair, then two singles. E.E. s arcade (the aisle pulled down). Quatrefoiled, keeled piers, double-chamfered arches with little broaches in the form of half dog-teeth. s doorway with thin keeled doubled nook-shafts. N arcade of round piers and round abaci. Dec however the N aisle windows, with intersecting and reticulated tracery. – BENCH ENDS. Of about 1530–5, with plenty of initials of those who gave them and with poppy-heads. One of the latter is a frontal female bust in a roundel instead. – SCULPTURE. Late Anglo-Saxon interlace slab, figure of eight (nave w). – STAINED GLASS. Three small c15 figures (N aisle w). – PLATE. Chalice and Paten Cover, by *T.B.*, London, 1655.

NORTH WILLINGHAM   *1080*

ST THOMAS. Late Georgian, of W tower, nave, and lower chancel. The nave has arched windows, the chancel a Venetian E window. But the w tower is medieval – see the w window surround and the arch to the nave still visible inside the tower. Also, the rest of the church may still have its medieval lowest course of masonry. The top part of the tower Victorian, probably of 1895. The interior with a flat ceiling and a quite pretty WEST GALLERY.

WILLINGHAM HOUSE. Built in 1790 for the Boucherett family. Its neo-classical quality proclaims a London architect.* It stands prominently in flat fields and is now committed to some utilitarian purpose and forlornly decaying. Only two fronts are worth reading. That to the s of seven bays and two storeys, cement-faced with stone quoins and strings. Its forte is the

---

* Perhaps *Robert Mitchell*, whose style at Silwood Park, Berks (1796), is close to Willingham.

grand tetrastyle Ionic portico, unfluted with lovely *Coade* ston·
capitals. The portico wall pilastered and with arched groun·
floor windows. Round the corner on the w front two bow·
and, between, three bays of windows with four giant Ioni·
pilasters carrying a pediment. Another bow to the E. The hal·
occupies two storeys with the stair around three side·
Wrought-iron balustrade. Nice plaster ceiling. In one room
some more neo-classical decoration.

NORTON PLACE *see* BISHOP NORTON

OLD BOLINGBROKE

Bolingbroke in the Middle Ages was a market town. The mano·
came to John of Gaunt in 1363, and Henry IV was born here i·
1367 and took his name from the castle.

ST PETER AND ST PAUL. At first a confusing church, but th·
confusion ceases when one accepts that John of Gaunt buil·
the major part of the church. It now consists of a NW tower·
a wide nave to its s without a separate chancel, and a narro·
Victorian N aisle (by *James Fowler*, 1890). This N aisle replace·
a nave and chancel attached to what was a W tower. John o·
Gaunt then added a lavish s aisle, which is now nave an·
chancel. In doing so, he followed the example of the Willough·
bys at Spilsby. The church is of greenstone. The tower is Per·
and carries eight pinnacles by *Fowler*. The present nave ha·
large windows with exuberant flowing tracery, over-restored·
the best in this part of the county, three lights to the s, four t·
the w, five to the E. They have heads as label-stops outside a·
well as inside. The s doorway has shafts with fillets, small lea·
capitals, and heads as label-stops. Above the doorway a quatre·
foil niche for an image. The bust corbel of this is all tha·
remains. The N arcade is of four bays with tall, slim piers·
their mouldings continuous with the arches. They are of fou·
shafts with fillets and four thin shafts with fillets in th·
diagonals. Sedilia with shafts set diagonally, leaf capitals·
nodding ogee canopies, little vaults, buttress-shafts, and muc·
crocketing. To the l. and r. of the E window inside traces o·
chopped-off niches. All this is Dec at its height, yet – if John o·
Gaunt is responsible – would be of as late a date as *c.*1365–70·
– STAINED GLASS. W window by *Kempe & Tower.* – MONU·
MENT. In the churchyard E of the church column to Edwar·
B. Bosanquet † 1848 aged four months. On the column smal·

relief of a rose and a knife, on top of the column two cherubs' heads facing W and E.

CASTLE. Only the mounds remain. The castle goes back to William de Roumare, first Earl of Lincoln, i.e. the C11. Its rounded earthwork and polygonal masonry plan suggest that it was originally a palisaded platform of no great height, and that it was given masonry defences only at a comparatively late date. The site is very suitable for wet defences, and a lake covered the whole S side. The castle was much enlarged in the C14 and again in the Elizabethan period and slighted in 1643–4. The gatehouse stood up longer than the rest but collapsed in 1815. Excavations are highly desirable.

E of the church a Georgian house of three bays with four Venetian windows and a thin porch. At the E exit BOLING-BROKE HOUSE, with a medievalizing part of about 1810. It consists of three polygonal projections, the middle one of three storeys with two turret-like chimneystacks, the side parts of two storeys and castellated. A builder's job but a lively one. At the S exit a Late Georgian three-bay house with a slightly gothicizing doorway: clustered shafts instead of pilasters or columns.

OLD CLEE   2000

HOLY TRINITY. Anglo-Saxon W tower. The W doorway has the typical blocks serving for capital and abacus together. The arch (and also the tall tower arch with its Norman-type imposts) has double voussoirs. Twin bell-openings with mid-wall shaft. The top of the tower is Perp, with nicely concave-sided battlements and eight pinnacles. The rest of the cruciform church is externally mostly new, but some of the lancets of the transepts are old, and the arches of the crossing tower as such of course are. Internally the story of the church is intricate and instructive. The Saxon nave was given aisles in the C12, but apparently in at least three stages; first on the N, and curiously enough not immediately E of the tower. The result is two bays, even more curiously, not with a pier but with two pairs of responds. They are quadruple-shafted, and have flat scalloped capitals with some modest decoration and triple rolls in the arches. Then followed, again with responds, the W bay, more ambitiously Norman, with zigzag and lozenge decoration in the arch and one of the familiar long-snouted label-stop beast-heads (cf., e.g., Malmesbury). The S arcade is of two bays with a circular pier with circular abacus and an arch decorated differently (pellets, billets, twisted rope). The arches have quadruple rolls. Then, and this is so special interesting, the crossing, transepts, and chancel were done apparently as one build. The style resembles that of St James Grimsby. There is a dedication inscription on the Norman pier. It refers to the function performed by St Hugh, Bishop of Lincoln, in 1192, the year when he began his new choir at the cathedral. So it can clearly not refer to the s arcade and must refer to the E parts. It makes them earlier than one would have thought, and yet they have absolutely nothing to do with the work at the cathedral. On the contrary, in some features such as the thick rolls in the arches they seem to continue the character of the arcades, which, after all, cannot have been more than ten or twenty years old when the *novum opus* began. The crossing arches have triple responds to N and keeled (and the same for the arch between N aisle and transept) triple responds rounded to E and W with a middle fillet (and the same for the arch between s aisle and transept). There are small differences between N and s. The s has dog-tooth up the hollow between the shafts, the N has not. And why are the capitals to E and W placed just a little lower than those to N and s? E.E. work is full of such inconsistencies, as is for that matter Norman work. – FONT. Norman, of tub-shape, with a rope band at the top.

CLEE HALL FARM. C17. L-shaped, with shaped gables containing circular blank lights.

OLD WOODHALL *see* WOODHALL

4060

ORBY

ALL SAINTS. Greenstone. Mainly Perp, but one lancet in the nave on the N side and one Dec s window in the chancel, which was rebuilt in 1888. The clerestory has six closely-set windows each side, not only on the s side, where there is an aisle, but also on the N side. The s porch is of brick, Jacobean. s arcade piers of an unusual moulding repeated in the arch: one hollow chamfer and one wave. Of the church preceding the present, witness is a most curious stone (s aisle w) which consists of a Norman capital with decorated scallops attached to a respond block, and this same respond block later partly carved into an E.E. capital upside down, so that then the Norman capital must have disappeared in the wall. – FONT. Octagonal, Perp, plain.

ORMSBY HALL see SOUTH ORMSBY

OWMBY

0080

2 m. NNW of Spridlington

ST PETER AND ST PAUL. Unbuttressed Norman W tower, see the arch to the nave. Higher up the details are E.E. Very crude N arcade of three bays, *c*.1200. Round piers, square but chamfered abaci, capitals with big stiff-leaves. Pointed double-chamfered arches. E.E. chancel, see the base and part of a keeled shaft in the vestry which probably come from the chancel arch, and also the E window of three lights with flat Geometrical tracery of foiled circles. Of the same date the N aisle, according to the E window. Intersecting tracery, the mullions with nice filleted shafts. Can the N window with bar tracery also be trusted? – PLATE. Chalice by *Richard Gurney & Thomas Cook*, 1742.

OWSTON FERRY

8000

ST MARTIN. Perp W tower, ashlar-faced. The hood-mould of the W window has on the l. a pretty group of two figures as a stop. Perp S porch with parapet decorated by blind quatrefoils. Nice S doorway with square hood-mould. Three-light Perp S windows. In the chancel also, on the S side, irregular Perp two-light windows. To the N a very different view – all yellow brick of 1840, though the old N aisle windows, identical with those of the S aisle, were re-used. The interior again very different. Four-bay arcades. The S arcade Dec with quatrefoil piers with fillets and small nailhead in the abaci. The N arcade Transitional between Dec and Perp. The piers also quatrefoil, but the foils connected by deep hollows. That is Dec, but the octagonal abaci are Perp. Also typical bell-shaped bases like those of the Perp tower arch. The nave ceiling has big tracery motifs. It looks Late Georgian, yet is as early as 1780 (Stonehouse). – STAINED GLASS. E window, three figures, 1836, by *J. H. Nixon* and *T. Ward*. – S aisle E by *Ward & Hughes*, 1861. – MONUMENTS. Several effigy-less Gothic tablets, notably J. Littlewood † 1821 and Edward Peart † 1824. – The churchyard GATEWAY is tripartite, of stone, and quite monumental. It looks with its black-letter inscriptions *c*.1830, but is not mentioned by Stonehouse (1839). So perhaps it is of 1840, like the parts mentioned above.

CASTLE, S of the church. The church itself may occupy the bailey of this 'castle of the Isle' (of Axholm). It was probably

dismantled in 1095, but was refortified in 1174 and lost t
Henry II by the Mowbrays in the same year. The motte ha
plainly been deliberately slighted.

CENTENARY METHODIST CHAPEL, ½ m. E, set back. 183⁊
Of brick, three bays, arched windows, but the upper midd⎰
window of the Venetian type.

BOURNE METHODIST CHAPEL, E of the former. Of the sam⬩
type, but more modest.

OWSTON CHURCH SCHOOL, yet further E. A pet. Probably ⎤
c.1840. Brick, lancets, bargeboards, a lantern, and nic⬩
lettering.

OWSTON HALL. Not up to much outside, but inside a small bu⬩
delightful staircase of Early Georgian date. Twisted balusters⬩
a very fat, boldly modelled newel post, simply carved ends
The stucco of the ceiling is of c.1775.

LOW MELWOOD, 1 m. N. An early C17 brick building with ⎤
doorway and a window at the side that could be C16 and ⎤
front doorway with a panel carrying a coat of arms. Melwoo⬩
was a Carthusian Priory. (In the cellar of the house is a ston⬩
column. So the house is built on the premises of the priory⎤
P. J. Hills)

KELFIELD, 1½ m. NE. A cottage carries the date 1689. This is i⬩
a semicircular pediment. The cottage has shaped gables an⬩
corbel-friezes of moulded bricks.

3070   OXCOMBE

ALL SAINTS. Built, according to White, in 1842. The style ⬩
indeed that of Haugham and the allied churches of c.1840, a⎰
by *W. A. Nicholson*, who must be the architect of Oxcomb⬩
too. It is a tiny church, of brick, cemented, with octagonal ⮣
tower with open bell-stage, a nave of two bays, and a polygon⬩
apse. – Inside, the Gothic FAMILY PEWS have survived, an⬩
some of the crude coloured GLASS in the windows. – MONU
MENTS to members of the Grant family, first half of the C19⎤

OXCOMBE HOUSE. Built in 1845, and evidently by *Nicholson*
too. The house lies alone with the church and some farm⬩
buildings in a beautiful, remote little valley. It is Tudoresque⬩
with mullioned and transomed windows and buttress shaft⬩
crowned by turrets l. and r. of the porch bay.

1070   PANTON

ST ANDREW. Disused, and at the time of writing disgracefully
neglected. The chancel is of greenstone and evidently Georgia⬩

– see the arched windows. The WEST DOOR is of bronze, a job
of quality, classical and probably of about 1925–30. – PULPIT.
With panels of beaten metal of the time when *Christopher
Turnor* restored the church in memory of his uncle (1905).
He probably did the panels, and very probably designed the
door and the pulpit. He lived at Panton till 1907 and at Stoke
Rochford from 1913 to his death in 1940. – (STAINED GLASS.
C18 German panels.) – PLATE. Two Patens, by *Philip Roker*,
1719. – MONUMENT. Upper half of the effigy of a Knight, no
doubt originally cross-legged. His hands are joined, and there
were angels by his pillow. His shield shows his arms in relief.

PANTON HALL. A house was built here about 1720 for Joseph
Gace. It has been attributed to *Nicholas Hawksmoor*. It was
thought to have been demolished and a new house to have
been built in 1775 by *John Carr*. Demolition of this at the time
of writing revealed the 1720 house still extant and only enlarged by Carr. Recent research suggests that *William Talman*,
not Hawksmoor, was the architect, supplying designs before
1719. The present STABLES are by *William Legg*, 1777, and
about the same time either Legg or Carr built the farm
buildings at GODDARD HILL. The grounds were laid out by
Mr *Eames*.

PARTNEY

4060

ST NICHOLAS. W tower of greenstone, Dec to Perp, i.e. the
doorway ogee-headed, but the five-light W window and the
three-light bell-openings Perp. The nave with clerestory and
aisles outside all by *C. E. Giles*, 1862, but the ogee-headed
S doorway with the remarkably well preserved statuette of
St Nicholas in a niche is Dec. The chancel of brick, 1828,
but with victorianized windows. Inside, more original work.
The tower arch, triple-chamfered, confirms the date of the W
doorway. The arcades are Dec on the S, Perp on the N side.
Four bays, slender octagonal piers, double-chamfered arches.
The S piers have bands of lush nobbly leaf, the N piers only
small leaf-bands and also small fleurons and heads. The
chancel arch stands on big busts and has small fleurons and
heads in a moulding. – FONT. Octagonal, of the pattern-book
type. The patterns all Dec, except for one which is Perp. –
PULPIT. Of stone, portly, and no doubt of the Giles time. –
SCREENS. Of the rood screen the dado tracery is intact. – The
N aisle screen has single-light divisions with cusped ogee arches
and panel tracery over. – STAINED GLASS. Still in the style of

the earlier C19, though no doubt of the restoration of 1862.
CROSS, S of the church. The base has the Symbols of the Fou
Evangelists on shields. Part of the shaft remains also.

PILHAM

8090

ALL SAINTS. Georgian, of before 1794 (the date of the Natte
drawing). It is a funny little building, with a small W tower,
very short nave (only about 21 ft inside), and an apse. Th
apse has a Venetian window. The nave windows are arched
of two arched lights with a solid tympanum, not a usua
design. – COMMUNION RAIL. Of the time of the church, bu
conservative. – PLATE. Chalice and Paten Cover, by *Joh*
Morley of Lincoln, 1569.

POOLHAM HALL
1¼ m. W of Woodhall

2060

Close to the farmhouse and in a corner of the moat are the ruin
of a small C13 domestic chapel. A lancet in the W wall.

RAITHBY

3080

ST PETER. 1839 by *W. A. Nicholson*, and a sister church t
Haugham. The style is Gothic, just pre-archaeological, i.e
very ornate, with what we would call all the gimmicks, i.e
openwork parapets in different patterns, pinnacles, and flowing
tracery at least in the windows of the polygonal apse. Th
tracery motifs by the way are not to be found in the real De
style. Like Haugham the church is of brick, cemented. Unlik
Haugham, however, it has inside a real, probably late C13, N
arcade of three bays, with octagonal piers and double-chamfered arches. Keeled responds. The roof and also most of th
FURNISHINGS are of the time of the church, namely WEST
GALLERY, ORGAN CASE, BOX PEWS, and also the STAINED
GLASS in two apse windows, obviously by the same maker as
at Haugham. In the other windows oval medallions with
German C16 glass. The organ incidentally is a BARREL
ORGAN.* – FONT. Octagonal, Dec. On a cluster of shafts with
fillets. Panels with quatrefoils exclusively.

RAITHBY-BY-SPILSBY

3060

HOLY TRINITY. Mostly rebuilt by *Sir G. G. Scott*, 1873. Only
some tracery details medieval. The tower renewed by *Hodgson*

* So Canon Binnall tells me, and it still has its original working instructions
and a list of thirty tunes.

Fowler in 1895. The tower is green, the rest grey. It would be valuable to know exactly what the s arcade was like before Scott. It looks as if there had been a two-bay Norman arcade with round pier and scalloped capital and arches with a slight chamfer. They were probably round and later made pointed. But was the abacus round? The thick square pillar would have represented the former w wall, and the chamfering and the double-chamfered arch a lengthening. s arcade of stubby octagonal piers. Pretty, no doubt C19, chancel decoration. – STAINED GLASS. Window by *Kempe*, 1896. – PLATE. Paten Cover, inscribed 1569; Chalice, London, 1654.

RAITHBY HALL. The date of the house is not known. It looks of the 1760s and was certainly built before 1792.* The s front has three-storeyed canted bays right up to the parapet and between them a wooden doorcase with open pediment. There was once a cupola. The wings each side appear of the C17, with segmental and broken pediments. To the unwary it looks as if an earlier house had been broken apart by the Georgian one. Drawings show this not to have been the case; for the wings were added after 1848. In the range of offices is a plain CHAPEL fitted up in 1779 for John Wesley. (It is an upper room reached by twin curved staircases and provided with a canopied PULPIT.) The small park is romantically landscaped.

RANBY 2070

ST GERMAN. 1861 by *Fowler*. Of grey stone, in the Dec style, nicely ivy-hung on the s side. In the outer vestry wall the head of a Late Perp four-light window set in. – FONT. Octagonal, Perp, with six big leaves, one shield, and one panel with the column and two scourges. – PLATE. Waiter used as Paten, by *John Law*, 1823.

RANBY HALL. 'Erected about 1868' says White, yet it is still in a Late Georgian style with pediment to the s front and *porte-cochère* on the w front.

RAND 1070

ST OSWALD. Broad w tower, not high. The bell-openings are Dec, but the w window has as a label-stop a Norman long-snouted monster-head. The nave was rebuilt c.1820, so the straight-headed Perp windows must all be Victorian. The chancel was rebuilt in 1862 by *R. J. Withers*, yet the chancel arch seems E.E., and the hood-mould of the E window with

* This is the date of a drawing by Nattes.

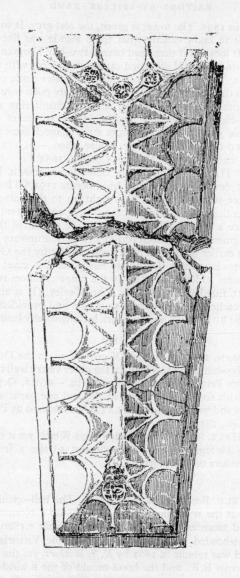

Rand, coped coffin lid, c.1200

head-stops cannot be later than early C14. Therefore the cusped intersecting tracery could also be correct. Inside an uncommon number of MONUMENTS, but only two really memorable. First a coped coffin-lid, 6 ft 9 in. long, of a dark grey stone, perhaps Purbeck. Up the spine runs a shaft like that of a cross. At its base a roundel, at its top three set so that two fork out from the third. The roundels have small foliage, perhaps of stiff-leaf affinities. Otherwise all along the four borders run arches, and on the long sides they have gables over. It is a most unexpected piece, and its most likely date is about 1200. – The second memorable monument is the effigy of a Lady, late C13, inspired by the Angel Choir of Lincoln Cathedral. She is praying. A shield lies on her middle. Two angels with incense by her pillow. Unfortunately her features appear to be re-cut. – The other monuments are Elizabethan to Jacobean. First (and most interesting) Sir Vincent Fulnetby and wives, probably of 1593. Large stone tablet without any figures, but with some rather bald strapwork and a total of twenty-two shields with coats of arms. – Brasses, a mixture of three, the legs of an early C16 Knight, and two Elizabethan Ladies. – Mrs Anna Metham † 1602. Alabaster, small, kneeling figure, her children kneeling close to her. – Dorothy Leigh † 1613. Alabaster, also small, also with kneeling figure. – Charles Matham and his wife who died in 1628. Alabaster, the two figures kneeling and facing one another. – Sir Sapcote Harington † 1630. The two kneeling figures in the same position, the children below as usual. – PLATE. Chalice and Paten Cover, London, 1570(?); Paten, London, 1732; Flagon, by *John White*, 1732.

REASBY HALL *see* SNELLAND

REDBOURNE

ST ANDREW. A Perp church with Dec arcades. They are of three bays with octagonal piers and double-chamfered arches. But is the w tower really Perp? It is unbuttressed and has a rectangular staircase projection which seems to indicate an earlier date. As for the Perp features, they include battlements and pinnacles on aisles, chancel, and clerestory. About 1775 the two E attachments to the chancel were built, in the Gothic style, with quatrefoil E windows. The southern one serves as the family mausoleum of the Dukes of St Albans. Of the same

time the charming coved plaster ceiling of the chancel (1777
and groined plaster vault of the nave. Nattes shows an C1
Gothic w porch and windows which may all be C18 too.
FONT. Good big baluster; *Richard Hayward* paid for it i
1775. – STAINED GLASS. The E window with a horrific scen
of Sodom and Gomorrha under quite harmless canopies an
the aisle windows with the Apostles are of *c*.1840 and b
William Collins. The scene of horror is very much in the styl
of John Martin, who as a young man worked for Collins.
Medieval bits in the aisle windows too. – PLATE. Chalice an
Paten Cover, by *John Morley* of Lincoln, 1569; Chalice an
Paten, by *Paul de Lamerie*, 1750. – MONUMENTS. Incise
slab of Sir Gerald Sothill † 1410 (chancel s). Foreign, accord
ing to Greenhill. – Low tomb recess in the chancel N wal
with cusped ogee arch. – Tablets to William Carter † 1752 an
Roger Carter † 1774, both probably of *c*.1775 and very fine
Probably by *Hayward*. Both have reliefs, the former a scen
of tree-planting, the latter a Chinese harbour and a ship.
Lady William Beauclerk † 1797, Grecian. – Duchess of S
Albans, 1838 by *Chantrey*, a draped Grecian altar. She wa
the widow of Thomas Coutts and had earlier been Harrie
Mellon, one of the most charming of English actresses.
Ninth Duke of St Albans, 1851 by *Lough*. Big relief o
mourning mother with two children. Gothic surround.

CASTLE HILLS, SW of the church. The very fragmentary
remains of an earthwork castle of two wards.

REDBOURNE HALL. Now straggling and incoherent, dwindling
out at the tail end with castellated farm buildings. Accounts
show that *John Carr* was employed for improvements in 1773
The W front has five bays of tall windows on the ground floor
and lower ones above. At the s end is a three-window bow
In 1778 a carver and gilder called *Hudson* and a joiner called
Bunning were paid for work. In the outbuildings are two
reliefs of Harvest and Autumn, one dated 1734. What may be
Carr's design is the GATEWAY, building in 1776, tripartite,
with castellations and arrow slits.

In the village the Georgian-Gothic BROOK COTTAGE and two
mid-C18 ranges, perhaps once ALMSHOUSES. Pediments to
the three-bay centres.

See
p.
767
0070

REEPHAM

ST PETER AND ST PAUL. 1862 by *Michael Drury*, with a poor
w tower with steep pyramid roof. But the arcades are medieval,

of the late C12 and the early C14. The S aisle has been pulled down, but it is clear that the arcade has waterleaf capitals, one somewhat enriched. The shape of the piers is not clear. Was it a Lincoln octagon with four shafts? If so, one would have to advance the date to the early C13. The Dec arcade has quatrefoil piers with fillets and with thin shafts in the diagonals. – PLATE. Paten Cover, London, 1569.

ICARAGE. Small box with an overhanging cornice. By *John Hartley* of Lincoln, 1838.

REVESBY

ST LAWRENCE. 1891 by *C. Hodgson Fowler*, a big Dec church with a recessed spire, built at the expense of the Rt. Hon. Edward Stanhope and James Banks Stanhope. Joseph Banks, a London lawyer, had bought the estate in 1714 (*see* below). Sir Joseph Banks, the naturalist, spent much time at Revesby Abbey, and the Banks estate housing will also be referred to. The house was called Revesby Abbey after the Cistercian ABBEY, ½ m. S of the church, which was founded in 1142. Nothing remains on the site, but it is known that the abbey had a nave and aisles, octagonal pier bases, a S transept, a straight E end, and the monastic premises on the S side. The most remarkable find was an area of TILE PAVEMENT of bold patterns in strips running W–E between the piers of the nave. It is on good grounds assigned to the C13, and a small part of it, about 4½ by 6 ft, has been re-set in the new church. This part is, as illustrations in the church show, only a portion of one of ten different arrangements. It is a complicated pattern of large six-pointed stars with incised lines and lilies and smaller black undecorated stars. The colours are green and buff, apart from black.* In the new church also many other FRAGMENTS from the abbey (under the tower and in the vestry), mostly later medieval, but also two small Norman double capitals with different patterns, probably from the cloisters, part of a respond with nailhead enrichment, and lengths of arches with dog-tooth along one moulding. – PULPIT. Incorporated in it three small Flemish reliefs of the late C16. – RELIQUARY. Of glazed earthenware; a cross-shaped little building; C14. – MONUMENT. Joseph Banks, 1727 by *Nost*. Bust, rather flat, above the grey sarcophagus. Evidently not in its complete setting.

* I owe this description and some valuable comments to Miss Norma Whitcombe.

The village is planned horseshoe-wise s of the church with
spacious green in the middle. The buildings are gabled and
bargeboarded. There are a SCHOOL (1858), ALMSHOUSE
(1862), and cottages, mostly semi-detached.

REVESBY ABBEY. Not to be confused with the Cistercian abbey
(*see* above). Craven Howard built a house here soon after the
Restoration, and this was enlarged by the Banks family. In
1843 *William Burn* designed the present house for J. Banks
Stanhope. In character it is close to South Rauceby (*see* p. 642)
with shaped gables, mixed sub-Renaissance details, and strapwork crestings. The house is E-shaped. The central stroke of
the E is the porch bay with a big Dietterlinesque *porte-cochère*.
Inside, Burn appears in his Baroque Harlaxton mood, though
less lavish. Note the ceiling of the staircase and the Viennese-
style plasterwork. Much furniture in a full-blooded Rococo
style. But the hall chimneypiece is dated 1659. The Continental
theme carried on in the gardens with much German C17
STATUARY. The SCREEN and GATES on the road with urn-
topped piers are dated 1848.

ROUND BARROWS. W of Home Farm are two large bowl
barrows, both surrounded by clearly visible quarry ditches
and standing on slightly raised platforms. The larger barrow
is 65 ft in diameter and 8 ft high.

1000

RIBY

ST EDMUND. Cruciform, perhaps already at the time when the
Norman nave N doorway was made, with a twisted, beaded
rope as a hood-mould. The present crossing arches, however,
are of *c.*1300, the chamfers partly continuous. s arcade of
three bays with octagonal piers and double-chamfered arches,
perhaps also of *c.*1300 or perhaps somewhat later. The exterior
of the church mostly by *Ferrey*, 1868. His vaulted chancel is
quite successful. – PLATE. Chalice and Paten Cover, by *John
Morley* of Lincoln, 1569; Paten, 1691; Flagon, by *Wm
Darkaratt*, 1730; Plate, by *John Richardson*(?), London, 1735;
two Flagons, 1735 (from Little Waldingfield, Essex). –
MONUMENTS. William and Elizabeth († 1773) Tomline. With
a free-standing wreathed urn in a niche. – Above it a small
tablet with a woman by an urn and drapery cascading down
from above. This is signed *L. Tomline* delineavit. The Tom-
lines were the family at the manor. – John Parkinson † 1840.
White marble; Gothic.

he Palladian Tomline seat has gone. Next to the church a Georgian five-bay, two-storey HOUSE with segment-headed windows.

RIGSBY

T JAMES. By *James Fowler*, 1863. Neo-Norman, with an apse. But the w rose window is really post-Norman and the bell-turret, corbelled-out and with a spirelet, is just High Victorian. Inside, however, Fowler re-used a real Early Norman arch (to the vestry). – FONT. Octagonal, Perp, each side with three thin cusped arches and above them six little panels of panel tracery, also cusped arches. – PLATE. Chalice, by *Wm. Howlett*, c.1640.

RISEHOLME

Iouse and church lie close to each other, separated from the oad by a lake.

▸T MARY. By *Teulon*, 1851. Small, of nave with a w bellcote and chancel. Elaborately decorated in the Dec style, e.g. E window of five, w window of four lights. – STAINED GLASS. Of the time of the building of the church the chancel windows by *Gibbs* (TK).

RISEHOLME HALL. A small late C18 house enlarged in 1840–5 by *William Railton*. He created a seven- by six-bay block, two storeys with a balustraded parapet. Projecting from the S front a Tuscan colonnade, bowed in the centre. The earlier house can be seen partly obscured at the E end. The STABLES are effective and unlike Railton. Can they be by *Teulon*, though classical and not Gothic? Their composition is a cubic, geometric one with little relief except for rusticated entrances and lucarnes.

RECTORY. By *Teulon*, 1873–4.

ROMAN BARROW, $\frac{1}{2}$ m. NW of the church, near the N boundary of the parish. The barrow is a round one, 60 ft in diameter and 9 ft high. It is steep-sided and has a markedly flat top. There are no traces of a surrounding ditch, and the site now supports a stand of half a dozen trees. Excavation revealed beneath the barrow and at its centre traces of burning, and a trench in which a single corpse appears to have been cremated. Sherds of Romano-British pottery were found in association with this burial. A secondary cremation in a Romano-British vessel was inserted on the SW. The finds suggest a date in the C1 A.D.

1090

ROTHWELL

St Mary Magdalene. Anglo-Saxon w tower. The w door-way, much weathered, has plain chamfered imposts, a plain tympanum, and a hood-mould. The twin bell-openings with the usual mid-wall shafts. The capitals are of the German Romanesque (and Early Norman) block or cushion type. Tall tower arch also with chamfered imposts. The moulding continues along the nave w wall to the s. Outside the Saxon nave the sw quoin remains, with long-and-short work. This nave was given three-bay arcades in the c12, at one go. Sturdy circular piers, multi-scalloped capitals, square abaci, the w arches with zigzag; the next with three rolls on the s, two and a square projection on the N, the third with a half-roll between two hollows. The s aisle has E.E. lancets at the w and E ends, the chancel a s lancet. The chancel was restored by *Seddin* in 1892. – PLATE. Chalice and Paten Cover, inscribed 1569; Paten, by *John Schofield*, 1781.

2060

ROUGHTON

St Margaret. The nave is of greenstone and has two Transitional doorways, plain, with segmental arches. Their position shows that the nave was later lengthened to the w.* The chancel is of the late c13, see the windows, one with Geometrical tracery (at the top two cinquefoiled circles and one trefoiled circle) and one with intersecting tracery. The w tower is Perp and in its lower part greenstone, but above brick. Brick two-light bell-openings with straight tops and brick battlements. – FONT COVER. Nice, simple, Elizabethan. – PULPIT. With nice Late Georgian stair railing. – BENCH ENDS. Some with minimum lozenge-shaped poppy-heads. – SCREEN. The tops of the dado panels with their tracery re-used. – PLATE. Chalice, by *Hammond Blake*(?), 1832.

Roughton Hall. The house is a delight to look at. It closely resembles the former Archdeacon's House in Lincoln (*see p.* 136), which is of *c.*1760. All that matters is the entrance front. Five bays, three storeys, white-painted stone quoins, strings, and window heads. A nice contrasty effect. In the centre bay is a tall door with segmental pediment, a Venetian window, and a tripartite lunette above this.

* In the nave NW quoins an odd stone is used which seems to be a section of a double-shafted corner, two shafts to one side, two shafts at r. angles to the other. Norman double-shafting does indeed exist.

ROXBY

ST MARY. Short, unbuttressed W tower, Saxon, on the evidence of one small S window. The SW quoin of the old nave is visible, with very big stones. Dec S and N aisles and chancel. In the aisles straight-headed windows. The S aisle has a pretty doorway, one specially pretty S window with subcusping, and a three-light E window with flowing tracery. In the chancel priest's doorway with ogee head and gable, nice gablets on the set-offs of the buttresses, and sedilia with cusped and sub-cusped ogee arches, buttress shafts, and crockets. In the S aisle a tall pointed-trefoiled tomb recess. The S arcade is low and has octagonal piers and double-chamfered arches. The N arcade is Victorian, probably by *James Fowler*, 1875, who rebuilt much of the church. – PLATE. Chalice, by *John Morley* of Lincoln, *c.*1569; Flagon, by *Wm. Grundy*, 1774; Cover, by *Wm. Elliott*, 1824. – MONUMENTS. C15 effigy of a Priest. – Robert Holgate † 1822. Arrangement of urn and a long branch.

ROMAN(?) VILLA. A mosaic pavement, discovered in the C17, is still preserved intact beneath a garden on the S side of the churchyard.

RUCKLAND

ST OLAVE. 1885 by *W. Scorer*. Of the smallest chapel size, yet with a rose window in the W wall. – MONUMENT. Inside, the upper half of a coffin-lid with foliated cross.

SALEBY

ST MARGARET. 1850 by *Stephen Lewin*. Nave with bellcote and chancel. Of a beige brick looking from afar exactly like stone. On the N side fancy Dec tracery, on the other sides correct. Are they later? – MONUMENT. An excellent effigy supposed to be William de Hardreshull who died in 1303. Cross-legged, with praying hands. He wears chain-mail and a surcoat. His shield has his arms carved on. At his pillow two angels. At his feet a lion. He seems to lie on a bed of flowers: at least there are flowers and leaves where one can see them. The effigy is in a low recess. The stops of the arch are big leaf (of the post-naturalistic kind) and a shield.

(THORESTHORPE HALL. Small manor house; C17. PB)

SALMONBY

ST MARGARET. Of greenstone, nave and chancel. Perp, but largely rebuilt in 1871. In the NE corner a small shingled

broach-spire of that date. In the chancel a Perp window with
segmental head. – STAINED GLASS. E window by *Clayton &
Bell*, 1876. – PLATE. Chalice, by *Alex. Saunders*(?), London
1769.

SALTFLEET

4090

The CHURCH of Saltfleet was washed away into the sea a long
time ago.

MANOR HOUSE. Built before 1673. Plain and gabled. Inside, a
spacious C17 staircase with heavy balusters and oak rails.

NEW INN. Its size, larger in fact than that of the manor house
opposite, indicates the past prosperity of this fishing village.
The N wing of four bays and three storeys is attached to an
earlier, higher, gabled wing. This extends E to form a T.

SALTFLEETBY ALL SAINTS

4090

ALL SAINTS. The sign manual of the church is its leaning
tower, Perp above, but Early E.E. below. To the w two lancets
one above the other, and traces of the round-arched bell-
openings below the present ones. They presumably originally
had twin pointed arches under the round arch. To the nave
the tower arch has keeled responds with stiff-leaf capitals and
a triple-chamfered arch. Springers in the corners indicate a
low quadripartite rib-vault. When the Perp top was added,
extra buttressing became necessary, and this, to the E, cut into
the s aisle, which is indeed E.E. too. It is of five bays with
round piers, round abaci, and double-chamfered arches. But
the chancel arch is older than what we have seen so far. Its
responds are Norman, semicircular with square abaci and
scalloped capitals. And the Norman chancel to which these
responds belonged received a Norman two-bay s chapel too –
see the round pier with scalloped capital and square abacus.
However, this place is evidently disturbed. First, the responds
of the chapel arcade are E.E., and the arcade is in line with the
aisle arcade. Secondly, the chancel arch is wider than is to be
expected. Could the Norman responds as well as the pier be
re-used? Anyway, the chancel windows are in the style of 1300
(plate tracery, Y-tracery), and at that time the relatively
narrowly set two-bay arcade to the chapel was considered old-
fashioned and a new arch built to its N, pending the demolition
of the old arcade, which however was in the end not carried
out.* Of *c.*1300 also the windows of the very wide s aisle (Y-

* The case repeats exactly at Willoughby.

tracery). Perp additions and alterations are the s porch, its entrance with three shields, and a donor's inscription, the s window of the s chapel, and – last but not least – the N front with a doorway set halfway between two symmetrically placed straight-headed three-light windows. They are delightful with their transoms and the small tracery of hanging arches below. Inside, there are original roofs in s aisle and nave, in the latter with tie-beams and queenposts. The nave roof has a notably high pitch. It was repaired in 1611. – REREDOS of stone in the s aisle, with buttress-shafts and gable, not as elaborate as those in the two Theddlethorpes, but earlier. No form demands a date later than the *c.*1300 of the s aisle. – PULPITS. One, in use, is Jacobean, with the usual stumpy blank arches, the other, at the w end, is a beautiful, probably Elizabethan, piece with pedimented panels, and in the panels, arches in perspective. – PLATE. Chalice, by *John Morley* of Lincoln, *c.*1569.

SALTFLEETBY ST CLEMENT   4090

ST CLEMENT. Mostly 1885 by *W. Mortimer* (PF). w tower, nave and chancel. But also some genuine lancets (chancel E, chancel s, nave s), simple E.E. w doorway and s doorway with rounded instead of chamfered jambs, and a tall Perp s window. The interior reveals that the church had an E.E. N aisle. Its five-bay arcade is preserved, with narrowly-set circular piers (circular abaci) and double-chamfered arches. – FONT. Of a former Perp font one piece of the stem remains, with a little saint with the extraordinary hair-do occasionally to be found in fonts around here, and faint traces of a second (cf. Covenham St Bartholomew). – PLATE. Chalice and Paten Cover, by *A.*, London, 1569; Paten, by *W.E.*, London, 1723.

SALTFLEETBY ST PETER   4080

ST PETER. The tower of the old church stands ½ m. NE of the new church. It is of greenstone and white ashlar, quite substantial, and entirely Perp. Big four-light w window. The new church is of greenstone and consists of nave with bellcote and chancel. It is mostly by *James Fowler*, 1877, but inside much of the old church was re-used. E.E. N arcade of five bays with circular piers and abaci and double-chamfered arches. The E respond with upright leaves, the w respond with stiff-leaf and a horrifying head, mouth wide open. The s arcade also E.E.

Responds with a little nailhead, arches with broaches in the form of half-dog-teeth. Also one small whorl stop. Externally Fowler repeated much that had been there in the old church, namely the w lancets of the aisles, and the fine Dec s window straight-headed, with reticulation units. But the E.E. chancel lancets are Fowler's. – PLATE. Chalice, by *A.*, London, 1569

PROSPECT TOWER, belonging to Saltfleetby House, ¼ m. NE of the new church. Who can be the architect responsible for this? Ground floor square with a blank arch in each face. Above this an ironwork railing and another storey, also square but with thin square turrets at the angles. Then the top storey an octagon pierced with circular lights. The conception is slightly Soanian. According to the A.P.S. Dictionary *Wyatville* designed a TOWER in Lincolnshire in 1812. Can it be this?

SANDTOFT GRANGE *see* BELTON

SAUSTHORPE

3060

ST ANDREW. 1842 by *Charles Kirk*. Of stock brick and typical of its date, i.e. a tall, rather narrow nave with tall windows, their tracery Perp. Battlements. The tower also of brick, but crowned by a Louth spire with turret pinnacles and flying buttresses like the churches of about 1840 by Nicholson. The WEST GALLERY is original. – STAINED GLASS. Chancel s two *Morris* windows, but of 1908, i.e. after the death of both Morris and Burne-Jones. – PLATE. Paten, by *John Jackson*, 1697; Paten, by *John Berthelot*, 1758; Flagon, by *Alex Johnston*, 1759.

SAUSTHORPE OLD HALL. Looks Later Georgian with its two storeys and two-bay slightly projecting wings. The interior is earlier. It has a date 1711.

SAUSTHORPE HALL. A chaste stone house of 1822. Two storeys and parapet. N front with Ionic porch and w front with a tripartite window. The continuation E on the s front is an earlier C18 wing with hipped roof and dormers.

SAXBY

0080

53 ST HELEN. Probably of *c.*1775 and surprisingly ambitious, though small. Red brick with ample stone dressings and a complete portico *in antis*, the width of the front. Tuscan columns. The portico is lit by circular windows from the sides.

The nave and apse have large arched windows; for the nave angle pilasters as well. Bell-turret, balancing on the portico, square with an ogee cap. Angle pilasters. Bell-openings with Gibbs surrounds. Nice interior with panelled dado, Ionic pilasters on it, and the low apse with a diagonally coffered vault. – PULPIT and READER'S DESK, the former with tarsia, the latter with fluted pilasters. – FAMILY PEW, also partly original. – STAINED GLASS. One S window by *Powell's*, 1874. The two scenes nicely stylized, with the kind of hieratic gestures as in the very earliest Pre-Raphaelite compositions. – PLATE. Chalice, mid C18. – MONUMENTS. Tablets of no special merit to three Earls of Scarbrough, the sixth † 1832 (by *Wray* of Lincoln), the seventh † 1835 (by *Theakston* of Pimlico), and the eighth † 1856 (by *C. R. Smith* of Marylebone), and also the seventh Countess † 1850 (also by *Smith*).

SAXBY ALL SAINTS 9010

ALL SAINTS. 1845–9 by *George Gilbert Scott*. Clean, white, of small, regular stones. The S tower, a less correct piece with its pyramid roof, is not by Scott. It was added in 1873 by *Neville* and looks as if meant for a town hall. Scott's style is latest C13. The motif of the pointed-trefoil-cusped lancet may have been taken over by him from original evidence, see the N aisle W and N windows. – STAINED GLASS. In the E window original, crude but quite impressive glass with large figures. The same style chancel N, also nave W (of 1859). – N aisle E by *Kempe* and very early: 1876. A Madonna, very gently done. – PLATE. Chalice and Paten Cover, by *John Morley*, 1569.

SAXBY HALL. The W block is late C18, with bow windows and a veranda between. On the S side a canted bay. A wing continues in this direction adjoining the road.

DRINKING TROUGH. To commemorate sixty years of Queen Victoria's reign. A column on a pedestal surmounted by the royal crown.

SAXILBY 8070

ST BOTOLPH. A complicated building history. It starts with the small, simple N doorway, Norman, the arch only with a slight chamfer. It is no doubt re-set. Then follow the E.E. responds of the N arcade, with capitals decorated by upright stiff-leaf. They are earlier than the piers of the arcade, which are quatrefoil in section with deep hollows between the foils and fillets

on the foils. That is Dec. Double-chamfered arches. T
chancel arch with keeled responds looks plain E.E. But t
real problem is the w tower. It has a Georgian-Gothick
doorway* but genuine lancet windows, and to the nave a wi
triple-chamfered arch, too wide for a tower arch. The arch
start with broaches. The hood-mould has heads to the w, n
the E. Can this be evidence of a free-standing tower wit
buttresses in all directions, including E, of before the tim
when the nave and aisle were built? And when was that
They are externally essentially Perp, embattled, with simp
windows and with roofs. The latest part, judging by the d
based tracery of the E window, would be the N chapel. Insid
this has to the chancel two-bay openings with a characteri
tically Perp pier. It would then be possible that the Norma
E.E., and Dec parts were all re-used when the church wa
rebuilt to communicate with the tower. The Perp tower top
C20. – FONT. Octagonal, Perp, with flatly carved coats o
arms. – SCREEN. Good Perp work with wide ogee-heade
openings and lively tracery to the l. and r. of the elongated
crocketed ogee tops. – SCULPTURE. Loose under the tower
Saxon stone with interlace, very damaged. – PLATE. Chalic
and Paten Cover, by *I.C.*, London, 1569. – MONUMENT
Knight and Lady, alabaster, *c.*1400, on a tomb-chest decorate
with much foiled and sub-foiled tracery.

2070

SCAMBLESBY

ST MARTIN. 1893 by *R. H. Fowler*. Of greenstone, nave wit
bellcote and chancel. Inside a considerable surprise. One pie
re-used from the demolished church of Cawkwell, combines i
the frankest way the Norman and the E.E., without a trace o
the Transitional. It is a pier of the Lincoln type, with octagona
core and four detached shafts. But the pier has horizontal zig
zag bands all along, i.e. a purely Norman motif. E.E. also th
NE and SW responds, and perhaps some more pieces. – Outsid
the porch lies a stone which may well be the head of an Anglo
Saxon window with a slight moulding. – BENCH ENDS. Wit
poppy-heads. – PLATE. Chalice, London, 1568; Paten
London, 1802. – Also, from Cawkwell, Chalice, by *Samue*
Godbehere & Edward Wigan, 1791.

CAWKWELL HOUSE. Plain, stock brick, with a Greek-Dori
porch.

* Of after 1793; *see* the Nattes drawing.

SCAMPTON

9070

ᵗ JOHN BAPTIST. Perp three-bay N arcade. Octagonal piers, double-chamfered arches. Coarse Perp chancel arch and arch into the N chapel. The exterior with small W tower looks Victorian, but, according to the Nattes drawings, there was a rebuilding or thorough re-modelling in 1794. – STAINED GLASS. N aisle and chancel by *Bodley & Garner*, 1876–7. – PLATE. Chalice and Paten, given 1692 (remodelled 1869).

CAMPTON HALL. The house preserves an early C17 gateway reminiscent of Jacob Francart's engravings. Paired studded Doric columns, broken segmental pediment with a raised pedimented panel, obelisks and decorative Jacobean trimmings. It was probably built for Sir John Bolle after 1603.

ʰe OLD RECTORY. Georgian. Bow on the W front.

CHOOL. Victorian, red brick, by *Ewan Christian*.

ᴿOMAN VILLA, NE of the junction of Lincoln Edge Road and Till Bridge Lane. The site was discovered in the C18 by workmen digging for limestone. Finds include portions of a tessellated pavement. The site has since been ploughed over.

SCARTHO

2000

ᵗ GILES. Anglo-Saxon W tower. The W doorway with double 4b voussoirs (cf. Old Clee). Twin bell-openings with mid-wall shafts, the capitals with uncommonly civilized foliage. In the S wall of the tower an E.E. doorway, and above it another E.E. arch, too narrow to be the remains of the arch to a S chapel. The Saxon arch to the nave is tall and has the familiar block-shaped capitals and abaci in one and the familiar opening above. Short S aisle with a blocked W doorway. The arcade is of two bays; E.E. Quatrefoil pier, or rather square with four broad semicircular projections. Double-chamfered arches. The proximity of Scartho to Grimsby has called for a larger church, and so, in 1955–8, *T. J. Rushton* built a whole new N side and chancel, though keeping the chancel arch and E wall of 1859. – SCULPTURE. Several panels of a C15 Nottingham alabaster altar retable. The scenes and their treatment are as usual. – PLATE. Chalice, by *W. S.*, London, 1661; Flagon, by *Thomas Farrer*, 1718.

SCAWBY

9000

ˢᵗ HYBALD. Medieval W tower, but its doorway etc. and all the rest of the church of 1843 (by *W. A. Nicholson*) and of 1870

(*James Fowler*). The style is E.E., the material small stones
give an appearance as if of grey brick. – PLATE. Chalice,
P.B., London, 1635; Paten and Flagon, by *John Cory*, 170
– MONUMENTS. To the Nelthorpe family (*see* below
Richard † 1640, two frontal busts in arched recesses. T
children kneel small below. – John † 1669, a handson
ornamental tablet. – Edward † 1781, nice, with an urn in fro
of an obelisk. – Amaziah Empson † 1798, by *Fisher* of Yo
also with obelisk and urn. – Sir Henry † 1830, Grecian, with
draped altar; by *George Earle Jun.* of Hull.

SCAWBY HALL. Mostly of a rambling appearance. A date f
the building of the house may be 1603, when Richard Ne
thorpe married. E front with tall projecting porch and a broa
chimneybreast to the S. To the N, a canted bay window wa
inserted between 1795 and 1806 in place of a similar chimney
breast. Then the house was crenellated and re-fenestrate
Where the N part of this front returns back to its continuatio
there projects another chimneybreast, but this replaced
canted bay: that is, chimney and bays were interchanged – a
odd alteration. The rest of the front was rebuilt in 1913. Th
S front is the show front, with a symmetrical late C18 face-lif
Two-bay, three-storey projecting wings and a lower three-ba
centre. The W front with two projecting chimneybreasts. N
these parts is a courtyard with the date 1686. The interior ha
two ingeniously devised staircases, one returning back upo
itself through two storeys.*

(OLD VICARAGE, Garage Lane. Late C18 front. Three bay
Rubble. Doorway with Roman Doric demi-columns. Two
storeyed canted bay windows on either side. MHLG)

SCAWBY GROVE. A mixture of styles. Big winged Frenc
Gothic dragon corbels. Built in 1884–90. There is a date 189
(BRIDGE. Medieval, though known as the Roman Bridge. P

SCOTHERN

ST GERMAN. Perp W tower with six pinnacles, but the arch
the nave on two E.E. responds, probably re-used. The nav
(Geometrical tracery) is of 1861, the chancel (Dec tracery) c
1904. But the chancel arch has two spectacular late C1
responds, of triple, fully detached shafts with waterlea
capitals. – PLATE. Chalice, Elizabethan.

---

* The house is notable for its collection of paintings by *Stubbs*, to whos
the Nelthorpes of the time were patrons and friends.

SCOTTER

ᵣ PETER. Of the Norman church mainly the s doorway remains.
It is tall and has an arch with roll mouldings. The tympanum
may be partly older than the rest. The s masonry of the nave
is Norman too (see the flat buttress). It can be seen that the
wall at that time was lower than it is now. To the late C13
belongs the N arcade. Four bays, quatrefoil piers with deep
hollows and fillets on the foils. One pier has triple projections
instead of the filleted foils, and the responds have thin shafts
between the foils. Stiff-leaf capitals, double-chamfered arches.
The church was then very soon lengthened, see the N arcade E
bay, not much different from the other bays, and also the one
SE window with intersecting tracery and a tall chancel window
of two lights with a quatrefoil above. In the chancel an ogee-
arched aumbry. Then the Perp W tower, or perhaps only its
top parts, the clerestory, and the bigger nave s window, set
strangely high, though not at clerestory level. The coarse,
broad, and rather low arch E of the s doorway which probably
went into a chapel is most likely to be Perp too. – FONT.
Perp, octagonal. – SCREEN. With two-light divisions and
small panel tracery above. – PLATE. Beaker, by *H.B.*, London,
1604; Paten, London, 1715.

ᵣₕe village is a long street of brown-brick and colour-washed
cottages, expanding near the church. From here a vista to the
Lower Green and the river Eau, where stands the Late
Georgian MANOR HOUSE.

COTTERTHORPE, 1 m. NW. The tall brick farmhouse may be
the hunting box built for Mr Hutton by *Joseph Fowler* in 1827.

SCOTTON

ᵀ GENEWYS. That unusual thing in Lincolnshire, a church
all of a period. The period is the late C13. Of the W tower only
the top is later, i.e. Perp. To the s formerly a W bay of the s
aisle. To the nave the arch is blocked. It is said to be Norman
(Cox). In the N aisle doorway with shafts and dog-tooth and
windows with Y-tracery. In the s aisle windows with intersecting tracery and an odd E window, nicely moulded outside
and with a straight-sided hood-mould arch. The chancel has
lancets and one tall two-light window with a quatrefoil in a
circle. Rere-arches inside. Slender three-bay arcades with
double-chamfered arches, on the s side ᴏn slender circular, on

the N side on slender octagonal piers. Nice head-stop
including three now on the gate of the former Vicarage NW
the church. In the S aisle a tomb recess. – FONT. Circular an
really terrible, yet said (by Kelly) to be by *Street*, who restore
the chancel in 1866. – PLATE. Chalice and Paten Cover, b
John Morley of Lincoln, 1569; Paten, by *P.B.*, London, 166
– MONUMENTS. Effigies of a cross-legged Knight and a Lad
*c.*1300 (the date of the church). They must once have been
good quality. – Effigy of a Priest, early C14. Only the hea
carved; sunk in an enriched ogee quatrefoil.

ROMAN SETTLEMENT, on Hardwick Hill. *See* Laughton.

4060

SCREMBY

ST PETER AND ST PAUL. Built in 1733. Brick, laid in Flemis
bond, and greenstone dressings. W tower with doorwa
pedimented and with Gibbs surround. The top parapet of th
tower curves up at the corners. Nave with two arched window
each side, polygonal chancel with a primitive Venetian window
Flat ceiling. – WEST GALLERY. – The chancel has PANELLIN
like a living room. – PULPIT. With fluted angle pilasters.
STAINED GLASS. E window by *O'Connor*, 1861. – PLAT
Paten, with vernicle, London, 1512 (only one other piec
of plate hall-marked in this year is known); Chalice, Eliza
bethan. – MONUMENT to Charles Brackenbury † 1816. B
Walsh & Dunbar of Leeds. Sarcophagus in relief above th
inscription.

SCREMBY HALL. Only the S wing remains, that is, part of
canted bay and the portion behind it. This mid-Georgia
house once stood in a landscaped park laid out with rusti
buildings. On the S vista a prettified FARMHOUSE and NW
on the road, a thatched COTTAGE ORNÉ. Also, on the A roa
S of the Hall, two Gothic COTTAGES, one with ogee-heade
windows, and a house with two thatched pavilions, almost lik
rondavels.

GREBBY HALL, ¾ m. NW. Late Georgian with added bo
windows. The whole a local builder's job, noticeable in th
clumsy pediment to the tripartite window.

2060

SCRIVELSBY

ST BENEDICT. In a field, set against a wood. Externally al
Victorian (restoration 1860). Nave, N aisle, and chancel. Th

NW tower with recessed spire is entirely of 1860. Greenstone except for the grey steeple. In the chancel real Perp windows and doorway. The N arcade is real E.E., somewhat primitive. Three bays; octagonal piers with four attached shafts. Double-chamfered arches. Two-bay N chapel of the same date and details. – FONT. Octagonal; in each panel just a small concave-sided crocketed gable. – SCREEN. A nice conceit. Two-light divisions. The lights are round-arched but an ogee arch rises above them so that parts of the round arches become the cusping of the super-arch. The doorway has two hanging ogee arches, and in the spandrel a big circle with a multitude of minute tracery. – STAINED GLASS. E window, three figures under canopies. By *Thomas Willement*, 1860. – PLATE. Chalice, by *John Swift*, 1776; Paten, by *Samuel & George Whitford*, 1805. – MONUMENTS to the Dymokes of Scrivelsby Court, except for the pre-Dymoke effigies of a Knight and a Lady, *c.*1300, probably Marmions. He is represented cross-legged and praying. The Dymokes came into the estate by marriage in the mid C14. – Sir Robert Dymoke † 1545. Tomb-chest with the typically bald forms of the ending Gothic style. On the lid brass effigy, bearded, a 2 ft 6 in. figure. – Lewis D. † 1760. Standing wall-monument of white and beige marble. By *W. Atkinson*. Against the base a beautiful emblem of a snake biting its tail (an emblem of Eternity) and two extinguished torches. In the centre of the monument an outstandingly good bust. Trophies l. and r. Open pediment at the top. – Emma D. † 1884. In the churchyard E of the church. Romanesque table-tomb with eight legs.

SCRIVELSBY COURT. The house of the Dymoke family, hereditary champions of England ever since the time of Richard II, has gone. What remains is the brick office range with mullioned windows, a gateway, now filled in, in the middle, the date 1574 above, and just one C14 or C15 window at the r. end of the front. This is straight-headed and has ogee arches to its three lights. Otherwise the present building is mainly Georgian. At the entrance to the park is the LION GATE with some shields and a bit of tracery. The greenstone four-centred arch is obviously re-done. The gate was indeed rebuilt early in the C19, when the stone lion was replaced, probably by *C. J. Carter* of Louth, who made designs for a new gate in 1833. *Humphry Repton* laid out the grounds before 1791, when Lord Torrington saw a thatched rectory, 'The Minister's house lately repair'd upon Mr R's plan'. Also to

'Mr R's' plan are probably the pair of octagonal LODGES tha
stand by one side of the Lion Gate.*

8010　　　　SCUNTHORPE

Scunthorpe, Frodingham, Brumby, Ashby, Crosby are all one
a town of nearly 70,000, grown together by virtue – thougl
visually it certainly cannot be called virtue – of ironstone an
smelting. The steelworks now employ well over 20,000. Th
industry is just over a hundred years old, and the grime o
Victorian industrial growth still lies over the old Scunthorpe
Unfortunately the new Scunthorpe up to the Second World Wa
has not been visually more responsible, and a change for the ver
much better is only just becoming noticeable. Conditions bein
what they are, we thought we would be justified in taking th
exceptional course of a perambulation including everything
except the old village church of Frodingham.

ST LAWRENCE, Frodingham, Oswald Road. A medieval churcl
with a new nave and chancel added on the N side by *Sir Charle*
Nicholson in 1913. The old chancel, now S chapel, is E.E. witl
a group of three stepped E lancets and three widely spaced
lancets. E.E. also the S porch entrance, formerly shafted an
with dog-tooth up the jambs and arch. The inner S doorway i
Georgian. The W tower must be E.E. too, or even C12. It i
square, and though its bell-openings seem Perp, they posses
nook-shafts. The small tower arch confirms the dating. The ol
N arcade, now between the old and the new nave, is of the C12
without a doubt. Three bays, round piers with many-scallopec
capitals, square abaci. The arches are Dec, see their ballflowe
decoration. The S arcade is Perp. Octagonal piers, double-cham
fered arches. Good E.E. chancel arch with triple responds. Si
Charles Nicholson's piers to his N aisle are square, set diagonally
and slightly chamfered in the main directions. The arche
characteristically die into them. Altogether the enlargemen
of the church places it of course in the Scunthorpe context. –
FONT COVER. A modest, but pretty, later C17 piece. – PLATE
Chalice and Paten Cover, by *John Morley* of Lincoln, 1569.

PERAMBULATION, including CHURCHES, CHAPELS,
and PUBLIC BUILDINGS

One ought not to start by St Lawrence; for of Frodingham
village nothing survives. Instead one should be honest and

* A STATUE of a warrior in Roman costume, standing by a pond, is signed
and dated *F. V. Frese* 1723.

begin by looking at the grim, grimy centre of Scunthorpe, the
E part of the HIGH STREET, with not a single redeeming
feature and the side streets turning at once cheap suburban.
It is all brick, except for the parish church.

ST JOHN, Scunthorpe. By 1891 the steel industry had generated
enough prosperity for the first Lord St Oswald to give to the
town this large, lavishly built church. The architect was
Crowther. It is still the most ambitious church of Scunthorpe,
and one is sorry to see it in the least patronized part. The style
is Perp. Tall W tower with coupled two-light bell-openings.
The rest all with battlements and fleuron friezes below (cf.
Althorpe). Very high interior, double the number of clerestory
windows as of arcade openings. Six-light E window. – Ornate
FONT.

The character of the HIGH STREET changes W of Wells Street.
The shopping is now more West-End. Soon one reaches the
main crossing. One can turn N, up FRODINGHAM ROAD, and
pass along by the CENTENARY METHODIST CHURCH (1908
by *W. H. Buttrick*), red, dull, with a (ritually) NW tower with
spire, and the HOLY SOULS CATHOLIC CHURCH of 1917,
red, with a NW tower, a bargeboarded gable, and a rose
window, to the parish church of Crosby.

ST GEORGE, Crosby. 1914–25 by *H. C. Corlette*. Brick, to the W
still unfinished. With tall, lancet-shaped windows with a little
Dec tracery. In the aisle good groups of lancets. Interior with
wide arches, low octagonal piers, and a high canted ceiling.
All around is red suburban housing of the same years as the
church, i.e. E of Frodingham Road *c.*1900–10, W of it 1920 etc.
If one returns by one of these back streets to the main crossing
and now walks W along DONCASTER ROAD the building gets
looser. One passes the Tudor MUNICIPAL BATHS of 1931
and 1960 and the featureless recent YOUTH CENTRE, and can
then turn N up HENDERSON AVENUE and have a look at
Scunthorpe's first housing estate, laid out with its central
circus by *Sir Patrick Abercrombie* in 1920, or go on to the end
of Doncaster Road, down the hill, to reach the BERKELEY
ESTATE, built W of Scotter Road in the thirties, E of it in the
fifties. The housing is quite uncommonly unenterprising.
Once more back to the main crossing and now S, along OSWALD
ROAD. At the corner of Doncaster Road the CONGREGA-
TIONAL CHURCH of 1912 (by *W. H. Buttrick*), red, with a
NE tower, lancet windows, and some free Gothic detail. Then
at once again suburban houses. A little S the church of St

Lawrence. This now stands as one entry to a more mode:
Scunthorpe. The approach to the railway bridge is flanked k
two recent brick buildings, the POST OFFICE and the BRIDGE
HOTEL, both again quite depressingly amorphous. Then tl
bridge and across to an open space. To the w, off BRUMF
WOOD LANE, lies BRUMBY HALL, the only old and wortl
while domestic building of Scunthorpe. It has a three-storeye
C17 porch with pilasters, strapwork motifs, and a sundi
dated 1637. The house was extended E and W in the C1
Inside, the staircase has pretty, thin, Late Georgian decoratio
s of the railway bridge, along ASHBY ROAD is the be
building of Scunthorpe, the new town hall.

CIVIC CENTRE. 1957–63 by *C. B. Pearson, Son & Partners*
Lancaster. Yellow brick, with grey slate posts. The curve:
stone-faced council chamber rises above. To the s the pier
in front of its curve, stand detached.

See
p.
768

s of the town hall the crossing with Kingsway and Queensway. I
KINGSWAY the NORTH LINDSEY TECHNICAL COLLEGE
1949–63 by the County Architect, *A. R. Clark*, quite ur
eventful. Continue s from the crossing further along Ashb
Road and you will soon be between St Mark's Methodi:
Church and St Hugh Old Brumby.

ST MARK'S METHODIST CHURCH, Ashby Road. 1960 b
Fisher, Hollingsworth & Partners of Hull. A little outré, bu
certainly not uneventful or unenterprising. Porch to the stree
with tapering skeleton tower. The church itself with the saw
tooth walls of Coventry Cathedral throwing all the light on t
the altar. Ample premises behind.

ST HUGH, Old Brumby, Ashby Road. Completed in 1939. B
Lawrence Bond. Concrete structure and brick. Nave an
chancel in one. The big pantile roof tapers into a gambre
shape. The s tower repeats the tapering outline in its top par:
All the detail tends to be playful, except the portico of fou
unrelieved pillars. – PLATE. Paten, by *John Cory*, 1711.

W of the churches in OLD BRUMBY STREET a very little o
Brumby village is left. SE of the churches in the maze of th
housing a fourteen-storey block of flats (Langland House, ir
Bridges Road). This is by *Jellicoe, Ballantyne & Coleridge*
1961–2. At the s end of Ashby Road one ought to turn E alonç
ASHBY HIGH STREET. There is new shopping here, bu
again architecturally valueless, except for the CO-OP SUPER
MARKET, which deserves praise. It is by *Derek Brown*, 1958
Soon on the r. St Paul's.

T PAUL, Ashby. 1925 by *H. C. Corlette*. Tall, of brick, and with
a still incomplete nave. Impressive E front. Prominent bellcote
on the E end of the N aisle. Low vestries on this side. Wide nave
and a steep, canted painted ceiling.

inally, w of Ashby, between Messingham and Burringham
Roads the RIDDINGS ESTATE, with more recent and acceptable housing and with the excellent SECONDARY MODERN
SCHOOL by *D. Clarke-Hall, Scorer & Bright*, 1958. Two-
storeyed blocks. The classroom block linked by a vestibule to
the dining room, gym, etc. The kitchen and ancillary rooms
are screened by an effective, very heavily rusticated or em-
bossed wall. A tall water-tower with glazed cistern provides
vertical emphasis.

CUNTHORPE STEEL WORKS. The company took the unusual
step of asking an architect to be consultant for new buildings,
and the result is *Frederick Gibberd*'s Steel Rolling Mill, Office
Building, and Electricity Sub-Station, all completed in 1949.

LABORATORY for RICHARD THOMAS & BALDWIN, Red-
bourn Works, $1\frac{1}{2}$ m. E of St John. An interesting structure
with fifteen concrete mushroom pillars. Hence the roof comes
forward in lobes. Designed by *H. S. Scorer* and built in 1958.)

SEARBY

ST NICHOLAS. Built in 1832. Grey brick. W tower, nave, and
polygonal apse. – WEST GALLERY dated 1832. – The other
WOODWORK mostly High Victorian and made by the then
vicar, *T. J. M. Townsend*.* – PLATE. Chalice and Paten Cover,
London, 1684. – MONUMENTS. Two unusually lovingly
detailed tablets by *G. Earle* of Hull, to Richard Roadley † 1825
and Richard Dixon Roadley † 1828. Both have urns, the latter
with garlands, the former also a small relief of hourglass and
branch.

MANOR HOUSE, N of the church. Red brick. Early C19. Tall
bows flanking a doorway with Tuscan columns. The windows
embellished by stone heads.

SIBSEY

ST MARGARET. A surprising interior. Arcades of five bays, with
Norman, many-scalloped capitals, square abaci, and single-
step arches, but the piers far too long. It gives the whole an

* Who also supplied the Gothic SHELTER w of the church, which is
dated 1866. It is of red brick, has a pillar and two arches and a rough length
of a tree trunk as a seat.

1840 look. In fact it can be seen that the original piers wer
only 7 ft long. The SE and NW responds have leaf crocke
instead of the scallops. Norman also the N doorway with or
order of shafts, a lively variation on the crenellation motif i
the arch. Hood-mould on two dragon heads. The W tower
clearly E.E., see the lancets below and the very overdone dog
tooth about the twin bell-openings. They are shafted, wit
shaft-rings, and have a pointed quatrefoil in plate tracer
under a round arch. Above this a Perp bell-stage, two ligh
with a transom. The W window is a Dec alteration, and at th
same time the arch towards the nave was altered. Tripl
shafted responds with fillet. Two sunk wave mouldings. Th
chancel is E.E. in style too, but was rebuilt in 1855 (by *Kirk*
But the lancets and especially the partly blocked low-sid
lancet can probably be trusted. The E window of course can
The aisles also were rebuilt. Early Perp clerestory of two-ligh
upright windows. The S porch with its round-arched entranc
and its archaic hoop-like transverse arches or ribs is date
1699. – STAINED GLASS. E window by *Ward*, 1856 (TK).
PLATE. Flagon, by *Thomas Parr*, 1719; Chalice and Paten, b
Sarah Parr, 1730.

RECTORY. 1822. By *George Smith* and *John Tyler*, builders c
Boston.

SIBSEY HOUSE. Early C19 with a Doric porch. The stables loo
late C18.

PORCH HOUSE. Fen Artisan-Mannerism. Brick with erratic
string courses, wayward details, and a crude pilastered an
pedimented door.

(WAYTEFIELD, Boston Road, A good, large house, probabl
C17. PB)

WINDMILL, 1 m. NW. Tower mill with complete gear, sails
and fan-tail.

SIXHILLS

1080 ALL SAINTS. By *James Fowler*, 1869. E.E., rock-faced, wit
lancets, internally shafted. The tower masonry is probabl
medieval, though the tall shafted bell-openings are of cours
Fowler's (1875). Inside, the former N aisle arcade appears
Three bays, octagonal piers, double-chamfered arches.
PLATE. Chalice and Cover, given 1720; Paten, by *Thoma
Parr*, 1720.

THE GRANGE, ½ m. W. Of the Gilbertine Priory which wa
founded here in c.1150 the pleasant farmhouse of 1747 exhibit
in its walls four small head-stops, their date probably the C1

SKEGNESS

1060

eland in 1540 wrote that the old town of Skegness 'is clene
onsumid and eten up with the se. Part of a church by it stood
late'. The Skegness that stands now is a recent growth, and the
arish church of today is clearly the church of a village
urrounded by C20 housing.

T CLEMENT, Lincoln Road. Squat, unbuttressed w tower, C13
or a little later. The tower arch is triple-chamfered. The rest
is Latest Middle-Ages, altered and polished up with brick in
the C18. – FONT. Octagonal, Perp, with panelled stem and
shields on the bowl set in barbed quatrefoils. – PULPIT.
Georgian. – PLATE. Chalice, London, 1720.

he story of the present Skegness starts about 1873–5, when the
ain streets of the town were laid out as a grid, wide enough for
ee planting and with a central circus, in the middle of which a
ew church was placed.

T MATTHEW. 1879–80 by *James Fowler*, completed 1884 by
W. & C. A. Bassett Smith. It is a prosperous building in the
E.E. style with a polygonal apse and a bell-turret.

METHODIST CHAPEL, Algitha Road. The date here is 1881,
the site less prosperous, but in the same genteel grid. The
style is also C13 Gothic. But *Charles Bell*, the architect,
handled it much more crudely.

he new town is marked as a seaside resort by the JUBILEE
CLOCK TOWER of 1899, brick, architecturally negligible, and
with a Big-Ben top. It stands at the SE corner of the laid-out
estate with, to its l. and r. along the front, a few bigger brick
buildings still in the High rather than the Late Victorian style,
and at the E end of LUMLEY ROAD, which leads straight to
the railway station and the Lumley Hotel. The station was
opened in 1875, and without it of course Skegness could not
have developed. The LUMLEY HOTEL was built between
1879 and 1883 and belongs to the early crop of architecturally
ignorant buildings of the town. More refined is HILDRED's
HOTEL of 1897 (by *A. Coke Hill*), halfway down Lumley
Road, eleven bays and only two storeys, in the Norman-Shaw–
Ernest-George style. It actually stands back a little and at an
angle; for it belongs to the HIGH STREET, whose name proves
it to be old and not new Skegness and which indeed does not
run in conformity with the grid.

ST PAUL's BAPTIST CHURCH, 1911 by *John Wills & Sons*,

stands next to Hildred's Hotel. It is the typical free Gothic ·
Nonconformist chapels of its date, with the equally asym
metrical s w (ritually s w) tower.

Here we have gone beyond 1900. By then Skegness had develope
from modest brick to brick with half-timber gables and ba
windows. The style at its more ambitious is illustrated by th
LINKS HOTEL, 1902 by *Brewill & Bailey*, the SEACROF
HOTEL, 1904 by *E. A. Robson*, and the NORTH SHOR
HOTEL, 1909 by *Bridge*.

So to the NORTH PARADE and the SOUTH PARADE. Both ar
C20 and illustrate a type of seaside boarding house with broa
bay windows and verandas which is functionally perfectl
sound and not at all gaudy. The same is true of the glazed-ove
PIER of 1881, by *Head, Wright & Son*. On the other han
there is of course the vast entertainment area with building
in a variety of meretricious modes, including some castellate
ones. Skegness at present can accommodate about 80,00
holiday-makers at a time.

SKENDLEBY

ST PETER AND ST PAUL. Restored by *Sir G. G. Scott* in 187
and consequently very scraped-looking. However, a cedar tre
to the E helps considerably. Grey stone, except for the mor
original-looking chancel, which is partly of greenstone. Th
windows now all with flowing tracery. Is that correct ? Reall
original, i.e. untouched, the hood-mould of the aumbry in th
chancel. The strangest thing about the church is that the v
tower in relation to the nave presupposes a N aisle whos
arcade has disappeared, but the chancel and chancel arch pre
suppose the full width. Was then the arcade taken out befor
the chancel was built ? – FONT. Octagonal. Panelled stem
moulded bowl on big heads and with a top band of fleuron
and small heads. – STAINED GLASS. E window by *Kempe &
Tower*, c.1908. – PLATE. Chalice, London, 1682.

SKENDLEBY HALL. Mid C18; that is the centre, E–W wing
The additions, including a chapel, are of 1913.

HOME FARM. Long, low, and L-shaped with a gabled porch and
a massive chimneystack growing from the centre. Probabl
late C17 Vernacular.

GIANT'S HILLS LONG BARROWS. These consist of tw
long barrows on the E slope of a valley, ¾ m. N W of the church
The N barrow is 200 ft long and still stands to a height o
5 ft. The side ditches, which are clearly visible, run roun

both ends of the barrow. Excavation revealed the latter to
be 8–12 ft deep and 15–25 ft wide. The barrow covered a
timber enclosure 189 ft long with a façade at the E end. Within
this mortuary enclosure traces of hurdle-work were found,
and beneath a small cairn the remains of eight disarticulated
skeletons which were presumably stored in the timber enclosure before the erection of the long barrow. The second
long barrow, 250 yds to the s, has been almost levelled by
ploughing.

SKIDBROOKE

4090

ST BOTOLPH. Alone on the flat marsh, with some trees as its
sole accompaniment. E.E. doorway, the hood-mould with
dog-tooth, and also E.E. the four-bay arcades. On the s side
short octagonal piers, later heightened, stiff-leaf capitals and
double-chamfered arches. On the N side very plainly moulded
capitals. E.E. also the chancel arch with roll mouldings. In the
Dec style a straight-headed N aisle window (tracery of reticulation units) and probably also the w doorway and the aisle w
windows. Perp w tower, but its lower part to the E the w wall
of the C12 church, before aisles were added (see the original
roof-line). Perp clerestory with three-light windows, Perp five-
light E window with a crude transom across the panel tracery
at the top. But there is other evidence in and around the
chancel which is decidedly obscure. Quite clearly there were
N and s chapels, but on the N side, visible from outside, there
is also the arch of a blocked opening, just possibly a tall lancet
of the E.E. aisle. Inside however there is half an arch much
higher up and cut by the line of the aisle. Whatever can it have
been? And is there not another such arch on the s side? The
interior of Skidbrooke is impressive in its size and scale. –
PULPIT. 1628, in a disarmingly rustic style, with a distinct
flavour of Gothic Survival, but also with big flowers, straight
vertical branches with leaves l. and r. On the back panel the
lion and the unicorn, but no coat of arms for them to protect.

SNARFORD

0080

ST LAWRENCE. Small w tower, C12 below, but above C13 or
C14. The tower has at a height above the arch to the nave four
mysterious round arches; that to the E has a billet band and is
segmental. The supports of these arches are shapeless. No
indication corresponds to these arches externally. The area is
too small to have been a crossing, and the height of the tower

not sufficient to call for a catching up of its weight. – Nothing else worth while architecturally, but there is the FONT (octagonal, Perp, with four shields referring to Christ's Passion: a large head, an arrangement of leaves and an IHS in branches), and there are the MONUMENTS, three of them, and all three worthwhile indeed. Sir Thomas St Pol † 1582 and wife. Alabaster. A six-poster, the corner posts bulbous and jolly like bed-posts, the posts between tapering and decorated with fish-scales. The tomb-chest has shields in juicy wreaths flanked by short fluted columns. The effigies are recumbent and hopelessly badly done. At his feet a cushion carved with a symmetrical daisy pattern, as they appear in embroidery work. Flat top and on it the kneeling children, the eldest son on a high plinth of his own. The inscription is still in black-letter. The composition of the monument reflects that of the monument to the second Earl of Rutland at Bottesford in Leicestershire, † 1563. – Sir George St Pol † 1613 and wife. Big standing wall-monument. Both effigies lie stiffly on their sides, the head propped up by the elbow. He lies behind and a little above her. A flat arch, columns l. and r., and at the top obelisks and an achievement. – Robert Lord Rich, Earl of Warwick, † 1619, and his last wife, widow of Sir George St Pol (see above). Alabaster tablet with a medallion in the centre in which his bust nearly frontal and hers behind in profile – an unusual and successful composition, like a boldly enlarged miniature. Good poem beneath. The medallion might well be by *Epiphanius Evesham*, who did the Rich Monument at Felstead in Essex, where the Earl of Warwick was in fact buried. – Also a brass inscription of 1597, recommended to latinists. – PLATE. Chalice and Cover, Dordrecht, 1622.

The St Pol mansion has long disappeared. It stood SW of HALL FARM (C17) and was surveyed by John Thorpe. Excavations have, however, recently revealed a different plan, with a front about 120 ft long, circular turrets at each end, and the doorway leading directly into a hall.

SNELLAND

ALL SAINTS. Very fully restored by *Edward Browning* of Stamford in 1863. Nave with bellcote and chancel. Late C13 details. Browning built the N aisle afresh. Medieval the plain C13 S doorway, the early C14 S window with ogee lights and a lozenge still in plate tracery, some of the ogee heads of the straight-topped N and S windows, and the small transomed Dec E window of the N aisle. By Browning the curious arrangement of the N arcade, where the piers have no capitals and the arches stand on corbels with heads and naturalistic foliage. – FONT. No doubt also of *c.*1863, as it is identical with that at Cold Hanworth. – PLATE. Paten and Flagon, by *T. S.*, London, 1695; Chalice and Cover, by *H.E.*, London, 1703.

EASBY HALL, 1¼ m. SW. There are arms of an Earl of Scarbrough and the date 1708 above the porch. E front of nine bays and two storeys, porch in bay six. Side elevations of three bays.

SNITTERBY

t NICHOLAS. 1866 by *Fowler*. W tower with rather mannered details. Nave and apse. Interior red brick, with some yellow and black bricks. The church preceding this was built in 1780 and had a clerestory with big quatrefoil windows.

SOMERBY

t MARGARET. In the trees, above the Hall, on the hillside. A rough building. The W tower reaches hardly above the roof. Its W window is a domestic mullioned C17 affair. So are two nave windows. Nave and chancel are in one. In the E wall of the chancel a blocked C18 window. But the chancel arch is E.E., and so are the stumps of a N and S chapel, unless the three arches belonged to a crossing. – PLATE. Chalice and Cover, inscribed 1569; Dish, C17(?), given in 1752. – MONUMENTS. Late C13 Knight, cross-legged, two angels by his diagonally placed pillow. At his feet not only the usual lion but also a tiny curled-up puppy. – C18 tablets to Westons, and one standing monument: Edward † 1770. Small urn on top of the usual obelisk.

OMERBY HALL. The Parliamentarian Sir Edward Rossiter built an ambitious brick house here in 1660. Its style was the usual Artisan Mannerism, but also owed something to Scandinavia. The present building is early C19, with some fragments that might be due to *John Carr*, who worked here in 1768. A square stock-brick block linked to pavilions. In the park a COLUMN with an urn, erected in 1770 by Edward and Ann Weston, to celebrate twenty-nine years of happy marriage.

3070

SOMERSBY

St Margaret. Of greenstone. Except for the connexion wit
Lord Tennyson, of no special interest. Short, rough w towe
nave and chancel. In the nave s wall a Perp window wit
segmental head. The position of the chancel arch shows th
former existence of a s arcade. – PLATE. Chalice, by *W. H*
1653. – In the churchyard a CROSS, complete including th
castellated knob at the top of the shaft and the carvings of th
Crucifixus and the Virgin.

48b MANOR FARM. Built in 1722 for Robert Burton and for goo
stylistic reasons attributed to *Sir John Vanbrugh*. The house i
in the embattled manner Vanbrugh used for small houses an
is remarkably close in plan to the Nunnery, built by him a
Greenwich before 1721. What seems to be the original desig
for Somersby is signed, however, by *Robert Alfray* ('*inv. e
delin.*'), of whom nothing is known.* Alfray was probably a
executant builder, claiming from his drawing more than h
deserved. There are four towers at the angles, each pierce
with circular and oblong windows. The N front between then
is castellated and has two rows of plain arched windows,
rusticated brick porch, and above this a partially blocke
Venetian window. The s front is spanned by a broad pedimen
and has segment-headed windows and a tripartite doorwa
and central window. The hall and staircase are ingeniousl
formed. Entry by a mock screens passage with an elliptica
arch (cf. Harrington Hall, p. 268). The hall with a partly
vaulted ceiling, and the staircase tucked into a narrow spac
by the 'screens', the stairs making two short turns.

SOMERSBY HOUSE, formerly the Rectory. This is the birth
place of Lord Tennyson. The E wing on the s side was i
'Carpenter's Gothic',‡ designed by *George Tennyson*. Th
bricklaying was done by his coachman, Mr Howlings. Th
main part of the house has an elegant, perhaps Late Georgian
staircase.

2070

SOTBY

St Peter. Nave with bellcote and chancel. Greenstone. Th
chancel arch is mid-Norman. In the chancel a low tomb reces
and a pointed cusped piscina. The nave masonry is medieva
too, but the arched windows and the doorway must be Late

* Banks Collection, Lincoln.
‡ Now trimmed of its Gothic bits.

Georgian.* The chancel was rebuilt (by *Drury*) in 1857. –
PLATE. Chalice and Cover, by *Matthew Cooper*(?), London,
1703; Chalice, gilt inside, by *Robert Hennell*, 1834.

SOUTH CARLTON

ST JOHN BAPTIST. An unpromising exterior, mostly by *Teulon*,
1860.‡ Unbuttressed W tower with pyramid roof, nave and
chancel in one with big slate roof in bands of two shades. To
the N the Monson Mausoleum by *Watkins* (GR), 1897–8, in a
fancy Gothic. Inside much more of historical interest. Plain
Early Norman W arch. Aisle arcades, rebuilt in the C19, but
with original materials. They are C13, of two periods. S arcade
of three bays, octagonal piers, capitals with pellets, double-
chamfered arches. N arcade of three bays, round piers, keeled
responds, double-chamfered arches. Hood-moulds with leaf
paterae. The separate bay to the E of the arcade (if original)
and the bay of the N chapel in the same style. – SCREEN.
With Perp parts. – BENCH ENDS. Perp, with tracery and
poppy-heads or figures in their stead. – PLATE. Chalice,
London, 1652; Paten, London, 1652; Flagon, London, 1676;
Alms Basin, by *E. G.*, London, 1676. – MONUMENTS. Sir
John and Lady Monson, 1625 by *Nicholas Stone*. Six-poster,
free-standing. Two white recumbent effigies, excellently
carved. The children kneel below along the tomb-chest. –
Sixth Lord Monson, 1864. By *Bartolini* and *Bencini* in Florence
to the design of *Insoni* (information from Mr R. Gunnis§).
The copy of a monument in the Annunziata in Florence. High
plinth in a neo-mid-C18 style. Above big coat of arms with
lush foliage. The monument is in the mausoleum. The E wall
of this inside is a big neo-Jacobean screen with recesses.

MANOR HOUSE. Early C18; of stone and clunch. Five bays,
two floors, pitched roof and dormers.

SOUTH COCKERINGTON

ST LEONARD. Of greenstone. W tower, nave and chancel. The
W tower is Perp, see the mouldings of the doorway and the

* The S side in the Nattes drawing is quite different from what it is now.
It shows e.g. the remains of a blocked Norman arcade.

‡ The work having been badly executed in 1851 (*Builder*, 1861, p. 12).
Information from GS.

§ Bencini I have not been able to identify. Is he not *G. M. Benzoni*? The
famous Bartolini died in 1850, and of Johann Insoni of Ortisei who also lived
in Florence nothing is known after 1831.

arch towards the nave. The mouldings of s and N doorway
also Perp. – FONT. Octagonal, Perp, with shields in pointed
quatrefoils. – SCREEN. Wide, one-bay divisions with crocketed
ogee arches and panel tracery. – PLATE. Chalice and Cover
1569. – MONUMENT. Sir Adrian Scrope † 1623. Very understandably attributed by Mrs Esdaile to *Epiphanius Evesham*
45 (cf. Snarford). Alabaster. Semi-reclining effigy, the features
exceptionally eloquent. His hand lies on his breast. Against the
tomb-chest kneeling daughters and a group of sons felicitously
composed in the typical Evesham way.

2080 ## SOUTH ELKINGTON

ALL SAINTS. Nave of 1843, chancel and N aisle of 1873. Ironstone and chalk. Perp w tower. s aisle with Perp windows.
The N aisle w window of late C13 style also seems original. Of
the s arcade the piers, C13 too, are in order, and two round
moulded capitals. N aisle and chancel are characterized by
their naturalistic foliage. The nave roof is supposed to be
medieval. Alternating tie-beams and hammerbeams. Angels
against the latter. Also decorated bosses. – FONT. Octagonal,
Perp, with shields in quatrefoils. – STAINED GLASS. The
smallest medieval bits in the s aisle. – PLATE (also of North
Elkington). Paten, London, 1704; Plate, London, 1748.

SOUTH ELKINGTON HALL. Italianate, by *W. A. Nicholson*,
*c.*1841. Its dullness architecturally is perhaps further indication that Nicholson was not the designing hand behind the
vigorous style of Bayons (*see* p. 185).

9020 ## SOUTH FERRIBY

ST NICHOLAS. The church lies a little above the road on the
hillside, overlooking the Humber. The Norman tympanum
over the porch entrance may well represent St Nicholas. The
figure is a bishop anyway. To his l. and r. crosses in roundels,
to the l. and r. of his head smaller roundels. South Ferriby
church is baffling in that *C. Hodgson Fowler* in 1889 gave it a
new chancel and ran it to the s, a very poor brick piece, by the
way. So the porch is a w porch, though its entrance seems a
re-set genuine C14 piece. This w wall exhibits early, perhaps
Norman, masonry. The tower, of brick and probably C18, was
a NE tower. Inside, the chancel arch seems to remain, with
interfered-with E.E. responds. Are the bases round abaci?
Remains of a Norman N doorway can also still be seen, and a

Perp window in the E wall. – PLATE. Chalice and Cover by *Edward Mangie* of Hull, 1666; Paten, London, 1728.

THE HALL. An estimate for rebuilding for Sir John Nelthorpe is dateable c.1800. The present house looks of that date. The front with no fewer than four projecting bays, two bowed, and in the centre, adjacent to paired entrances, two others with columned windows. The grounds once stretched to the Humber's edge.

SOUTH KELSEY

0090

ST MARY. Much weathered ironstone W tower. The date probably c.1300–30, see the triple-chamfered tower arch and its responds *vs.* the bell-openings. The rest of 1795, tall ashlar nave and tall polygonal apse. But the windows were made genteel Gothic by *Butterfield* in 1853. Bald interior. – PLATE. Chalice, Elizabethan; Chalice, by *John Morley* of Lincoln, c.1569. – MONUMENTS. Cross-legged early C14 Knight. – Brasses to a member of the Hansard family, c.1410–20, and wife (chancel N). The figures are 4 ft 9 in. long.

SOUTH KELSEY HALL. The site partly surrounded by a wide moat. Within this stood a large Tudor house, with a courtyard and towers at the angles. Attached to the present farmhouse of c.1610 are the remains of a SE tower. Octagonal, brick with stone quoins, and part of one pointed cusped light. Other Tudor fragments are built into barns.

MOORTOWN HOUSE, 2 m. SE. A small early C19 park with a plain house.

SOUTH ORMSBY

3070

ST LEONARD. At the W end of the s aisle, re-set, a Norman doorway, single-chamfered, with billet in the hood-mould. This is said to come from the demolished church of Calceby, but was already at South Ormsby in 1835. The W tower of the church is of greenstone, Perp, and has a tall arch to the nave. The chancel and chancel chapel are over-restored, but, if this was done correctly, must both be Dec. The chancel is in fact dateable to before 1384 (built by the rector who died in that year), a late date for flowing tracery. Good, stately Perp windows in the nave on the N side, one of them of four lights. The s aisle was rebuilt by *Fowler* in 1871–2. Inside, however, the s arcade of three wide bays is E.E. The piers and arches are of greenstone, the capitals of limestone. The piers and abaci are round, the capitals have upright stiff-leaves. The arches are double-chamfered, and the label-stops are whorls of various kinds. The chancel arch may well be E.E. too, but the two-bay arcade to the chapel is later, and fits a C14 date. Short octagonal pier, the arches dying into the E and W imposts – FONT. Octagonal, Perp, very lavishly carved. Panelled stem, angels against the underside of the bowl, shields on the bowl with the symbol of the Annunciation, the Instruments of the Passion, the M for Mary, the I H S, and arms. All these shields are held by angels with hair standing out from their heads. The inscription at the foot refers to the donation of the font by Rudulphus Bolle and his wife. – STAINED GLASS. In the chapel many German or Netherlandish C16 and C17 medallions. – The E window by *Clayton & Bell*, 1873. – PLATE. Paten, by *Ed. Cornock*, 1724; Chalice, by *J. Denzilow*, 1783. – MONUMENTS. Brass to a Lady, a dog sitting at her feet. Early C15, the size 3 ft 2 in. – Brasses to Sir William Skipwith † 1482 and wife, 3 ft figures. The three brasses are on the floor of the S chapel. – Anthony Floyer † 1834, with draped urn. By *Jos. Earle* of Hull. – Charles Burrell Massingberd † 1835. By *Westmacott*, according to W. O. Massingberd's *History*. A seated mourning woman and by her feet a broken-off Corinthian capital – a conceit a little out of the ordinary.

ORMSBY HALL. By *James Paine*, 1752–5. There are enigmatic plans in the County Record Office inscribed 'Paine's plans of Ormsby house with Carr alterations'. In its present condition the house has an E front of three generously spaced bays, l. and r. with a tripartite window under a blank arch and in the middle a canted bay which contains the entrance. Originally this front was crowned by a giant pediment spanning the whole width of the façade. The Roman Doric porch is a later addition, perhaps by *John Carr*. The S front is quite irregular with a canted bay at the E end and a sunk basement. Additions to the rear by *P. Atkinson & Son*, 1803. Interior typically Paine with, on the back wall of the ENTRANCE HALL, a chimneypiece and above it a Roman bust on a bracket flanked by garlands. The excellent Rococo ceiling in the DRAWING ROOM and other plasterwork in the house was executed *c.*1775 by *J. Rose Senior* and '*Signor Pedrola*'. The chef d'œuvre of the house, however, is undoubtedly the STAIRCASE, superbly carved in mahogany, taking four sides of a well and having an arcaded gallery on the upper floor. The style of this is still Kentian. The carpenter was *William Lumby*. His balusters are

quite specially beautiful. The LIBRARY with grisaille panels
over the bookcases looks later and might be by *Carr*.

RECTORY. By *C. F. Penrose*, 1849. RIBA lists)

SOUTH RESTON

4080

ST EDITH. By *James Fowler*, 1864–5. Rock-faced and apsed.
With a bellcote and plate tracery. Inside brick-lined, red, with
bands of stone and some vitrified bricks. Naturalistic foliage
of course, and, also of course, nailhead up the arrises of the
chancel arch to spike it. – FONT. Octagonal, Perp, eight heads
supporting the bowl, eight different large leaves filling the
panels of the bowl. – STAINED GLASS. The one panel in a N
window with Christ exhibited to the people is good and looks
as if it might be by *Powell's*, designed by *Wooldridge*. – PLATE.
Chalice, by *James Salkeld*, 1827. – Also, from Castle Carlton,
Chalice, Elizabethan.

SOUTH RESTON HALL. Late Georgian, conservative, with
arched and keystoned windows. On the S front of the E wing a
canted bay and a tripartite window.

CASTLE CARLTON, Carlton Hill, ⅝ m. NW. Of the castle of
Hugh Bardolf, Justiciar under Richard I, the remains are so
completely covered in dense undergrowth that little of them
can be made out. However, the motte is a good specimen by
Lincolnshire standards. It and its two large baileys are surrounded by a wide circular ditch. (The church of Castle
Carlton was demolished in 1902. Cox)

SOUTHREY

2 m. SE of Bardney

1060

ST JOHN THE DIVINE. Built of wood by the parishioners in
1898, and like the church of an outpost of the Commonwealth.
Painted white, with a W porch, a sweet little bell-turret, and
on its top a big weathercock.

SOUTH SOMERCOTES

4090

ST PETER. A stately church. E.E. arcade of five bays, circular
piers with octagonal abaci; double-chamfered arches. Of the
same date the chancel arch and the N doorway into the chancel.
Then the low W tower, which has angel busts in the spandrels
of the doorway and Dec bell-openings. On the tower an elegant
recessed spire, the lucarnes successfully kept under control.

Spires are almost absent in this part of the county. Perp aisle windows and straight-sided arches. The original clerestory was suppressed in 1893. The interior is pleasantly unspoilt. The floor is partly tiled. – FONT. Big, octagonal, Perp. Fleuron frieze, shield with the Instruments of the Passion, heads on the underside. The COVER is Perp too, quite simple, but with a finial. – SCREEN. With wide, ogee-arched, single-light divisions. The tracery patterns vary, but are all Perp except for one which is purely Dec, i.e. flowing. Should one call this Early Perp? – PLATE. Chalice, London, 1773.

SOUTH THORESBY

4070

ST ANDREW. 1735–8. Of brick, still laid in English bond. Nicely and not immoderately overgrown with ivy. W tower, nave, and short chancel. The windows are arched and keyed-in. The E window is of the Venetian type with very broad pillars between the three parts (cf. Hannah, 1753). The entry is by a doorway with Gibbs surround and pediment in the S wall of the tower. Flat ceiling inside. – FONT. Octagonal, Perp, of the pattern-book type so frequent around here. Five panels with window patterns, Dec and Perp, two with bigger tracery patterns, one now invisible. – PULPIT and READING DESK. From a former three-decker. Probably of c.1738; simple. – PLATE. Almsdish, London, 1663; Chalice, by *John Swift*, 1746. – MONUMENT. Willoughby John Wood † 1786, aged 18. Tablet. Obelisk with an oval relief, showing a rose bush with one rose fallen to the ground.

RECTORY. 1853 by *Teulon*. Of rough red brick with smoother, redder bands and lozenges. Gables, one half-hipped, and a polygonal corner bay with pyramid roof. Picturesque and yet robust.

SOUTH WILLINGHAM

1080

ST MARTIN. Of greenstone. Perp W tower. Nave of 1838 with windows filled with Y-tracery. A N aisle has disappeared, and of the details of the arcade nothing can be said any longer. The chancel is late C13, if the very curious ironstone windows can be trusted. Three lancet lights and a quatrefoil in plate tracery over, the whole under one arch. The chancel arch is not medieval anyway. – FONT. Square, with chamfered angles, on nine shafts with fillets and on the bowl two quatrefoils on each side. – A panel with three such quatrefoils in the chancel N wall. – SCREEN. Perp. Three-light divisions with ogee-headed lights and panel tracery above. The springing of the coving is original too. – PLATE. Chalice and Paten Cover, by *John Morley* (?), 1571.

SPILSBY

4060

T JAMES. Externally the church is disappointing; it looks all Victorian, owing to *W. Bassett Smith*'s rebuilding of the chancel, adding of a S aisle, and scraping generally (1879). Only the W tower has a true appearance. It is tall, of greenstone, and has to the nave an arch with concave-sided semi-octagonal responds and to the outside a base frieze of quatrefoils with shields, polygonal embracing buttresses, bell-openings of the latest Perp type, and eight pinnacles. Money was indeed left to its building in 1529. To call the tower the W tower – and the tower arch an arch to the nave is in fact not correct. It was built as a W tower, to go with a Dec nave, but soon after a new nave was built and the old made into an inner N aisle with the old N aisle as an outer N aisle. Bassett Smith finally added his new S aisle. There are thus three arcades inside, one Dec, the other also C14, the third C19. They are all of four bays and have octagonal piers and double-chamfered arches. The Dec arcade has tiny ballflowers in the abaci, the later C14 arcade is sturdier. Of the same moment or a moment between the two the N chapel arcade in the new terms, S chapel arcade in the old. It is the Willoughby Chapel now, and since a chantry was endowed by the will of the first Lord Willoughby in 1348, there is no reason to doubt that that is the date of the arcade. It is likely that converting the old chancel into the family chapel implied providing for a new chancel, and so for the new nave, and in that case the five-light E window with reticulated tracery can be dated to *c.*1350 too. The W window of the new aisle has the same tracery. Otherwise the tracery is Perp.

MONUMENTS. The principal reason to visit the church is, however, not this architectural puzzle, but the Willoughby and Bertie monuments in the chapel. They are chronologically as follows: Effigies of a cross-legged Knight and a Lady, first half of the C14, on a tomb-chest on which buttresses divide panels of two quatrefoils in a fleuron border. The buttresses now carry heavy pinnacles, two at each corner, but they are not original. Presumably they replace a canopy. The details have ogees, which helps to fix the date. The presumed Willoughby represented is John, first Lord, † 1348 (*see above*).

– John, second Lord, † 1372. Tomb-chest with figures holding shields and standing against cusped fields. Alabaster effigy and l. and r. horizontal shafting with tiny figures of monks.

31 Robert, third Lord, † 1396 and his wife. Alabaster effigies much renewed, and on a tomb-chest which looks completely renewed. – Margaret Zouche, third wife of the third Lord † 1391. Brass; a fine 4 ft 1 in. figure. – William, fifth Lord † 1410 and his wife. Brasses under canopies. A much bigger surround with figures has disappeared. The figures are 3 ft 10 in. long. – Richard Bertie † 1582 and his wife, Baroness Willoughby de Eresby and former Duchess of Suffolk, † 1580. This is a most remarkable monument. It fills the w wall of the chapel, which is really the space of the chancel arch of the original church and so blocks the view from the w tower to

42 Here, as the back of the monument, a screen has been erected like a reredos. It has three fluted Ionic columns of fancy details separating two fields filled by six passages from the Bible, five in Latin, one in English. They are placed in strap-work panels. Below is an altar-like or tomb-chest-like projection with shields in scrolls. At the top is a frieze with foliage and medallions. To the E, i.e. the chapel, the arrangement is like this: Again a tomb-chest-like projection, with colonnettes here and shields in strapwork surrounds. Above three hefty, extremely coarsely carved standing figures, a monk and two wild men (the Willoughby emblem) and between them two niches with columns on baluster-shaped bases and a sweeping busy, all-over pattern of a kind of diapering, consisting of chains of circles and rectangles filled with flowers. The niches are quite tall, and in them stand, preposterously out of proportion, two alabaster busts, excellently done, obviously by a different sculptor and probably with a view to a different setting. Top frieze with fruit and leaves. – Peregrine Bertie tenth Lord, † 1601 and his daughter † 1610. She is represented semi-reclining. Black columns l. and r. Two flat arches behind. A baby (she died in child-bed) in a bed at her feet. So far this is nothing special, but above in an arched niche with strap-work l. and r. the splendidly upright figure of the tenth Lord under a broken segmental pediment. – PLATE. Chalice London, 1569.

The MARKET PLACE is a drawn-out rectangle with houses and shops along its centre. The w parts are cobbled and dominated by the statue of John Franklin, bronze, by *Charles Bacon*, 1861 Facing this the genial façade of the WHITE HART and the former TOWN HALL, the latter of 1764 and originally with open ground-floor arcades. From here two parallel streets run E, interrupted by another open space ending in a third, both with lopped trees. Or else one might call the whole a long market space interrupted by two islands, one being the town hall. On the open space farthest E the MARKET CROSS, perhaps C14, the base with tracery, the top knob also preserved. To its E the METHODIST CHAPEL of 1877–8 (by *Charles Bell**), stock brick, with Geometrical tracery and no tower. If this is the E accent of the town, the church, W of the market place, is the W accent. Beyond the church, however, one more, very unexpected, accent: the SESSIONS HOUSE,61b 1824 by *H. E. Kendall*, fluted Greek Doric portico slapped on to a plain stock-brick box behind as a challenge to the church.

ERESBY. The avenue to this lost great house begins just W of the church and runs S ending by a lonely but magnificent brick and stone quoined GATEPIER. It is over twenty feet high and is topped by a splendid urn. Near by the STABLES in a C17 brick Artisan Mannerism with straight gables and small oval moulded brick lights. Leland says of the Tudor Lord Willoughby 'I hear he intendeth to build sumptuously'. So that dates the lost house. *Stephen Switzer* was staying here early in the C18, presumably to order the gardens.

SPITAL-IN-THE-STREET
2 m. E of Harpswell
9090

ST EDMUND'S CHAPEL. Oblong with straight-headed mullioned and transomed windows, the lights with four-centred arches. Bell-turret. Above the doorway an inscription stating that this place was a hostel for the poor in 1398, but not in 1594, and again in 1616. To its S the hostel itself with a date 1620.

SPRIDLINGTON
0080

ST HILARY. 1875 by *James Fowler*, and more important than most of what he was commissioned to do. The church was built to commemorate an incumbent who had died in 1873. It was paid for by his widow and friends. Ornate NW tower with saddleback roof. Nave and chancel only, but wide and spacious. The detail late C13 in style. – PAINTING. Large C18 painting of Moses pointing to the Ten Commandments. – PLATE. Chalice, Elizabethan.

* Information received from Mr G. Spain.

OLD RECTORY. Looks Early Victorian Classical, but the plans are of 1878 (by *F. H. Goddard*).

SPRINGTHORPE

8080

ST LAWRENCE AND ST GEORGE. Anglo-Saxon w tower. The s window is curious; basically probably of the keyhole type. The w doorway is blocked and part of a window set in. Bell openings twin, as usual, with mid-wall shafts.* Norman doorway with two orders of shafts, two of them decorated with zigzag. Also decorated capitals and abaci. Arch with zigzag. The rest of the exterior all over-restored. Inside a low two-bay C14 s arcade. Octagonal pier, double-chamfered arches. Big heavy capitals. The chancel is in a coarse Neo-Norman, especially the chancel arch. The date probably 1845. – STAINED GLASS. Much of *c.*1865 (restoration). It is fairly close to the Morris style and probably *Powell's*. – MAIDEN'S GARLAND to Mary Hill, killed in 1814 while ringing a bell. – PLATE. Chalice and Cover, by *John Gibbons*, 1706.

STAINFIELD

1070

ST ANDREW. Built in 1711. Brick, in Flemish bond, and stone quoins. The church is not orientated, and what will here be called w is in fact N etc. Thin w tower with ogee cap, like a Jacobean stair-turret. Nave s side with two arched windows and in the middle between them a doorway with open segmental pediment on brackets. The N wall is of stone and has no windows. The chancel E window alas victorianized, i.e. gothicized (by *Fowler*). – Good REREDOS with big segmental pediment on fluted Ionic pilasters. The Commandments etc. in cross-stitch EMBROIDERY. – PULPIT. Plain. – ARMOUR, a helmet and gauntlets. – PLATE. Chalice and Paten, by *D. G.*, London, 1654; Cup, by *R. & S. Hennell*, 1808.

STAINFIELD HALL. In the C16 Sir Robert Tyrwhit built a great house here, and this is shown on a Buck engraving of 1726. All of it has gone except for C18 brick STABLES. They may be the addition carried out by *H. Stanley* in 1766. The present house is a dull substitute built in 1856. One forlorn rusticated GATEPIER stands in a field.

STAINTON-BY-LANGWORTH

0070

ST JOHN BAPTIST. Built in 1796. Grey stone, small w tower with low pyramid roof crowned by a knob, nave and lower

* But the Nattes drawing, showing the s side, has no such bell-openings.

chancel, arched windows. The sedilia and piscina in the church are partly re-used Dec, partly completed later. The C17 seems the most likely date. – FONT. Octagonal, very large, the base with spurs like the base of a C12 pier. – PLATE. Chalice and Paten Cover, London, 1568; Paten, by *I.A.*, 1679; two-handled Cup, *c*.1680. – MONUMENT. Sanderson family, three generations of men, 1619. They kneel one behind the other, facing E, under arches. In a roundel at the bottom a bone, a scythe, a spade.

FAIRLEA. In the garden of this cottage, 200 yds N, by the railway bridge, stands the base and half the shaft of a former church-yard CROSS.

STAINTON-LE-VALE *1090*

A charmingly secluded hamlet in the Wolds.

ST ANDREW. Small oblong W tower with a W porch in it and a W doorway, both triple-chamfered, i.e. probably of *c*.1300. But the N doorway into the nave is Norman, of the simplest. There was formerly a S aisle of four bays with quatrefoil piers, C13 or *c*.1300, and where the chancel E wall now is, the church continued, on a semicircular S and a semi-octagonal N respond.

STALLINGBOROUGH *1010*

ST PETER AND ST PAUL. Built in 1745–6. Brick with brick quoins, nave and chancel with round-headed windows, and a W tower with pyramid roof, keyed-in round-headed doorway and bell-openings, and a round W window. The interior disappointing. – PLATE. Chalice and Paten Cover, by *John Morley* of Lincoln, 1569. – MONUMENTS. Brasses to Sir William Ayscough † 1541 and wife, 18 in. figures (chancel floor). – Sir Edward Ayscough † 1612 and wife, alabaster, she stiffly on her side, propped up on her elbow. The children kneel along the tomb-chest. – Sir Francis, his father, above, also alabaster, a bust with both arms in an arched recess. His posture with cheek propped up by one hand and the other holding a baton is decidedly Mannerist.

DAISY COTTAGE, SE of the church. Cottage, dated 1601, of four irregular bays with formerly mullioned windows. Built into the wall is a medieval corbel head.

STENIGOT *2080*

ST NICHOLAS. 1892. Of red brick. Nave and chancel in one; bellcote. – FONT. Octagonal, Perp, with shields in quatrefoils.

– PLATE. Chalice, by *W. M.*, London, 1678; Paten and Flagon
by *C. A.*, London, 1678. – MONUMENTS. Two small alabaster
tablets with kneeling figures: Francis Velles de Guevara † 1591
and Sir John Guevara † 1607.

OLD CHURCH, ¾ m. NE, not on any road. Heaps of stones mark
w tower and nave, but the chancel stands with a Norman
chancel arch, unmoulded and on the simplest chamfered
imposts. Also one Norman s window with a Perp top. Perp
also the E window. No N window.

STENIGOT HOUSE. A sizeable Neo-Georgian house by *A. N.
Prentice*, 1911. Two colours of brick, seven bays, with a
five-bay attachment. Stables dated 1913.

STEWTON
3080

ST ANDREW. The church consists of nave with bellcote and
chancel and looks from a distance entirely unpromising. Yet
this is what one notices as one approaches and enters: a
Norman N doorway blocked, a Norman s window, the same
i.e. Norman masonry in the chancel too, a Norman s doorway
with the plainest chamfered imposts and a blank tympanum,
and an equally plain chancel arch, i.e. a whole Norman church
of the C11 or early C12. E.E. a bit of dog-tooth re-used above
the E windows. Below these windows a heavy block of stone
most probably the keystone of a rib-vault, perhaps from Louth
Abbey or Legbourne Priory, both in the vicinity. Victorian of
course the w window (*c.*1866 by *Fowler*). – SCULPTURE. One
fine bearded head, presumably a label-stop. – PLATE. Chalice
and Cover, by *R. A.*, London, 1624.

STICKFORD
3060

ST HELEN. E.E. four-bay arcades, first N, then S. The N arcade
has quatrefoil piers with more than semicircular foils and
fillets, double-chamfered arches and head-stops, the s arcade
octagonal piers with a little nailhead enrichment and also
double-chamfered arches. So the w and E lancets of the N aisle
may well be original. Otherwise most of the exterior is of 1881
Dec, however, the s porch entrance with angels holding shields
l. and r., and Perp the w tower of greenstone. Four stages
open formerly to N and s into w bays of the aisles. Early Perp
doorway, four-light w window, Victorian bell-openings. –
FONT. Octagonal, with quatrefoils whose centres are shields
or leaves. – PLATE. Chalice, London, 1585; Paten, by *Robert
Abercromby*, 1736.

WINDMILL, ¾ m. sw. Tower mill still with its four sails, though
the cap and the fan-tail are in decline.

STICKNEY

ST LUKE. E.E. four-bay arcades. Quatrefoil piers with more-
than-semicircular foils and fillets. Double-chamfered arches.
Nailhead decoration on both w responds and the N piers. The
capitals also differ between N and s. Dec s doorway. The s
porch with gargoyles and a pointed stone roof on hollow-
chamfered transverse arches. The porch was rebuilt by *Bassett
Smith* in 1887. Was he correct in this? He also half-rebuilt
the w tower in 1900. The tower is tall and Perp with three-
light bell-openings with transoms. The w doorway has immediately above its depressed arch a frieze of four quatrefoils.
Four-light w window. Triple-chamfered tower arch. Otherwise the N aisle (bands of stone and brick) was apparently
rebuilt in 1793. The chancel and the clerestory are of 1853
(*Butterfield*). – PLATE. Beaker, by *F. S.*, London, 1608.

STIXWOULD

ST PETER. Of medieval grey masonry. w tower with its upper
parts Victorian. The windows of nave and chancel also
Victorian.* – FONT. Octagonal, later C14, with the Signs of
the Evangelists and four representations of months: January
(warming a hand and a foot by an unrepresented fire),
February, March, and April (represented by a figure with a
cornucopia). – SCREEN. Of two-light divisions, the arches
rounded and clasped by a super-ogee-arch. Instead of the
usual panel tracery roundels with quatrefoils. – BENCH ENDS.
With poppy-heads, some of the common foliage type, some
with heads l. and r. – ORGAN CASE. Early C19 and very pretty.
– FRAGMENTS. The bits of moulded stone and probably also
the COFFIN LIDS come from Stixwould Priory, founded for
Cistercian nuns in the early C12 and re-founded at the twelfth
hour, in 1536, for Premonstratensian canonesses to pray for
Jane Seymour. – However, the COFFIN LID inside the church,
with its elementary sunk head and no other carving, comes
from St Andrew, Woodhall Spa. – CROSS. The base with
angle spurs; long shaft. – PLATE. Chalice and Salver Paten, by
William Colson, inscribed 1732.

* The church was considerably rebuilt in 1831 and enlarged in 1864, says
Cox.

ABBEY FARM. On the site nothing remains visible of the priory.
The present house is L-shaped and early C18. The E front of
nine bays.

STOW

ST MARY. Of the early parish churches of England Stow is one
of the most monumental, so much so that it has been attempted
to connect it with the cathedral of Lindsey which was founded
by King Eigfrith of Northumberland on the Roman site of
Sidnacaster in 678 and removed to Doncaster after the Danish
ravages had begun (*see* Lincoln Cathedral, p. 82). But this is
not proved, and indeed not likely. Yet the size of Stow church,
though now partly Anglo-Saxon and partly Norman, was very
probably already before the Conquest more or less the same
as today. The Anglo-Saxon remains are of two periods, as we
shall see, but they comprise the whole crossing and the transepts, and hence the sizes of nave and chancel are to a certain
extent determined. For the dating of the Anglo-Saxon work
we have little to go by. The only fact recorded is a rebuilding
by Bishop Eadnoth, and he could be Eadnoth I, who ruled
from *c.*1004 to 1016, or Eadnoth II, whose dates are *c.*1034–50.
The church was collegiate. To the C11 belongs most of what
we see, and in fact nearly all the noticeable features, but the
lower parts of the walls are different (see the less neat coursing,
the change in the quoins about 9 ft from the ground, and
especially traces of lesenes or pilaster strips), and they are in
places reddened by fire. This one would like to connect with
the Danes, but Dr and Mrs H. M. Taylor, who have done the
most recent investigation of Stow,* do not want to go back
further than the C10. This date is based largely on the fact that
these lower courses of the transept walls presuppose a crossing
much as it is now, at least in plan, and that such a crossing is
hard to believe as of the C9.

This crossing is remarkably spacious – about 26 ft wide and
long – and it projects slightly beyond the walls of the transepts
and of course of nave and chancel, so that its angles are exposed. The arches are only about 14 ft wide. In these two
ways the crossing differs from the mature Romanesque crossing, where the length and width is identical with those of the
arms and the arches are the full length or width of the arms
except for the responds. Now this mature type is first to be

* And to whom I am most grateful for having given me access to their
unpublished text.

found with certainty at St Michael at Hildesheim about 1000,
although earlier claims have been made (Mittelzell, Reichenau,
late C10 or earlier, e.g.). But even if these earlier examples had
not the perfection of Hildesheim, they were clearly on the way
to it, and more cannot be said about Stow either. Moreover, as
regards Stow, it must be seen primarily in an English and not
a Continental context, and there the situation is this. Except
for Norton in County Durham, Stow is the only Anglo-Saxon
crossing, i.e. a crossing with arches to the transepts as high
and wide as those to nave and chancel – the only, if one ex-
cludes Ramsey Abbey, whose chronicle described the church
built about 970 in the following terms. The church had two
towers, the smaller one at the w end, the larger 'in quadrifidae
structurae medio, columnas quatuor porrectis de alia ad aliam
arcubus sibi invicem connexas, ne laxe defluerent, deprimebat',
i.e.: the larger stood in the middle of the four-part (cruciform)
structure and pressed down four columns connected with each
other (so that they would not be deflected) by arches extending
from one to the next.*

We can now move on to the elevational features, and that 5a
means the unforgettable crossing arches. Their scale (30 ft
high) and consistency are unique. They are of the familiar
type of e.g. Wittering in Northamptonshire, Skipwith in
Yorkshire, and St Benet at Cambridge, i.e. with sturdy demi-
shafts and thin rectangular lesenes or pilasters accompanying
the arch openings but at a distance from them, an entirely
unstructural device, as the shafts have nothing to do with the
angles or the reveals. The arches have broad rolls. They and
their imposts exist complete to all four sides, although unfortunately their evidence is masked in the inner corners by
strengthening piers and in the arches by strengthening arches.
The date of these reinforcements seems the early C14. An
Anglo-Saxon crossing tower can be surmised, but it was
perhaps of wood and hence needed less in the way of supports.
Anglo-Saxon also is the masonry of the transepts, and in it are
one complete window in the w wall of the s transept, one
complete doorway in the w wall of the N transept (where did
this lead?), and traces of two windows in the N and w walls of
the N transept. The treatment of the surrounds, as indeed of
all quoins, is worth looking at. The s transept window has
single splays and a hood-mould with, on its lower surface,

* Rolls Series 83, pp. 38 etc., quoted by the omniscient Sir Alfred Clapham
who was, however, singularly quiet and inexplicit about Stow.

palmette ornament. The same ornament also occurs in t
hood-mould on the w side of the w crossing arch and is to
found in a few other churches as well (Barholm and Coleby
Kesteven, St Peter at Gowts Lincoln, Carlton-in-Lindri
Nottinghamshire). Anglo-Saxon finally some window su
rounds re-used when *Pearson* in 1865 restored the church a
built the stair-turret in one of the angles of the crossing.

To proceed now to the Norman work, we are told th
Bishop Remigius found the church ruinous and rebuilt muc
He installed Benedictine monks from Eynsham in Oxfordshir
That was in 1091, but already c.1094–5 (or in 1109?) Bish
Bloet removed them back to Eynsham and annexed the chur
to the see. That gives us a fairly precise date for the Ear
Norman activity at Stow. It is preserved in the nave – whic
like the chancel, is indeed not bonded in with the crossin
The nave has flat, broad buttresses and few plain window
high up and just above a string-course. To the w two window
and a circular one over. Circular windows are also in the gab
fronts of the transepts. The principal pieces of enrichment
the nave must be later, perhaps of the time of the Lincoln
portals, i.e. of c.1140, or even later. The w and s doorways hav
three orders of colonnettes with variously decorated scallo
capitals and arches with an abundance of zigzag. The shafts
the s doorway have horizontal zigzag too, and the s strin
course was given an enrichment of little scallops. The
doorway is simpler (one order of colonnettes).

5a   The chancel of Stow is a prodigious piece of Late Norma
display, at least if one can trust *Pearson*, who restored th
church well in 1853–64 and gave it its rib-vaults. They did n
exist in the C18, but Pearson may have seen indications tha
they had existed. The chancel is of three bays, divided outsid
by flat buttresses, inside by composite shafts. Along the inne
walls runs blank arcading with colonnettes carrying decorate
scallop capitals. The E wall is in its present form largel
Pearson's work. Above the blank arcading string-course wit
small scallops just as on the outside of the nave, on the s sid
Pearson's ribs and transverse arches are lavishly decorated. S
are the windows, outside with nook-shafts and zigzag at
angles to the wall and inside with zigzag also at r. angles to th
wall, alternating with a crenellation motif. When this chanc
was completed, the church was once again complete. It is 150
long, and may well have had that length in the C11 alread
Of post-Norman date only two additions need be referred to

First the E.E. two-light windows, one with plate tracery in the s wall of the s transept, others with bar tracery (s transept E, N transept E and W), and secondly the present crossing tower, which is Perp.

FURNISHINGS. FONT. E.E., octagonal, on nine supports. On each side of the plain bowl one small motif: stiff-leaf, a knot, a green man's head, a monster. Also in the corners of the base a head, leaf, and a largish monster. – SCREEN. Panels from the dado used in the chancel seats. – BENCHES. With square-headed ends decorated with tracery and embattled. – PULPIT. C17, with various panel motifs. – SCULPTURE. Two pretty Perp brackets in the transepts, one with two busts, the other with three heads. – PAINTING. Lower part of a figure of St Thomas Becket. Other figures have disappeared. Late C12 or early C13 (N transept, E wall, in a reredos recess). – PLATE. Chalice, London, 1624 (base Elizabethan); Paten Cover, Elizabethan, inscribed 1569 but the date altered to 1633. – MONUMENTS. In the chancel floor two C13 coffin-lids with the heads of two ladies carved sunk in roundels.

WESLEYAN CHAPEL, s of the church. 1824. Brick, simple.

STRUBBY

₄₀₈₀

ST OSWALD. 1857 by *Maughan & Fowler*, but the chancel 1874 by *Ewan Christian*. Brick and bands of greenstone. Open wooden bell-turret with spirelet. Medieval the s aisle E window, which must be of *c.*1300 and has a cinquefoiled circle in its head, and medieval also the four-bay s arcade (octagonal piers, double-chamfered arches). But is it Perp or is it Dec ? – FONT. Octagonal, with an assortment of window and other tracery patterns. – PLATE. Chalice, by *Edward Vincent*, 1728. – MONU-MENTS. Headless effigy of a Civilian, early C14. His head on a diagonally placed pillow and under a nodding ogee arch. – Small tablet to William Ballett † 1648, aged 99. Is it for that reason that he and his two wives are presented in Elizabethan dress ? They kneel, he facing his wives across a prayer desk. The children small, not below but above and behind the parents against the back wall of the tablet.

GRANGE FARM. Early C18. Brick, T-shaped, with a Venetian window.

WOODTHORPE HALL. The Ballett family house. A conservative Georgian essay. Gabled side elevations and a tall staircase light at the rear. The stairs also contemporary.

STURTON-BY-STOW

ST HUGH. By *Pearson*, 1879. Brick, and quite humble. Wi⟨th⟩ windows in the C13 style, a bellcote at the E end of the nav⟨e⟩ and a relatively wide apse. Decidedly dignified within i⟨ts⟩ modest means.

SUDBROOKE
2 m. SW of Langworth

ST EDWARD. 1860–2 by *John Dobson* of Newcastle. Ne⟨o-⟩ Norman, inspired by Streetly in Derbyshire, which, howeve⟨r,⟩ it need hardly be pointed out, has no bellcote like Sudbrook⟨e.⟩ Grey stone, tunnel-vaulted chancel, rib-vaulted apse. Norman PULPIT. – ARCHITECTURAL FRAGMENT. On th⟨e⟩ floor a good, large E.E. stiff-leaf capital with upright leaves. The GATEPIERS, though meant to be somehow Norma⟨n,⟩ manage to look a belated Grecian.

SUDBROOKE HOLME, a house where *Dobson* worked fo⟨r⟩ Colonel Ellison, has gone.

SUTTERBY

ST JOHN BAPTIST. A small, disused church in a tiny hamle⟨t.⟩ Bricked-up Norman or Transitional N doorway. The S porc⟨h⟩ entrance with a piece of flowing tracery. Nave and chancel ⟨of⟩ greenstone, wonky brick bellcote. – PLATE. Chalice and Pate⟨n⟩ Cover, Elizabethan, gilding later.

SUTTON-ON-SEA

ST CLEMENT, at Sutton-le-Marsh. The medieval church dis⟨-⟩ appeared in the sea. The new one is of brick and was built i⟨n⟩ 1818. W tower with saddleback roof. Modest nave with pointe⟨d⟩ windows with Y-tracery. But the lower courses are masonry and look like medieval masonry. Chancel 1860. – FONT Octagonal, of the pattern-book type, with blank windows a⟨nd⟩ Dec; so the font probably is Dec. – PLATE. Beaker, by *Wm⟨.⟩ Shaw & Wm. Priest*, 1762, stem 1879; Tankard, gilt inside by *Samuel Godbehere & Edward Wigan*, 1792.

METHODIST CHURCH, Sutton-on-Sea. 1910 by *John Wills &⟨⟩ Son*. Red brick, Gothic, with a (ritually) SW turret with spirele⟨t⟩ and a free, Arts and Crafts (ritually) W porch.

Several small recent HOLIDAY CAMPS with modern buildings Along the road at low tide stumps of trees can be seen belongin⟨g⟩ to a submerged forest about 4,500 years old.

(a) *Lincolnshire landscape:* Cowbit Wash

(b) *Lincolnshire landscape:* Tattershall church (L),
begun 1440, and the Wolds

(a) *Lincolnshire townscape:* Stamford, from the south-west

(b) *Roman Lincoln:* Lincoln, Newport Arch, *c.*200

Barton-upon-Humber church (L), tower, later tenth century

4

(a) Stow church (L), crossing, tenth century (?), and chancel, Late Norman

(b) Barton-upon-Humber church (L), tower arch, later tenth century

5

(a) Sempringham church, south doorway, mid twelfth century

(b) Bicker church, north arcade, early twelfth century

7

(a) Lincoln, the Jew's House, later twelfth century

(b) Boothby Pagnell Manor House, begun c.1200

8

(a) Whaplode church, capitals at the west end, c.1180-90

(b) Weston church, capitals, early thirteenth century

9

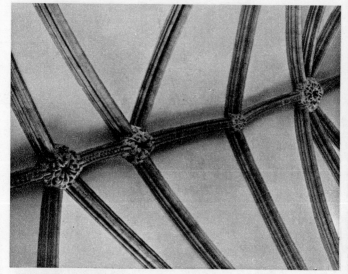

Great Grimsby (L), St James, nave, early thirteenth century

(b) Lincoln Cathedral, nave, vaulted in 1233

(a) Deeping St James church, south arcade, late twelfth century

Kirkstead Abbey (L), St Leonard, early thirteenth century

Vue de Cal... d.l... d.f...

14

(a) Lincoln Cathedral, Angel Choir, 1256–80

(b) Lincoln Cathedral, Angel Choir, 1256–80, capital

15

Lincoln Cathedral Angel Choir *page 80 way 1 via3 ...*

(a) North Rauceby church, tower Early English

(b) Sleaford church, tower *c*.1200, aisles *c*.1360–70

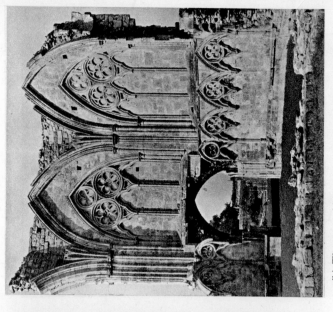

(b) Thornton Abbey (L), chapter house, 1282–c.1308

(a) Crowland, Croyland Abbey, west doorway, mid

18

(a) Weston church, font, Early English

(b) Greatford church, transept piscina, Decorated

19

(a) Kirkstead (L), St Leonard, monument to a knight, *c*.1250

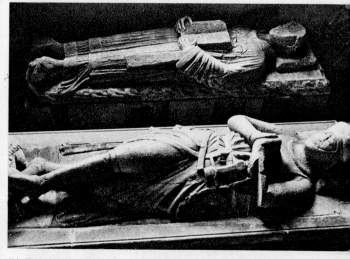

(b) Rippingale church, monuments to a deacon, mid thirteenth century and a knight, late thirteenth century

(a) *top left*, Ewerby church, steeple, Decorated. (b) *bottom left*, Brant Broughton
church, steeple, Late Decorated. (c) *right*,
Louth church (L), steeple, second half of
the fifteenth century

21

Boston church, begun 1309

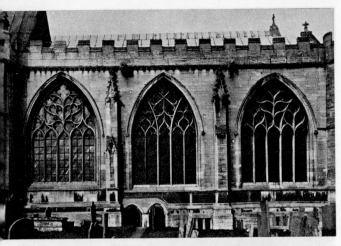

(a) Grantham church, south chapel, Decorated

(b) Wilsford church, east window, Decorated

(c) Billingborough church, south aisle west window, Decorated

23

(b) Claypole church, capitals, Decorated

(a) Lincoln, 'The Priory', No. 2 The Close, cornice, early fourteenth century

(a) Holbeach, All Saints, south arcade,

(b) Tattershall church (L), begun 1440,

26

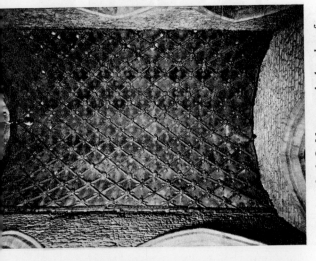

(a) Addlethorpe church (L), nave roof, Perpendicular

(b) Stamford, St Mary, north chapel roof, Perpendicular

27

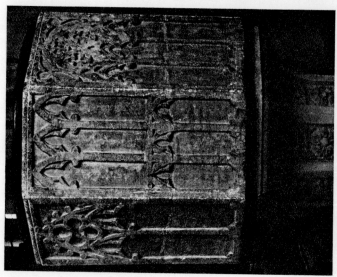

28

Ewerby church, detail of rood screen, Decorated

(a) Lincoln Cathedral, stalls, c.1365–70, misericord with Alexander the Great raised to the sky by eagles

(b) Careby church, cope used as frontal, fifteenth century

Spilsby church (L), monument to Robert, third Lord Willoughby, †1396, and wife

(a) Holbeach, All Saints, monument to Sir Humphrey Littlebury, late fourteenth century

(b) Stamford, St Mary, monument to Sir David Phillips †1506 and wife

(a) Crowland, triangular bridge, later fourteenth century

(b) Thornton Abbey (L), gatehouse, begun *c.*1382

33

Tattershall Castle (L), begun *c.*1440, keep

(a) Tattershall Castle (L), begun *c*.1440, brick vaulting in third-floor lobby of the keep

(b) Tattershall Castle (L), begun *c*.1440, chimneypiece in the keep

Gainsborough (L), Old Hall, begun c.1470
(*Copyright Country Life*)

(a) Irnham Hall, *c*.1510–*c*.1531

(b) Grantham, Angel and Royal Hotel, late fifteenth century

Wainfleet All Saints (L), Wainfleet School, founded 1484

(a) Stamford, Browne's Hospital, 1480s

(b) Lincoln, High Bridge, sixteenth century

(a) Torksey Castle (L), Elizabethan

(b) Doddington Hall, by Robert Smithson (?), 1593–1600

Snarford church (L), monument to Sir Thomas St Pol †1582 and wife

Spilsby church (L), monument to Richard Bertie †1582 and his wife
Baroness Willoughby de Eresby †1580

Stamford, St Martin, monument to William Cecil, Lord Burghley, †1598

Stallingborough church (L), monument to Sir Edward Ayscough †1612; detail of bust of his father, Sir Francis

South Cockerington church (L), monument to Sir Adrian Scrope †1623, by Epiphanius Evesham (?)

(a) Denton, Welby Almshouses, 1653

(b) Corby, Grammar School, 1673

(a) Belton House, by William Winde (?), begun 1685

(b) Gunby Hall (L), 1700

47

(a) Culverthorpe Hall, north front, c.1704 and c.1735
(*Copyright Country Life*)

(b) Somersby (L), Manor Farm, by Sir John Vanbrugh (?), 1722

(a) Grimsthorpe Castle, north front, by Sir John Vanbrugh, designed 1722

(b) Grimsthorpe Castle, great hall, by Sir John Vanbrugh, c.1725
(*Copyright Country Life*)

(a) Boston, Fydell House, by William Sands (?), 1726

(b) Stamford, No. 13 Barn Hill, 1740

Coleby Hall, Temple of Romulus and Remus,
by Sir William Chambers, 1762

(a) Gainsborough (L), All Saints, 1736–44

(b) Langton-by-Partney church (L), c.1720–30

Saxby church (L), c.1775

Stamford, St Martin, monument to John, fifth Earl of Exeter, by
P. É. Monnot, 1703

Frampton church, chandelier, 1722

(a) Edenham church, monument to the second
Duke of Ancaster †1741, by J. F. Roubiliac

(b) Belton church, monument to Viscount
Tyrconnel †1754, by Sir Henry Cheere

56

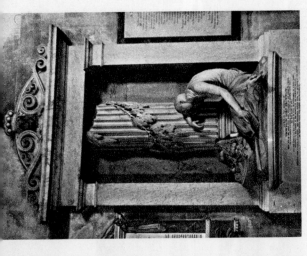

(b) Belton church, monument to Brownlow, first Lord Brownlow, †1807, by Sir Richard Westmacott

(a) Stamford, St George, monument to Sir Richard Cust and others, by John Bacon, 1797

Belton church, monument to Sophia, Lady Brownlow, †1814, by
Antonio Canova

(a) Brocklesby Park (L), Mausoleum, by James Wyatt, *c.*1787–92
(*Copyright Country Life*)

(b) Casewick Hall, west front, by William Legg, 1785

Brocklesby Park (L), Mausoleum, by James Wyatt, c.1787–92, figure of
Sophia Aufrère by Joseph Nollekens, c.1791 (*Copyright Country Life*)

(a) Folkingham, former House of Correction, by Bryan Browning, 1825

(b) Spilsby (L), Sessions House, by H. E. Kendall, 1824

(a) Bayons Manor (L), by Charles Tennyson and W. A. Nicholson, begun 1836 (*Copyright Country Life*)

(b) Harlaxton Manor, by Anthony Salvin, designed 1831 (*Copyright Country Life*)

Harlaxton Manor, stairwell, by William Burn, *c.*1840
(*Copyright Country Life*)

Cold Hanworth church (L), by J. Croft, 1863

1 m. WNW of South Thoresby

ST NICHOLAS. Of brick; 1828. Nave and small, low polygonal chancel. W porch and bellcote. The windows of the nave are arched and placed nicely in brick projections echoing the brick angle lesenes. Other windows are pointed. The bellcote has teeth rather than battlements. – PLATE. Chalice and Paten, by *F.W.*, London, 1668.

HOLY TRINITY. Unbuttressed W tower with pyramid roof. The bell-openings, needless to say, are neo-Norman (1868). Original Norman work the small W doorway, the plain tower arch, and one W window. A former S aisle and one-bay S chapel are still visible outside. They were probably C13, as is a capital not *in situ* inside and as is the N arcade of two bays. Round pier with round abacus, some dog-tooth on the W respond, double-chamfered arches. C13 also the chancel arch with a fillet and some small nailhead in the respond. – SCULPTURE. Upper part of a stone relief of Christ crucified; C14 or C15.

ST HELEN. Short, oblong W tower; nave and chancel in one. The tower has a porch as its ground-stage, and this has as its entrance two re-used quatrefoiled piers, the foils keeled, the abaci round, i.e. of C13 date. The inner doorway is pointed and has only a slight chamfer, i.e. *c.*1200. Then, as one enters, the baptistery to the S has responds of the same type as the entrance piers. So the medieval church (or the church before its restoration of 1860) must have had a C13 arcade of three bays, i.e. two piers and two responds. The W wall of the nave has moreover one lancet on either side of the tower, and there is still a N lancet. They might well have belonged to the former aisle. On the S side two-light Dec windows with a reticulation unit, and inside a pointed-trefoiled piscina. – PLATE. Chalice, London, 1728. – MONUMENTS. Frances Alington † 1828, aged 28, and the Rev. Henry Alington, her cousin and betrothed, who died nineteen months before her. 'Her health sunk under the efforts made by her pious and affectionate mind to bear but conceal the anguish of a broken heart and to submit with cheerfulness to the will of her creator.' The

monument is by *E. Gaffin*. – Mrs Pye † 1847. By *T. Gaffin*.
Nice relief of almsgiving.

SWINHOPE HALL. Its position on a terrace above a lake helps
an otherwise dull house. It was built in 1785 of stock brick
with pedimented centre-pieces on two fronts. The s front
faces the church across a distance.

OLD RECTORY. Late C18, with a curved bay to the w front.

CROMWELL'S GRAVE, in a small wood on HOE HILL. Fine
Neolithic long barrow, 180 ft long and 11 ft high at its broader,
E end. The barrow has been protected by the wood in which
it lies, and is one of the finest examples of the type in the
county.

LONG BARROW. *See* Normanby-on-the-Wolds.

3080

TATHWELL

ST VEDAST. The church lies above a lake in the sheltered Wold
village. Norman w tower, but with brick top. The tower arch
is of blackish greenstone and has triple responds with scalloped
capitals carrying a single-step arch, i.e. early C12. The brick
top is no doubt Georgian, as are the nave, chancel, and apse.
The windows were all plainly arched, but some have been
gothicized (made honest) in 1857. The timber s porch with
brick-nogging is straight out of Sussex and has no business in
Lincolnshire. – STAINED GLASS. Botterill memorial window
(† 1923) in a mildly Expressionist Eric Gillish style. By
Powell's. – PAINTING. Christ at Emmaus, Venetian, mid-C16,
in Titian's style. – MONUMENTS. Standing wall-monument
to Edward Hamby † 1626. An alabaster piece in four tiers: at
the foot the kneeling children in relief, then the couple kneeling and facing one another across a prayer-desk, then a kneeling
son who also died in 1626, and finally the achievement etc.
There are no columns, but three tiers of pediments. The
inscription says

> The Knot of love which twixt these two was knit
> It held full fast till death united it.
> Who so in true and honest love do live
> To such the Lord especial grace doth give
> Well may we hope they come to blessed end
> Whom for theyr truth and love we may commend.

– Thomas Chaplin † 1747. Obelisk with winged hourglass. On
the base relief of a mourning woman by an urn. By *Hoare* of
Bath.

TATHWELL HOUSE, ¼ m. w. The early building was long the seat of the Chaplin family, and *Thomas Archer* the architect often stayed here. The late C17 brick house in the vernacular style was replaced in 1842 by the present Grecian one of three by three bays and two storeys. It is somewhat severe, with a blocking course, crisp moulded windows, and a heavy porch of four square pillars. The centre of the other main front a tripartite window. The gatepiers are Georgian, decorated with Greek key.

LONG BARROW, in the NW corner of the parish. An unexcavated long barrow, 105 ft long and 5½ ft high at the broader, SE end. The barrow has a large tree growing on it (which is a useful landmark for locating the site) and has in the past been considerably damaged by rabbits.

BARROW CEMETERY, on BULLY HILL. This is one of the finest surviving barrow groups in the county. It consists of six bowl barrows arranged in a line, with a seventh a little distance away from the group, in the same field. The largest is 60 ft in diameter and 10 ft high. Two show traces of disturbance, although there is no record of their excavation. They are probably of Late Neolithic or Early Bronze Age date.

TATTERSHALL

2050

The Cromwells had been at Tattershall since 1367. The grandson of the first Ralph, also a Ralph, became Treasurer of England in 1433 and died in 1456. He was a tenacious man with a great gift for administration, a tidy mind, a faith in accurate records, and an ability to steer a safe course amid the intrigues of the age of Henry VI. It was he who built Tattershall Castle, and later the equally grand South Wingfield in Derbyshire, and also built the church, founded the college to serve it (in 1438–9), and built the premises of the college. They have gone completely, but the church survives in its entirety, and of the castle the keep remains also, an unforgettable group, more menacing than lovely, and one utterly different from what it must have been like in the C15.

HOLY TRINITY. Lord Cromwell's church, begun in 1440 and completed after the Treasurer's death by his executor Bishop Waynflete (see the arms of the Bishop over the N porch) in the 1480s,* is 186 ft long, built of Ancaster stone, and consists of nave and aisles, transepts but no proper crossing, and a chancel. It was evidently built regardless of expense and for a

1b

* The contract for the bell-frame is dated 1482.

man who wanted size rather than pretty decoration. It is i
fact almost gaunt in its absence of ornament – to the extent c
all windows being left without cusping. The difference thi
makes to the general impression will be admitted by anyon
who has noticed this detail. Another equally telling detail i
the liking for triangles instead of arches. They occur in th
panel tracery everywhere and also in the decoration of the v
doorway. The doorway has spandrels with simple tracery
shields above, a five-light W window, three-light bell-opening
and no pinnacles. The aisles have large four-light windows
the clerestory closely-set three-light windows – eight of ther
for the nave, and they are carried round the transepts (as a
Newark). The aisles have pinnacles, the N porch (to the oute
world) is modest and has its old roof, the S doorway and tha
to the S from the S transept are not in their original context
This context was the college, whose premises lay – the monasti
way – to the S. The transept end windows are of six lights, an
of enormous size. The buttresses l. and r. end in pinnacles a
the springing of the window arches. The chancel is a littl
lower but makes up for that and for the absence of clerestor
windows by having five immensely tall transomed three-ligh
windows N and five S. The E window, to finish with, is of seve
lights. The whole church is truly what is often said of Per
churches: a glass-house.

26b   The interior is consequently, and of course especiall
because little stained glass remains, extremely light, too ligh
perhaps for any *Stimmung*. One walks through it and stays i
it and never quite forgets the Treasurer's badge, which is a
purse. The tower opens to the E to the full height of the nave
The arch is broadly and simply panelled. The N and S arche
to the aisle W bays have broad mouldings and bases of th
crazy height of 7 ft. The bases of the arcade piers are only a
little lower. The piers are set lozenge-wise and consist of a
shaft to nave and aisle, thin triple shafts to the arch openings
and wide shallow hollows in the diagonals. The arch moulding
are complex and finer than between W bays and tower. Al
roofs are of low pitch and have thin, insignificant arche
braces. In the nave roof they alternate with angel figures. Th
transept arches rise again to the full height, but the chance
arch is a little lower. Passing through the door in the ston
screen (*see* below), one is partly prepared for the flood of ligh
coming in from N, S, and E. The roof here rests on stone ange
busts, and the arched braces have tracery in the spandrels

The sedilia and piscina have four-centred arches with ogee gables, a frieze with little beasts, and a cresting.*

FURNISHINGS. ROOD SCREEN. To the w three broad four-centred arches, cusped and subcusped and placed under ogee gables. The arches to the l. and r. were for reredoses of lay altars. The centre has the original DOOR with tracery and leads to a panelled passage. On the w side above the arches is also panelling, again rather bald. The loft has a canted projection to the E like a balcony, no doubt for the rood. – Bits of the dado of a wooden SCREEN are in the N transept. – Another old DOOR is the N door, with a wicket. – PULPITS. One of wood, Perp, in the nave, another of wood, finely traceried, in the chancel. Its traceries probably come from the chancel stalls. – FONT. The base has arcading which looks Dec and would in that case be older than the church. – STAINED GLASS. This dated from 1481-2 etc. Much of it is now at St Martin's Stamford and some in the Great Hall at Burghley House. At Tattershall there is original glass only in the E window, and this is reassembled. Among figures, scenes, and representations recognizable there are the following (from l. to r.): An Act of Mercy (Clothing the Needy), a Confirmation from a series of the Seven Sacraments, the Lord Treasurer's purse (occurring several times), the Virgin and Child, St James, Misericordia and Pax (two of a series of Virtues), a Baptism (again from the Seven Sacraments), a Veritas (from the Virtues), St Peter, St John Evangelist, angels playing music (several), Feeding the Hungry (Acts of Mercy). The names of several of the glaziers are known from the accounts: *Robert Power* of Burton-on-Trent, *John Glasier* of Stamford, *John Wymondeswalde* of Peterborough, *Thomas Wodshawe*, and *Richard Twygge*. The last-named worked at Malvern and Westminster Abbey about 1507. – BRASSES. Apart from that to Hugh de Goudeby † 1411 on the chancel floor (19½ in. figure), they are all in the N transept, and first of all Lord Cromwell, the builder of the church, † 1456 and his wife. The brass of Lady Cromwell and the head of Lord Cromwell have been stolen. They are (or were) modishly dressed, he with a feather in his hat. A triple canopy over both and strips of knights to his l. and her r. – Joan Lady Cromwell † 1479, their niece (they had no children), under a single vaulted canopy. She has her hair down. Saints l. and r. under high canopies. The figure is 5 ft 2 in. long. –

* Scattered about the church are quite a number of pieces of quatrefoil iezes.

Lady Maud, wife of Lord Willoughby de Eresby, † 14[
(but the brass earlier), also under a canopy, also with sai[
l. and r., but a broader strip. The figure is 5 ft long. – A[
William Moor, a priest of the college, † 1456, 27½ in.;
unknown priest of the college, c.1510, 5 ft long, with sai[
on his orphreys; and William Symson † 1519, another prie[
22½ in.

TATTERSHALL CASTLE. The castle was first built by [
Robert de Tateshall under a licence granted him in 1231.
had no keep but instead towers strengthening a curtain wal[
the new principle of fortification learned by the West in t[
Crusades. The bases of two round towers remain, adjoini[
the great keep to NE and SE. Between these two presumab[
stood the Great Hall. Traces of other curved bastions exist [
the middle of the S and E sides of the present inner baile[
Cromwell's castle, begun in 1434–5, was a much more comp[
affair. It consisted of an outer moat, an outer bailey, an inn[
moat (brick-lined), and an inner bailey. The two moats we[
connected by a cross-cut. The approach was from the [
corner along the N to the W, and across a bridge N of the ke[
into the outer bailey. Here, W of the castle, stood a bri[
GUARD HOUSE of which a gable wall with two-light windo[
remains. Then the approach carried on across a second bridg[
across the cross-cut, through a gateway into the E half of t[
outer bailey to its NE corner, where another GUARD HOU[
remains complete, though altered. It is also of brick a[
originally had its doorway on the S side and a second doorw[
on the first floor on the N side.* Then across a bridge, whe[
the present NE bridge is, the inner bailey was finally reache[
Here Cromwell must have built a variety of brick structure[
including KITCHENS in the moat to the SE of the keep,
building of unknown destination just W of the keep ([
which the put-holes are clearly visible), and of course t[
keep itself.

34   The KEEP must always have been as unmistakable as it [
now, though now it stands alone in the Fen fields, and then [
had at its feet a variety of other buildings. It is 110 ft high a[
87 by 67 ft wide and dwarfs the great collegiate church to its [
It is singularly menacing for the mid C15; for not only had t[
manor house by then replaced the fortress, but also, whe[
fortification was necessary such as along the S coast of Englan[

* The upper floor is now used as a museum of fragments, plans, phot[
graphs, etc.

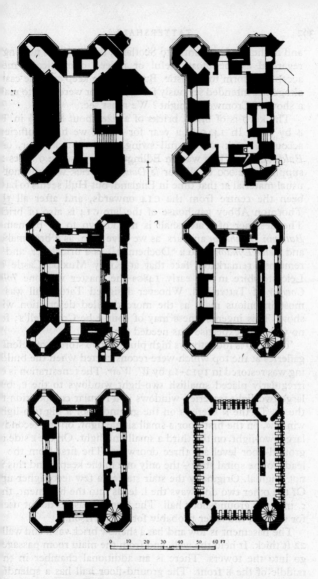

Tattershall Castle, keep, begun 1434–5: plans of basement, ground
floor, first floor, second floor, third floor, and fourth floor

and in the border country to Scotland, the keep was no long
regarded as the most useful or indeed domestically mo
acceptable form for a castle. But were the keep and the cast
altogether intended seriously for defence, or were they to ma
a show of Cromwell's might? We must see.

The keep is of brick, bricks of a size about 8 to 8½ in. b
4 by 2 in. In 1445–6, a year for which we have sufficien
accounts, work was in full swing, as the brickmaker, or
Baldwin whose kiln was on Edlington Moor some 9 miles N
supplied 322,000 bricks for *le Dongeon*. Brick was still not
usual material at that time in England, but Hull seems to hav
been the centre from the C14 onwards, and after all th
Thornton Abbey gatehouse of the late C14 is also of bricl
The designer of Tattershall is not known to us by nam
Baldwin Dutchman appears, as we have seen, as a brickmake
and *Peter Lyndon* (also a 'Docheman') as a bricklayer, and
remains a remarkable fact that at Kirby Muxloe Castle i
Leicestershire in the early 1480s the master was one *Joh*
Cowper of Tattershall. Whoever designed Tattershall was
most ingenious man, as the more detailed description wi
show. This ingeniousness may of course be Cromwell's; fo
no technical expertise was needed for it.

The keep is four storeys high plus the two storeys of defenc
galleries at the top which were reconstructed when the build
ing was restored in 1912–14 by *W. Weir*. The fenestration is o
irregularly placed smallish two-light windows to the E, bu
large two-light traceried windows in a regular composition t
the W. To the N there is on the ground floor a big two-ligh
window, on the first floor a small single light, on the second
large two-light, on the third a small one-light. On the E side a
ground-floor level are three doorways. The first from the
leads to the spiral stair – the only one in the keep – and this i
not original. Originally the stair started a few feet higher up
Of the other two doorways the l. leads into the basement, th
r. into the ground-floor hall. The former was no doubt use
for storage, the latter probably for the garrison.

The basement is low and has a shallow brick vault and wall
22 ft thick. It held the well, and from the main room passage
go into the towers. There is an additional chamber in th
middle of the E front. The ground-floor hall has a splendi
chimneypiece in the E wall, the first of four in the keep, al
harmonizing in style. This one has an ogee gable over its fla
four-centred opening, shields l. and r., and a crenellated top

There are large two-light windows, two to the w and one to N, one to s. In addition there are three corner chambers and a garderobe in the space between the staircase and the hall. The stair is not accessible from the hall, a security measure probably in case the garrison turned out to be the enemy and not outside aggressors.

The staircase, as has been said, originally started a little above ground level. It has a sunk hand-rail and had a doorway to the curtain wall (and perhaps the kitchens) just below first-floor level. On the first floor one reaches from the staircase a lobby, and from there enters the hall. The hall is lit by big windows from the w and the s. The fireplace, again in the e wall, has a row of shields above the opening and crenellation along its top. The soffits of the window embrasures to the w are simple brick rib-vaults of two different designs (four ribs and eight ribs). As for other chambers, a passage runs N from the lobby along the e front to an oblong chamber. Passage and chamber have pointed tunnel-vaults. To the sw and NW are cabinets, and on the N runs another passage e from the NW cabinet. All these have pointed tunnel-vaults.

On the second floor the basic arrangements are nicely varied. This time, as one steps off the staircase, one has to enter a long passage along the e front and reaches the doorway to the hall only at its end. This passage is brick-vaulted throughout with five quadripartite rib-vaults with heraldic bosses – quite an impressive sight. If, instead of turning l. into the hall, one continues straight one arrives in a tunnel-vaulted cabinet with a garderobe. The hall chimneypiece this time is in the w wall. The band above the opening has shields and the 3 Treasurer's purse in fields of panel tracery. The large windows go to the w and the N. NW and sw cabinets, again tunnel-vaulted, the latter converted into a dovecote in 1700.

On the third floor the lobby has a little brick vault much 35a more complicated than the others, quadripartite with ridge-ribs and lierne-ribs forming a star. The entry to the hall is at once to the l., but one can also continue into a short passage or cabinet along the e side. The hall again has rib-vaults in the soffits of the w windows, but now they have in the cells foiled roundels and mouchette wheels. The fireplace is again in the e wall. The frieze above the opening has panels of curious shape with shield and purse and again crenellation over. Cabinets to the NW and sw. From the NW cabinet a passage runs along the N side and ends in a garderobe. The NE corner

cabinet has an extension to the s along the E front of the tower
All these cabinets have pointed tunnel-vaults.

As to the functions of the three halls we have no guidance
They have been called the Great Hall, the Great Chamber
and the Solar or Lady's Chamber, but that is quite arbitrary
In fact the hall on the third floor is no doubt the decoratively
most distinguished one. It is on the other hand awkwardly
distant from the kitchen.

The top parts are most strictly for defence. They are very
instructive, but it must be remembered that they are partly
reconstruction. They consist of two low storeys. The first of
them is open to the sky for most of the area and surrounded by
galleries on all four sides with arcading to the inside and small
shuttered oblong openings to the outside. The galleries project
on big corbels, and between them the machicoulis or machicolation holes are open and operative. They are frequent in
C13 to C15 France but relatively rare in England. In the three
towers not occupied by the staircase are heatable polygonal
cabinets. On top of the arcaded galleries is finally the topmost
stage, the parapet walk proper. The towers have cabinets again
at this level. The three chimneys of the fireplaces on the E side
(ground floor, first floor, third floor) form an erection at the
back decorated by blank crow-stepping. The towers below
their tops have the usual frieze of small pointed arches.

So much by way of a description. In conclusion the question
must again be asked how far Lord Cromwell's keep was a keep
and how far it was a piece of demonstration. The large windows
to the w are unwise from the point of view of defence, yet the
machicoulis were certainly built to work as such and the access
to the keep could not be much more roundabout in any
medieval fortress. On the other side it might again be said that
brick is not a suitable material for a keep in an age of cannon,
yet Kirby Muxloe with its C15 gun-posts is brick. The political
situation in the 1440s made provision against attack quite a
wise precaution, especially if one was a man as powerful and
unpopular as the Treasurer. So perhaps the keep must be
regarded as built for defence, but with as much of the comforts
of space and lighting and heating as the greater probability of a
peaceful existence at the castle allowed. After all, South Wingfield, Lord Cromwell's other mansion, though a manor house
with a great hall and all the other appurtenances on no more
than two floors, has all the same a very substantial and
defensible tower.

ALMSHOUSES, N of the church. Single-storeyed, completely
plain and apparently C17. They cannot be the ones for which
a contract of 1486 with a carpenter exists.

SCHOOL. Parts of the medieval school are behind the houses on
the N side of the Market Place. PB)

TOM THUMB'S HOUSE. Miniature model of a house on the
ridge of a cottage on the E side of the Market Place. Supposedly
ancient. PB)

TEALBY

1090

ALL SAINTS. At the top of a terraced village. The material of the
church is ironstone. The oldest part seems the W doorway into
the mighty tower. It is small, with plain chamfered imposts
and an unmoulded arch. Above it a small window whose headstone is Later Norman. Carved on it are a small head, two
birds, and a hood-mould on two long-snouted monster-heads
– all tiny. Does this go with the tremendous tower arch towards
the nave with its multi-scalloped imposts and its one-step-one-
chamfer arch and whose only decoration is billets? But the
arch is pointed.* Above this arch, but pushed to the r., is a
round-arched opening, the size of a doorway rather than a
window. Where can it have led to? The thing becomes more
mysterious, as above this opening, in line with it, is another,
but appearing above the roof, and this has a moulded surround
and a pointed arch. Both find no explanation inside the tower.
Near in time a number of contributions of the early C14.
Intersecting tracery in the N and S aisle E windows and a
chancel N window,‡ reticulated tracery in another chancel N
window, also octagonal piers and double-chamfered arches (a
little differing) in the four-bay N and S arcades and semi-
octagonal responds in the tower arch. The bell-openings of the
tower are Perp, as are the clerestory with segment-headed
three-light windows, battlements, and pinnacles, and probably
the S porch (in spite of its C17 upper window). The nave roof,
no doubt of the time of the clerestory, has heavy tie-beams
alternating with arched braces with big pendants. The chancel
was remodelled inside by *Fowler* in 1872. It then received the
niches with the tablets to the Tennyson d'Eyncourts of Bayons
Manor and their sumptuously carved foliage. – COMMUNION
RAIL. A handsome C18 piece. – STAINED GLASS. In the side

* At Malmesbury pointed arches and the long-snouted monster-heads
appear together.

‡ In the chancel S wall a low-side window with original bars.

windows of the chancel remains of the canopies of glass of the early C14. – PLATE. Chalice, by *Thomas Hebden*, c.1690.

SCHOOL, s of the church. 1856. An effective asymmetrical composition; very Gothic.

BAYONS MANOR, *see* p. 185.

3070   TETFORD

ST MARY. Of greenstone. Perp w tower with thinly decorated parapet. The aisles were originally E.E., see the bases of the arcade piers and the w lancet of the s aisle. But the present piers are Perp (three bays), and in the w lancet a Dec gable has been inserted, probably from a sedilia or piscina. Perp clerestory; the earlier roof-line still visible. On the N side of the chancel blocked arch to a former chapel. The N aisle (windows with Y-tracery) is of 1826. – ARMOUR of the C17 nave E wall. – PLATE. Chalice, Paten, and Flagon, by *Joh Jackson*, 1700.

MANSION HOUSE. Late Georgian, with Roman Doric attachments.

3000   TETNEY

ST PETER AND ST PAUL. An impressive Perp Marshland tower high, of grey Lincolnshire oolite ashlar, with a high three-light w window and very high bell-openings in two-light twin under one ogee arch. The lowest part of the openings is blank and panelled. Blocked small s doorway E.E. The N aisle has windows of 1861 (*Withers*) except for the E window with its flowing tracery. The s aisle E window is Perp and pretty. The chancel was rebuilt in 1861. The interior is wide and spacious but not particularly poetical. Four-bay arcades, octagonal piers, not very high, double-chamfered arches. On one N pier that rare thing an inscription commemorating the date of the church or this part. It states that this work was done in 1363 Robert Day being vicar. The pier bases, except for two with Dec moulding, have the characteristic Perp bell moulding. The capitals might be of any date. – SCREEN. Parts now displayed under the tower. Cusped ogee arches with small panel tracery much like Marsh Chapel. – PLATE. Chalice, London 1787.

8010   THEALBY

1½ m. E of Burton-upon-Stather

A small hamlet of Georgian character and pretty in a picture postcard way. Close to a hill is a small green with two rows of low cottages.

See p. 768

THEDDLETHORPE ALL SAINTS

4080

LL SAINTS. The richest of the churches in this Marshland area. It is as varied in its architecture as in its furnishings. The building material is greenstone, ranging in colour from green to deep rust. The architecture begins with some Norman evidence, namely in the N wall of the nave many pieces of zig-zag from an arch and also masks from a corbel table, and in the sedilia in the chancel a round and a polygonal shaft with Late Norman capitals. All the rest is Early Perp, the result of one build, dateable about 1380 or even 1400. W tower, the arch to the nave of two continuous chamfers. Battlements to aisles and clerestory and moreover big gargoyles and crockets on the aisle W and E ends and, above a lovely pierced quatrefoil frieze, the E gable of the nave. The clerestory tracery still has a decided touch of the Dec. The N aisle windows with low four-centred arches, the s aisle windows with basket arches. s door-way with an ogee head, again more Dec than Perp. To these notes on the exterior must be added the fact that the s porch as well as the tower have a lot of brickwork which (as Cox spotted) is pre-Reformation. In the tower E wall it seems indeed used deliberately in alternation with greenstone, and if this means brick of the late C14 it is – as far as England is concerned – very early brick indeed. However, Hull was a centre, perhaps the centre, for C14 brick. The interior is large, with five-bay arcades (octagonal piers, double-chamfered arches), the original roofs (tie-beams, queenposts, bosses), and the chancel arch with concave-sided semi-octagonal responds. – FONT. Octagonal, Perp, fleurons against the stem, quatrefoils against the bowl, heads against the underside. – ALTAR TABLE. Of marble, Early Georgian, with baluster legs (N aisle W). – REREDOS, or rather reredos niche. At the E end of the s aisle. Very ornate, with fleuron bands, a top in the form of an almost straight-sided depressed arch, and above this a crocketed gable inside a bigger crocketed gable. Is this Early Perp too or is it later, as the s aisle windows may well be? – SCREENS. A splendid lot, as screens go in North Lincolnshire. The rood screen has two-light divisions, with Y-arrangement, but ogee arches below the forked division, and panel tracery as well. – The screens to the N and s chapels, or rather the E bays of the aisles, must date from c.1535, i.e. they are in Early Renaissance forms, tracery having been replaced by symmetrical scroll-work and also heads in profile. In the centre of the N screen,

two such heads, evil-looking, touch with their noses a roun
with the face of Christ. Arms of the Angevine family. – CO
MUNION RAIL. With dumb-bell balusters; Early Georgian
BENCHES. Of two types, the older in the N aisle, with
poppy-heads missing, the other straight-topped with trac
and crenellation. Of this type a complete bench front, like
dado of a screen, remains. – STAINED GLASS. Some lit
glass in the tracery of a S aisle window. – PLATE. Silver-
Chalice and Cover, London, 1637; Paten, by *Thomas Pa*
1712; Chalice, by *Gabriel Sleath*, 1730. – MONUMENTS.
the S chapel brass to Robert Hayton † 1424, a good 21
figure, and an extremely late case of bascinet with chain m
hanging from it. – In the chancel high up a funerary HELM
Nicholas Newcomen † 1703. Very good tablet with, at the t
garlands and, at the bottom, cherubs' heads and a skull
Charles Bertie † 1727. By *Andrew Carpenter*. Standing w
monument of black and white marble. Two busts on the bl
sarcophagus. Architectural background. The busts compet
but dull.

RECTORY. By *G. P. Kennedy*, 1864.

The HALL. Georgian, with short projecting wings and gabl

THEDDLETHORPE ST HELEN

4080

ST HELEN. Of greenstone; Early Perp, but nearly rebuilt
1864–7 by *Teulon*. Typically Early Perp especially the be
openings in the W tower and the clerestory windows.* T
tower arch has concave-sided semi-octagonal responds. T
arcades with the usual octagonal piers and double-chamfer
arches, the N arcade shorter, because a long stretch of w
towards the tower was left standing. In the E wall of the
aisle REREDOS niche, similar to that at All Saints, yet differe
Fleuron bands below, l. and r. as there, a depressed alm
straight-sided arch as there, but the top gable different a
crowned by a Crucifixus (now detached). The arch has a ba
of moderate zigzag on the l., undulation on the r., and at t
top of the fleuron band to the r. is a tiny couple, Knight a
Lady, and their dress dates the reredos safely to the late C1
i.e. Early Perp. – PLATE. Chalice and Cover, London, 168
Paten and two Flagons, by *John Newton*(?), 1722.

THIMBLEBY

2070

ST MARGARET. By *Fowler*, 1879. Greenstone, in the Dec sty

* Yet wills were made with donations to the steeple in 1529–31.

The w tower is octagonal in its upper stage and carries a spire. One Dec window-head on the s side is original. So are parts of the sedilia. They are pre-Dec, but only just. – PLATE. Chalice, by *John Morley* of Lincoln, *c.*1569; Paten, by *James Smith*(?), London, 1727.

ECTORY, E of the church. By *S. C. Lomas*, Surveyor; 1839.
he short main street pretty with thatched and whitewashed cottages and the view of the church front at the end.

THONOCK HALL
1½ m. NE of Gainsborough

8090

mid-Georgian house recased and stuccoed in the early C19. Four- by five-bay, three-storey block with projecting ground-floor window bays on the s front. Now forlorn-faced.

ARTHWORK, in CASTLE HILLS WOOD. This large earth-work, which is covered by dense undergrowth, may be a Norman motte and bailey.

THORESWAY

1090

ucked away in a fold of the Wolds.

T MARY. By *Fowler*, 1879–80, but on the w side the former E arch of a Norman tower with the plainest imposts, on the N side a simple, chamfered, round-headed doorway in the Transitional style, and the arcades of the former aisles of the late C13 (three bays, octagonal piers, double-chamfered arches). Fowler's own is the bell-turret with its spire.

ne good house at the E end of the hamlet. It has an early C19 bow with attached Ionic columns the full height of the house.

THORGANBY

2090

LL SAINTS. Low nave, N aisle and chancel; bellcote; all mostly of *c.*1900. Medieval the N arcade, in elementary C13 forms, circular piers, circular abaci, double-chamfered arches. Very rough chancel arch, the shafts cut down. They carry fillets. Double-chamfered arch. On the s side one original window with intersecting tracery. – BENCH ENDS. Square-headed, with tracery in big, bold forms.

HORGANBY HALL. Although most of the fronts look Late Georgian, there are remains of a former rebuilding of 1648. This can be seen on the E front (the stone plinth here and elsewhere) and the s front which, although Georgian in all its

details, has preserved the arrangement with projecting wing
and extruded corners on open arches. The original entranc
may have been in the l. one of them.

THORNHOLME PRIORY see APPLEBY

1010

THORNTON ABBEY

Thornton Abbey was founded for Augustinian Canons in 1139
But what remains now is Late E. E. and Perp, ruins of part of th
church and chapter house, and in addition the largest of al
English gatehouses.

The gatehouse is approached by a red-brick BARBICAN with tw
round turrets and walls with blank arches l. and r. It is 120 f
in length and seems to date from the C15. The GATEHOUSE

33b
itself is certainly a building for fortification as well as living
Licence to crenellate was granted the abbot in 1382, and th
building is called 'the new house over and beside the gate'
It is indeed a house, a gate keep one would be inclined to say
Or one might think of Harlech a hundred years earlier, wher
the main living quarters were above the main gate, or indee
of Wardour Castle of the later C14, where the great hall lies
as at Thornton, above a gateway, even if in a different context
The Thornton gatehouse is supposed to have been the abbot'
house. The only staircase admittedly would make a ver
awkward approach, but the approach to the upper halls o
Nunney (licence to crenellate 1373) and Wardour Castle
(licence to crenellate 1393) are no better. Alternatively, th
abbot may have had accommodation somewhere else as wel
and built the gatehouse just in case of need. But what woul
have made him consider that possibility in 1382?

The gatehouse stands 68 ft high. Its front consists of fiv
parts, the three centre parts faced with stone, the side parts o
brick – very early brick as England goes. However, Hull
where brick-making flourished already in the later C14, wa
near enough. The parts are separated by projecting turrets. Ir
the side parts the cornice rises pediment-like to the centr
part. This has a tall archway in, set recessed under a cuspe
and subcusped segmental arch. To the l. and r. are blank bays
under uncusped segmental arches. A fleuron frieze with head
etc. runs along above the arches. On the buttress-like turret
l. and r. of the archway are brackets and canopies for images
the brackets on crouching caryatids. The archway itself ha

three orders of shafts with small nobbly capitals. The arch has three rolls and two hollows. In one of them are fleurons. Above the whole ground-stage runs an outer wall-passage. The upper stage has in the middle part a display of poor sculpture on brackets and under canopies. There are large figures of the Virgin, St John Baptist, and St Augustine, and above them, small figures of Christ with angels carrying the Instruments of the Passion. One of them is missing. So are the figures for the single brackets and canopies in the side parts.

The archway inside has a most interesting vault. It looks a pointed tunnel-vault with a longitudinal ridge-rib and l. and r. of this four quadripartite rib-arrangements making eight saltire crosses in all. In fact it ought to be called a rib-vault of two bays without transverse arch, but with normal diagonal ribs plus tiercerons running up diagonally to the ridge-rib from springers half-way along either bay. A very similar vault is at Urchfont (Wilts.). All springers are expressed by little polygonal shafts with leaf capitals. The vault has big, coarse leaf bosses and just one head boss. This vault reaches three-quarters through the archway. It is then interrupted by another archway whose original DOOR is preserved. The tracery is – a memorable fact – still reticulated, i.e. purely Dec about 1385. Just before this big doorway the passage splits. The direct continuation (for carriages and horses) has a similar vault but with a transverse ridge-rib. But to the r. a skew passage for pedestrians, quite roomy, turns off. It starts with a doorway with fleurons and a hood-mould on head-stops, also with fleurons. It is vaulted in two parts on the same system. The first part has the ribs connected into arched panels and a head boss in the centre, the second is quite irregular. In a corner to bring it to life a little crouching demon.

The inner façade of the gatehouse is much more domestic. There are again projecting turrets. The middle part is entirely stone-faced and has on the first floor an oriel window on a head-corbel, on the second a two-light window. To the s the first-floor window is of four lights, the second is taller and of three. On the ground floor there are again arches in front of the actual front, the l. one deep, where the pedestrian passage comes out, the r. one shallow. In the turret between the two archways the staircase runs up. Its upper end has a flat ceiling carried on eight cusped ribs. The doorway is placed in a projection. At the top of the whole middle part a frieze of monster-heads. Above this there must have been a parapet, perhaps crenellated, and the turrets must of course have been crenellated too.

The high brick walls to the l. and r. of the outer, i.e. brick, pieces of the gatehouse, have arched recesses. The walls are later than the gatehouse.

The main chamber on the first floor is spacious (48 by 20 ft) and tall. The ceiling rests on big busts, much better than the outer sculpture. The oriel has an ante-bay with a transverse arch and the oriel itself rib-vaulting. Is the recess in the r. wall a lavabo? Or is it a piscina, in which case the oriel served as a chapel which, given its orientation, is entirely possible. Exits here and in the chamber on the second floor lead into a whole system of wall-passages with cabinets and also garde-robes. The second-floor chamber has a curious arrangement to the alcove which has the two-light window and stands above the ante-room to the oriel. In the main chamber is an ex-emplary display of finds from the church and monastic quarters, very instructive for those who want to study details under the best conditions.

The gatehouse lies in line with the church front, but 250 yards away from it. What buildings there were here – brew-house, bake-house, workshops, guest-house, stables, granaries – we do not know at all.*

The CHURCH which we see now in its foundations was started about 1264 and was 282 ft long, including the Lady Chapel to the E, begun in 1395. The nave was first intended to have no S aisle or no aisles. This is proved by the remains of outer wall inside the S aisle W of the crossing. To its E the responds of the arch from aisle to transept. The nave piers have octagonal bases, the chancel piers square bases. The transepts had an E aisle, divided into chapels, as in Lincoln Cathedral, by thin partition walls. To the N, beyond the transept, was the chapel of St Thomas Becket, a separate building of the C14 reached by a passage from the N choir aisle. The reredos was two bays from the E end, leaving space for an ambulatory and E chapels.

---

* The later history of the site is no less puzzling. The abbey was purchased in 1610 by Sir Vincent Skinner, who, according to De La Prymme, demolished the 'college' (probably an almshouse) 'and built a most stately house out of the same, on the west side of the abbey plot within the moat, which hall, when it was finished, fell quite down to the bare ground without any visible cause'. This house was surveyed by John Thorpe. The plan was spatially ingenious and the house looked an example of Gothic Revival – or Survival.

All this can only be read in the plan. But of the S transept
the S wall stands high up and shows us the S respond of the E
aisle with filleted three-quarter shafts and some grand blank
arcading on the S wall of the SE chapel. This is typical of its
date, about 1280–90. Three pointed-trefoiled lights and three
circles over, provided with four centripetal fleurs-de-lis in lieu
of quatrefoiling. Inside the transept a lump of masonry, part
of the support of the night-stair to the dormitory.

So to the MONASTIC QUARTERS. The dormitory lay as usual in
the E range on the first floor. Below it first a mysterious
corridor-like room with very elementary blank arcading and
two bays of equally elementary quadripartite rib-vaulting. The
Ministry of Works calls it the Parlour. To its S follows the
passage to the chapter house with, in contrast, fine ribs on
small corbels. The entry to the chapter house has five shafts
too. Of the octagonal CHAPTER HOUSE two bays stand, even 18b
more interesting for the study of dating than the S transept;
for it is known that the chapter house was begun in 1282 and
paved in 1308. There is blank arcading of the dado and of the
upper walls. In the dado pairs of pointed-trefoiled arches
carrying quatrefoils in circles, in the upper panels three lights
also pointed-trefoiled, and in the three circles above quatrefoils
and cinquefoils, their centres nicely marked by a flower.

To the S of the chapter house smaller rooms of earlier date,
including at the S end the WARMING ROOM with a C13 fireplace repaired later in brick. In the S range was the REFECTORY
with a row of octagonal piers along its centre, and in the W
range the STOREROOM also with piers along the centre. The
CLOISTER was rebuilt c.1322–37, and many of the pieces are
in the gatehouse museum. The openings were of four lights
with curious horseshoe heads to the lights, and the tracery had
ogee trefoils and ogee quatrefoils, all daintily cusped.

THORNTON-BY-HORNCASTLE

2060

ST WILFRID. Greenstone, nave and chancel. No bellcote, only
a timber frame for the bell in the gable. Also of timber the S
porch, both no doubt Victorian contributions (restoration *E.
Christian*, 1890).* – CURIOSUM. Fine wrought-iron HAT
PEGS with some minimum scroll-work and pegs for thirty-two
hats; presumably Late Georgian.

* In a drawing of 1792 in the Banks Collection the fenestration is entirely
Georgian.

ooio

THORNTON CURTIS

ST LAWRENCE. A memorable church, mostly of between 120
and 1300. The wide chancel comes first, with lancet-shape
but round-headed windows, a priest's doorway set in a buttres
which splays for it like a chimneybreast (one order of shaft
and a roll moulding), and a corbel table. All this looks *c.*120
Then the even, wide nave and the wide aisles. The s arcade c
four wide bays has quatrefoil piers, the foils a good three
quarter circle. Stiff-leaf capitals, double-chamfered arches. I
the responds and one pier dog-tooth runs up between the foils
The same motif in the excellent s doorway. The capitals hav
specially lively stiff-leaf. Many-moulded arch. The N arcad
has moulded capitals on piers with four keeled foils and thi
diagonal shafts between. Then the w tower. w lancet. Twi
bell-openings tall with a polygonal shaft and outer shaft-ring
The angle buttresses are chamfered, as are the w buttresses c
the nave. Tower arch with filleted foils and thin diagona
shafts between. Tower top with eight pinnacles Perp. The
aisle windows, if they can be trusted, *c.*1300–30 in their motifs
The s windows have simple flowing tracery, the buttresse
between them niches. – FONT. One of the few black Tourna
marble fonts in England (cf. Lincoln Cathedral). It is, like al
the others, square. On the sides affronted birds and beasts
two pairs to each side. Five supports. – PULPIT. Jacobean
with blank depressed rounded arches. – SOUTH DOOR. Wit
medieval ironwork. – COLLECTING SHOE, really a smal
shovel or alms-pan. Dated 1661. – INSCRIPTION PANEL. I
commemorates the working of the stalls in 1532 and is still i
black letter. – PLATE. Chalice, by *Peter & William Bateman*
1807. – MONUMENTS. On the floor of the s aisle Lady o
*c.*1300. Only head and bust appear, sunk in a pointed-trefoile
surround. – William Skinner † 1626. Bust in a circular niche.
Of the CHURCHYARD CROSS part of the shaft remains, wit
fleuron decoration.

THORNTON HALL, ½ m. E. Sir Rowland Wynne came here i
1695, and the present house is said to have been built soo
after this. Brick; E front of seven bays and three storeys, th
third storey as an attic (now heightened) above a cornice. Th
façade proper is of five bays, the end bays lying back a littl
and carrying the main chimneys. These end bays are larg
enough to provide closets at first-floor level. Stone details ar
restricted to the window surrounds and quoins. Segmenta

pediments to the lower windows, an open segmental pediment
to the door. On all sides of the house are low three-bay
pavilions. One rainwater head is dated and inscribed 'Chapman
fecit 1769'.* *Thomas Mawson,* the landscape gardener, laid *See*
p.
768
out the gardens.

RECTORY. By *Arthur Ashpitel,* 1855 (GA).

THORNTON-LE-FEN *see* WILDMORE

THORNTON-LE-MOOR   *0090*

ALL SAINTS. Of ironstone. Basically Norman, see that extremely
rare survival, the bellcote, twin with a middle shaft,‡ see also
the S doorway, of the first half of the C12, with one order of
columns, two-scallop capitals, and an outer band of zigzag
round the arch, and see the remains of the nave corbel table
too. A length is at the SW end, and more heads are built into
the walls inside. Otherwise E.E. (one W lancet) and with an
E.E. or Dec clerestory of tiny quatrefoils. There was a N
arcade of four bays with low octagonal piers and double-
chamfered arches; E.E. too. – SCULPTURE. Part of an Anglo-
Saxon cross shaft or slab with interlace at the back of the
square recess in the chancel N wall. – PLATE. Chalice, by
Gabriel Sleath, 1715; Paten, by *I.N.*(?), refashioned 1860. –
MONUMENT. Defaced coffin-lid in the S porch with the
demi-figure of a man, too damaged for dating.

THORPE ST PETER   *4060*

ST PETER. Of many periods, starting with the simple S doorway
probably of *c.*1200, moving to the late C13 W windows of the
aisles (Y-tracery) and the W respond of the N arcade (demi-
quatrefoil with fillet), the only surviving element of the arcade
of that date, and so to the Dec of the rest of the arcades (four
bays, octagonal piers, double-chamfered arches), of the chancel
arch, and of the W tower, short, with typical bell-openings. It
opened originally by arches into W extensions of the aisles.
Much of the other windows is Victorian, especially in the
chancel. The clerestory windows are rough and without

* The design for these pavilions is in the Newby papers signed by 'J.B.'
and dated 1760. Mr Howard Colvin convincingly suggests *John Bell,* James
Paine's understudy on Wynne projects.
‡ That is, if it was correctly rebuilt in 1862.

pretence, and so is the nave roof with tie-beams and queen posts. – FONT. E.E., with pointed-trefoiled arches on colonnettes. Heads against the underside. – PULPIT. Jacobean, with panelled sides and arabesques. The door is preserved. SCREEN. One-light divisions, round arches with ogee arches over, panelled tracery, and pretty detached buttress-shafts. PLATE. Chalice, Paten, and Flagon, by *Thomas Cook & Richard Gurney*, 1755. – MONUMENT. At the W end of the nave a coffin-lid with a cross and the inscription around it Orate pro anima Ricardi Markeby capellani.

THWAITE HALL *see* WELTON-LE-MARSH

0080

TOFT NEXT NEWTON

ST PETER AND ST PAUL. 1891 by *Hodgson Fowler*. Nave with bellcote. Chancel without structural division. Of the medieval church the following pieces: two Late Anglo-Saxon blocks with interlace (now a base in the churchyard, SE of the church) perhaps of a CROSS, one stiff-leaf capital, one head-stop, and block with bold C14 foliage. – PLATE. Chalice and Paten Cover, by *Joseph Ward*, 1704.

8070

TORKSEY

At the junction of the Trent and the Roman Foss Dyke. There was an important Roman port here. In the Middle Ages Torksey possessed a castle, three churches, and two religious houses, one of Augustinian Canons founded before 1216, the other of Cistercian nuns (Fosse Priory) founded *c*.1218. The CANAL, said to be the oldest navigable waterway in the country, has been in operation for over a millennium.

ST PETER. Perp w tower with a charming crouching figure above the w window. Nave, N aisle, and chancel of 1821. Windows with Y-tracery. But inside a beautiful E.E. three-bay arcade. Quatrefoil piers with fillets. Stiff-leaf capitals. The w respond has a capital left unworked. Double-chamfered arches. E.E. also the chancel arch, see the heads of the corbels supporting the arch. – FONT. Big, E.E., of tub-shape. Lively stiff-leaf frieze along the upper part of the bowl. – SCULPTURE. Small figure with thin legs, set, not *in situ*, in the S wall, high up. Is it C14? And what does it represent?

40a CASTLE. In name only. Now the impressive remains of Sir

Robert Jermyn's Elizabethan mansion. The W front stands in glorious isolation, a melodramatic fragment right on the edge of the river and like a scenic backcloth. Four sturdy octagonal towers divide the façade into three parts, the middle one wider. There may have been a gateway or portal here. The tower to its r. had a spiral staircase. The house was three storeys high, half the height of the façade stone-faced, the rest brick with stone quoins and dressings. Two stepped gables remain, and the windows range from two to six lights with a transom. There is in addition a big ten-light window (i.e. a canted bay with three-four-three lights) in the N tower. The plan of the house is unknown. Behind the front are simple fireplaces and a detached corner fragment of brick. The kitchen fireplace adjoins it. Sir Robert was rebuilding his family seat at Rushbrooke in Suffolk c.1559 and perhaps he got on to Torksey immediately after that.

TOTHILL

4080

T MARY. Built in 1778 and consisting of nave and apse. The bellcote is Victorian, the stone base of the church medieval. The Georgian work is of rough brick; arched windows, their surrounds of rubbed brick.

MOTTE AND BAILEY – the Toot Hill* from which the parish takes its name. It seems to be of almost entirely natural formation, standing as an island amid swampy ground.

TOOT HILL. An early C19 farmhouse close to the motte and bailey.

TOYNTON ALL SAINTS

4060

ALL SAINTS. Georgian. Brick, still laid English bond. W tower, long nave, and chancel, the windows victorianized. The surprising length of the nave finds its explanation inside. The church has only a Georgian envelope. Inside the four-bay N arcade and the three-bay S arcade of the medieval church are all but intact. The N arcade is Late Norman or Transitional, see the W respond with scalloped capital. Round pier, pointed double-chamfered arches. The S arcade has octagonal piers instead. – BENCH ENDS. Two, with poppy-heads. – PAINTING. Oil-painted copy of *Rembrandt*'s etching of Christ healing, the so-called Hundred-guilder-piece. – PLATE. Chalice and Paten Cover, Elizabethan.

* From the Old English *tótian*, to peep out.

TOYNTON HALL (Spilsby R.D. Offices). Built in 1908. In th
garden is the early C19 Greek Doric porch from the old house

TOYNTON ST PETER

4060

ST PETER. Perp w tower of greenstone. All the rest 1876 by
Fowler, except for the C14 N arcade of four bays. Low octagona
piers, double-chamfered arches. – FONT. Octagonal, with
square leaf motifs against the stem and four shields and fou
simple blank arches against the bowl. – CROSS. W of the towe
The base is the bowl of a square font. – PLATE. Chalice
Elizabethan.

TRUSTHORPE

5080

ST PETER. Of brick, with a chancel of 1931. The w tower is o
1606. Doorway in a debased Gothic, the bell-openings pointed
Nave of 1842, 'pre-archaeological', pointed windows with Y
tracery. The chancel arch is the one medieval piece. Is i
Perp? – FONT. Panelled stem; the bowl of the pattern-book
type with blank windows, Dec and Perp. – INSCRIPTION. I
the tower, referring to the building of the porch in 1522. –
PLATE. Chalice, London, 1782.

Along the coast at low tide the remains of a submerged forest ca
be seen which extended all along the coast from the Humbe
to Skegness. It is dated to about 2500 B.C.

TUPHOLME ABBEY

1060

1¾ m. SE of Bardney

Of the Premonstratensian abbey founded *c.*1160 there survive
the S wall, i.e. the outer wall, of the refectory. It dates from the
first half of the C13 and stood on a low vaulted undercroft, an
to this there is access from the S by a small doorway with a
single-chamfered segmental arch. The windows were smal
and oblong. The refectory itself has higher lancet windows
Five and a half are preserved, and to their l. the Reader'
PULPIT, a beautiful piece in two bays, recessed in the wall and
partly corbelled out on the outer wall in order to gain space
without destroying the flushness of the inner face. The two
bays are separated by a pair of slender shafts, and the arche
are pointed-trefoiled. In the spandrel a pierced quatrefoil. T

the l. of the pulpit a Norman window. In the wall of the farmyard stones from ribs, the same profile as in those from
Bardney Abbey in Bardney parish church.

TUPHOLME HALL, ½ m. N. Shown in a Buck engraving of 1726.
A tall, elegant cubic silhouette now unfortunately marred by
the addition of two-storeyed early C19 wings. The house was
originally linked to small pavilions, which remain. They are
delightful examples of a rustic bricklayer's style. A moulded
stone doorway is linked by its keystone to the lower keystone
of an *œil de bœuf* above. There are good panelled rooms and a
good staircase. The Vyner family lived here before they moved
to Gautby (*see* p. 247).

TWIGMOOR HALL
5½ m. w of Brigg

9000

Georgian, but the E and S walls incorporate material from an
earlier house.

ULCEBY
3½ m. sw of Alford

4070

ALL SAINTS. 1826. Of brick with a bellcote. This was altered
when the w porch was built in 1893. The nave of two bays has
pointed windows. The chancel is lower. Inside a tripartite
division between nave and chancel, also with pointed arches.
To the l. and r. of the porch, outside, parts of an E.E. pier
with a cluster of eight attached shafts. They were dug up in
the churchyard. – FONT. Octagonal, Perp, with a panelled and
buttressed stem and plain shields (with letters carved on them)
set in quatrefoils. – PLATE. Chalice, Elizabethan(?).

ULCEBY
3 m. NW of Brocklesby

1010

ST NICHOLAS. The ironstone w tower structurally C13 to C14,
but the bell-openings Victorian, and the fine, tall, grey recessed
spire with rolls up the edges Perp (rebuilt 1928). Spires are a
rarity in the north of the county. Much of the rest Dec,
clerestory Perp, but all over-restored. Inside, E.E. chancel
arch and later three-bay arcades with octagonal piers and
double-chamfered arches. – SCREEN. Partly original; Perp. –
PLATE. Chalice and Paten Cover, by *Kath. Mangy*, c.1680.

UPP HALL *see* MANBY

UPTON

ALL SAINTS. C11 chancel, the s side entirely of herringbone
coursing. On the N side little of it is preserved. The nave
doorway is partly Norman. Plain tympanum. C13 two-bay
arcade. Circular pier, keeled responds, double-chamfered
arches. The N aisle windows lancets and paired lancets. Also
E.E. the chancel lengthening and E wall with two lancets and
an almond-shaped window above. Or is all this the work of
Ewan Christian, who 'rebuilt' the church in 1867 (*R. & P.*
1867), or of *James Fowler*, who 'added the N aisle' in 1874–5
and 'restored the chancel' in 1880? Moreover, the tower with
its keyed-in circular w window is Georgian. Murray gives 1770
as the date. It was drawn by Nattes in 1793. – Of the C13
sedile one simple, impressive stone arm remains. – PLATE
Chalice and Paten Cover, by *John Morley* of Lincoln, 1570
(gilded *c.*1875); Paten, London, 1720.

USSELBY

ST MARGARET. An unpromising little building. The masonry
medieval, but what did *Hodgson Fowler* do to it in 1889? The
windows with thin brick arches cannot be his. Is the answer
that what he took over had already been remodelled in the
C18? An inscription inside makes that probable. It reads
QUEEN ANN'S Bounty fell to this CHURCH IN MDCCXLIX. –
PLATE. Parcel-gilt Chalice and Cover, London, 1811.

UTTERBY

ST ANDREW. A rough-looking building of ironstone and chalk.
Dec w tower, Dec s transept, Dec N aisle E window, but Perp
chancel and Perp s doorway. In the hollow of its mouldings
fleurons, heads, a wild man, an animal. Hood-mould with
crockets and finial on head-stops. The N arcade is of three bays
and has concave-sided octagonal piers and double-chamfered
arches. The same arches for chancel arch and transept arch.
So all this is Perp (cf. Marsh Chapel). The tower arch triple-
chamfered and dying into its imposts. At the E end of the N
aisle an elaborate, very pretty canopy with a little vault. –
(FONT. With a drain in the floor. PB) – STAINED GLASS. Bits
in chancel windows. – MONUMENT. Slab with the effigy of a
Rector, late C14. Only the demi-figure visible, i.e. sunk relief
in pointed quatrefoil surround.

UTTERBY MANOR. There was a C17 house here, see the date-stone 1639 and perhaps the coat of arms of the Elye family. Then considerable additions were made in the C19, but these have disappeared again, and the house now has a three-bay front with a middle porch, a shaped and scrolled gable, and dormers, all this and more of 1900.* (Original C17 staircase inside.)

RECTORY. 1863 by *James Fowler*, in red brick patterned with yellow stock brick.

BRIDGE. Packhorse bridge with stone chamfered arch. Probably C14.

WADDINGHAM   *9090*

ST MARY AND ST PETER. Broad W tower, the details Perp. E.E. three-bay arcades. The piers on the N side quatrefoiled keeled, on the s side quatrefoiled with fillets. Double-chamfered arches. The chancel arch has fillets on the responds too, and capitals with crockets and a few upright leaves. With the arcades go the s aisle W and E lancets, the plain, single-chamfered N doorway, and the very restored S doorway with shafts and dog-tooth up the jambs and round the arch. Altogether most of the exterior is restoration (*c*.1860). Can the N aisle E window be exempted? It has bar tracery with a trefoil at the top, i.e. could be later C13. – PLATE. Chalice and Paten Cover, by *John Morley* of Lincoln, 1569.

WADDINGWORTH   *1070*

ST MARGARET. Greenstone, of nave and chancel. The E window Dec of two lights, transferred from the s side by *H. F. Traylen* when he restored the church in 1913. He also made the s windows with their brick arches, which look as if they might be part of the church as it was rebuilt in 1808. The PANEL-LING, PULPIT, and BENCHES no doubt of 1808. The division between nave and chancel by two posts and three arches by Traylen. – PLATE. Chalice, by *W. L.*, London, 1661; Paten Cover, by *R. H.*

WAINFLEET ALL SAINTS   *4060*

ALL SAINTS, High Street. 1821, by *R. H. Sharpe* and *P. Atkinson* (Colvin). Of stock brick with tall, thin Perp windows.

* Yet Burke, *Visitation*, says built in 1718 for John Sapsford and 'greatly altered' before 1854.

Broad gabled porch with a funny leaded bell-turret. Th chancel was lengthened and the N transept added in 1887. FONT. Octagonal, Perp, fleurons on the stem, tracery an Instruments of the Passion on the bowl. – STAINED GLAS Chancel s 1891 by *Mayer & Co*. of Munich. – PLATE. Chalic and Flagon, by *Joseph Fainell*, 1725; two Patens, by *M* London, 1726 and 1728. – TABLET commemorating the tran fer of the church and the monument to William of Wayneflete father from the old to the new church. Elegantly neo-classica with garlands.

The little town, once a prosperous port, has not much characte In the rather large and featureless MARKET PLACE th MARKET CROSS, base, whole shaft, and knop medieval, seems, and on it a weathervane, and the CLOCK TOWER • 1899, brick and with nothing to recommend it. From th Market Place N along the High Street for a glance int BARCUMBE STREET because of its two odd, entirely townis two-and-half-storeyed terraces of High Victorian date, facin one another. From the Market Place s, again along the HIG STREET, past the church and past the railway, to the nice houses around the embanked WAINFLEET HAVEN, e.g. or with a Roman Doric porch, and another (BRIDGE HOUSE facing E, which is thatched and has a rare fretwork fence and Gothick doorway.

But the chief monument of Wainfleet is of course WAINFLEE SCHOOL, founded in 1484 by Bishop Waynflete of Wincheste a native of Wainfleet, as a school to go with his other founda tion Magdalen College Oxford, as William of Wykeham Winchester College was to go with New College Oxford an Eton with King's Cambridge. On 25 April 1484 *Henry Alsbro* contracted with him to make the ceiling and floor. Mr Joh Harvey suggests *John Cowper* as the mason or designer. H work at Esher and at Buckden Palace are in a comparab brick style, all influenced from Tattershall. The school is • brick and lies like a ship at anchor in the fens. The w front flanked by broad, three-storeyed polygonal towers. Centr doorway with depressed head, and above this a four-light Per window. Entrances also to the towers. The long N front has si irregular bays of brick with moulded-brick single and doub lights, and two projecting chimney-flanks. The E front has n towers but a five-light window. The great first-floor room still the original static oblong space. The wide splayed windo recesses do not yet come down to the ground (cf. Thornto

Abbey). Two chimneypieces with castellated decoration and corbelled angel heads are blatantly and unashamedly Victorian Gothic.

WAINFLEET ST MARY

4060

ST MARY. An impressive Marshland church, yet going back in its architectural history to the Norman and E.E. periods. Late Norman the responds of the tower arch (scalloped capitals, semi-octagonal abaci). The double-chamfered arch E.E., like the lower parts of the tower otherwise, i.e. the w doorway with two slight chamfers, the lancet windows, and the handsome blank arcading higher up. The tower was heightened in the Perp style. E.E. also the nave arcades. They are of five bays on the N, four wider bays on the S, and have double-chamfered arches. The N arcade has as its w respond a detached shaft, as its first pier a round one with hollows in the main directions and detached shafts set into them, and simple round piers with round abaci after that. Big label-stops of stylized leaf. The S arcade is simpler. Round piers and round abaci and a little nailhead enrichment. The rest mostly Perp and mostly Victorian rebuilding of 1875–92. Original the arch of the nice S doorway with heads set radially in a broad hollow (and one grotesque crouching figure). The arch does not match the jambs. – FONT. Perp, octagonal, leaves on the stem, four tracery panels and four shields with the Instruments of the Passion on the bowl (just as at Wainfleet All Saints). – COMMUNION RAIL. With twisted balusters; early C18. – PASCHAL CANDLESTICK. A very handsome mid-C18 piece with an eagle at the top and other birds. Not ecclesiastical and brought in recently. – PLATE. Chalice, two Patens, and two Flagons, by *Richard Bayley*, 1724. – MONUMENT. Edward Barkham † 1732. White and grey marble tablet; pilasters and an open pediment.

WAITHE *see* WAYTHE

WALCOT HALL *see* ALKBOROUGH

WALESBY

1090

ALL SAINTS. Alone on the hill top, with wide views to the w, of ironstone, rough, very tactfully restored. E.E. w tower with big diagonal buttresses. Twin bell-openings with chamfered shafts. N and S aisles of *c.*1300 (see the intersecting and Y-tracery). The chancel S doorway looks E.E., and there is one N

lancet, but the s windows include one with reticulated tracer
Perp clerestory. However, as one gets ready to enter, o
observes the round-arched, slightly chamfered s doorway, a
this is clearly Transitional. But it is scant preparation for t
Transitional display inside. Wide nave, again unrestored. T
N arcade has circular piers with circular abaci and capitals, o
scalloped, one with early upright stiff-leaf, one with two tie
of small stiff-leaf, and one plainly moulded. The arcades a
round but double-chamfered, the bases of the 'water-holdin
type – i.e. all is literally in transition from Norman to E.
The piers of the s arcade are octagonal, the arches pointed a
double-chamfered. One capital has small heads and tref
leaves, two are unmoulded and have a little nailhead. E.
chancel arch and tower arch. – FONT. C13? Drum-shape
defaced, originally with angle shafts up the bowl. – PULPI
Dated 1626. From St Leonard's Chapel, Kirkstead (PB). T
top panels have arabesque decoration. Pretty tester with han
ing arches. – Some BOX PEWS. – PLATE. Chalice and Pat
Cover, by *I.P.*, London, 1569.

ST MARY. All Saints being so far to go, a new church was bu
in 1914. It is by *Temple Moore* and deserves a visit, though t
outside is not specially interesting, even if the square tow
top and the paired oblong bell-openings and the use of pla
mullioned windows of Elizabethan and Jacobean type ma
one watchful. Inside, the nave is divided lengthwise by tv
piers reaching right up to the ridge of the roof and thus cuttir
across the chancel arch. Temple Moore must have got the id
from Caythorpe. Also he used two genuine Perp windows
placing them like a screen inside two of his mullioned window
a remarkably successful device. – FONT. Is the stem, flut
alternatingly with round and square projections, C17? T
bowl is octagonal and undecorated.

WALMSGATE HALL
1¼ m. SSE of Burwell

The house, crisply Grecian, in the style of Smirke has recent
been pulled down. It dated from after 1824. The remarkab
chapel has been re-erected at Langworth (*see* p. 293).

LONG BARROW, ½ m. s of the entrance to the Hall, in BEACC
PLANTATION. The site lies just N of the main Louth
Spilsby road, from which it is clearly visible and easily acce
sible. 257 ft long, 64 ft wide, and 7 ft high at the broader s

nd, it is the largest long barrow in the county. It has un-
ortunately been considerably damaged by stone robbing.
Areas of burnt earth were discovered when digging in the
barrow in the C19. It is therefore possible that the barrow
covers a cremation trench similar to those found beneath a
number of barrows in Yorkshire.

WALTHAM   2000

L SAINTS. The ambitious neo-E.E. tower is of 1887 (prob-
bly by *J. Fowler*). Nave and aisles were rebuilt in 1867 and
874. The chancel over-restored too, but the s windows, the s
aisle doorway (with three continuous chamfers), and of course
he interior are of about 1300. Only the tower arch may be a
little earlier. Then, of *c.*1300 the three-bay arcades with
quatrefoil piers and double-chamfered arches. But the arcades
are not identical. The piers have two little steps between the
foils on the N side, whereas on the s side the steps are chamfered. Also the capitals on the s side are simpler. The bases of
he piers are oddly set diagonally. The chancel arch is wide. Its
details, the stepped chamfer and the capitals of the responds,
are clearly E.E., earlier probably than the arcades, but then the
arch was heightened by a vertical piece and the arch dies into
his. In the chancel simple sedilia and part of the piscina of
*c.*1300. – FONT. Perp, octagonal, ornate. On the bowl angels
holding shields, also some big flowers. Against the underside
busts of angels. – BRASS. Joanna Waltham † 1420 with grown-
up son and daughter. Demi-figures, the mother 12½ in. long,
he children 9 in.

f the church the tall GARDEN WALL of a former house. Grey
brick, with blank arches. Early C19 no doubt.

1. s a working WINDMILL. Brick, of the tower type, with cap,
four sails, and fan-tail. At the time of writing this was the only
working windmill in North Lincolnshire.

WAYTHE   2000

MARTIN. The Anglo-Saxon central tower is the interest of
the church. It has twin bell-openings with the familiar mid-
wall shafts. The capitals are of the Norman or Romanesque
block or cushion type, i.e. clearly C11. The tower has a narrow
arch to the W and one to the E, i.e. was preceded and followed
by other rooms, a W porch probably and an E chancel, i.e.
belonged to the type of Barton-upon-Humber, though it has

the slenderness of Late Saxon w towers. The arches reveal
useful detail at all, and the church around this central tower
of 1861 (by *Fowler*). Victorianly speaking its remarkable p
is the chancel, whose walls are covered with hatchment-shap
commemorative tablets to the Haigh family. The aisles ha
their walls faced with brick. The arcades of the nave (two bay
are in fact E.E. work. Quatrefoil piers, the foils more th
semicircles, on the N side keeled and with a big circular abac
on the s side with a little nailhead in the abacus. But of cou
the corbels for the hood-moulds are Fowler's, with th
naturalistic leaves.

⁴⁰⁷⁰ WELL

WELL HALL (Wellvale House). The house is said to have be
built for James Bateman before 1725. If so, then it is uncol
monly advanced. Its style did not really become comm
property until Gibbs's *Book of Architecture* came out in 172
Forgetting the one-bay extension added for Samuel Dashwo
*c.*1760, Bateman's house is a seven-bay, two-storey brick blo
with hipped roof and pedimented dormers behind the parap
Minimal decorative details, just a front projection with
pediment and a Doric porch. Of the interior little need
said. *Guy Elwes*'s rearrangement left a few chimneypieces
vaulted corridor, and a Gibbsy-looking ceiling. Could t
house be by *Gibbs*? The family employed *Thomas Archer*
build Monmouth House, and Archer married into the Chapli
of Tathwell not far away. But Well would be plain Archer p
Yet the GATEPIERS are quite bizarre and Borrominesq
bases of fluted tapered cylinders with lion masks, supporti
obelisks richly decked with garlands, scallop shells, and orr
mental motifs. The iron GATE was bought in Italy early in t
C20. The PARK is the greatest attraction. To the E and w
the house a chain of lakes, and opposite the E front as its *po
de vue* the church. Was this house–church relationship fix
by 1733? If so, this would again show pretty advanc
thinking.

ST MARGARET. Built in 1733, and emphatically in the spirit
the Palladian or, to be more correct, the Inigo Jones reviv
Four Tuscan columns and far-projecting eaves. Victorian be
cote (unfortunately). The E window Venetian, the side windo
pointed with wooden Y-tracery and presumably La
Georgian. The stucco work of the ceiling looks definitely la
C18. Perfect interior with PEWS facing the gangway, in t

college-chapel fashion, three-decker PULPIT in the middle of the s side, with tester. – COMMUNION RAIL. – The FONT is a wooden baluster. – PLATE. Chalice, two Patens, Flagon, and Almsbasin, probably by *John Wirgman*, 1755.

WELTON-BY-LINCOLN   0070

ST MARY. W tower 1768 by *Thomas Bell*. Pretty Gothick w doorway with ogee gable. The rest of the church, including the polygonal apse, of 1823–4 by *E. J. Willson*. The windows are victorianized. Large N vestry by *Temple Moore*, 1912. The arcades inside are the one survival of the medieval church, though they are much re-managed. To the s three bays, to the N four bays. Octagonal piers; double-chamfered arches. The s arcade looks C13, the N arcade C14, but the E respond corbel is C13 again. It may in the C13 have belonged to a N chapel. – PLATE. Chalice, by *R.H.*, London, 1676; Paten, by *Thomas Parr*, 1713.

WILLIAM FARR CHURCH OF ENGLAND SECONDARY SCHOOL. By *Roy Bright* of *D. Clarke Hall, Scorer & Bright*. Straightforward two-storeyed block, but to relieve the shape, a bold outer staircase to the upper floor on one side, a detached cistern with a glass wall on the opposite side.

WELTON-LE-MARSH   4060

ST MARTIN. Brick on a medieval chalk base. Brick w tower. The building dates from before 1792 (Nattes drawing), but the windows were altered in 1891. – FONTS. One octagonal, Perp, crenellated, the other a job of the time when the church was built. – PLATE. Chalice, by *Thomas Evesdon*, 1718.

BOOTHBY HALL, 1 m. E. Early C19, with two canted bays on the s front and a stone porch to the E.

HANBY HALL, ¾ m. NE. L-shaped and mostly C18. The site is picturesquely moated.

THWAITE HALL, ¾ m. NW. In the middle of a wood the remains of a small Augustinian house recorded in 1440. Attached to an C18 cottage is a stone building measuring 30 by 21 ft. In the N front a pointed doorway and a small two-light window. In the E gable the head of another window. The interior possesses three single-light blocked windows with deep splays. It has been called a chapel, but characteristics suggest a domestic use.

WELTON-LE-WOLD

In nicely rolling and wooded country.

ST MARTIN. 1850. In the Dec style, as Dec is probably the original w tower, though its w window is Perp.

WEST ASHBY

ALL SAINTS. Large, of greenstone and of all styles. The s doorway is Early Norman (chamfered imposts, unmoulded arch, hood-mould). The N arcade of four bays is E.E. (elementary piers of the odd shape of a square placed diagonally and chamfers with shafts attached to the chamfers; double-chamfered arches). Dec N aisle windows with straight tops but a little flowing tracery. The Dec windows of the chancel are Victorian. Perp w tower, the parapet with a lozenge frieze. Perp s porch entrance with castellated capitals and Perp N doorway. – FONT. Octagonal, Perp. Panelled stem and panelled bowl. – PLATE. Chalice, London(?), 1758.

WEST ASHBY HOUSE. Behind the yew trees of the churchyard and visually entirely satisfying. The house must be of the early C18. L-shaped with an E front of five bays, two storeys, bracketed eaves cornice, pitched roof, and pedimented dormers. The doorway has Roman Doric pilasters, the frieze the typically Early Georgian parallel horizontal lines leading up to a point in the middle; the straight canopy rests on carved brackets. The doorway is said to have come from Captain Cook's house in London. Big Ionic Venetian window in the s wing, also an addition, and a finely carved s doorway decorated with cherubs' heads (another addition).

THE GROVE. Gothic; C19. Perhaps by the same architect as THE MANOR. Brick Gothic of the 1840s.

WEST BARKWITH

ALL SAINTS. Perp w tower, an original Dec window-head in the s aisle near its E end. Otherwise all features *Withers*'s restoration of 1867-8.[*] – PLATE. Paten Cover, inscribed 1569; Chalice, by *S.P.* or *S.R.*(?), London, 1663.

RECTORY. A typical *Charles Kirk* of 1875.

WEST BURTON POWER STATION
see GAINSBOROUGH

[*] Canon Binnall tells me that a very early Norman gargoyle was found on the tower when this was rebuilt about 1930.

WEST BUTTERWICK

8000

ST MARY. 1841, by *Briggs* (GR). Of beige brick. Thin w tower with octagonal bell-stage and even the spire of brick. The tower stands eccentric to the nave. Tall windows with Y-tracery, short chancel. The exterior as well as the interior evidently intended for unemotional worship. – PLATE. Modern Ciborium made out of old Chalice, York, 1807; Cover, by *Robert Cattle*, 1836.

WEST HALTON

9020

ST ETHELDREDA. Little of the more distant past remains. In the w tower the masonry and the Perp top, in the chancel arch part of E.E. responds, in the nave a window of *c.*1300 with intersecting tracery (or parts of it), and also Perp windows in nave and chancel. But the restoration of 1876 has obliterated much. The medieval church in any case had previously undergone changes after a fire of 1692. This is witnessed by the tower s window and doorway from tower to nave, and also by the s doorway to the nave. – PLATE. Paten, by *Joseph Clare*, 1716; Flagon, by *W. & J. Priest*, 1766; Chalice, 1770.

To the sw of the church a late C17 HOUSE, of L-shape, with nice wooden cross-windows (and the original staircase; MHLG). See p. 768

WEST KEAL

3060

ST HELEN. With a wide view s over the plain. Tall Perp w tower (rebuilt in 1881–4). The bell-openings of three lights with surrounds decorated with fleurons. s aisle with much brick repair. Perp clerestory. The s porch has gargoyles, an entrance of two continuous chamfers, a gable moulding with fleurons, and a niche over. Inside, pitched stone roof on single-chamfered transverse ribs. They are carried by angels with shields, and also two by heads. The s doorway has fleurons and big heads too. Both aisles have the narrowness of pre-Dec and pre-Perp styles, an indication of what the interior has to show. The N aisle is now all Victorian. The chancel with bleak plate tracery by *Street*, 1867. The five-bay arcades inside are a replacement of E.E. arcades – see the responds. That at the NW end has stiff-leaf, the others leaf and heads. The replacement is Dec. Octagonal piers, double-chamfered arches. Their capitals are impressive, especially those on the N side with broad bands of leaf uniting capital and abacus. Heads and animals appear

among the leaves, the latter especially in one pier, where on
can find a monkey on a chain, a fox holding a chicken, and a
owl. On another a long serpent winding round in the foliag
Yet another has angels and busts. The s capitals are le
exuberant. They have single leaves and single grotesque mask
The capitals of the chancel arch are similar to the latter, bu
have busts of human figures and of monsters. The shaft
however are E.E. and keeled. But the earliest evidence in th
church is a Norman scalloped capital with square abacus bui
into the N aisle w corner. – PLATE. Chalice and Paten, b
Sarah Parr, 1729.

0090

WEST RASEN

ALL SAINTS. Of ironstone. Unbuttressed w tower. The (new
bell-openings Dec, the pinnacles of an unusual turret shap
with projecting crenellations. The church had a Norman
arcade of which the arches and the square abaci can be recog
nized in the N wall. The s arcade is E.E. with octagonal pier
keeled responds, and double-chamfered arches. Then a fourt
N and s bay were added, making the church cruciform. The
are even traces in the piece of wall to the w of this bay on the
side, as though a real crossing with a w arch had existed corre
sponding to the E arch which is now the chancel arch. Th
looks late C13. To such a date corresponds the pretty N windo
set in the wall of the former N transept. It has pointed-trefoile
lights with two pointed trefoils and a trefoil over. Of the sam
type, all late C13, the s aisle windows including a w lancet, an
one single-light chancel N window. On the chancel outsid
inscription referring to work done in 1828 and 1829. But th
Victorian forms must belong to the restoration of the 185c
and 1860s. Nice clerestory windows, the frieze of shields o
the s side said to come from a tomb-chest. – BENCH END
Straight-topped with simple arched and traceried panels.
PLATE. Chalice and Paten Cover, by *John Morley* of Lincoln
1569; Beaker, by *H.B.*, London, 1654.
PACKHORSE BRIDGE. C14. With three arches.

WEST RAVENDALE *see* EAST RAVENDALE

1080

WEST TORRINGTON

ST MARK. By *R. J. Withers*, 1860. Nave with bellcote, an
chancel. Old masonry was used. Is not for instance the double

bellcote old? – FONT. Norman, of the tub type, with intersected arches. – SCREEN. Fragments of the screen of St
Benedict, Lincoln. – PLATE. Chalice and Paten Cover,
London, 1568. – MONUMENTS. An amorphous lump is the
remains of an effigy.

WHITTON   9020

T JOHN. Well placed above the Humber. Norman w tower,
with genuine tower arch, but not-so-genuine bell-openings.
This and the nave and chancel with windows of late C13 type
is by *W. & C. A. Bassett Smith*, 1892–7.* – PLATE. Chalice,
by *John Morley* of Lincoln, *c.*1569; Chalice, Paten, and Flagon,
by *Charles Fox*, 1830.

WICKENBY   0080

T PETER AND ST LAWRENCE. Dignified w tower by the
younger *G. G. Scott*, 1868. The N side of the church mainly of
1878, but with a Transitional doorway, with single-chamfered
round arch. Also one Perp three-light window. The S arcade
C13. Three bays. Octagonal piers, double-chamfered arches.
The piers differ in detail. Note the angle pieces of the base of
one of them. Dec S windows, straight-headed, and E window of
the S aisle of four lights under a low four-centred arch, the
tracery with reticulation units. Inside the S aisle an ogee-
headed piscina. Perp chancel S window. – SCREEN. Perp parts
are used. – ARCHITECTURAL FRAGMENTS. A number of
small heads, re-set. Also heads for the S aisle roof-corbels. –
STAINED GLASS. Original bits in the tops of the four-light
window. – PLATE. Chalice and Cover, by *W. M.*, London,
1663; Chalice, two Patens, and Flagon, by *Edward Barrett*,
1717. – MONUMENT. Henry Millner † 1635. Brass plate with
inscription and corpse in a winding sheet. Modest alabaster
surround.

WILDMORE   2050
2½ m. NNW of Langrick

T PETER, Thornton-le-Fen, at Frog Hall. Dated 1816. Perhaps
by *Jeptha Pacey*. Red brick with a pedimental gable. Nave and
chancel. No bellcote. Three pointed side windows with
Y-tracery. The compartments defined by pilaster strips.

* But the Nattes drawing does show twin Norman bell-openings.

8090

WILDSWORTH

ST JOHN. 1838. The architect, according to GR, is *Charles Bigg*
Yellow brick. A polygonal w tower with a small spire and a
doorway. Tall windows with Y-tracery and between them th
polygonal buttresses with minimum finials. Short chancel.

2060

WILKSBY
⅝ m. SW of Moorby

ALL SAINTS. Late Georgian. Two-bay nave, the s wall of bri
with arched windows with wooden Y-tracery. The N wa
stone, as are the chancel walls. (The chancel arch is called E.)
in Walter's *History of Horncastle*.) – FONT. Octagonal, with
big trefoil-leaf in each panel and small heads at the corner
Is it Dec? – PLATE. Chalice, by *G. S.*, London, 1661.

8080

WILLINGHAM

ST HELEN. In the unbuttressed w tower a small Norman
window. The rest 1880 (by *Brodrick & Smith*), as is most
the church. But the blocked simple N doorway is Transitiona
the s doorway has an early C13 arch and hood-mould, and th
ample chancel arch looks late C17. Is that the date of th
'classical' church preceding that of 1880? The Nattes drawir
does not tell. – FONT. Norman, drum-shaped, with pointe
little arches on coupled shafts. – BENCH ENDS. Some a
Perp; square-headed, with tracery. – MONUMENTS. In th
tower two nice C18 tablets: † 1741 and † 1781.

WILLINGHAM HOUSE *see* NORTH WILLINGHAM

4070

WILLOUGHBY

ST HELEN. The village is on the edge of the Marsh, and th
church partakes of the Marsh character, i.e. it is Perp and a
of a piece. The style here is Early Perp, as certain details
mouldings and tracery show which are still close to the De
style, e.g. the doorway mouldings and those of the s por
entrance and the tracery of the chancel side windows and th
bell-openings. The latter are high and have a transom. The
wall of the tower also has a niche with a nodding ogee arc
and a window with an ogee head. The church is big, as th
Marshland churches are. Five-bay arcades and a clerestor
Octagonal piers, double-chamfered arches. The tower arc

triple-chamfered and dying into the imposts. The N chancel chapel sets a problem. It has towards the chancel two arches, one behind the other. The outer one, i.e. the one towards the chapel, is in line with the aisle arcade, the inner one is in its E respond clearly E.E. The capital of the W respond is a late, debased replacement. The most likely thing is that there was an E.E. chapel and that a C14 replacement was built and given its own arch with a view to pulling down the old arch and widening the choir, but that the plan was later given up (cf. Saltfleetby All Saints). – In the tower a wonderfully primeval LADDER. – PLATE. Chalice, by *Thomas Watson*, c.1805. – MONUMENT. Defaced effigy, praying. Only the bust appears, sunk, in a pointed-trefoiled niche. The rest of the slab is bare.

RECTORY. By *Benjamin Broadbent*, 1856, with additions made by *James Fowler* in 1875.

OGSBECK HOUSE, 1 m. SE. Dated 1796. Large square windows, Doric porch, contemporary STABLES and DOVECOTE.

ROUND BARROWS, 1½ m. E. Seven bowl barrows, arranged in two widely-spaced rows running E–W. They vary in size from 30 to 80 ft in diameter and from 2 to 4 ft in height. All have been considerably reduced by cultivation, and they are still under the plough.

WILLOUGHTON

9090

ST ANDREW. The only medieval features the chancel arch and the remains of a Perp two-light S window in the chancel. The rest of 1794. W tower with victorianized doorway. Big circular bell-openings. Pyramid roof with a knob. Arched windows in nave and chancel. White interior with flat ceiling. – COMMUNION RAIL. Later C17. – VAMPING HORN (W wall). Six feet long. – PLATE. Chalice and Paten Cover, by *John Morley* of Lincoln, c.1569. – MONUMENTS. Nicholas Sutton † 1602. Only fragmentarily preserved. The back wall with strapwork and a rhymed inscription.

WILLOUGHTON MANOR. Mostly a rebuilding in Early Victorian stock brick.

NORTHFIELD FARM. Rubbed brick dressings to the windows and such decorative embellishments as oval and blank windows. They all look early C19.

WINCEBY

3060

ST MARGARET. Built in 1860. Disused. E.E. style with a W rose window of ugly plate tracery. – PLATE. Chalice, London, 1569.

PATCHETT'S FARM. Early Victorian in stock brick, thre
storeyed, with a big Roman Doric porch.

9020   WINTERINGHAM

ALL SAINTS. The four-bay arcades are both rewarding an
baffling. That on the N side is rich Norman, that on the s si
Transitional. The N side has sturdy round piers with mult
scalloped capitals and square abaci, the s side slimmer rou
piers with smaller multi-scalloped capitals and octagonal aba
Both sides have decorated arches, with pellets, lozenges, et
but the earlier side has them pointed, the later round –
example perhaps of the inconsistency of a transitional phas
Good E.E. chancel, the E wall with three widely-space
stepped lancets and a Victorian circular window over. Th
stepping is Victorian too. In the Nattes drawing they are ev
and carry three incongruous pediments. Victorian also th
details of the aisles. But the s transept is again E.E. The
tower on the other hand may basically well be Norman. Its to
is Perp. The early date is suggested by the identity of mason
with the W quoins of the nave before aisles were added. –
SCULPTURE. Tiny figure of a man in what looks like a c
niche (s transept E wall). – PLATE. Chalice and Paten Cove
by *John Morley* of Lincoln, 1569; Paten, by *John Carter*, 176
Flagon, by *W. & J. Priest*, 1769. – MONUMENT. Under
segmental arch in a recess a C13 cross-legged Knight, tw
angels at his diagonally laid pillow.

As in so many of the Humber villages, the visual effect is
consistent early C19 one, yet few houses are worth speci
mention. EASTFIELD has a plaque inscribed: 'Pray play an
See
p.
768
sing God save the King 1796.'

ROMAN(?) JETTY. In the C19 the remains of a wood an
timber jetty were noted when the Humber was very low
the result of a dry summer. It was tentatively ascribed to th
Romans. This jetty has been subsequently noted on a numb
of other occasions, although not recently.

9010   WINTERTON

ALL SAINTS. Anglo-Saxon W tower, embraced by the late
aisles. One s window looks into the s aisle. Wide tower arch
the simplest imposts. The familiar doorway or window abov
it. Bell-openings with mid-wall shafts as usual. Above th

Saxon top an E.E. heightening. Tall twin bell-openings with shaft and nook-shafts. Finally, on top Perp battlements and eight pinnacles. Next in order of date the arcades with their very strange piers. They are tall and octagonal and have a strong shaft-ring or waist-band, on the S side with dog-tooth. The capitals have small flat leaves of excellent varieties, quite original and inventive. They are unfortunately over-restored, but the capital in the S transept shows how finely they were done. The abaci have a little nailhead decoration. The arches are double-chamfered. The responds are interesting too. The SW respond is triple and has a semicircular abacus, the NW respond is keeled. NE and SE have broad fillets, but the capital of the NE respond is a re-used Norman fragment with a dragon. All this must be early C13, and there is indeed a dedication reported for 1203. A little later the whole generous composition of transepts and chancel. First the transepts with tall lancets (one in the S transept has a dog-tooth hood-mould inside). This transept may be what was consecrated in 1245; for the chancel must be as late as the late C13. The E window is Victorian, but one S window has two lights with a circle and without foiling or cusping. Again a little later, i.e. c.1300, the S doorway with two orders of thin shafts, and the S aisle and N aisle W windows, both with intersecting tracery. The N aisle otherwise redone in the C18, see the pedimented porch and the wide pointed window. The porch has, however, curiously enough, a pointed tunnel-vault, and so the C18 may only have remodelled it. Of the second third of the C14 the bold transept end windows, of four lights with flowing tracery like broad leaves branching off a bough. The boughs are uprights between lights one and two and three and four and reach right up into the arch. The upright between lights two and three does not quite touch the apex. A small drop shape is inserted. – SOUTH DOOR with Perp ironwork. – ARCHITECTURAL FRAGMENTS. Intricately traceried Perp stone panels under the tower. Are they from a stone screen? – PAINTING. Above the altar Holy Family by *Anton Raphael Mengs*. May it some time be cleaned. – STAINED GLASS. Chancel S and N by *Kempe & Tower*, 1913. – PLATE. Two Patens, by *Mary Barrett*(?), Dublin, c.1726; Chalice, by *R. Hennell*, 1836. – BRASS. Two ladies, 25 in. long, the wives of John Rudd † 1504.

TRINITY METHODIST CHURCH. 1961–2 by *Derek Brown*. Simple and convincing, with flat roofs and a skeleton tower. Simple internally too; no gimmicks.

A Humber village, and predominantly Early Victorian in character. The houses worth mention are as follows.

THE CHAINS, No. 35 West Street, built in 1827 by *William Fowler* for himself. It has lost its gabled roofs. Fowler called it Parva Domus.

DENT COTTAGE, No. 56 Park Street, built for Joseph Dent in 1830 by *H. F. Lockwood* of Hull, is in a spiky Gothic manner of buttressed wall and tall pointed gables. In the garden is the tomb of Jonathan Dent. It all evokes The Priory at Louth (*see* p. 306).

The OLD HALL, Park Street, is in the mid-C17 Artisan Mannerism with pedimented and pilastered Ionic gable-ends.

See p. 768 THE HALL is later C18. Front of five bays, two storeys, quoined angles; one pediment.

ROMAN VILLA, at the foot of Lincoln cliff. Roman occupation in this area was noted as early as the C17, and in the C18 wall foundations, three tessellated pavements, and quantities of bricks, tiles, and small finds were uncovered. No details are known concerning the layout of the buildings, but at least one of the mosaic pavements survives intact beneath the ground.

5060

WINTHORPE

ST MARY. A Perp Marshland church, but the successor to an earlier one of which some fragments are displayed in the church: late C12 pier bases, a late C12 capital with flat upright leaves, and a mysterious stone with a sunk circle. The church is of grey stone. W tower with Late Perp bell-openings and a lead-covered spike. Three- and four-light windows in the aisles. N doorway with traceried spandrels. Ornate S porch similar to that at Addlethorpe. It was given, according to the inscription, by Robert Langay and William Palmer (who died in 1520 – *see* Ingoldmells). Entrance with fleurons up two mouldings. A niche above, a charming rising parapet with a trail of feathery leaves (quatrefoils and shields over the W and E walls), and top pinnacles. The clerestory has battlements, pinnacles, a delightful little open Sanctus-bell turret on the E gable, and two-light windows, except for the last one to the E which is of three lights to light the rood. Five-bay arcades with octagonal piers and double-chamfered arches. The chancel arch the same. Nave roof of low pitch with tie-beams, arched braces, and bosses. Good bosses in the N aisle roof at the E end. – FONT. Octagonal, Dec, with a base decorated with shields, a panelled stem, and on the bowl pattern-book forms of window tracery. – SCREENS. The rood screen has one-light divisions with ogee arches and panel tracery. So have the parclose screens, but it is remarkable how different they yet are. The rood screen has as its speciality a pretty band of openwork arcading at the top of the dado. The dados of the parclose screens on the other hand are specially richly traceried. – CHANCEL SEATS. With the return seats – a splendid set. Intricate tracery on the ends, but on one St Hubert and the Stag instead. A great variety of poppy-heads, including one with little men beating down acorns. Beasts on the arms. – BENCH ENDS. Also with good poppy-heads. – DOOR. The valve of the original S door, now leaning against the chancel arch, is Dec, not Perp. – SCULPTURE. Head of the churchyard cross with the Virgin and the Crucifixus (S aisle W). – STAINED GLASS. Original bits in the N aisle. – PLATE. Chalice and Paten, C17 Flemish(?). – MONUMENTS. Brasses to Richard Barowe † 1505 and family, 2 ft 5 in. figures. – To Robert Palmer † 1515, a 1 ft 8 in. figure. – CROSS. S of the church, base and part of the shaft. For the head *see* above.

WISPINGTON

₂₀₇₀

ST MARGARET. By *John Bownas Atkinson* of York, 1863. Of grey stone. Lancet windows and a steeple with a broach spire. It stands inside on two columns and three arches. – FONT, PULPIT, and a RELIEF of St Margaret were all carved in stone by the then vicar, the *Rev. Charles Pratt Terrot*. – PLATE. Chalice and Paten Cover, by *Thomas Folkingham*, 1711. – MONUMENTS. Philips family, last death recorded 1715, and John Philips † 1720 – an interesting comparison, the former still Baroque, with putto heads and a skull, the latter classical, purely architectural, with pilasters and without figures.

WITHCALL

₂₀₈₀

ST MARTIN. In a secluded spot in the Wold. By *Sir Arthur Blomfield*, 1882. Nave, with high bellcote over its E gable, and chancel. Brown and grey stone. Lancet windows and windows with plate tracery.

WITHERN

₄₀₈₀

ST MARGARET. The chancel may be medieval (restoration 1875), the nave dates from 1812. It is of brick and as broad as the C19 liked it. The roof does not reveal the fact that insid[e] the Perp three-bay arcades were kept (octagonal piers, double chamfered arches). The intersecting tracery of the windows i[s] again typical early C19; but the bellcote must be later. – FONT Octagonal and probably C14. A pattern-book of window designs, mostly Dec, but also one Perp. – Coloured GLASS i[n] crude colour in some of the windows, no doubt of 1812. PLATE. Chalice, by *John Spackman*, 1692; Paten, by *Georg[e] Wicks*, 1729. – MONUMENT. Grantham Hodgson † 1858. B[y] *Tyley* of Bristol. Draped urn.

CASTLE HILL. The house of the Fitzwilliam family was insid[e] the moated area to the E of the church.

WITHERN HALL. Late C17; of five bays with a narrow two storey pedimented porch projecting from bay four.

EARTHWORK, at the W end of the village. Trapezoidal in plan and very strongly banked and ditched. It appears to be [a] medieval castle of an unusual type.

WOLD NEWTON

ALL HALLOWS. A little above the village, nicely placed agains[t] the hill and nicely landscaped. 1862 by *James Fowler*. Nav[e] and apse and a polygonal bell-turret with spirelet roguishl[y] corbelled out. – FONT. Dec, with inscription recording th[e] donors. Band of horizontally placed reticulation units cusped i.e. really two wavy wands. – STAINED GLASS. Some Nether landish C17 panels. – A number of ARCHITECTURAL FRAG MENTS collected recently, e.g. a Norman capital from Bardne[y] Abbey, another Norman capital, two E.E. capitals, all small and a larger and good Dec foliage capital. – Also many smal[l] items which *The Buildings of England* cannot list. – PLATE Chalice, Elizabethan; Spoon, with the Apostle St Joh[n] c.1620.

The MANOR. A fine brick and stone-quoined BARN represent[s] a style of building prevalent throughout the village.

WOOD ENDERBY

ST BENEDICT. 1860 by Mr *Hackford* (PF). Grey tower wit[h] broach spire, neo-E.E. Nave and chancel of greenstone; ol[d] masonry but new windows (except perhaps one N window straight-headed with ogee lights). The arcade inside als[o] appears entirely Victorian. – PULPIT. Attached to it an iro[n]

relief of the Noli me tangere; German, C17. – ARCHITEC-
TURAL FRAGMENT. The fluted capital of a pillar piscina;
Norman. – PLATE. Chalice, by *F. T.*, London, 1634; Paten,
mid C18; Alms Plate, London, 1771.

WOODHALL

2060

ST MARGARET. Alone with the farmhouse and the business-like
modern barn, both bigger than the church. The base of the
church is of greenstone but the rest mostly of brick. Nave and
chancel and thin Perp w tower, buttressed also into the church.
The w front is odd. Two buttresses with the w window
squeezed between them. They carry an arch high up, and on
this stands the bell-stage, decorated to the w with panelling
and shields l., r., and at the top. Above the bell-stage a thin
spire with a waist-band and thinner spirelets. – FONT. Round,
with a kind of elementary angle volutes. Most probably E. E. –
PULPIT and LECTERN no doubt by the *Rev. J. Conway Walter*
(*see* Langton-by-Horncastle). – PLATE. Beaker, probably
North European, *c.*1660.

WOODHALL SPA

1060

The spring, which is beneficial to people suffering from gout or
rheumatism, was discovered in 1824, and at the back of the spa
premises there are indeed still Georgian brick chimneys and
buildings, one with lunette windows. The Spa itself is singularly
modest but lies in trees, and close to it is the Kinema. There is
nothing festive or glamorous about the Spa. But there is about
the rest of Woodhall Spa, which is mostly early C20 and much
like a suburb of Bournemouth, tree-lined streets, large, affluent,
and soporific-looking houses for retired people who have not
done too badly for themselves, pines, birches, other trees, and
shrubberies everywhere, and the few principal hotels (GOLF
HOTEL by *R. A. Cann* and PETWOOD HOTEL) highly half-
timbered, as if Woodhall were near Droitwich.

ST PETER. 1893 by *Hodgson Fowler*, brick inside and out, and
also of a type familiar from wealthy suburbs. Nave and wide s
aisle; no tower; windows of three stepped lancet lights.

TOWER ON THE MOOR. The impressive fragment of a tower
built in the C15 by Cromwell s of Tattershall, a little later than
Tattershall Castle (*see* p. 390. The same craftsmen may have
been employed. The tower was smaller, and the remaining

octagonal NW stair-tower is nearly 60 ft high. There were fou
floors. The stair tower is nearly detached from the corner o
the main tower.

WELLINGTON MONUMENT, near Waterloo Wood, 1½ m. N
This wood was planted 'from Acorns Sown Immediately Afte
The Memorable Battle Of Waterloo', according to the inscrip
tion upon the monument. The obelisk is 36 ft high and sur
mounted by a bust of Wellington. It was erected in 1844 b
Colonel Richard Elmhirst.

WOODTHORPE HALL see STRUBBY

0010

WOOTTON

ST ANDREW. Perp W tower of ironstone. Elementary E.E.
arcade of three bays. The N arcade looks later. Externally a
details Victorian, except for one straight-headed N windov
with ogee lights. – PLATE. Chalice and Paten Cover, by Pete
Carlill, 1569 (the earliest dated piece of Hull silver extant)
Tankard, by William Shaw & William Priest, 1751; two
handled Cup, by John Kentember(?), 1767; Chalice, gil
inside, by L.I., London, 1786. – MONUMENT. John Uppleb
† 1839, with a portrait head in profile below. – Several C 1
tablets.

WOOTTON HALL. The W front presents an essay in two planes
an effect of blank arches and stepped-back wings. Of brick
five bays wide, and of three storeys. The centre three bay
pedimented and the middle bay like a giant blank arch th
height of the front. In this is a stone Doric porch, a Venetia
window, and a semicircular window. On the S and N ends ar
two-storey canted bays facing outwards. The design is un
usually sophisticated, and James Paine has been suggested as
possible candidate. A nice touch is the ha-ha formed aroun
the house in the shape of a trefoil.

See p. 768

VICARAGE. Later Georgian. Pointed gable-ends to the wing
and a fat canted bay projecting from two bays of the centr
part. In the garden is a jolly castellated FOLLY of brick t
screen a pig sty.

0010

WORLABY
1½ m. SE of Bonby

ST CLEMENT. 1877 by W. Scott Champion, but the tower arch
towards the nave Anglo-Saxon, the S arcade with Dec quatre
foil piers and keeled responds and the N arcade with octagona

piers at least partly medieval. – FONT. Disused, under the tower. Circular. How can these strange depressions and blobs be dated? – STAINED GLASS. E window apparently by *Kempe*. – PLATE. Chalice, by *John Morley* of Lincoln, *c.*1569. – MONUMENTS. Incised slab to a Civilian and wife, under the tower. Very defaced. Greenhill dates it *c.*1325 and calls it foreign. – Effigy of a Lady, late C14, very defaced (behind the organ).

WORLABY HALL. In the C17 Lord Bellasis built here a bizarre brick house in the familiar Fen Artisan Mannerism. Its decorative details were of the weirdest. The present house is of *c.*1799. C17 gatepiers.

WORLABY HOSPITAL. Quite on its own, some distance E of the church. This was also built by Bellasis. The date is 1673. Though more restrained, it provides a key to the style of his house. The front of five bays and two storeys divided by giant Doric pilasters. Flat projecting surrounds and strange hoods to the door and ground-floor windows. The pilasters and all the frames dotted with studs. The style is not Fen Artisan Mannerism but rather a Humber brick style (cf. Wilberforce House, Hull). The roof has been altered. There were once Dutch gables and a fat studded cornice. The foundation was for four poor widows, yearly endowed with £3 10*s.* 0*d*, a blue gown, and a cauldron of coal.

WRAGBY

ALL SAINTS. 1838 by *W. A. Nicholson*. Yellow brick, quite large, of the Commissioners' type. W tower, wide nave, short chancel, never lengthened, lancet windows, mostly in pairs. The WEST GALLERY remains. – Norman PILLAR PISCINA with a decorated scallop capital; found in a garden at Wragby and probably from the old church. – PLATE. Paten, by *R.C.*, London, 1676.

OLD CHURCH, ¼ m. SE. Only the chancel has been preserved. Brick, laid in Flemish bond. Arched, keyed-in windows. But the chancel arch is E.E.

The early C19 TURNOR ARMS, Tudoresque ALMSHOUSES of 1840, and a tower WINDMILL of brick, painted white, dated 1831, are all that need be recorded.

WRAWBY

ST MARY. Unbuttressed C13 W tower with good triple-chamfered arch towards the nave. The hood-mould has dog-tooth.

Nave with clerestory. The easternmost N and s windows are
larger than the others to throw more light on the rood. Four
bay N arcade, perhaps late C13 (octagonal piers, double-chamfered arches), as the N doorway seems to be. Perp s arcade, but
the capitals perhaps interfered with in the C17 – cf. the odd
caryatid bust of the w respond. – CHANDELIER. Brass; dated
1820. – TAPESTRY. Christ and the Children, said to have been
shown at the 1862 Exhibition. – MONUMENT. Sir Robert
Tyrwhitt † 1548. Tomb-chest with shields in quatrefoils
separated by arched panels. Back arch with almost straight-
sided four-centred arch. The brasses below it are missing.
Top quatrefoil frieze.

RECTORY. By *W. A. Nicholson*, 1830 (GA).

WINDMILL. Post-mill with four sails.

KETTELBY HOUSE. An ancient Tyrwhitt seat demolished in
1697. The present house dates from 1769.

WROOT

7000

ST PANCRAS. 1878. Probably by *James Fowler* (see below).
Small, of brick, with lancet windows and a s porch tower. –
PLATE. Chalice and Paten Cover, by *John Morley* of Lincoln,
1569.

(RECTORY. According to GA, the house was first designed in
1793 by *John Hibberd*, then rebuilt in 1878 by *James Fowler*.

WYHAM

2090

1¼ m. w of Ludborough

ALL SAINTS. Chalk and ironstone. Nave with bellcote and
chancel. So far nothing of interest. But there is herringbone
masonry in the chancel s wall, and so the chancel must be C11.
In the w wall a Dec window with reticulated tracery, a blocked
shapeless C17 or C18 window over, and above that one Norman
stone with zigzag.

YARBOROUGH CAMP *see* CROXTON

YARBURGH

3090

ST JOHN BAPTIST. Built shortly after a fire of 1405. Perp w
tower of ironstone. The doorway quite ornate. In the spandrels
the Fall on the l., shields on the r. In a hollow of the mouldings
fleurons, a branch, a bird on its nest, and an inscription: 'wo
so looks thys work upon, pray for all that yt begun'. Upper

windows with embattled transom. The tower is very similar to that of Market Rasen. The S aisle has been demolished. Nothing of the arcade can any longer be verified. Perp windows set in. Perp also the S doorway. Perp N aisle too. Arcade with octagonal piers and double-chamfered arches. – SCREEN. Now under the tower. One-light divisions. – BENCH ENDS. With poppy-heads; very rustic. Also one bench back with linenfold panelling. – PLATE. Remains of a Paten Cover, Elizabethan; silver-mounted Coconut Cup, c.1635.

KESTEVEN AND HOLLAND

*

ALGARKIRK

ST PETER AND ST PAUL. An over-restored church (*R. C. Carpenter*, 1850–4), once no doubt very beautiful. Cruciform, the crossing tower with Victorian E.E. twin bell-openings. Victorian recessed lead pyramid roof. The W, E, N, and S windows are all very large and elaborate and all Dec, but in their present form Victorian. However, those visible in the Nattes drawing – i.e. N transept N and S transept S – are as they were then. But can the Dec aisle windows be trusted, under their segmental arches? They seem different in the Nattes drawing. The transepts have a W aisle, a very unusual thing, here probably derived from Spalding. The nave clerestory of ten Perp three-light windows. Perp clerestory also in the transepts. The chancel E wall shows E.E. buttressing, i.e. is older than it appears. The interior is a purer pleasure. Five-bay arcades of the early C13. Round piers, octagonal abaci, moulded capitals, except for the two NW piers, where stiff-leaf appears. Double-chamfered arches. The transept W arcade of the same type, but the outer responds with stiff-leaf. The crossing piers are curiously indistinct. Round with keeled projections. One pier still has waterleaf capitals, i.e. a form definitely pre-1200, one has proper stiff-leaf. To the same moment belong or belonged transepts and chancel. The N transept had a small E chapel. Of this the double-chamfered round arch exists, where again stiff-leaf (and an engaging monster) and waterleaf are used side by side. The S transept also had such a chapel (see the N respond), but later the whole transept was widened to the E. N of the N chapel entrance a tall lancet, shafted inside. The form of the chapels must have been odd; for the chancel, to give it greater breadth than the nave, splays out E from the crossing so that the narrow arcade arch from the N chapel is skew. Then a lancet. The rest of the chapel E.E. in proportion though Dec in most details (e.g. the ballflower frieze under the roof). But the sedilia and double piscina are E.E. The piscina in the s transept is a handsome Dec piece. – REREDOS. Very sumptuously Dec. By *Crace*. – STAINED GLASS. Bits in the N chapel N side. – E window by *Hardman*. Other windows by *Clayton & Bell*. – PLATE. Chalice and Paten, by *H.S.* 1613; Paten and Flagon, by *Wm. Lukin*, 1700; Paten, by *Wm. Barrett*(?), 1718. – MONUMENT. Brass to Nicholas Robertson † 1492 and two wives, $37\frac{1}{2}$ in. figures. – Stone effigy of a priest C14. – Stone effigy of a Civilian, C14, the head under an ogee canopy. – Charles Beridge † 1782. Big urn on a square base.

SCHOOL. Gothic, by *Sir G. G. Scott*, 1857.

ALLINGTON HALL *see* WEST ALLINGTON

AMBER HILL
$4\frac{1}{2}$ m. NNW of Swineshead

2040

ST JOHN BAPTIST. 1867 by *E. Browning* (GR). Red brick and rubbed brick, nave with high roof, polygonal apse, bellcote, lancet-shaped but round-headed windows and in the w wall even a composition of three of them with three plain circles over. In fact the church is not without individuality. Wide interior, yellow brick, with a red dado and a black band, big heavy timber roof, and – the most surprising detail – naturalistic foliage capitals cut in red brick. The capitals of the s porch prepare for this feat.

ANCASTER

9040

ST MARTIN. Ashlar-faced w tower with recessed spire. Two-light bell-openings. In the spire three tiers of lucarnes in alternating directions. Norman chancel, recognizable by the traces of shafted windows in the E wall and the corbel table. In the s wall a late C13 window with cusped lights and an encircled quatrefoil. In the E wall Dec window with reticulated tracery E.E. N aisle, the doorway altered but preserving its dog-tooth up the jambs. Also lancet window in the w wall. In the E wall Dec window with, in the tracery, two circles filled by two mouchettes each. E.E. s doorway with a boldly pointed-trefoiled head. Dec s aisle windows. The s aisle has Perp battlements with much decoration and pinnacles. The same on the clerestory with its four pairs of windows on the s side, four single windows on the N side. As one enters, one is back at the beginning. Not only the chancel, the N arcade is Norman too, of *c*.1160–70. It is of four bays, the tower cutting into the first. Sturdy round piers, multi-scallop capitals, octagonal abaci, round arches. The w arch just one step, the next a step and rolls, the third just an absurdly fat roll covered with billet, the last zigzag. The s arcade is E.E. Three wider bays, octagonal piers with four attached shafts in the main directions. Double-chamfered arches. The chancel arch is the same in style. Dec tower arch with shafts connected by continuous hollows. Arch with three sunk quadrants. Of the Perp roof only some flattish primitive figures are preserved. – FONT. Norman, drum-shaped. With thin intersecting arches. – PLATE. Chalice and Cover, c.1569; Chalice, London, 1771. – MONUMENTS. In the s porch two effigies of priests, the earlier early C14. The other is carved so that the draperies of the lower part merge into the unelaborated slab and only his feet come out of this. – Elizabeth Long † 1743 (N aisle). Tablet with a trumpeting angel in relief at the top. Very conservative. – John Roe † 1796. By *King* of Bath. Standing woman by an urn in front of an obelisk – the common subject treated very nicely. – Many more tablets.

Ancaster was the ROMAN STATION of CAUSENNAE, mentioned in the Antonine Itinerary. Good stretches of the town rampart and ditch, the latter some 60 ft wide, can be seen in fields on the s and E sides, and traces can also be detected of the w portion of the wall. A conspicuous mound at the NE corner of the defences marks the position of a large, stone-built, circular bastion projecting from the line of the defences. In addition to a large number of small finds, the site has produced a number of pieces of Roman SCULPTURE, including an altar, portions of an inscribed milestone of Constantine I, and figures of Mother Goddesses (now at the Grantham Museum).* ERMINE STREET passes from N to s through the town on its way to Lincoln, forming today's main street.

The village is visually rewarding in its grey Ancaster stone, and only C20 cottages have the temerity to break away from the vernacular tradition. The three best houses are, from the church N: ANCASTER HALL, a georgianized C17 house, the street front of four bays and two storeys, with two-light windows and a tall pedimented doorcase; the ANGEL INN, a Georgian six-bay, two-storey house; and LAUNDE HOUSE, with a nice panel of Rococo ornament above a heavy early C19 acroterion-topped doorway.

* Two more fragments, one small head with moustaches and two heads together, probably female, were found in 1960.

SUDBROOKE HALL, 1 m. NW, really in Sudbrooke village
    Dated 1610 and L-shaped. One front C18 with four pedi-
    mented windows with a pulvinated frieze.
In the village a HOUSE of 1843 with an elegant doorcase that mus
    be *ex situ*. Elongated fluted Doric columns with rose motifs in
    the necking. It looks late C16, and may have come from
    Grimsthorpe.
WILLOUGHBY HALL, 1⅛ m. W, a tall, gaunt, French-styl
    house of 1873, said to be by *Watkins*, is in ruins.

1050   ANWICK

ST EDITH. The church has an E.E. N doorway (dog-tooth an
    nailhead) and E.E. to Dec arcades (four bays, low). The pier
    are quatrefoil with thin shafts in the diagonals, all foils an
    shafts filleted. The N arcade is earlier, with flatter bases an
    some nailhead and dog-tooth. The S arcade and all the rest i
    Dec, including the N aisle windows. The aisles as well as th
    tower are ashlar-faced. The tower has a typical arch to th
    nave, with triple responds, the middle one filleted, and sun
    quadrant mouldings in the arch. The bell-openings are Dec too
    and then there is a frieze of leaves, monsters, etc., and a spir
    not high and with three tiers of lucarnes in alternating direc
    tions. Their gables have figure stops, and they have finials a
    well; so too much sticks out for the spire to be satisfactory i
    outline. The S porch has a Dec entrance, the S doorway fin
    shafts and fine mouldings, and the S windows are the same a
    those to the N. The S arcade was built at the same time as th
    s aisle wall. Eight filleted shafts, four major, four minor, an
    arches with sunk quadrant mouldings. The chancel arc
    belongs to the S arcade, and the priest's doorway in the chance
    too. – Norman PILLAR PISCINA. – SCULPTURE. Headles
    Virgin with Child, early C14, and once no doubt very beauti
    ful. – MONUMENTS. A number of C17 and C18 tablets.
    CROSS. E of the church, fragmentary as usual. The shaft i
    fluted.
POST OFFICE AND SMITHY. Two early C19 Gothic cottage
    with conical roofs joined to each other by a straight range
    They stand S of the church at the road junction. A little furthe
    W a third with a thatched roof.
HAVERHOLME PRIORY. A Gilbertine house founded in 1139
    In the 1780s a Gothic house was built and then in 1835 re
    built in Tudor style for the Earl of Winchelsea. The architec
    was *H. E. Kendall*. The centre and the porch remain

KITCHEN GARDENS also C19, and a fine BRIDGE dated 1893. A crazily asymmetrical LODGE to the SE.

ASGARBY

1040

T ANDREW. A church with a Perp exterior and a Dec interior. So we start inside. The pier principle is the quatrefoil with deep unbroken hollows between the foils. So it is done in the three-bay arcades (double-chamfered arches*) and so in the five-shafted responds of chancel arch and tower arch. The tower then continues Perp. It is a very tall, ashlar-faced tower, attached to a relatively small church. Perp bell-openings, a lozenge-decorated band below the parapet, and then the rather over-crocketed spire zone, i.e. pinnacles with crockets, pretty but ineffectual flying buttresses of little open arcading with castellation – like lace – and then the spire itself. Perp chancel, the windows with crenellated horizontals in the panel tracery. Perp clerestory of an unusual and very successful type. The windows are of three lights and straight-headed. So the result is an almost continuous band of glazing similar to what you may find in timber-framed houses. Also an E window, but this with a four-centred arch. Battlements and pinnacles. – PAINTINGS. In the N aisle a young kneeling figure with an inscription scroll; background of stylized flowers; C15. – Also a C17 wall painting above the tower arch, with a cadaver upright and big cross-bones. The inscription reads 'Redeem the time' and 'Prepare to die'.

SGARBY HALL, S of the church. Early C19, Gothic, rough-cast, of three widely-spaced bays. Windows and doorways and the windows of the two canted ground-floor bays all with four-centred arches. Rusticated corners contrived with pebbles. Pretty little Gothic eaves frieze.

ASHBY-DE-LA-LAUNDE

0050

T HIBALD. Unbuttressed W tower, probably older than E.E., as the masonry changes and the tower recedes below the E.E. bell-openings. This is probable, though the arch towards the nave is E.E. The bell-openings are two of one light each, still with a continuous roll. Heads l. and r., also heads in the span-drels to the N and a little man. Corbel table and gargoyles. It all looks suspicious. Minor recessed spire. No crockets, one tier of lucarnes. Nave and chancel of 1854 (by Mr *Huddleston*).

* One pier stands on a circular base.

E.E. N doorway with dog-tooth in arch and hood-moul
Inside, the Dec former N arcade is exposed. Three bay
Low quatrefoil piers filleted with three shafts in the diagonal
Double-chamfered arches. – FONT. Octagonal with squar
leaves. – SCULPTURE. A Guardian Angel and a Saint, woo
Continental, Baroque. – PLATE. Chalice and Paten Cover, t
Wm. Colson, 1719; Flagon, by *Aug. Courtauld*, 1719. – MONU
MENT. Edward Kinge † 1617. What survives is six kneelin
figures, the three daughters in relief.

ASHBY HALL. Much altered. Exterior recased in the C19. Onl
the W front reveals the original conception of projectin
gabled wings and a two-storey porch with crockets and obe
lisks. The oriel may be C19, but the entrance has Dori
columns, an equilateral pediment, and the date 1595. E of th
C19 S front is a nicely rounded late C18 bow.

ASLACKBY

0030

ST JAMES. The chancel is of 1856, but the N lancets are origin
E.E. work. The W tower is puzzling in that it has, besides th
high arch towards the nave, equally high blank arches to N, s
and W. Are they really relieving arches or just decoration
To the W above the doorway a tall three-light window wit
two castellated transoms (one in the zone of the tracery) – a
below this giant arch. The date is C14, see the responds wit
shafts connected by continuous hollows, polygonal abaci, an
triple-chamfered arches. The buttresses carry square shaf
ending in pinnacles below the tower top. The chancel
exactly like the tower arch, the arcades of three bays ar
similar. Quatrefoil piers with continuous hollows and fillet
Arches with sunk quadrant mouldings. Dec N and S aisle win
dows, the N aisle E window (four lights) grander than th
others. The S aisle carries an oddly clumsy parapet. Is it C17
It was called Saracenic in 1835. Perp clerestory. Three pai
of close windows. Lozenge frieze, battlements, and a rood
stair turret with spirelet. – PLATE. Chalice and Paten Cove
*c.*1570; Chalice, London, 1635.

VICARAGE, NW of the church. Late Georgian, with, on th
ground floor, attractive blank arcading. This is taken up als
in the adjacent stable block.

THE MANOR, W of the church, a little farther away. One win
stone and the other, shorter, wing brick, in the wildest Artisa
Mannerism. Dutch gable, and pilasters, and hood-mould

changing into crenellation, and shields, all in crudely cut brick. GATE to the Green, of the same date.

TEMPLE FARM, E of the church. There was a preceptory of Templars at Aslackby, founded in 1154. The round church still stood throughout the C18. The gatehouse remained until 1887, and so did a vaulted undercroft. Now there is nothing but the head of a two-light C15 window and a pinnacle (in the garden of the farmhouse).

ASWARBY

0030

ST DENIS. The church has a splendid Transitional S doorway, or rather a doorway with Norman and, side by side, E.E. motifs. Norman the inner order of shafts with six rings (cf. Coleby, and also the W transept of Ely Cathedral) and the arch treated in the same way, and also the zigzags meeting at r. angles at a roll. E.E. the dog-tooth. In between waterleaf and crocket capitals. Dec four-bay arcade. Quatrefoil piers with fillets and tiny hollows in the diagonals. Arches with two sunk quadrant mouldings. Dec also the N aisle windows. Perp W tower with recessed spire. The chancel by *Blore*, c.1840. – FONT. Transitional. Circular with four corner shafts. They have ribbed leaf capitals and these, in a very unusual way, send out horns or spurs to clasp the round bowl. – BOX PEWS, early C19. The ends rise in a kind of battlements and sink trough-like. – In the NW corner a platform above the Which-cote family vault. The iron RAILINGS look C17. – PLATE. Chalice, Paten, and Flagon, by *Thomas Evesdon*, 1726. – MONUMENT. Lady Whichcote † 1849. By *Thomas Campbell*. Large relief of a seated young woman reading a book. By her side a standing oil-lamp with a snake coiling round its shaft. The snake means eternity.

An ESTATE VILLAGE with cottages dated 1845 and 1851.

ASWARBY PARK. The seat of the Tudor Carres and later the Whichcotes, a picturesquely gabled affair, has been demolished. The remaining STABLES are probably those built c.1836 by *H. E. Kendall*. Also Tudor LODGES. Two Georgian columns with urns stand alone in a field. Torrington in 1765 called the park a 'moorish flat'.

MOUND. In Aswarby Park is a large mound of roughly pear-shaped plan which superficial examination suggests might be a barrow. It has been reported, however, that it was raised in the C19 to cover an elephant which died in a travelling circus!

AUBOURN

St Peter. 1861–3 by *J. H. Hakewill*. E.E. with a SE steeple wit
a shingled broach spire. Round apse and transepts. – PLATE
Chalice and Paten Cover, by *John Morley* of Lincoln, 1570
Paten, by *John Cory*, 1700.

Old Church, close to the Hall. The plan is laid out in th
ground, with NE tower, S porch, and short, two-bay N aisl
What remains standing up is the chancel, with a tower adde
on the N side presumably about 1862. The chancel is E.E.
see the S lancet. The other S window is Dec; the late C13
window of two lights with a trefoil over is said to come from
Scotton Hall Lincoln. – FONT. Octagonal, with shields i
quatrefoils. – COMMUNION RAIL. C18. – MONUMENTS. Si
Anthony Meres † 1587. Small kneeling figure; the origina
setting destroyed. – Sir Christopher Nevile † 1692. Table
with columns and an open scrolly pediment. – Mrs Elizabeth
Nevile † 1745, with bust in profile in a medallion.

Aubourn Hall. The Tudor house may have followed th
present L plan; for there are bits of rubbed brick mullions i
the NE angle.   Then Sir John Meres altered and added con
siderably, some time between 1587 and 1628. He formed a
inordinately high, completely flat S front. Three storeys o
brick, stone-quoined, and with five bays of squarish cros
windows. Round the corner, the W front is of three bays. Th
question is whether the asymmetrically placed S doorway is
Mere job. Its jumped-up pediment and Doric pilasters etc
point to a state after 1628, i.e. the period of Artisan Classicisn
of the mid C17, and the period when the house was owned b
the Nevile family. The INTERIOR is also distinctly of tw
periods. Chimneypieces in the STUDY and DRESSING ROOM
one with tiers of pilasters with waist-bands and wilful detai
– seem late C16. The DRAWING ROOM and BEDROOM loo
mid C17. One chimneypiece has ovals with four keystones,
leitmotif of this period. The STAIRCASE deserves better docu
mentation. It cannot be Elizabethan, as has been suggested
Up three flights round a square well with tall newels droppin
below the risers.   The decoration is grotesque: entwined lea
thery foliage and serpents all in a Gothic-Viking tradition. Ye
the balustrade is *avant-garde*, with openwork panels of strap
work. The question to ask here is whether it anticipates th
maturer classical type of balustrade as at Ham House Surrey
of c.1638, or whether it is a provincial survival of the mid C17

AUNSBY

0030

ST THOMAS A BECKET. A specially rewarding church. Examination ought to begin inside with the Norman responds of the chancel arch. They are triple, and the scallop capitals indicate the first half of the C12. Of the same time the one-bay N chapel arch. Again scallop capitals. The arch here is original and has one step and one chamfer. To this church, later in the C12, a N aisle was added. Two bays, circular pier, square abacus, uncommonly good leaf capitals, partly unfinished. The round arches of one step and one chamfer are rebuilt. Then, a century later, the W tower. The arch to the nave is triple-chamfered. The responds are triple with continuous hollows between the foils and with fillets. The bell-openings have Geometrical tracery with a trefoil in a circle, a quatrefoil in a circle, Y-tracery, and a pointed-trefoiled head instead of other tracery. Shortish broach spire with two tiers of lucarnes in alternating directions. Y-tracery. The very top of the spire is Perp and has the inscription Ave Maria. The tower buttressing shows that the rebuilding of the aisles was begun after the tower. The S aisle has three-light windows with flowing tracery. The window surrounds go lower down than the window openings, leaving the bottom part blank. Pretty mouchette decoration of the parapet. Very nice S doorway. One moulding beset with fleurons. Thin buttress-shafts l. and r. Crocketed gable. The S arcade of three bays with slender piers on the borderline between Dec and Perp. Quatrefoil with hollows in the diagonals between the spurs. Bases and abaci already polygonal. Varied leaf capitals. Arches with sunk quadrant mouldings. Corbelled-out piscina on a head. Dec also the one-bay S chancel chapel. The arch has the same mouldings. They die into the imposts. Perp N aisle. – FONT. Circular, of c.1200. At the corners four polygonal shafts. The capitals have ribbed leaves, waterleaf, crockets. Spurs extend from them to embrace the bowl. They are small and leaf-shaped, except for the horizontal heads (cf. Aswarby). – PLATE. Chalice and Paten, by H.S., 1569.

BARHOLM

0010

ST MARTIN. The small S doorway E of the principal doorway is Anglo-Saxon, cf. especially the spoon motif below the imposts, and on the r. abacus the traces of interlace or a rather Viking dragon. The little rows of rectangles on the imposts are curious

too. Norman the responds of the chancel arch. This arch
perhaps widened, and the arch itself was certainly mac
pointed later. The scallop capitals and other details still heav
Then the N arcade, also Norman, but probably a little late
Three bays, round piers, many-scalloped capitals, squa
abaci. Arches with a big half-roll and smaller mouldings, als
zigzag at r. angles to the wall. Hood-mould with two rows
lobes or scallops. Two pieces of such a hood-mould are r
used over a tower window. The tower arch uses the sam
motifs, but appears all Victorian. The S doorway seems
belong to the N arcade. Two orders of colonnettes, scallope
capitals, tympanum with incised bands of zigzag, arch wit
zigzag, also at r. angles to the wall. Small, plain N doorwa
probably of the same time. Late C13 chancel, see the sedil
and piscina and the S window with Late Geometrical tracer
(pointed-trefoiled lights, a pointed quatrefoil above) and the
window with intersecting tracery. The nave S side has a wir
dow of three stepped lancet lights which goes with this dat
The W tower rebuilt in 1648 and heightened in 1855. Belo
the date 1648 the moving and telling inscription: Was eve
such a thing since the creation. A new steeple built in the tim
of vexation.* – FONT. Octagonal, Norman, with the oddes
jumble of unconnected, isolated motifs: a short length of dog
tooth, rows of small circles, five-petalled flowers, a spiral, etc
– PLATE. Chalice and Paten, by *Thomas Folkingham*, 171
(from Stowe); Almsbasin, by *John Wakelin & Willia*
Taylor, 1785.

OLD HALL. A slightly more sophisticated example than usual c
the small late C17 manor house. L-shaped with pairs c
moulded stone chimneystacks on the gable ends. The E fror
with a protruding chimneybreast and a similar protrusion o
the opposite wing, capped by a timber gable.

    DOVECOTE. Contemporary. Gabled and finialled.

9040

BARKSTON

ST NICHOLAS. Well-proportioned W tower of ironstone. Un
buttressed. Shafted Norman window to the W, with a roll an
a wavy motif in the arch. Twin E.E. bell-openings, one with
lozenge in the tympanum. Recessed crocketed Perp spire c
Ancaster stone with two tiers of lucarnes in alternating direc
tions. Early C13 S arcade. Three bays. Circular piers wit

* But the Rev. R. Burman points out that the lowest courses of the towe
seem to be Anglo-Saxon.

circular abaci. Double-chamfered round arches. Nailhead in
the hood-moulds. In the s wall a simple tomb recess. Early
C13 also the N doorway. Hood-mould again with nailhead.
The N windows are Perp. The chancel was of *c.*1300, see the
frame of the E window and the new, intersecting tracery, if
this can be trusted. In the s wall part of one window uncovered. Plain tomb recess in the N wall. Dec s aisle, with
ornate Perp top. Parapet decorated with cusped lozenges.
Pinnacle. Niche to the w. The Perp s porch cuts into aisle
windows. Inscription commemorating Thomas Pacy, i.e. a
mid-C15 date. Perp also the s chapel. One-bay opening to the
chancel. – STAINED GLASS. The E window has early *Kempe*
glass. Date of death 1885. – s aisle E by *Hughes*, 1866. – PLATE.
Chalice and Paten, by *Robert Garrard*, 1804; Almsbasin, by
William Fairbee, 1808. – MONUMENTS. Effigies of a Priest,
C14, and of a Civilian, C14, the latter under an ogee arch with
censing angels in the spandrels.

ALMSHOUSES, N of the church. 1839, in the Belton Estate style.

BARROWBY   8030

ALL SAINTS. Of ironstone. The N aisle has a late C13 W window
of two lights with a trefoil over, and the N doorway has continuous double-chamfering. Inside, the N arcade consists of
two parts, each of two bays, separated by a piece of wall left
standing. Octagonal piers. Double-chamfered arches. The details however seem later than those of the exterior. The s
arcade is of four straightforward bays with octagonal piers.
The aisle windows are Dec with minor but all different patterns of flowing tracery. Good s doorway. Only the w window
is a plain small lancet. Ballflower frieze below the eaves. Dec
w tower, the arch towards the nave with ballflower in the
abaci. Dec bell-openings. Recessed spire with two tiers of
lucarnes. In the chancel the earliest remaining piece, the boldly
and barely trefoiled head of the priest's doorway. Otherwise
in the chancel Dec and Perp windows. Perp also the N aisle N
windows. – FONT. Octagonal, Perp. The stem has the surprising and delightful feature of being transparent and reveal-
ing through its little two-light windows a devil inside. On the
bowl eight different patterns of three-light windows, mostly
Dec but also one Perp. – PULPIT. Victorian, but perhaps with
Perp parts. – SCREEN. Perp, with two-light divisions. –
SCULPTURE. In the outer s wall of the chancel a length of
Anglo-Saxon interlace, probably from a cross-shaft. – PLATE.

Chalice and Paten, by *R.C.*, 1696; Almsbasin, by *Peter*
William Bateman, 1808. – BRASSES. Nicholas Deen † 147
Also the wife of James Deen † 1508 (he died in 1498), bo
35 in. figures.

There are some cottages dated 1691, all with two- and thre
light windows with flat tops.

BARROWBY HALL. The street front dated 1691. Stone-face
five bays and two storeys. Mullion-and-transom-cross wi
dows. In the garden an octagonal Gothic SUMMER HOUS
Opposite, a house with mullioned windows. In the gable fro
to the street they are, from bottom to top, four-light, thre
light, three-light.

BARROWBY OLD HALL. C17, L-shaped and much altered in t
C19. Medieval fragments in the front wall.

RECTORY. Dated 1588. Stuccoed and gothicized in the ear
C19.

9050   BASSINGHAM

ST MICHAEL. The W tower was rebuilt by *Thomas Bell* in 178
But, surely, the small N window is a genuine C11 piece, ar
the bell-openings, single lights, shafted, are at least essentia
E.E. Norman N arcade (rebuilt by *J. H. Hakewill*, 1860),
three bays, the piers round with scalloped capitals and squa
abaci. The first of the arches has zigzag at r. angles to the wa
the others are clearly not to be trusted. The S arcade is of abo
the same time, but of two bays, again with round pier an
square abacus. The capital is impressive, with broad ribb
leaves. The responds have scallops. The double-chamfer
arches are later. Is the S doorway contemporary or Trans
tional ?* To the E of the arcades pieces of wall left standing, b
not so that they would face one another. Then, about 1300,
new chancel was built, with Y-tracery in the side windows ar
an E window of five lights with intersecting tracery. Th
priest's doorway looks Transitional, but can it be ? Perhap
after all, such elementary details went on being applied. Th
chancel arch is by *Hakewill* and terrible. The new chancel w
linked to the Norman N arcade by a two-bay chapel. Keele
responds and nailhead, i.e. also *c.*1300. Later another one-ba
N chapel was added. The S chapel of one bay is Dec, so th
the linking took place here later. The S aisle at that tin
received its straight-headed windows with ogee lights. Per
clerestory, embattled, with quatrefoiled parapet, gargoyl

* In the chancel a Norman PILLAR PISCINA, also with a ribbed-le
capital.

and pinnacles. Windows and parapet are by *Hakewill*. – FONT. Octagonal, Perp, with quatrefoils. – PULPIT. One panel of it survives loose. It is dated 1674 and still entirely Jacobean. – The same is true of the ALMS BOX, dated 1668. – BENCH ENDS. Square-headed, with linenfold panelling. – SCREEN. Bits, under the tower. – SCULPTURE. In the s aisle at the E end two blocks with Anglo-Saxon interlace. – PLATE. Chalice, by *John Morley* of Lincoln(?), c.1571; Paten, by *T.S.*, 1683; Chalice, London, 1765.

ᴛhe nicest house faces s towards the Green. Three bays on the ground floor and five above with an oval light. The overhanging eaves cornice and steep hipped roof suggest an early C18 date.

ᴀSSINGHAM MANOR. Early C18, with a later face-lift on the s side. Canted bays and a decorative iron balustrade along the roof.

BASSINGTHORPE

9020

ᴛ THOMAS. Norman chancel arch. Triple responds, the main capitals with rosettes. Arch with one step, one chamfer, and one big half-roll. Three-bay s arcade of c.1200. The piers are round, one abacus octagonal, one of a chamfered Greek-cross shape. Double-chamfered round arches. A little nailhead decoration, also on one waterleaf capital. Unbuttressed E.E. w tower. Bell-openings with Y-tracery. Short spire with tiny broaches, really just three stepped courses. Late E.E. chancel. The E window has curious tracery and may be of the C19. The chancel originally had a one-bay s chapel. Two four-light windows of the church are Elizabethan (nave N, s aisle). – PLATE. Chalice and Paten Cover, London, 1584; Flagon, by *William Cripps*, 1761.

ᴀNOR HOUSE. A curious, unconventional building, quite small, but with swagger details. Also, it is dated 1568, which is a rare date, before the Elizabethan style really spread. The house was built for Thomas Coney, and his punning sign, the rabbit, as well as his and his wife's initials, appear outside. The house is an oblong facing N on to the churchyard and with a small, lower w extension and nondescript s extension. The house perhaps went on to the s. The main range has stepped gables and splendidly moulded chimneystacks, a group of four, two square, two diagonally-set over the middle, and two singles on the E gable. In this gable a window with a pediment. To the N the lower windows have apparently been made in the

c19 more Tudor than they were (arched lights), but the up
windows are intact. They are of three lights, transomed, a
with their straight entablatures entirely classical. To thei
is an oriel window placed on a flat wall-shaft. Its dado ha
simple, also Early Elizabethan, decoration of squares a
oblongs connected by links. The top is a semicircular pe
ment or gable with two halves of such a pediment merg
into the roof. This identical motif is found at Dingley
Northamptonshire, also dated 1568. The small w extensi
is lower and originally also probably had a stepped gable. T
two-light window now has a segmental pediment qu
detached from it. This may be an alteration; for this side v
altered. A chimney was placed to its r., cutting off half
stepped gable and set so in front of the main range that
window in the gable gets hardly any light. Among the featu
on the L-shaped s side the most baffling is the gable of a p
jection in the re-entrant angle which is medieval, not Eli
bethan.

BASTON

1010

ST JOHN BAPTIST. E.E. chancel arch, but the chancel
built c.1860. Otherwise mostly Perp, and the best piece the
corner of the s aisle, which was probably the chapel of
Mary founded in 1403. w wall with its own low-pitched ga
with a fleuron-frieze and its own bellcote. It also has a bla
quatrefoil above the w window and blank panelling l. and
of the window. This continues also on the s side, E of t
porch. The porch has an elaborate niche above the entran
The aisle continues Perp and with the fleuron-frieze. Th
tower is Perp too. The arch towards the nave has castellat
capitals. Dec to Perp arcades of four bays. Sturdy octago
piers, double-chamfered arches. On the s side the arcade
disturbed. After two bays a stretch of wall, where no dou
the original w wall of the predecessor of this church ra
Then the pier to the E with four polygonal projections, i
more Perp than the rest. – PLATE. Chalice, by *Richard Bayl*
1730.

MANOR HOUSE. Like Barholm (*see* p. 444), c17 and L-shape
of stone with some brick and stone bands in the N front. P
of a moat borders the village street. The DOVECOT is da
1802, yet looks c17. Much conservatism elsewhere. A near-
BARN is dated 1795, and a small c17-style HOUSE with fo
light windows is probably Late Georgian.

BAYTHORPE see SWINESHEAD

BECKINGHAM

ALL SAINTS. The church possesses a Norman and a Transitional doorway. The N doorway has one order of shafts, a little nailhead, zigzag at r. angles to the wall, lozenges broken round the angle of a step, and in the triangles towards the circumference little faces, animals, leaves. The S doorway is already pointed and has keeled shafts, dog-tooth between the orders of shafts, and both dog-tooth and zigzag in the arch. Next the arcades, which are E.E. They are of four bays and have thin compound piers, first with four shafts and four spurs in the diagonals, then with four keeled shafts and dog-tooth in the diagonals, then again as the first. Double-chamfered arches. The S porch was built at the same time. Entrance richly shafted with nailhead in the capitals, arch with many mouldings, dog-tooth on the hood-mould. The chancel also was rebuilt at this time, or perhaps a little earlier. It has lancet windows throughout (but the E windows are of the restoration of 1888) and an arch to the nave with triple responds, shaftrings, a little nailhead, and a moulded arch including fillets on rolls. The clerestory was provided in the C14, and the aisle walls and windows were also rebuilt. Dec windows under depressed four-centred, almost segmental arches.* Finally the Perp W tower, ashlar-faced. Twin two-light bell-openings with transoms, an ogee arch over both together, and on its top diagonal corbels carrying pinnacles, so that the top has eight pinnacles in all. – STAINED GLASS. In a S lancet early C19 fragments. – N aisle E window by *Gibbs*, *c.*1855. – PLATE. Paten Cover, Elizabethan; Chalice, by *D.G.*, 1652. – MONUMENT. Effigy of a Lady, early C14, defaced.

RECTORY. A Late Georgian refacing with stone window surrounds and quoins. The N front pedimented. Fine cast-iron entrance GATES with Greek key and acroterion ornaments (*see* Skellingthorpe, p. 632).

BELTON

ST PETER AND ST PAUL, N of the house, between garden and village street. A small church, badly over-restored, and brim-

* Hamilton Thompson draws attention to the foundation of chantries in the church early in the C14 by Thomas of Sibthorpe, the then rector, and Canon Binnall kindly told me of the chapel of St Mary being called newly built in 1347.

ful of Brownlow (i.e. Cust) monuments. Externally the churc
presents itself like this: Unbuttressed w tower of *c*.1200. Th
top is dated 1638. Perp s porch with crockets and pinnacles
The stone roof on transverse ribs. Perp clerestory wit
battlements. The chancel is of the early C18, and the mortuar
chapel on the N side of 1816. It was designed by *Sir Jeffr
Wyatville*, and has battlements and pinnacles and on the
wall a large stylized cross in relief. Inside, the chapel has
fan-vault and a triple-canopied niche in the E wall. Perp ceilin
to the N chapel, Perp chancel arch. But the two-bay N arcad
is original Norman work and differs from others in the neigh
bourhood by only one motif, but this outstanding: the incise
lozenge decoration of the massive pier, entirely à la Durham
or Norwich or Waltham. Scalloped capital, octagonal abacus
single-step arches. – FONT. To accept this as a Norman fon
demands much credulity. These figures, the bell-ringer, th
squirrel, the knight with his square helmet must be romanti
reconstruction, even if the bishop or the man and bird ma
well be original, and altogether the placing of figures i
arcading.* – PULPIT. With small tester; C17. – COMMUNION
RAIL. With twisted balusters; early C18. – SEAT. Under th
tower. Made up of early and later C17 bits. – SOUTH DOOR
Traceried; C15. – STAINED GLASS. In the large s window
heraldic C19 glass, probably given in 1823. – PLATE. Chalice
by *C.F.*, 1637; Flagon, by *W.M.*, 1656; Paten, London, 1682
Paten, by *Benjamin Gignac*, 1773.

MONUMENTS. There are so many that a topographical arrange
ment seems best, starting under the tower and working
anticlockwise. – Tower: Sir Richard Brownlow † 1668. Larg
architectural tablet with achievement in an open scrolly pedi
ment at the top. – s wall: William B. † 1726. By *Edward
Stanton* and *Christopher Horsnail*. Architectural tablet wit
two columns and standing putti outside them. – Alice Lady B
† 1721. By *Edward Stanton* and *Horsnail*. Tablet with flute
pilasters, an oval inscription plate, and three fine putto head
57b   at the top. – Chancel s: Brownlow, first Lord B., † 1807. B
Westmacott. Standing monument of white marble. Semi
circular plinth and on it kneeling maiden by a broken column
The capital lies by her on the ground. Reredos background. –
56b   Viscount Tyrconnel † 1754. By *Sir Henry Cheere*. Standin
monument of white and pink marble. Seated figure of Hope

* The font was illustrated as original in 1825 by F. Simpson.

holding a portrait medallion. Richly decorated reredos background. – Chancel N: Sir John Cust, Speaker in the House of Commons, † 1770. By *W. Tyler*, and a specially good work of his. Standing monument of white, black, and brown marble. Seated figure holding a key. To her r. medallion, and on it in relief the Speaker's Chair. At her feet an open book. In it recorded the year 1768 in the Journal of the House of Commons, when Sir John was re-elected Speaker. – Etheldred Ann Cust † 1788, aged seventeen. By *John Bacon*, 1793. Tablet with a charming roundel of a young girl with a lamb. – Katherine Cust † 1827. Small tablet with pretty arrangement of flowers round the frame. – Hon. Rev. Richard Cust † 1864. By *W. Theed*. Big white tablet with Christ and a kneeling shepherd. – N chapel: Sir John and Dame Alicia B. † 1679 and 1676. By *William Stanton*, 1679. Standing monument. Black and white. Against the reredos background two frontal demi-figures holding hands. Columns and an open segmental pediment. Inscription on a draped cloth. Stanton received £100 for this monument. – Richard B. † 1638. By *Joshua Marshall*. Alabaster. Frontal demi-figure in an arched niche. Complex surround. – Mortuary chapel: First Earl B. † 1853. In the centre. By *Marochetti*. Tomb-chest with white recumbent effigy. – Caroline, Countess B., † 1824. Standing white monument with a seated lady. Pilgrim's staff and pilgrim's hat on the ground. Putti in the sky. – Adelaide, Countess B., † 1917. By *Lady Feodora Gleichen*. Tablet with white profile against dark blue mosaic. Surround of green marbles. – Sophia, Lady B., † 1814. Standing monument. By *Canova*. Upright 58 Grecian woman, one hand raised, the other on a portrait medallion. This stands on a short Greek Doric column (not quite – it has a base). But the plinth has a band of nobbly Perp foliage. – Viscount Alfred † 1851. Designed by *Sir. G. G. Scott*. Tomb recess in the w wall. Brass cross on the sarcophagus lid. – N aisle: Sir John B. † 1697. Architectural. Standing monument with two columns and a segmental pediment. By *W. Stanton* (Mrs Esdaile). – Henry John Cokayne Cust † 1917. Recumbent effigy on a slab supported by disagreeable stumpy red marble pillars with equally disagreeable beige marble capitals.

he village is a paramount example of benevolent estate activity. The whole very complete and visually very satisfying. The style is Tudor to Jacobean. Cottages are dated 1828 and 1839. That dated 1839 consists of a r. half with that date and a l. half

with the date 1470. Beneath the date is indeed the re-erect
bay window of the Chantry House in Watergate, Grantha
Arched lights to the windows. Around the VILLAGE CRO
are grouped the ALMSHOUSES (1827)* and cottages. Oppos
a PUMP as an obelisk. The former smithy of 1838 has a sto
horseshoe fitting nicely into a shaped gable. The RECTO
lies on its own to the N. Early C19, in Ancaster stone. Five
five bays and two storeys with a three-bay pediment. T
WESLEYAN CHAPEL is by *T. Brownlow Thompson*, 1879.

BELTON HOUSE. Belton is perhaps the most satisfying amo
the later C17 houses in England. It is a house of fulfilme
rather than innovation, built nearly a quarter of a centu
after its prototype, Pratt's Clarendon House in Piccadi
(1665). This established the influential form of 'double pile
that is suites of rooms back to back, with projecting end ba
(H-plan), equally-proportioned storeys, hipped roof wi
dormers, balustraded platform, and a cupola. Belton has a
these characteristics, although it is perhaps more smoothly ne
classical, owing to the face-lift of 1777 by *James Wyatt*. T
now rich grey-golden Ancaster stone was being dug at He
dour in 1684 by 'Mr Marsh', probably *Samuel Marsh Jun*
and in March 1685 the first stone was laid by the owner, S
John Brownlow. His master mason was *William Stanton*,
London man. That he was not the architect, and that Wre
was not the architect, is now generally accepted. Mr Geoffre
Beard has plausibly suggested *William Winde*, whose favouri
plasterer, *Edward Goudge*, is mentioned by Winde as havir
worked here. The house has a basement, two main storeys,
hipped roof, dormers with alternate segmental and triangula
pediments, and a – rebuilt – octagonal cupola. The centre
47a   seven bays, wings of two bays, projecting two bays on the
and three bays on the N. Both fronts are pedimented on th
slightly advanced three middle bays. The S wings have to th
inside arched niches instead of windows. The doorway no
neo-classical Doric by *Wyatt*. In the N pediment big cartouch
with swagged oval lights. The side elevations, that is E and v
present a mason's rather than an architect's face. The ba
spacing is: 2–break in cornice–quoined flank–1–4–1–quoins
break–2.

The INTERIOR is best described in the order of public view
ing, starting by the S door. First the MARBLE HALL, with
floor laid in black and white lozenges, and panelling of *c.172*

* Piae Senectae Domus.

when Viscount Tyrconnel made interior alterations. But over
the paired late C17 chimneypieces are pendants of naturalistic
foliage, fruit, and game, in a wonderfully fertile style, though
not quite as good as the best of Grinling Gibbons. In fact
Edward Carpenter was paid for the carving, and he may be
Belton's Watson. Next door, progressing clockwise, is the
TAPESTRY ROOM, with a chimneypiece of *c.*1722 in a Kentian
style, more naturalistic carved wood pendants, and a luscious
plaster ceiling by *Edward Goudge*. Beyond this in the W wing
(private apartments) is the BIG DINING ROOM, decorated
with wall paintings by *Hondecoeter*, and a chimneypiece from
Ashridge Park Hertfordshire. Back to the circuit. The RED
DRAWING ROOM is in *Sir Jeffry Wyatville*'s style. Then,
across the centre of the N front, the SALOON, a room of
restrained Carolean splendour. Segmental and broken pediments to the doors, bolection surrounds to the chimneypieces,
and cascades of wood carving to the overmantels, overdoors,
and intermediate wall panels. The ceiling by *Goudge*. Adjacent
is the TYRCONNEL ROOM, notable for its elaborately painted
C18 floor. Then the CHAPEL DRAWING ROOM, marbled in
dark green and gold (*Vanderbank* oriental-style Soho tapestries), and then the CHAPEL in the NE angle. At the entrance
end a tripartite arched gallery where the wood carving reaches
an apogee of sumptuousness, particularly the decorated Corinthian pilasters on the side facing the altar, the cherubs of
almost Renaissance quality. More carving around the altar
frame. The reredos is of coupled Corinthian columns, carrying
a segmental pediment in which the cherubs sit rather pre-
cariously. The ceiling by *Goudge* is his *chef d'œuvre*. The BLUE
BEDROOM in the SE corner, which has its name from the
colour of the tremendous bed canopy and the bed hangings,
opens to the LITTLE MARBLED HALL, where the stairs are
modern and the ceiling is of *c.*1722.

On the first floor the LIBRARY, by *James Wyatt* (1777), who
raised the height of the old room to take a shallow tunnel-
vaulted ceiling. The Adamesque plasterwork is perhaps by
Joseph Rose, the inset paintings perhaps by *Biagio Rebecca*.
The caryatid marble chimneypiece with two windows has
been attributed to *Sir Richard Westmacott* (Gunnis). Next
door (private) is the BOUDOIR, also by *Wyatt* and richer in
style. The ANTE-LIBRARY is marbled, and beyond this is the
QUEEN'S ROOM, and beyond that the CHINESE ROOM with
imitation C18 bamboo wallpapers.

The W forecourt has two ranges of offices: that to the W
what can be described as *Stanton*'s style. The windows squar
of two lights, a flattish moulded stone archway, and a rustical
bulbous cupola. To the N the range is Victorian, but sympa
thetically designed and incorporating the old C17 S door
the house. The pediment open and scrolled. Across the for
court, an iron SCREEN and GATEWAY is *ex situ* and early C1
It has been attributed to *Thomas Robinson* but may be by *Joh
Warren*, who is known to have worked for Stanton at Denha
Place Buckinghamshire. By the same hand are the CHURCH
YARD GATES, the WILDERNESS GATE (from Hough Hall, s
p. 581n.), and the splendid LONDONTHORPE GATES an
SCREEN, removed from the S parterre in 1722. The STABLES ca
also be attributed to *Stanton*. Eleven-bay fronts advanced at th
ends and pedimented over the centres. The W entrance
typical mason's job with the doorway made tripartite an
tightly pushed up by niches. At the end of a dried-up can
is a little Kentian TEMPLE with a rusticated and pedimente
centre arch and niches to the lean-to and intersecting sid
bays. The GREENHOUSE is by *Sir Jeffry Wyatville*, of 181
Nine bays, the outer ones narrower than the others. Ston
piers, top architrave and balustrade, all the rest glass. In th
N vista is a SUNDIAL of Father Time and a cupid supportin
a column. Mrs Esdaile attributes this to *C.G. Cibber*. Near th
stables, the C18 CASCADE and the Gothic RUIN. Sited on th
hill to the E is the BELMOUNT TOWER, built in 1750. No
really a tower, but a tall arch with an upper part containing
Venetian window, masonry buttresses, obelisks, and an iro
balustrade. The park landscaped to SE and S, in the style
Brown, but by *W. Eames*.

3040

BENINGTON

ALL SAINTS. Essentially an ashlar-faced church. The long four
bay chancel appears Perp, but there are four lancets on the
side, and they are the only preparation one gets for a grea
surprise inside. The chancel is E.E. indeed, and it was in
tended to be vaulted. The lancets are shafted inside with stif
leaf capitals, and between them there are, very low down, th
springers for a steep rib-vault. Moreover, as one examine
them, it becomes clear that they were to be two sexpartit
vaults, not four quadripartite ones, i.e. the French Earl
Gothic system taken over at Canterbury in 1175 and then i

the Lincoln transepts. The vault at Benington was never built, or else rubble masonry would appear in the spandrels. Also the chancel arch is much too high to allow for the vault. But it is an E.E. chancel arch, the responds with three detached shafts, shaft-rings, and a semicircular abacus. Moreover the stiff-leaf capitals are like those of the lancets. The answer is probably that the chancel arch was heightened to match the nave arcades when these were built, and they are Dec. Six bays, octagonal piers, double-hollow-chamfered arches. On the N side the bases are circular and may be those of the E.E. predecessor arcade. The arcade goes with the Dec S aisle windows (reticulated W, straight-headed S), the S doorway with four groups of fine mouldings and a hood-mould on big flower stops, and the straight-headed N aisle windows. Dec also are the sedilia, piscina, and the tomb recess in the chancel, all with the same fine mouldings. The chief Perp additions are the clerestory with six big Perp three-light windows and battlements, the NE rood-turret, and of course the W tower. The doorway has a charming continuous moulding of quatrefoils and niches l. and r., the W window is of four lights, on the buttresses are gablets supported on busts (a Boston motif), the bell-openings are of two lights, and there is a flower frieze under the plain parapet. The tower arch has concave-sided semi-octagonal responds, the nave roof tie-beams on arched braces alternating with angels against principals. – FONT. The base with two kneeling stones (cf. Freiston). The font is octagonal, of ironstone. Big leaves on the foot. On the stem and the bowl small, pretty, but elementary figures under crocketed gables. On one panel the Trinity with two angels. – SCREEN. Of one-light divisions. Rounded arches, used as the foils of a trefoiled ogee arch over. The doors are preserved. – PLATE. Chalice, by *John Payne*, 1755; two-handled Cup, by *Peter & Anne Bateman*, 1796.

LMSHOUSES, by the churchyard. Built in 1728 'by the charity of Mr Wm Porril'.

AY HALL, ¼ m. W. A Georgian cube silhouetted in the flat landscape. Five by five bays, three floors, and a parapet.

BICKER

2030

T SWITHUN. A cruciform and truly amazing church. It has a Norman nave so ambitious and yet so short that it seems con- 7b vincing that it was originally continued westward. As it is, it is two bays long. Very fat round piers with heavily scallop[ed] capitals and cruciform abaci. That looks emphatically ear[ly] C12. So does the clerestory, with two windows shafted insid[e] but outside placed in a blank arcade of stepped groups of thre[e]. Here again the capitals are of the early block shape. Typica[l] Norman corbel table (cf. Freiston). However, the NE respon[d] inside has nailhead, and the arches not only rolls but also zi[g]zag at r. angles to the wall surface and lozenges broken rou[nd] an angle, i.e. Late Norman motifs. On the capitals stan[d] sturdy wall-shafts to support the roof principals. And the si[ll] line of the clerestory windows is also emphasized by a rol[l] course. The Norman nave is divided by a Dec crossing fro[m] an E.E. chancel. The chancel has tall lancet windows (and [a] Dec s window), the group of three in the E wall shafted insid[e] with shaft-rings. Inside, the sedilia are E.E. too, and so is t[he] fine recess in the N wall with its cusped arch and trefoi[l] leaf cusps. The chancel has a three-bay chapel, as if it were [a] nave again and more of a nave than the nave. It h[as] round piers and double-chamfered arches, and there is a cler[e]story of alternating small lancets and large round window[s]. The abaci of the piers vary, and the second pair has a curio[us] projection to the nave, perhaps for the Lenten veil. One mo[re] C13 piece, late C13 probably, is the doorway to the s aisl[e] with fine mouldings. This leads on to the crossing. The two [s] piers oddly differ from the N piers. The latter are more nor[-]mally Dec than the former, though it is the former that hav[e] some nailhead enrichment. The arches have many hollo[w] chamfers. A variety of details distinguishes the arches into th[e] transepts and from the chapels into the transepts, but they a[ll] fit the Dec date of the crossing. One anomaly needs pointin[g] out: there is a quatrefoil pier and an arch with three hollo[w] chamfers in the E wall of the s transept, and this is proof of th[e] intention of providing that transept with an E aisle (cf. Spald[-]ing). Externally the Dec date of these parts can be read o[ff] without effort. The s transept has a s window with reticulate[d] tracery, though the N window of the N transept is a replace[-]ment. The s chapel has reticulated windows; those of the [N] chapel are less distinctive. – FONT. Quatrefoil, with polygon[al] shafts in the corners and a little stiff-leaf; E.E. – Very elab[o]rate Flamboyant tracery from a SCREEN (N chapel altar). CHOIR STALLS. Ends with some tracery. Nice little niches a[t] the corners. – BENCHES (N aisle). Plain and square-heade[d]. One with Jacobean back panels. – SCULPTURE. Stones wit[h]

Anglo-Saxon interlace in the s and N aisles at their w ends and in the porch. – PLATE. Chalice, c. 1570.

ℝED LION INN, ¼ m. s, on the A road. Dated 1665. Brick, with modest details of the Fen Artisan Mannerism.

BILLINGBOROUGH

1030

ST ANDREW. Ashlar-faced. Tall NW tower with a recessed spire c.150 ft high. The position is most unusual in Lincolnshire. The style is Dec. Thin flying buttresses connect the pinnacles with the spire. This has three tiers of lucarnes in alternating positions. The arches to nave and N aisle have shafts connected by continuous hollows and triple-chamfered arches. Vault of eight radiating ribs and a circle high up. Early C14 N aisle with later battlements. Geometrical tracery of unusual kinds (e.g. ogee-topped rounded trefoils). The N doorway matches the style of the windows. Of the same date the w end of the s aisle (three stepped lancet lights under one arch with a solid tympanum). The s doorway again matches. But the s aisle w window must be a replacement made when 23c the other s aisle windows were given the same shape. In the tracery large quatrefoil with four long concave-sided barbs. That is Dec proper, even if without ogees. The same motif occurs at Great Bedwyn in Wiltshire and Whitby Abbey in Yorkshire. Dec proper also the large, a little bleak nave w window. Four lights, reticulated tracery. Dec moreover the four-bay arcades and the chancel arch. They have the same mouldings. Quatrefoil piers with fillets and deep continuous hollows between the foils. Double-chamfered arches. Four bays on the s, three only (because of the tower) on the N. Original roof in the N aisle. Perp clerestory of eight closely-placed windows. The chancel is of 1891. – STAINED GLASS. Small fragments in the top of the s aisle E window. – PLATE. Chalice, 1829, and Paten, 1830, by *William Bellchambers*(?). – MONUMENT. Mary Wayet † 1831. By *Crake* of Chelsea. The inscription in black-letter capitals.

The GEORGE AND DRAGON INN is C17 and looks odd with the dormers to the canted and corbelled bays lopped off. The RECTORY is mostly by *Thomas Pilkington* of 1847 (GA). The village is mainly one street, quite townish for a short stretch.

BILLINGBOROUGH HALL, NW of the church. By tradition built for William Toller in 1620. A six-bay N front of two floors with three gables. Bay windows have been added to the ground floor. On the first floor mullion-and-transom-cross windows, in the gables three-light windows. A one-bay, two-storey gabled addition to the W (with a four-light window on the ground floor, a three-light window above) is duplicated on the W end of the S front. Between the two angles thus formed is the entrance side of the house, with a three-storey gabled porch hidden by an early C19 addition. The doorway is of the early C18 and has a bolection moulding and keystone. Of the same Early Georgian date is the S or garden front, a symmetrical seven-bay front of two floors with gables over the end bays. Segment-headed windows, parapet to the centre, and triangular pediments to the dormers. The interior is unusually grand: staircase with twisted balusters with groups of six at the turn. In the vestibule doorways with three varieties of pediment.

1050

BILLINGHAY

ST MICHAEL. The church has an E.E. W tower (low arch towards the nave with keeled responds) with Georgian bell-openings and a broach spire without any parapet. The date of these additions is 1787.* Late E.E. the S arcade of four bays. Quatrefoil piers with fillets and deep continuous hollows between the foils; double-chamfered arches. The N arcade is later (octagonal piers). Is it Dec? Dec indeed the S aisle windows (ogee-headed lights under a segmental head) and the porch entrance (keeled responds) and also the chancel, see the flowing tracery. The piscina is ogee-headed at any rate. Perp clerestory with gargoyles and tie-beam roof with arched braces and bosses. Painted roses in the spandrels. A blocked arch in the E wall of the N aisle indicates a former N chapel. The N aisle itself was rebuilt in 1856. – FONT. Octagonal, with the simplest Perp panel tracery. – BENCH END. One with a poppy-head in the porch. – PLATE. Chalice, c.1569. – MONUMENTS. Slate headstones in the churchyard.

9020

BITCHFIELD

ST MARY MAGDALEN. The nave is C11 work – see the herring-bone masonry. Early C13 N arcade of three bays. Round piers and abaci, round, double-chamfered arches. Plain early C13 doorway with one continuous slight chamfer, dog-tooth on the chamfer. E.E. W tower, the twin bell-openings with Y-tracery. Recessed spire. The triple chamfers of the tower arch die into

* The spire was rebuilt in 1912.

the imposts. Varied windows, e.g. an early C14 nave s window with intersecting tracery and ballflower in a niche in its jamb. The s porch also C14. It has a stone roof on transverse arches with sunk wave mouldings. The nave roof has Perp bosses and angel figures. – FONT. Octagonal, Perp, with flat quatrefoils with shields and above them a nice frieze of fleurons and trails. The stem has an arched panel with a tiny chalice in it. – PLATE. Chalice, Paten, and Almsbasin, by *S.H.*, 1805.

BLANKNEY

ST OSWALD. Proud w tower of 1805–7 of a type with paired bell-openings and eight pinnacles (cf. Beckingham). The tower arch and the w window are of 1878–81. Much else is Victorian too, but apparently genuine E.E. lancets on the s side, Dec s porch entrance, Perp N chapel with decorated parapet, and more genuine features inside, especially the arcading. Three-bay aisle arcades with octagonal piers and double-chamfered arches; E.E. seats round the piers. E.E. chancel arch in the same style. E.E. also the sedilia with detached circular shaft. And E.E. most probably the N chapel arch from the chancel too. That from the aisle with dog-tooth is indubitably E.E. – LECTERN. With a splendid mid-C18 eagle putting one claw on a serpent. Brought in. – PRAYING DESK (s aisle). This seems to incorporate four Georgian table legs. – (ALTAR FRONTAL. Embroidered; from Seville; assigned to the C16.) – PLATE. Silver-gilt Chalice and Paten, Antwerp(?), early C16. – MONUMENTS. John de Glori; effigy of a bearded man praying, late C14. Only the bust and the feet appear in sunk relief. They are framed by oddly cusped windows including ogee details. – Lady Florence Chaplin † 1881. By *Sir Edgar Boehm*. Kneeling life-size figure in relief, white marble, in a Gothic stone surround. – The LYCHGATE is by *Bodley*.*

BLANKNEY HALL. The ruin of the grand Palladian house of the Chaplin family still stands, under demolition. The STABLES are by *E. J. Willson*, 1825.

The village is eminently picturesque. It was laid out by *W. A. Nicholson* in the 1830s and 1840s, mostly in the Tudor style. All the houses are of stone.

RECTORY, ¼ m. SW. By *R. W. Edis*, 1881 (GA). Competent Tudor, essentially symmetrical.

* This information and the date of the tower were kindly given me by the Rev. P. D. Stephens.

GREEN MAN INN, 3½ m. w. Mid C18, a long range with a high
wing at one end boasting a big Venetian window. Behind th
window was a Georgian clubroom with busts of its membe
in ovals on the walls. These have been destroyed.

BLOSSOM HALL see KIRTON-IN-HOLLAND

oo5o

BLOXHOLM

ST MARY. Both arcades seem to date from about 1300. Thre
bays, octagonal piers, double-chamfered arches. Round seat
The N responds keeled, the S piers with some nailhead. Th
Perp tower is built into the nave, which makes it a thin piec
Open parapet and pinnacles. The N aisle W window is a lance
the N doorway is single-chamfered with a segmental arch, an
both are probably earlier than the arcade. The nicest featur
of the church is the alterations and additions made by Gener
Manners in 1812. His coat of arms is over the porch entranc
made of Coade stone and signed *Coade & Sealy*, 1813. He als
gave to nave and chancel their surprising plaster rib-vault
and the chancel E window is probably his too. – PLATE. Chalic
Paten, and Flagon, by *A.F.*, 1771; Chalice, by *A.F.*, 1772.
BLOXHOLM HALL. Although a ruin, the skeleton of the mic
C17 house, erected for Septimus Ciprian Thornton, and as ye
unrecorded in architectural literature, is still clearly visibl
Its style is that christened by Sir John Summerson 'Artisa
Mannerism'. The S front, which has now collapsed, consiste
of five bays, a semi-basement, three storeys, and an attic. Th
Venetian window with squiggly lugged and half-scrolle
pilasters was highly uncommon in domestic architecture of th
time. The unusually high and big dormer windows in the
and N fronts were quoined with rustication and topped b
alternate triangular and segmental pediments. The centr
gable once supported a magnificent stone peacock dated 177
and one of *Mrs Coade*'s finest works. It toppled to the groun
Of about the same date are the elegant GATEPIERS, of char
nelled masonry, by the churchyard.   The wings adjacent t
the house are additions of 1827 by *Lewis Vulliamy*. Also b
him are the STABLES dated 1825.

9o5o

BOOTHBY GRAFFOE

ST ANDREW. 1842 by *W. A. Nicholson*. Neo-E.E. tower, nec
Dec the rest. – MONUMENTS. The Rev. Peniston La Tou

† 1851 and Mrs Peniston La Tour † 1851. Both by *Sanders* of New Road, London, both still entirely in the Georgian tradition, both with draped urns, but the urns and the draping differ.

he best house is BRANKLEY HOUSE, Georgian, with dressed stone bays to the ground floor and a crude stone Doric porch.

BOOTHBY PAGNELL

9030

T ANDREW. Late Norman W tower, the much restored W doorway with waterleaf capitals. The bell-openings are twins and still have the Saxon motif of mid-wall shafts. The top with battlements on heavy corbels and eight pinnacles is of course Perp. Is the low groin-vault inside original? Norman certainly the arcades. Two bays. The S arcade comes first. Round pier with square abacus. Capitals with scallops and also with broad flat leaves. The N arcade is different, but also Norman. Round pier, abacus square but with nicked corners. Scalloped capitals. The arches on both sides are single-stepped, i.e. all this looks second quarter of the C12, and certainly earlier than the tower. Of the Norman chancel arch one respond shaft has been exposed on the S side. Dec chancel. The E window is of five lights and has flowing tracery worth memorizing. The three-light side windows have a rare type of reticulation, where the ogee bottom tip of the unit points downward, but the top tip radially outward instead. N aisle and N chapel also Dec and with normal reticulation. Dec nave clerestory. Perp S aisle, the windows with triangular heads. – FONT. Norman, tub-shaped. Flat intersecting arches and a kind of crenellation below. – ORGAN CASE. The ornate case in the N chapel is by *Pearson*, who restored the church in 1896. – STAINED GLASS. C15 fragments in the porch windows. – PLATE. Chalice, London, 1571. – MONUMENT. Elizabeth Tyrwhit, later Litchford, † 1696. Tablet with two free-standing busts. A curtain is looped up to reveal them. Not very good.

OOTHBY PAGNELL HALL. Stone Tudor house, built by *Lewis Vulliamy* for J. Litchford in 1824. It is still essentially Georgian, but the windows have hood-moulds and there are low-pitched gables.

OOTHBY PAGNELL MANOR HOUSE is in the grounds of the 8b Hall. It is the most important small Norman manor house in England. A manor house emphatically, not a castle. It was

built about 1200 and had as its only defence a moat. The hou
is rectangular and has a vaulted ground floor and above th
hall and solar. The walls are built of oolite rubble with ash
dressings and are very massive – in the lower parts about fo
feet and above an average of two. The W wing and the ro
and gables can be omitted in a description, as they are pro
ably C18 and later. From the approach one sees the E fro
with external stairs at its S end. These stairs have been r
stored. At their top a round-headed entrance with chamfer
jambs led directly into the hall.* The windows on this si
are from l. to r. as follows. First a C15 four-light one replaci
the C12 original which is now inserted in the S front. It follo
the pattern of the next one along, that to the solar. Two arch
lights divided by a polygonal colonnette with simply-c
capital and a solid tympanum. The S front now has two of th
C12 windows, one *in situ*, the other the re-set hall windo
already referred to. On the W front only the high cylindric
chimney with plinth and stepped buttress deserves mentio
and the N front is plain except for the signs of a blocked wi
dow that may have lighted the solar. In the lower storey th
windows have been re-cut, but the entrances are original. Th
have (as also the doorway from hall to solar) a lintel on quarte
circle corbels. Inside on this ground level an undercroft und
the hall with two bays of quadripartite rib-vaulting, the ri
being simply single-chamfered. Under the solar a tunne
vault at r. angles to the front. Inside the hall the most notab
piece is the fireplace. Projecting hood on joggled lintel a
tapered corbels. Both hall windows (one behind later par
tions) have seats in the jambs. E of the fireplace are signs of
blocked niche, and in the N wall is a triangular aumbry.
the solar another aumbry.

3040

BOSTON

INTRODUCTION

Boston in the Middle Ages was a port of considerable impo
tance. In a levy of 1205 the town paid only a little less tha
London and more than any other port. In 1369 it was given th
privilege of the staple for wool and other goods. The Hanseat
League had an establishment, a so-called steelyard, at Bosto
No wonder one still gets a sense of generous scale as one wal

* Now there are some timber-framed partitions.

rough the streets, even though few actual buildings of the
Middle Ages survive – apart of course from the prodigious church
which, incidentally, was up to the C14 a chapel of ease to Skirbeck. As in all thriving medieval towns, the friars settled here,
but remains exist only of the Blackfriars (*see* p. 473). The Greyfriars were behind the Grammar School, the Austin Friars S of
this near St John's Road, the Carmelites on the other side of the
river between West Street and Liquorpond Street. The C16 saw
sad decline. Leland calls the steelyard hardly occupied, and a
letter of the Corporation written in the 1570s speaks of the port
, 'destitute of ships and trade of shipping'. Later Boston rallied
again, but the prosperity of the C18 was moderate and far from
spectacular. The specialities are neat brick terraces trimmed with
white-painted brick and doorways of elongated proportions,
sometimes on two steps (flood precautions), and with a great
variety of surrounds (e.g. the inturned capitals of Nos 47–49
High Street). Population in 1801 was 6,000, and it rose steadily
though slowly to 15,000 in 1851 and 25,000 in 1961.

CHURCHES

ST BOTOLPH. St Botolph is a giant among English parish
churches. It is 20,070 sq. ft in area, as compared with Hull
20,040, Newcastle 20,110, Coventry (St Michael) 22,000, and
Yarmouth 23,000. St Botolph is 282 ft long, and the Stump,
the most prodigious of English parochial steeples, is 272 ft
high. It was apparently begun in 1309, or at least the steeple
was, i.e. all that there is is Dec and Perp, and by and large one
can say that the steeple is Perp and the body of the church
Dec. The best views are those which allow the length as well
as the height to be seen. The most usually photographed view
boosts the steeple, which needs no boosting, at the expense of
the nave and chancel. The chancel asserts itself towards the
market place, the steeple with unforgettable force towards the
river, that is the port, source of Boston's wealth and hence of
the church being what it is.

The description naturally starts with the STUMP in all its
elaboration and daring. The W doorway is placed in a projection and is Dec. Two tiers of niches l. and r. An arch,
cusped and subcusped and with foliage all over, and an ogee
gable protect the doorway. Decorated battlements. Perp panelling around the doorway and on the main buttresses in several
tiers. Very tall W, N, and S windows, the former of eight lights,
the other two of four. Then on each side two tall two-light

windows with transoms, each under an ogee gable. Blar
arcading over; decorated parapet. This was no doubt intende
to be the bell-stage and a spire to follow – exactly as at Louth
If that had been done, the length of the church would hav
spoken more dramatically than it does now. But *hubris* grippe
the Bostonians, and they decided to heighten their tower.
next stage was put on, of different masonry, with thinn
buttresses and with big four-light windows with transom
wholly transparent but uncusped – an undeniable coarsenin
And then, yet later, the boldest move was resolved on, th
adding of the top stage, again wholly transparent, but no
handled with grace as well as boldness. A highly decorate
transparent parapet and turret pinnacles sending up tran
parent flying buttresses to an octagon. This has two-ligl
openings with two transoms on each side. On top again
transparent parapet stepped up in the middle, and the fin
eight pinnacles. It is a veritable lantern, and one reason (
pretext) for building it no doubt was that it could serve as
beacon to the sailors entering the port. Was a spire meant
heighten the tower yet more? The closest parallels to Bosto
All Saints Pavement at York and Fotheringhay and Lowi
in Northamptonshire, have none. Yet how would the traditic
of calling the steeple the stump have arisen if there had bee
no intention of a spire? The exceedingly high tower was
universal ambition of the Late Middle Ages. One need on
think of two Continental parish churches such as the Minst
at Ulm, with its spire reaching up 630 ft and only complete
in the C19, the highest European building before the Eiff
Tower, and what is now the cathedral of Antwerp with i
tower 306 ft high, i.e. almost exactly as high as Boston. Y
at Boston the height is excessive. One cannot overlook th
fact that tier followed tier to changed plans, and if one cove
with one's hand the upper stages, a more harmonious relatic
between church and steeple appears at once. But harmony w
not the aim of an age so bent on excesses. One is natural
curious to know who designed the Boston Stump. Howeve
nothing can be said with certainty. Mr Harvey sugges
Reginald Ely as the designer. He designed King's Colleg
Chapel Cambridge in its first form, died in 1471, and le
6s. 8d. to the Guild of Our Lady at Boston. More than this w
do not know, except that for the completion of the spire
Louth in 1515 a *John Tempas* of Boston was called in. Was h
then the master of the Octagon?

Having had the experience of the steeple, we can now turn to NAVE, AISLES, and CHANCEL. We walk along the s side first, the N side later. The s aisle W window of five lights is a Perp insertion (as is the N aisle W window). Then the COTTON CHAPEL, three bays, buttresses with gablets on bust stops, three windows of three lights with reticulated tracery. At the SW corner of the aisle is a prominent turret pinnacle. The s porch is two-storeyed, Dec below, Perp above. Buttresses with three tiers of niches and with pinnacles. Typically Dec entrance. Fine shafts and fine mouldings, a head at the apex. Above a protecting four-centred arch, cusped and subcusped. The upper floor, which houses the library, has a five-light Perp window under a four-centred arch with fleuron decoration. Bust stops and a bust at the apex. Parapet with quatrefoils. The inner s doorway has three thin shafts belonging to three groups of mouldings. As the s aisle continues, the first buttress has another niche, but then they stop. Gablets on bust stops. The parapet varies between three patterns: undulation, lozenges, and a kind of pointed undulation. The windows are of four lights with flowing tracery in two alternating designs. A pinnacle on the SE corner. The aisle E window is again a Perp insertion, of five lights. Rising openwork quatrefoil parapet. The clerestory has fourteen closely-set upright two-light windows. They are Dec too and alternate in design, and – this may be anticipated – they also, with one exception, alternate across, so that one design on the s faces the other on the N. Quatrefoil parapet, a flower frieze under, and at the E end an openwork quatrefoil parapet and angle turrets. The chancel has three Dec and two Perp windows, the latter expressing a lengthening, imperative indeed, as the heightening proceeded. They are all of four lights, the Dec ones different from either aisle pattern. Parapet of alternating sexfoils and panelling. Pinnacles on plain buttresses. The priest's doorway cuts one window short. It is surrounded by panelling and has battlements above. But other details suggest an C18 remodelling. The chancel E window is glorious Dec, but a copy after the Carlisle E window (in a Lincolnshire church an insult, if in this case not an injury). The choice was *Scott*'s, who restored the church in 1856–7.* E gable with open quatrefoil parapet and two turrets. The N side is in most ways a repetition of the s side. The exceptions are the projecting W bay

* First, it seems, in 1843 (*Builder* ,p. 487). Then he was appointed consulting architect in 1851 (GS).

of the chancel with blank tracery containing a staircase, the more ornate filigree parapet over the E side of the N aisle (with three statuettes under canopies), the absence of a N porch, and the simpler doorway.

The INTERIOR is unified to the degree of uniformity. But before it is perambulated, everybody will be curious to see how the tower is managed inside. The curiosity pays: the entry under the tower will never be forgotten. The tower is open inside to the top of the second stage, 137 ft, and right up there is a lierne-vault, a star, consisting of four stars ingeniously worked into each other. Many bosses. The walls are organized like this: a high dado, many fine shafts in the corners, with little polygonal capitals. The sills of the lowest windows are rolls, and the roll mouldings of the surrounds of the N and S windows cross them and stand a little lower down on bust corbels. The upper string has plain panelling. The tower arch is complex: the responds to the nave are blunt half-octagons, but to the tower there are panelled imposts. The arcades between nave and aisles are of seven bays. The piers stand on high bases and are quatrefoil, filleted, and with thin filleted shafts in the diagonals. The abaci are still round, the arches of two wave mouldings. At the top of the clerestory a flower frieze. The roofs are of 1928–31, replacing pretty C18 wooden rib-vaulting. The Cotton Chapel has an arcade of two bays to the S aisle. The pier is quatrefoil too, but with a deep hollow without a break between the foils, and the capitals have more mouldings – more layers, as it were. Many-moulded arches. The little doorway to the tower has label-stops still with naturalistic foliage. Along the S aisle the following details. First the S doorway, with two wide chamfers and a hood-mould on head-stops. Then the doorway to the porch staircase, the doorway into the demolished chapel of the Corpus Christi Guild, a wider opening into that former chapel, a shafted tomb recess, the doorway to the rood stairs of the former Lady Chapel, a more ambitious tomb recess with a gable, and l. and r. high buttress-shafts carrying niches for images. Thickly foliated corbels, canopies with nodding ogee arches, and finally the sedilia, with cusped arches without any ogees on quatrefoil shafts. The chancel arch is moulded only to the W – on the same principle as the arcade arches. In the chancel, as in the nave, a flower frieze just below the ceiling. However, the ceiling here is still the thin-ribbed C18 vault. Little to be added on the N aisle. The label-stops to the windows as on the s side. In the E bay a low tomb recess, and two more further w. That is all.

FURNISHINGS. FONT. Elaborately decorated Victorian Dec. By *Pugin*, and given by Beresford Hope in 1853. – REREDOS. By *W. S. Weatherby*. 1890, but finally completed by the weak statuary only in 1914. – STALLS. A fine set of *c*.1390, especially important for their MISERICORDS. The canopies are of 1853–60, but go well with the original work. Among the misericords the following may be singled out: return stalls N: a man catching a lion; s: two antelopes; upper stalls N: an owl, a bear playing the organ, a couple in their kitchen, a pelican, St George, a knight and griffin, virgin and unicorn, another St George, a baboon, and a fox; upper stalls s: stag, two eagles, knight on horseback, lion and dragon, dragon and griffin, Sir Yvain's horse cut in two by the portcullis, mermaid and sailors, helmet, wreath and mantle, woman chasing a fox, bear-baiting, rose-bush; lower stalls N: two swans, schoolmaster birching a boy, two jesters with cats, hunter with knife, man with an axe, buck between trees; lower stalls s: hunter with bow and arrows chased by his wife, hunter and stag, wolf preaching to hens, wild man fighting a lion, man eaten by wolves, the Pillar of Christ's Flagellation, the crowning of a queen, bird on a tree. – Also poppy-heads with faces affronted and ad-dorsed, excellently composed animals, a pair of tumblers. – The elbow-rests are decorated too (bear-baiting, hare and hound, beggar and dog, cat and mouse; fox eating a chicken, swan, beggar, woman with bellows, man and dog, fox as a priest). – COMMUNION RAIL. A beautiful, courtly wrought-iron job, *c*.1740. – COMMUNION RAIL (s aisle). Of wood, sym-metrical openwork acanthus panels. – PULPIT. 1612. On a polygonal shaft. The typical low blank arches, but at the cor-ner fluted Ionic columns and also Flemish lambrequin work, almost as if it were C18. Door, back panel, tester – all is pre-served. Fine Georgian stair with sparse thin balusters. – The s, w, and N DOORS are all original Dec with almost Flamboyant-looking intricacies of ogee work. – DOOR KNOCKER to the s tower door, inside the nave. Probably C13. Lion's head and a ring of two lizards. – IRON GATES, now under the tower, originally further E in the nave. Made in 1743. – STAINED GLASS. All that needs looking at is Victorian. E window by *O'Connor*, 1853, Nathaniel Hawthorne in 1855 called it 'the richest and tenderest modern window that I have ever seen'. – s aisle E by *Kempe*, 1891. – s aisle first and second from E by

Hardman, 1883 and 1876. – N aisle E again by *Hardman*, 1868.*
PLATE. Paten, by *Thomas Mason*, 1727; Set, by *Nick Dumee*
1776; Strainer Spoon, by *S.J.*, 1810(?).

MONUMENTS. At the W end of the N aisle large incised slab
of Tournai marble to Wissel Smalenburg of Münster † 1340,
Hanseatic merchant. Praying figure 6 ft long. To the l. and r.
buttress-shafts, and above the cusped and subcusped arch a
thick canopy. The slab comes from the Greyfriars Church.
To the l. and r. of the altar two major brasses of *c.*1400: Walter
Pescod † 1398 and wife, 4 ft figures under triple canopies and
with figures up the buttress-shafts. – A priest, *c.*1400, a 5 f
3 in. figure with saints on the orphreys. – Civilian and two
wives, *c.*1400 (S aisle). Only partly preserved. 12 in. figures. –
Alabaster Knight, C15. On the tomb-chest four frontal angels
holding shields. They stand under flat ogee arches (S aisle). –
Alabaster Lady, C14. Puppies nibble at her dress (S aisle). –
Part of the canopies and the buttress-shaft of a large brass of
*c.*1500 (nave floor). – Richard Fydell † 1780. Big tablet of
coloured marbles. Obelisk with profile in oval medallion. By
James Wallis of Newark (chancel N wall). – Thomas Fydell
† 1812. Sarcophagus with inscription. Two joined urns above.
By *Crake* of London (chancel N). – James Hollway † 1828
Very Empire in style (chancel N). – John Carrington, designed
by *Scott*, 1873. Gothic tablet with the Resurrection in relief
(chancel S).

ST JAMES, George Street. 1861–4 by *George Hackford* (GR)
Stock brick with stone E front to the street. Nave and aisle
almost as wide. An oddly personal, anti-archaeological church
not attractive. Arcade of thin circular piers. Plate tracery of a
completely incorrect kind. – PLATE. Two chalices, by *John
Robins*(?), 1787; Chalice, Paten, Flagon, and four Almsplates,
by *Charles Fox*, 1821.

ST MARY (R.C.), Horncastle Road. 1826, much restored in
1884. Front with pedimental gable and an enclosed porch with
Tuscan pilasters.

ST THOMAS, London Road. 1912 by *Temple Moore*. Chancel
etc. only 1933. Inside not un-Lincolnshire, but with most of
the windows mullioned and the W window mullioned and
transomed.

HOLY TRINITY, Spilsby Road. 1846–8 by *Sir G. G. Scott*.
Quite big, neo-Dec, without a tower, an archaeologically

* Canon Ellis mentioned to me also one window in the Cotton Chapel
and three in the N aisle as by *Grylls*.

Boston Church, monument to Wissel Smalenburg
of Münster, a Hanseatic merchant, † 1340

convincing job with flowing tracery in the windows. Th
capitals are not yet naturalistic, i.e. Scott before the Secon
Pointed got hold of him entirely.

NONCONFORMIST CHAPELS, *see* Perambulation.

CEMETERY, *see* p. 472.

PUBLIC BUILDINGS *see* PERAMBULATION

PERAMBULATION

(A) *Market Place – Church precincts – Wormgate – Witham Ban*
East – Red Lion Street

We start in the MARKET PLACE, which lies immediately SE (
the church and has a nice irregular shape. On the E side fron
N first, in STILL LANE, the early C19 STILL PIT, and then
back in the Market Place, the grander PEACOCK AND ROYA
HOTEL, the market place hostelry *par excellence*. Late Georgia
façades and nice ironwork. But inside one is at once surprise
by remains of C17 panelling in Sir John Summerson'
'Artisan Mannerism': see especially the chimneypiece in th
ground-floor lounge. Keyed ovals and the *leitmotif* of verti
cally halved pilasters supporting a lugged angle and scrolle
at the base. The date must be 1670–80. The pattern goes wit'
such slightly earlier North West Anglian buildings as Thorp
Hall Peterborough and Wisbech Castle. Note the Gothi
details of the adjacent wing, No. 26. No. 30 has a good C1
staircase with three varieties of baluster, twist-straight-twis'
almost identical with that of Fydell House of 1726. On the 1
side of the Market Place Nos 32–33 dated 1777, then No. 34
a Regency house, then the EXCHANGE BUILDINGS, formerl
Corporation Buildings, an especially grandiloquent essay
Fifteen bays, three storeys, recessed arched ground-floor win
dows, and a three-bay pedimented centre. In the tympanun
a cartouche with the town's arms and the date 1772. The bac'
towards the river is pedimented too. Next come the ASSEM
BLY ROOMS of 1826. Pedimented front, a canted first-floo
bay supported on Tuscan columns with a veranda, and ta
windows lighting a big assembly room. Again a dignifie
façade to the river. An island site intervenes (passage t
Church Street N to church) and, following the line of th
Market Place, one arrives at LLOYDS BANK of 1864. Vermi
culated rustication. Lloyds Bank overlooks the church pre
cinct with a bold half-oval screen of railings and Dec crockete

piers (utilized from a church restoration in 1774). In this area
the STATUE of Herbert Ingram by *Alexander Munro*, 1862,
with an allegorical figure cast by *Elkington*. Now S of the
church to No. 28 CHURCH STREET, timber-framed, black
and white. Then between the Stump and the river to CHURCH
HOUSE at the corner of Wormgate, Boston's paramount
example of Fen Artisan Mannerism with lots of wilful details
all in brick. Chunky brick quoins to angles and entrances,
peculiar tongue-shaped pediment, and an arched brick-cut
pediment hanging like a coathanger from the centre of the
rectangular frame of a string course. Instead of being over a
window, it – and the one below – just touches the centre of
a pair of windows. N of the church is the SESSIONS HOUSE,
built in 1841–3 by *Charles Kirk*. Tudor-Gothic, but not grim
like Kirk's mock-heroic Sessions House at Spalding. The
Gothic theme is continued by the adjacent COUNTY HALL of
1925–7 and by BARCLAYS BANK with a face S towards the
Market Place. This is of 1835 and was designed by *Lockwood
& Mawson* of Bradford. Now up Wormgate and on to
WITHAM PLACE, with Nos 5–10 all with pedimented doorways on thin Tuscan columns, and beyond to the GRAND
SLUICE (first built 1764 by *Langley Edwards*, engineer) with
its watery view of Dykeland. At the end of Witham Place,
opposite the sluice, the BARGE INN, red brick, five widely
spaced bays and some nice fanlights. On, yet further N, to
WITHAM BANK EAST, where Nos 11 and 12 are quite grand.
Both are red brick and both are early C19. No. 11 a nicely
proportioned three-bay and three-storey house with pretty
cast-iron work to porch and garden front. No. 12 perhaps
slightly later, with big Doric porch, handsome doorway,
balcony above, and also balconies to the first-floor windows.
From here all the way back to the junction of Wormgate and
Witham Place and off to the E into RED LION STREET, where
the choice item is the startling Edwardian CENTENARY
METHODIST CHAPEL, somewhat megalomaniac. Big square
W towers with Ionic lanterns and drawn-up Wrenian domes.
Between them a convex two-storey front with attached columns
to the ground-floor entrances and a thin glazed colonnade to
the first floor. The stock brick church behind this with giant
pilasters is probably that of *Stephen Lewin*'s chapel of 1839.
This also had two W towers. Between them was an Ionic
colonnade *in antis*. Then, after a fire of *c.*1910, Messrs *Gordon
& Gunton* rebuilt the front with Lewin in mind, but only just

in mind. To the S of the Methodist Church the horribl
CONGREGATIONAL CHURCH of 1868, by *Innocent & Brown*
yellow and red brick, Transitional, with a monstrous plate
tracery rose window. So back in a few minutes to the Marke
Place.

(B) *Market Place – Pump Square – Windsor Bank – Bargate*

From the Market Place E along Dolphin Lane to PUMP SQUARE
Note the odd rythm of window-spacing of Nos 7–10
A–B–C–D–C–B–A, and the elegant Bostonian doorway of
No. 2. From Pump Square to MAIN RIDGE, mostly early
C19 (e.g. Nos 2–4) and the smashing neo-Egyptian FREE-
MASONS' HALL, quite late, built in 1860–3, and based on the
portico of the Temple of Dandour in Nubia. This pinch from
Denon's *Voyages* screens a plain stock-brick box. WIDE
RIDGE cuts through this part of the town to the MAUD
FOSTER DRAIN. Consistent groups of visually satisfying
cottages (e.g. Windsor Bank seen from the bridge). Beyond
Vauxhall Street is VAUXHALL HOUSE, once a miniature
Vauxhall Gardens, laid out *c.*1815 with a Maze, Arboretum,
Bowling Green, and Playhouse. Now all has disappeared.
From Windsor Bank to Bargate Bridge and BEULAH'S
CANNING FACTORY, *c.*1870, with lots of patterned and
coloured bricks. Then from Bargate Bridge NE into SPILSBY
ROAD. No. 5 Late Georgian, and the QUEEN'S HEAD with
a profile portrait above the door; *c.*1840. From Bargate Bridge
N along the Drain run two parallel roads. First WILLOUGHBY
ROAD with the MAUD FOSTER MILL: a five-sailer tower-
mill with ogee cap, built in 1809. It is in working order. If
walking, one can cross the Drain by the HOSPITAL ROAD
BRIDGE, an elegant single-span iron bridge cast by the But-
terley Company in 1811.* Further on in HORNCASTLE ROAD,
which is the road parallel with Willoughby Road, is the Late
Georgian LEA HOUSE, and then the CEMETERY, laid out in
1854 by *J. P. Pritchett* of Darlington. An avenue aligned upon
a central mortuary chapel and avenues to r. and l. to chapels
with small naves and stumpy towers over open arches. Retrace
your steps to Bargate Bridge and then enter the WIDE BAR-
GATE. This is the largest communal space in the town, now
the centre of the cattle market and in the C18 known as the
Sheep Fair. It is funnel-shaped and goes from genteel to
rustic, from the War Memorial to the cattle market. From the

* Another at Cowbridge, 1½ m. N.

NE corner, i.e. BARGATE END, clockwise, Nos 84–88 are early
C19 with Tuscan doors and open pediments. Past the cube of
BARGATE LODGE to the former UNITARIAN CHAPEL of
1804 with a pedimented façade and pilasters 1–2–1 dividing
the façade into two bays. Turn off S into CHENEY STREET,
with an eight-bay, three-storey group at the angle. Along this
street (note the tall doorcase of No. 10) into GROVE STREET,
the centre of a compact development of c.1840, almost unspoilt. Back to Wide Bargate, having lost nothing in the
diversion. Nos 27–29 are Late Georgian with a projecting
ground storey. This is Regency and has a cast-iron balustrade.
Nothing merits comment until one reaches the N side and No.
20, probably Early Victorian, but still in a nice Georgian style,
five bays and three storeys with a Doric doorcase carrying an
open pediment. No. 22 has recessed segment-headed windows
with flat fanlights, rather Wyattish, and No. 24 is a bland,
six-bay house of the same date. Past a pretty group of three
houses, including the RED COW, to an attractively genteel
terrace with arched entrances and open pediments. Wide Bargate ends here and becomes Bargate. Off Bargate in MITRE
LANE something of a puzzle, the so-called PESCOD HOUSE,
timber-framed, with brick infilling, and probably the fragment
of a C15 hall. So again back to the Market Place.

(c) *Market Place – South Street – Hussey Tower – Skirbeck Road*

In SOUTH STREET, Nos 2–4 is the SHODFRIARS HALL, the
ghost of a C16 timber-framed building. It must now all be of
J. Oldrid Scott's restoration of 1874. A double overhang and
two gables with elaborately fretted bargeboards. The eight-bay
timber-arched ground floor looks a little more authentic. To
the l. of Shodfriars Hall is SIBSEY LANE, with a small decaying Late Georgian cul-de-sac. Above the door of a warehouse
note the Green Man corbel, probably Dec and perhaps from
the BLACKFRIARS, established before 1288; for as we walk
back to South Street and proceed to No. 12, in a passage off
No. 12 we are met by a C14 doorway in a stone wall and,
entering through it, by one and a half bays of a low arcade with
octagonal piers, thin moulded capitals, and single-chamfered
four-centred arches. Immediately behind one arch appears
mysteriously another identical one. The spandrels show that
there once was vaulting. So this was the undercroft of a room
running N–S. Then at once the CUSTOMS HOUSE of 1725.
Just three bays, two floors, and a parapet, but neat mercantile

trim. Stone quoins to the angles, stone strings, and a nice
royal coat of arms over the doorway to the l. in bay one.
After that one must note the endearing jumbled-up vista of
warehouses and house backs on the edge of the river Witham.
Next is SPAIN LANE, with a ten-bay, two-storey pedimented
front that may have been a Late Georgian warehouse. It has
a classical pediment, but in the familiar roundel a Gothic rose.
Then the almost totally ruined stone shell of the BLACK-
FRIARS HALL. What survives is about 90 ft long, with several
plain chamfered entrances and the remains of upper two-light
windows. This building of course runs W–E. Its upper floor is
supposed to have been the refectory. SPAINS COURT is a small
early C19 front like the one in Sibsey Lane. Further on is the
UNITARIAN CHAPEL of 1819, three by three bays, red brick,
the front with arched doorway and arched windows and segment-headed windows over, modest but dignified. Returning
to South Street, to the r. is the Late Georgian WAREHOUSE of
T. H. Lincoln & Sons,* to the l. the GUILDHALL or Guild
of the Blessed Virgin Mary, a late C15 hall much rebuilt
externally and altered internally, a poignant reminder of
Boston's medieval prosperity. The front to the street has stone
quoins and the remains of an ornamented coping to the gable.
On the ground floor a triplet of two windows with segmental
heads and a pointed doorway, all under a continuous mould.
The show-piece is the five-light window above, with the
curious but not unique motif of lozenges instead of normally
curved shapes. One moulding with fleurons. Nothing else
is worth comment on the exterior. The brickwork is mostly
Georgian, but the further gable-end crow-stepped. Inside
Georgian alterations: Tuscan supports and an arched door
to the main stairs (sturdy turned balusters); the Museum
with a Georgian gallery but a C15 kingpost roof with trusses
and arched braces springing from grotesque corbels; also
Georgian the Old Council Chamber with chimneypiece and
overmantels and a remarkable C15 linenfold-panelled cupboard with original ironwork. Adjacent to the Guildhall is
FYDELL HOUSE, undoubtedly the grandest house in town.
Built in 1726 for William Fydell, it is still persistently attributed to Henry Bell, who died thirteen years earlier. There is
no reason why it should not be by *William Sands* of Spalding,
'architect' of the Spalding Gentlemen's Society. Six-bay
front divided 2–2–2 by giant Doric pilasters, two floors, full

50a

* Called 'new erected' in 1816.

entablature and balustraded parapet. The provincial hand is
apparent in the composition of the ground-floor centre: tall
Doric columned doorway with scrolled open pediment push-
ing up a small niche between the upper windows, and arched
windows squashed between the doorway and the pilasters.
Nice ironwork screen in front with gateway and overthrow.
The rear elevation also six bays, but quite plain, except for a
projecting single-storeyed three-bay Doric porch and pediment. Wooden balustrade and gable-ends with dormers.
Inside the Doric theme continues with bold woodwork and
a fluted order. The staircase with alternating twisted–fluted–
plain balusters taking three flights and a landing. Much mid-
century Rococo decoration: panels of plasterwork on the staircase walls, frieze in the corridor; and an especially pretty
chimneypiece with a genre relief in a ground-floor room;
'Chippendale' fret china cabinet above it with pediment.

Opposite, the river front of SOUTH SQUARE is taken up by the
best of Boston's warehouses, mostly Late Georgian, especially
HURST & SONS, LINCOLN & SONS (with some C15 stonework on the ground floor), and the grandest, JOHNSON &
SON, fourteen bays and five floors. Then No. 4, of red brick,
dated 1809, and No. 5, later C17. Then, just in GREYFRIARS
LANE, so called after the Greyfriars (house founded before
1268), the entrance to the yard of the GRAMMAR SCHOOL.
The one old building is dated 1567. It is of brick, symmetrical,
with a middle bay window, canted and with a stone parapet
and battlements. To the l. and r. two widely spaced bays each,
and that is all. Renewed roof and renewed interior. Additions
to the N and S 1866. South Square here becomes SOUTH END.
No. 1, SCHOOL HOUSE, is dated 1827 and has an open pediment on Greek Doric columns; HAVEN HOUSE is C17 but
remodelled in the C18. The latter is in a cul-de-sac. On into
the SKIRBECK ROAD, and there, neglected at the time of
writing, is the HUSSEY TOWER, similar in type to the Rochford
Tower (cf. Skirbeck). Brick, square in plan, of three main
floors; octagonal stair-turret at the NE angle, and crenellated
parapets. Rib-vaulted ground floor. The tower was being dismantled as early as 1565. On the Skirbeck Road a little further
on is the old UNION WORKHOUSE, attributed to *Sir G. G.
Scott* (1837). The usual composition of low frontage pavilions,
an entrance courtyard, and a high main composition. The
front part with a pedimented archway is rendered. The back
red brick and still classical.

(D) *Market Place – High Street – London Road*

Across TOWN BRIDGE (*John J. Webster*, 1912, replacing *John
Rennie*'s bridge of 1807) to the happily juxtaposed buildings
of the WHITE HART, L-shaped, the l. part quiet and Georgian
the higher r. part Italianate and Victorian, all in a robust
Victorian classicism. This is the best viewpoint in town
(Stump – rear of Assembly Rooms – Witham vista – lively
waterscape). A judiciously placed tree shelters the DRINKING
FOUNTAIN in coloured bricks, 1860 by *Samuel Sherwin* of
Liverpool. Then into HIGH STREET, and at once a detour
into WEST STREET to sample the MUNICIPAL BUILDINGS
1902 by *James Rowell*, low, of two storeys, yellow and brown
terracotta, with Dutch strapwork gables, a French pavilion
roof, Italianate windows, and a touch of Gibbs.* Off West
Street in TRINITY STREET a swagger factory of 1877 pre-
sided over by a swan. Back and now along High Street, with
mostly Late Georgian façades. No. 45 is the odd man out:
C17 with stepped gable and four- and five-light windows with
straight hoods. Opposite a nice warehouse – tall, five storeys –
dominating the river front. Nos 47–49 has Late Georgian
inturned volutes to the entrance (note the view from here of
the warehouses on the E bank). The LORD NELSON has two
pretty allegorical figures. Sited back from the road the
GENERAL BAPTIST CHURCH of 1837, stock brick and a nice,
unusual composition. Broad front of five bays, bays one and
five with gables and a larger, higher gable over bays two to
four. Glazing bars like intersecting tracery, i.e. still the pretty
insouciant Early Gothic Revival. No. 114 is early C19, with
recessed arched windows and an arched doorway to the ground
floor, and No. 116 Late Georgian, of five bays, two storeys,
and dormer roof. Arched entrance with side lights and fanlight. No. 120 is the best house in the street: probably late
C18 (cf. the similar Frampton House of 1792). Five bays, three
storeys, projecting centre bays with pediment, partly balustraded parapet, a splendid Rococo cartouche and long garlands of flowers in the pediment, and a good pedimented
Ionic doorway. To the r. and l. lower canted wings, perhaps
later. Next comes Nos 124–136, an unusual terrace group.
Three storeys and eighteen bays divided by giant pilasters in
a 6–6–6 rhythm, two houses for each group. The middle six

* REGALIA. Seal of the Court of Admiralty, 1573; Tazza; silver-gilt,
1662; Admiralty oar Mace, s.-g., 1725; Punch bowl, s.-g., 1740; Cruet,
1744; Salver, 1821; Spoons, before 1837.

breaks forward just slightly with paired pilasters at each end.
Pilasters also to the side elevations. The bays created by the
pilaster division can also be regarded as a series of blank arcades.
Did the architect take his idea from the C17 Grimblethorpe
Hall (Lindsey)? Not much else worth comment in High
Street, except for No. 152, a Late Georgian pair of eight bays
and three storeys. Into LONDON ROAD and, overlooking the
river, Nos 2–3 mid-Georgian, No. 4 early C19, and No. 5 a
Late Georgian warehouse. Then the SHIP INN, mid-
Georgian, and No. 10, early C19. No. 12 is mid-Georgian
with a modern bay. The CROWN AND ANCHOR has a nice
sculptured bas-relief sign dated 1803. Beyond the level crossing, Nos 36–39, early C19, are worth noting with their porches
and elaborate ironwork to the stairs.

URTON HALL, Wainfleet Road. Of brick, probably mid C17.
Shallow H with three storeys to the gabled fronts: three-,
four-, and five-light windows. Between the wings the three
bays of the centre of the same height and mullion sequence.

BOULTHAM   9060

T HELEN. *See* Lincoln City, p. 143.

OULTHAM HALL. Only the gatepiers and lodges of 1872 are
left.

OULTHAM LODGE. Now by the railway crossing, but built in
1846 as a Gothic cottage, 'harmonizing well with the surrounding rural scenery'.

ARTSHOLME HALL, 1 m. NW. Demolished, but once an
expensive house. By *F. H. Goddard*, in a landscape by *Milner*,
all of c.1862. A column beside the lake was erected in 1902
'To commemorate the establishment of the Lincoln waterworks 1846'.

BOURNE   0020

T PETER AND ST PAUL. The church is what remains of a
priory of the Augustinian canons founded for Arrouaisian
canons in 1138. Of the quarters of the canons nothing survives
at all. They lay to the N, and all that reminds one of them is
some blank arcading to the NW of the church at its W end,
where the W range of the claustral buildings joined.* To understand the architecture of the church it is best to start inside.
The four-bay arcades are Norman. They have round piers with

* But in the S aisle lie a number of Norman fragments, including many
mall zigzag arches. They may belong to the domestic premises.

many-scalloped capitals and square abaci with nicked corner
The arches have a single step. Then to the E are the remains
a taller flat pier shafted at the angles, the former supports
a crossing arch or chancel arch. To the w also remains. Th
are of a N pier with shafted angle and a semicircular projectio
to the s, the start no doubt of some special treatment of the
front. But this fragment is insolubly linked with a more am
bitious rebuilding scheme of c.1200, a scheme for a two-tow
front. Only the sw tower was built. Both tower halls hav
blank arcading inside. It is not the same, and on the s si
e.g. there are some stiff-leaf capitals. The N hall has springe
for a vault which was never built. They rest on head corbe
The oblong centre bay between the towers has arches to E,
and N. They have compound responds, some with fillets, and th
arch to the s tower again has stiff-leaf capitals. The place whe
the remains of the Norman w pier stand is specially interestin
It shows that the E.E. responds were gained by cutting aw
from the more solid Norman pier, and that for some reaso
the work was left unfinished and the Norman pier, and inde
the Norman arcades, allowed to stand. Externally this E.
front has blank arcading for the tower fronts, that of the
tower of a very odd giant intersecting form. Above are paire
lancets. The triple lancet in the middle was only put in in 187
to replace a Perp w window which was instead made the
window. But the Perp w doorway was allowed to remain. The
much later, it was decided to build up at least one of the tw
towers, and the result is the Perp sw tower with its pairs
transomed two-light bell-openings. This additional heig
made the canons doubt the safety of the supports, and so th
NE pier of the tower was strengthened (and made shapele
thereby), the E arch to the NE of the tower was given a ne
Perp shape (one chamfer, one hollow chamfer), and the w ba
of the s arcade received a different arch. More E.E. wor
remains in the s transept, but it is later. There is half a doo
way in the w wall, and there is the large s window with Geo
metrical tracery (three unfoiled circles), set back when th
transept was shortened, and there is the arch from the transe
into the s aisle. The s porch entrance is Dec, the aisle window
N and s and the tall three-light clerestory windows are Per
The N aisle is specially wide. The chancel was rebuilt in 18c
(see the inscription on the w wall). Its walls are very bar
No more than one straight-headed three-light window
one s.

FURNISHINGS. FONT. Octagonal, Perp, with the inscription: Jesus est nomen quod est super omne nomen. The inscription is spread over the eight fields. – CHANDELIER. Of brass, a glorious piece, of three tiers, dated 1742. – PLATE. Chalice and Paten Cover, London, 1569; Chalice, by *D.G.*, 1657. – MONUMENTS. Tablet by *Edward Sharman* of Peterborough, † 1798, with a woman by an urn; by *Gaffin* of London, † 1836, with a mourning cherub.

ARKET PLACE. Only the TOWN HALL of 1821 is distinctive, but in a special way. It is stone-faced, only three bays wide, and not detached. *Bryan Browning* wanted a grand exterior staircase. To provide this in the restricted space he ingeniously recessed his horseshoe flights within the front, framing the space with a screen of Doric columns *à la* Roman baths. The bases are the height of the ground floor, and above the correct entablature is a bit of elliptical arch to add the genuine touch. The DRINKING FOUNTAIN in canopied Gothic is by *Edward Browning*, 1860. In WEST STREET are a number of Georgian houses with pleasant doorcases, the BAPTIST CHURCH of 1835, stone-faced, of three bays, with arched windows, and the BOURNE INSTITUTE, probably of *c.*1860–70, High Victorian Gothic, also of stone. This is at the corner of ST PETER'S ROAD, and in this is a row of Late Georgian WAREHOUSES. Brick and stone trim, of twelve bays and three storeys. Back to West Street again, and on to the MALTINGS, Late Georgian, and to the MANOR HOUSE with a stone front. Back to the Market Place and now into NORTH STREET. This has been much mutilated, but No. 17 shows on the upper floor that it was once a good early C18 house; brick and stone quoins. No. 22 is C17 with a later bowed shop-window. Again to the Market Place and for a moment into ABBEY ROAD (which should really be East Street), to see the dignified façade of the METHODIST CHURCH. Giant Doric pilasters and a pediment running right across the three-bay front. Then from the Market Place into SOUTH STREET, which is in a modest way more eventful than the others. First an early C19 WAREHOUSE, then beyond this THE CEDARS, of the same date. It has a nice porch with fluted columns and a Gothic fanlight. The E front is C17 with a C19 face and fronts on an elegant cast-iron BRIDGE which connects the house with the front of the church. In South Street follow TUDOR COTTAGES, probably old almshouses. They are dated 1636, but have no feature of such antiquity. Brick, one storey, with dormers, stone quoins, and

stone gable-ends. Wooden mullion-and-transom-cross wi
dows. From here a footpath to the churchyard and through
round the church, to the FREE SCHOOL of 1678. Pitched ro
and in the gable-ends big six-light windows. More or le
opposite Tudor Cottages a Gothic lodge marks the start of t
former drive to RED HALL, the grand early C17 mansion
Bourne. It now stands forlorn, immediately by the railwa
Three gabled bays to the S front, two-storey porch with
round-arched doorway flanked by Tuscan columns. The por
has rounded merlons at the top. The principal windows of t
house have mullions and transoms. Inside a good stairca
with turned balusters and tall newel finials.

RECTORY. By *F. H. Goddard*, 1878.

CASTLE. To the S of the town lie the very extensive earthwor
of a C11 castle. It consisted of a motte and bailey, with at le
two large outer enclosures. It had masonry defences, and the
is a copious water-supply for its ditches. Of all this little r
mains; the ditches are largely dry, the masonry has be
removed, and the motte has almost entirely vanished
probably dug for gravel.

CASTLE FARM. Within the earthworks of Bourne Castle, i
NW of Red Hall. A plain C18 stone house with a large barn.

AUSTERBY MANOR HOUSE, ¼ m. S. Early C17, Victori
gothicized.

DYKE, 2 m. NNE. BRITAIN HOUSE has an early C19 fro
hiding C17 gables.

CAWTHORPE, 1½ m. NNW. CAWTHORPE HOUSE is in a co
servative Georgian style with gables, and CAWTHORPE HA
is also Georgian, with a stone pilastered front and canted c
bays.

HANTHORPE, 3 m. NNW. HANTHORPE HOUSE has be
demolished, but the stable court remains. It was built in 17
and has been attributed to *C. H. Tatham*.

BRACEBOROUGH

ST MARGARET. The tower raises a problem. Externally w
its clasping buttresses it may be of *c.*1300. Broach spire w
one tier of lucarnes. But internally it has a double-chamfer
arch with continuous mouldings not only to the E, but also
the N and S, and the E arch is flanked by half-arches all of t
same mouldings. The answer is of course that the church
*c.*1300 had a nave and aisles embracing the tower. The cutti

down was done in the C18, when the tower arch also received its lower and narrower arch. The Perp side windows must then have been set back. The curious flat panels in which they sit are C18 anyway. They have hood-moulds, some with beasts, their fore-paws hanging down. The same motif in the s doorway, which now leads into the tower. The polygonal chancel dates from 1859 (*C. Kirk*). – FONT. Square, Norman, but completely re-cut, or an imitation. Angle-shafts. In the fields zigzag, lozenge, tree, and blank-arch motifs. The latter are of the standard Purbeck type. Along the top, frieze of loops. – STAINED GLASS. In a s aisle window *Kempe* glass of 1895.

RECTORY. 1848, in *William Thompson*'s Tudor style.

IVY FARM, SW of the church. In a gable-end a late C13 window re-set. Two lights and a circle at the top.

MANOR FARM. C17 vernacular, i.e. L-shaped with moulded stone stacks, and the usual two- and three-light windows.

BRACEBRIDGE

9060

ALL SAINTS. Anglo-Saxon nave; the long-and-short quoins are perfectly preserved. In the N aisle also a (re-set) blocked Saxon doorway, tall and narrow. The chancel arch again Saxon, and again tall and narrow. The two large squints to the l. and r. are of course later, but defy dating. The W tower C11, and possibly also pre-Conquest. Plain W doorway and arch to the nave. Coupled bell-openings with the typical mid-wall shaft, but capitals approaching Norman forms. Later pyramid roof. Lowish E.E. chancel with three s lancets of moderate size. Pointed-trefoiled sedilia niche. E.E. s aisle, externally with smallish and small lancets and a simple doorway decorated with dog-tooth, internally with a beautiful Lincoln arcade, whose openings incidentally do not tally with the windows. Three bays, circular piers with four detached shafts. Shaftrings, moulded capitals, double-chamfered arches. The responds are keeled. N aisle, N transept, N chapel by *Pearson*, 1874–5. – FONT. Norman, of drum shape, decorated with intersecting arches. – MONUMENT. Mrs Katherine Ludington † . .79. Simple tomb-chest.

ST JOHN, Bracebridge Heath. 1908 by *C. Hodgson Fowler*. – PLATE. German Cup, *c*.1630; Paten Cover, also *c*.1630.

ST JOHN'S HOSPITAL, London Road. Built as the County Pauper Lunatic Asylum. The contract was drawn up in 1849

with Messrs *Hamilton & Holland* of Gloucester, but the wor▮
executed by *Hamilton* and *Thomas Parry*, the Kesteven Count▮
Surveyor. The tender was for £32,870 (GS). It represents th▮
grand manner in mental hospitals, grimly severe, in a Palla▮
dian style of Venetian windows and rustication. The plan is ▮
grid of pavilions and the s front is over 780 ft long. The to▮
floor was added in 1850. Other additions 1865, 1880, 191▮
1932, 1935, 1939.

0030   BRACEBY

ST MARGARET. Nave and chancel. The gabled bellcote ▮
clearly C13. It is supported as usual on a middle buttress. Th▮
s side had a three-bay arcade. No details are recognizabl▮
The early C14 windows (Y-tracery, flowing tracery) wer▮
probably set back when the aisle was pulled down. The ▮
arcade remains and is C13 too. Also three bays. Semi-octogon▮
w respond (spell out the inscription on it). One pier quatrefo▮
with fillets, the other octofoil, but with a waterleaf capital, i.▮
earlier than the quatrefoil pier. Fine C13 chancel arch with ▮
lively grouping of the shafts. Two of them are detached. Per ▮
clerestory. – PLATE. Chalice and Paten Cover, by *John Morle*▮
of Lincoln, 1569.

MANOR FARM. Dated 1653, and a remarkably regular fron▮
Two storeys, six bays, the doorway (with a four-centred hea▮
in the fifth. To its l. and r. evenly placed mullioned window▮
of three lights on both floors.

9040   BRANDON
              1¾ m. NW of Hough-on-the-Hill

CHAPEL. Mostly of 1872, by *Kirk* of Sleaford, but with plent▮
of old materials. Nave and chancel in one, and bellcote. Sever▮
re-used windows and a good Norman s doorway. The lintel an▮
the tympanum have chip-carved St Andrew's crosses in rows▮
but the hood-mould has a motif of radially placed simpl▮
leaves or loops which is really an Anglo-Saxon motif (see e.g▮
Stow, Lindsey). Inside a N arcade made up of one E.E. roun▮
pier and two semi-octagonal responds, one with nailhead▮
Two Dec N chapel responds. One Dec or Perp image niche i▮
the N chapel.

OLD HALL. Dated 1637, and texturally an attractive essay wit▮
bands of grey stone alternating with golden ironstone. Thi▮
texture carries through to the garden wall extending s. Th▮

original L-shape has been truncated and the fenestration altered: now with three C19 Gothic lights and five three-light windows.

BRANSTON

0060

LL SAINTS. The SW quoin of the nave shows unmistakable *See* p. 768 long-and-short work, i.e. is Anglo-Saxon. So is probably the W tower, though there are no Saxon features at once visible. The W doorway is Norman, with moulded arch and volute capitals, but it is remarkably narrow, and that may be Saxon. To the l. and r. of the Norman portal Norman blank arcading, two bays each, starting half-way up the doorway. On the S side the same arcading must have existed. A round, probably Transitional, arch cuts into it. The bell-openings are twin, with block capitals. Recessed Perp spire without crockets. Three tiers of lucarnes in alternating positions. E.E. chancel. The Dec E window is by *M. Drury*, 1863. There was a composition of lancets here too, as there are lancets on the S and (blocked) on the N. A course runs inside below the windows, and round the priest's doorway it forms a round arch. The stops of the course are stiff-leaf. Nice sedilia. Chancel arch with some nailhead. The two doorways in the N and S aisles may be of the same date or a little earlier. The aisles themselves are Dec, see the W windows and the arcades. They are of three bays with octagonal piers and double-chamfered arches. Two capitals have bold broad leaf bands, one has wooden branches with single leaves. The outer N aisle belongs to the restoration by *Sir G. G. Scott* (1876). Perp clerestory with battlements, pinnacles, and three-light windows. – COMMUNION RAIL, with twisted balusters. – BENCH ENDS with simple poppy-heads and coarse tracery, mostly of one pattern. Also occasional figures, e.g. a chained bear, a fox, and two women. – STAINED GLASS. Bits in the outer N aisle, including some of the C15. – The E window is by *Kempe*, c.1899. – SCULPTURE. In the outer W wall of the porch a small Crucifixion. – PLATE. Chalice, by *T.A.*, 1669; Paten, by *J. Walker*, Dublin, 1714; Paten, by *J. Elston*, Exeter, 1720. – MONUMENTS. Sir Cecil Wray † 1736, but erected before his death. By *Thomas Carter*. Obelisk of mottled marble with coat of arms attached. To the l. and r. busts with fat and phlegmatic faces. – Lord Vere Bertie, 1770. Noble sarcophagus on big lion's feet, obelisk, and arms in a roundel. of the church a plain Georgian house of seven bays and two and a half storeys with a three-bay pediment.

BRANSTON HALL. A *J. MacVicar Anderson* job of 1884 f
Lord Vere Bertie. In the late Burn style, with shaped gabl
and a big strapwork-studded *porte-cochère*.

STONEFIELD. A bizarre Victorian folly house of yellow bri
with black stone quoins and strip decoration, like a zebra. A
array of steep pointed and shaped gables and castellation
The garden piers are a conglomerate of rough stone, up
which squat monkeys.* In SILVER STREET is a pair of hous
also in a *Lovely* style.

LONGHILLS, I m. ESE. The house is said to be by *George Base*
1838 (Colvin), but is an architectural puzzle. There are on t
ground floor of the w front three Venetian windows. The re
of the fenestration is odd. To the three bays of the w fro
with the centre recessed correspond three bays on the N fro
with a pediment, and seven closely spaced bays on the S fror
The roofscape looks Victorian, as does the *porte-cochère*.

MERE HALL, 1½ m. SW. C17 farmhouse on the site of a mediev
hospital of the Knights Hospitallers (founded *c.*1240).

9050   BRANT BROUGHTON

21b ST HELEN. The spire of Brant Broughton is one of the mo
elegant of Lincolnshire. It is 198 ft high‡ and, with the tow
on which it stands, ashlar-faced and Late Dec throughout, s
the tower arch and the two-light bell-openings. Under t
tower vault of diagonal ribs and ridge-ribs ending in a lar
circle. Above the bell-openings gargoyles and a fleuron friez
Then parapet and pinnacles and the spire recessed just t
right distance. It is crocketed, but not excessively, and has s
tiers of lucarnes, but they are tiny and quatrefoil so as not
disturb the outline (cf. Caythorpe). The rest of the churc
can be described chronologically. The aisle w windows are
*c.*1290 at the latest (two pointed trefoiled lights and a quatr
foil over), and in the vestry is a capital with nailhead used as
bracket which points to the same time. Next the arcade
probably a little later, but not necessarily. They are of thr
bays, tall, with octagonal piers and double-chamfered arche
The chancel arch may be of the same time, and also the tow
arch. The former is of the quatrefoil type with deep continuo
hollows between the foils, the latter is quatrefoil with sm
projections in the diagonals. The chancel itself with its wood

---

* The builder of this *bizarrerie* was Mr *Lovely*, about whom is t
anecdote: 'There'll be a good monkey in that house (meaning a mortgage
says one. Says Mr Lovely, 'I'll show them where the monkeys will be.'

‡ Measured by the R.A.F. in the Second World War.

lierne-vault is by *Bodley*, 1876. But the rest of the church is Early Perp, or Transitional from Dec to Perp, i.e. late C14, i.e. a date to which the steeple may well belong. And all this rest of the church is most lavishly detailed. The aisle windows with thin castellated transoms above ogee-headed lights are Perp. Fleurons in jambs and (two-centred) arches. The buttresses have niches, the battlements quatrefoils with shields and pinnacles. In the S aisle at the E end two brackets, one with an animal, the other with a crouching figure. The porches, however, are the real show-pieces. They are not identical twins, but twins. The entrances are still close to the Dec (round abaci). The N porch then has an entrance arch with fleurons, a shield over and a niche over that, an openwork parapet and pinnacles, and a frieze of faces, beasts, etc. at the level of the foot of the gable. Decorated cresting of the roof. The S porch is a little simpler. In the niche above the entrance an original seated figure. Both porches are vaulted inside, two sexpartite bays on wall-arches. These arches stand on leaf brackets, and at the apexes of the arches are little figures holding on to them. Bosses, including the Lamb and the Pelican. Of the doorways that on the N is more elaborate, with two mouldings of fleurons, tiny ballflower (still!) and heads in the hood-mould, and even a moulding of fleurons and heads inside. The only Late Perp contribution is the clerestory (and the angel roof, which is largely in its original state). Three-light windows, battlements decorated with shields in quatrefoils, pinnacles. The pre-clerestory roof-line is visible inside against the tower. – FONT. Octagonal, with quatrefoils and big leaves against the underside. – CANDLESTICKS and CANDELABRA, by *F. Coldron & Son*, probably of c.1876. – STAINED GLASS. Nearly all of it designed by Canon *F. H. Sutton* and made by *Kempe*. – But the E window by *Burlison & Grylls*. – SCULPTURE. In the vestry a length of Anglo-Saxon interlace. – Also a beautiful C14 Trinity, the upper half of God the Father however missing. – PLATE. Silver-gilt Chalice, German(?), late C15; Chalice and Paten, by *I.M.*, 1634.* – MONUMENT. Tomb-chest in the N chapel with shields in barbed quatrefoils.

ESLEYAN CHAPEL. A modest brick box with hipped roof and arched windows, entirely Georgian, yet dated 1862.

* Mrs Cundy mentioned in a letter in addition the silver-gilt (later) ten to go with the Chalice, and a Victorian Chalice and Paten made from dy Augusta Sutton's jewels.

FRIENDS MEETING HOUSE. 1701. Plain oblong, about 40
by 15 ft, but with the humble furnishings completely preserve

THE OLD RECTORY, s of the church. It looks mid C18, wi
wings with canted bay windows, extruded angles, and a Dor
veranda.*

THE PRIORY, N of the church. Three-bay stone house with cro
windows, a hipped roof, and rusticated gatepiers. The hou
carries a date-stone 1658.

THE OLD HALL, N of The Priory. Mid C18, in brick, with
gabled one-bay projection and a rusticated doorway covered
a big segmental pediment.

MANOR HOUSE, ½ m. N. At the N end of a spacious late c
street. Much altered.

Several more nice houses in the village, both stone and brick.

BRAUNCEWELL

0050

ALL SAINTS. Probably of the early C19. The chancel rebuilt
1857. Nave and chancel and stone bell-turret. In the w gab
a round window. The other windows with Y-tracery. – FON
Octagonal, Perp, with flowers in pointed quatrefoils. – PLAT
Paten, by *William Peaston*, 1748; two-handled Cup, by *Willia
Sheene*, 1766.

BRAUNCEWELL MANOR. In attractive unison with the churc
A much modified L-shaped C17 house.

BROTHERHOUSE BAR see COWBIT

BROTHERTOFT

2040

1 m. s of Langrick

ST GILBERT. 1847 by *S. Lewin*, the chancel 1854. Stone, in t
Perp style. Hammerbeam roof in the nave. – STAINED GLAS
The E window by *Wailes*. – PLATE. Chalice, *c.*1580.

BROTHERTOFT HALL. Built out of the profits from cultivatin
woad. In the flat Fens it looks larger than life. The E front
five bays and three storeys, the side elevations as canted bay
All this must be *c.*1780. C19 additions are cement-renderin
ground-floor bay windows, and a pilastered extension to the

BULBY

0020

3 m. E of Corby

BULBY HALL. Built for William Watson Smyth in 1840–2. Th
style is Tudor-Gothic, and the stables are dated 1864. A fi
avenue of elms aligned on the house front.

* *F. H. Goddard* made plans in 1875 (GA).

BURTON COGGLES

9020

т Thomas à Becket. The w wall of the nave has a Norman window with deep splay. This must be a relic of the time before the church received its w tower. The date of the tower is c13. It is unbuttressed and carries a short broach spire. The spire has two tiers of lucarnes both in the same direction. The lower has twin openings with plate tracery. Also E.E. the three-bay s arcade with octagonal piers and double-chamfered arches. The comparison with the Perp octagonal piers of the N arcade is instructive. The s aisle windows are of c.1300 (three arched lights under one arch, and Y-cusped), and so the arcade is perhaps also late. In the N aisle one window with Y-tracery too. So the N arcade was a replacement. Dec chancel, except for the Victorian E window (1874). Remains of a double piscina with a little nailhead decoration. In the s aisle roof old timbers, including two angels. – STAINED GLASS. In the chancel by *Hardman*, 1874. – PLATE. Chalice, Paten, and Flagon, by *I.S.*, 1668. – MONUMENTS. In the porch two effigies of cross-legged Knights, both early c14. One has his hand at his sword, the other prays. The head of the latter is under a close-fitting projecting canopy with an early ogee arch. – Brasses of Cholmeleys of 1590 and 1620.

ECTORY, s of the church. By *Thomas Blashill*, 1838 (GA).

BURTON PEDWARDINE

1040

т Andrew. 1870–1 by *C. Kirk*, except for the N transept. Nave and chancel; bellcote. The transept has a three-light N window with Geometrical tracery (trefoiled circles) but also ogee arches. Blocked arch to the former N aisle. Niches with ogee heads in buttresses. This motif and the N transept N window are confirmed as existing in the medieval church by Nattes's drawing. – SCULPTURE. Notable Late Anglo-Saxon fragments at the w end. They are of interlace patterns and seem to come from at least two crosses.* – PLATE. Chalice and Paten, by *W.S.*, 1638. – MONUMENTS. In the N wall of the transept low tomb recess beneath the window; no doubt the monument to the founder of the transeptal chapel. On the lid of the tomb-chest was a bust not in brass but in a composition. It was a Knight in chain-mail; early c14. Lombardic script. – Sir Thomas Horseman † 1610. Standing alabaster monument with recumbent effigies.

* There are also architectural fragments at the w end and in the transept.

BURTON HOUSE. C19, but the stables look C18. *William San*
carried out work here before 1751.

3040

BUTTERWICK

ST ANDREW. Georgian brick W tower (according to Pish
Thompson of 1714, but on the clerestory rainwater heads tl
date 1770) and Tudor brick clerestory. Also a circular bri
NE turret with spire. The N aisle W and E walls and the S ais
W wall also brick. Arcades of four bays. Octagonal pie
double-chamfered arches. They are supposed to be E.E., b
that can only be true of the N arcade. However, the W respon
of the S arcade is definitely E.E. too, see the primitive stin
leaf capital. It ought to be added that Pishey Thompson ca
'scarcely any portion of the building . . . original'. – SCREE
One-light divisions with ogee arches and two-light trace
over. – PULPIT. Plain C17, probably late. – DOOR to the roc
stair; Perp and traceried. – PLATE. Chalice and Paten, 1
Thomas Rusk, 1738.

PINCHBECK'S SCHOOL. Founded in 1665. Only bits look tl
date.

9060

CANWICK

ALL SAINTS. The interior is more interesting than the exterio
Two-bay Norman N arcade. Sturdy circular pier, squa
abacus, many-scalloped capitals, unmoulded round arch
The chancel arch Norman too, with three orders of colo
nettes and zigzag at r. angles to the wall. Then the E.E. ar
from the chancel into the N chapel, double-chamfered on cc
bels. The fragmentary W arch into the chapel seems earlie
and what is the date of the priest's doorway E of the chap
arch? In the C14 the nave was lengthened, see the one W b
of the N arcade. The arch dies into the imposts. The W tow
has Georgian bell-openings. Its E wall is the W wall of the c
lengthening. – FONT. Elementary E.E. Four corner colum
carry and embrace an octagonal bowl. The thicker mid
support is Perp. – ARCHITECTURAL FRAGMENTS. N of t
tower, outside, a late C12 capital and a Norman stone wi
four rosettes in relief. – PLATE. Chalice, by *John Morley*
Lincoln, c.1569. – In the churchyard WAR MEMORIAL,
Gothic canopy. It looks c.1870 but commemorates the Fi
World War.

CANWICK HALL. The severe stone front to the N is a rebuildi
of 1810 by Colonel *Waldo Sibthorpe*, who is said to have be

his own architect. It has a pedimented, only one-storeyed portico of four Tuscan columns. The whole front is squashed between two other parts: to the E recased old offices, and to the W a competently designed wing built shortly before 1810 to contain a collection of paintings. Of this, one front is pedimented, the other has bows.

CANWICK HOUSE. 1889. In *Watkins*'s favourite red brick Dutch Renaissance. Gables and panels in terracotta relief, the hallmark of his style.

CANWICK DOWER HOUSE. By *William Burn*, 1876, and one of his duller inventions.

ALLMAN HOUSE. Characteristic of recent small single-storey houses. Felicitously sited on the Jesus College estate. By *Parker & Roberts*, 1957.

CAREBY   0010

ST STEPHEN. At the far end of the village; on its own. Norman chancel, see the plain single-chamfered priest's doorway and one original N window. The W tower was started early in the C13. The tower arch is round and has two chamfers and one step. Clasping buttresses. The staircase runs up in the thickness of the wall. Twin bell-openings under round arches. E.E. the S porch entrance. Stiff-leaf capitals and a steep double-chamfered arch. Inside, a steep stone roof on two transverse stone beams, meeting at the apex. The N chapel arch still has E.E. bases but a sumptuous leaf band in the capitals which must be after 1300. Perp windows, Perp clerestory, Perp arcades. Three bays, the piers with polygonal projections to the nave, demi-shafts to the arch openings. But the most memorable feature of the interior is the Victorian wooden tierceron-vault with all ribs performing three-dimensional curves. Its date seems to be unknown. – DOOR KNOCKER. C14. Head of St Stephen with lizards whispering in his ears (Cox). – COPE. Beautiful crimson cope changed into a frontal. Assumption of 30b the Virgin, feathered angels, double eagles. – PLATE. Chalice, by *John Morley* of Lincoln(?), *c.*1571; Paten and Flagon, by *Thomas Tearle*, 1732. – MONUMENTS. In the N chapel memorial of a C13 heart burial. Pointed quatrefoil, the rim with stiff-leaf and dog-tooth. A shield, and above it two hands holding a heart. – Cross-legged Knight, two angels by his pillow (chancel). – Knight and Lady, only their busts visible, surrounded by cusping. The bodies disappear not under a blanket, as at South Stoke, but into the solid slab, which is

however fluted. His shield lies on the slab. The monumer
is probably of *c*.1300.

OLD RECTORY. By *Thomas Boyfield*, 1827 (GA).

HILL-FORT. A small oval fort, defended by two banks an
ditches. The two lines of fortification are about 130 ft apar
the outer being barely visible on the ground, the inner sti
standing to a height of 3 ft. The site is unexcavated but
probably of Iron Age date.

0010

CARLBY

ST STEPHEN. E.E. W tower. The bell-openings have Y-tracer
on a detached shaft with a capital. Broach spire with two tier
of lucarnes in the same directions, both apparently pre-1300
The arch to the nave has a little nailhead enrichment. A door
way is placed asymmetrically above. E.E. three-bay arcade
N before S. Both have round piers with round abaci and bot
have double-chamfered arches, but the N arches are round, th
S arches pointed. Yet S was begun like N – see the W and
responds. The N aisle has a pair of small lancets to the E an
a plain N doorway. Perp chancel arch and chancel E and
windows. – PULPIT. Plainly panelled; C17. – BENCHE:
Two plain old benches remain. – WALL PAINTING. Remain
of a Doom above the chancel arch; C14. Better recognizabl
in illustrations than in the original. – PLATE. Chalice, by *I.I*
1672; Paten and Flagon, by *I.C.*, 1675. – MONUMENT:
Low tomb recess in the N aisle. In it a coffin-lid with a foliate
cross, singularly ornate, with big cabbagey leaves to l. as we
as to r.

9050

CARLTON-LE-MOORLAND

ST MARY. The church has an Anglo-Saxon W tower. This ap
pears from the blocked arch in the W wall with its unstruc
turally laid shale-stones intended to act as voussoirs, from th
tower arch with plain chamfered imposts and unmoulde
arch, and from the opening above the tower arch, which
round-headed and plain inside the tower. The nave has n
aisles now, but at the NE corner inside the marks of a forme
respond appear, and also of an arch into a N chapel. Thi
exists, though not in its medieval form. From these arche
and the arch from the chancel into the chapel (keeled respond
the E.E. date of these parts is evident. Dec chancel (see th
two-light low-side window). Otherwise much Elizabetha
remodelling. Mullioned and transomed windows in the nave

Mullioned windows in the tower and the vestry. – SCREEN.
One-light divisions; bits of the dado tracery; also plain return
STALLS. – COMMUNION RAIL. C17. – STAINED GLASS. In
the E window, by *Kempe*, 1890. – PLATE. Chalice and Paten
Cover, Elizabethan.

CARLTON SCROOP

9040

T NICHOLAS. Norman W tower, see the brown rubble masonry,
one W window, and the arch towards the nave. Big capitals
with clumsy pellets. The ashlar-faced upper parts of the tower
are dated 1632. Norman also the plain, single-chamfered N
doorway. E.E. S porch. It has a pitched stone roof on single-
chamfered transverse ribs. Is the chancel entirely of the late
C13, or is the N lancet earlier? The E window is of four lights,
intersecting, but the top left out of the intersecting pattern and
filled by a quatrefoiled circle – a piece of wilfulness typical of
the moment when people had grown tired of the perfection
of the E.E. style. Dec S aisle and N aisle windows. The low
two-bay arcades with octagonal pier and wide double-chamfered arches probably also Dec. The N details look a little
older. – FONT. Octagonal. With eight models of Dec windows.
– PULPIT. C17; plain. – STAINED GLASS. In the tracery of
the E window two original figures of donors, though one with
a wrong head. The (restored?) figure of Christ comes from
another church. – In the S aisle E window early glass by *Kempe*
(date of death 1890). – PLATE. Chalice and Paten, by *D.G.*,
1633.

CASEWICK HALL

0000

1¼ m. NE of Uffington

few houses in the county fill one with such delight. The story
is this: there was an earlier quadrangular building with a gatehouse on the N side of the moat. This was bought in 1621 by
William Trollop of Thurlby, who commenced to rebuild it.*
His is now only the S range. Then in 1785 *William Legg* of
Stamford began to gothicize Trollop's W range. This is now 59b
the show front: fifteen bays and two main storeys. Pairs of
crocketed gables with three-light windows at each end. Otherwise the windows sashed, except for the Rococo-Gothic centrepiece: a tripartite window of moulded pointed lights on the

* His masons were *John Cole* and *George Beaver*, according to the Casewick papers.

ground floor, and a tripartite window above, its centre oge
arched. A crenellated parapet at the top forming a pediment
Round the corner to the E the three-bay side of this rang
continued by a decorative GATEWAY dated 1651. This has
curvaceous outline, three obelisks at the top and in the midd
a pierced oval. The s front is still intact in its C17 Trollc
form. Four widely-spaced bays, two and two, four-light wit
dows with a transom, and three-light windows without in th
tiny gablets over each bay. The rainwater heads are date
1789, but the windows must be the result of a C19 restoratio
The range is continued by a small Gothic ORANGERY, bi
if one wants to know what its details were like originally, o
must enter a small courtyard behind the s range. The windov
here are mullioned, of three lights, with a straight entablatur
To the N of this small courtyard the service range, and the
side of this takes one to the forecourt or entrance court, i.
the space between the C17 and the C18 work. Legg's range ha
here five completely plain bays, Georgian without any Gothi
and the original C17 windows were mostly altered in the late
C17 (wooden mullion-and-transom crosses). But here also on
original two-light window remains. The DINING ROOM ha
carved wood Rococo *sopraporte* and portrait ovals. Th
chimneypieces by *Edward Bingham*.

DOVECOTE. Early C18. Square with octagonal lantern.

₉₀₁₀

CASTLE BYTHAM

ST JAMES. Unbuttressed E.E. w tower. Twin bell-opening
The top Perp. Lozenge-frieze and battlements. In the wall t
the nave a trefoil-headed doorway above the tower arch ar
another, asymmetrically placed. The N arcade is earlier tha
the tower, say of *c.*1200. Three bays, responds with waterle
and flat upright leaves. Double-chamfered round arches. Th
piers are octagonal. The arch to the transept however ha
nobbly leaf on the impost and will be Dec. E.E. the N porc
entrance with triple responds and the N transept with i
strange N window (three stepped lancet lights under one arcl
solid tympanum with blank trefoils and quatrefoils). Of abot
the same date also the chancel E window with Geometric
tracery (three stepped lancet lights and two unfoiled circle
and the N aisle w window (three stepped and cusped lanc

* It is curious that the windows in the gables are not sashed but mu
lioned (three lights). They may well be a survival of the w front of the hou
of the 1620s.

lights under one arch). The other windows of the long chancel
are Dec. Dec also the s side of the nave. The s transept was
rebuilt in 1857. – FONT. Octagonal. Patterns in flat raised
bands, a star, IHS, etc. Is this 1660s? – CHANDELIER.
In the nave. Brass, two tiers. Dated 1810. – SCULPTURE. In
the porch parts of an Anglo-Saxon slab with a rope moulding
and an inscription. – PLATE. Chalice, by *John Morley* of
Lincoln(?), *c.*1580. – MONUMENT. In the chancel a large
recess, also or exclusively used as an Easter Sepulchre. It is
Dec. Low tomb-chest with seven crocketed ogee-headed
panels. Canopy on shafts. In the arch openwork cusping and
in one moulding ballflower. Ogee gable. Buttress-shafts with
crocketed finials.

residing over the village are the impressive earthworks of the
CASTLE. It stands on a projection towering above the stream,
the main ward occupying the point of the prominence on the
w; on the level E side it is protected by a small outlying mound.
Since its masonry defences, like those of the castle in general,
have vanished, it is impossible to say whether the latter was the
emplacement for a keep-tower or simply a barbican protecting the approach to the main ward. The whole is surrounded
by a powerful ditch and bank, double in places, and on the E
side is a large bailey, apparently divided across the middle
by a curtain. There are abundant indications of former
masonry defences, but nothing remains above ground. The
castle was almost certainly built in the C11; the date of its
vanished stonework is unknown. It was demolished in 1221,
after a futile outbreak against Henry III by William de Forz,
count of Aumâle. Leland still saw great walls. From the
castle one gets the best view of this texturally attractive village,
particularly the roofscape of red tile and grey Collyweston
slabs. By the castle a C17 CONDUIT HOUSE.

HE PRIORY, E of the church. A C17 front. From the r. first a
gabled bay with a shallow bay window with six lights on the
ground floor, six on the upper floor. Then a three-light window on the ground and the upper floor and above them a
small gabled dormer. The house is nicely composed with the
church.

ANOR HOUSE. In the main street. Also C17, but probably a
little later. Symmetrical three-bay front. The windows to the
l. and r. of the doorway of five lights, above of three.

CAWTHORPE see BOURNE

9040

CAYTHORPE

ST VINCENT. A tall, somewhat austere church with a crossin
tower. The nave is banded Ancaster stone and ironstone. T
tower has Dec bell-openings, an openwork parapet with
undulating pattern, pinnacles, thin flying buttresses, and
spire, achieving a total height of 156 ft. The spire has a slig
entasis, which was however greater – cf. the sugar-loaf effe
at Welbourne – before *Scott* in restoring the church in 18
softened it.* Crockets up the edge. Six tiers of lucarnes, b
quatrefoil and so small that they do not mar the outline (
Brant Broughton). All this is Dec, and Dec is indeed the sty
of the church, but at its very earliest and emphatically of
moment before flowing tracery became the fashion. T
church is in fact a pattern book of Late Geometrical tracer
say of *c.*1290–1300, from the purely E.E. of the S transept
window to the odd details of the two W front windows, t
S windows, and the N aisle W (former N) window (a cross in
circle, three circles in a circle, trefoils and pointed trefoils
circles, the barbs like long thorns, cf. Billingborough). On
in the S windows mouchette wheels in circles occur, i.e. og
shapes. The S doorway is cusped and slightly ogee-heade
Above a seated figure under a gable. Buttress-shafts l. and
Of later details there is the wide Perp E window, starting hig
up, the Perp NE window, the N transept N window, and t
barren Perp S window. The Geometrical varieties of trace
are interesting enough, but far more interesting is the interio
As one enters one notices with amazement that this is a tw
naved church.‡ Along its middle runs a three-bay, or rath
two-and-a-half-bay, arcade. The piers of course must be ve
high. The arches start in the middle of the W front – hence t
two W windows – and end in a half arch above what appea
to be the chancel arch. The piers are octagonal and the arch
double-chamfered. But – and this increases the surprise an
leaves one puzzling – the chancel arch is no chancel arch b
the W arch of a crossing, and the rest of the church is perfectl
normal in plan. The two-naved part would be even more im
pressive if *Scott* had not added an outer aisle. The crossin
arches are Dec, five shafts connected by deep hollows, and t
middle one filleted, arches of three sunk waves. – ARCHITEC
TURAL FRAGMENT. An E.E. capital (N transept NE).

* And reduced the height by *c.*10 ft.

‡ Others in England are e.g. Hannington Northants, Stretford Herefor
shire, and Wootton Bassett Wiltshire.

ARMOUR (chancel). C16. – PLATE. Chalice, by *John Morley* of
Lincoln, *c.*1569; Cover, 1675; Paten, by *I.I.*, 1693; Paten and
Flagon, by *Thomas Tearle*, 1732. – MONUMENTS. Sir Charles
Hussey † 1664, but clearly of *c.*1730, and anyway signed by
W. Palmer. Bust under open scrolly pediment. Pilasters with
hanging stylized flowers and top volutes. – Sir Edward Hussey
† 1725. Purely architectural, with pilasters and a broken pediment. Garlands below it. – Nice slate headstones in the churchyard. – CROSS. S of the church. Square base with scooped-out
top corners and part of the shaft.

village of rich golden ironstone. Cottages dated 1833, 1836,
and 1839 in a C17 vernacular style.

ICARAGE. By the church. Probably the house built by *William
Fowler* for the Rev. Woodstock in 1827 (Colvin).* Plain, with a
central canted bay. In the garden a Gothic crenellated garden
house.

OME FARM, NW of the church. C17. Three widely spaced bays,
two storeys and Dutch gables. Three-light windows with flat
entablatures. In the NW angle an early C18 doorway and an
oval keyed-in window.

AYTHORPE HALL. This was once a Hussey seat, and of Hussey
splendour. Now only the magnificent brick walls of the park
remain. The present house was built in 1823 by *William
Parsons* for Colonel G. H. Packe. A cleanly detailed, five-by-
five-bay block of two storeys. On the S front the centre bay is
slightly recessed, and the end bay slightly advanced. Ionic
portico to the ground storey, windows with lugged upper
corners, a cornice and blocking course. The E front with centre
bow and tall lower windows. Stables of the same date.

Y HOUSE, High Street. Dated 1684. Projecting gabled wings,
three-light windows.

OLYCROSS, ½ m. S. One gabled C17 wing with later windows
and parapet. To the E another wing added late in the C19 in a
convincing Queen Anne style.

AYTHORPE COURT (Kesteven Farm Institute), 1¼ m. E. By
Sir R. Blomfield. Built in 1899 in Ancaster stone with bands of
ironstone (cf. Denton) and gables. Early C17 style strongly
influenced by the local vernacular. S front with three-storey
projecting wings.

CHAPEL HILL   2050

OLY TRINITY. 1826; restored (and remodelled) 1884 by an
architect given as Mr *Knight*. Red brick. Nave with bellcote

* According to the Rev. J. E. Draper, this was only a refronting.

and chancel. – PLATE. Chalice, by *John Read*(?), 1714; Pate
by *Thomas Parr*, 1770.

Lincoln. A 1609; Cover, 1675; Pate
Flagon, by *Thomas Tearle*, 1732. – MONUMENTS. Sir Charle
Hussey † 1664, but the inscription . . . . . and away signed c 17

8040

CLAYPOLE

ST PETER. A proud church. w tower, below late C13, abo
Perp. w window with Y-tracery. Tower arch with triple
sponds and capitals, on the s still stiff-leaf, on the N going boss
The tower top has a frieze of cusped lozenges below tl
battlements, pinnacles, and a recessed crocketed spire with tw
tiers of lucarnes in alternating directions. The rest mostly D
and of high quality. Externally the tall, noble chancel wi
side windows of three lights (a five-petalled flower motif in tl
tracery), the aisles embracing the tower with their intersectii
ogee tracery, the N transept with the same motif, the smal
transept s doorway (or is this late C13 ?), the clerestory wi
tall, three-light windows with intersecting tracery (no ogee
and the s doorway with bossy leaf capitals – a preparation f
more to come. Substantial Perp alterations to make the chur
yet lighter, namely the five-light E window with a transom a
cusping below and the s transept s and N transept N windows
four lights and arches below. Also Perp the battlements a
pinnacles of the s transept and the lively s porch with
cusped lozenge frieze, its battlements, and its pinnacles. T
interior is very fine and very unified. Dec arcades of four bay
The piers of four shafts and four slimmer diagonal shaf
Double-chamfered arches, those to the transepts higher. T

25b
capitals are broad bands of infinitely varied foliage. The sar
applies to the arches from the transepts to the aisles and to t
chancel arch. The voussoirs of the chancel arch are interrupt
by two lively little caryatid figures, once probably supportii
the rood. However, there is one significant difference in deco
ative style. The tower arch, we have seen, has responds of
different section and still one naturalistic capital. The N r
spond of the N arch from aisle to transept and the s respond
the corresponding s arch have the same section as the tow
arch, and the N respond has a delightful naturalistic capi
(with heads in the leaves). All other capitals are bossy, i.e.
after 1300. Are there then two phases revealed here ? There
indeed a roof-line against the tower which disregards the ea
C14 clerestory. Also the s doorway of the s transept has be
mentioned as perhaps still C13, and in the s transept are pla
sedilia and a double piscina which are obviously C13. Alte
natively these could be from the E.E. chancel and re-set wh

the Dec chancel was built and received its sumptuous sedilia with tall niches with ogee arches, openwork cusping, a head frieze, and a crenellated top. To the same style belong the vestry door and the aumbry opposite. Nice panelled nave ceiling with decorated principals; Perp no doubt. – FONT. Octagonal body; no distinction between stem and bowl. Two-light panels with Dec tracery and crocketed gables, i.e. a piece of the date of the arcades and chancel. – PULPIT. Perp body, the back panel, lectern, and tester made up with Perp pieces, especially of a dainty quatrefoil frieze. – SCREEN. Big one-light divisions. Ogee arches with tracery over. – SOUTH DOOR. With tracery. – PLATE. Chalice and Paten, 1699, and Paten, 1704, by *John Jackson*.

RECTORY, off the E end of the village street to the N. (Inside a staircase with barley-sugar balusters and the date 1683. MHLG)

(BRIDGE. Of two arches; C14. NBR)

COLEBY

9060

ALL SAINTS. Unbuttressed W tower built in the C11. To the S a keyhole window, the hood-mould with radially placed leaf (cf. Stow, L). The tower arch to go with this window is blocked, but enough has been exposed to show that it had the same type of hood-mould. The present, smaller tower arch is Perp. The bell-openings are Perp too, and so are the decorated parapet and the pinnacles, the thin flying buttresses, and the crocketed spire with its two tiers of lucarnes in alternating directions. After the Saxon the Norman contributions. N arcade of two bays. Sturdy round pier with scalloped capital and square abacus, billet in the hood-mould. Ornate Late Norman S doorway. Two orders of shafts, capitals with leaf decoration. Arch with lozenge-chains, also at r. angles to the wall. Hood-mould with a chain of V-shapes broken round the moulding. The inner arch with a roll, and in a hollow a kind of leaf dog-tooth. Then the chancel arch, which must also be Late Norman. Slim round respond, but still square abacus. The S arcade is E.E. Respond triple and keeled. The pier of the Lincoln Cathedral school, i.e. octagonal with the sides to the main directions hollowed to hold detached piers. A seat round the pier. Stiff-leaf capitals, double-chamfered arches. Also E.E. the chancel. All lancets, in the E three stepped. Sedilia of two seats with round shaft, only partly original. The arch into a former N chapel is a little ahead of the S arcade, see the excellent, more agitated stiff-leaf capitals. Little more need be said architecturally. The S W view is odd, because the S aisle has no W window and the S porch carries on its W wall flush and also without windows. The porch was originally two-storeyed. The N aisle windows are Latest Perp, and the strange N window of the vestry is of course Victorian (restoration by *Kirk & Parry* to designs by *Penrose*). – FONT. Drum-shaped, Norman, with intersecting arches, but with four E.E. polygonal angle-shafts. – BENCH ENDS. Plain, with poppy-heads. They come from Hackthorn (Lindsey). – SOUTH DOOR. Heavily studded. – PLATE. Chalice, by *P.D.*, 1666.

COLEBY HALL. By 1628 William Lister had built his house. Of this the remarkably flat E front is intact. Brick with stone dressings. Six steep gables and a rebuilt and heightened porch. The windows now sashed, but in the porch still hood-moulds of the former mullioned windows. The C19 N front replaced an C18 front, and the S front expresses the restorations of 1892 and 1910. In 1762 Thomas Scrope called in his friend, *Sir William Chambers*, to design the TEMPLE OF ROMULUS AND REMUS placed at the end of an avenue. It is a composition of great monumentality and ought to be better known. Circular, with two projecting apses and two pedimented porches. Tuscan columns. Beneath the central dome a splendid honeycomb coffered ceiling of white on blue – the design a distant echo of Borromini. *Scrope* himself was an amateur architect and designed the small semicircular TEMPLE TO PITT. In June of 1774 Scrope asked Chambers 'to reconnoitre an old bad mansion, either to pull it down or to add, as you think proper . . .', and in July he asked for a sketch of a gateway, 'truly elegant and chaste', and he then referred to Coleby as his 'hobby horse'. The present GATEWAY is an imitation-ruined Roman arch based upon the Lincoln Newport Arch – of whose preservation Scrope was a strong supporter. *John Yenn* exhibited a design for a new house at Coleby in 1782. It was about then that the N front was rebuilt.

COLSTERWORTH

9020

ST JOHN BAPTIST. Inside first. The nave has exposed herring-bone masonry, an C11 feature. The N arcade is a C12 addition in two stages. First two bays of about the mid century. Circular pier, circular abacus (an early case), multi-scalloped capital, unmoulded arches, one of them with incised zigzag. No responds, only imposts. Then the w bay was added, w of the former w wall. This also has an unmoulded arch, and the responds even have the early motif of square abaci. But the ribbed crocket capital and the waterleaf capital are unmistakable. The extension may have been done with a view to a w tower, though the details of the tower are somewhat later. A date 1305 is cut into the fabric of the tower. The top is Perp with eight pinnacles, the intermediate ones on rounded not on square battlements.* E.E. also the N doorway, simple, with one order of shafts. The upper rood-stair doorway has a little nail-head decoration. If it is really of c.1200, it is, according to Aymer Vallance, the earliest record in existence of a rood stair (but cf. Thurlby). Dec s arcade of three bays. Quatrefoil piers with fillets, the foils more than semicircular. Double-chamfered arches. Perp s aisle and Perp ashlar-faced clerestory. The chancel was rebuilt in 1876 (by J. Fowler). – SCULPTURE. Three parts of an Anglo-Saxon cross shaft. Two with interlace, the third with the top cross. – PLATE. Chalice and Paten, by W.G., 1667; Paten, by S.R., 1679.

WOOLSTHORPE MANOR, ½ m. NW. Famous as the birthplace of Sir Isaac Newton, but architecturally undistinguished. A conventional T-plan of c.1620, with one-, two-, and three-light windows all with straight hoods. There is a form of semi-basement on the w front where the ground has been built up. The E base of the T is a later addition. Inside are a few moulded chimneypieces of the period.

COMMONSIDE see OLD LEAKE

CORBY

0020

ST JOHN EVANGELIST.‡ The N aisle must date from the late C13, see the windows, one with quatrefoils in circles in the tracery, one with intersecting tracery, one small and just a quatrefoil (W). Single-chamfered doorway. The s doorway is Dec (two continuous wave mouldings), and so is the aisle (see below) though the windows are Late Perp. Perp also the s porch. Late C14 four-bay arcades with tall piers. Their moulding is four shafts and four hollows. The piers have polygonal

---

* On the s side of the tower, on the base moulding of the w buttress, nscription naming the mason *Thomas de Somersby*.

‡ Are the quoins of the nave a sign of Norman date, asks the Rev. C. Tayler.

bases and capitals, the arches two sunk waves. It is likely tha
the arches are Dec, like the s doorway, and were re-used. Th
tower arch is similar to the arcades, but the chancel arch has
most oddly, two plain Norman imposts, perhaps *ex situ*. Perp
w tower with a quatrefoil frieze. The chancel is mostly o
*c.*1880. Late Perp clerestory and N chapel. The chapel arcade
with a polygonal projection to the chancel, demi-shafts to the
arch openings. – COMMUNION RAIL. C17. – STAINED GLASS
In the quatrefoil N aisle window figure perhaps of St John
C15. – Also small fragments in other windows. – WALL
PAINTINGS. Very extensive remains, discovered in 1939
The most easily visible are the figures in the clerestory: shep
herd, shepherd, King Herod, Magi, Virgin and Child. They
are of the early C15. Less enjoyable mostly what remains in the
aisles. N aisle: St Anne teaching the Virgin. A delightful figure
of *c.*1325. – Gigantic St Christopher, originally nearly 11 ft high
*c.*1350. – Seven Deadly Sins and Warning to Swearers. In the
centre Pietà. The devils and elegantly dressed youths are easily
recognized. Early C15. – In the s aisle, to the r. of the E window
a scroll pattern of *c.*1325. – Remains of a figure of the same
date to the l. of that window. – In the SE corner of the s aisle
wall Tree of Jesse in a beautifully interlaced ogee pattern
mid C14. – PLATE. Chalice, by *T.S.*, 1609.

OUR LADY OF MOUNT CARMEL (R.C.), High Street. 1855–6
Asymmetrical w front. The style of *c.*1300.

RECTORY. The elevation to the church shows a massive late C16
or early C17 chimney-flank. The chimneystacks bear out such
a date. The garden front rebuilt in the C19. Near by, a
HOUSE dated 1619.

46b GRAMMAR SCHOOL, *c.*200 yds SW. A satisfying composition in
a golden brown stone, its silhouette dominating the skyline
An oblong of five by one bays, steep hipped roof and dormer
to an attic above the schoolroom. Tall pedimented porch with
a doorway with broken triangular pediment, and a keyed
horizontally-oval light to the 'parvise'. The main windows o
the school proper with mullion-and-transom crosses. Inscrip
tion of the entablature in Roman lettering: 'Carolus: Read
Generosus: Hanc: Scolam: Disc . . . ratam: Fundavit: Anno
Domini: 1673.'

MOTTE. About 200 yards NW of the church is a large, low motte
oval in plan, with no sign of a bailey.

SECONDARY MODERN SCHOOL, ½ m. s, at Corby Glen
1960–2 by the county architect *J. W. H. Barnes.*

COUPLEDYKE HALL *see* FREISTON

COWBIT

2010

ST MARY. A confusing church. It is Perp, of brick, with low walls but signs of a much higher former roof. The centre part of the church is supposed to have been built by Prior de Moulton of Spalding *c.*1400. It was lengthened to the W, no doubt to link it up with the W tower, when this was built. The tower is quite stately, ashlar-faced, and usually connected with a consecration in 1487 by Bishop Russell of Lincoln. It has a quatrefoil frieze at the base. The W doorway has spandrels with tracery, and there is a five-light window over, and a niche above that. Also the tower is vaulted inside with diagonal and ridge ribs round a big circle for the bell-ropes. The rubble-built short chancel is also attributed to Bishop Russell, but its masonry makes an earlier origin likely. The only certain signs of a much earlier church are the enormous stones re-used in the S porch side walls and the heads from a corbel table re-used for the chancel roof. – PLATE. Chalice, 1697/1720.

ST GUTHLAC'S CROSS, 2 m. S, at Brotherhouse Bar. About 3 ft of a shaft with roll-moulded l. and r. framing of an inscription reading HANC PETRA GUTHLAC. This is supposed to mean that this stone marked a boundary of St Guthlac's Abbey Crowland. The shaft looks Norman (see the l. side moulding with a spur between two rolls), but is supposed to be one of those set up by Abbot Thurketyl early in the C10. (Another stone not far away, in a field, is about 2 ft high and known as KENULPH'S STONE.)

CRANWELL

0050

ST ANDREW. A small church, of nave and higher chancel. On the nave W gable the oddest of bellcotes. The wheel for the bell is placed vertically in a W–E direction and the bellcote itself curves up and ends in a semicircle. Is this C17 work? The NE angle of the nave, not now visible, has Anglo-Saxon long-and-short work. What is however visible enough and impressive enough is the Norman three-bay N arcade which was opened out of this Saxon nave early in the C12. Circular piers, cruciform abaci, round arches of a step, a chamfer, and a half-roll. Capitals with big scallops, the responds with upright leaves and volutes (E) and volutes and scallops inorganically combined (W). Billet-frieze on the hood-mould to nave as

well as aisle. The w bay was added E.E., and E.E. also th
w lancet, the n aisle w lancet, and one s lancet. On the s sid
also a Dec window. The chancel arch is E.E., but the chance
Perp. – SCREEN. Simple, Perp, of narrow one-light division
– BENCH ENDS. The panels set in are probably C17. – SCULP
TURE. Four interlace lengths of an Anglo-Saxon cross shaf
– STAINED GLASS. Odd bits in the w lancet. – PLATE. Chalic
Elizabethan; Paten, by *Daniel Garnier*(?), 1697.

ROYAL AIR FORCE COLLEGE, 1¾ m. w. The style – a red brick
stone-dressed Neo-Georgian Baroque – is what one woul
expect of the official grand manner of 1933. The plan consist
of a roughly rectangular central block linked by narrow corr
dors to quadrangular blocks open on one side, making a fron
tage of over 800 feet. The quadrangles are too sprawling an
affirmative to lead up naturally to the centre as it ought to b
in a Baroque composition. The main s front of the centre i
nineteen bays wide and has a giant Ionic order throughou
embracing two storeys; a hexastyle projecting portico, and
dome above a square substructure. Although this dome has a
the usual appendages – pilastered drum, columns breakin
forward and paired at the angles – it lacks sufficient statemen
The architect was *J. G. West*. In 1952 part of the main win
was converted into St Michael's Chapel, to designs of *Lawrenc
Bond*. It is small, just 50 by 15 ft, and its unity of design ha
produced a wholly satisfying effect. It achieves repose in th
same way as a chapel by Sir Ninian Comper. The surround
ings of the college are laid out with lime trees and lawns and
as is to be expected from a military establishment of thi
nature, they are immaculately kept.

0020

CREETON

ST PETER. Small, at the end of the village. Late C12 chance
arch with waterleaf capitals. Late C13 w tower. Twin bell
openings, the shafts – an unusual enrichment – with lea
capitals. Broach spire. Two tiers of lucarnes in the sam
directions. The tower arch has some dog-tooth. Above it
doorway not in axis. Late C13 also the s transept, see the
lancet. The s window is Victorian (restoration 1851–4).
PLATE. Paten, by *I.M.*, 1638; Chalice, by *I.Y.*, 1691.
SCULPTURE. In the churchyard two substantial pieces o
Anglo-Saxon cross shafts. One has the curious pattern of two
roundels connected by a staff and close patterning of chip

carved St Andrew's crosses l. and r. The pattern may be a
Norman alteration. The other has mostly interlace, but also
very bald scrolls of vegetable origin. (A third stone in the
wall by the s doorway.)

The hamlet huddles against the ancient boundaries of Grimsthorpe Park.

RECTORY. By *Edward Browning*, 1851 (GA).

CRESSY HALL see GOSBERTON

CROWLAND

2010

CROYLAND ABBEY. Croyland Abbey was founded in 716 to
commemorate the place on the island in the fen where St
Guthlac had made his habitation. His landing on the island
is illustrated in the bottom scene of the quatrefoil of the w
portal. His cell w of the w end of the s aisle was excavated
in 1908 but filled up again. The abbey, after Danish raids,
was rebuilt by Thurketyl early in the C10 and again after a
disastrous fire which took place in 1091. The fire and the beginning of the rebuilding are described in one of the most lively
accounts in any of the English medieval chronicles (*Historia
Croylandensis*) by Ingulph, the abbot himself under whom
they took place. However the rebuilding proper only started
under his successor Geoffrey of Orleans. The date of the start
is 1114, the architect the lay brother *Arnold*, to whom the
chronicle refers as 'cementarie artis scientissimo magistro'.
An earthquake interfered in 1117, a fire in 1146. Completion
is attributed to abbot Robert, who died in 1190. The solemn
translation of the relics of St Guthlac took place in 1195. In
1236 abbot Henry died who 'had renewed nearly the whole
church'. The E end was remodelled by Abbot Radulphus
before 1281. So much for the documents. They do not help
the architectural chronology much, as it is at once presented
by the w front of the church.

The s aisle front is Norman. No doorway. Four tiers of
blank arcading, the bottom one with small zigzag arches, i.e.
a good deal later than 1114, an upper one intersecting. To the
s the rubble walling where the w range of the monastic
quarters adjoined. To the N enough to recognize the shafted
Norman buttress, now hidden by a mighty Perp buttress.
This was in fact the N wall of the cell built w of the Norman
s aisle w wall, see its former doorway and an upper window.

The nave w wall was completely remodelled in the mid C13
18a The style is close to Westminster Abbey. w portal with fou
orders of shafts with stiff-leaf capitals. The doorway itse
divided by a renewed trumeau. Tympanum with a quatrefoi
containing four scenes from the life of St Guthlac surrounde
by stiff-leaf trails. To the l. and r. of the portal tall blan
panels with trefoiled arches. In each of the panels stood
figure on a corbel. Both corbels remain, but only one figure
She is similar to the mid-C13 work at Westminster and th
work of c.1260–70 at Lincoln, as is also the angel of the
corbel with its small round head and smiling face. The
followed the stage of the E.E. w window. Its tracery is gone
and its top too. But to the l. and r. are two tiers of two figure
each, below under gables, above in panels with Geometrica
tracery à la Westminster and Lincoln. The former springing
point of the E.E. window can be surmised. It was heightene
and received the Perp tracery of which signs remain. At th
same time the tiers of smaller figures in niches went up,
lower tier of two l. and two r., and an upper of eight and tw
smaller niches. The shape of the top gable is unknown. It i
assumed that the seated Christ now on the bridge (see below
was once in this gable.

The N aisle front was completely changed when the paro
chial N aisle received its mighty w tower in the second quarte
of the C15 (Abbot Lytlington, 1427–70). Of the Norma
buttress signs can again be seen, including some in the ce
off the present w porch to the s. This porch projects beyond
projection of the w tower. The latter makes it flush with th
big buttress between nave front and s aisle front. The porc
itself is two-storeyed. Inside, below, are the springers of
two-bay fan(?)-vault. Deep-panelled w doorway. All th
arches four-centred. The upper room is cruciform and has
window to the aisle. The w tower itself has on top of th
buttresses detached, diagonally-placed square buttress-shaft
connected with the tower by dainty flying buttresses. Ver
large six-light w window, five-light N window, six-light
window. Then, higher up, blank arcading including the lo
bell-openings and a short, rather stunted, recessed spire.

In the porch are many ARCHITECTURAL FRAGMENTS
Quite a number of them are Norman, and with fragments i
other places they allow the reconstruction of plenty of details
But as one walks round the tower one does not return ye
to Norman evidence. The N side is entirely the Perp parochia

aisle which was made out of the old aisle in 1405 when the
nave was also remodelled. It is widened in its w parts by three
chapels. These were provided by a will of 1394. Two have their
original four-light windows. Then, as if it were the chancel of
a parish church, three four-light windows, tall, with a transom up in the tracery. However, this seeming chancel is in
fact the E part of the N aisle. At its E end, still without entering,
one can see where the Perp aisle had its (panelled) arch into
the transept and also where its preceding Norman aisle had
its arch into the Norman transept (the s respond is exposed)
and where the gallery was above. Then the former Norman
crossing W arch and the start of the crossing N arch. They
are of course very tall. Zigzag in the arches. Nothing further
E, i.e. nothing of the late C13 chancel, remains above ground.
So we can now enter the ruined part, by crossing the Perp
pulpitum by one of its two doorways. We now look down the
nave westward. All seems here Perp, i.e. of the work of Lytlington, though it is not quite. On the N side the respond and
arch of the first Norman bay of the aisle arcade and gallery
arcade remain visible. On the s side only the gallery arch; for
in the C13 the lower part seems to have been replaced by a
giant (triple?) respond and an arch nearly up to the Norman
gallery arch. The gallery arches had a pretty motif on the
hood-moulds: flat, radially-placed leaves. The rest Perp. On
the N side a half-arch plus six arches plus the tower arch, all
compound piers with continuous mouldings. On the s side
the piers still stand detached, while on the N the enclosing
of the present parish church does not allow their N side to be
seen. Above the tall arcade was a wall passage, and then a
broad band of blank wall and high tall clerestory windows.
Their Perp tracery was all still there on the s side in the C18.
Now there is nothing of this left. The nave was vaulted, see
the springers. The aisles were also vaulted (and the N aisle still
is, as we shall see presently), see the springers in the s aisle.
Again a panelled arch to the transept.

Nothing else Norman; only the s aisle W wall with just one
blank shafted arch and the base of one pier underpinned with
a *mixtum compositum* of drums and shafts. E.E. of course the
inner wall of the W front. The segmental arch of the portal is
characteristic (cf. again Westminster).

Now into the parochial aisle. Through the broad panelled
tower E arch into the aisle itself. The vault is preserved. It is
a simple, uncomplicated tierceron-vault. The outer chapels

were also vaulted; see the springers. At the E end the arch
opening to the Norman transept is also visible inside. Of the
monastic premises nothing at all remains. The abbey in the
C14 to early C16 had between twenty-four and forty-one
monks, fewer than the layman would imagine, though more
than most other Lincolnshire monasteries.

FURNISHINGS. FONTS. An E.E. font, round with corner
shafts, is built into the tower arch as a stoup. – Simple octagonal Perp font. – COMMUNION RAIL. Georgian. – SCREEN
Partly Perp. One-light divisions. Some old colour. – PAINT-
ING. Panel with Moses and Aaron, C18, primitive. – PLATE
Chalice and Paten, by *T.S.*, 1681; Paten, by *John Stocker*(?),
1713; Almsbasin, by *Abraham Buteux*, 1725; two Cups (used
as vases), by *Robert Garrard*, 1830–1. – MONUMENTS. Under
the tower parts of a Perp tomb-chest. Also the large early
or mid-C14 incised slab to an architect, see his L-square and
dividers. Ci gist mastre William de Warmington, etc., is the
inscription. Above his head an ogee arch.

A view of the town from Welland Bank Bridge still provides an
intimate picture of its early monastic seclusion. The tower and
ruins of the abbey rise above the trees, and the road into
town follows the line of the embankments built to keep the
waters out. The wide streets were planted in the late C18
with islands of trees that swing through the village in a
serpentine line – an unusual treatment of great beauty. As
one walks w from the abbey façade one soon has the MANOR
HOUSE on the l. This is dated 1690. It is a modest piece,
typical for its date anywhere in a small provincial place. Five-
bay front, below stone, above brick. Two storeys. Wooden
mullion-and-transom-cross windows. Hipped roof. The
garden front is really a 'Great Room', a brick addition,
perhaps of 1775. The centre a tripartite doorway with a semicircular window above. The style is possibly that of *William
Sands the Younger* of Spalding, as is that of the STABLES dated
1775. Then almost at once the TRIANGULAR BRIDGE, called
by Gough 'the greatest curiosity in Britain, if not in Europe'.
Three arches joined to each other at an angle of 120 degrees.
The function of the bridge was to serve three streams at the
junction of the Nene and Welland. Its date is the later C14,
although in 943 a similar bridge is mentioned.* The bridge
may also have been the base of a great cross. The mouldings
of the arch ribs partly hollow chamfers, partly wavy chamfers

33a

* 'A Ponte de Croyland triangulo per aquam de Weland.'

– SCULPTURE. Large seated figure, probably Christ, and quite possibly from the gable of the abbey w front. The date certainly seems to be that of the w front.

SCHOOL, Postland Road. 1856. Brick, one-storeyed, but the boys' and the girls' parts joined by a crazy, completely asymmetrical centre piece with steep gable, oriel, and spirelet.

CULVERTHORPE HALL

0040

A late C17 house mostly remodelled in the C18, and l. and r. of its s front two detached ranges of office buildings at r. angles. That to the E is possibly of the early C17. It has traditional features such as two-light windows. That to the w has arched doorways in pedimented projections, cross windows, and steeply gabled dormers. This may be contemporary with the bones of the centre part of the present house, rebuilt c.1679 for Sir John Newton. The house is two and a half storeys high and had originally probably seven windows to the s and seven to the N. To it, today, the steep-pitched roof and a pair of centrally placed stacks probably belong. The type may have conformed to a fairly advanced Artisan Mannerism such as that of 19 St George's Square, Stamford (see p. 676). John and Susanna Newton succeeded in 1699 and improved the N front 48a in a delightful and individual way: they added a grand staircase and gave it a projection in the centre of the old N porch. Quoins at the angles, fluted Ionic columns to the door, a taller staircase window above with pendant fruit swags, scrolls at the base, and a panel of fruit and flowers over. The modillion brackets to the cornice are grouped 3–2–2–2–3, each one elaborately scaled and decked with an acanthus leaf. The cornice and parapet provide added height above the coping level of the attic. The mason-contractors (and probably designers) of this addition were *William* and *Edward Stanton*, employed in 1704–5.* By 1734 Sir Michael Newton had begun extensions taking the form of lower wings attached to the E and w sides. The wings have to the s a Venetian window each, a lunette window below in the basement, and a sculptured roundel above. To the N they appear two-storeyed. Sir Michael also began colonnades to extend from these wings outward. A start was made with a pair of large attached columns on the w and E sides and smaller pedimented doorways between them. But nothing followed. The state with the colonnade is shown in a view by Badeslade dateable to c.1740. Sir Michael further

* According to family papers studied by Mr Colvin.

also altered the fenestration of the S front, giving it five more
generously spaced bays, the ground-floor windows with
pediments, and added an entrance porch. All this work is
Palladian in character, and Palladian also are the obelisk
chimneys.* The compressed Ionic elevation of the porch is
articulated with niches, sculpture, and moulded arched
windows. The architect may have been *Robert Morris*, who
dedicated to Sir Michael the 1734 edition of his *Lectures*. In
both this book and the *Select Architecture* there are plans
similar to Culverthorpe as projected.‡

The interiors are competent. The staircase is of c.1699 with
a spacious open well, three twisted balusters to the tread and
nice details such as inlay panels to the risers. The walls were
painted before 1704 by *Louis Hauduroy* with the story of
Psyche. Only the Marriage remains, but now whitewashed
over. The old centre of the S front is entirely taken up by a
tripartite HALL with two screens of paired fluted Corinthian
columns. From the middle part access is direct to the staircase. To the r. of the hall the DINING ROOM (former morning
room) with an odd demi-screen behind the Venetian window
i.e. just the entablature jutting forward from the walls as
far as two Corinthian columns, but not continued, so as not
to interfere with the arch of the Venetian window. In the other
wing the DRAWING ROOM, a fine white and gold room. The
decorative ensemble of Culverthorpe Hall is in a rich mid-
Georgian style. One chimneypiece was supplied by *John
Bossom* of Greenwich in 1740. A secondary STAIR remains
from the 1679 house: a composition of leathery interlacing
openwork panels. The garden was rearranged in 1912. Two
wrought-iron panels on the N vista came from the CHAPEL,
where they were probably altar rails. This building was
designed in 1691, and its façade has been re-erected at the
end of the E ride in a wood close to the road from Culverthorpe
village to Rauceby. Tetrastyle Ionic portico and pediment.
Such temple fronts for chapels were still rare in the late C17.

3030

DAWSMERE
4½ m. NE of Gedney

CHRIST CHURCH. 1869. Yellow and red brick, nave and semicircular apse under one slate roof and without structural

* Obelisk chimneys appear at Chiswick c.1725.
‡ For this information I am indebted to my wife. Mr Colvin has also found
that Morris was employed on Sir Michael's London house in Burlington
Street in 1731–2.

division inside. Small lancet windows. Wooden flèche. The interior faced with red rick. Thin timber roofs, but all the same a little church of some character. – Original BENCHES, very functional and well and truly pegged.

IOUSE, ⅝ m. E. Georgian, five bays, two storeys, parapet.

DEEPING GATE see DEEPING ST JAMES

DEEPING ST JAMES

T JAMES. The church was the church of a Benedictine priory founded from Thorney Abbey in 1139. That explains its size and certain unparochial features. Externally one thinks at first one is concerned with a church of the Norfolk–Lincolnshire border country, long and Perp, but one or two things do not fit from the beginning. One has nothing to do with the monastic past either. It is the w tower of *c.*1730 at the latest,* a very interesting piece in that it clearly tries to be medieval, though all is done with blunt round arches, Vanbrughian rather than Kentian. The three-light w window and the pairs of two-light bell-openings deserve particular notice. The tower also carries, though behind a balustrade, a proper spire *du pays* with two tiers of lucarnes in the same directions. *Portwood* may be suggested as its architect, on the strength of the tower of Witham-on-the-Hill. The other surprising details of the exterior prepare for what the interior is going to demonstrate. Along the N side of the nave runs a Norman zigzag frieze. That gives a date, and it also establishes that this priory church never had a N aisle. So now first inside. There is the astounding S arcade, seven bays long and continued by a long chancel. It has its problems. The w respond and the first pier are quatrefoil with slenderer shafts in the diagonals and have Norman scallop capitals, perhaps not made for them. There are round abaci embracing the whole quatrefoil, and moulded round arches, Late Norman or rather late C12. The second pier is the same but has a plain moulded capital. Then the piers keel the diagonal shafts, and the abaci have a square stepped plan, and so they carry on. On the N side are now large Perp windows, but their shafted surrounds inside are E.E. Where they end to the E follows the arch of a chapel or transept which has responds of the same type as the E piers

12a

* *Reports & Papers* 1871 say 1735, but a date 1732 is scratched into the wall outside. Canon Binnall's date is 1717.

of the s arcade and waterleaf capitals. To continue with the
s arcade, the strangest thing is the two springers of transverse
arches from the third and fifth piers. Whatever they had been
meant to perform, they can never have been built; for above
the s arcade runs a wall passage of pointed arches on shafts
in front of single-lancet clerestory windows. These lancets
also continued originally further E, i.e. where the arcade was
replaced by the plain wall of the chancel. Externally one sees
nothing of the clerestory, as it lies below the present aisle roof.
Externally indeed of all this early work there is nothing visible
except for two tall, shafted, round-headed chancel windows.
Inside, between the end of the arcade and these windows
there is one bay of close blank arches on corbels (sedilia?)
then the double piscina and above a tall blank arch with stiff-
leaf capitals. Then two windows follow and are richly shafted.
There is also big dog-tooth here, i.e. we are in full E.E. E.E.
also the s porch entrance, its hood-mould with dog-tooth.
Then the C14. To its beginning belong the two s aisle
windows. Their tracery, all with rolls, strikes one at first
as Geometrical, but ogee forms are used. Inside two piscinas,
i.e. the wall was indeed provided with two altars. The other
s aisle windows are different, much more the ordinary Lincolnshire Dec. Dec also one two-light N window and the pretty
chancel N doorway. Its ogee arch is formed by two mouchettes
– a nice conceit. Finally what gives the church its external
character: the large three-light Perp N and S windows. –
FONT. Circular, Norman, with intersecting arches. – PLATE
Paten, by *Benjamin Watts*, 1715; Chalice, by *Richard Bayley*,
1728; secular Cup, by *W. Bellchambers*, 1834. – MONUMENTS
Early C14 Knight, his head under an ogee canopy. His body
is hidden or covered and only his feet stick out. – The other
effigy is later C14, though there is still dog-tooth in the rim.
Was it earlier and remodelled? – CURIOSUM. The church
preserves one of the rare GRAVESIDE SHELTERS for the
parson to keep dry during rainy burial services.

OUR LADY OF LINCOLN AND ST GUTHLAC (R.C.), NE of and
  a little distance from the bridge (*see* below). The building is
  of no interest, but in it are two pieces of SCULPTURE. One is
  a moving wooden Crucifixus of *c*.1330, said to come from
  Belgium but in its style dependent on Cologne. The other is
  a wooden Virgin of *c*.1500 from the old cathedral at Boulogne.
  – FONT. Octagonal, Dec. Shallow fields with ogee arches and
  in the spandrels heads, beasts, etc.

HE PRIORY, N of the church. Mid C17, H-shaped, with a central two-storeyed, gabled porch. The windows of two, three, and four lights. The early stair remains.

ECTORY. By *Edward Browning*, 1839 (GA).

ARKET CROSS. C15 and once ambitious. A high square base with two tiers of steps at the angles. Tracery, ogee-cusped panels and crenellations. The shaft was destroyed when the cross was converted into a lock-up in 1819.

ARN, N of the Cross. C17. Of stone. Nine bays, buttressed.

rom Deeping St James to DEEPING GATE cottages run on both sides of the Welland. Nos 40–44 CHURCH STREET has two projecting wings. It is dated 1688, but rebuilt. At Deeping Gate the BRIDGE. Three nearly semicircular arches with two slight chamfers. (Dated 1651. MHLG) Near by, and also C17, a cottage with canted-out oriel.

ROGNALL, ½ m. NE. A particularly attractive grey stone and clunch hamlet, almost purely vernacular. One C17-style cottage dated 1744.

DEEPING ST NICHOLAS

T NICHOLAS. 1845–6 by *C. Kirk*. A substantial, rock-faced edifice in the Dec style. Four-light E and five-light W windows with flowing tracery. N tower with pinnacles and a broach spire with lucarnes. – MONUMENT in lieu of an Easter Sepulchre. Also Dec with its ogee canopy. It commemorates William and Nicholas Clarke Stevenson † 1844 and 1843 and was designed in 1847 by *R. C. Hussey*.

HE HOLLIES, ½ m. NE. Brick, of two and a half storeys. Doorway with fluted columns and broken pediment. Late Georgian.

DEMBLEBY

¾ m. SW of Aunsby

T LUCIA. 1867–8 by *C. Kirk* of Sleaford. Norman, rock-faced. Nave and chancel with apse. Twin bellcote. No-one would expect to find in such a church what may well be the finest PILLAR PISCINA in the country. The shaft has a polygonal front with horizontal zigzag. On the bowl three scallops with rosettes and above them a band of three tiers of very small St Andrew's crosses. The chancel arch is original Late Norman work and has waterleaf capitals. It is far too rudely scraped.

DENTON

ST ANDREW. Tall, five-stage Perp W tower with several decora
tive little niches. Twin three-light windows below the be
stage, tall pairs of two-light bell-openings. Quatrefoil frie
battlements, pinnacles. The N doorway with three slig
chamfers probably Transitional (cf. the two early bases
piers of the N arcade inside). The N aisle windows – thr
lights, with intersecting tracery – of c.1300. The chan
sedilia and piscina Dec. So the Perp windows (E four light
must be an alteration. The clerestory windows look Dec, b
seem to go with the arcades of octagonal piers inside who
castellated capitals spell the Perp style. The arcade is of fo
bays on the S side, but starts one bay further E on the
Double-chamfered arches. The two-bay N chapel arcade, t
chancel arch, and the tower arch all have the castellated capit
too. – FONT. Octagonal, Perp. – ORGAN CASE. By *Bentle*
1887. The front in Renaissance forms, which is interestin
but the sides with quite original details only describable
Arts and Crafts, which is equally interesting. – STAINI
GLASS. Original fragments in a chancel S window. – T
adjoining window by *Kempe*, 1901. – PLATE. Chalice, Spanis
C17; Paten, by *John Becke*, 1707; Almsdish, by *Benjamin Pyn*
1710; Chalice and Cover, by *Humphrey Payne*, 1712; Flago
by *Alex Roode* or *John Ruslem*, 1712; Almsbasin, by *Thom*
Ewesdin, 1714. – MONUMENTS. Effigy of a Priest, sunk, und
a trefoiled canopy; C14 (chancel). – John Blyth † 1602. Stor
with a recumbent effigy on a half-rolled-up mattress. Agai
the tomb-chest the children standing frontally, their nam
marked above them. Back panel with big inscription, colum
and a pediment. – Richard Welby, erected 1714. By *Gre*
of Camberwell. Life-size statue on a base. Reredos backgrou
with pilasters. Outside the pilasters two mourning putti (n
the tears). Above the statue two putti holding a metal coron
– Susanna Gregory, erected before 1755. Tablet with volu
l. and r. At the foot skull, bats' wings, a serpent biting
tail (a symbol of eternity), and an hourglass. By *Thomas Tayl*
Below the church lies the lake of the Welbys' DENTON MANO
Sir Arthur Blomfield's house of 1883 has gone, except for
stabling. At the time of writing it is being replaced by one
Marshall Sisson. The Georgian parkscape is notable. In it
two SPRINGS. One pours from a lion mask set in a rusticat
wall and guarded by Flora; the other is called ST CHRIST

PHER'S WELL and is a dim dank GROTTO opening on to the lake. Inside are ammonites, coloured stones, and verses ending:

> 'Approach you then with cautious steps
> To where the streamlet creeps
> Or Ah! too rudely you may wake
> Some guardian nymph that sleeps 1823'

Also in the park, but close to the church, to the s, are the Welby Almshouses.

WELBY ALMSHOUSES. In the nature of a folly or conceit. 46a Dated 1653 and built of ironstone with grey stone dressings. The roofs end in pairs of shaped gables, each with its outline accompanied by a stone ribbon ending in a double-curve flourish. In the gables large horizontally-oval keyed-in windows. Below on the N side a sham doorway and a three-light window each side. On the W front is a smaller beribboned gable of the same variety. A massive array of six chimney-stacks rises from between the two roof ridges.

KEYS HOUSE. Immediately E of the church. Once the school-house. In the traditional Queen Anne style, an oblong of two storeys with a hipped roof, dormers, and a central stack. Quoins and window heads of dressed stone, and a big stone doorway with an open triangular pediment enclosing the Welby armorial and the inscription 'Learn to know God and Thyself 1720'.

RECTORY. It looks 1840s and may therefore be that known to have been built by *A. Salvin* (GA).

OLD MANOR HOUSE, at the SE end of the village. Now L-shaped, but perhaps the fragment of a larger house. Gables with three- and four-light windows and three projections to the street. One piece of display a Serlian garden gate with alternately blocked pilasters and three stone balls on square bases. House and gate are of about 1640.

The village is long and L-shaped, spreading around the confines of the park and the patronage of the Welby family. It belongs in character rather to Leicestershire and the Belvoir country than to Lincolnshire. The predominant stone is a warmly rich golden ironstone. Among the vernacular cottages are admirable examples of C19 and C20 estate building, showing the appreciation among firmly-rooted local builders of the *genius loci*.

DIGBY   005a

ST THOMAS MARTYR. The SE quoin of the nave can only be understood as Anglo-Saxon long-and-short work. Otherwise there is nothing Anglo-Saxon, but there is the Norman doorway. One order of shafts with decorated scallop capitals. Zigzag and lozenges in the arch.* So we turn to the tower, o *c.*1200 in its lowest parts, see the ground-floor W lancet and the single-chamfered tower arch, and see also the fact that according to its E wall, the tower was originally narrower to the N than the present N arcade. Yet this N arcade is not much later than the tower. Both arcades are of three bays. They have quatrefoil piers with fillets and thin shafts in the diagonals and double-chamfered arches. The capitals differ, and those of the N arcade are earlier. Yet a little later the W bay of the N aisle, which projects W as far as the tower. But even this still has lancet windows to W and N. The S aisle has a W lancet too, and this has nailhead decoration in the hood-mould. Earlier E.E. again the chancel, see the chancel arch with stiff-leaf capitals and the lancet windows. The chancel was rebuilt in 1881. Later than the E.E. contributions are the bell-openings of the tower, the S aisle E window with its flowing tracery, and the N aisle windows (E reticulated tracery). Finally Perp the clerestory of six closely-set windows arranged in pairs and the tower top with its decorated parapet, pinnacles, and recessed crocketed spire (one tier of lucarnes). – SCREEN. Of one-light divisions with ogee arches and panel tracery over. – PULPIT. Minor Jacobean. – BENCH ENDS. Many, with rather coarse tracery and poppy-heads. – AUMBRY. With bits of Early Renaissance and late C17 woodwork. Another length of the Early Renaissance frieze in the N aisle at the E end. – STAINED GLASS. In the N aisle E window some fragments. – PLATE. Chalice and Paten Cover, Elizabethan.

SE of the church a restored VILLAGE CROSS and SW of the church a LOCK-UP like a pepper-pot, hardly high enough to stand up in.‡

₉₀₇₀
DODDINGTON

ST PETER. 1771–5 by *Thomas and William Lumby*. A very remarkable building, Gothic more than Gothick, except for the W tower, which still has all the Strawberry Hill prettiness: W doorway with niches l. and r. and lushly foliated and crocketed ogee gables. A circular window above, and bell-openings with Y-tracery. What made it possible for the architects to

* The Norman-looking head of the chancel N low-side window is not original.

‡ In a private garden are the remains of a CROSS with acanthus decoration attached to spiral bands. *Arch. J.* LXXXIII.

produce so convincing a nave and aisles and chancel is that they could copy a part of the N aisle which had remained from the Dec building (engraved by Kip). The S aisle was built entirely afresh, both W windows are of the 1770s too, and the battlements were continued in the original form. The chancel E window is more doubtful. It is supposed to date from 1729 but may be a Victorian replacement. The N and S aisle windows are straight-topped, of three ogee-headed lights to the N and S and to the E and W of four lights with flowing tracery. Inside, the two-bay arcades have octagonal piers and double-chamfered arches, and only the capitals are not correct enough for a Victorian date. – FONT. E.E., tub-shaped, with, along the top part, a wide band of simple, diagonally placed stiff-leaf. – PLATE. Chalice, by *John Morley* of Lincoln, *c.*1569; Almsbasin, by *D.R.*, 1670; Flagon, by *John Bodington*, 1706; Paten, by *William Fawdery*, 1706.

DODDINGTON HALL. To come across Doddington in the remote Lincolnshire fields is a surprise. The house belongs in fact to that group of advanced Late Elizabethan Midland houses which includes Worksop Manor, Wollaton, and Hardwick Hall. All are by *Robert Smithson*, and there is good reason to attribute Doddington also to him.* It was built between 1593 and 1600 for Thomas Taylor, the Bishop of Lincoln's Recorder. It has changed little since then, or since the engraving of *c.*1705 by Kip. Entrance to the forecourt is gained by a gatehouse in the vernacular style. This has shaped gables, two-light windows, and a renewed flattish archway. The style is Late Tudor, that is conservative, rather than in the advanced spirit of the house. Spreading cedars prevent an immediate comprehension of its façade. It is sophisticated and austere. The plan is an elongated H. The projections run E and W. On the entrance, i.e. E, front in the corners to the wings are extruded square bays, and in the centre is a porch bay of the same proportions. The l. extruded corner houses the secondary staircase, the r. one is there for symmetry's sake. All three bays rise above the parapet and finish with tall, octagonal, bulgy domed cupolas, each one big enough for a summer house, and each leading on to the flats. Only the porch with Tuscan columns and finials and cresting is a little fussy.‡ Otherwise the effect is broad and

* And he was designing for Lord Sheffield in the N of the county, perhaps Normanby, cf. p. 324.

‡ Kip shows little peaks protruding up from the parapet.

smooth. The fenestration is quite regular, with equal
spaced transomed three- and four-light windows. On t'
N and s fronts are paired projecting chimney-flanks. The
are quoined and chamfered, and support moulded bric
columns. In addition, the stairwell projects deeply on the
front. The overall fenestration here was slightly re-arrange
40b   in the c18. The w (garden) front repeats the system of th
E front, except for the extruded angles and the replacement
window bays three and seven by chimney-flanks. Also on th
ground floor the windows of the centre (except for one whic
may be altered) are much smaller and set higher up. What ma
be the reason? Smithson's Worksop Manor (before 159.
is an obvious parallel to Doddington, but Doddington ca
be compared to several other Smithson houses as we'
Equally, the low undecorated silhouette of Doddington ant
cipates the N front of Hatfield (c.1607) or the façade
Quenby. Of the original INTERIOR little remains. Entranc
is still into the hall at one end, that is into the tradition
screens passage, but the screens have gone. Now the notab
rooms are those altered for Sir John Hussey Delaval in 176
and they are by the Lincoln carpenter *Thomas Lumby* (s
above). His joinery is excellent, and he reveals his skill in th
manipulation of the stairs, rising by a single flight and return
ing by a double one. For economy of line it is remarkab
advanced. The long gallery is also Georgian and extends th
length of the w front on the second floor. In the small garde
are two rusticated gatepiers.

2030   # DONINGTON

ST MARY AND THE HOLY ROOD. Except for the priest's doo
way in the chancel, which has a little nailhead decoration an
is E.E., this is a Dec-cum-Perp church. Dec is its outstandi
feature, the s steeple standing proudly detached so that,
one passes through it – for it acts as a porch – one enters th
aisle, not the nave. The steeple is 143 ft high. The porc
entrance with its responds and finely moulded arch shows th
date. Niches in the buttresses and above the entrance. Ta'
two-light bell-openings. The spire is recessed and has thre
tiers of lucarnes in alternating directions. Inside a strang
vault, a combination of a two-bay quadripartite rib-vault
not unusual in porches and a ring as usual in towers. Th
mouldings of the s doorway are very dainty. Ogee-heade
niche over with a seated figure. The w doorway into the na

is Dec too. It is placed under a protecting depressed ogee arch with thick square leaves. The N aisle W window is a piece of uncommon Dec design with four ogee-headed lights, but otherwise cusped intersecting which is not at once recognizable, because the head of the window is a four-centred arch. Finally Dec the s aisle windows: the E window of four lights, flowing tracery and slim shafts inside as well as outside; the s window with ogee-headed lights and no further tracery, under a depressed four-centred arch. Only the W window is Perp (four lights too), and so is the five-light nave W window, the E window of the chancel (five lights), the embattled clerestory, and the impressive long line of the N aisle and chapel, eight bays altogether, with nine buttresses. Inside, seven-bay arcades, also Perp, with tall octagonal piers and castellated capitals. The W end instead of responds has two corbels. They are specially enjoyable little figures. The E corbels are two shield-holding angels. L. and r. of the altar are two doorways, now blocked. They may have led into a low E vestry as they occur in Norfolk (e.g. Little Coates, Lindsey),* or into a relic chamber which visitors to the church could pass through. The N recess with the remains of steps was connected with the upper room of another vestry, perhaps a priest's room or a watching loft for those who wanted to visit the relics or relic. The dedication of the church suggests that a relic of the Holy Cross may have been kept here. – FONT. Dec, octagonal, stem and bowl in one, Dec window patterns under crocketed gables. – The upper part of another FONT near by. This also had blank window patterns.‡ – Square-headed BENCH ENDS with tracery; s aisle. – MONUMENT. Matthew Flinders † 1814, the explorer. Tablet by *Whitelaw*, with a ship in the 'predella'; draped urn at the top. – CURIOSUM. One of the few GRAVEYARD SHELTERS, which allowed the parson to stand dry by the graveside during funerals in the rain.

n CHURCH STREET an C18 house with Venetian windows and an Ionic pediment over the door. No. 22 is Late Georgian, in local brown brick, with single-bay side wings and sloping side walls.

RAMMAR SCHOOL. Founded in 1719 and rebuilt in 1812. Porch with segmental pediment.

* And also several places in Norfolk and All Saints Hereford.
‡ The Rev. F. C. Hodgkinson tells me that the second bowl is the original ne, the first a Victorian replacement.

DORRINGTON

ST JAMES AND ST JOHN. The church has a Transitional towe
arch with stiff-leaf capitals and already a double-chamfere
pointed arch. The simple N doorway could be of the sam
time. Then the C13 arcades. Two bays, the N pier quatrefoi
with dog-tooth up the diagonals, the S octagonal with ele
mentary capitals. C13 also the chancel, see the side lancet
and the chancel arch. The E window with its reticulate
tracery, the roll moulding applied externally to mullions an
tracery, and the shafted ogee-headed niches l. and r. inside, i
of course Dec, as is the W tower higher up. It is a tall towe
ashlar-faced and with impressively little in the way of fenes
tration. The Dec bell-openings are tall and of two lights. Th
top parapet looks bald now, but originally there was a spire
Dec also the N and S aisle windows, the latter under segment:
arches. The mouldings of the S doorway are characteristicall
Dec too, as is the ogee-headed niche by the E window. Lat
Perp clerestory with uncusped windows. – SCULPTURE
Outside, above the E window, two lengths of a frieze or
tympanum of the Last Judgement, clearly C13. The l. piec
shows figures climbing out of their graves, the r. piece th
mouth of hell. Where do they come from ? – BENCH ENDS. I
the chancel, with poppy-heads. Two of them are heads.
PLATE. Chalice, by *John Morley* of Lincoln(?), *c.*1571.
MONUMENT. Anthony Oldfield and family, erected accordin
to a will of 1715, but so chaste and purely architectural wit
its pilasters and segmental pediment that a date about 1725–3
seems more likely.
Several cottages – e.g. KEW COTTAGE – show the conservatis
of the Lincolnshire Vernacular as late as the C19. One three
bay, cemented house in the main street has giant pilaste
starting at first-floor level.

DOWSBY

ST ANDREW. Perp W tower, the arch to the nave with castellate
capitals. E.E. N arcade of three bays, quatrefoil piers (mor
than semicircular foils) with fillets. Moulded arches. Patera
with stiff-leaf of a former hood-mould. The S arcade (octa
gonal piers, double-chamfered arches) is later. – SCULPTURE
Parts of an Anglo-Saxon cross shaft with interlace, now i
the S aisle E wall outside. C10 or C11. – PLATE. Chalice an
Cover and two Almsplates, by *Arte Dicken*, 1720; Flagon, b

Robert Cox, 1755. – MONUMENT. Effigy of the C14 under a nodding ogee canopy, angels to its l. and r. Angle-shafts, angle-buttress-shafts, and finials. The effigy, probably a Civilian, has been mercilessly converted into an Elizabethan Lady.

DOWSBY HALL. What remains of Sir William Rigdon's house, built between 1603 and 1610, is uncommonly interesting, because as Sir John Summerson has shown, it was probably designed by *John Thorpe*. There are two plans of Rigdon's house in the famous Thorpe Album (Thorpe 27, 28) that are patently designs rather than surveys. The problem presented by Dowsby is its s front, for this is entirely blank wall and most unusual if the house has not been truncated at some time, possibly in the C18. What one would expect is some sort of duplication, or doubling, of the present house so that the E front would present a symmetrical elevation. Yet curiously the plan of Dowsby today is close to those by Thorpe. The s front shows clearly the two gables of a double ridge roof with an impressive row of chimneystacks in the valley, paired 3–2–2–2. The E front provides a better idea of Rigdon's interpretation of Thorpe's designs: a soaring elevation of three bays with ample fenestration. Bays one and two, grouped as a pair, have on the ground floor twelve lights with two mullions and three (now two) transoms; above are six lights of two mullions and one transom. Bay three is canted but has similar fenestration plus the addition of single lights to the canted faces. The two gables surmounting this 2–1 sequence of bays have respectively a four- and five-light mullion under a flat cornice, and finial terminations. Gable two, because of the canted bay, is corbelled out. Oddly the N and s fronts are of brick, not stone. The N has an unsatisfactory array of windows of two, three, six, and eight lights; the W front a canted bay similar to that on the E but now minus its gables, and adjacent two storeys of six-light windows, quite plain. The interior much altered.

DRY DODDINGTON

ST JAMES. Unbuttressed W tower with early C14 bell-openings. The spire proudly started with big steep broaches, but then finished humbly. Nave of 1876–7, but Norman doorway with flat zigzag on jambs and arch. In the N aisle a small E lancet. Four-bay arcades with octagonal piers and double-chamfered arches. The N capitals plainer than the s; both late C13 to

early C14. Richly leaf-carved chancel arch of 1876–7 – th
whole of the vicar's garden and a bird for good measure.

DUNSBY
1020

ALL SAINTS. In the chancel, visible from the N chapel, a fla
buttress which may be Norman. E.E. the S doorway wit
damaged stiff-leaf capitals. E.E. also the S arcade. Four bays
round piers with octagonal abaci. Double-chamfered arche
The N arcade has octagonal piers. The chancel (with a littl
nailhead) also E.E. Dec N chapel; see the nobbly foliage c
the capitals. Dec W tower. The arch to the nave also wit
bands of nobbly foliage. Triple-chamfered arch. Crockete
gablets on the buttresses. In the niche to the W with it
crocketed gable stands a STATUE of Christ, C15 it seems
Two-light bell-openings. The fenestration of the clerestor
and much else of the restoration of 1857. – FONT. Octagona
Perp, in the fields an inscription carried right round (c
Bourne). It reads 'Jesus Christ Maria Baptista', and in th
eighth panel what Cox interpreted as '*in principio*'. – PLAT
Chalice and Cover, by *D.R.*, 1671.

DUNSTON
0060

ST PETER. Mostly 1874–6 by *R. H. Carpenter*, paid for by th
Marquis of Ripon (*see* Nocton). But the following medieva
parts remained or were re-used. Unbuttressed W tower wit
(renewed) two-light W window. Transitional S porch entranc
with round hood-mould decorated with dog-tooth. E.E. S door
way with two orders of shafts and stiff-leaf capitals. Als
probably the N arcade of four bays. Quatrefoil piers an
double-chamfered arches. Carpenter's work is remembere
for the strange cusping of his Y- and intersecting tracery.
PLATE. Chalice and Paten Cover, London, 1569; Chalice, by
John Morley of Lincoln(?), *c.*1571.

DUNSTON PILLAR, 4 m. W. Square, tapering pillar. Built as a
lighthouse in 1751 by Sir Francis Dashwood to guide traveller
over the desolate heath. Inscribed on the W side: 'Columnan
Hanc Utilitati Publicae D·D·D· F Dashwood M·DCC·LI'. I
1810 the Earl of Buckingham substituted a statue of Georg
III for the lantern. This was by *Mrs Coade* and modelled b
Joseph Panzetta. It seems that the mason for this later wor
was *John Willson*, who fell off the pillar to his death:

'He who erected the noble King
Is here now laid by Death's sharp sting'.

His tomb is in Harmston churchyard (*see* p. 566). In recent years the statue has been removed.

DYKE *see* BOURNE

EAGLE

3060

LL SAINTS. Unbuttressed w tower E.E.; the bell-openings pairs of small lancets. The rest by *J. T. Lee*, 1904. – FONT. E.E. circular shaft with angle spurs. Of the drum-shaped Norman bowl only the lower part is preserved. It had blank arcading with coupled shafts. A few fragments of the upper part built into the E aisle w wall inside.

ʜᴇ JUNGLE, 1 m. NNE. Spidery and vegetable-like, an ancestor of Gaudí, if ever there was one. Built *c*.1820. There is no better description than one of 1826: 'Samuel Russell Collett Esq has had erected a very singular but tasty and handsome Residence. It is composed of overburnt bricks until they run together in large masses, these are built up in that rough state forming a centre and two circular corners in the manner of a castle & has a grotesque but not inelegant appearance.'* The frames of the windows and doors are made from oak branches formed into Gothic arches. Have we here another confection by Mr *Lovely* of Branston (*see* p. 484)? At the time of writing most of the front is heavily hung with ivy. Collett acquired a Zoo that included deer, pheasants, buffalo, and kangaroos.

EASTON PARK

9020

ʜere has been a medieval house, one of 1805, and a later Victorian one. All have gone. The terraced gardens are still spectacular in the French formal way in which they were laid out in the C19 for the Cholmley family. Seven terraces descend one side of a valley to a stream. Then the *allée* continues to an iron grille flanked by pavilions, then yet further to gates on the Grantham road. It must all have been in emulation of near-by Stoke Rochford, as that was in emulation of near-by Harlaxton. On the hill to the E of the main axis is a tall archway with an open pediment. Behind this is a startlingly sinister pit. The visitor wades through deep grass, stumbling over stone dogs peering up at him.

* By Major-General J. H. Lofts, quoted from Barbara Jones's classic on llies.

0020

EDENHAM

ST MICHAEL. The church has E.E. arcades of four bays. Th
w part has quatrefoil piers with fillets, thin diagonal shaft
with shaft-rings, and over the whole one round abacus. The
piers are a little different (shaft-rings e.g. right round the
piers), but not significantly so. The chancel arch goes with th
E bay. E.E. also the s doorway. One order of shafts, stiff-lea
capitals. Arch with many mouldings. Some dog-tooth. De
N aisle windows with transoms. Perp w tower. Clasping but
tresses, doorway with traceried spandrels. Five-light w win
dow. Four-light bell-openings, of two plus two with the middl
mullion reaching up into the apex. Quatrefoil frieze. Tal
pinnacles. Ornate Perp s porch. Frieze with various motifs
Perp s aisle windows. Perp clerestory. – FONT. Large, drum
shaped without a stem. Around, shafts carrying oddly two
lobed arches. Late C12? – LECTERN. A brass eagle assigned
to the C17. – BENCH ENDS. With poppy-heads; few.
STAINED GLASS. In the N aisle. By *Baillie & Mayer*, c.1865-
70. – SCULPTURE. In the s aisle at the w end, high up an
probably re-used, a large Anglo-Saxon roundel with fou
scrolls in it. It is 2 ft or 2 ft 6 in. in diameter. What can it hav
been? – Equally mysterious a part of a cross shaft at the v
end. On one a St John, half man half bird, early C9. On th
other piece in a niche seated figure holding something. I
could be a Virgin. Clapham considers her a later alteration. –
PLATE (all silver-gilt). Oval Dish, by *Friedrich Hirschvogel*
Nuremberg, 1619; Chalice, Dutch, inscribed 1692; Chalice
Augsburg, early C18, knop by *C. T. & G. Fox*, 1847; pair o
Italian Candlesticks, C18; Incense Boat.

See
p.
768

   MONUMENTS. The church contains the monuments t
Berties, Lords Willoughby of Eresby (cf. Spilsby) and late
Dukes of Ancaster – a series larger than that in any othe
Lincolnshire church. Of c.1300 the following stone effigies
Civilian and Lady (tower). – Lady (E of the tower). Very larg
angels hold her pillow. – Later C14 Knight and Lady (tower)
she under a nodding ogee canopy, he already with the low
belt of the later C14. They lie on a tomb-chest with shields in
lively foiled and cusped fields. – Two HELMS above. – Bras
of an Archbishop (18 in.), not an effigy, rather meant to b
St Thomas Becket, and said to come from the w face of th
tower. It looks, however, as if it were part of a brass, of th
type with the deceased praying by means of a scroll up t

such a figure. – Robert Bertie, first Earl of Lindsey, † 1642 (N aisle). Black and white marble. Large double inscription plate surrounded on all sides by white military still-lifes. – Richard Bertie † 1686. White, with scrolly surround, also flower chains. Two putto heads at the foot. – First Duke of Ancaster † 1723. Signed *L. I. Scheemaeckers and H. Cheere inv. et fec.* Standing white figure against a grand black reredos background. – Robert Lord Willoughby and others, 1738. Black and white. Mighty sarcophagus on an inscription base. Urn on the sarcophagus, and to l., r., and above seven busts. – Second Duke of Ancaster † 1741. By *Roubiliac.* Standing figure, the type of Guelfi's Craggs in Westminster Abbey. His elbow leans on an urn. Below a medallion with the profile of his wife. To the l. a putto. – Third and fourth Dukes † 1778 and 1779. By *Charles Harris* of London. An interesting group. Two standing figures and the medallion of the wife of one. Against the convex-sided back panel small medallion of a child. – Hon. Frederick Burrell, † 1819 as a baby. White relief. Angels carry the baby up. Behind them an oval with palm trees and a shield. Another angel seated on the oval. – First Lord Gwydyr † 1820. By *Nollekens.* Bust on a round pedestal, just as it would be in a house or museum. – In the churchyard High Victorian monuments of more members of the family.

There are a Georgian VICARAGE, a Tudoresque SCHOOL of 1816, and, by the church, a vernacular stone COTTAGE with a finial-topped gable.

MITCHELL FARM or Manor Farm, Scottlesthorpe, I m. SW. An old Bertie seat. In a decaying barn a C12 DOORWAY said to come from Vaudey Abbey. Two orders of shafts, scallop capitals, arch with two roll mouldings. Tympanum with scratched-in scallop and zigzag.*

ELLOE STONE *see* MOULTON

ERMINE STREET *see* ANCASTER *and* STAMFORD

EVEDON

ST MARY. Low W tower, the very wide W window filled in with inappropriate tracery in 1898. Even later some equally inappropriate tracery was put in the opening to a former S

* But the MHLG regards the doorway as *in situ,* observes remains of medieval detail inside the barn as well, and so suggests that it may have been a chapel.

chapel. The details of the arch are Dec. Inside, the arcade to t
former N aisle is preserved. Two bays, late C13. Quatrefoi
piers with fillets and thin shafts in the diagonals. Nailhead i
the abaci. Double-chamfered arches. The chancel arch is i
harmony with the arcade. – FONT. Octagonal, Perp, wi
shields in cusped fields. – SCREEN. A little of the dado unde
the tower. – ARCHITECTURAL FRAGMENTS. An extraordin
ary charnel-house of pieces in the chancel S wall, e.g. a bit o
a gable with an angel, a polygonal shaft with stiff-leaf capita
and also parts of two responds in the style of the N arcade.
PLATE. Chalice and Paten, by *R.S.*,* *c*.1635. – MONUMENTS
Brass to Daniel Hardeby † 1630, with the kneeling family.
Sir Peregrine Bertie and wife, 1705. Cartouche with flower
and arms, inscription on marble drapery. – Rowland Fox
1722, still in the late C17 tradition. – William Bailey † 1801
white and gold, with a classical urn. Signed *Brown*.

MANOR HOUSE. Once a Bertie seat. An L with the front dresse
up in the C19 but retaining a mid C17 Tuscan porch.

1040

EWERBY

ST ANDREW. Essentially a Dec church, of the Sleaford family
W tower with Dec bell-openings of odd tracery. The buttress
es have decorated gablets half-way up. A fleuron frieze belov
the start of the slender broach spire which brings the heigh
of the steeple up to 172 ft. The three tiers of lucarnes i
alternate directions are well managed. The aisles, also Dec
with minor flowing tracery, embrace the tower. The S porch
entrance is the showpiece of the church. A leaf trail up on
moulding, thick nobbly leaf up another. Gable on top. Th
N doorway has six fine mouldings all dying into the jambs. Th
N chapel is of rougher stone. Its windows are all renewed
This was probably a chantry chapel; for in it is the MONU
MENT to Sir Alexander Aunsell who died in 1360. Effig
under a low, finely moulded arch. The date may refer to th
church as a whole. Arcades of three bays. Quatrefoil pier
with fillets, the foils flowing into one another. Double
chamfered arches. The W tower arch is of the same type an
triple-chamfered. In the tower a vault of eight ribs and
big ring. One Dec arch to the N chapel. No chancel arch, bu
in the chancel plainish Dec fitments: sedilia and piscina, an

---

* The Rev. J. Gordon Cox suggests that this is *Robert Sanderson*, th
first English silversmith to work in America.

tomb recess and aumbry opposite. – FONT. The base is
part of a Norman font with intersecting arches. The bowl is
Dec, six-sided with blank windows. – ROOD SCREEN. A very
fine piece. Ogee-headed one-light divisions, but the doorway
with two ogees and the tracery above of close and busy 29
reticulation, e.g. mouchette wheels. Probably Dec. – PAR-
CLOSE SCREEN, to the N chapel. Plain ogee arches formerly
on shafts or muntins. Three such units form a division. Is
this pre-Perp? – COMMUNION RAIL. C17.* – CHEST (N aisle
w) with arches and many rosettes, chip-carved, probably C14.
– PLATE. Chalice, Elizabethan; Paten, by *William Bateman*,
1818. – MONUMENTS. Anglo-Saxon slab with a plain Latin
cross surrounded on all sides by interlace; an impressive
piece, 58 in. long. – Twelfth Earl of Winchelsea † 1898.
Recumbent effigy in stone. The sculptor seems unrecorded.

n front of the W end of the church a piece of lawn, the
VILLAGE CROSS (base and *c*.6 ft of shaft), one judiciously
placed tree, and a pair of Early Victorian Tudor houses.
Ewerby in the Middle Ages was a market town, not a·village.

FENTON

8050

ALL SAINTS. Perp W tower of grey ashlar. Below the parapet
a cusped lozenge frieze. Square pinnacles, crocketed spire
with two tiers of lucarnes in alternating directions. The aisle
walls of ironstone with Ancaster stone bands. In the N aisle
a plain, single-chamfered Transitional doorway. The interior
is more rewarding. Norman N arcade of two bays. Strong
round pier, square abaci, scalloped capitals. Arches with two
slight chamfers. Late C13(?) s arcade. Octagonal pier, double-
chamfered arches. The chancel was rebuilt in 1838. At that
time probably the E bay of the arcades was interfered with
too. The N chapel belongs to the S arcade. – PULPIT. Perp,
with arched panels. – SCREEN. Perp, with one-light divisions.
– BENCH ENDS. With tracery and poppy-heads. – PLATE.
Paten Cover and Chalice, by *William Mascall*, York, 1667;
Paten and Flagon, by *Wimans*, 1697.

FISHTOFT

3040

ST GUTHLAC. The church must have been large already in the
C12; for the width of the chancel was the same then as it is

* The Rev. J. G. Cox draws my attention to STALLS, also of the C17, and
ells me that the rood screen is *ex situ*.

now, see the Norman priest's doorway (one scallop capital, one reeded capital) and opposite the Norman window. The Norman chancel was remodelled about 1290; see the excellent five-light E window with three circles in the top, the top one with pointed quatrefoils set radially, the lower two with pointed trefoils. Shafted mullions. Also in the side walls not only Perp windows but one lancet. The arcades of the nave are later but must have been preceded by E.E. ones; see the one head of a clerestory lancet above the s arcade in the nave. The s arcade is Dec. Five bays, with filleted quatrefoil piers and double-chamfered arches. The N arcade is later; see the Perp capitals. With the Dec arcade goes the Dec s doorway, with the Perp N arcade the N windows. But the s windows are Perp too, and Perp is the present clerestory (three-light upright windows with panel tracery). Finally the w tower, ashlar-faced, as is all the rest. Shields on the buttresses at ground level; four-light w window with transom, a niche above it with a figure looking earlier than the tower. The tower arch starts Perp, but was broken off and an arch a little further w set on brackets, probably because it was regarded as a structurally better position. – FONT. Octagonal, Perp, with restless blank tracery including bits of crenellation. – SCREENS. The rood screen has tall, wide crocketed ogee arches and Dec tracery around them in the side divisions, but Perp in the middle division. The divisions are emphasized by detached buttress shafts. – The screen under the tower was brought from Freiston. It has ogee arches too, but yet wider. – PULPIT. Perp, of wood, with small tracery to the blank arches. – ARCHITECTURAL FRAGMENTS. Built into the walls. – STAINED GLASS. Original bits in the clerestory windows. – PLATE. Chalice and Cover, Paten, and Flagon by *John Payne*, 1757.

OLD RECTORY. Big, rambling, and very plain. By *H. E. Kendal* 1827.

3020

FLEET

ST MARY MAGDALEN. A wholly Dec church as far as the exterior is concerned. Detached steeple with spire, but the body of the church alas over-restored. It is called 'lately much repaired and beautified' in 1798. The steeple is *c.*120 ft high. The spire is recessed behind battlements and has three tiers of quatrefoil lucarnes. The tower buttresses have nice decoration in the gables, with blank Y-tracery. Below the battlements bold gargoyles, whole figures and pairs of figures. The ground floor of the tower is windowless. Then a stage with ogee-headed lancets. Then two-light bell-openings with transoms, the members roll-moulded. The church is ashlar-faced too. s porch with Dec entrance. All aisle windows have Victorian tracery. Then a blocked doorway into a former two-bay chancel chapel. Only the E bay of the chancel stood free, see the foliage frieze below the roof. In the SE buttress a niche. The E window is entirely Victorian. The N side had a three-bay chancel chapel. The windows seem again all Victorian. In fact the chancel was rebuilt in 1843. But was it done correctly? The N chancel windows, if representing those of the N chapel, are interesting. Two have mullions up into the arch, but above the pointed-trefoiled lights round trefoils. The nave w window finally is of five lights and the one Perp item. Inside, however, the church has a different character. The piers are round, the capitals are round, their details and those of the bases are E.E. Only, the piers were heightened to suit the Dec requirements. The Dec roof corbels are preserved, exceedingly fine busts of great variety. The responds of the chancel arch are also E.E. and heightened. Dec sedilia and piscina with steep trefoiled ogee arches and heavily crocketed gables. – FONT. Octagonal, Perp, with simple panels. – REREDOS. 1790, with fluted pilasters and a scrolly open pediment (now under the tower). – PLATE. Chalice, by *I.H.*, 1596; Paten, by *A.M.*, 1674. – MONUMENT. Defaced miniature effigy of a Civilian, early C14 (W wall).

ECTORY. High, of red brick, forbidding. By *Ferrey*, 1854.

IOTTE, SW of the village, near Battle Bridge. It is badly ploughed down. Late C11 and C12 pottery has been dug out of it.

FOLKINGHAM

0030

T ANDREW. Ashlar-faced, except for the ironstone chancel. Fine tall Perp four-stage w tower. The doorway has a kind of tympanum with shields and tracery. Four-light w window with castellated transom. Niches l. and r. A vault high up inside. Tierceron-star, cusped. Four-light bell-openings grouped as two plus two. No mullion up into the apex. Two decorated friezes, decorated battlements, and sixteen pinnacles. Chronologically first in the church is the N chancel chapel. One bay, triple responds, the middle shaft keeled, many-scalloped capitals. It is likely that this was the chancel

arch of the Norman church. The chancel now is late C13
and much renewed (*Kirk & Parry*, 1857). Geometrical tracery.
The capitals of the sedilia seem to be between naturalistic
and bossy, i.e. *c*.1300. Dec N aisle, the windows alternating
between straight-headed with reticulated tracery and shallow-
arched. Of the latter one has still three stepped lancet lights,
the other already flowing tracery. Dec S aisle. Straight-headed
windows. S doorway with one order of slim colonnettes.
Piscina with crocketed gable on heads. Finally the three-bay
arcades. Are they Dec too, or Perp? Octagonal piers, arches
some moulded, some double-chamfered. Perp two-storeyed S
porch. Battlements, pinnacles. Inside the porch a tierceron-
star vault. – FONT. C18. A heavy baluster and a fluted bowl. –
SCREEN. Excellent, with two-light divisions under trefoiled
ogee arches. Nice decoration of the doorway arch. – STALLS.
Arched panels on the fronts.* – STAINED GLASS. Bits in a N
aisle window. – The village STOCKS are exhibited in the S aisle.
The centre of the village is the exceptionally spacious square,
a long oblong going gently down the hillside. Its scale is due
to the fact that Folkingham used to be a seat of Quarter
Sessions. At the top, in the NW corner, the access to the
church, which lies back a good deal. In the middle of the N
side and dominating the square is the GREYHOUND INN, of
brick, two-storeyed with parapet. Five spacious bays, and
in the middle the former archway in. This is stone-lined. On
the r. an assembly room was added. It is marked by the
Venetian window. The houses flanking the square are of
brick or, more often, of stone. Nice doorcases. Torrington
in 1791 mentions building activity at Folkingham. At the
bottom on the r. is the MANOR HOUSE, a Restoration type of
house, though the doorcase suggests an early C18 date. Yet
the windows are still of two lights, mullioned, with a straight
entablature, and the roof is still steeply hipped. Three-
storeyed porch with top pediment. The best rooms are at
piano nobile level.

61a In the Billingborough Road the remains of the former HOUSE
OF CORRECTION,‡ dated 1825, and by *Bryan Browning*,
architect of the equally interesting Town Hall at Bourne (*see*
p. 479). What is preserved is the Gatehouse-cum-Governor's
House, an emphatic, apotropaeic composition, stone-faced, of

* Originally part of the benches (F. R. Money).
‡ PLATE (now in Lincoln Museum). Cup and Cover, by *Peter & William*
Bateman, 1811.

three bays. The centre a deeply-chamfered niche leading to a tunnel-vaulted entry at the end of which is a much smaller doorway. The arched side windows blank except for the top lunettes. The sides and back are brick, and there were of course more buildings. The stone front has an illustrious pedigree: Sammicheli's town gates, Ledoux's toll gates, and of course Vanbrugh – especially for the details at the back. The House of Correction lies where Henry de Beaumont's Folkingham CASTLE stood. Remains of this consist of a very strong, square moated site, with a powerful outer bank, and on the N a large outer enclosure.

FOSDYKE 3030

ALL SAINTS. 1871–2 by *E. Browning*. A sizeable and respectable church. Very red brick. The steeple s of the w end of the s aisle. Broach spire. E.E. style, lancet windows and windows with Geometrical tracery. Quatrefoil clerestory windows. Interior with round piers and rich stiff-leaf capitals. The church replaces a Georgian church of 1755. – FONT. If this is Perp, the panels of the bowl anyway are completely re-cut. The underside and the stem are more convincing. – FONT COVER. Tall, Perp. – PLATE. Chalice and Cover, by *Matthew Lofthouse*, 1713; Paten, by *George Lambe*, 1717; Flagon, by *Ed. Fennell*, 1782.

FOSTON 8040

ST PETER. Narrow Norman chancel arch with scallop capitals and zigzag in the arch. Early C13 N arcade of three bays. Octagonal piers, round, double-chamfered arches. The s arcade is later E.E. To it belong the s doorway and the irregular s lancets. In the chancel one N lancet. The w tower is E.E. too. Twin bell-openings with plate tracery under a round arch. Blocked w doorway, also round-arched. Some small dog-tooth. The transeptal s chapel has a small quatrefoil E chapel and a very curious coffin-shaped s window. Tiny C16 or C17 clerestory. – MONUMENTS. Many enjoyable slate headstones, mostly after 1800. The names of the carvers are e.g. *G. Neale* and *R. Neale* of Grantham, *C. Sheppard* of Newark, *Wood*, *Collingwood*. Other churchyards in this district may be just as rewarding, if one makes a point of seeking out the best of these headstones.

Straddling the edge of a hill, the village spreads like a dog-leg from the church to the former INN. The latter is long, with three faces to the street. Opposite is the OLD HALL, with a datestone 1616. Of BODKIN HALL near by the lodges are early C19, with ogee niches and blank windows.

FRAMPTON

ST MARY. The w tower, embraced by the aisles, is a strong and impressive job, from Norman to E.E. The ground floor inside has arches to the aisles and the nave which are Late Norman, i.e. they have scalloped capitals (except for one moulded E.E.-looking one), but double-chamfered pointed arches. The w doorway is round inside, but pointed with two rounded chamfers outside. The responds of the arch to the nave are really too tall for Norman responds in this place, and so one can assume that the change of heart from Norman to E.E. took place while building was still at ground level. There are indeed lancets here. The continuation upward is a robust, somewhat blunt E.E. Flat clasping buttresses. Twin bell-openings shafted but still without plate tracery. A blank arch l., a blank arch r., bits of vertical dog-tooth. And then a broach spire, one of the earliest (cf. Sleaford and North Rauceby). Big broaches, three tiers of lucarnes in the same directions, the lowest with dog-tooth, the upper with Y-tracery. The nave arcades are E.E. too. Five bays with circular piers and abaci, in the w part octagonal, in the E part round. The bases E.E. for the N arcade, Perp for the s arcade. Double-chamfered arches. The last arches to the E are higher than the others, and this is one indication of transepts. The s transept was indeed built, and of the N transept a joint still gives evidence. There are also the arches from the aisles to the transepts. Half-arches divide the w bays of the aisles from the rest. The northern one stands on a specially good bust. Then there is a mysterious low and narrow extra arch w of the w respond of the s arcade. Now externally. The s transept is Dec with its large reticulated windows (s five lights). On the SE angle-buttress a portrait head, a man showing his teeth, and the inscription: 'Wot ye whi I stad her for/I forswor my Savior/ego Ricardus in angulo'. Dec also the aisle windows (those of the N aisle Victorian), the ogee-headed N aisle doorway, the s doorway and s porch, and the chancel. Windows with flowing tracery, priest's doorway with crocketed ogee head and a lot of lush decoration inside. Priest's doorway with fleurons up jambs and arch, sedilia (proving incidentally that the chancel was shortened) and Easter Sepulchre. All crocketed ogee gables, buttress-shafts, finials, etc. The tomb-chest of the Easter Sepulchre has a wavy pattern familiar from parapets. – FONT. Octagonal, Norman, with intersected arches. – SCREEN. Very tall, ogee arches with panel tracery over. At the top of the dado pierced tracery (cf. Winthorpe, L). – CHANDELIER. Brass, with three 55 tiers of arms. Dated 1722. – PLATE. Two Chalices and two Patens, by *R.C.*, 1642. – MONUMENTS. Early C14 effigy of a Civilian. – Samuel and Hannah Tunnard † 1818 and 1816. By *Chantrey*. Draped sarcophagus with two linked wreaths.

ST MICHAEL, 1½ m. W. By *Fowler*, 1863. Stone outside, brick showing inside.)

FRAMPTON HALL. One of the grander houses of the district and of complicated architectural history. The main block was built for Coney Tunnard in 1725. Of this date is the S front. Five bays, three storeys divided by stone strings and affirmed by heavy rusticated stone giant pilasters at the angles (i.e. quoins all of even length). Nicely disposed stone trim: stone-faced central bay, door with open segmental pediment and fluted pilasters. Upon this the first-floor window with a grotesque head to the keystone, above that a voluted window, and above that again a small semicircular pediment. To the r. and l. two-storey wings, three bays to the W and two bays to the E. If the odd third bay is Victorian, then it is most skilfully adapted to the rest of the house. The N elevation has symmetrical two-bay wings. The *chef d'œuvre* of this front, and in fact of the house, is the gorgeous rainwater heads, among the finest in England. Square tanks with pilasters, cornices and lions in relief. The wall ties and plates decorated with armorials and figural subjects. The Victorian phase of alterations seems to have taken an odd form of quasi-mediev-alism. Garden ornaments and walls are decorated in a mixture of Romanesque and Tudor styles, and barns with stepped gables also look Tudor Revival. Inside, a good staircase with balusters in groups of two twisted and one fluted; carved tread-ends. The wrought-iron forecourt screen to the S has putti of the Seasons on the piers. Also in front of the house a splendid yew pyramid. In the garden two archways with re-used Norman shafts and scalloped capitals.

FRAMPTON HOUSE, 1½ m. WNW. Dated 1792. With an elegant sophisticated front that does not look provincial (but cf. 120 High Street, Boston, p. 476). Roman Doric porch and a stone

pedimented centre of three bays. Adjoining the road a goo
castellated brick wall.

3040

FREISTON

ST JAMES. If one approaches the church from the N, as is th
usual thing, it is a Perp church, i.e. it has a Perp W tower wit
an inordinately big W window of five lights and a niche ove.
with a headless statuette. Then there is a brick N aisle, bu
of C15 bricks of the Tattershall type and with Perp window
Some of these are so debased in their details that they mu
be post-Reformation replacements. And the clerestory wit
eight closely-set three-light windows with simple tracery
of course Perp too. But then comes the first puzzle. Th
corbel table of the clerestory is of a type unmistakabl
Norman (see e.g. Bicker, p. 456). The second puzzle is that th
S porch entrance has E.E. responds. Then, walking round th
tower to the S side, this turns out to be all imitation Norma
It is in fact of 1871. But there is an imitation Norman doorwa
in the E bay. How can that be? The only answer is the doo
way out of a monastic nave into the cloister. And indeed, i
now inspecting the E side this is revealed as the W side of
Norman crossing with triple shafts facing E. Freiston Prior
was founded from Croyland in 1114 and was never a bi
house. The crossing need not be much later. So one enter
with curiosity, and there is the Norman nave. Arcades o
nine bays, the six E bays with stubby circular piers (4 ft i
diameter), plain scalloped capitals (except for one with volutes
and cruciform abaci. The arches differ: some have one ste
and rolls, others one step with a thin roll on the next, yo
others a step, a hollow, and a roll, and the easternmost on th
S side has (later) zigzag at r. angles to the wall. Hood-mould
on long-snouted monsters.* The W crossing arch belongs t
the zigzag arch just referred to. It cannot be earlier than th
late C12. It is pointed and has several ornamental moti
including again zigzag at r. angles. The E window is of 1871
There were Norman transepts too, see the blocked arche
from the aisles to the E. This Norman nave was lengthene
to the W by three E.E. bays with circular piers, circula
abaci, and triple-chamfered arches. The capitals are moulde
but those of the four responds have early stiff-leaf. It deserve
special notice that this Norman monastic nave had apparentl

* The interruption in the N arcade is due to the former rood-loft stair.

no gallery or triforium, a most uncommon thing. Tall Perp tower arch. Perp nave roof with alternating tie-beams and angels against the principals. There are also original bosses. – FONT. Perp, octagonal, with nice very narrow, slender blank arches, four to a panel, and tiny quatrefoils over (cf. Leverton). The font base has two kneeling stones (cf. Benington). – FONT COVER. A Perp piece with Perp windows set radially or fin-wise as buttresses and with intricate canopies (cf. Fosdyke). – SCREENS. To the N and S aisles, the S screen with trefoiled ogee arch specially good. – NORTH DOOR. Traceried. – PLATE. Chalice and Cover, by *John Jackson*, 1698.

FREISTON PRIORY, S of the church. Mostly C17, but with a Georgian seven-bay W front of two storeys, plain windows, and a stone string. The E front has two projecting chimney-flanks.

COUPLEDYKE HALL, ½ m. SSE. A Late Georgian refacing of an earlier L-shaped house.

WHITE LOAF HALL, 1¼ m. E. Dated under one window 1613 and in the gable 1614, but seems late C15 by the style of windows (straight-headed, with the lights ending in four-centred cusped arches). The gable of 1614 is stepped. The crude brick string and cornice relate to the local Fen style.

FRIESTON
9040

½ m. S of Caythorpe

An unusually large hamlet without a church. The GREEN visually pleasing with groups of small houses. Just S is a low one-storey range of COTTAGES with three-light windows and a blocked doorway. They might once have been C17 ALMS-HOUSES. The OLD HALL is Georgian but received a Gothic front early in the C19. Within its gable area a castellated screen. FRIESTON HOUSE, near by, has an earlier wing but is mostly late C18 with thin Georgian details.

FROGNALL see DEEPING ST JAMES

FULBECK
9050

ST NICHOLAS. Perp W tower with eight pinnacles, the middle ones on diagonal projections starting above the transomed twin two-light bell-openings. The arcades of three bays with round piers and double-chamfered arches, much renewed, but probably of *c.*1300. So anyway are the S and N doorways.

To the church in this state probably belonged a clerestory o
circular windows, see one part of one blocked one on the
side. The clerestory as it is now is Perp, with a lozenge friez
on the parapet and pinnacles. But what is the strange en
crusted canopy at the SE corner? The aisle windows, also Dec
are all over-restored. Only the S aisle E window is Perp. Entirel
of the restoration (by *Charles Kirk*, 1887) is the beautifu
five-light chancel E window in the style of 1300. – FONT. *
splendid piece, due, however, perhaps to re-tooling. Transi
tional, of drum-shape, with four polygonal angle-shafts
In the fields between intersecting arches, a leaf band above
and above that a rope moulding, except in one quarter wher
there is dog-tooth instead. – ARCHITECTURAL FRAGMENTS
Half a Norman capital used as a shelf in the chancel. Wit
two scallops. – A strip of Norman arches with saltire crosse
over, perhaps from a square font. This is behind the pulpit.
SOUTH DOOR. With tracery; Perp. – STALLS. Two in th
chancel, one of them with a leaf MISERICORD. – PAINTING
Former altarpiece, Christ and the Woman of Samaria. Stot
hard style. – PLATE. Chalice and Cover, by *W.S.*, 1626; Pater
1724. – MONUMENTS. A group of *c.*1680, oblong, with curve
tops and no figures, namely Nevile Fane † 1680 (in the centr
an urn on a plinth with heraldic shields), Thomas Bell, 167
(a faithful Fane servant who travelled with his master, so w
are told, over most European countries), and Timoth
Thorold, Doctor of Physick, and members of his family t
1680. Also other nice tablets.

VILLAGE CROSS, SE of the church. Base and restored shaft.

The unwary will miss the best of the village. It lies off the mai
road to the W, where a green opens to the church, an inn, an
S to a hill, and where cottages, judiciously placed trees, and
village pump contribute to the scene. In this part is ERMIN
HOUSE. The parapet, brought up to a peak and having sid
scrolls and an ornament on the top, occurs also at Wyberto
(*see* p. 718); thus the house may be by *William Sands th
Younger*. Here is also the MANOR HOUSE, the old Fan
family seat, basically C17, but too much restored.* On th
main road proper lie the grander houses.

FULBECK HALL. Built in 1733 for Francis Fane, and in its styl
proclaiming the hand of a Stamford architect. The 'Stam
fordian' front is partially obscured by the porch, which cam
from Syston Hall (by *Vulliamy*?). The 1733 front is of fiv

* The MHLG gives the date 1737.

bays and two storeys divided by giant Doric pilasters. The
entablature and parapet broken over the order. First-floor
windows with Gibbsian surrounds and built-up keystones,
centre window pilastered and with a deep triangular pediment.
The three-bay wing to the N was added shortly before 1800.
Its upper storey is later. Vernacular mullioned windows with
flat hoods in the outbuildings. Inside, good joinery to the
hall and stairs, all of c.1733. The entrance GATES fronting
the avenue have been attributed to *John Warren* (cf. Belton).
Opposite is a gateway in the wall, dated 1583. It came from
Tudely in Kent.

FULBECK HOUSE, ¼ m. N. Perhaps early C18, but much restored.
A convincing silhouette in the traditional hipped-roof style.
Five bays, two storeys. Doorway with segmental pediment.
The curious modillions to the doorway look suspicious.

GARNSGATE HALL *see* LONG SUTTON

GEDNEY   4029

ST MARY MAGDALEN. A splendid church of a Norfolk Fen
type, splendid in all styles from the E.E. tower to the Perp
clerestory. It belonged to Croyland Abbey. All ashlar-faced
of course, to show that throughout the centuries only the
best was good enough. The tower first. It is at the W end and
has strangely complicated clasping buttresses with further
shallow chamfered buttress-shafts attached and an angle-shaft.
On the ground stage there is only a lancet to the W and one to
the S, both with a little dog-tooth. The arch to the nave has
triple responds like the tower arches of Long Sutton. The
hood-mould again with dog-tooth. The next stage has blank
arcading, also like Long Sutton. Then follow the original bell-
openings, two twins, tall, with much shafting and shaft-rings
and much dog-tooth. Up to here Hamilton Thompson dated
the tower as of c.1280. All arch mouldings are rolls. Above this
is a Perp stage, again very tall, so that the tower comes to 86 ft.
Also two twin bell-openings. They have transoms and ogee
gables. Cusped lozenge frieze below the parapet. Then the
start of a stone spire which unfortunately was never continued.
The little lead spike is the one disappointment of Gedney.* Inside, the E.E. bell-openings were once exposed to the E. The

* From it, however, the height of the intended spire can be calculated.
Mr John Welch has done so, and arrives at a height of c. 40–50 ft.

earliest roof-line is below, and under its gable is a former doorway-like opening with a shouldered arch as its head. Then there is a second C14 roof-line, below the present one, which is probably Early Tudor.

But first the examination of the exterior must be continued. It is, except for the clerestory, entirely Dec. Some of the windows have fully developed flowing tracery, others still have cusped intersecting tracery, and there seems no system in the distribution. The flowing tracery is in the aisle windows, except the last two on the NE and SE, and in the chancel only in the E window, and here it is reticulated rather than of the leaf mouchettes of the other windows. So there is no chronology to be gained that way.* The chancel is tall and appears so from outside. The church has a two-storeyed S porch rather later C14 than the rest. The entrance arch is still Dec, but the windows above look a little later. S doorway with fine mouldings, partly renewed. Doorway to the former upper floor with ogee head.

The clerestory is spectacular. Twelve windows, very closely set, of three lights under flat four-centred arches. Panel tracery, battlements, pinnacles. On the E gable a Sanctus bellcote. Inside, the clerestory windows are divided by shafts standing on busts, heads, animals. The roof has alternatingly tie-beams on arched braces and arched braces supporting principal direct. But in one place this system is broken and a pair of hammerbeams introduced to replace the arched braces. Or are they a tie-beam cut off? At the E end of the roof the E wall of the clerestory appears above the chancel and has a most curious circular window, made up, it seems, of bits of re-used tracery. This dates from 1860. But this is anticipating. We must, on entering, first look at the arcades. They are of six bays with octagonal piers and double-chamfered arches, rather disappointing really.

FURNISHINGS. PILLAR PISCINA (N aisle E). One remaining piece of the E.E. church. Triple shaft, stiff-leaf capitals. – FONT. The base is dated 1664, but the bowl is either Perp and almost entirely re-tooled, or Victorian with one Perp panel, the Virgin and a donor (a boy?). – SOUTH DOOR. A wonderful piece, full of surprises. The door itself is Dec, with upright buttresses all decorated with pellets or ballflower and an in-

* The N aisle W window is a C17 replacement of the type of Gothic paraphrasing, as familiar from French late C16 and early C17 windows and Oxford chapel windows of before 1660 or 1670.

scription board across: Pax Christi sit huic domui et omnibus habitantibus in ea hic requies nostra. But the wicket door has its own inscription 'in hope' and a tiny French early C14 ivory set in. It represents the Crucifixion and is sadly rubbed off. And on the inner side of the door is a lock with inscribed metal strips of bell metal. The lettering (John Pette auyseth beware before), it has been observed, is much like that of the C14 bell at Glapthorne Manor near Oundle. – PULPIT. Of *c*.1700, panels and cherubs' heads. – STAINED GLASS. In the five lights of the N aisle E window substantial remains of an early C14 Jesse window. A whole figure and large parts of several others. The colour still with some deep red and blue but essentially the typical yellow–green–brown. The same in the fine canopies of one N window. In others and in s windows many smaller bits. – PLATE. Two chalices, by *T.*, 1569; Paten, by *I.A.*, 1683; two-handled Cup, by *Ed. Pocock*, 1731. – MONUMENTS. In the s aisle at the E end torso of a C13 effigy of a Knight, not too late, though with crossed legs. The drapery must once have been fine. On the hollow-chamfered edge of the slab individual stiff-leaves. – The slab lies on a Perp tomb-chest, big and defaced. – Also in the s aisle a 5 ft brass effigy of a Lady of about 1400, a puppy at her feet. When the canopy and the side pieces with their small figures were still complete, this was an outstanding piece. – Adlard Welby and wife, erected 1605. Large tablet of alabaster with kneeling figures facing one another, columns and nicely naive sprays of foliage. – Mrs Millington † 1844. Tablet with a figure of Hope.

OVENDEN HOUSE, 1¼ m. NNW. 1912 by *Nicholas & Dixon-Spain*. Neo-Georgian. The door surround of a curious stone, boldly marbled brown and greyish blue.

GEDNEY HILL

HOLY TRINITY. Perp w tower with two-light bell-openings. The arch towards the nave suggests a C14 date. Bold mouldings. The body of the chancel by *James Fowler*, 1875, and very progressive and attractive. Arcades on wooden posts. In the roof Perp tie-beams used. In the wall between chancel and vestry a re-set Perp three-light window – STAINED GLASS. E window by *Ward & Hughes*, only too unmistakable. – CHURCHYARD CROSS. s of the church. High base, plinth, and shaft preserved.

GOSBERTON

ST PETER AND ST PAUL. A cruciform church, Dec and Perp,
with one inconspicuous exception which, however, establishes
that the church received its shape already in Norman times.
There is a thin Norman nook-shaft just N of the NW crossing
pier facing into the N transept. This must be connected with
the entry from a Norman N aisle into a Norman N transept.
So to the Dec parts of the church. The three-light transept
window is a good piece of flowing tracery. It has shafts with
fillets inside. The flowing tracery of the N aisle windows is
much coarser and also more elementary. But what is the date
of the plain, round-headed double-chamfered N doorway?
Then the crossing steeple, 160 ft high. Dec bell-openings,
battlements, crocketed pinnacles connected by thin, pretty
and useless flying buttresses to the recessed crocketed spire.
Three tiers of lucarnes in alternating directions, the lowest
with embattled transoms. Among the gargoyles of the tower
(E wall) is an elephant. The spire is of course Perp. So are the
lierne-vault under the tower, and the transepts (the S transept
S window with its elaborately crested transom is Perp, the N
transept N is not). The S aisle windows are Perp too – note the
two outer tomb recesses – and the S porch is again Perp.
Entrance with fleurons up the jambs, three niches, pinnacles,
S doorway with two of the mouldings decorated by square
leaves, an ogee gable and two niches. Five-light Perp W window, and roof parapet with lozenges. In the W doorway a
moulding has a nice sparse twig decoration. Perp clerestory of
eight closely-set two-light windows. Parapet again with
lozenges; battlements. The chancel was rebuilt and lengthened
in 1896–7. Perp four-bay aisle arcades. The piers of a typically
Perp, complex form. Lozenge shape. A flat projection to the
nave, then a diagonal wave, a hollow, and semicircular shaft
to the arch opening. Only these have capitals at all, and they
are castellated. The crossing is Perp too, not a usual thing.
Inventive lierne-vault: basically a ring in a square set diagonally in another square, though the distortions by means of
the curvature of the vault do not allow one to recognize at once
how simple the basic shapes are on paper. Dec S chancel chapel
of two bays, the pier square with semicircular projections

* Excavations have revealed more of this Norman church: the foundations
of the W wall across the third pier line, circular bases of two N arcade piers,
and the S nave wall. The E.E. base in the S arcade is probably not *in situ*.

filleted; double-chamfered arches. The sedilia and piscina are Dec also, ogee-arched but simple. But the finest internal piece of Dec decoration is the tomb recess in the s transept, low and ogee-headed, with censing angels l. and r. of the arch, cusps to the arch, and buttress-shafts. In the recess MONUMENT, no doubt to the donor: cross-legged early C14 Knight, praying. – The MONUMENT to his wife also survives. – FONT. Octagonal, Perp, a large and plain piece. – SCREEN, to the N chapel. With ogee arches and panel tracery over. – PLATE. Chalice with Paten Cover incorporating traces of pre-Reformation Paten, by *Edward Noddall*, Boston, 1619; Paten, London, 1635; Paten, Dublin, 1683; Flagon, by *Gurney & Co.*, 1742.

t GILBERT AND St HUGH, Gosberton Clough, 2½ m. wsw. By *Bucknall & Comper*, 1902–4. Small and very attractive. Timber-framed nave, pebbledash facing. Wooden Late Perp windows, straight-headed and with round-arched lights. Two of them in the w front, one above the other. Only in the chancel cusped, more churchy windows. Inside tie-beams below a canted ceiling painted white.

GOSBERTON HOUSE (HOLLAND COUNTY COUNCIL SCHOOL). Built for Mrs Jane Smith in 1826, and strangely conservative. A Palladian brick cube of four bays and three storeys; semicircular porch, pediment, and small cupola. School additions of 1956.

GOSBERTON HALL, ¼ m. SE. Unfortunately derelict at the time of writing. An interesting early C19 villa with an ingenious plan. In the centre of the w front is a deep square recess containing the bowed wall of the staircase. On the opposite front a similar recess contains the Doric porch.

MONKS HALL, ½ m. NW. *William Sands* made extensions in 1729, but of these only the outbuildings remain.

CRESSY HALL, 1½ m. sw. Moats to the SE mark the medieval house of the Cressy family. This was burnt in 1791 and the present house built soon after. A finely finished brick block of five bays and three storeys with low adjacent pavilions. Windows recessed in blank arcading and open triangular pediments above them. Nice Rococo cartouche on entrance front.

WOODLANDS FARM, 1¼ m. NE. Of red brick, three storeys, five bays, with canted bay on the ground floor, l. and r. of the doorway. This has Greek Doric columns, i.e. is of *c.*1820–30.

GOSBERTON CLOUGH *see* GOSBERTON

GRANTHAM

Grantham was a royal manor and may have had a castle E of the
street still called Castlegate. It was a prosperous town in the
Middle Ages, as is witnessed not only by its proud church but
also by the existence of a house of the Greyfriars, as settlements
of friars always and nearly exclusively developed in towns of
some consequence. The original market place was immediately
w of the church.

CHURCHES

ST WULFRAM. Many connoisseurs of English parish churches
would list Grantham in their first dozen. In Lincolnshire it is
inferior only to Boston, and even that might be denied, on the
strength of its perfect steeple and the clarity of its interior.
This is a simple parallelogram including the tower and mea-
sures 196 by 79 ft. The height is moderate. The aisles are
nearly the same width as the nave. The piers are not too thick
to prevent free views in all directions, and the three identical
wagon roofs (of the restoration of *Sir G. G. Scott*, 1866–9)
stress the equal value of the three vessels. Even the fact that
this interior is historically not at all of one piece, does not at
once obtrude itself. Yet it will soon be noticed. The three
middle bays of the nave belong to a late C12 church of which
the round arches of the clerestory are visible just above the
present arches, but nothing else survives. The piers are round
(or rather of four shallow lobes) with attached shafts in the
diagonals, the latter with shaft-rings. The capitals are some
unworked, some with crockets, one with fine leaves which may
betray acquaintance with the work of 1175–80 at Canterbury.
The steep, double-chamfered arches are a later alteration.
This late C12 piece must in fact have been preceded by yet
another building; for the stretch of herringbone masonry in the
bay of the chancel where now the organ stands tells of the C11.

At the w end of the late C12 piece the former w wall is
marked. Then, stimulated by what was being done at Newark
not far away, a *novum opus* was embarked on, and in connexion
with this the arcades were extended w to link them with a new
tower. But before that was done a s doorway was provided
and a s porch. Both the doorway and the porch entrance survive, though re-set. The s doorway has stiff-leaf capitals and
probably dates from about 1230 or so. The new work to which
reference has just been made must have been started about
1280. It meant the rebuilding of the whole church outside the

existing one, and a beginning was made with this on the N
side. The six N windows of four lights are a direct copy from
the Angel Choir at Lincoln, begun in 1256 and completed in
1280.* Above the four lights, as at Lincoln, are three circles,
one sexfoiled, the others quatrefoiled. The W window of the
aisle is yet larger. It is of six lights, and the super-arch of the
two middle ones sticks up a little higher than the others, a first
sign of a wish for individuality or capriciousness. There are
seven circles now, the three plus three below cinquefoiled, the
very large one above with seven small quatrefoiled circles
inside. Above this window a little gable with a blank trefoiled
spherical triangle, oddly enough not in axis with the window.
While the wall with these windows was built, a sumptuous
new N portal was also provided. This survives inside the later N
porch. It has rich shafting, rich stiff-leaf capitals, and exquisite
arch mouldings. Blank arches l. and r., and above all three
three steep gables. But of these only the stiff-leaf paterae remain and some very fine ornamental detail. The rest was mutilated when the porch was added. The aisle has a frieze of small
heads at the top and also battlements which are later additions.

Meanwhile the S aisle had also been begun. Here the five-
light W window has the middle light sticking up higher than the
others and in the large top circle a new little irregularity: eight
trefoiled foils. The gablet above here has a foiled spherical
quadrangle, and again it is out of true with the window. Then,
round the corner, the windows have intersecting tracery (uncusped). So we must now have reached c.1300. Then the
entrance to the S porch to which reference has already been
made. While this is of c.1230, the inner doorway with bits of
nailhead is again of c.1300. This part of the building must have
been completed after 1300; for the frieze above has ballflower
below the battlements, i.e. an early C14 motif – ballflower
whose 'quaint medlar-like twist and sourness' Ruskin praised.
The moment when ballflower came in is also the moment when
the steeple was begun. The motif appears at once in the W
doorway and in excess, inside as well as outside, in the surround and the intersecting tracery of the four-light window
above. The tower has angle-buttresses connected by a diagonal. The doorway has five orders of shafts and exquisite arch
mouldings. To the l. and r. of doorway and window and also on

* But Hamilton Thompson has also recalled the equally similar chapter
house of Salisbury Cathedral – a comparison suggested by the fact that
Grantham church was a prebend of Salisbury.

the face of the buttresses are three tiers of niches with pointed
trefoiled heads. The figures are of course recent. Above th
two tiers of steeply gabled small blank arcading, also pointed
trefoiled. With the upper tier the steeple comes free of th
embracing aisles. Another band of blank motifs, four tiers
quatrefoils, making a broad patterned band all round th
tower, E.E. in character rather than Dec. It is above this th
the exquisite elegance of the rise comes to full effect. The ne
stage has two tall twin windows. The stage after that also h
two twins, but gripped more closely together by a super-arc
into the apex of which runs the dividing mullion of the twin
Then polygonal pinnacles above the buttresses and th
beautifully slender crocketed spire, starting from negligib
small broaches. Four lower lucarnes with ballflower and in th
diagonals tight tabernacles with statues. Then a second tier
lucarnes, open in the diagonals, blank in the main directions. I
the top tier this is reversed.* The total height is about 272 f

We must now return to the interior. As the new work pr
ceeded, the old W wall was pulled down and the two bays
arcading built to connect with the mighty free-standing E pie
of the steeple. These bays have the same piers in plan, b
capitals typical of *c*.1300. The steep double-chamfered arch
suit that date, and they were now also provided for the old
bays instead of whatever arches there may have been. The tow
piers are enormous. They are placed diagonally and are strong
shafted all round. The farthest-projecting shafts have fille
The piers carry high up the arch between nave and tower a
lower down the W arcade arches and to the N and S the arch
into the W bays of the aisles. All is identical here, i.e. work beg
c.1280 and reaching the ballflower details of the W wall aft
1300. The tower has a vault of twelve radiating ribs round th
big circle for the bell-ropes. The ribs touch the outer walls
that there is in each cell a blank arch as a penetration.

Now what happens further E inside ? The old bays are co
tinued by a wider bay.‡ The arch is later, as it stands on th
W side on a short piece of semicircular respond with sem
octagonal capital above the abacus line. Hamilton Thomps
suggests the second half of the C14. But what does concern
already now is the telling fact that the transepts were not r

---

* The top was rebuilt in 1664 and repaired in 1797 and again in 1945-
‡ Not representing the former transept, as foundations of this have be
found one bay further E. Information kindly provided by the Rev. D. V
Owen.

built in the new scheme. Evenness of outline and of internal flow were now valued too highly.

To continue our story, we must now move from the style of c.1300 to the mature Dec. It is most impressive to watch that step on the outside. The two-storeyed embattled s porch to which reference has already been made is Perp and of rough masonry, though its crocketed stair-turret is of ashlar. Then follows a Perp five-light window, then the Perp rood-loft turret, with pretty little windows and a crocketed spirelet,* and then the glorious flowing tracery of the three-bay s chapel. The s windows are of five lights, the E window has six. That 23a the wilfully undulating details of the tracery differ from window to window needs no mention. The E window is flanked by round, purely decorative turrets without spires. All this may be 1330 or anything up to 1350–60. Then, to complete the external story, the Perp parts of the building: the enormous six-light chancel E window with transom and the N chapel with a seven-light E window between polygonal turrets and five-light N windows. To the N the Late Perp chapel of St Katherine projects with three closely-grouped small three-light windows to the E, three to the w. The four-light window to the N is flanked by niches. Small doorway from the E with a niche over. Battlements and pinnacles. This was the family chapel of the Hall family (see Grantham House, p. 548). The tomb of the founder must have stood in the panelled arch between the chapel and the N aisle, and the small doorway to its r. was the entrance. A N turret is covered by this chapel. Finally comes the N porch, which was added about 1330 or so. It is deep and has archways from the w and E as well as the N. Polygonal façade turrets with crocketed spires. Windows with reticulated tracery. Blank arcading inside in two bays, damaged. The former vault has disappeared. The archways to the w and E have sunk wave mouldings, that to the N many finer mouldings. From the former upper storey a window in the form of a large arch-head gives on to the N aisle. It has the weirdest tracery, including two transoms, a wavy frieze below the lower, a frieze of somewhat irregular squares with pointed quatrefoils between the two.‡

* The upper storey of the s porch has just such a window looking into church. It projects box-like and is carried by the bust of an angel.

‡ It has been considered post-Reformation. Above this window, in the ch, is a large STATUE of Christ in ample drapery. It cannot easily be a, but seems C15, not too late, and of high quality. It ought to be made ilable.

Inside the chancel the Dec s chapel has piers of a strang
section and with a stranger, though perfectly logical, bas
Four filleted foils and four fillets only in the diagonals. Flatti
capitals. On the N side there is first a bay of a similar style
the s chapel. Of the second bay the organ hides the detail
The further bays are of course Perp. Pier section compl
with a projection to the chancel of two wave chamfers leadi
to a kind of fillet. Normal shafts to the arch openings.

So to the crypt, which is below the s chapel. Access from t
chancel is from a strange Perp box like a chantry. It projec
into the s chapel. Perp panelling and the doorway with fleuro
in one moulding and an ogee gable. The crypt itself is of t
date of the s chapel. Middle pier of a strange section. Fo
concave sides and in the diagonals four thin shafts with f
lets. Bold single-chamfered ribs making four quadriparti
compartments.

FURNISHINGS. In topographical order. Chancel: RERED(
By *Sir Arthur Blomfield*, 1883, enlarged 1901. – STAIN
GLASS. By *Heaton, Butler & Bayne*. – ROOD SCREEN. By *
G. G. Scott*, 1868. – PARCLOSE SCREEN. By *J. Oldrid Sco*
1886–7. – N chapel: nothing. – s chapel: STAINED GLAS
Second window from the E by *Clayton & Bell*, 1875. – MA
SCREEN. Of wrought iron; *c*.1766. – STAINED GLASS. E and
windows by *Kempe & Tower*, 1920 and 1932, yet still t
style of the late C19. – Nave: FONT. Perp, octagonal. Statuett
against the stem. Against the bowl religious scenes, e.g. A
nunciation, Nativity, Baptism of Christ, three seated Kings.
The tall Gothic FONT COVER is by *Sir Walter Tapper*, 189
– STAINED GLASS. W window by *Wailes*, 1856. – N aisle fro
the E: ORGAN CASE. By *Sir Walter Tapper*, 1909. – STAIN
GLASS. Window by *Kempe*, 1891, typical of his early colours
MONUMENT. Mrs Middlemore † 1701. Tablet with conv
inscription plate, three putti above and columns l. and r.
STAINED GLASS. Another *Kempe* window, 1897. – MON
MENTS. Lord Chief Justice Sir Dudley Ryder † 1756.
Henry Cheere. Seated figure with reversed torch. Medalli
standing on the ground. Black obelisk behind. Of very fir
delicate quality. – Sir Thomas Bury † 1722. Architectu
composition, very restless, with an urn as its centre. – STAIN
GLASS. W window by *Wailes*, 1853. – s aisle from the
MONUMENT. So-called Harrington Tomb. Recess of *c*.136
80. Cusped. The main cusps are angels with the Instrume
of the Passion. Helm and shields in the spandrels. Much mu

lated. – STAINED GLASS. By *Kempe*, 1885. – MONUMENTS. William Cust † 1747. Standing monument. Bust before obelisk. Military still-life at the foot of the bust. On the base relief with a man of war. Understandably attributed by Mr Gunnis to *Cheere*. – Edward Turnor † 1769. Minor standing monument. Rusticated base. Signed by *Bingham*. – Richard Saltby, according to a former inscription 1369. The composition exactly like that of the other tomb recess. – William Thorold † 1808. With a white profile bust just like a silhouette at the foot. – STAINED GLASS. SW window by *Clayton & Bell*, 1875. – W window by *Wailes*, 1855. – In the S porch the CHAINED LIBRARY, given in 1598. – PLATE. Pair of Chalices, by *Edward Fennel*, 1785; Chalice, by *William Pitts*, 1808; two Flagons and Almsbasin, by *Peter & William Bateman*, 1808.

T JOHN SPITTLEGATE, Station Road. By *A. Salvin*, 1840–1. In a plain E.E. style. Ashlar the short W tower with clumsy pinnacles. Wide aisles, widened tactfully in 1883–4, when also the chancel was rebuilt. Low circular piers. Open roofs, in the rebuilt aisles frankly in a utilitarian way.

T MARY (R.C.), North Parade. By *E. J. Willson*, 1832. Classical, ashlar-faced. Bell-turret with stone cupola. Side walls smooth with few classical windows.

HAPELS. *See* Perambulation.

PUBLIC BUILDINGS

ee Perambulation, and at the end of the Perambulation.

PERAMBULATION

he MARKET PLACE, of pleasing irregularity, was once dominated by the Palladian Grantham Grange, but this has now gone. There are still two C18 INNS (especially the BLUE LION, five bays, two and a half storeys, rendered, with pedimented doorway). The CONDUIT is dated 1597. A square with stepped buttresses at the angles, a crenellated parapet, and obelisks. The MARKET CROSS retains only the early steps and a steeply pyramidal base. The PRIORY to the N has medieval fragments (from a church restoration?) in the garden. Much window tracery, bits of jambs, a three-light Dec window with cusped heads and a Perp one with intersecting tracery. In WESTGATE at the entrance from the Market Place the former CORN EXCHANGE, 1852, of stone, three spacious bays, the ground floor with Tuscan columns, the upper floor with large pedimented windows; top balustrade. Then minor Georgian brick

houses. At a widening on the l. the OLD MALT SHOVEL, one
bay, gabled, timber-framed. To the l. on a detour, starting in
STANTON STREET. The visual appearance of this and the
WHARF ROAD area is due to the establishment here in 1815
of Richard Hornsby's Spittlegate Iron Works, and later
to the coming of the Great Northern Railway in 1852. All
utilitarian red-brick terraces, two- and three-storeyed. Past
the NATIONAL SCHOOL of 1853 to COMMERCIAL ROAD,
aligned on the Gothic tower of St John's. In Commercial
Road a METHODIST CHAPEL, red brick, three bays, with
arched upper windows and three-bay pediment. The date is
1867. Then a small breathing space of quiet backs and so to
the clamour of the LONDON ROAD. Turning N, typical early
C19 brick terraces, wealthy, whereas in the Wharf Road area
they were poor. The wealthiest of the houses is No. 12, of the
later C18, detached and lying back, five wide bays, two and
a half storeys. (Good interiors. MHLG) Into ST PETER'S HILL
with its island of trees and two statues: J. F. Tollemache, 1892
by *George Simmonds*, and William Newton, 1859 by *William
Theed the Younger*. They stand in excellent company with
William Watkins's TOWN HALL of 1867–9. Symmetrical,
brick and much stone. High-pitched French roofs of the most
unexpected outlines. A triple curved central oriel *à la* Hengrave
Hall above the entrance and a tall clock lantern finished off by
a gay coronet of wrought iron.* On the N side of St Peter's
Hill a terrace of brick houses with altered ground floor but a
nice iron veranda on the upper floor.

From here into the HIGH STREET. At the start (No. 42
St Peter's Hill) a three-bay brick house with a central
Venetian window and a tripartite lunette window over. Then,
after a bit, the elegant and remarkably large GEORGE HOTEL
of 1780. Brick, seven bays, three storeys, thin cornice and
parapet. The end bays have blank giant arches the whole height
of the front. In the centre, the now filled-in rusticated carriage
arch. Inside, a spacious and traceried stair light in the Adam
style. It ought to be remembered what spacious inns the Great
North Road needed in the later C18. That it needed very fine
inns already much earlier will be seen presently. But first the
NATIONAL PROVINCIAL BANK, with giant Ionic pilasters
of rather provincial proportions. So to the ANGEL AND ROYAL
HOTEL, one of the grandest of English pre-Reformation inns

* REGALIA. Seal, 1613; Loving Cup, 1678; two silver-gilt Maces and
Mayor's Chain with silver-gilt medallion, 1766.

and with a remarkably rich late C15 façade.* Two storeys; stone-37b
faced. To the l. and r. of the centrally placed archway, first stepped buttresses, then a narrow bay, then a canted bay window.
The windows now sashed but retaining their drip moulds. Those
on the first floor corbelled with armorials and figural subjects.
Over the archway a small canted oriel is bracketed on animal-
ized corbels. There is a rich decorative overlay: the cornice,
grotesque gargoyles, and a parapet of flat, diamond-patterned
panels. The façade is not symmetrical. The canted bay to the
r. is wider than that to the l., and the archway is just off-centre.
Inside, all the bay windows and the oriel windows have panelled or ribbed soffits of varied patterns. The prettiest is that on
the ground floor on the r., with a pelican as its boss. To estimate the importance which an inn could have already in the
Middle Ages one should remember that Richard III signed
the death warrant of the Duke of Buckingham and sealed it
with the Great Seal at the Angel, not at the castle. The inn was
originally Templars' and later Hospitallers' property. So it
was probably already then a place where travellers could receive
hospitality. At the rear there is a long brick range dated 1776.
It is the replacement of whatever there was of stabling. The
replacement is a townish terrace, fourteen bays long and three
and a half storeys high. Nice staircase with slim turned
balusters.

Continuing along WATERGATE, No. 6 is a five-bay stone
mid C18 house, built for the Whichcote family. (It has a very
good staircase. MHLG) Nos 16–17 is of brick with two-storey
canted bays and a doorcase with Doric pilasters and a pediment.
Outer bays with tripartite windows and tripartite lunettes over.
In NORTHGATE and NORTH PARADE is plain early C19
speculative terrace housing. North Parade is rightly called
Parade; for, apart from the presbytery of the Catholic church
and one terrace of four late C18 houses with canted bay windows immediately N of the church, all is on the other side. To
the w it must have remained un-built-over into the C20. Then,
turning towards the town again, off to the E into BROWNLOW
STREET, where No. 10 was built in 1643. It now has an altered
stone front. The s continuation of Brownlow Street is SWINE-
GATE. This presents a gently ascending vista of brick houses.
Turn r. into VINE STREET. At the corner a long upper floor
of exposed timber-framing, narrow overhang, and stone-faced
ground storey. In Vine Street is VINE HOUSE, dated 1764

* Illustrated by *Pugin* in his *Contrasts*.

and probably by the Grantham architect *John Langwith*, wh
designed the vicarage (*see* p. 549). Venetian windows, triparti
lunette windows, and a Doric porch. On the other side a litt
further on a small C16 stone doorway with a four-centred hea
and a hood-mould. Turn back to Swinegate and along its
continuation Elmer Street North to the corner of FINKI
STREET. A glance to the r. produces *Salvin*'s SAVINGS BAN
of 1841, in a wayward Jacobean style of gables and fat Ion
columns dropping below the string. Turn E and immediate
the WESLEYAN CHAPEL of 1840, a massive cubic twir
towered affair broadly reminiscent of Vanbrugh's pavilion
Swinstead (*see* p. 692).

Into CASTLEGATE. First on the E side Elysian Terrac
dated 1873, and such an ordinary terrace. Then Middlemo
House, No. 55, late C18, stone, more formal than it appea
from the street, and with panelled rooms. No. 49 is mid C1
stone, of five bays. Progressing N the garden of Grantha
House and opposite the Gothic NATIONAL SCHOOLS
1859. They overlook to the N the churchyard. Opposite the
end of the church is GRANTHAM HOUSE, with a core
c.1380. It was the house of the Hall family. The extent of tl
great hall on the S front and the old entrance to the scree
passage in the N wall are all that can definitely be allocated
this period. The next phase of building may have been arour
1574 (date on a chimneystack), and the W front is characteristi
ally Elizabethan. Two- to five-light windows and flat hood
The N front towards the courtyard has three-light window
In an angle of the W wing an extruded corner looks C1
Within it are the stairs. E of this, the main part of the W front
a later screen for a corridor and disguises the old hall entran
and the remains of a C16 window. The garden front is said
be a reconstruction after 1734. Yet the centrepiece loo
stylistically c.1680. Tall pedimented door and big rectangul
mullion-and-transom-cross windows. The window hea
formed by the pulvinated frieze. In the garden wall a C13 doo
way. The STABLES follow. They are C16, restored by *Dawb*
& *Tapper* in 1930 and later by *L. Bond* for himself. Did the
originally belong to Grantham House? N of the church facir
the churchyard, in CHURCH STREET, Nos 1–2, re-fronte
handsomely in the early C18 with seven bays, two storeys, an
a parapet. Windows with moulded surrounds and keystone
doorway with triangular pediment on brackets. In No. 2 is
C17 painting above a fireplace. Masonic subjects in grisai

against an architectural background. Adjoining this is the
KING'S SCHOOL, chiefly two ranges. The s range facing the
church is the school room, built in 1497. Six two-light windows with depressed-arched lights. Open roof with collar-
beams on arched braces and two tiers of wind-braces. To the r.
of the s front a small doorway. This now leads into a passage from which the main doorway opens into the schoolroom.
The main entrance, however, was from the w. The doorway
is blocked. The N range was master's house and what else?
The front is of five irregular bays with one-, three-, and four-
light windows and a canted bay with a quasi-five-light oriel.
The later school buildings, seen best from BROOK STREET,
are of 1904, by *John Bilson*, the great architectural historian.
To the l. of the school is the VICARAGE, 1789 by *John
Langwith* (GA).* Brick, Venetian windows, doorway with
open pediment, and hipped roof. Then, before one reaches
Swinegate again, HURST'S ALMSHOUSES in a pretty C19
Gothic.

GRANTHAM COLLEGE OF FURTHER EDUCATION, Avenue
Road. 1949–59 by *J. W. H. Barnes*, the county architect.

KESTEVEN AND GRANTHAM GIRLS' SCHOOL, Sandon Road.
1911 by *H. H. Donn*, plus extensions 1956–7 by the county
architect *J. W. H. Barnes*.

HILL VIEW HOSPITAL. By *Valentine Green*, 1891. In accommo-
dating groups of small pavilions. It cost £26,000 and was much
trouble to its architect.

BARRACKS, St Catherine's Road. Of *c*.1858 and 1872, perhaps
by *Goddard*. Castellated and very forbidding.

ARNOLDFIELD, Gonerby Road. 1820. Neo-Greek. Three by
four bays and two floors with a projecting pedimented centre.
Crisp clean lines. Tuscan porch to the w front.

GREATFORD

0010

THOMAS A BECKET. Essentially an E.E. church. First the
chancel. Lancet windows to N and s. Piscina with pointed-
trefoiled head and dog-tooth on the hood-mould. Plain priest's
doorway. But, as a Dec alteration, the E window with reticulated tracery, the low-side window with transom, and one
other s window, which has inside a pretty frieze of trails of
ballflower. The N doorway and the NW lancet also E.E. On
the s side the doorway E.E. too, with a little nailhead. But the

---

* It cost £801 12s 0d, as Mr Savidge kindly tells me.

s porch entrance is again Dec, see the flat nobbly leaves of t
capitals. E.E. to Dec the most impressive part of the churc
the s tower, in a transeptal position. Lancets and shafted la
cets. Arch to the nave with triple responds and a little nailhea
Bell-openings of two lights with plain bar tracery (unfoil
circle). Broach spire with two tiers of lucarnes in the sa
directions, the lower still late C13, the upper Dec. Late C1
window in the s aisle (bar tracery with a pointed quatrefo:
The one-bay s chapel also looks late C13. Dec N transept, see t
arch to the nave as well as the reticulated tracery of the N wi
dow. To the E of the arch to the nave a squint of two lights w:
19b   ogee heads. One of them was the transept piscina. Six radiati
oak leaves round the drain.* – STAINED GLASS. E window
Ward & Hughes, 1882, really hideous. – PLATE. Chali
London, 1578; Paten, by Timothy Ley, 1689; Paten, by Geo:
Smith & Thomas Hayter, 1798. – MONUMENTS. The R
Francis Willis, M.D., † 1807. By Nollekens. Bust and boc
against an obelisk above the inscription (which ought to
read; it refers to the curing of George III's first attack
lunacy). – Mrs Francis Willis † 1797. By Nollekens too. L
before an obelisk. – John Willis, M.D., † 1835. By T. Gaf
Relief. Recumbent on a couch with two angels about him.

GREATFORD HALL. Dr Francis Willis, famous for cur:
George III in 1788, lived and maintained a private asylum
Greatford. A large C17 house burnt down in 1930 b
sympathetically rebuilt. Of a straightforward vernacular ty,
The out-buildings are impressive but owe much of their eff
to the C20.

SHILLINGTHORPE HALL. The Willis reputation was such t:
another asylum was opened here. But the house designed
Sir Robert Smirke in 1833 for Dr John Willis has been den
lished. 'So carefully were unhappy patients excluded fr
observation that his guests were never pained by their obt
sion.'‡ A pretty but decayed cast-iron BRIDGE in the park
The VILLAGE is wonderfully crazy. Someone obviously has b
tremendous fun with it. He was Major C. C. L. Fitzwilli
who carved all the obelisks, mushrooms, Norman basi
elephants, giant coronets, etc. He did this in the 1930s, a
used the exhibitions at the Chelsea Flower Show to obt

* But Cox calls it an offertory basin and compares it with East Kirk
Bridlington in the East Riding, and Speeton in the East Riding.

‡ The Willis–Smirke papers were kindly communicated to me by M
Crooks.

orders for the embellishment of people's gardens. His *magnum opus* is to be looked for on the roof of Messrs Derry & Toms of Kensington.

GREAT GONERBY

¶ SEBASTIAN. An unusual dedication. Of ironstone and grey stone. All early C14 except for the Perp w tower, clerestory, and some details. The tower has a frieze of shields below the battlements and a fine recessed spire with two tiers of lucarnes in alternating directions. The clerestory has a frieze of shields in pointed quatrefoils, battlements and pinnacles. The N aisle, which embraces the tower, also has such a frieze, battlements and pinnacles. At the NW corner a niche carried on the demi-figure of a dignified gentleman with chain; early C16, it seems, and perhaps representing the donor. However, the windows of the N aisle are early C14, first cusped intersecting and Y cusped, then, further E, even uncusped intersecting and uncusped Y, i.e. perhaps pre-1300 (cf. Grantham). The s aisle is almost exactly the same. The chancel has plain battlements, plain sedilia and piscina inside, and windows with Y, intersecting, and also reticulated tracery, i.e. a later form. The interior has a C13 S arcade which is cut into by the Perp tower. Three bays now. Round piers, round abaci, double-chamfered arches. The N arcade is Perp. Piers with a polygonal projection to the nave and demi-shafts to the arch opening. This arcade of course takes notice of the tower. But the history of the building is more complicated, as the fourth bays show. They are wider than the others. That on the N is earlier than anything so far. The capitals have recut leaf motifs typical of the late C12, and one base has spurs. The s bay is not so different from the other s arches, but the capitals are evidently muddled. It looks as if parts of two capitals were put one on top of the other. What may have happened is that the preceding church had no aisles but transepts. Then the N transept arch would be *in situ*, the s transept arch altered, and the transepts would explain the width of the bay. – FONT. Dec, octagonal, stem and bowl in one. With eight different patterns of Dec windows, like a pattern book. – STAINED GLASS. One piece: the hare riding the hound (chancel s). – PLATE. Two Chalices, by *R.C.*, 1630; fine pewter Flagon with portrait after van Dyck of Charles I on horseback.

he OLD MANOR is Georgian, stone, Vernacular, MANOR FARM is Victorian Tudoresque. In GREEN STREET a pair of cottages designed for agricultural workers by *H. Roberts* in 1848 under the auspices of the Society for Improving the Condition of the Labouring Classes. An identical pair is attached to ELMS FARM.

SCHOOL. Dated 1841. Tudor style with a porch-cum-bell-turret similar to that at North Rauceby, of 1842 (see p. 613).

GREAT HALE
1040

ST JOHN BAPTIST. Anglo-Saxon W tower, the bell-openings of the familiar type with mid-wall shaft. Plain arch towards the nave. The S window has some defaced decoration round the arch. On the N side one small circular window. (This looks into the staircase which is in the thickness of the wall and only 15½ in. wide. Cox) Perp top of the tower with eight pinnacles. The arcades inside are E.E. Five bays, tall circular piers, circular abaci, double-chamfered arches. There is no structural division to the present chancel; for the medieval chancel collapsed in the mid C17. Most of the rest *c.*1300 to Dec. First S porch entrance, steep-arched S doorway with continuous chamfers. S aisle windows with intersecting tracery. So far this might still be the same build as the arcades. Then Dec S aisle E window of four lights (cusped intersecting, but with ogees, odd Dec N aisle E window. The N aisle windows all Dec, but all over-restored by *C. Hodgson Fowler* in 1896–7. A chantry was endowed in the church in 1334. Then the minor N doorway. This could again go with the arcades. The doorway in the E wall below the intersecting E window confirms that this is not the original E end. – FONT. Octagonal, big, Dec or Perp and of a very unusual design. In each side a plain cusped arched panel flanked and surmounted by a frame of sunk quatrefoils. – SCREEN (N aisle). One-light divisions. Tracery above the ogee arches with a variety of motifs. – COMMUNION RAIL. Later C17, with dumb-bell balusters. – PLATE. Chalice by *T.C.*, 1619; Paten, by *Thomas Holland*, 1709. – MONUMENT. Robert Cawdron † 1665 and others. Small tablet with kneeling couples in two tiers, one above the other. Erected 1668, and very conservative for its date.

GREAT HUMBY
0030
1½ m. SE of Ropsley

CHAPEL. There was a Brownlow mansion here, but now nothing tells of it but a forlorn chapel, 30 by 15 ft. It was built in 168

Oblong with solid bell-gable. The windows mullioned, of three lights, the mullions concave-sided. Doorway with four-centred head but a big blank keystone, i.e. entirely pre-classical. – FONT. Elementarily fluted circular bowl. – PLATE. Silver-gilt Flagon, by *G.B.*, 1671; silver-gilt Chalice and Paten, by *I.C.*, 1673.

MOORE FARMHOUSE, Little Humby, ¼ m. NW. A nearly symmetrical street-front, mullioned windows of three to six lights. Doorway with four-centred head. Above it the string-course rises to form an oblong panel. This carries the date 1631 and three very stylized, flatly carved fleurs-de-lis – a West Riding rather than a Lincolnshire composition.

GREAT PONTON

9030

HOLY CROSS. The church has a big W tower, *c.*80 ft. high. Frieze of quatrefoils, mouchette wheels etc. at the base. Niches in the buttresses. To the l. and r. of the W doorway inscriptions. On the S and N walls inscriptions also. They read: Think and thank God of all. Above, only to the S, there is one big window. Then the bell-openings. Two twins under one arch with the dividing mullion rising into the apex of that arch (the Stamford motif). Below to the W the arms of Anthony Ellis, merchant of the Staple of Calais, who built the tower in 1519. The tower buttresses are recessed, but join to turn polygonal at the bell-stage. There is then a change of plan. The decorated battlements and eight pinnacles do not quite fit the stage below. The earliest features of the church are the chancel arch and the two-bay arcade from chancel to N chapel. The E arch is blocked. The details indicate the late C13. The chancel E end must be shortened. Also late C13 and re-set the S porch entrance. Otherwise all is Perp. Three-bay arcades with octagonal piers and double-chamfered arches. The tower arch corresponds. In the S aisle near the W end a C16 fireplace. – PLATE. Chalice and Paten Cover, inscribed 1569. – MONUMENT. In the N chapel walls three shields of Anthony Ellis †1520, suggested convincingly by the Rev. H. Grundy to be part of Ellis's former tomb-chest, which was quite probably set up in this favourite place.

RECTORY. Built by Anthony Ellis. It may have just been completed then. Roughly L-shaped with a high gable-end dominating the street side. This is crow-stepped with triangular finials. A two-light window in the gable and two four-light

ones below. They have arched lights. The windows on the
side of a Late Perp type with square drip moulds. On thi
front the staircase projects and is corbelled out on a bracket
Round the corner are additions of 1920. Round the corne
again, to the s, where there are two-, three-, and four-ligh
windows all of the C16 type and an early C19 entrance.* The
interior is much mutilated. The entrance must always hav
been through the door in the N front. This probably led int
a small hall with the newel stair adjacent. The present stair
are C17. In the E room are a C16 chimneypiece and tw
blocked doorways. A third immediately to their l. This now
leads into the semi-basement of an attachment which ma
well be original. Were the three doorways then the usua
kitchen and offices access? That can hardly be so, as th
chimneypiece just mentioned and a second standing back t
back with it would be in their way. Upstairs, corresponding t
the latter, yet another big chimneypiece, this time with a hood
It probably belonged to the solar. The highlight of the hous
is an exciting and almost complete scheme of early C16 WALL
PAINTINGS. They travel round the whole upper floor, ignor
ing the later partitions. Red and yellow. Columns form panel
in which stylized trees spread large, lush leaves. In some of th
space between peacocks and deer. It is a rare English inter
pretation of French verdure tapestries.

GREEN MAN INN see BLANKNEY

0020

GRIMSTHORPE CASTLE

The house is set in a parkscape which has been rightly compare
with the spacious expanses of Touraine. Its early history i
connected with the Cistercian Abbey of Vaudey (Vallis Dei
founded in 1147, which stood to the s of the lake,‡ and th
castle built in the later C13 by Gilbert de Gant. This had fou
ranges round a courtyard and four square or oblong angl
towers of differing sizes. They as well as the courtyard stil
exist. In the C16 Leland mentions a gatehouse and grea
ditch, castellations, and the 'new building of the second court
About this time Grimsthorpe had been granted to William
tenth Lord Willoughby, whose daughter married Charle
Brandon, Duke of Suffolk. It was this Duke who enlarged th
castle, as we shall see; for shortly before 1541, when Henr

★ *J. Langwith* made alterations in 1826.
‡ Excavations in 1851 revealed the four crossing piers of the church.

VIII visited, Fuller says that Brandon made 'an extempore building set up of a sudden', which may be Leland's 'second court'. In 1685 a brand-new N front was provided by Robert, third Earl of Lindsey. This was again rebuilt by *Sir John Vanbrugh*, who intended to rebuild the whole castle. Work ceased in 1727, not to be taken up again until 1811, when the fragments of *Vanbrugh's* partly built W front were demolished and a new Tudor-style front designed by *Henry Garling* and *Samual Page* for Lord Gwydir. Brandon's work seems to have been the insertion of state rooms in the E and W ranges and is best seen on the E, where the centre has five bulgy canted extrusions. All have C19 windows and crenellated parapets. To its N the three side bays of Vanbrugh's N front, of which more anon. In the SE corner is the mightiest of the four C13 towers, KING JOHN'S TOWER, and inside it two rooms with quadripartite rib-vaults are preserved. On the S front, between the two towers, is an irregular sequence of twelve bays with projecting chimney-flanks and eight gables. The windows are mostly Georgian. SUNDIAL on the SW tower dated 1757. Turning round to the W front one turns to *Henry Garling's* work of 1811, characterized by the rhythm of narrow chimney-flanks with chimneystacks rising above the parapet. However, at the N extremity of this range is another and bigger bay window of Brandon's time, set against the C13 NW tower. Then the three side bays of Vanbrugh's N front, corresponding to those already noticed at the N end of the E front.

And so to the N front, Vanbrugh's last work. Oddly enough, 49a this was the replacement of a grand front put up less than forty years before, in 1685.* The first Duke of Ancaster had probably earlier employed Vanbrugh at Swinstead (*see* p. 691); in the winter of 1722 the designs for Grimsthorpe were made. In July 1723 the Duke died and Vanbrugh wrote in August 'but shall wait upon his new Grace of Ancaster in my way, having the honour of an invitation from him, to consult about his building; by which I believe he is inclined to go upon the general design I made for his Father last Winter and which was approved of by himself'. The complete plans were published in the third volume of *Vitruvius Britannicus*, i.e. in 1725, and included a hexastyle Corinthian portico to the S front influenced directly by the Palladian Colen Campbell's Houghton. Otherwise Grimsthorpe is out of Seaton Delaval (*c.*1720) by Lumley

* According to Mr Gunnis, *Ezra Horson* and *Joseph Warrington* were making window cornices then.

Castle (*c*.1722), the latter confirming the plan of a four-towere
medieval castle, the former the type of forecourt with long sid
walls covered by heavy blank arcading and summer houses a
the N ends (as if we were back in Elizabethan England). Als
from Seaton Vanbrugh's original synthesis of Palladian ele
ments. The Grimsthorpe front is successful as a compositio
only if viewed frontally – an objection that can also be raise
at Seaton. The angle towers – Seaton towers in little – are o
three storeys, with emphatic quoins, heavy modillion cornice
balustrade, and noble circular swagged terminations at th
angles. There are three bays to the sides and one bay to th
front. The window sequence: rusticated, Venetian, triangular
pedimented to the N; and rusticated, straight-hooded, tri
angular-pedimented to the E and W. Locked between th
towers is Vanbrugh's hall front. It is one of his most seren
compositions. The centre of two equivalent storeys. First, from
l. to r., a single bay of arched windows, then a paired Dori
order, the most magnificent exposition of the theme in Eng
land. Banded free-standing columns under great chunks o
entablature. Above them equally massive pedestals supportin
Rape groups. Between the columns are seven bays of arche
windows formed as a continuous arcade. Above this a balus
trade with parapet, urns, and in the middle the Ancaster arm
on a true Vanbrughian scale. The doorway looks odd. Cor
rectly Doric, with triangular pediment, and good enough fo
any Palladian – as are the Venetian windows in the tower. Bu
Vanbrugh's original design omitted these 'correct' element
His doorway pediment was intended to die into the fron
below it, and in place of the Venetian windows he wanted
continuation of the single-arched theme. The reason for th
palladianizing of this last design has never been fully eluci
dated. There may have been less built, when Vanbrugh die
in 1726, than has been realized, or *Hawksmoor* may have com
pleted the front (cf. below). Much else of the front is, Palladio
wise, unethical. The juxtaposition of towers and centre mus
horrify any purist. Strings miss each other, pediments die int
the wall. The forecourt is also Vanbrugh, at least in the con
ception of the plan. Low walls of twenty-six bays of rusticate
niches, linked to two-storey pavilions, the main angle tower
in miniature. Connecting them is the great iron GRILLE an
GATES upon which *Edward Nutt* was working in 1730. Th
inner courtyard is positioned as shown by Kip and Knyff abou
1705. Successive restorations to these parts have disguised th

early fronts. They are best seen now on the s, where the c16 predominates but with the hipped roof and dormers of the 1680s.

Of the INTERIOR a perambulation would proceed from the GREAT HALL clockwise. This is unquestionably Vanbrugh's 49b finest room. A reflection inside of the outside wall treatment, that is, two storeys of arcading. The N wall seven bays of windows, the s wall, above, seven English Kings in grisaille (from l. to r: William I, Edward III, Henry V, George I, William I, Henry VIII, Henry VII) by *Sir James Thornhill*, and below, six deeply sunk niches. The E and W walls are spatially a *tour de force*. Triplets of superimposed arched openings divide the hall from the stairs at each end. The ceiling has a concave oval centre, probably intended for a painting. The whole arrangement reflects the black and cream patterns of the marble floor below. The inner doorcase in a supreme fluted Doric with Willoughby heads as triglyphs, and the same Willoughby head appears on the overmantel of the chimneypiece opposite. This defies description. To the l. out of the hall, and beneath the vaulted aisle of the arcade, first to the EAST ENTRANCE HALL, a tripartite vaulted space allied to Vanbrugh's Lumley undercroft, and then back again to the STAIRS ascending r. and l. and returning to the central doorway. The iron balustrades are masterpieces of smithery by *Bell* of Sheffield. The ceiling above, Apollo and Muses, by *Thornhill*. The Michelangelesque theme of the narrowed pilastered doorway is odd for Vanbrugh and more of a Hawksmoor trait. Through the doorway, into the STATE DINING ROOM, the first floor of the NE tower and the first of the rooms on the E front. The ceiling with Liberal Arts is attributed to *Francesco Sleter*. From now on the decorative ensemble is of the late 1730s and later, rather than of the 1720s. Next is KING JAMES'S DRAWING ROOM, including the first of the c16 bows, making little alcoves. Fluted Corinthian pilasters, a coved ceiling, arched doorways, and *sopraporte*. Then the STATE DRAWING ROOM, with two of the c16 bows. In blue, white, and gold, the walls decorated with portraits in carved frames and lots of Rococo foliage pendants. The ceiling an oval in a square, the bows treated with flattish arches, and a delicate chimneypiece, perhaps by *Sir Henry Cheere*. Then comes the noticeably lower TAPESTRY ROOM with two more bows. An essay in subdued brown and gold, the ceiling a triad of octagons, and the walls hung with Soho tapestries made by *J. Morris* for Normanton Park, Rutland. This is the end of the main suite of State Rooms. They

must have been designed and supervised by an absolutely firs
class London architect. His name ought to be known. At the
angle of this range in King John's Tower the BIRDCAG
DRESSING ROOM. The vault paintings are attributed to Cle
mont, and the walls covered with Anglo-Chinese wallpape
The rooms on the s front are mostly by *Detmar Blow*, 1911–1
His is the TAPESTRY BEDROOM with a mid-Georgian chin
neypiece, not *in situ*. Only two other rooms need be describe
The CHINESE DRAWING ROOM occupies the N end of the
front next to the chapel. Octagonal coffering to the cove ar
a ceiling with divisions decorated perhaps by *Clermont*. Th
woodwork has been regarded in the past as Regency. It lool
the highest quality mid-Georgian Chinese Chippendale. Blac
and gold fretwork, and inset lacquer panels. Of the same da
is the wall mirror and lacquer commode. The window is
Brandon bow, that is C16, but the fan-vault, cusps, and centr
pendant must be of 1811. Just before the chapel is the sta
exit and the stairs with another painted ceiling, an assembly
gods, attributed to *Francesco Sleter* or a Venetian (Crof
Murray). The CHAPEL has a gallery at one end. The order
a fluted Corinthian; windows with broken triangular ped
ments, and rich joinery for the Venetian window in the N wa
The ceiling with quatrefoil centre and lusciously decorate
beams is almost in a Jonesian style. All below the order is Ne
Georgian and probably by *Blow*. It is not known who w
responsible for this chapel. Designs are recorded in *Hawk
moor*'s sale catalogue, and the style is mid-way between th
Vanbrugh work and the fitting-up of the State Rooms.

The STABLES were the C17 Riding House and have no
in 1959, been given a sympathetic Vanbrugh-style face 1
R. J. Page. The GARDENS were originally laid out by *Geor
London*, that is, for the pre-Vanbrugh house, with militar
style bastions. They remain on the s front and s front vist
There were park works by *John Grundy* about the mid centur
and then, in 1772, *Capability Brown* landscaped the par
naturalizing the formal canals.

GUNBY ST NICHOLAS

¾ m. SE of Stainby

ST NICHOLAS. 1869, probably by *R. Coad*, who built Stain
church for the same rector. The w tower Perp in style, th
rest c.1300. – WOODWORK by the Rev. *W. Thorold* after 187

– PLATE. Chalice, London, 1706; Flagon, by *Thomas Tearle*, 1722.

GUY'S HEAD *see* SUTTON BRIDGE

HACCONBY

T ANDREW. We start with the priest's doorway, which seems to be of *c*.1200. Then the E.E. arcades. Three bays, circular piers and abaci, double-chamfered arches. After that the W tower, of banded ironstone and grey stone. It is of the late C13 to early C14; see the W window, the triple-chamfered arch to the nave dying into the imposts, the twin bell-openings with the thick leaf capitals of the separating shaft, and the pointed quatrefoil in the tracery. Then a Perp lozenge frieze and the recessed spire which has four polygonal pinnacles at its foot, but not at the corners of the tower. Three tiers of lucarnes in alternating directions, all with crocketed gablets. Perp S aisle, the doorway with a quatrefoil band over, Perp N aisle, Perp clerestory, and Perp also the N chapel, which is the stateliest part of the church. The arches are of the basket type. In one bay the doorway is flanked by the mullions of the windows above, carried down for the purpose. Inside, the mullions all descend below the window openings. A bench runs along the N and E walls. To the chancel the four-centred arch provided for the monument of the founder of the chapel and a small doorway with leaf and shields in the spandrels. Outside at the NE corner a handsome niche. – PULPIT. Perp. The panels were formerly painted. The pulpit stands on a polygonal spreading base. – COMMUNION RAIL. Probably early C18. – CHEST. C14. Tracery and foliage on the front. On the posts l. and r. panels with dragons. – STAINED GLASS. The E window by *A. K. Nicholson*, 1937. Quite terrible in its total neglect of the revival of technique and style to respond to the essence of stained glass. – MONUMENT. Inscription brass under twin canopy to Samuel Hopkinson † 1841. Designed by *Pugin* and made by *Hardman & Iliffe*.

HACEBY

T MARGARET. Early Norman, completely unmoulded chancel arch on the plainest imposts. Norman W tower, unbuttressed, see the small round-arched windows. The arch to the nave E.E. The bell-stage ashlar-faced and Dec. E.E. chancel with

c 17(?) E end. Lancet windows, including one 'low-side'. On(
window with Y-tracery. Perp s arcade (octagonal piers, double
chamfered arches). Perp windows. Perp clerestory. – PLATE
Chalice and Paten Cover by *R.W.*, 1641; silver-gilt Chalice
Cover, and Almsdish, by *William Fawdery*, 1718.

ROMAN VILLA. The remains of a large villa lie partly in thi(
parish and partly in that of Newton. Examination in the c 1(
revealed six rooms, including a bath house at one corner of th(
site. Some of the rooms had tessellated pavements. The vill(
was probably of courtyard type.

HANTHORPE see BOURNE

3030
HARLAXTON

ST MARY AND ST PETER. Mostly of ironstone and, especially
inside, grossly over-restored (1856 and – by *Oldrid Scott* ·
1891). The w tower is Dec below, Perp above. Battlement(
with crocketed, recessed spire. The rest externally all Perp(
except for the s porch and s doorway, which are imitation
E.E. But inside the N arcade is really E.E. It consists of thre(
bays plus one w of the former w wall. This bay has exactly
the same details as the w respond of the other part and can thu(
not be later. Perhaps they re-used the chancel arch? All th(
capitals are unworked except for one with crocket-like ribbe(
leaves, still Late Norman in character, but all re-carved. Th(
s arcade probably Dec. The w respond has a little nailhead(
Chancel chapels of two bays, both Perp. The N pier with th(
familiar four-shafts-four-hollows section, the s pier with (
polygonal projection to the nave and demi-shafts with capital(
to the chapel openings. To the l. and r. of the s chapel (
window and of the chancel E window Perp niches. – FONT(
Octagonal, Perp, all entirely re-cut. – PLATE. Chalice and(
Paten Cover, by *John Morley* of Lincoln, 1569; silver-gil(
Chalice and Cover and Paten, by *David Willaume*, 1711(
silver-gilt Flagon, by *John Ward*, 1713; silver-gilt Almsbasin(
by *John Ward*, 1714; Waiter, by *Daniel Smith & Robert Sharp*(
1780; secular Flagon, by *J. Denzilow*, 1781. – MONUMENT(
In the N chapel monument said to represent Sir Richar(
Rickhill and wife, early c 15. Alabaster and quite good.

Of the old HARLAXTON MANOR no more is preserved than a(
Elizabethan archway about 150 yds SSE of the church.

The village can boast quite a number of crazily detailed cottage(
starting from the one SE of the church with an assembly o(

brought-in timber colonnettes, arches, etc. Other cottages
with strange brick motifs, the outcome of the activities of the
lord of the manor. He was guided by the best advice. The
principles, listed by Loudon, deserve to be quoted here in full:

1. To bestow the principal expence on the main features,
such as the porch, the chimney pots, and the gardens.

2. Always to have some architectural feature in or about the
gardens as well as the cottage.

3. Never to employ two styles of architecture in the same
cottage, or at all events not to do this so frequently as to lead a
stranger to suppose that it has been done through ignorance.

4. Not altogether to omit objects purely ornamental, where
they can be introduced with propriety.

5. To indicate the occupation of the inhabitant, where it can
be done.

HARLAXTON MANOR. Before 1830 George de Ligne Gregory
lived at Hungerton Hall (*see* p. 718), where he had a large
architectural library and a collection of works of art. Oddly, as
we shall see, in view of his monster house, he was not *nouveau-
riche* but rather old landed gentry. He also owned Harlaxton
Manor, a substantial early C17 house, then in a decayed condition. Two factors may have determined him to build: his
increasing art collection, and the buildings undertaken at near-
by Belvoir Castle. Although the designs for the new Harlaxton
are dated 1831, the house's origin is much older; for Loudon
in 1832 says: 'Mr Gregory having determined to build a new
family mansion, informs us that he studied the subject for
several years previous to commencing it.' Loudon then refers
to the country houses seen by Gregory. They included Burghley, Montacute, Rushton, Wollaton, Cobham, and Audley
End. All contribute details to the present structure, whose
designer was *Anthony Salvin*, at the time aged only thirty-two.
There are no Salvin designs for the interiors and outworks, as
by 1838 he and his builder, Mr Weare, had been replaced by
William Burn, then forty-nine, and his builder Mr Nowell.
Harlaxton must be seen to be believed. It is without any doubt
the wildest and most fanciful mansion of the 1830s – High
Victorian, one would be tempted to say, rather than Early
Victorian – and it has certain interiors again so gloriously and
thickly Baroque that the 1830s seem an unbelievably early
date.

In terms of silhouette Harlaxton exploits the potentialities
of the site to the full. The approach is planned as a crescendo

of effects. From the entrance gates the drive drops into a valley
and crosses the splendid BRIDGE (perhaps by *Salvin*), and
then, beyond the KITCHEN GARDENS with massive stone
banded piers and walls articulated by rusticated stone niches
(perhaps by *Burn*), a gentle ascent leads to the GATEHOUSE
which is in a Baronial Tudor style. Through the gatehouse for
another descent and ascent, and up to the pyrotechnic display
of the FORECOURT GATES and SCREEN. These prelude Salvin's towering façade, and prelude, in a stylistic way, the
Baroque effusion of the interior. They were not built by 1840
and must therefore be by *Burn*. There is nothing like them in
England at this time, and only Vanbrugh and Blenheim bear
comparison. Before Harlaxton Burn showed no inclination for
this style; so perhaps Gregory's tastes started him on his eclec-
tically Baroque career. The scale of the gates is gargantuan.
The outer lodges, strapwork-banded, support scrolled con-
soles with sarcophagi on top. The openings circular or square
all massively identified by mouldings and cornices. The inner
lodges pierced with arched openings and carrying terminations
like a group of chimneystacks in the form of a square indented
twice at the angles. This synthesis of Continental and Jacobean forms is highly singular and, once again, Vanbrugh is the
only parallel. To the r., that is S, an ogee-cupolaed GAZEBO
like those at Montacute. Its placing is judicious, as from a
distance its vertical value is equivalent to that of the OFFICE
WING on the N side. This is dated 1843. It is a variation on the
theme of the angle towers of Wollaton.

62b   The house is built in glowing golden Ketton stone, the plan
a combination of E and H. On the W front the ogee gables and
strapwork-crested bow windows of the wings derive from
Rushton, and the tall octagonal angle-turrets marking the four
extremities of the block from Cobham. The centre stroke can
almost be regarded as a building within a building. Its power
and strength within the composition is a Baroque rather than
a 'Jacobean' gesture. The two-storey oriel and polygonal bay
windows with spired cupolas are the Burghley theme, and the
oriel with a lusciously decorated arch between the turrets is
the theme of Northumberland House, London. In the balustrade by the arch, 1837 is lettered. Salvin's design has 1831 in
the same place, so building took from 1831 to 1837. But the
culmination of the centre is yet to come. Behind the cupola
and arch is a massive square base burrowing back into the body
of the house. Upon it a towering octagonal arcaded turret with

stone-banded cupolas. They look like the C17 ones at Stoney-hurst. Attached to the turret is a gigantic clock with strapwork. To the r. and l. the roof ornaments create a Burghleyesque sky-line. The s front is a restrained, masterly essay in balanced asymmetry. Four bays between two angle-turrets. Bay one of ogival plan with a canted projection; bay two with a deeper canted projection with an arcaded ground floor – a theme from old Harlaxton; bay three with plain mullioned and transomed windows; and bay four repeating the gable of bay one but with a semicircular bay window added to a square projection, that is, the w front oriel in little. Round the corner to the E front for Salvin's masterpiece. The two projecting wings have shaped gables and canted bays following the s front roof-line. But here the house is built on a terrace from out of the hill, and Salvin could not give height to his central elevation with-out imposing upon the silhouette line. He therefore dug out the hill between the wings to achieve sufficient depth. The result defies analysis and might be called abstract asymmetry. It has rightly been compared with Lutyens's Edwardian-Tudor phase. In one angle a tall polygonal oriel with two windows divided by stepped buttresses. Then a keeled bow window creating an acid contrast, and next to it the N angle entrance. This has a profusely decorated window with strapwork balcony. The roof-line unaffected, just three small stepped gables.

THE INTERIOR. Entering through the w porch one finds oneself in a dark VESTIBULE. But a Baroque stream of light pours down from the staircase on the l. It is separated from the vestibule by two rows of heavily rusticated tripartite arches, one behind the other. The front one with top-heavy scrolled brackets supporting the main roof beam and draped about with gargantuan iron trophies of trumpets, lances, and shields. The chimneypiece sounds an alien note. It is classical and of the early C19, quite excellent in quality. White marble, as tall as the vestibule and with pairs of Ionic columns and a gene-rously full entablature. A bas-relief signed by *A. J. Smith*.* The stair balustrade is a *tour de force* of the bronze-worker's art. The arcade at the top of the stairs has fluted and banded pillars in a French late C16 style, the ceiling star compart-ments and pendants. From this point a short passage leads to the DINING ROOM (at the time of writing the CHAPEL), two-storeyed and taking up the centre of the E front. A splendid

* A similar chimneypiece at Malahide Castle, Dublin.

free paraphrase of Jacobean forms by *Burn* rather than
Salvin. The source is Audley End, and for the stair gallery
perhaps Wollaton. But at neither place are there patterns for
the Michelangelesque terms supporting the roof trusses, and
the gargantuan chimneypiece with four waisted pilasters –
beating the Jacobeans at their own game. Beyond the chimneypiece the hall bay with a pendant in the vault and heraldic
glass by *Willement*, dated 1837. The present DINING ROOM
is entered from the stairs and is placed immediately below the
central tower on the w front. The view from this point is the
finest contrived view in the county. At the far end appears the
spire of Bottesford church. The walls of the room are restrained, the ceiling and chimneypiece lavish. It must be *Burn's*
design. The ceiling is like his at Stoke Rochford (*see* p. 645)
and the chimneypiece of white and mottled red marble with
black columns derives from either Hatfield or Cranborne. Of
equal sumptuousness are the door surrounds – white against
pink marble. The overdoors with putti and a profusion of
shields. The next room is an anteroom – for the ballroom to the
s, the staircase to the E. The room is not Jacobean but French
Dixhuitième, more Louis Quinze than Quatorze. Gregory or
Burn must have seen the work of Benjamin Dean Wyatt in
that style at Belvoir. But Harlaxton is entirely different and
perhaps better. It has more vitality, is less copyist, and possesses indeed almost an Edwardian lushness. Berainesque ceiling with scallop-shell heads and lots of reversed scrolls and
S-curves. The door furniture by *Gibbons* of Wolverhampton
and as good as the best C18 work. Then comes the BALLROOM
for the whole length of the s front, again in a French style. The
doors are the best of Burn. Panelled walls, with bas-relief compartments to the overdoors and lovely sculptured angels in the
form of half terms. To the s and E door surrounds with free-
standing white marble columns, the capitals and bases in
simulated bronze. The doors lead to the s terrace and to the
conservatory. But first back to the anteroom and r. to the
STAIRCASE, to a world of Italian Baroque opulence, quite
alien to anything else in England. The first Baroque feature is
deceit. The effect of three main floors is obtained by raising
the upper part in a tower not visible from the fronts. The
lower compartment is relatively restrained. Kneeling Michelangelesque slaves on the returns and a luxurious white marble
portal with barley-sugar columns and a gyration of putti in the
pediment. Pairs of terms support the first-floor balcony, each

with a big scrolled bracket looping itself up and draped with
hanging fruit clusters on real rope. Between the terms the
windows filled with mirrors. Then at the landing begins the
real movement, the panoply of theatric effect. Swagged cur-
tains interlaced with thriving putti blowing trumpets and
grasping ropes with huge tassels. Above this is an arcade with
more plaster decoration right up the blue scintillating pseudo-
sky. Here are six balconies like Jacobean pendants cut in half.
Then more putti and a pair of Fathers Time, both grasping
real scythes, one draped with a flag incised with a plan of
Harlaxton, the other holding the relief portrait of a woman.
Beyond the stair are more rooms in the French style, notably
one as good, or better, than any Louis XV ones at Belvoir;
then the Baroquely detailed CONSERVATORY. Upstairs are
more rich effects. Each attic room has its Jacobean ceiling and
its marble chimneypiece.

In the GARDENS the hill provides a setting for display. The
Baroque terraces to the E are by *Burn* and perhaps also the
SUMMER HOUSE. The STABLES look neither Burn nor Salvin.
Their style is mixed and unsuccessful.

HARMSTON

9060

ALL SAINTS. CII W tower, probably not pre-Conquest; for the
twin bell-openings have among the capitals of their mid-wall
shafts one with unmistakable scallops. Also a block and a volute capital. Maybe the date is even later than 1100, or would the
tremendous, clearly early C12 tower arch be an afterthought?
Triple responds with capitals with a band of leaves standing
up and volutes above. The arch has several strong rolls. Perp
tower top with decorated parapet and eight pinnacles. The
rest of the church externally all by *Withers* 1868 (plate tracery).
He rebuilt a church of 1717, but what was that church like?
One would like to know, because the arcades and the chancel
arch with round piers and round abaci are all wrong in their
mouldings, impossible for the Middle Ages, impossible for
Withers, yet unlikely for 1717. – FONT. Circular, but the underside octagonal. With large flat arches or scallops, again decidedly odd. – SCULPTURE. A part of an Anglo-Saxon cross
shaft, 41 in. long, with a small primitive Crucifixion at the top
and interlace below and on the other sides. – ARMOUR (w
wall). C17–C18 funeral pieces. – PLATE. Chalice, Paten, and
Flagon, by *Edward Pocock*, 1736. – MONUMENTS. Sir George

Thorold † 1722, former Lord Mayor of London. Standin
monument. Bust with wig, columns l. and r., weeping put
outside them. Open curly pediment. – Sir Samuel Thorol
† 1738. The same composition exactly, but an open segment
pediment. – In the churchyard headstone of *John Willson*, wh
made the statue on Dunston Pillar (*see* p. 520).

HARMSTON HALL. To an earlier C18 house, Samuel Thorol
added a tall N front in 1775. This was demolished in 189
The S front seems to preserve the rebuilt shape of the earl
house, where there is a rainwater head dated 1710. Insic
a gorgeous Edwardian Rococo chimneypiece in coloure
marbles.

HARTSHOLME HALL *see* BOULTHAM

HAVERHOLME PRIORY *see* ANWICK

1040
HECKINGTON

ST ANDREW. A large town church in a village, in fact one of tl
dozen or so grandest churches of Lincolnshire. Like Sleafor
it is a church remembered for Dec exuberance. It is moreov
all of a piece, even if certain details in the N aisle and N tra
sept differ from the rest and may indicate the earliest activi
(base mouldings, continuous string-course, less promine
buttresses). The church is built of Ancaster stone and is 1(
ft long. The spire reaches a height of *c.*180 ft. There are tra
septs as well as aisles, but the transepts are strangely undete
mined in that they keep well below the height of the na
clerestory and are followed by what looks like the E bay of tl
nave, before the chancel starts.

EXTERIOR. The detailed description can start at the towe
The buttresses have niches under gables at ground level (o
original figure to the S). The gables stand on figure-stops. T.
buttress top gables again have these figure-stops. The
window of three lights with shafted mullions, the bell-openin
of two lights. Broach spire with big polygonal pinnacles, n
standing on the broaches but merging oddly into them. Thr
tiers of lucarnes in alternating directions with gable-st
figures and finials. Tall clerestory of three-light windows, t
tracery with two encircled trefoils and one reticulation un
On the N side the tracery is different, an odd mixture of re
culation and quatrefoils on quatrefoils, surprisingly ambiguo
and perhaps not original. The S aisle windows have reticulat

tracery. So have the N aisle windows, but here they are un-cusped and look like a late, poor remodelling. The S porch has buttresses with niches as we have seen them on the tower. 24a Up the gable rises a parapet with a delicious band and in the spaces two shields, then two angels, then two kneeling figures, and finally Christ (a replacement), all against a leaf back-ground. The doorway inside the porch is E.E. rather than Dec. The N doorway on the other hand is typically Dec. Many fine arch mouldings dying against the jambs. Then the transepts. The S transept S window is a glorious piece of flow-ing tracery. Five lights and of daring irregularities. The tran-sept buttresses have once more the niches with gables and figure-stops like tower and S porch. The E windows of the transept are the same as those of the clerestory. The N tran-sept N window is a replacement of 1866, and it is odd that *Kirk* should have chosen forms of *c*.1300 rather than Dec forms. Did he believe so fixedly in the Second Pointed that he thought he could improve Heckington? The E windows are strange too, with trefoils in the head which have an ogee at the top of the top foil. The transept has plain buttresses and a plain parapet. After the transepts the extra nave bay to which reference has already been made. The tracery is not reticulated here. At the E end of this bay on the S side the crocketed spirelet of the rood-stair turret. The chancel finally has three-light windows, niches in the buttresses, a parapet with wavy tracery and end pin-nacles. There are three S windows with shafted mullions and a small S priest's doorway with an ogee head and the *clou* of the whole building, the six-light E window, one of England's greatest displays of flowing tracery. As at Sleaford, one never ceases to be amazed at the fertility of invention displayed in these windows with their ogees, reticulation units, and mou-chettes in infinitely varied combinations. Even the NE vestry has the motif of the niche in the buttress, the parapet frieze of monsters etc. and pinnacles. It is of two storeys, the lower rib-vaulted.

INTERIOR. The interior resembles Sleaford, but whereas there the stage of the polygonal abaci prevails, here the abaci are all still round, that is more purely Dec. The tower arch has the same five shafts with deep hollows and filleting as Slea-ford, but a triple-chamfered arch and a vault of eight ribs with a ring. The arcades are of four bays, the piers not really quatre-foil but a square with four demi-shafts almost covering it and no fillets. The arches are double-chamfered. The transept

arches are higher and wider, but the responds are the same
Towards the w side of the transept the third pier is continued
by a short piece of wall covered by a blank arch. This again is
as at Sleaford. In the s transept are sedilia with round shafts
nobbly capitals, and arches with openwork cusps, and no
ogees. (In the N transept wall, behind the organ, is a recess.
In the E bay of the nave, the bay which follows after the transept and was meant perhaps for a special screen and rood, the
beautiful corbels for the rood survive. The chancel arch has
responds of three shafts, the middle one with fillet, and separate hollows between. The arch has two sunk quadrant mouldings. The chancel is long, and in it are the four fitments which
have made Heckington famous in England. They are sedilia,
piscina, Easter Sepulchre, and a tomb recess. All have the
most exuberant ogee and crocket work, plenty of nobbly
foliation, buttress-shafts, gables, and finials. In the high
sedilia one ought to observe specially the little vaults inside,
the beautiful figures of Christ, the Virgin, two angels and St
Margaret and St Katherine at the top, and the four delicious
genre scenes at the springers of the gables, all connected with
feeding – a woman feeding a dove, another feeding a dog, a
man on all fours eating, a bearded man feeding someone else.
The piscina has plenty of ogee and again figures at the gables
and leaf capitals to the shafts even towards the interior of the
piscina. The tomb recess, cusped and subcusped, contains
the MONUMENT of Richard de Potesgrave who was installed
in 1307, became chaplain to Edward III, and of whom it was
said in a lost inscription that he rebuilt the chancel. The loca-
tion of his monument indeed confirms this statement. It has
also been suggested that the chancel was built shortly after the
abbey of Bardney had appropriated Heckington, which was in
1345. The two versions contradict one another, and the former
is more likely to be an indication of date. The Easter Sepulchre
is a show front around a simple triangle-headed recess no
larger than two foot high. Below, as in Lincoln Cathedral, a
base like the front of a tomb-chest and against this in relief
the seated soldiers. They are separated by buttresses, and out
of these rise four buttress-shafts, creating a triptych effect
and leading right up to the horizontal top cornice with small
figures, a mermaid, a piper, a bagpiper. The centre of the
triptych is of course the triangle-headed opening. To its l.
and r. in the side pieces of the triptych the three Maries and
the Angel, exquisite little figures in relief. Above the triangle

angels and Christ risen. Steep gable above this group. In the
l. and r. compartments above the women and the angel gables,
and above them rising parapets with wavy tracery. Their lines
and that of the top gable will not match. The whole upper part
of the composition is filled by close foliage in shallow relief.
Again there is no ogee in all this.

FONT. Six-sided, Dec, stem and bowl in one. Much
crocketing and foliage. – PLATE. Chalice, by *John Morley*
of Lincoln, *c*.1569. – MONUMENT. Effigy of a Civilian; only his
bust in sunk relief appears in a quatrefoil. For the rest the slab
is plain (s transept).

HIGH STREET. The best house is No. 63. Late C18, of five bays
and three floors. The NAG'S HEAD has a gable dated 1684.

HECKINGTON HALL, E of the church. Late C19 Carolean
Revival, but possibly a recasing of an earlier house.

HECKINGTON MANOR, ESE of the church. A conventional type
of *c*.1700, on an H-plan and with a hipped roof. It was rebuilt
in 1909 in new brick and with stone window surrounds. The
centre wall of the E front looks *c*.1700, as does the open string
stair round a square well.

VICARAGE. Red brick box by *William Barnett*, a builder, 1822
(GA).

WINDMILL. Black and white tower mill dated 1830. Eight-sailer
with an ogee cap. The gear comes from a mill at Boston.

HEIGHINGTON 0060

SCHOOL CHAPEL. A curious survival. Part of the village school
of Heighington is a medieval church with W tower, nave, and
chancel which has preserved its Late Norman tower arch with
waterleaf capitals. The church fell into decay and was revived
in 1619 as a chapel founded by Thomas Garrett, one of the
Fen Drainage adventurers. Of this second life nothing can be
seen any longer. The third is *Michael Drury*'s, who in 1865
gave the building its present form and added for the purposes
of the school. – PLATE. Chalice and Paten Cover, by *John
Morley* of Lincoln(?), *c*.1570.

HEIGHINGTON HALL. In 1872 *White's Directory* said that the
grounds had 'recently been tastefully laid out by Mr *Milner*
of Norwood' (who laid out Hartsholme, *see* p. 477).

HELPRINGHAM 1040

ST ANDREW. A fine church, all ashlar-faced, with a W tower
embraced by the aisles. W doorway with four orders of shafts.

w window with flowing tracery. Bell-openings of two light
with fine rolls. Square panelled pinnacles connected with the
spire by flying buttresses. Two tiers of lucarnes in alternating
directions. Spire and pinnacles, the spire crocketed. s aisle
windows reticulated tracery, N aisle cusped intersecting
tracery. The s and N doorways of the same style as the w doorway. The steep arch of the s doorway is under a gable. The s
porch is Perp. Clerestory of three-light windows also probably
Dec. The clerestory is embattled. At its SE end a little rood-
stair turret with pinnacles. The chancel may be somewhat
earlier than the rest. Low-side lancets, also Y-tracery, and
the E window of three stepped lancet lights under an arch.
This window is shafted outside and inside. Inside, the sedilia
in the chancel are indeed decidedly C13 and not C14. Trefoil
arches, only that of the adjoining piscina pointed. Hood-
mould with capitals with naturalistic leaf, a safe sign of *c.*1275–
1300. The four-bay arcades and the tower arches Dec, the
latter with deep continuous hollows between the shafts, the
former quatrefoil with thin shafts in the diagonals and all foils
and shafts with fillets. The arches with sunk quadrant mouldings. – FONT. Circular, with four polygonal corner shafts,
*c.*1200. On three sides plain blank pointed arcading, on the
fourth a tree, a bird, a quadruped (Tree of Life?). – PULPIT.
The tester late C17. – SCREEN. With wide one-light divisions.
– BENCHES. Two Perp benches with straight-topped ends.
More of the C17, probably mid C17, with ogee tops to the ends
crowned by knobs of various forms. – ARCHITECTURAL
FRAGMENTS. Inside the s wall a beautiful Norman frieze of a
shallowly undulating trail with ribbed leaves. The same leaves
in an equally beautiful capital(?) now in the NE corner. –
PLATE. Chalice, by *Thomas Wallis*, 1779.

MANOR FARM, E side of the Green. Late C17 front with a big
hooded porch on coarse, oversized scrolled brackets. There
is a later C18 wing.

THORPE LATIMER HOUSE, 1 m. s. Now looks early C18, a
traditional L-shaped stone building. The s front dressed up
with bows.

HERONSHAW HALL *see* OLD LEAKE

HEYDOUR

ST MICHAEL. A large and rewarding building. E.E. chancel
with three single-stepped lancets in the E wall and single

smaller lancets rather high up in the N and S walls. Priest's
doorway with cinquecusped head. Inside plain sedilia also
with cinquecusped arches. Opposite a low tomb recess. Dec
W tower with recessed spire, the ground floor perhaps still
E.E. Inside over the doorway to the staircase a re-set length
of Norman zigzag. Also inside vault of eight ribs radiating
from the circle round the bell-ringers' hole. Dec arcades of
four bays. Quatrefoil piers but with polygonal projections.
The abaci however are those of normal quatrefoil Dec piers.
Double-chamfered arches. Dec N and S aisle walls and windows. But inside, the roof-line of an earlier N aisle is visible.
The windows have interesting tracery, especially a variation
on the theme of reticulated tracery, with the units developed as quatrefoils. Also a motif of four radially placed arches
meeting in the middle. Big S porch, inside with a stone roof
on transverse ribs. Perp clerestory of six windows. Decorated
battlements; pinnacles. The N chapel must have been built
in the C17, see the straight-headed E window of four lights
with a transom. It was probably built as a funerary chapel
and is this now. – FONT. Octagonal, with patterns of Dec
tracery. – CHEST. Of c.1530–50. With three heads in profile
set in roundels. – PAINTING. In the chancel ornamental
painting. Lozenges with a flower and feigned ashlar with a
flower. Later Victorian. – STAINED GLASS. In two N aisle
windows original Dec figures, fairly well preserved. – The
adjoining window by *Wailes*. – The chancel E, N, and S windows by *Kempe*, 1899. – PLATE. Chalice, Cover, and Flagon,
by *George Wickes*, 1727. – MONUMENTS. An exceptionally
good set in the Newton family chapel (cf. Culverthorpe Hall).
Abigail Newton † 1686. Large tablet with convex inscription
plate flanked by columns. Good floral carving. No figures. –
Sir John, 1734 by *Rysbrack*. Also no figures. Tablet with
excellent classical architectural detail. Inscription and open
pediment above. Then urn before a grey obelisk. – Lady Newton, 1737 by *Peter Scheemakers*. Standing monument. Black
sarcophagus with putti l. and r. and a bust on the top. Reredos
background. – Sir Michael † 1746. Also by *Scheemakers*. All
white. Two life-size seated figures, one reading, the other
holding an extinguished torch and a ring with a snake curling
round. Between them sarcophagus with an urn on. Reredos
background. – Margaret Countess of Coningsby (Sir Michael's
daughter-in-law), 1761 by *Rysbrack*. A simple architectural
tablet.

The house immediately w of the church looks as if it must have once been the RECTORY. Of this we know that it was built in 1800. The date fits the plain, modestly classical house. Above the door the large C14 stone FIGURE of a young Musician with cymbals. This is said to be from the castle which stood w of the house.

The remains of the CASTLE itself consist of a low circular enclosure with a wet ditch, together with some remnants of masonry defences. Nothing stands above the foundations and no coherent plan can be recovered.

THE PRIORY, s of the church. C17. Three irregularly spaced bays and three- and four-light windows. Projection on the front for the stairs.

HOLBEACH

3020

ALL SAINTS. A large, even church, all Dec and open with its N side to the main street of the town. The ambitious and consistent building may have been the result of the Bishop of Lincoln having acquired the advowson in 1332 and promised in 1340 to rebuild the chancel. W tower with battlements and a recessed broach spire (not a usual thing). The spire has four tiers of lucarnes, their gablets on gargoyle-like animals. The total height is c.180 ft. The bell-openings are of two lights with a transom. The W front of the tower is given a shallow gabled porch panelled inside and with a cusped panelled vault, and above that a strange W window of five lights. The three centre lights each with a pointed arch concentric with the window arch and between the two arches cusped shapes separated by mullions rising to the window arch. Windows of the same design and yet larger to the N and s. These details are the latest of the church. They are Perp rather than Dec and may be a remodelling (cf. the tower arch inside, for which se below). The aisle windows are all of the same three-light design with flowing tracery. The s porch has a very steep tall entrance arch, the N porch a delightfully lacy ogee-cusped and subcusped arch. Both doorways are Dec too. But to the l. and r. of this N porch entrance stand two round towers, not at all ecclesiastical-looking and not bonded with the porch. They must either come from a castle (Moulton Castle has been suggested) or be in imitation of castle architecture. The upper windows of the porch are certainly c.1700 or early C18 in style. Were the towers then imitated or imported? Nothing seems

to be known.* The clerestory is of fourteen closely-set two-
light windows in pairs, each pair separated from the next by
a buttress. Battlements on clerestory and aisles. Sanctus bellcote on the clerestory E gable. The chancel windows of Holbeach are most elaborate. To the E four lights, to the N one
four-light of the same pattern as the E, to the S two, and to the
N the other of three lights, all with flowing tracery. The tower
arch to the nave is decidedly early C14, see the deep continuous hollows between the shafts, and also the fillets. Tierceron-star vault inside. The arcades on the other hand, seven 26a
bays, slender piers with polygonal bases and capitals, and thin
triple projections between diagonal hollows, look rather mid
than early C14.‡ Yet the arches with sunk quadrant mouldings
are the same for tower arch and arcade arches. The chancel
arch is different. Continuous mouldings, two chamfers and
one printer's bracket.

FURNISHINGS. FONT. Octagonal. Perp. Panelled stem.
Bowl with angels holding shields and the Instruments of the
Passion. Unfortunately the representations are defaced.
– SOUTH DOOR. Original, i.e. Dec, with reticulated tracery. –
PLATE. Chalice and Paten, and another Paten, by *W.I.*, 1766.
– MONUMENTS. Sir Humphrey Littlebury, late C14. Ascribed 32a
to Bristol craftsmen (cf. Lord Berkeley † 1368, Bristol Cathedral). Stone effigy, praying. His head on a big helmet with
a head as a cresting. The tomb-chest has deep niches with
trefoiled ogee tops coming forward. In plan the niches are as
deep as kneeling niches and have chamfered inner corners. To
the S they are diapered. – Brass to a Knight, early C15, headless figure, 30 in. long. – Brass to Joanna Welby † 1488, on a
tomb-chest, the figure 34 in. long. – Philip Ashby † 1794
(chancel N). Tablet with books on top. By *Henson* of Spalding.

The CHURCHYARD has to the S of the church a magnificent
fern-leaf beech-tree and a catalpa, to the N a screen of silver
birch to separate it from the High Street.

To walk the town one should first go up BOSTON ROAD, i.e.
N, as far as CEDAR HOUSE on the l. Georgian, five bays,
doorway with an apsed hood on carved brackets. Then W
along WEST END; on the l. STUKELEY HALL, 1922 by
W. E. N. Webster. On the site of William Stukeley's, the antiquarian's, family house – an example of Fen-Mannerism. The
garden in typical Corporation manner. It would not receive

* In Nattes's drawing of 1791 they are there.
‡ Under the three W piers of the N arcade Norman bases have been found.

Stukeley's approval. Opposite THE PRIORY, Georgian, wit
a dainty doorway. Segmental pediment on fluted pilaster
Then to the E. No. 45 is brick and Early Georgian. Five bay
small pediment over the centre, and a high roof with a centr
chimneystack. No. 63 is dated 1785 and has tripartite wir
dows. Nos 71–77 is of c.1840, perhaps by the same build
as houses in Chapel Bridge Road, Long Sutton (*see* p. 599
From here s into BARRINGTON GATE. A few nice house
and at the end in its garden SERPENTINE HOUSE. The co
is of 1831. Enlargements of the 1860s. At the N end an elega
porch with fluted Doric columns and nicely detailed rusticat
stone steps curving up to one side. On the garden front
happy juxtaposition of styles and a Regency cast-iron verand

Back to the High Street, and continuing E past the ALMSHOUSE
of 1845 (brick, long, low, with middle gable) to the WORE
HOUSE (now Fleet Hospital). Brick, no doubt of c.1835, i.
still Latish Classical. Two-storeyed and long, the centre tw
and a half storeys.

CEMETERY CHAPEL. Really two chapels, Dec, and separat
by a very peculiar spire over an archway. They are of 185
Could they be by *Pritchett*?

GEORGE FARMER SECONDARY SCHOOL, ½ m. N. By *L. Ba
low*, 1958. A main two-storey teaching block with lower anc
lary wings. Brick with glass infillings.

PENNY HILL, 1 m. N, opposite the Bull's Neck. Brick, lat
C17, with the pediment of a former window in one gable-en
and moulded brick string courses.

MANOR HOUSE FARM, 2½ m. N. Dated 1737. A five-bay, tw
storey front with dormers and a small pediment breakin
above the parapet and pierced with an *œil-de-bœuf*. The hou
was raised three feet in the 1870s. STABLES dated 1736 ar
1865.

3010   HOLBEACH DROVE

CHURCH. No doubt of the 1860s. Brick. Nave and chancel
one. Bell under spirelet on the E end of the nave. Small land
windows, all like Holbeach St Matthew. Brick-faced interior
BENCHES. The functional Gothic benches as at Dawsmere, et

3020   HOLBEACH FEN

ST JOHN BAPTIST. 1840 by *Robert Eliot* of Fleet (PB). Goth
Brick. Nave and short chancel. Tallish lancets. w front with
highly incorrect shallow porch and a bellcote.

HOLBEACH HURN   3020

ſ LUKE. 1869–71. Nave and chancel, red brick, with a bellcote
and lancet windows. – PAINTING. Large Adoration of the
Shepherds, English, early C19. No doubt the altarpiece of an
important church. Two shepherds l. and r. They could be
portraits. The Virgin higher up.

HOLBEACH ST MARKS   3030

ſ MARK. 1868–9, by *Ewan Christian* (Kelly). Almost a copy of
Dawsmere. Red brick with stone bands. Small lancets. Nave
and apse in one. Slate roof. Bellcote. Inside brick-faced too.
Later N chapel. – BENCHES. The same functional High
Victorian Gothic type as at Dawsmere.

HOLBEACH ST MATTHEW   4030

ſ MATTHEW. 1868–9, by *Ewan Christian*. Brick. Nave and
chancel in one. Bell under spirelet on the E end of the nave.
Lancet windows. – BENCHES. The functional Gothic type as
at Dawsmere.

HOLLAND FEN   2040
2¾ m. SE of Chapel Hill

ſ LL SAINTS. 1812. Red brick, with a cupola, the side windows
with pointed arches in a rhythm of two-centred, four-centred,
two-centred arch. The chancel 1880. Nice WEST GALLERY on
iron shafts. – PULPIT with fluted pilasters. – PLATE. Chalice,
by *William Bell*(?), 1812.

HOLYWELL   9010

ſ WILFRID. It stands S of the house as one of its garden ornaments. It was built about 1700 and has a short bell-turret on
the W part of the nave. The keyed horizontally-oval window
is original. The other windows are an unfortunate alteration
of 1863–4. But the original builder used parts of the medieval
chapel of Aunby, 1 m. W, and used them well. His W doorway
is of *c.*1300. Shafts with nobbly leaves. His E window has
reticulated tracery, and he placed the E wall of his bell-turret
boldly on two sturdy late C12 piers. Round, with flat crocketty
capitals. – STAINED GLASS. The E window a mosaic of small
fragments from the C15 to the C19, English and foreign. –
PLATE. Paten, by *M.*, 1662; Chalice, by *R.A.*, 1662.

HOLYWELL HALL. There seem to be three phases, the first th.
of a largish L-shaped house of which the core remains and on
gable-end; the second of 1732 or 1764; and the third of th
early C19. Samuel Reynardson married in 1732, at which tim
he may have laid out the gardens and built the temples. Thes
are in a competent London-Palladian style, in contrast to th
w front, which may be of 1764 – a date suggested by tradition
Five bays, moulded window surrounds, and a wooden cornic
The S and E fronts are early C19. The S front is a plain six bay
plus a seventh on the l. which is the gable-end of the W rang
Here a tripartite window was put in to harmonize with the
front. This is a much more sophisticated affair, of three wid
bays, the centre with Tuscan columns *in antis*, the sides on th
ground floor with tripartite windows under solid segment
arches. The uprights of the windows are delicate colonnette
There remains a wing to the N containing offices. Its decorativ
motifs are square, keystoned, semicircular windows, an
rusticated entrances. Facing the drive are the Palladia
STABLES. Seven bays with a central archway, pediment, an
blank walls pierced only by semicircular lights. Above is a
octagonal domed stone lantern. The themes are Burlingtonia
and they are continued in a side entrance, where an arc
is topped by three ball finials.

DOVECOT. C17. Gables and a small gabled dormer with
three-light window.

GARDEN TEMPLES, SW of the house. By the water is th
FISHING TEMPLE with a pedimented Roman Doric portic
in antis and rusticated windows in the side bays. The quoir
are also rusticated, as are the inner portico doors. It is ident
cal with the menagerie designed by *James Gibbs* at Hackwoo
and published in his *Book of Architecture* (1728).

ORANGERY, W of the house. A loggia of five bays, the en
pilastered, and the centre bays pilastered and supporting
broken pediment enclosing a bust.

BRIDGE. On the road between two easterly lakes. Thre
arches and a balustrade.

₉₀₄₀ HONINGTON

ST WILFRID. Interesting Norman work inside. Two-bay
arcade. Round pier with a square abacus, multi-scallope
capitals. Round arches of one step and one chamfer. Then th
chancel arch, not the present neo-Norman one, but the high
original one of which traces are visible in the W wall of th

chancel. Traces also of a Norman chancel s window. In addition the one-step arch of a Norman N chapel. Capitals with two tiers of small upright leaves and a top tier of scallops. The chancel was evidently remarkably long, all the more so as the position of the Norman chapel shows that it has at some time been shortened. The unbuttressed w tower is E.E., see the twin bell-openings and the arch to the nave. In the chancel s wall late C13 windows, two with Y-tracery, one with a circle in bar tracery. In the nave on the s side a contemporary window with intersecting tracery. Perp tower top. Cusped lozenge frieze, concave-sided battlements, pinnacles. Perp clerestory also with a lozenge frieze and pinnacles. Perp s porch with pinnacles. Its stone roof rests on six transverse ribs. In the chancel w of the Norman chapel an early C16 Perp chapel of one bay. The capitals are decorated. In the former arch of the Norman chapel an Easter Sepulchre with three pinnacles. In the E wall of the chapel two diagonally placed niches, differing in detail. – COMMUNION RAIL. Of c.1700, good, with nicely turned balusters. – PLATE. Gilt covered Beaker, by *W.H.B.*, 1577; Paten and Flagon, by *Benjamin Godfrey* (1732). – MONUMENTS. In the N aisle heavy tomb-chest, badly treated, and as its lid an incised slab to William Smith † 1552, bearded. – Thomas Hussey † 1697. Architectural background and lifeless bust with big wig. – Dame Sarah Hussey † 1714. Architectural, with pilasters and, above the inscription, three cherubs' heads. – FUNERAL HELM.

HONINGTON CAMP, ¾ m. SE. The only major Iron Age fort in the county. The camp lies on a limestone plateau at a strategic point immediately s of, and guarding, the approaches to the Ancaster Gap. The site, of roughly rectangular plan, is defended by two banks and ditches, with a third, counterscarp bank beyond the outer ditch, which enclose an area of a little over an acre. The ramparts are in an excellent state of preservation, standing to a height of about 5 ft. They are broken by a single entrance of simple form in the middle of the E side. There are no visible surface features in the interior, although in the C17 an urn was found inside the camp containing a hoard of Roman coins.

HORBLING
1030

ST ANDREW. First there was a cruciform Norman church. To this belong of the present fabric the w wall (remains of the outer wall arcading, flat buttresses), the chancel (two original

shafted windows with billet, buttressing at the bottom of th
E wall), the crossing tower (shallow buttresses with angle
shafts to and including the bell-stage), and perhaps the but
tressing of the S transept S wall. The twin bell-openings ar
later C13, a curious shape with Y-tracery in round arches bu
quatrefoils in plate tracery above them to fill the tympanu
of a pointed arch. Perp battlements and pinnacles. Dec th
N aisle and the N transept N windows, with flowing tracery
Perp the S aisle and S transept S window. As one enters, th
Norman date is confirmed by the chancel sedilia (large roun
arch – a rarity) and piscina with continuous rolls, just lik
the rolls round the windows, by the zigzag frieze below th
Victorian E lancets of 1852, if this is original, and by th
responds of the W and E crossing arches. But they lean so badl
that it is not surprising to see that their arches were late
rebuilt (though the three-roll mouldings are probably origi
nal), and the N and S arches were entirely rebuilt early in th
C14 – see the typical shafts connected by continuous hollow
The same type of arch between N transept and N aisle. Th
nave on the other hand is a surprise. It is early to mid C1
The N arcade comes first. Four bays, hexagonal piers, earl
stiff-leaf capitals (i.e. stiff leaves on high, clearly visible stalks
arches with two slight chamfers. The S arcade has one roun
and two quatrefoil piers (with the foils more than semicircular
moulded capitals, arches partly one chamfer and one hollo
chamfer, partly one chamfer and one keeled roll. In the
transept a nice bracket for an image. – FONT. Octagonal, wit
cusped fields. Shields in them with the Instruments of th
Passion. – STAINED GLASS. In the W window single figures o
1854. – PLATE. Two Patens, by *John Cory*, 1706; Chalice, b
Edward Vincent(?), 1713; Flagon, by *Humphrey Payne*, 1731
Almsdish, by *John Crouch*(?), 1840. – MONUMENTS. In th
N transept front of a tomb-chest with quatrefoils etc. This i
in front of a recess which it has nothing to do with. Above thi
a lunette with a relief of two figures flanking Christ, who i
rising out of his tomb. – The Rev. Thomas Brown † 184
Brass plate, designed by *Pugin* and made by *Hardman*. – B
the same probably also the brass to Benjamin Wilkinso
† 1848.

A village mostly Georgian. HORBLING HALL was tudorize
*c.*1880.

SPRING WELL, *c.*150 yds N of the church, in a side lane, is a nea
relation of the southern communal washing trough. A dee

open cistern feeds water to three adjacent troughs and they compose like a piece of abstract sculpture. At the bottom of the cistern are coins and photographs of loved ones.

HOUGHAM

8040

ALL SAINTS. The visible history of the church begins with the exposed jamb of a window in the former s wall, i.e. before there was an aisle. The jamb has a two-step profile and may well be pre-Conquest. Anyway the s arcade, i.e. the providing of an aisle, is Norman. One plus two bays, the bit of wall left standing marking probably the original sw corner. The style of the three bays does not differ. One-step arches. Round pier with square abacus, capitals scalloped and also one with crockets. Only the e respond is a Dec remodelling. The n arcade is entirely Dec. Of about 1300 the w tower (Y-tracery, some dogtooth). Only its top, with eight pinnacles, is Perp. Dec s aisle windows. Perp clerestory, large Perp n aisle windows. Perp s porch with pinnacles. Stone roof on four transverse ribs. Georgian chancel with large arched windows, the e window Venetian but bare in the details. – SCULPTURE. Inside, above the s doorway, a length of Anglo-Saxon cross shaft, with interlace decoration. – MONUMENTS. In the n aisle cross-legged Knight, hand on sword, the other raising the shield. – The Rev. George Thorold † 1823. By the younger *P. Rouw*. With a still-life of books and a chalice. – Arthur William Thorold † 1853. By *Boucheau* of London. Marble monument with cross on the lid, very clumsily done.

MANOR HOUSE. The exterior is Early Georgian and a refacing of a house of c.1620. The present main façade is N. Windows of c.1620 in the e gable-end. But there are also remains of a much earlier date, notably a completely mysterious huge respond in the room at the SE corner. It is a triple respond, doubtless C13 and probably early. The floor has been raised. Originally it was about 7 ft high. It is about 5 ft 6 in. in diameter, i.e. of cathedral size. Above the capital it is three times corbelled out, and to its l. in the wall is yet another corbel. What on earth can it have served for? It seems *in situ*, and moreover in the wall opposite it is a small oblong window, and if this and the wall are *in situ*, the room was small, not a vast undercroft. Further e from this SE corner and more or less flush runs a wall to the e and in this are the traces of three large Perp windows, probably of a former chapel. The site seems to be that of a de Bussey mansion, and for this an oratory was licensed in 1405.* The moat of the mansion is all else that remains.

OLD RECTORY. A typical grand early C19 rectory. It was built for the Thorold family.

9040   HOUGH-ON-THE-HILL

ALL SAINTS. The w tower in its lower parts is Anglo-Saxon and, with its semicircular stair projection, belongs to Barworth, Brigstock, and Broughton. Rough masonry, irregular quoins. Small arched windows to s and N, but in the stair projection tiny round, oblong, and arched windows, and even a lozenge-shaped one.‡ The stair projection incidentally does not continue the string-courses of the tower. Is the projection then an addition? Narrow arch to the nave with a slight chamfer. Above it, in fact very high up, a triangle-headed doorway. It shows that the nave had the characteristically Anglo-Saxon excessive height. The upper part of the tower is Perp. Two two-light bell-openings with transom under one broad basket arch. Decorated concave-sided battlements and eight pinnacles. The intermediate ones should really (cf. e.g. Beckingham) stand on an ogee gable above the basket arches. Plain E.E. s doorway and s porch. E.E. also the s aisle E lancet and the tall two-bay arcades (octagonal piers, double-chamfered arches), the chancel arch, and the two-bay N chapel arcade. The s aisle s windows oddly placed. Perp clerestory with battlements and pinnacles. The chancel has a decorated parapet too. Perp nave roof of flat pitch. N chapel windows C18. SCULPTURE. In the N chapel an Anglo-Saxon stone with interlace decoration. – STAINED GLASS. N aisle E window by Kempe, 1901 (see his trade-mark, the wheatsheaf). – PLATE. Chalice, Elizabethan, with Paten Cover by Richard Bayley, 1731; Paten, by C.H., 1707; Flagon, by John White, 1726. MONUMENTS. Edward † 1728 and Thomas Payne † 1741. Identical standing monuments with white sarcophagus in front of a black obelisk.

The bold ridge on which the church stands ends in a sharply defined point, where stands a small and rather damaged MOTTE. Building has obscured any bailey it may have had.

The village lies on the edge of the cliff with a long S-bend encompassing the BROWNLOW ARMS (C19 Tudoresque).

* Information supplied by Mrs Joan Varley.
‡ One oblong window of the same size in the s porch ex situ.

Hough House, a view of the church, and a drop into the valley with cottages and the Tudor Gothic SCHOOL.

OUGH HOUSE is mid C17 with, to the street, a high three-storey gable-end, with four-, three-, and two-light windows. It looks the truncated part of a larger house perhaps with a symmetrical wing. The doorway is C18: lugged angles and a scrolled keystone.*

OUND BARROW, on LOVENDEN HILL. A small, flat-topped barrow, 28 ft in diameter and 4 ft high. Excavation revealed four Pagan Saxon inhumation burials and forty cremations, the latter in urns. Associated grave goods included an iron knife, two pairs of bronze tweezers, and part of a chatelaine.

HOVENDEN HOUSE see GEDNEY

HOWELL   1040

OSWALD. Plain and over-restored Norman S doorway. N arcade of three bays of *c.*1200. Round piers with round abaci; double-chamfered round arches. Tiny W lancet in the aisle. E.E. double bellcote. The nave and chancel details Dec. Off the chancel Dec N chapel, i.e. Dec arches from aisle and chancel, a Dec E window (cusped intersecting tracery with ogee details), and a quatrefoil in a circle as a W window, a conservative form to choose. Low tomb recess in the chapel with ogee cusping. – FONT. Octagonal, Perp, with shields in pointed quatrefoils. – STAINED GLASS. With original bits in the N chapel. – PLATE. Chalice, by *Nathaniel Lock*(?), 1707. – MONUMENTS. Anglo-Saxon slab with crosses, very elementary (S porch). – Slab in the S chapel, C14; the slab is plain, but at its top an arch with pointed trefoil cusping and in it in sunk relief bust of a lady praying. Below on the slab the same is repeated much smaller, and there the little daughter is praying. The small trefoil is placed below the l. half of the larger. – Incised slab to John Croxby, rector, † *c.*1470. Well preserved. The figure is under a canopy (chancel floor). – Sir Charles Dymok, Jacobean, with the two usual kneelers.

HUNGERTON HALL see WYVILLE

INGOLDSBY   0030

BARTHOLOMEW. Short, broad W tower, embraced by the aisles, probably E.E. The W window is evidently C17, as is

Hough Hall, drawn by Nattes in 1803, does not quite fit these remains.

the s aisle w window. Much was done to the church then,
we shall see. The round-arched blocked s aisle doorway e
may well be C17. The s aisle is otherwise of c.1300, see the
window (later cut down at the top) and the tomb rece
inside. The N aisle windows may be C17 too, or could be C1
In the chancel Dec and Perp windows. The E end is shortene
but the window may be re-used. It is of an interesting desig
and the sickle-shaped hood-mould terminals are surprisi
indeed. The dominant element of the interior is the thre
bay N arcade. It belongs to the late C12. Round piers, squa
abaci with nicked corners. The capitals have upright leave
still Norman, but on the way to stiff-leaf. One also has wate
leaf. Round, double-chamfered arches. But what has happen
to the s arcade, the tower arch, and the chancel arch ? Th
may have been E.E. (the tower arch has keeled responds) b
as they are now, they must be an attempt at approximati
them to classical columns. So here is the C17 again. – FON
Octagonal, Perp or Dec. Barbed quatrefoils containi
shields. – STAINED GLASS. In the s aisle E window so
original early C14 fragments. – A few bits also in a chan
N window. – PLATE. Flagon, by *John Bodington*, 17
Chalice, by *John Kentember*, 1772.

RECTORY. Gothic, with an octagonal tower; by *Charles Ki*
1847.

EARTHWORK, 1 m. w, and just N of Ingoldsby Wood.
roughly circular earthwork of about 2 acres, surrounded b
single bank and ditch. Bank and ditch are of modest dime
sions. Nothing is known regarding the date of the site.

IRNHAM

ST ANDREW. A large church, hidden by the trees of the groun
of the Hall. The lower part of the w tower is Late Norm
see the w doorway with only a slight chamfer and the a
towards the nave with waterleaf and upright leaf capitals a
a round, double-chamfered arch. Next follows the chanc
which has to the s two windows with Geometrical trace
i.e. late C13. The triple responds of the chancel arch and
sedilia confirm the date. The N aisle is of the same time.
also has windows with Geometrical tracery (three lights, th
entirely quatrefoiled circles) and a doorway matching
windows stylistically. The N arcade was built together w
the walls and windows. Three bays, octagonal piers, doub

chamfered arches. The s aisle, which has been demolished, also seems contemporary. There were certainly round abaci to the piers, and the s doorway has one order of shafts and dog-tooth. The chapel arcade of three bays is only a little later, say c.1300 (round piers, double-chamfered arches). Externally the chapel appears Late Perp. It is embattled, as is the Perp clerestory. The upper parts of the tower are Dec, but below them are pairs of twin E.E. bell-openings which were shafted. Inside the church the great surprise is the former Easter Sepulchre, one of the finest in England and almost a match for Heckington. It is of the same time as Heckington, i.e. fully mature Dec. It is now incongruously set at the E end of the N chapel. But where can it have been originally? Its proper place is the N wall of the chancel. But there is the N arcade there which is older than the Easter Sepulchre. Can the chancel have been longer? It is long as it is. Or can the E bay of the arcade have been copied late in the c14 when the brass went into place? Or can the Sepulchre have been in the N chapel? One can hardly believe that. Anyway, it is most ornate and most inventive. Three bays with nodding ogee arches. Inside, little vaults which are pierced so that one can look up beyond them to behind the gables etc. The sides of the Sepulchre have reticulated grilles to the outside encrusted with leaf. Above the nodding arches all is encrusted too. Top with crenellation and little hanging canopies. The aumbry is of the same time (ballflowers and fleurons). – BENCHES. The ends straight-topped with simple tracery. – STAINED GLASS. E window, date of death 1859. Big scene of the Crucifixion. – PLATE. Chalice, by *John Smith*, c.1710; Paten, by *Edward Holaday*, 1711. – MONUMENTS. Late c13 tomb recess in the chancel, the upper part all renewed. – Brass to Sir Andrew Luttrell † 1390, a fine 5 ft 5 in. figure under an ogee canopy (N chapel). – Brass to Sir Geoffrey Hilton(?), c.1440 (chancel; 25 in.). – In the churchyard big Grecian sarcophagus to William Hervey Woodhouse † 1859 – a late date for the Grecian taste. In axis with the N porch.

NHAM HALL. Grandiose and almost unknown to architectural literature. The builder was Sir Richard de Thimelby, and the date is between 1510 and 1531. The long, low, picturesque group of grey stone is seen from the churchyard. It forms a big L with roughly equal wings, one running parallel with the churchyard w–e, the other behind it N–s. In detail the house is still unaffected by the Renaissance and much like 37a

the slightly later Thame Park, Oxfordshire. Unfortunatel
unlike Thame, Irnham was gutted by fire (in 1887), and i
interior is now all of that date. The N front which one se
from the churchyard is all C19, though it has an Elizabetha
or Jacobean entrance with bulgy pilasters. The focus of intere
is behind, where one can see the E side of the N–S range an
the S side of the W–E range. Reading from the extrude
stair-turret in the angle there are first on the S side of th
W–E wing nine bays with C19 fenestration. Bay two cants ou
bay nine repeats bay two, bay six is occupied by a thre
storey octagonal stair-turret rising above roof level. Th
escaped the fire and has its original two-light windows wi
depressed-arched lights. They are repeated all over the façad
and may in some other cases also be original.* Rainwat
heads are dated 1765, when alterations were made for th
Conquest family. The E façade of the N–S range has one ba
and then a canted bay window. Then, after two more bay
the façade comes forward, and at the corner is an Elizabetha
porch, a recessed porch, with columns and an arch to N
well as E. After that more of the early C16 windows. A litt
set back behind the not projecting front are three gabl
with Elizabethan or C17 windows. The inner doorway of th
porch looks pre-Elizabethan. To this date the crenellate
parapet must belong. The W front is totally C19 but retai
its gabled roof. There was once a front of 1765 with Veneti
windows, which may have been gothicized only after 188
The INTERIOR has kept its screens passage with the paire
stone entrances to the serveries. The passage lies behind th
Elizabethan porch. So this must always have been the ma
entrance. The hall is now lit from the upper gables. Is th
original? The fenestration is, but perhaps before the fire th
windows lit an attic storey above the hall. Bits of the chap
remain. This was designed in 1822 for Lord Clifford b
Joseph Ireland. The park in Georgian landscape style, b
neo-Tudor GATEHOUSE, and a splendid castellated wall ne
the church.

The VILLAGE deserves commendation. Its sequestered positi
adds to its delight. Essentially grey stone enlivened by mu
leafage, and a sprinkling of vernacular estate cottages. W
the church will be found the MANOR HOUSE, C18 and
shaped; N will be found the grander NEWTON HOUS

---

* It must be remembered how many have their arched lights already
Nattes's drawing of 1804.

possibly the Dower House to Irnham Hall. It would be tempting to date this *c.*1765, when the Hall was being altered. What attracts is the front added to a C17 house: five bays, three storeys, cornice, and later parapet. All stone-faced, the windows with moulded surrounds and each keystone nicely decorated with a carved flower. The second-floor windows rest on scrolled acanthus brackets, and there are similar brackets as modillions to the cornice. Doorway with open segmental pediment. NE of the church the GRIFFIN INN, facing the confluence of three roads. Mostly Georgian and later, with bits of castellation.

THE JUNGLE see EAGLE

KELBY

T ANDREW. A smallish church and externally very muddled. W tower with recessed spire. What is its date? It is unbuttressed, and the nook-shafts at the bell level appear E.E. at the latest. The ground-floor windows have triangular heads inside. Has this any significance? The puzzling thing is that above the chancel arch, inside, the wall has herringbone masonry, an C11 sign and in this case the sign of an C11 crossing tower. Was it at once replaced by a Norman W tower, or were parts from the crossing tower re-used when the W tower replaced it? The big heads at the top of the tower look re-used certainly. The former crossing tower would also explain why such a short nave received so high a Perp clerestory. The N windows are original, the S windows Victorian. The S aisle has small windows of *c.*1300. Above the S porch entrance a monster-head, again re-used. To the N beyond the N aisle arches of a former outer aisle or two chapels. The chancel dates from *c.*1825. The interior has much more to offer. Early E.E. two-bay N arcade. Round pier, round abacus, double-chamfered round arches. The chancel arch and the tower arch Dec. The S aisle has the rare distinction of being vaulted. Quadripartite bays with longitudinal ridge-ribs and signs of former transverse ridge-ribs. The piers are Dec. Octagonal, without capitals and with double-chamfered arches. This, the pattern of the vault, and especially the excellent figure carving towards nave as well as aisle, proves a Dec date. Specially enjoyable the little contortionist King and Bishop. – BENCH ENDS. With poppy heads and tracery patterns. A fine set, particularly so because unrestored. One

end has a woman in a costume of c.1530. – STAINED GLASS.
In the s aisle E window small figures: Dec too. – PLATE.
Baptismal Bowl, German, second quarter of the C17, by
Heinrich Friederich of Hamburg; Chalice, foreign(?).

A small group of farmhouses of vernacular types. The gabled
porch, the mullioned windows with straight hoods, and the
L-plan are characteristic.

0050
KIRKBY GREEN

HOLY CROSS. Built in 1848. Nave and chancel in one. Bellcote,
w porch. The E wall according to Bonney accurately repro-
duced from the medieval predecessor. Two lancets shafted
with shaft-rings and a vesica window over, i.e. E.E. The
piscina shaft also is original C13 work. The attitude of copying
the old church is an antiquarian attitude which was still a
very recent achievement in 1848. – PLATE. Paten Cover and
Chalice, by *John Morley* of Lincoln, 1569.

0040
KIRKBY LAYTHORPE

ST DENIS. w tower, not high, nave and low N aisle, and chancel.
Norman s doorway with one order of shafts, the whole almost
entirely restoration. Transitional four-bay arcade. Round
piers and abaci, the arches almost round. In the s wall of the
nave two lancets. w tower, unbuttressed, but the w window
Dec. N aisle windows also Dec. The chancel was rebuilt in
1854, in the E.E. style, but the priest's doorway is Transitional.
– FONTS. One octagonal, Perp, with pointed quatrefoils, the
other (Kirkby had originally two churches) also octagonal,
also Perp, with tracery with much small crenellation. –
SCREEN. Part of the Perp screen now in the tower arch. –
BENCH ENDS. Bits of tracery etc. made up into a choir seat. –
SCULPTURE. Two small pieces of Anglo-Saxon interlace in
the w tower w wall just below the string-course. – STAINED
GLASS. Original bits in the w and a s window. – PLATE.
Pre-Reformation Paten with the Agnus Dei, c.1490–1510,
the stem added by *I.G.*, 1665; Chalice, by *I.G.*, 1665;
Flagon, by *I.S.*, 1682.

(THE GRANGE. A moulded beam inside bears witness to a C1
to early C16 house. MHLG)

0020
KIRKBY UNDERWOOD

ST MARY AND ALL SAINTS. Unbuttressed E.E. w tower.
Traces of a w lancet. The tower arch dies into the imposts.

Perp bell-openings. Perp clerestory. Otherwise externally not much of interest. Internally the blocked N arcade was E.E. too. Three bays, quatrefoil piers (the foils more than semicircular), one without, one with fillets. The S arcade is essentially the same except that one pier was replaced or remodelled in the C14 and received a capital which is a broad band of leaf. – PULPIT. Simple; C17. – SCULPTURE. A bit of Anglo-Saxon interlace carving in the outer chancel wall. (Also other Anglo-Saxon bits.) – ARCHITECTURAL FRAGMENT. A capital with a leaf trail and a head; probably of c. 1300 (cf. Little Bytham).

KIRTON-IN-HOLLAND

3030

ST PETER AND ST PAUL. A town church in a village. But Kirton was in fact a market town. The church is of substantial dimensions, and a baffling church too, which must originally have been yet bigger. For the story of the church is that its Perp W tower was rebuilt in 1805 (by *William Hayward* of Lincoln) out of the materials of what was a crossing tower, that crossing and transepts were demolished and the chancel shortened. It is an unlikely story, but the fact is that it is confirmed by Nattes's drawing of before 1804 and by documentary evidence. One is amazed how neatly the tower fits its position, the chancel fits the nave, and the aisles end in blocked E windows, not in arches to transepts. Is it due to *Hodgson Fowler*, who restored the church in 1900, that any unevennesses were smoothed over? In detail the ground-floor niches of the W tower buttresses with two early C14 statuettes e.g. must be original. Above, the tower appears Perp. But inside it, in its E wall, there is indeed the W doorway of a cruciform Late Norman church. Two orders of colonnettes, zigzag at r. angles to the wall, lozenges broken round an angle. The S doorway is Late Norman too. Two orders of shafts with shaft-rings, and in the arch the same motifs and also bobbins. The N doorway is a little, but only a little, later. Again shafts with rings, but a fully E.E. finely moulded arch. Late E.E. six-bay arcades. Circular piers with circular abaci and double-chamfered arches.* They were originally lower, and their heightening must be connected with the provision of the crossing. What remains after the demolition is the crossing piers shafted with deep hollows between the foils and

* The bases of the W part are square, of the E part circular.

already polygonal capitals, i.e. later C14. The capitals are a
the height of the heightened arcade capitals. There is also the
blocked arch to an E chapel. The Perp capitals and semi-
octagonal lengths of shaft to the W are no doubt connected
with the rood. Externally the N aisle is Early Dec. Windows of
three stepped cusped lights under one two-centred arch
Decorated gablets on the buttresses. Battlements. The S aisle
is Dec too. Splendid four-light windows with flowing tracery
Again decorated buttress gables. Battlements with shields in
quatrefoils – a busy pattern. The clerestory is the one chief
Perp contribution. Twelve closely-set windows, battlements
decorated like those of the aisle, pinnacles, inside coarse
panelling of the arcade spandrels below the clerestory. Tie
beam roof. Embattled E gable, as are the E roofs of the aisles
The other Perp contribution is the chancel – whatever its
story. Four-light side windows, five-light E window. Frieze
with heads, flowers, etc. – FONT. Octagonal, given in 1405 (see
the re-cut Orate inscription). Simple panels with shields. –
SCREEN. A part with elaborate Flamboyant tracery at the N
aisle W end.* – WEST GALLERY. 1907. – PLATE. Chalice and
Paten Cover, Boston(?), 1569; Paten and Flagon, by *John*
Payne, 1757.

The KING'S HEAD INN is an example of Fen Artisan Manner
ism. Brick rusticated windows, door frames, and lugged
corners. Dated 1699 and conservative for that date. BLOSSOM
HALL, 1½ m. SE, is also in this category but grander. Prob
ably early C17, with a group of four moulded and twisted
brick chimneys. A brick house on the GREEN is dated 1657.

Outside the funny TOWN HALL (of 1911) a statue of William
Dennis, local magnate, by *P. Lindley Clark*, 1930.

LANGTOFT

ST MICHAEL. Ashlar-faced E.E. W tower. Clasping buttresses
W lancets. The bell-openings are Dec, tall and shafted, and the
S attachment to the tower of which a blocked arch tells also
seems to have been Dec. Recessed spire with rolls up it
angles. Two tiers of lucarnes in the same direction, the lower
ones with transom. E.E. also the chancel and the chapel off it
The E window is of 1859, but the chancel arch is eloquent
enough and so is the aumbry (though the paterae are Victo

* The Rev. F. M. Buffett kindly tells me that this came from the organ
screen of a London church.

rian). The one-bay chapel arches to chancel and aisles are also
easily dated. After that the arcades, which must be late C13.
On the N side four bays, quatrefoil piers with circular abaci
embracing the whole quatrefoil; double-chamfered arches.
On the S side only one pier is of this type. Another has a
quatrefoil abacus. A third was completely altered in the late
C14 (polygonal base and capital). The responds have leaf-band
capitals, the piers moulded capitals. The N chancel chapel
was continued E by one more bay at this time or a little earlier.
But the S chapel of two bays is fully Dec and sumptuous.
Quatrefoil pier with thick leaf-band capital. The W respond
has a little carrying man in leaves, the E respond a three-
quarter figure in leaves and below him the chancel piscina
with a crocketed gable. The chapel piscina has such a gable
too. Perp aisle windows and battlements. Perp embattled
clerestory with big three-light windows. The nave roof with
its angels against the wall-posts looks as if it might be C17.
The S porch with paired Doric pilasters is clearly C18.
– FONT. C18; square stem set diagonally; fluted bowl (cf.
Wilsthorpe). – PULPIT. C18; with tarsia panels. – CHAN-
DELIER. Of brass; three tiers of arms; dated 1759. – PLATE.
Chalice and Cover, c.1600; Flagon, by *I.A.*, 1685; Paten, by
Robert Cooper, 1703; Chalice, by *Nick Hearnden*, 1807. –
MONUMENT. Elizabeth Moulsworth † 1618. Tablet with a
tiny kneeling figure.

LAVINGTON see LENTON

LEADENHAM

9050

ST SWITHIN. A Dec church with a dominating Perp spire
and a poor Dec clerestory. The W tower is very bare below
to the N and S, but has a Perp W window. Yet it is Dec below,
see the tower arch. Perp however the bell-openings of two
lights and the whole stage below, which has tall blank
windows, two of one light, but as wide as if they were of two
lights. Recessed spire, not very high in comparison with the
posts below. Crocketed edges and two tiers of lucarnes in
alternating directions. Dec aisle windows with ogee-headed
lights under depressed four-centred, almost segmental arches.
The gablets of the buttresses carry a little decoration. The N
doorway has thin shafts, nice mouldings, and a crocketed
gable with a blank arch on shafts under. The S doorway and

s porch entrance are similar. In the s aisle an ogee-heade
piscina and two brackets with little caryatids l. and r. of the
window. Dec also the aisle arcades: three tall and wide ba
with quatrefoil piers filleted and with thin, also filleted shaf
in the diagonals. The hollows between are deep and co
tinuous. Finely moulded arches. The arch to the chanc
belongs to the arcades, and also probably the clerestory. C
the clerestory outside, on its E corners, turret pinnacles, a
another pair on the E corner of the chancel. Inside the chanc
the ceiling was painted by *Pugin* in 1841, and his motifs ar
manifold black-letter inscriptions are well preserved. Finall
the Perp N porch with a parapet decorated with shields
saltire crosses. Small niche under. – STAINED GLASS. In t
E window Flemish early C16 glass in the tracery head
Christ and angels. All the rest by *Hardman*; c.1880–90.
PLATE. Paten, by *I.I.*, 1690; Chalice and Paten, by *Christoph*
Ridley and *William Gamble*, 1703; Flagon, as Chalice and Pate
with *R.I.*, *G.A.*, and *John Porter* on handle. – MONUMENT
In the chancel E wall Elizabethan tablet: coat of arms in le
surround and framing. Above, the letters C.B. – Lady Ja
Sherard † 1851. Mourning kneeling woman by an urn. Sign
Gaffin (s aisle). – Frances Reeve † 1858. Kneeling you
woman. Signed *T. Gaffin* (N aisle). – General John Reeve a
wife, both † 1864. With figures of Faith and Hope. By *Buri*
– Nice slate headstones in the churchyard.

The village has two Georgian-Vernacular pubs: FEATHER
YARD and the GEORGE HOTEL. The latter with a rustica
doorway carrying a broken segmental pediment. The RE
TORY may be that which *William Fowler* is known to ha
built in 1823. A DRINKING FOUNTAIN, a hexagonal Goth
canopy, is dated 1867.

LEADENHAM HALL. One of a group of houses sited on T
Cliff and commanding spacious views. According to an accou
book it was building between 1790 and 1799. A squa
chastely detailed block with relieving decoration only on
w front, namely slight recessions, a tripartite window, an
projecting canted porch. An E wing terminates in a tw
storey arcade. Perhaps this is the known addition by
Vulliamy of 1829. The interior now mostly by *Detmar Bl*
c.1903. The STABLES are a successful composition of bla
arcaded walls and were designed by *E. J. Willson* in 1833.

LEADENHAM OLD HALL, ½ m. N. Visually one of the m
enchanting houses in the county. A Charles II essay; in beau

ful golden ironstone. The date may in fact be slightly post-
Charles II, say *c.*1690. It is a nearly square house, five by five
bays with four on the N front. The proportions on the E are
odd, with ground-floor windows placed low and the doorway
top-heavy. A basement seems needed. The effect of depth
nicely judged: windows recessed in moulded frames and
joined vertically by projections. The pediment over the doorway is a rustic delight; broken double scrolls enclosing a
cascade of miscellaneous grotesque masks, fruit swags, and a
cartouche, and topped by putti that would do credit to Marino
Marini. Good staircase with balusters nearly vertically
symmetrical and with a little acanthus. The newel posts carry
urns. Pedimented doorways and discreet stone chimneypieces.

LEASINGHAM

T ANDREW. The tall W tower is a puzzle. It starts with a good
doorway with two orders of shafts, waterleaf capitals, and
a round, moulded arch. So that is late C12. Above it is a
circular window, foiled (but the foiling may be Victorian),
and to the S a shafted E.E. lancet. The arch towards the nave
has five shafts as responds. The twin bell-openings also seem
to be E.E., at least in their upper parts with the circle above
the two lights. But what are those two rising stone beams
forming a flattish triangle on which the shaft between the
two lights stands? Is all this an awkward emergency alteration? The broach spire is E.E. for certain. It stands bluntly
on the tower and has lucarnes in three tiers and alternating
directions, projecting too far for the outline of the spire. Of
the same date as the tower doorway the S aisle doorway, which
is pointed.* Of the same date as the upper parts of the tower
one N aisle window of two lights with Geometrical tracery
(a sexfoiled circle). Dec the three-bay S arcade. Quatrefoil
piers with fillets, thin shafts between the foils, double-
chamfered arches, seats around the piers. With this arcade
goes the cusped W lancet of the aisle and the interesting window
of three lights, where cusped intersecting tracery is given an
ogee turn throughout. Perp N windows with castellated transom above the centre lights and Perp vestry (former N chapel ?)
with a frieze of square leaves and monsters. The chancel is of
1863. – FONT. Octagonal. Base and stem E.E., but the bowl
carved with unidentified subjects (except for Christ on the

* And also, it seems, the blocked N doorway.

rainbow) early in the C16 in an unbelievably rustic style. –
PULPIT. Victorian, of stone, the lectern of it on a detached
shaft with ivy twining round it. – STAINED GLASS. Bits in
nave and vestry windows. – PLATE. Chalice, by *C.H.*, 1783;
Paten, by *Edward Jay*, 1783; Flagon, by *John Naylor*(?)
1783.

ANCIENT HOUSE, NW of the church. A four-bay two-storey
front with a gabled dormer containing a two-light window
and the date 1655. Other three-light windows with straight
hoods.

LEASINGHAM HALL. The S wing in Tudor Gothic, dated
1836. The NW wing looks even later, although there are C17
bits. Nice Georgian gatepiers, and by them a box tree inscribed 'This Boxwood Grew in the Garden of Houcomon
during the Battle of Waterloo, 18th June 1815'.

LEASINGHAM MANOR HOUSE, opposite Leasingham Hall.
The street front is deceptive, just plain clunch with moulded
window surrounds, and a Late Georgian Gothic-detailed
porch. Hidden behind the garden wall is the grand S front
identical with No. 13 Barn Hill, Stamford (see p. 668), of
1740. Five bays and two storeys with rusticated quoins, a
modillion frieze, and a panelled parapet pierced by three oval
keyed openings. Rusticated ground-floor windows with
stepped keystones, and upper windows with triangular pediments. The doorcase with Doric pilasters. The house was
originally L-shaped and dated from the C17.

OLD HALL, ¾ m. NE. L-shaped, stone, and mostly C17. Gabled
and buttressed W front.

ROXHOLME HALL, 1 m. N. In bleak stock brick and said to be
dated 1874. The N wing is C18, with a fine pedimented Doric
doorcase of stone. There is also a circular gabled DOVECOTE

0030

LENTON

ST PETER. Dec W tower with broach spire. Three tiers of
lucarnes in alternating positions. The S aisle has Dec windows
but a W lancet. The latter goes with the E.E. S arcade. Three
bays, octagonal piers, double-chamfered arches. One of the
piers has a stiff-leaf capital, the W respond has sparse stiff-leaf
knobs, the E respond more such knobs in two tiers. The intermediate wooden floor in the tower seems to have as stone corbels
E.E. capitals. Large Perp N windows; Perp clerestory. In the
S porch pretty little Perp niche with a vault. – FONT. Octagonal, Perp, with shields in pointed quatrefoils. – SCULPTURE

Small relief of a standing figure; Roman. – PLATE. Chalice and two Patens, by *P.M.*, 1689. – MONUMENT. Armyne family, erected 1605, but looks as if it were of *c.*1570. Altar table at the foot on short square pillars. Then two bays, two tall tiers of back panels, slender, baluster-like Corinthian columns, with foliage in their lower parts, fluted in the upper. The panels between have inscriptions on the upper tier, shields on the lower. The panels are surrounded by egg and dart. No figures at all.

SCHOOLHOUSE, SE of the church. A plain, single-storey, three-bay cottage. Over the door the date 1790 and an inscription telling all posterity that the building cost £112 5s. 8d. and that Sir Gilbert Heathcote contributed 10 guineas, the Rev Dr Wright 5, Thomas Forsyth Esq 5, a levy on Lenton and Hanby £17 16s. 0d., and seven years' salary (the schoolmaster's?) £33 9s. 8d.

LEVERTON   4040

ST HELEN. The church can boast an extremely lavish chancel, the buttresses with gablets on busts and fine tracery, a frieze of flowers, monsters, etc., pinnacles, three-light side windows, and a five-light E window. The building no doubt was connected with that of the chapel attached on the S side, which is of two bays with straight-headed windows. This was, it can be assumed, the chantry chapel of the person who paid for the chancel. Inside the chancel there are sedilia with little vaults, all three of different patterns, and with crocketed ogee gables, buttress-shafts, and a cresting. The doorway to the chapel is odd – round-headed of lots of continuous mouldings. The chancel arch has the usual Perp form with concave-sided semi-octagonal responds. Perp also the W tower with its tall four-light W window, its three-light transomed bell-openings, and its plain parapet,* and Perp the N aisle windows. The clerestory looks Perp too but is of 1892. But step inside, and you will find not a Perp but a Dec church. The arcades are of five bays, and the tower was started a little further W than their responds. The S arcade was built first. The piers are of four filleted main and four filleted subsidiary shafts, the arches of two sunk waves (the Boston motifs). Building went on from W to E, see the simpler capitals of the W respond and the first pier. The arch mouldings also change after the first

---

* It is known that money was spent on it in 1498–1503.

two arches. The N arcade piers have four shafts and fo▮
diagonal hollows, i.e. the section which became a favouri▮
with the Perp masons. The S doorway with groups of fir▮
mouldings harmonizes with the S arcade, and so do the oge▮
arched, straight-headed S aisle windows.* The E window h▮
reticulated tracery. L. and r. of it inside niches. – FON▮
Octagonal, Perp, each panel with four small, very slim arch▮
and four small quatrefoils over (cf. Freiston). – SCREEN. ▮
two-light divisions, with an ogee arch over every two. Clo▮
panel tracery over. – PLATE. Chalice, by *A.B.*, inscribe▮
1569; Paten, by *Richard Green*, 1705; Paten, by *Gabri*▮
Sleath, 1713; Flagon, by *Charles Fox*, 1829.

LITTLE BYTHAM

ST MEDARD. A rare dedication. The church was Anglo-Saxo▮
in its architectural beginnings – see the NE quoin. Then follow▮
the chancel arch, a Norman S window, and a S doorwa▮
uncommonly ornate for a priest's doorway. It has a tym▮
panum with birds in two roundels l. and r. of a central round▮
which is sunk and empty. The tradition is that it once held▮
relic. Round the tympanum a billet frieze and an outer frie▮
of little squares with ribbed leaves. A stone bench runs roun▮
the chancel inside. The steep double-chamfered chancel arc▮
is C13 and probably late. The double piscina may be contem▮
porary. Norman again the tower arch. It is unmoulded and th▮
hood-mould rests on two beast's heads. Above it, in axis,▮
doorway. The upper parts of the tower carry on into the C1▮
Twin bell-openings under a round arch. Perp top with▮
lozenge frieze. Recessed spire. Two tiers of lucarnes in th▮
same directions. Back to the late C12 and so to the nave▮
doorway. Norman lozenge chains in the arch, but also▮
continuous roll moulding and dog-tooth running parallel to ▮
both l. and r. The hood-mould again on two beast's head▮
Above the arch small relief of a man. The S arcade is earl▮
C13. Round piers, a little nailhead, round, double-chamfere▮
arches. The W respond has a fillet. Seats round the piers. ▮
the same time or a little later the S porch entrance. Shaf▮
with shaft-rings. But the E window of the aisle must hav▮
been inserted later. It has intersecting tracery, i.e. dates fro▮
*c.*1300. Of the same moment the piscina in the aisle. Pointe▮
trefoiled head. The Easter Sepulchre in the chancel is De▮

* The tracery of the W window is Victorian.

and regrettably coarse. Ballflower in the gable. In the N aisle a curious arrangement of three niches, one above the two others. – PULPIT. The stone base is dated 1590 and has the inscription Orate et Arate. – BENCH ENDS with poppy-heads; a few. – ARCHITECTURAL FRAGMENT. A capital with oak leaves; good; Dec (S aisle w end; cf. Kirkby Underwood). – PLATE. Chalice and Paten Cover, by *John Morley* of Lincoln (?).

LITTLE HUMBY *see* GREAT HUMBY

LITTLE PONTON

9030

ST GUTHLAC. The problem of the church is the chancel arch. In the literature it is called Norman, but is it not rather of the so-called Saxo-Norman overlap? The responds are shafted, and the shafts carry capitals with volutes, rosettes, and scrolls. The bases are extremely steep and also shapeless. And instead of an arch moulding there is accompanying the arris a shallow half-roll and a shallow raised band – a typical Saxon arrangement. The abaci also are more Saxon in their ignorant mouldings than Norman. Other Norman evidence is two re-used capitals in the S porch entrance. As for the rest, the church consists of a nave and chancel and a N aisle added in 1850. In the w gable the date 1657 and some re-set heads. The N arcade is E.E. Three bays, circular piers with circular abaci. The simple S doorway is E.E. too. Late C13 chancel, see the Geometrical tracery of one S window (pointed trefoiled lights and a trefoil over). The nave once had a one-bay S chapel. – PLATE. Silver-gilt Chalice, Paten, and Flagon, by *Richard Goldwire*, 1776; Paten, by *Robert James & John Schofield*, 1776.

LITTLE PONTON HALL. There was once an Early Georgian E front of seven bays with a three-bay centre, two storeys, and a row of dormers. This was later reduced to the centre plus the two S bays, and a prolongation S again was added of three slightly higher bays, filling in an angle between the old S and E fronts. The curved bay of the S front is externally late C18, the room behind is early C19. The w front may have work coeval with that on the S. Moulded stone window surrounds and a pedimented doorway. Of the same period are the five pedimented entrances to the stable yard.

DOVECOTE. Octagonal and Georgian.

ROUND BARROW, ¼ m. N, just E of the Great North Road.
large round barrow with steeply sloping sides and a markedl
flat top. Unexcavated, but possibly Roman (*see* Riseholm
Lindsey, p. 343).

9030   LONDONTHORPE

ST JOHN BAPTIST. Early C13 S arcade of three bays. Keele
quatrefoil piers with thinner shafts in the diagonals. In th
capitals rather raw upright stiff-leaf. Double-chamfere
arches. Only the E respond is Dec. The N arcade is of *c.*130
The foils of the quatrefoil carry fillets and are connecte
by continuous hollows. Double-chamfered arches. In the
wall a tomb recess. The stump of the tower is perhaps a litt
earlier. Responds of the arch towards the nave triple, th
middle shaft keeled. Triple-chamfered arches. The tow
has a W lancet with a round rere-arch, and that looks like a y
earlier beginning. The bell-openings typical of the late C1
To the E two single lights, to N and S two pointed-trefoile
lights carrying a trefoil or a spherical triangle. Perp S porch wit
battlements and pinnacles. Perp S aisle, also with battlemen
and pinnacles. Perp clerestory. The N aisle is dated 1852, and th
chancel looks all Victorian too. – PLATE. Chalice and Pate
by *Daniel Sleath*, 1708. – MONUMENTS. A fragmentary C1
coffin-lid with an exceptionally fine and well preserved foliate
cross. – Cross-legged Knight (N aisle).
N of the church the HALL. Mid C18 (MHLG). Stone W front
five bays with a one-bay pediment.
SE of the church a good three-bay C18 house, also of stone.

Londonthorpe is a typical Lincolnshire village composed almo
entirely of a close group of farms, agriculturally working ou
wards from this nucleus. Estate cottages are dated 1849, an
there is a grandiloquent CONDUIT HOUSE with a big arch an
rustication.

8040   LONG BENNINGTON

ST SWITHUN. The S doorway has polygonal shafts wit
scalloped capitals, but there is nothing else Norman le
though the three-bay arcades are only a little later. Roun
piers, octagonal abaci, round arches with fine moulding
The last N pier and the NE respond have flat leaves on th
capitals. The other capitals are all moulded. E.E. the rest
the S doorway, the S porch entrance, and the lower parts

the tower (shafted, clasping buttresses, w lancet). The top is
Perp with eight pinnacles. Two two-light bell-openings with
transom. Ogee gables carrying the subsidiary pinnacles (cf.
Beckingham). Inside the tower quadripartite rib-vault with a
big ring in the centre. Dec aisle windows, those of the s aisle
with reticulated tracery including a strange variety where a
transom cuts through the reticulation units. Spacious Perp
chancel windows, that to the E Victorian. Wide sedile inside.
Perp clerestory of three-light windows with low-pitch triangular heads. – FONT. Octagonal, plain bowl on three short
polygonal pillars. Between the capitals and the underside of
the bowl bunches of stiff-leaf. So it seems to be E.E. –
PULPIT. C17. With tall, simple, arched panels. – SCREEN.
Of two-light divisions with trefoiled ogee arches. – STALLS.
Five, plain, in the chancel. – PLATE. Chalice, by *Nicholas
Gossen* of Nottingham, c.1570.

Although on the A1, the village has not received the notice it
deserves. It is remarkably straggling, perhaps the longest
village in the county, with nearly half a mile of unspoilt
Georgian houses disposed behind strips of green. Most of
the houses are of brick, but some are of coursed rubble.
The village centre is off the A1, to the E. Here is the most
notable building, PRIORY HOUSE, Georgian, of coursed
brick, with a three-bay, four-storey front. Later castellated
bows on the ground floor, coeval perhaps with rainwater
heads dated 1798. In an outbuilding part of a C13 doorway,
the only relic of the Cistercian grange which existed here.
In another outbuilding C19 panelling from a palace at Karachi.

LONGHILLS see BRANSTON

LONG SUTTON

ST MARY. The early C13 tower is one of the most exciting of
its date in Lincolnshire. It was originally detached like that
of West Walton across the Norfolk border, and has one of the
earliest well preserved lead spires in England. The tower
itself has angle-buttresses with a nook-shaft in the corner for
two stages. Then they turn into octagonal turrets, and these
turrets carry rather naive, slightly inward-leaning lead spirelets to accompany the main spire, which rises to 162 ft. The
ground stage of the tower was originally open to all four sides.
Triple responds and simply stepped arches. Inside in the

corners shafts rise sheer without carrying a vault. The seco
stage of the tower to the outside has blank arcading, the thi
the bell-openings, slender, of two lights with Y-tracery,
detached in front of twin openings with shafts. Of the chur
to which this tower was added the exterior tells us nothi
or near to nothing. The only promise is two flat, obvious
Norman, buttresses separating nave and aisles on the w fro
The s aisle to which they belonged was then widened, a
we have evidence of this Dec aisle: the over-restored
window with flowing tracery and two s windows with re
culated tracery. The nave w window of five lights is also D
and rich but, as it is now, all Victorian (*Slater*, 1864,
W. & C. A. Bassett Smith, c.1895). We can take in the Pe
parts as we go round the building. Two-storeyed s porc
coarsely decorated outside, but with a fine two-bay vault
tierceron stars with bosses inside. Nice projecting polygo
stair with windows above as in a domestic bay window. E
the porch all large three-light windows with transoms a
lively tracery. The s aisle E window must be Victorian. T
chancel projects by one bay only and has a Victorian fi
light E window. However, its surround seems original, a
this has ballflower. That would mean that the Dec rebuildi
extended right to the E end. Adjoining the NE corner the u
expected addition of a polygonal two-storeyed vestry (cal
Vestiarium in a deed of 1411). It has a steep stone roof. The
aisle E window is again Victorian. The N side is like the
side except that the windows here have no transoms and t
there is no original porch. The N doorway on the other ha
is impressive. But is it Dec or Perp? It is surmounted
indubitably Perp panelling, but the doorway itself with
steep ogee head and the coved voussoirs panelled with a la
band of quatrefoils seem more Dec than Perp. So we are ba
at the w front, and the flat buttresses prepare for the surpr
of the interior.

It is Norman to beyond the chancel arch, and close
style and character to Walsoken across the Norfolk bord
The nave arcades are of seven bays. They have circular pi
(except for numbers three and four from the w, which cor
spond to the doorways and are octagonal) with many-scallop
capitals and square abaci with nicked corners. The arches
round with one step and one slight chamfer. E and W respon
are triple. Moreover, the complete clerestory is now inside t
Dec and Perp building. To what always was the inside it h

small shafted single-splayed windows, but to what was originally the exterior there is fine blind arcading all the way along.
The chancel arch is Norman too, but was heightened. The w
respond of the Norman N chancel aisle is still partly preserved. The rest of the chancel aisle arcades is Perp, with
very tall, slender octagonal piers. Hence the heightening of
the chancel arch. The Norman chancel corbel table above the
chancel aisle roof also survives partly on the N side. The
aisles of the nave are wide, that on the s side, in order to reach
out as far as the tower, especially so. The vestry has a vaulted
ground-floor room with a shield in a circle in the centre and
radiating ribs of a gently hollow-chamfered section. It is of the
C14. More surprising is the date of the Norman parts. A
document tells us that William, son of Loneis, about 1180
gave to the priory of Castle Acre 3 acres of ground to build a
parish church. Must one then really accept as of after 1180
what looks like 1170 at the latest?

REREDOS. The former reredos of c.1700 is in the N aisle.
Classical, with fluted pilasters and some carving. – COM-
MUNION RAIL. Also of c.1700, and also in the N aisle. With
exceptionally pretty turned balusters. – PULPIT. The sounding board of the former pulpit of Lutton church is now used
as a table in the children's corner. It dates from c.1700. –
POOR BOX. Dated 1712. A square, heavily profiled piece. –
LECTERN. Perp. A brass eagle of a familiar East Anglian type.
– STAINED GLASS. Many original fragments in the s and N
chancel aisles and the N aisle. In the s chancel aisle also the
figure of a Knight. – PLATE. Chalice, Elizabethan; Chalice, by
Peter Petersen, Norwich, 1568; Plate, by *T.F.*(?), given
1687; silver-gilt Chalice, by *C.O.*, 1715. – MONUMENTS.
Tomb recess in the s aisle. – Many tablets, e.g. Nicholas
Wileman † 1752, with an urn in front of an obelisk.

To the w of the church the MARKET PLACE. Here, at the place
where it continues as WEST STREET, a long late C18 front of
three storeys, rusticated ground floor, fluted pilasters above.
The Market Place is continued at its N end to the w in Market
Street, to the E in High Street. Beyond Market Street is
CHAPEL BRIDGE ROAD, which has first on the N a nice if
rustic Late Georgian terrace of fourteen bays, then on the s
the SCHOOL of 1835 (seven bays, arched windows, middle
pediment), a terrace of three three-bay houses, and then the
WESLEYAN CHAPEL of 1839. Three bays, three storeys,
also arched windows, but a pediment right across the front.

Between High Street and Churchyard is the stately forme[
VICARAGE. Early C19, stone front, yellow brick sides. Thre[
storeys, five bays, Roman Doric porch. Further E, in LONDO[
ROAD, a number of nice doorcases, all Late Georgian.

EAST ELLOE MAGISTRATES COURT. 1960–1 by *L. Barlo*[
Holland County Architect. Red brick, single-storeyed, wit[
a raised slate-faced centre. Detached pedimented porch o[
black posts.

PEELE COUNTY SECONDARY SCHOOL, 1 m. N. 1957 by th[
Architects' Co-Partnership and the county architect *L. Barlo*[
Certainly the most successful of the few modern Lincoln[
shire schools. The main block is a cube, three storeys i[
height, with curtain walling and reinforced glass infilling[
On the E one-storey ranges extend S and E forming a grid c[
two courtyards. The hall is inserted in the S side of the mai[
courtyard, and the gymnasium extends from its outer angl[
Both these units are higher than the rest of the ranges.

WINDMILL, ¾ m. SE. Tower mill with six sails.

GARNSGATE HALL, ⅞ m. WSW. (Dated 1724. MHLG) Seve[
bays, the windows l. and r. of doorway and upper midd[
window very narrow, a typical Queen Anne and Early Geo[
gian motif.

LOVENDEN HILL *see* HOUGH-ON-THE-HILL

LOW FULNEY *see* SPALDING, p. 655

4020

LUTTON

ST NICHOLAS. A Perp brick church. Only the arch of the [
tower to the nave and the recessed spire are of stone. One ti[
of lucarnes giving an odd outline from a distance. Height c[
the spire 159 ft. The arcade inside is of course of stone to[
The profile of four semicircular projections and four sma[
hollows in the diagonals is still Dec, but bases and arch[
(with two pairs of small hollow chamfers) are Perp. To th[
arcade belongs a roof-line against the tower earlier than th[
present one, which takes in a clerestory in which even th[
windows and even the cusped arches of their twin lights ar[
of cut brick. Most of the other windows are Victorian (1859[
Nice nave roof of moderate pitch with tie-beams and quee[
posts. – FONT. Octagonal, Perp, with little decoration. [
PULPIT. 1702. Given by Dr Busby of Westminster Schoo[

With nicely shaped and inlaid panels. – COMMUNION RAIL. With twisted balusters. Probably of about the same date. – PLATE. Chalice, c.1570, with remains of date letter 1522; Paten, by *S.C.*, 1826.

MANTHORPE
1½ m. N of Grantham

ST JOHN. 1847–8 by *G. G. Place* of Nottingham. Obviously a Brownlow gift, a typical estate church, sizeable and well built. Beige ashlar. Nave and chancel and a central tower between. The tower carries a broach spire. The detail in the style of c.1300. – STAINED GLASS. The W window by *Willement* in the style of Holbein. The E window also original, but Gothic and more sombre in the colours.

Like Belton, Manthorpe is a perfect C19 village with estate cottages, a school and conduit, all in a picturesque red-brick or stone Tudor style. The SCHOOL dated 1865 and COTTAGES 1849, 1853, etc. The roads, a nice effect of two levels.

MANTHORPE
2½ m. WSW of Thurlby

BOWTHORPE PARK FARM. C17 stone house with three- and four-light windows and a buttressed stack. The place is more famous for the 'Great Oak' once here. According to Howlett 'frequently twelve persons have dined in it with ease'.

MARKET DEEPING

ST GUTHLAC. One enters the church by a doorway – the S doorway – of the late C12. One order of shafts with waterleaf capitals. Arch with roll mouldings. Waterleaf also in the arch to the former N chapel. But the arch is pointed. The three-bay N arcade is of the early C13. Quatrefoil piers with undetailed capitals. The abaci circular, embracing the whole quatrefoil. Double-chamfered round arches. The S arcade is of c.1300. The quatrefoils have continuous hollows between the abaci and the foils, the arches are pointed. The chancel arch is by *Fowler*, 1878, but the sedilia, the former priest's doorway, and the ogee-arched piscina are Dec. The two vaulted niches l. and r. of the Perp E window are Perp too. The window has a transom. Perp clerestory, Perp S aisle windows, Perp W tower. It has clasping buttresses, a deep niche in the sw buttress, and four-light bell-openings in pairs of two with the middle mullion reaching up to the apex of the arch. Castellated transoms. The N aisle exterior must all be of the restoration. – FONT. Octagonal, Perp. With foiled or cusped fields. – DOOR. With ironwork of the C13. – SCULPTURE. An Anglo-Saxon interlace panel in the s porch. – STAINED GLASS. s aisle E by *H. Hughes*, 1880. – N aisle (Vergelle window), 1920 by *H. Hendry*. Two large figures. Good, in the English wood-engraving tradition, still based on the 1890s. – PLATE. Chalice and Paten, by *Samuel Courtauld*, 1750. – MONUMENTS. Many coffin-lids with foliated crosses.

RECTORY. The N front and the interior are what matters most. The doorway has continuous mouldings of Dec type. The DOOR with its ironwork is original too. As one enters there are on the l. two plain chamfered doorways to the kitchen and offices. On the r. is the hall. One of its windows is original,* an interesting, very original design, straight-headed, of two lights, each with a cross at the top whose side arms are rounded. Below, the lights have a shouldered top taking up the form of the top half of the cross. Lower down a transom and the same shape repeated. The hall has its original roof timbers, though it was later horizontally subdivided. There is an alternation of hammerbeams and small pseudo-hammer-beams, all with little figures. The bay window was replaced in the late C16 or early C17 by a bigger and taller one, three storeys, i.e. rising above the medieval part, and with mullioned windows.‡ Round the corner to the w alterations of 1761, again altered by *Thomas Pilkington*§ in 1832. The s front is almost totally of the Pilkington period. Two projecting wings, buttressed and gabled, and over the centre a tall, dated gable. The pair of pointed entrances may not be C15, as they are similar to a triplet in the 1761 part of the house. The hall now contains a staircase of 1761, ingeniously contrived to serve three levels.

From the rectory and the church s runs CHURCH STREET, a wide street with grass verges and mostly stone houses, none disagreeable, not even the ALMSHOUSES of 1877 (which are

* See e.g. Hudson Turner, vol. 2, 1853.

‡ Tradition has it that the house was the refectory (or dormitory?) of a monastic cell of Thorney (or Croyland? or Sempringham?), but nothing of such a cell is known.

§ Who, according to Mr Howard Colvin, made designs for the Town Hall here in 1833.

probably by *Edward Browning* of Stamford). The MARKET
PLACE has alas recently become 'the roundabout'. In it, facing
us, on the l. a neo-Tudor house of 1880, on the r. the best
house in the place, early C18 in the Stamford Georgian style,
five bays, two and a half storeys, with segment-headed
windows. Further E the NEW INN, dated 1802, but conservative for its date. A good deal further W, about ¾ m. out
of the town, the MILL, three storeys, also of stone, with a
handsome wooden four-column porch.

MARSTON

8040

ST MARY. Of ironstone. Good E.E. s doorway. One order of
shafts and a second of three clustered shafts. Early stiff-leaf
capitals. Arch with beautifully elaborate mouldings. E.E.
also the three-bay s arcade. Round piers with round abaci.
Double-chamfered arches. In the spandrels pierced almond-
shaped openings. Are they an unusual piece of decoration,
or clerestory windows of a former aisled church? Both
suggestions are equally improbable. On one capital stiff-leaf
carving has been started. It was never continued. The same
pier has in its base a re-used chip-carved Norman stone. The
N arcade is of c.1300. Quatrefoil piers, the foils a little more
than semicircular. Fillets on them. Double-chamfered arches.
Also of c.1300 the intersecting tracery of the N aisle windows
and the doorway with continuous sunk quadrant mouldings.
Dec w tower with slender broach spire. Excessively tall
broaches. Three tiers of lucarnes in alternating directions.
The tower arch goes with the date. Triple responds, arch
with two sunk quadrant mouldings. Are the straight-headed
s aisle windows and the s chapel windows with trefoils on
pointed trefoiled heads of the lights Dec or Victorian? Perp
s porch with three small niches above the entrance. The
rich chancel is of 1878, by *C. Kirk*. – PLATE. Chalice and
Paten Cover, by *John Morley* of Lincoln, 1569; Chalice, by
R.C., 1692; Chalice and Paten, by *James Sutton*, 1780. –
MONUMENTS. William Thorold † 1569. Wall-monument
of Purbeck marble without any figures. Tomb-chest with
three shields in medallions. Back wall with shafts carrying a
straight lintel with rounded corners. Top quatrefoil frieze
and cresting. – Sir Anthony Thorold † 1594. Standing alabaster monument with recumbent effigy on a half-rolled-up
mat. No arches. – Anne Lady Hodgson † 1719. Signed *Stanton*

& Horsnail. Architectural, with two columns and an open segmental pediment. Inscription on a cloth.

MARSTON HALL. What remains of the late C16 house of the Thorold family is an oblong block of two storeys, seemingly the centre stroke of an H-shaped building.* Disregarding everything W of the porch on the S front and reading from l. to r.: first the square projecting porch of two storeys, then three bays, then a shallow but wide one-bay projection. Georgian windows and the stone rain-pipe circlet suggest a complete refacing of the centre part, when the hall mullions were destroyed. If this flank represents half the composition, Marston must originally have been a large house. The projection looks like an extruded stair angle, rebuilt with a thinner wall. The E front shows obvious marks of dissection. The N front is confused. Here the chimneybreast, later broadened, and the tall blocked hall window are original. A blocked window in the upper part at the E end points to a stair in this NE angle. The W gable looks Georgian, the result of an attempt to juggle with unequal levels, possibly because of the ruined W parts. W of the porch the base moulding dies into the wall, and beyond this the continuation is a Georgian and later rebuild. Inside, the hall has the blocked remains of a screens entrance. Perhaps *c.*1720 can be suggested as the date of the Georgian alterations; for such a date would accord with the fine moulded stone chimneypiece and the heavily moulded woodwork. The chimneypiece looks *ex situ*, but where would it come from? Its overmantel is Elizabethan, lavish with caryatids and strapwork. In the garden a piquant GAZEBO with a Gothick front. Built in 1962 for Henry Thorold by *John Partridge*; the pinnacles by *Christopher Blackie*; and the interior with murals by *Barbara Jones*.

MARTIN

HOLY TRINITY. By *T. H. Wyatt*, 1876, but the tower built in 1911. An odd choice of architect for Lincolnshire. S porch tower with pyramid roof. Nave and chancel and polygonal apse. Lancet windows. Transepts, and consequently a proper crossing, expressed inside in the roof timbers. The capitals round the crossing were obviously meant to be carved, probably with foliage, but in the end remained as raw chunks.

MERE HALL *see* BRANSTON

* Such a building is shown on a survey of 1615.

METHERINGHAM

0060

T WILFRID. Unbuttressed w tower, the bell-openings twin with separating shafts under a round arch. One s lancet. But what signifies the roof-line of a puzzlingly tall attachment against the w wall of the tower? Low blocked w arch. The middle buttress of the tower is dated 1601 and was put up after a fire had damaged the church in 1599. At the same time the piers inside were replaced by Tuscan columns. The mason was *John Tirrell,* who was much patronized by Sir Thomas Tresham (*see The Buildings of England: Northamptonshire*). The arches with the discoloration due to the fire are still medieval. The clerestory with two-light windows, the lights depressed arches, is also of after 1599. Nice Dec s doorway. Dec also the ogee-headed piscina. The Dec-looking E window is Victorian. The chancel E window was Perp and was re-used in the chancel s wall. Wide N aisle of 1870. – SOUTH DOOR. Of *c.*1601. – BENCH ENDS. Two with simple poppy-heads outside the church on the N side. – PLATE. Chalice and Paten, by *Gabriel Sleath,* 1716. – MONUMENT. Sir Thomas Skipworth † 1763. Quite a swagger piece. White, grey, and pink marble. Obelisk with a good relief of kneeling Hope and a putto. At the foot a large cherub's head.

MANOR HOUSE, ¼ m. E. Built by a Skipworth late in the C17. Greek cross plan with stepped gables.

MITCHELL FARM, SCOTTLETHORPE *see* EDENHAM

MOAT HOUSE *see* OLD LEAKE

MONCY BRIDGE HOUSE *see* PINCHBECK

MONKS HALL *see* GOSBERTON

MORTON

0020

T JOHN BAPTIST. The most interesting feature of the church is the N arcade. Four bays, octagonal piers, double-chamfered arches, but capitals of lively naturalistic leaves, of a fern character. This must be late C13. E.E. also the entrance to the deep w porch. The w doorway in it is Dec. But the porch otherwise is Perp and has nice openings to the l. and r., two lights, in pairs. This goes with the rest of the w front, which

is also Perp. The w window of the nave is of four lights wi
an embattled transom, the w windows of the aisles ha
three lights. The church has no w tower, but a crossing tow
instead. This is Dec below, Perp above. Pairs of two-lig
bell-openings with two transoms. The tower rests on D
arches inside with continuous mouldings. The w arch
much higher than the others. The cusped fan-vault insi
belongs of course to the time of the Perp finishing. A spire w
intended, as squinches in the bell-chamber prove. This crossi
must have replaced an earlier one; for the s transept ha
besides its Perp w and E windows, a s window which c
hardly be later than 1300. Three stepped lights and thr
spherical triangles over. The chancel also, in spite of
modest Dec N and s windows (the E window is Victorian), h
sedilia which must be pre-Dec.* Equally, the arch from t
N aisle to the N transept has the same pre-Dec leaves as t
N arcade. The s arcade incidentally is also Dec, and the ar
from it to the s transept has the characteristic nobbly leav
Perp s aisle, N aisle, and N transept windows. – FONT. B
octagonal, Perp. Shields in fields with low ogee arches.
them the Instruments of the Passion. – SCREEN. Under th
arch of the crossing the remains of a stone screen. – WE
DOOR. With tracery and an ogee-headed wicket. – STAIN
GLASS. By *Powell & Baillie*, probably of the time of t
restoration of the church, i.e. 1860. In sombre colours. T
representations still pictorial. They include a High Victori
version of Reynolds's New College window.

VICARAGE. Arched doorway with Venetian windows and fi
bays above. Date 1796, architect *John Andrew* (GA).

THE GRANGE. Probably C17. L-shaped. The pair of circu
lodges with conical roofs each side of the entrance may al
be of this date.

Opposite a three-bay Georgian stone HOUSE with a one-b
pediment.

₃₀₂₀
                              MOULTON

ALL SAINTS. Ambitious Perp w tower, one of the finest
the county. Four stages and the spire. Low w doorw
castellated frieze over, tall, steep, four-light w window wi
charmingly crested transom. Niches with canopies in t
buttresses. A second stage with small niches under t

* In fact the priest's doorway appears late C12, as Mr L. Bond remi
me. Is the chancel masonry then that old?

gables to the w, windows to the N and s. Two-transomed two-light bell-openings. Frieze below the battlements. Square panelled pinnacles connected by lacy flying buttresses with the crocketed spire, which has three tiers of lucarnes in alternating directions. Total height about 165 ft. Long, low aisles, the windows with Geometrical tracery all Victorian. Embattled chancel. Victorian E window. Earlier evidence, to prepare for the interior, is as follows. The clerestory is E.E. Triple clusters of shafts with stiff-leaf capitals carry alternatingly narrow round and wider segmental arches. The windows are no longer E.E. The N doorway is minor E.E., and the s doorway is decidedly late C12. Clustered shafts with capitals whose leaves belong to that date. So do the arcades inside, a splendid set, characteristic of, say, 1180–90.* Five bays plus a w bay. The piers are, except for one circular pair, all circular with four attached demi-shafts not yet clearly separated from the core. The E responds have some keeling and are perhaps the end of the operation. The capitals have one row of close upright leaves on the way to stiff-leaf but not quite stiff-leaf yet (cf. the E part of Whaplode nave). In some capitals also a few heads. The double-chamfered arches must be later. The w bay is something special. It is separated from the rest by a tall demi-shaft to the nave. Then follows another bay, the w responds a little more advanced in style. What must have happened is that a tower was projected here and was to be embraced by the aisles but never carried on with. The chancel has its simple E.E. sedilia and a plain C14 Easter Sepulchre opposite (ogee arch). The poor chancel arch is probably of 1777. – FONT. Stem and to its l. and r. Adam and Eve. Bulgy bowl with Baptism of Christ. Made in 1719 by *William Tydd*, of course on the Gibbons pattern.‡ – SCREEN. Largely renewed. One-light divisions with trefoiled ogee arches. Detached buttress-shafts. – PLATE. Chalice, early C17(?); Flagon, by *Matthew Lofthouse*, 1716; two Patens, London, 1724.

ᴐ the s of the churchyard the tower-house of a brick MILL ᴌooks much like a giraffe.

ᴏulton is the most satisfying village in this neighbourhood. A Green with old trees adjoins the church tower immediately

* There is in fact a document of c.1180–90 which shows that the church s building then.

‡ This information was conveyed to me by the Rev. Paul Cory. Tydd was ᴅ £7 3s. 0d.

to the W. On its W side the GRAMMAR SCHOOL HOUS brick, three bays, dated 1792. At the S end of the Gre BAYFIELD, dated 1805, with a porch with fluted Dor columns. A little further S, on the E side of the street, MI HOUSE, with delicately detailed dormers and, in a wing the front, a Venetian window which has Gothic glazing ba

ELLOE STONE, ⅞ m. NE. The stone marks the meeting-place the Court of the Wapentake. Probably of pre-Conquest dat but the inscription now indecipherable.

CASTLE. At King's Hall Park there is an oval moat which probably the site of the castle of Moulton mentioned in 121 Its other defences are not likely to have been considerable.

2010
MOULTON CHAPEL

ST JAMES. 1722, by *William Sands Sen.* of Spalding (accordi to a former inscription). The church is (or was) a brick oct gon. The chancel etc. added in 1886. Each side has a pair giant brick pilasters. The windows and the doorway arche Domed interior. The type is decidedly Dutch, and it has be suggested that this Dutch influence came with the fen draine of the later C17.* – FONT. Marble. A square pillar and octagonal bowl. – WEST GALLERY. Probably early C19. PLATE. Cup, gilt in bowl, by *George Beech*(?), Edinburg 1788.

3020
MOULTON SEAS END
2½ m. NE of Moulton

MISSION ROOM. 1867. Nave and apse. Bell under a spire at the E end of the nave. Red and yellow brick. The windov are cusped lancets.

The name, and the stretches further W marked 'sea banks' black letter on the ordnance maps, show how far inland t Wash went.

9050
NAVENBY

ST PETER. Three different parts and a *crescendo* to the E. Po W tower, a replacement after a fall in the mid C18. Go Perp clerestory with battlements, decorated by shields quatrefoils, and closely-set three-light windows, but on five of them, and taller Dec chancel with large windows. T side windows have reticulated tracery, the E window (part

* Mr John Harris found drawings by *John Talman* at the Spaldi Gentlemen's Society showing that he intended to finish the church with cupola.

rebuilt in 1875–6 but, it is said, correctly) a six-light composition with in the head two very large mouchettes nodding to each other and a very large reticulation unit at the top. Of the interior more later. First, still regarding the outside, the odd s aisle w and tower w windows with tracery one would call C17, if they were not clearly of after the fall of the tower and must therefore be extremely belated in style. Now the arcades. They are of three bays. The w respond and the first pier on the N side are good E.E. work, the pier quatrefoil but set diagonally so that the thin detached shafts between the foils come in the main directions. Round abacus, round seat. The second pier, the E respond, and the s arcade normal quatrefoil with fillets, i.e. late C13. That date goes with the s aisle windows with intersecting tracery. The N aisle windows are Dec, but Victorian. Just s of the chancel arch a charming corbel of a lady wearing a wimple. It must have been for the rood, and is a nice introduction to the glorious chancel interior. Here the Dec style really showed what it could do: founder's tomb, Easter Sepulchre, piscina and separate sedilia all have ogee arches, crocketed gables, crocketed buttress-shafts, big finials, and the variety of bossy leaf shapes with occasional small figures is prodigious. The finest piece is the Easter Sepulchre, although it is small and upright, not horizontal. The opening is only less than 3 by less than 2 ft. But at the foot stand three Roman soldiers in relief (cf. Lincoln Cathedral and Heckington), and in the spandrels above two and two exquisitely swaying draped figures, the three Maries and the angel. The sedilia have tiny vaults inside. – FONT. By *Charles Kirk* of Sleaford; lavish. Shown at the London Exhibition of 1862. – PULPIT. Jacobean, with flat decoration. The door is preserved. – PLATE. Chalice and Paten, by *Daniel Rutty*, 1655; Flagon, by *Humphrey Payne*, 1750. – MONUMENT. Late C13 slab with inscription in Norman script: 'Pray for Richard de Lue' (Louth). The shape is odd, a reversed pointed trefoil.

•LD RECTORY. By *H. A. Darbyshire*, 1859. Stone, gabled.

CHOOL. The main building dated 1816 but inscribed 'The Benefit Society 1821'.

NEWTON
2¾ m. NW of Folkingham

T BOTOLPH. The tower arch has a Norman shaft with scallop capital, an E.E. shaft, and a pointed arch with one chamfer

20—L

and one roll. It does not seem in original order. The towe
otherwise is E.E. Bell-openings with Y-tracery. Later a nev
Perp bell-stage was put on. Late C13 s chapel. Geometrica
and Y-tracery. The arches into this chapel die into thei
imposts. The same is true of the arches into the N chapel
The chancel seems of c.1300. The E window of four lights ha
intersecting tracery all finely roll-moulded. The chancel arcl
is Victorian. In the chancel a piscina with a partly origina
gable, decorated with dog-tooth. The tomb recess opposit
must be a little later; for it has ballflower and an ogee arch
Dec also the N aisle and N doorway. The windows have ogee
headed lights and nicely filleted shafts. Are the three-ba
arcades also Dec? Octagonal piers, double-chamfered arches
The E respond on a head corbel. The s aisle wall must be of th
restoration of 1865. – STAINED GLASS. In the s chapel sma
bits in the tracery of two windows. – PLATE. Chalice an
Cover, by *A.M.*, 1668.

Newton lies nicely in a valley. It has an extremely attractiv
centre with the church, the quite ambitious SCHOOL of 1874
and cottages round the (much restored) CROSS.

NEWTON HALL. 1839–41 for Sir G. E. Welby Gregory wit]
additions of 1870.

ROMAN VILLA. *See* Haceby.

NOCTON

NOCTON HALL. A fire in 1834 destroyed the magnificer
Jacobean and Carolean house of the Ellys family. In 1841 i
was rebuilt for the first Earl of Ripon by *William Shearbur*
His style is a late Vernacular Tudoresque. Near by, 100 yds i
of the church, facing the wood, as the E wall of a house, is a
impressive fragment of the later C17. A composition of thre
bays, brick and stone-quoined. Tall windows with straigh
entablatures to the ground floor and above each a bolection
framed horizontal oval with four scrolls.

ALL SAINTS. By *Sir George Gilbert Scott*, 1862, for the Coun
tess of Ripon, in memory of the first Earl. A typical estat
church in its setting against a backcloth of wood and in i
ambitiousness and unvillagey character. Purely architecturall
speaking one of Scott's major works. Of Ancaster stone
in the E.E. style at the plate tracery stage. NW steeple 13
ft high. Porch below, octagonal bell-stage with stiff-lea
shafting, spire. Tall, short nave, s aisle with vaulted s porcl
s clerestory, chancel. The nave roof of a trefoil section wit

collar-beams, more Italian than English. The arcade capitals are moulded, but the hood-mould stops are completely naturalistic passion-flowers, roses, lilies, etc. The chancel is yet richer. The windows have marble shafts and all the capitals thick foliage. – REREDOS. Marble and alabaster, with religious reliefs. – CANDLESTICKS. Tall and Gothic; of brass. – COMMUNION RAIL. Of brass. – PULPIT. Of Caen, Ancaster, and red Mansfield stone with green marble columns. – FONT. Caen stone, also with green marble columns. – PAINTINGS. All along the walls red-outline drawings of figures and religious scenes. – STAINED GLASS. By *Clayton & Bell*, except for the palish E window, designed in a belated kind of Nazarene Italianism by Miss *Hobart*, daughter of the Dean of Windsor (*see* below). – MONUMENTS. Under the tower Sir William Ellys † 1680. Mrs Esdaile attributed this monument to *William Stanton*. White and grey marble. Tall standing monument, yet of a type more suited to the tablet. Columns frame a large oval inscription plate; flowers in the corners. Above, big scrolly open pediment with an urn, excellently carved garlands. No figures. – Robert, Earl of Buckinghamshire, † 1816. White marble, with a plain, broad, and flat pointed framing. Inside, sarcophagus in relief placed at an angle and draped with the Earl's robes. At the foot the Charter of the East India Company, 1813. – Rev. H. L. Hobart † 1846, son of the Earl and Dean of Windsor. White marble. Arched surround and two kneeling praying women. – First Earl of Ripon † 1859. Designed by *Scott*, the recumbent, white-marble effigy by *Matthew Noble*, 1862.

SCHOOL. Gothic. By *Sir G. G. Scott*.

NORMANTON

9040

ST NICHOLAS. Small. Unbuttressed w tower, probably Dec; for though the w window is mostly Victorian (and ignorant), some of the ballflower decoration is original. Late C12 aisles, see the w lancets.* The rest of the N aisle outside of 1845, when also the chancel was all but rebuilt. Short Perp clerestory with busily decorated battlements, also Victorian. Late C12 S arcade of two bays; low. Round pier, waterleaf in the capitals. Round arches of one step and one chamfer. The N arcade is late C13 to early C14. Octagonal pier, abacus with a little nailhead, double-chamfered arches. – PULPIT. C17; entirely

* In the rere-arch of the S aisle lancet a stone with small decoration much like dog-tooth.

plain. – PLATE. Chalice, by *John Morley* of Lincoln, *c.*1569
Flagon, by *Richard Bayley*, 1731.

9060   NORTH HYKEHAM

ALL SAINTS. 1858 by *Michael Drury*. Low, rock-faced, in th
late C13 style. SW tower with short spire and the oddest bell
openings: circular, set out with foiled circles and place
under pointed arches.

1050   NORTH KYME

ST LUKE. 1877 by *Drury & Mortimer*. Of brick; nave an
chancel and oddly corbelled-out wooden bell-turret. Th
windows are oddly detailed too.
W of the church, by the school, CROSS, base and about 6 ft c
shaft.

0040   NORTH RAUCEBY

17a ST PETER. A church of moderate size, but very beautifu
Ashlar-faced. Well-proportioned E.E. W tower. The bell
openings twins with plate tracery of unusual, complicate
shapes under round arches. To the l. and r. a blank pointe
arch – much as at Sleaford. Broach spire with big, stee
broaches. Three tiers of lucarnes in alternating directions. De
aisles with reticulated tracery, also cusped Y-tracery wit
ogees and in one case tracery with two circles filled by tw
mouchettes. At the w end of the S aisle a stair-turret and
half-hipped stone roof looking curiously 1960. Perp clere
story of five bays. Three-light windows with low-pitch tr
angular heads. Decorated battlements. The chancel wa
rebuilt by *Teulon* in 1853. It originally had N and S chapel
S porch entrance later C13, with two orders of shafts and
triple-chamfered arch. Of about the same date the towe
arch inside. Above it appears asymmetrically a round-heade
doorway. To the tower arch correspond the responds of th
N arcade. The arcades are of three bays, and both are De
They differ N from S, but both have shafts connected b
continuous hollows, N quatrefoil with fillets, S octofoil wit
four fillets. At the E end of the S aisle a tomb recess. Th
chancel arch of the same type as the arcade piers. – FONT
Octagonal, Perp; re-cut. Flowers in cusped fields. – BENC
ENDS. In the aisles, with tracery patterns and small poppy
heads. – STAINED GLASS. Some original glass in the tracer

of a N and a S aisle window. – E window by *Ward*, *c*.1853. –
MONUMENTS. Effigy of a Priest; C14; defaced (N aisle). –
Brass to William Styrlay † 1536, a 20 in. figure (vestry).
CROSS, SE of the church. Complete with a small lantern taber-
nacle at the top and a crocketed pinnacle.
SCHOOL. Dated 1841. Symmetrical. The porch gablet is com-
bined with a bell-turret as at Great Gonerby (*see* p. 552).

NORTH SCARLE

8060

ALL SAINTS. Essentially E.E., but with the following exceptions. In the W corner of the N aisle lies a big Norman capital
with ribbed leaves, similar to that at Bassingham. The N
doorway seems to be of *c*.1200, with its one slight chamfer,
but may of course link up with the E.E. work. The S doorway
on the other hand remains a puzzle. It is round-arched, but
cannot possibly be Norman. Is it Elizabethan ? To continue
with the not E.E. features, the bell-openings of the W tower
are Dec, but with its lower parts the E.E. work begins. It is
an unbuttressed tower anyway, and the responds are keeled.
The castellated capitals of course are a later alteration,
probably Perp. E.E. also the chancel, as proved by one low-
side lancet, even if the rest appears Perp. To this chancel at
once a N chapel of one bay was added, an important chapel,
considering the strikingly high arch. When the chapel was
demolished, so one may assume, its N doorway was re-set
in its present position. It is very handsome with its dog-tooth
and nailhead enrichments. The sedilia are plain E.E. and in
the N, not the S wall, a grave anomaly. The date of the arch
to the S chapel is less easily decided, but could be E.E. too.
E.E. also the S arcade of four bays. Keeled E respond, octagonal piers, very elementary capitals, double-chamfered
arches. The aisle was narrower than it is now, see the old
roof-line on the outer E wall. The N aisle is by *Comper*, who
restored the church in 1895–8. – By him also the pretty
chancel roof and the STAINED GLASS in the chancel. –
SCREEN. Little of it is old. – BENCH ENDS. Some with poppy-
heads. – PLATE. Chalice and Paten, by *John Cory*, 1702.

NORTH WITHAM

9020

ST MARY. Narrow Norman chancel arch. On the imposts
leaves like little flutes and billet. The arch is unmoulded.

Later medieval openings l. and r. to facilitate the seeing
the altar. Norman also the N and S doorways. The former l
one order of shafts, one crocket and one waterleaf capi
and an arch with one step and zigzag on it. The S doorway
simpler. The arch has one step and one slight chamfer. E.
chancel, see the one partly uncovered lancet. The rest of
windows here Perp. C14 S porch entrance, the capitals w
little heads. The N chapel entrance from the chancel ha
steep triple-chamfered arch, perhaps re-used. Perp W tow
ashlar-faced. Recessed spire. Vault inside of eight radiati
ribs round the circle for the bell-ropes. – FONT. Circul
with pointed-trefoiled arches on shafts, all re-tooled. Origina
probably late C13. – SCULPTURE. A part of an Anglo-Sax
cross shaft with interlace. – Also, in the chancel, a stiff-l
patera, *ex situ*. – STAINED GLASS. In the S aisle by *Kem*
1903. – PLATE. Gilt Chalice and Paten Cover, Lond
1577; Paten, by *Robert Cooper*, 1695; Flagon, by *Thon*
Tearle, 1724. – MONUMENTS. William Misterton † 14
Small, only the bottom half of the figure. – Otherwise mos
the Sherards of Lobthorpe near by.* Elizabeth S. † 16
Signed by *Joshua Marshall*. Oval tablet with rich scro
surround. – Richard S. † 1668. Large tablet with restl
surround. White demi-figure in an arched niche. The inscr
tion below flanked by fragments of a pediment. – Thon
Johnson † 1697. Also an oval inscription plate. Drape arou
– Sir John S. † 1724. By *Edward Stanton & Horsnail*. La
architectural tablet. The inscription between two colun
and below a baldacchino of drapery. – Sir Richard S. † 17
Also by *Stanton & Horsnail*. Large tablet. Columns carry
segmental pediment. Also putto heads at the foot. –
Brownlow S. † 1736. By *Edward Sharpe* of Stamford. Lar
very monumental sarcophagus on a square base. – HEL
and GAUNTLETS collected on it.

NORTON DISNEY

ST PETER. Unbuttressed E.E. W tower (see e.g. the tower arc
with later (Dec) bell-openings and a lavish top: many g
goyles and eight pinnacles. Also E.E. the N arcade of two ba
Circular pier, cruciform, chamfered abacus (an odd ide
double-chamfered arches. Late C13 the important N cha
It has windows to the N with pointed-trefoiled lights, t

---

* But of their mansion nothing remains.

foils over, and an encircled quatrefoil at the top. The original
E window is blocked, as is that of the chancel. In the chapel
the replacement is straight-headed with arched lights, a C15
form which occurs also in other places in the church, especially
strangely in the S wall of the S transept or chapel where two
such windows are one on top of the other as in a house. The
arch into this transept is four-centred and probably late C14,
as is the narrow E arch of the N arcade added to bring this in
line with the chancel arch, and as are the two arches of the
arcade to the N chapel. But what can be the date of the two
beautiful corbels l. and r. of the S transept E window? One of
them has big, rich leaves, the other leaves and a smaller
caryatid figure. The window is Perp, but can the corbels be
so late? A date about 1300 seems more probable. Low N aisle
with gargoyles. It looks Perp, but the doorway is plain ogee-
headed. – FONT. Octagonal, Perp, with simple lozenge-shaped
poppy-heads. – SCREEN. Perp, humble, of one-light divisions.
– COMMUNION RAIL. C17, and not too late. – BENCH ENDS
in the chancel. With poppy-heads, including faces. – In the
nave straight-headed and plain. – STAINED GLASS. Bits in
the N chapel. – PLATE. Chalice and Paten Cover, by *A.K.*,
1571; Snuffbox for hosts, Rotterdam, 1747(?). – MONU-
MENTS. Several early effigies to the Disney (d'Isigny) family. –
Knight on a later tomb-chest. Straight legs, in chain mail,
praying, his shield carved with his coat of arms and held high
up; later C13. – Slender Lady, *c.*1300. – Lady, mid C14, her
head under a nodding gable. She prays. Only her bust is
visible, in sunk relief. Then the slab continues carved with a
cross and shield, but the foot of the shield is an ogee arch
and inside this, once again in sunk relief, her feet appear.
The lettering is Norman. – Hantascia Disney, late C14. She
is praying, a beast at her head and her feet. Angels by her
pillow. Shields on the coping of the stone and on one side of it
the inscription. – Brass to William Disney and family, *c.*1580;
an interesting palimpsest. On the back a Flemish inscription
of 1518 of which the completion is at West Lavington, Wiltshire. – Fourth Viscount St Vincent, 1887. By *J. S. Westmacott.*
Angel with a wreath hovering over a flag. Still in the Georgian
tradition of the Westmacott family.

OMAN VILLA, on POTTER HILL, 200 yds SE of the Fosse
Way. A ploughed out, fortified villa site surrounded by a
ditch system. Excavation revealed a complicated structural
history divisible into five periods.

0030   OASBY
                        ¾ m. sw of Heydour

MANOR HOUSE. The w wing is of the c15 and has in its s gabl
end a canted oriel window corbelled-out on an angel figur
The lights of the window are two-centred and cusped. To tl
r. of this the façade continues c17 with two dormers. Tl
windows, no doubt normal mullioned types, have been mac
to look older.

4050   OLD LEAKE

ST MARY. Quite a large church, and it was probably as lar
already in the c12. For, though the six-bay arcades of tl
wide nave are Dec, the responds are Norman, on the w sio
triple-shafted, on the E side just sturdy, single and sem
circular. So, unless they have been re-used in the c15 in
shifted position, the Norman and the Dec nave length mu
have been the same. The arcades themselves have quatref
piers with fillets and thin shafts with fillets in the diagona
The necks of the capitals are polygonal, the capitals ar
abaci round. The arches have two sunk wave mouldings. /
this comes from Boston. The clerestory harmonizes with tl
arcades. Yet the upright two-light windows alternate betwe
a purely Dec and a purely Perp form. Only the first windo
from the w is in a simpler Perp. Niches in the buttress stri
and a decorated frieze. Gable-end with openwork quatref
parapet. SE turret with spire. And as the clerestory tries
combine what were old with what were new forms, so do
the church otherwise. Take the s aisle. Windows have thr
stepped lancet lights under one arch, i.e. a motif of the la
c13, but one has reticulation, i.e. a Dec motif; yet anothe
incidentally, is a Perp alteration. Dec s doorway with ;
elaborate niche to the l., a simple niche over. In the N ais
all Dec windows, including reticulation, but again also Pe
remodelling. Again the chancel (restored by *Temple Moor*
appears externally all of *c.*1300, but has a decidedly Dec ar
towards the nave with leaf capitals. The chancel is four ba
long and the large three-light side windows have cusp
intersecting tracery. The four-light E window is in keepin
It consists of two parts on the Y-principle and two quatrefo
and a sexfoil in circles over. Battered sedilia and piscir
Short, broad Perp w tower, the buttresses with many set-of
Six-light transomed w window, three-light bell-openings,
with late, schematic panel tracery. The tower was begun

1490 and not finished until 1547. It cost £359 14s. 10d. In the aisles two low tomb recesses. In the s aisle also a little niche in the jambs of a s window and niches l. and r. of the E window, one of them double. – REREDOS. All of divers Victorian tiles, probably of the restoration of 1873–5. – PULPIT. 1734. With fluted Ionic columns, back panel and tester. – PLATE. Chalice and Cover, inscribed 1678; Almsdish, by *F.S.*, 1679. – MONUMENT. Effigy of a Knight; alabaster; c15.

CHURCH, Commonside, 1¾ m. NW. 1875. Nave and chancel in one. Of stock brick, with lancet windows. The church is curiously like a crisp job of about 1820, see e.g. the wide pointed windows and the glazing bars all forming intersecting tracery. To the sides three-light, to the E four-light windows.

ERONSHAW HALL, ¾ m. SSW of the church. Brick, T-shaped, with c18 windows. A plaque dated 1576.

MOAT HOUSE, 1 m. SSE of the church. Once called St Lawrence's Chantry. c16 or early c17, but rebuilt in 1835. The plan a stubby T with corbelled gable-ends and a ground-floor bow to the s front. There are fragments of early coffin lids and corbel heads. It needs investigation.

OLD SOMERBY

9030

ST MARY MAGDALEN. The church has a Norman chancel arch with semicircular responds and nook-shafts, scalloped capitals, and zigzag in the arch, set diagonally. Then the E.E. contribution: the s arcade of two bays with quatrefoil piers with keeled additional shafts in the diagonals, fillets on the main foils, and double-chamfered arches, and the w tower with twin bell-openings having in the tympana blank foiled circles. Dec N side and (entirely renewed or Victorian) chancel windows. Perp s aisle and clerestory. The three-light clerestory windows have triangle heads of low pitch. The arch from tower to nave is also Perp. – SCREEN. The dado panels are re-used in the altar panelling. – PLATE. Chalice, Cover, and Paten, London, 1683; Flagon and Almsbasin, 1684. – MONUMENTS. Effigy of a Knight, early c14, his legs crossed, his hands praying. Against his feet – a charming and unusual conceit – his saddled horse. – Dame Elizabeth Brownlowe † 1684. Marble tablet. The top an urn set in an open scrolly pediment. Garlands around. The monument (according to Mrs Esdaile) is by *William Stanton*. – John Hotchkiss † 1744. Architectural tablet.

0030

OSBOURNBY

The village opens out suddenly from the main road and turns
out to be ambitious and satisfying, similar in character to Folkingham (*see* p. 528), but with more vernacular stone building.

ST PETER AND ST PAUL. Mostly Dec. First the chancel with
tall lancets of two lights; Y-tracery but also ogee details. The
E window is of 1873. The W tower with its flat clasping buttresses may look earlier still, but the doorway to the staircase
inside has an ogee head and the bell-openings and the top are
Dec anyway. Typically Dec S aisle,* see the windows, some
with reticulated tracery, some with cusped intersecting tracery.
Nice S porch with blank ogee arcading l. and r. inside. Perp
N aisle. The arcades again Dec. Four bays, quatrefoil piers,
the foils flowing into each other. Double-chamfered arches.
Fine Dec chancel sedilia, also with ogee arches. Amusing
head corbels. – FONT. Norman, drum-shaped, with inter-
secting arches. – SCREEN. Only the dado is preserved.
BENCH ENDS. A specially good set. The ends have poppy-
heads of many varieties and below tracery as well as scenes
such as the Crucifixion, Adam and Eve, St George and the
Dragon, the Fox preaching to the Geese. – PAINTINGS.
Moses and Aaron, from a former reredos. Signed *T. Phillip
Pinx.* Bourne. Are they the worst paintings in the county?
Anyway one cannot help liking them. – PLATE. Chalice and
Paten Cover, by *John Morley* of Lincoln, 1569; Flagon, by
Humphrey Payne, 1719.

SW of the church a COTTAGE with a mullioned window and
remains of more.

The SCHOOL is dated 1845 and, like some of the cottages,
Aswarby Estate work (*see* there).

PENNY HILL *see* HOLBEACH

0030

PICKWORTH

ST ANDREW. A Dec church. Heavy W tower with broach spire.
Three tiers of lucarnes in alternating directions, the top tier
too close to the top. There is however a round-headed W
window which seems Norman. The tower arch is no more
than a small doorway (two continuous chamfers). Does that
also connect with Norman precedent? Dec chancel, the

* The W bay which embraced the tower has been demolished.

window of four lights, the side windows with reticulated tracery. One small low-side window. Minor sedilia and piscina. Dec aisle and s doorway; Dec s porch entry. But the oversized battlements are presumably a Perp addition. Dec N aisle, as is the s aisle, with straight-headed windows. The clerestory could be Dec too. Arcades of four bays. Round piers, double-chamfered arches. Pretty piscina in the s aisle. Crocketed and on a horizontal figure. – PULPIT. Two-decker, dated 1693. Simply panelled. – COMMUNION RAIL. Dated 1767 and signed *Jos. Dabell fecit*. But the slender, vertically symmetrical balusters look C17 rather than later C18. – SCREEN. One-light divisions. Very pretty tracery above the ogee arches. – BENCHES. The square ends with simple tracery. – SCULPTURE. Headless female Saint, *c.*1400. – PAINTINGS. They are really what matters at Pickworth, and as so often in England they are far too badly preserved to be enjoyed. If one wants to enjoy or indeed to study them, one must look at reproductions. Above the chancel arch the Doom, continued on the nave s wall (three figures in a cauldron). On the nave N wall first the Ascension, then the Three Quick and the Three Dead, then St Christopher. In one of the N arcade spandrels a Weighing of Souls. Backgrounds of stencilled sexfoils and cinquefoils. The suggested date is the late C14. – PLATE. Chalice and Paten Cover, by *John Morley* of Lincoln, 1569.

PINCHBECK

2020

ST MARY. An ashlar-faced church of considerable size. The w tower, C14 to C15, has no spire, which suits the character of the building. Two friezes at the foot of the tower. w doorway with cusping and subcusping and an ogee gable. Niches in the buttresses. Tall four-light w window with transom. Tall three-light bell-openings with transom. The chancel was rebuilt by *Butterfield* in 1855. His is the spectacular E window with its Geometrical tracery. The side windows are Dec. The aisle windows of the church are Perp. The N chancel chapel has one four-light Late Perp and one pretty Dec window (reticulation with little fancy infills). Perp clerestory: ten closely-set windows. Decorated battlements. Perp s porch with springers for a vault. But the s doorway is Dec and very ornate. Trefoiled ogee opening with many mouldings. Fleurons in one order and the hood-mould. Ogee gable. Inside, the church is much more varied and tells of a much

longer stretch of time. First the arcades. They are of five bays
chronologically divided four plus one. But they are chronologically divided further in that one arch on the s side re-use
Norman lengths of zigzag and billet. Once one has seen that
are not the roll mouldings of other arches also Norman? Th
arcade piers are E.E. Round or octagonal in an alternatin
rhythm, with round abaci. The piers were presumably no
originally as high as they are now. The hood-moulds wit
dog-tooth. The fifth bay is separated from the others, and th
N arch is simply double-chamfered. But this also is still C13
as is the uneventful chancel arch and the three-bay arcad
to the N chapel which has quatrefoil piers with oddly indeterminate undulating of one foil into the next. Very tall towe
arch with much deeper undulating hollows, i.e. Dec. Se
also the ogee-headed stair doorway. A vault was intended
Fine nave roof of low pitch with alternating tie-beams o
arched braces and hammerbeams with angel figures. Prett
tracery over. The N aisle and N chapel roofs are original too

FURNISHINGS. FONT. Prettily decorated Perp stem (cf
Surfleet). – SCREEN to the N chapel; with two-light divisions
partly old. – NORTH DOOR. Traceried. – STAINED GLASS
C14 bits in the N aisle E window. – In the other N aisl
windows many small C15 figures in the tracery. – The v
window by *O'Connor*, 1861, with large figures. – PLATE
Sweetmeat Dish, by *H.S.*, 1634; Chalice, by *F.W.*, given i
1656; Flagon, by *Thomas Mason*, 1736; two Patens, b
Abraham Peterson, 1810. – MONUMENTS. In the s aisle at th
E end tomb-chest with many shields under little steep gables. –
In the N chapel Edward Walpole † 1725. Boldly moulde
sarcophagus with an unusual peaked top. – CURIOSUM. A
graveside shelter, probably early C19 (cf. Deeping St James
Donington, and Friskney (L)).

VICARAGE. Large and pleasant to look at. Red brick (C17 back
C18 front and side; MHLG). The STABLES have Georgia
Gothick details.

GRAFF HOUSE, NW of the church. Early Georgian, five bays
of brick. Segment-headed windows. Doorway with a she
hood.

MONCY BRIDGE HOUSE, 1½ m. w. Dated 1772. Five bays
brick. Segment-headed windows, doorcase with pediment o
fluted pilasters.

PUMPING STATION, Pinchbeck Marsh. It contains a beam
engine dated 1833.

PODE HOLE *see* SPALDING, p. 655

POTTER HANWORTH   *0060*

ST ANDREW. Built to replace a church of 1749. The *Journal of
the R. Institute of British Architects* in 1854 said: 'And when
we state that the late fabric was of the date 1749 and that the
present one is built after the design of Mr *Hussey*, we need
not further remark that no comparison can be made between
the two.' Nave, N aisle, and chancel. Geometrical to Decorated
tracery. Genuine Dec w tower, see the bell-openings. But the
openwork parapet is probably R. C. Hussey's. – PLATE.
Chalice, Tuscan, C14.

POTTER HILL *see* NORTON DISNEY

QUADRING   *2030*

ST MARGARET. In a field, a very complete building, almost
like a model. The w tower is Perp and wondrously leaning.
The buttresses stop just above the sill of the bell-openings,
which results in an oddly tapering outline. The tower arch
towards the nave is still Dec rather than Perp, but the w
window, tall, of three lights, with an embattled transom, is
Perp. The bell-openings also have embattled transoms. Recessed spire with two tiers of lucarnes in alternating directions.
Perp of course also the impressive clerestory: eight closely-set
upright three-light windows and decorated battlements. There
was an E window too, but it is blocked. The chancel has a
Perp four-light s window, again with an embattled transom,
but the shallow buttresses on this s side prove that basically
the chancel is a Norman survival.* Perp N aisle but Dec s
aisle windows (reticulation motifs under depressed arches).
The s doorway has continuous mouldings. This s aisle is
very wide, and as one enters it one expects to find a Dec
arcade as well. However, both arcades (of four bays) are
identical, and they are of the date of the N aisle. Perp piers of
lozenge shape, consisting of a flat front to the nave, a diagonal
wave and a semicircular projection to the arch. The rood-stair
turret is oddly and attractively placed right in the nave and
has nice decoration round the doorway. – MONUMENTS.
Incised slab to Richard Peresone, vicar, † 1472, much defaced

---

* It was almost rebuilt in 1862.

(chancel). – Thomas Ducket † 1822. Tablet with stran
details. By *Blackwell*.

QUARRINGTON

St Botolph. E.E. three-bay N arcade. Circular piers ar
abaci. Double-chamfered arches. Dec W tower, the arch
the nave triple-chamfered. Recessed spire. The chancel wi
polygonal apse dates from 1862. The S side of the nave
puzzling. The doorway is clearly the re-set priest's doorwa
Nice work of *c*.1300. At the apex head of a man putting h
tongue out. But are the large S windows Victorian fancy
correct restoration? They certainly have the oddest pattern
The tracery is of three hexagons with barbed pointed tr
foils. Yet they are (except for the westernmost) considered
be Dec. The N aisle is of the 1850s. – FONT. Octagonal, th
bowl with tapering sides. Simple motifs. Probably Perp.

RAUCEBY HALL *see* SOUTH RAUCEBY

RIPPINGALE

St Andrew. The most interesting feature of the church is th
long S aisle, carried on all along the chancel. No structur
division between nave and aisle either. The arcade is of *c*.130
Six bays. Quatrefoil piers with fillets and continuous hollow
Double-chamfered arches. Good windows of the same da
with Geometrical tracery of unusually large forms. In the si
windows four pointed trefoiled lights carrying a trefoil,
the E window the same motif doubled and with a trefe
upside down above the others. Priest's doorway with thr
orders of shafts and many mouldings. Pointed-trefoil-head
piscina. The N windows of the church are Dec, of thr
lights with [simple flowing tracery. Dec also the S porc
Tall Perp W tower, ashlar-faced. Quatrefoil frieze with shiel
at the foot. Tall arch towards the nave, with castellated capita.
Two two-light bell-openings with transom. Tall pinnacle
– FONT. Octagonal, Perp, with motifs in pointed quatrefoils
Of the ROOD SCREEN the most exceptional part survive
the coving of the loft. It starts with palm-frond ribs and th
spread into lierne ribs. – PLATE. Silver-gilt Flagon, by *T.M*
1669. – MONUMENTS. Deacon. This is of the mid C13 and
very rare type of monument. His hands hold an open bo
with an inscription on the pages. Stiff-leaf along the rim. H

feet against stiff-leaf whorls. – Cross-legged Knight, late C13. –
Completely defaced cross-legged Knight. – Lady on a tomb-
chest. Ogee canopy over her head. Above the whole tomb
ogee canopy with ballflower decoration. Early to mid C14. –
Roger de Quincey and two wives, late C15. Effigies on a
tomb-chest with panels in which angels hold shields; also
suspended shields.

ROCHFORD TOWER see SKIRBECK

ROPSLEY

9030

T PETER. The nave is Anglo-Saxon, as the long-and-short SW,
NW, and NE corners reveal. So the exposed W wall inside is
also essentially Anglo-Saxon. Then the Normans built a new
chancel and added a N aisle. Of the chancel one S window is
preserved. The E window must be C17 (cf. Ingoldsby), and
the chancel was shortened probably at that time. The N
arcade is of three bays. Circular piers, square abaci with
nicked corners. Heavily scalloped capitals. Round arches with
one step, one chamfer, and a heavy half-roll. Next followed
the S chancel chapel, early C13, of one bay, with triple responds and a double-chamfered round arch. So to the full
E.E., i.e. S arcade, chancel arch, and W tower. The arcade has
keeled responds (originally triple) and a round pier. Double-
chamfered arches. The octagonal pier is, according to its
inscription, a replacement of 1380 (by *Thomas Bate*, mason of
Corby). The chancel arch corresponds to the S arcade. The
tower has twin bell-openings with a colonnette and blank
foiled circles in the tympana. Dec broach spire, the broaches
of moderate size. Three tiers of lucarnes, two in the main
directions, the third in the diagonals. Dec S chapel with
irregular fenestration. Is the clerestory Dec or Perp? Perp
aisles and S porch. The porch has pinnacles and a parapet
with shields in pointed quatrefoils. An inscription inside
records its building in 1486. The inscription outside reads:
Hac non vade via, Nisi dicas Ave Maria. Inside the chancel a
tomb recess of *c*.1300. It is its position which shows that the
chancel was shortened. Inside the S aisle a plain tomb recess.
At the E end of the N aisle a curious arch to carry the passage
to the rood-loft. Stone faces support the nave roof. – FONT.
Octagonal, Perp, with shields in pointed quatrefoils. –
BENCH ENDS. With minor poppy-heads. – STAINED GLASS.

Original bits in the N aisle. – MONUMENTS. C14 effigy of a
Lady under a nodding ogee arch. In the S aisle recess.

ROWSTON

ST CLEMENT. In the N wall is a small doorway with Norman
jambs. Its width fits exactly a Norman tympanum built in
under the tower. It has a cross in the middle and around it a
barbaric assembly of motifs, leaf chains, interlace, rows of
saltire crosses, a lion, a whorl. It is no doubt by the same
workman as the tympanum at Haltham-on-Bain (Lindsey).
The second remarkable thing about Rowston is the E.E.
W tower, as thin as only Early Victorian towers dare to be.
It has a W lancet, shafted one-light bell-openings, and even
a spire with pinnacles standing on the broaches. The spire is
crocketed and has two tiers of tiny lucarnes. E.E. also the
four-bay N arcade, a job of remarkable variety. On the W
corbel stiff-leaf, the first pier round, the second quatrefoil
with fillets and nailhead, the third the same but with thin
diagonal shafts. The arches are double-chamfered. The
doorway is all Victorian but may represent the E.E. truth
and E.E. certainly is the chancel, see the exposed N lancet
with a low-side attachment. Finally the Perp clerestory with
battlements even up the E gable and with pinnacles. There
are clerestory windows also on the S side where there is no
aisle. But this S wall is very disturbed. – REREDOS. Painted
and now in N aisle and vestry. With the pilasters and garland
of a Wren church, but the Royal Arms of George II. – FONT.
Perp, octagonal, big leaf and flower panels. – SCREEN. The dado
tracery still used in the present reredos. – SCULPTURE. Head
of Christ under a gable. From a gable cross? – PLATE.
Chalice and Paten Cover, Boston(?), c.1569, the Cover the
damaged pre-Reformation Paten, c.1450; Flagon and Almsbasin, by *Jonah Clifton*, 1716.

MANOR HOUSE. Of stone, dated on a rainwater head 1741.
Seven bays, the doorway with a segmental pediment as its
hood, placed on plain brackets.

ROXHOLME HALL *see* LEASINGHAM

RUSKINGTON

ALL SAINTS. The exterior would not make one expect the powerful Norman tower arch, mid C12 probably. It has sturdy tripl

responds and an arch of one step and two chamfers. Scalloped capitals. The s arcade also is impressive with its two piers of Lincoln Cathedral character but quite different details. The first pier is an octagon with the main four sides hollowed out and detached shafts set in them. The abacus is a square with rounded corners set diagonally. The second pier has four keeled foils set diagonally, thin shafts in the main directions, and dog-tooth to accompany them. Double-chamfered arches. The N arcade is normal Dec: quatrefoil piers with fillets and thin shafts in the diagonals.* That matches the aisle w window (a pointed quatrefoil) and the N doorway. The s aisle is also Dec, see the E window (cusped intersecting tracery with ogee lights) and the s porch entrance. The s doorway though corresponds rather to the s arcade. It has two orders of colonnettes and much dog-tooth, but is largely Victorian. On the aisle w wall the E.E. and the Dec outlines can be distinguished. E.E. also the chancel with its lancet windows (but the E windows are Victorian) and the two low-side windows with continuous roll mouldings. The chancel arch also E.E. The w tower collapsed in the early C17 and was rebuilt in 1620. Typical posthumously Gothic tracery. – FONT. Octagonal, with pointed quatrefoils and in them flowers and on two shields Instruments of the Passion. – STAINED GLASS. In the s aisle E window beautiful *Morris* glass of *c.*1873–4. Three lights, three figures, the Ascending Christ and two angels in white robes. Lovely flowers, pale yellow, on the quarries below and around the figures. – PLATE. Chalice, by *H.N.*, 1662; missing from the parish since *c.*1840, returned in 1962. – MONUMENTS. Headless Priest, C14, much defaced, in the churchyard s of the church. – Tablet to Matthew Stow † 1710. With two naive little figures l. and r. holding palmfronds. – Enjoyable slate headstones in the churchyard.

brook runs along the middle of the main street due E of the church.

ST IVES' CROSS see SUTTON ST JAMES

SAPPERTON

ST NICHOLAS. Ashlar-faced w tower with a short recessed spire. Early C14 w window and triple-chamfered arch to the nave. Late C13 s doorway (dog-tooth in the arch). Are the

* Seats round all the piers, even those of the chancel arch.

late C13 s windows genuine with their intersecting tracery,
and is the one N window with Geometrical tracery? Late C12
three-bay N arcade now blocked. Octofoil piers, double-
chamfered round arches, except for the w arch, which is
pointed. One capital has waterleaf. Shortened chancel. –
PLATE. Chalice, by *M.K.*, 1683; Paten, 1683, and Flagon
1684, by *G.W.* – MONUMENTS. Long early C14 effigy of a
Lady, her head under an ogee arch. – Two tablets, † 1683
and † 1685, the former with oval, convex inscription plate
and scrolly surround, the latter classical, black and white
with two columns and an open segmental pediment.

The approach to the church is gay with the brightness of the
orange-red tiles of the barns.

OLD MANOR HOUSE. L-shaped; C17 vernacular, with mullioned
windows under straight entablatures. The garden walls are
built of stone from a house begun here by the Saunders
family and demolished in 1710 before it was complete. It
was grandiose, possessed a saloon with a double staircase
at one end, and cost £15,000.

SCOPWICK

HOLY CROSS. Although it all looks at first of the time of the
restoration and rebuilding of 1852, there is plenty preserved.*
The w tower is E.E. below, see the w lancet, the flat buttresses,
and the triple-chamfered tower arch. The top with the bell-
openings looks C17. Also E.E. the s doorway with dog-tooth in
the hood-mould, and both arcades at least partially. On the
s side the two keeled responds convince. On the N side the
quatrefoil piers with fillets and thin diagonal shafts also look
medieval. Yet the aisles were rebuilt in 1852. Similarly the
chancel was rebuilt in 1884, and yet the capitals of the chancel
arch do not look that date. The s capital has stiff-leaf, the
N capital a strange sort of hanging leaves. Lovely Dec niche
s of the chancel arch. – MONUMENT. Effigy of a cross-legged
Knight, not at all the usual type. Very flat carving. Gable
above the head.

(VICARAGE. In the garden an E.E. arch from Kirkby Green
church.)

SCOTTLESTHORPE see EDENHAM

* The *Gent. Mag.* calls the church 'almost wholly new' in 1833.

SCOTT WILLOUGHBY

0030

1 m. SE of Aunsby

ST ANDREW. Built in 1826, but remodelled in 1863. Much laurel on the s side. Nave with bellcote and chancel. – PULPIT and READING DESK. C17, with lozenges in oblong panels. – COMMUNION RAIL. With thin twisted balusters, probably Early Georgian. – PLATE. Parcel-gilt Chalice, Paten, and Almsdish, by *Robert Hennell*, 1829.

SCREDINGTON

0040

ST ANDREW. 1869. Nave and chancel and a funny polygonal sw turret with a long needle spire. But many medieval parts survive, notably the low three-bay N arcade. Octagonal piers, double-chamfered arches. Probably Dec. Also the two doorways. – PLATE. Chalice and Paten Cover, Elizabethan. – MONUMENTS. Recess with crocketed gable, badly made up now. In it monument to Thomas Wyke, a priest, C14. – Also a tomb-chest with three big shields in quatrefoils.

CROSS. Part of a cross shaft in Marcham Lane, the Roman road, 1¼ m. NW, on the E side of the road, opposite the middle of three single oak trees.

SEDGEBROOK

8030

ST LAWRENCE. Of ironstone, with Ancaster stone bands, all Perp, and all built more or less at the same time, culminating in the s chapel and the chancel. These were provided by Sir John Markham, whose licence dates from 1468. From the s the s chapel stands out, by being higher than the s aisle and by being separated from it by means of a stair-turret all of Ancaster stone. The w tower has two two-light bell-openings under an ogee gable, but this does not, as one would expect, carry intermediate pinnacles. The aisle windows are interesting in one way. On the N side one of them is raised above the porch, i.e. it is as big as the others, but placed higher. To the s chapel corresponds a N chapel, but this was cut short at the E side by a former vestry. Hence the high clerestory-like placing of the E windows of the chapel. The chancel projects by only one bay, but it has very tall windows with specially dainty tracery, transoms and ogee arches below. The E window is of five lights. To the former vestry three closely-set two-light clerestory-like windows. Inside, the chancel and the

chapel are so lavishly adorned that the effect is almost barbaric
Sedilia with six little pendant gables, vaulted under. Small pis
cina with shelf. Two very tall niches with high canopies se
diagonally l. and r. of the E window. The same arrangemen
of niches in the chapel. The chapel is separated from the
chancel by a two-bay arcade. The E pier and E respond
have, two-thirds of the way up, a shelf facing E and W respec
tively and carried by big angel busts. Rich piscina and, oddly
enough, a second small piscina just E of the stone screen which
divides the chapel from the S aisle. The screen has a two-ligh
window, i.e. is not like the wooden screens of the period. Now
at last the rest of the interior can be looked at. The S arcade i
Perp like the rest (three bays, tall, octagonal piers) but the n
arcade is much older. Its date must be the early C13. Circula
piers, octagonal abaci, round, double-chamfered arches. -
FONT. Octagonal, Norman, with heavily scalloped underside
eight scallops altogether. – PULPIT. Jacobean, the panels with
twin pendant arches. The framing is diamond-cut, the pen
dant nice and rotund. Dated 1634 on the door. – SCREENS
Of two- and one-light divisions. – BENCHES. Two with Perp
panelled parts. The poppy-heads include a feathered angel
Also the form of the poppy-heads is unusual. – PLATE. Chalice
by *W.G.*, *c.*1571; Paten, London, 1681; Chalice and Pate
Cover, London, 1684. – MONUMENT. Poor, small incised
slab to Dorothy Markham † 1494 (S chapel).

SEDGEBROOK MANOR. The house lies to the NW of the church
and is composed with it. To the onlooker it seems C18, bu
behind the front is a structure of *c.*1632. The long rectangula
body with slight projections on the N front is of this period, in
the vernacular tradition of stone with dressings and moulded
stone chimneystacks. About 1716 the house was sold t
Sir John Thorold, who may have faced it with the present
front. Although a note of Palladian uniformity is struck by the
line of six pedimented first-floor windows, the details ar
remarkably conservative. The doorway with a flat leather
frieze, the urn on a grotesque head, and the scrolled cartouch
of the sundial are all in a C17 idiom, as is also the curiousl
ill-proportioned candelabrum on the parapet. The hall ha
C17 panelling, a pattern of square motifs indented at the angle
and set diagonally inside larger panels. The pilasters of th
overmantel grotesquely decorated with fish-scales, strapwork
and a kind of flame pattern, showing the C17 building to hav
been as conservative as the C18 rebuilding.

SEMPRINGHAM

mpringham is famous as the birthplace of the order of the
lbertines, the only monastic order founded in Britain. It is
aracterized by canons and nuns living in the same establish-
nts, with churches divided along their length by a solid wall
d with two cloisters. The order was founded by St Gilbert of
mpringham in the 1130s. St Gilbert, son of the lord of the
anor, was over forty when he founded it. As, in its years of
vour, it grew remarkably quickly, he wanted to place his group
maidens and men under the Cistercians, then the most active
the new orders. He went over to Cîteaux in 1147, and St Ber-
rd of Clairvaux became his friend. The new order could not,
wever, be accepted by the Cistercians, largely probably because
the combination of sexes in one house on which Gilbert in-
ted. But he almost at once obtained sanction for his order from
e pope. When Gilbert died in 1189, there were about twelve
uses established, apparently ten of them double houses, and
e number of nuns is variously given as about 1000 to 1500.
e church of Sempringham was largely excavated in 1938-9.
originally built it was c. 250 ft long. In 1301 a radical rebuild-
; began, which was not completed until early in the C15. It
tended the length of the church to 325 ft. The s side was the
ns' church, long, narrow (35 ft), and without aisle or transept.
e canons' church was more articulate. W of the long narrow
) ft) chancel was a transept with three E chapels, and the nave
d a N aisle. The shrine of St Gilbert stood astride the wall
tween canons' and nuns' chancels. The church and the con-
ntual quarters were after the Reformation superseded by the
ge mansion of Lord Clinton, three ranges round a courtyard.
ae mansion was 200 ft long and built before 1585, the year when
rd Clinton died. It may never have been finished.

ANDREW. A proud Norman church, unfortunately shorn of
ts chancel and transept (pulled down in 1788) and unfortunately provided with an apsed chancel of 1868-9 (by
Browning). At the same time the N aisle wall was rebuilt and
extended to the E to cover the area of the former N transept.
So what remains is the Norman nave and N arcade and the
crossing tower. The latter has nothing Norman left. The
arches to all four sides are C14 (round capitals, polygonal
abaci), and the ashlar-faced superstructure is Perp. Battlements and eight pinnacles. That leaves the Norman work,

thrilling throughout. The N arcade is of four bays, in an alt
nating rhythm. The responds are triple and keeled. The mid
pier repeats the same pattern l. and r. of a flat piece,
appears as two responds grown together. The intermedi
piers are circular and sturdy with square abaci but nic
corners. The arches have a single step. In the N aisle W v
a blocked Norman window. In the s wall two beautifully
Norman windows, round-headed lancets really. Also
three-light Dec window. The Norman corbel table is co
pletely preserved. It does not run through but is divided i
four separate lengths by lesenes which form panels in wh
the windows are set – a motif reminiscent of the lesenes
so-called Lombard friezes in C11 and C12 North Italian
German work. Preserved also are – the only places on wh
decoration was lavished – the doorways. The s doorway i
situ, the priest's doorway has been reassembled in the s por

7a   The s doorway has three orders of shafts. The capitals h
ribbed leaves, but also waterleaf. In the arches zigzag, also
r. angles to the wall, and incised scalloping. Arch with m
mouldings. The motifs of the N doorway are much m
remarkable. There is a tympanum here filled by a shell or
strangely classical. In the arch a beautiful beaded band
almond-shapes, each meeting-point surrounded by a bea
circle. Now what is the date of all this? Is it really the chu
in which St Gilbert's order started and which was the chu
of his conventual house before it moved into the valley 350
to the SW? As this move took place in 1139, one can say
to this question, unless building was slow. Neither kee
shafts nor waterleaf capitals can be assumed before the 11
– BENCH ENDS. With poppy-heads and divers tracery mo
– SOUTH DOOR. With beautiful iron scrollwork of the e
C13. – SCULPTURE. Small piece of Anglo-Saxon inter
work. – MONUMENTS. Many slate headstones, mostly sig
as they are to be found in this whole neighbourhood.

The village of Sempringham lay to the NW. Bumps in the g
show where it was.

SILK WILLOUGHBY

0040

ST DENIS. A very fine steeple, bare below, ornately Dec ab
The bell-openings fully shafted, the buttresses with decor
gables, a fleuron frieze below the openwork parapet with
undulating pattern (cf. e.g. Heckington). Small pinnacles
flying buttresses. Spire with two tiers of lucarnes in alterna

directions. Dec the aisles, their tracery reticulated or cusped
intersecting. Big s porch entrance with Dec mouldings. s doorway with ballflower, also in the hood-mould. The niche above
it, however, seems Perp. In the N aisle a five-light post-
Reformation window. The chancel was rebuilt in 1878. The
spaciousness and height of the three-bay Dec nave inside
are reminiscent of Swaton, not far away. Quatrefoil piers with
fillets, the foils connected by continuous hollows. Double-
chamfered arches. The tower arch has shafts connected by
deeper continuous hollows and a triple-chamfered arch. The
chancel arch simpler but of the same date. Rich Perp sedilia
with crenellated top, and little lierne-vaults above the seats.
Also a long, simpler Perp niche l. of the E window. – FONT.
Norman, of drum-shape, coupled shafts carrying coupled
intersecting arches with a rope pattern. The cover is Victorian
in imitation of Jacobean. – The SCREEN is mostly reconstruction. – PULPIT. Jacobean. – BENCH ENDS. Many, with poppy-
heads and tracery patterns. Also more or less complete benches.
– Some roof BOSSES in the N aisle (E end). – PAINTING. An
Italian (Tuscan?) early C17 painting of the Annunciation,
painted on agate, its many colours ingeniously made use of. –
STAINED GLASS. Bits in the tracery of the chancel (s). –
PLATE. Chalice, by A., 1569; Paten, by R.H., 1675.

MANOR HOUSE. C17, but restored. E front of five irregular bays
and a two-storeyed gabled porch. A similar porch on the W
front makes the plan into a Latin cross.

OLD RECTORY. The N wing built in the C17, the E wing some
time in the C19, and the W wing in 1813 (by *William Hayward*).

VILLAGE CROSS, W of the church, by the main road. Only part
of the shaft, but a mighty base, carved with the Signs of the
Evangelists.

SKELLINGTHORPE

9070

ST LAWRENCE. 1855 by *Kendall & Pope*. The top parts of the
nave burnt in 1916. Quite a big church; E.E. in style. Tall W
tower with a higher stair-turret. Nice group with the SCHOOL
to the s. – PLATE. Chalice, Cover, Paten, Flagon, and Almsdish, by *F.H.*, 1693.

SKELLINGTHORPE HALL. A Greekly august house of *c.*1830.
The porch is particularly good, pilasters at the angles and
fluted Greek Doric columns *in antis* with a finely carved
frieze behind them above the entrance. Notable also are the

cast-iron entrance GATES with Greek-key pattern and acan
thus motifs.

SKILLINGTON

ST JAMES. The NE corner of the nave shows Anglo-Saxon long
and-short quoining. The two-bay S arcade is early C1:
Circular pier with circular abacus. The capital with minimum
crocket leaves. The respond capitals are undetailed. Th
double-chamfered arches are later. With this arcade go th
arch into the S transept chapel and the arch from this into th
chancel. The chancel arch follows at once. This now ha
full-blooded stiff-leaf capitals and an arch with roll moulding
The N arcade is later C13. Circular pier and octagonal abacu
Nailhead enrichments. Also of the later C13 the chancel. I
the N wall there is a small window with Y-tracery. In the
wall a pointed-trefoiled piscina. Again later C13 the S aisle, se
the S window with Geometrical tracery (two lights and
quatrefoiled circle). The S porch entrance has leaf capita
with the leaves going naturalistic, i.e. also late C13. The sam
stage of foliage in the sedilia of the S transept, rebuilt at th
time. The W tower has late C13 bell-openings (Y-tracery) an
a Dec broach spire with low broaches and two tiers of lucarne
Perp, ashlar-faced, embattled clerestory. – FONT. Octagona
Perp. The stem mostly with square leaves, the bowl wit
quatrefoils and crenellation. – PLATE. Chalice, London, 156
THE ABBEY, W of the church. Small stone manor house dated c
a gable 1637. Its shape is almost a Greek cross. Symmetric
s façade with two gables, balustered finials, and three-ligh
windows, all this much restored.
The Green is dominated by a severe looking METHODIS
CHAPEL dated 1847.

SKIRBECK

ST NICHOLAS. A large church, but one looking too new an
indeed with a N aisle of 1875 and a chancel of 1933. The be
thing in the church is the wide nave with its E.E. six-ba
arcades and its E.E. clerestory with circular windows (ov
the spandrels, not the arches). The arcades have piers with a
octagonal core hollowed out in the main directions and d
tached shafts set in – a Lincoln Cathedral motif. The N base
are circular, and there are seats around them. Stiff-leaf cap
tals and pretty moulded arches. The chancel arch has E.E

corbels too, and the very tall tower arch with its continuous double chamfer is more probably Dec than Perp, though the w window looks Perp (but is Victorian), and the top of the tower certainly is Perp (and is also much restored). – FONT. Plain, moulded, octagonal, and dated on the stem 1662. – PULPIT. Jacobean; the reading ledge on flat cut-out cockerels. – PLATE. Dish, by *William Gamble*, 1709; Almsbasin, London, 1791.

OLD RECTORY. Late Georgian in style, though of 1847. By *Edward Lapidge*.

ROCHFORD TOWER, 1½ m. NE. A red-brick tower resembling Hussey Tower, Boston (*see* p. 475), and also probably of *c.*1510. Embattled parapet and turrets corbelled out at the angles. The octagonal stair at the SE angle communicates with three floors. Some windows are of stone, and two have a little tracery. The ground-floor room is brick-vaulted. On the first, traces of mural PAINTINGS: the Annunciation; the Virgin and St Anne; and St Michael and St Anthony.

SLEAFORD

ST DENYS. Sleaford church is of course remembered for the flowing tracery of its windows, but it represents three periods. The w tower comes first, late in the C12 and early in the C13, the Late Dec glories second, the Perp clerestory and Perp remodelling of the chancel, dateable to about 1430 (inscription below the E window: *orate* for Richard Dokke, his wife and children and other benefactors), last. The church is built of Ancaster stone and the steeple is 144 ft high. Its w portal is clearly still Transitional, i.e. late C12. Three orders of shafts, the completely renewed capitals stiff-leaf, but the arch still with zigzag at r. angles to the wall. The next stage is of 1884. It is the replacement of a Perp w window which was re-erected as a picturesque object NE of the church. The bell-stage is pure E.E. Twin bell-openings with a blank arch l. and r. Shafts with stiff-leaf capitals and rings. The broach spire is one of the earliest in England. It is broad and solid with the lucarnes starting right at its foot. It was rebuilt in 1884.

When the great Dec rebuilding began, they did at Sleaford what they had done at Newark and Grantham and embraced the tower with their work. The date of the Dec work is doubt-ful. It certainly is late, as the interior will show. Hamilton Thompson dated it *c.*1360–70. Meanwhile the exterior must

be described in detail. The aisle fronts are encrusted with
decoration, i.e. the N doorway has three orders of shafts with
bossy and square leaves in two mouldings, a hood-mould with
roses, and a gable standing on a goat and a lion and provided
with crockets and a finial. The S doorway is simpler and unrestored, but has a big niche to its l. with the gable on monsters. The N gable reaches up into the zone of the five-light
window, the first of the great Sleaford windows. Their detail
varies infinitely, but their elements remain the same, ogee
arches, reticulation units, and mouchettes. It is a prolonged
delight to follow the mason's inventiveness along the building.
The S window has only three lights. Niches high up l. and r.
of the windows, on the N side with their original statuettes,
then a rising parapet with leaf decoration, a pierced wavy
parapet, a whole canopy with gables and spirelet stressing
rather unhappily the step in the parapet, and at the angle
buttresses with decorated niches, their gables on supporters
figures, and as the final flourish an angle turret, again with
gables and a spire – all crocketed whenever possible. It makes
the old tower look very glum.

But what does more damage to the tower than the Dec W
front is the Perp clerestory. There are eight three-light windows, unadorned, and there is a decorated parapet with
pinnacles. All this stands up higher than the sill of the bell-
openings.* But of course something fairly high and dominant
was needed to act as a finish to the Dec aisles and transepts.
The outer N aisle is an addition of 1853 (*Kirk & Parry*; GS),
but the windows were re-used. They are of four lights and
again of a new pattern. The mullions incidentally are shafted
which the W windows were not. But between these Dec windows stands a doorway which must derive from the church
for which the tower was built; for with its two orders of colonnettes and its two slight chamfers in the arch it is Transitional.
The S aisle S windows are of four lights too, and their mullions
are shafted, but the tracery does not repeat the pattern of the
N side. Above the windows a frieze with leaves and monsters
and then a parapet with shields in lozenges. On the S side is a
surprisingly plain porch protecting the S doorway with its
buttress-shafts and its crocketed gable.‡ So to the N transept,
for there is none on the S side, and the S aisle E window repeats

* Pinnacles on the S side only. This and the following notes were kindly
contributed by the Rev. Philip Mann.
‡ Under the S porch is a bone-hole.

one of the designs of the s windows.* The N transept N window
is one of the great flowing designs in the country. It is of six
lights, 34 ft 8 in. high, and can be read in several ways. The
appearance of two quatrefoils in circles near the top is a
reminder of the E.E. The transept E windows are of four lights
again and again novel. All these have mullions with shafts too.
The transept has a parapet decorated with quatrefoils. The
chancel was re-windowed in the Perp style. That it is essentially Dec is proved externally by the priest's doorway and also
internally. The windows are of three lights and the E window
of seven in a pattern of four and four interlocking. The
mullions include a large cross. In the panel tracery are two
castellated horizontals. The vestry is original too.

As for the INTERIOR, it is as unified as any. The same
design was carried through except for a few minor features.
They are first a billet hood-mould inside above the w doorway,
and secondly in the E wall of the N transept at its s end the
moulding of a window jamb which only makes sense as part
of a nave aisleless at least in this place. The plan must have
been changed when aisle and transept were built. The connexion between the two is in fact the earliest Dec feature of
the church; for, whereas throughout the rest of the church
pier shafts have the polygonal abaci of the Perp or the transition from Dec to Perp, the arch from the N aisle to the N
transept has them round, as is the Dec rule. The rest of the
description is quickly done. The tower has a tierceron-star
vault inside and arches to the aisles as well as the nave. The
latter is five-shafted with deep hollows and no breaks between
the shafts. The arches are finely moulded. The w bay of the s
aisle is separated from the rest of the aisle by a half-arch
resting on a flying buttress (cf. Finedon and Rushton in
Northamptonshire). On the N side there is a strainer arch
instead on the pattern of Wells Cathedral, and this dates from
1853.

The arcades are of four bays with tall quatrefoil piers with
fillets, the foils flowing into each other, and with many-
moulded arches. The four bays include on the N side the entry
into the transept, which is thus not marked in any special way.
But running N from the third pier is a narrow piece of wall
with a blank arch to introduce to the transept (cf. Heckington).
In the s aisle w bay is a tomb-recess and a piscina, in the E bay
another piscina. The chancel arch responds are just like the

* So do windows in St Hugh's Chapel and the Baptistery.

arcade piers, and the chancel arch has the same height a
the arcade arches. In the chancel the sedilia have trefoiled
ogee arches and little lierne-vaults inside (even with bosses).

FURNISHINGS. FONT. Dec and much repaired. Stem and
bowl in one. Octagonal, with blank two-light Dec windows
and leaf spandrels. – ROOD SCREEN. Tall, of spacious one-
light divisions with ogee arches, cusped and subcusped, and
panel tracery over. The coving, loft and cornice are also
original. But the rood itself is by *Sir Ninian Comper*, 1918. –
COMMUNION RAIL. From Lincoln Cathedral. A fine piece
with ample balusters partly decorated by acanthus and hanging garlands on the posts. – DOLE CUPBOARD (N transept)
C17, with two tiers of small balusters. – DESK with fifteen
chained books in the passage to the vestry. – STAINED GLASS
In the chancel N and S signed *H.W.*, Warwick, 1857. – In the
s aisle E window very Gothic glass by *Hardman*, probably of
about 1853. – In the N transept SE window by *Ward & Hughes*
with much pink, and terrible. – Over the chancel arch rounde
by *O'Connor*. – In the s aisle s window by *Morris & Co.*, 1900
Four angels in white and pale green, and many of Morris'
pretty quarries each just with a yellow flower. In the tracery
heads fruit and leaves.* – In the N aisle E window by *Kempe*
1906. – TAPESTRY. A small piece of early C17 Sheldon tapestry with Judith and Holofernes in the N aisle. – NEEDLEWORK
An early C17 Dorsal in the N aisle at the W end. – PLATE
Silver-gilt Almsdish, by *Frederick Kandler*, 1758; two Paten
and two Flagons, by *John Bayley*, 1760.

MONUMENTS. Slab in the N transept to Yveyt wife of W. de
Rouceby. A foliated cross, but in the middle of its head he
face appears in sunk relief in a roundel, lower down the stem
her praying hands appear in an almost almond-shaped slit
and at the foot of the cross her little feet also come out in a
roundel. – Brass to George Carre † 1521 and wife. 20 in
figures. Chancel floor. – Robert Carr † 1590. Alabaster; no
figures. Pilasters l. and r. and an achievement at the top. –
Sir Edward Carre † 1618 and family. By *Maximilian Colt*, se
the design at the College of Arms. Two alabaster effigies
recumbent, he on a half-rolled-up straw mat. In the back wall
still-lifes of death and two cherubs. At the top obelisks and
an achievement. – In the N aisle John Walpoole; erected 1631
Tablet without figures but made probably for two kneelers
– Sir Robert Carr † 1682, plain tomb-chest of black and white

* The Guide of 1907 gives this glass to *Hamilton Jackson*.

marble, and next to it, not *in situ*, the excellent bust of his son Sir Edward Carr † 1683. Its sculptor ought to be recognizable. N aisle E end. – Many C18 and C19 tablets, e.g. Ann Bankes † 1834, chancel, by *Sir R. Westmacott*. A young woman sinking to the ground, remarkably tender and with a touch of the Rococo.

NONCONFORMIST CHAPELS. They are singularly unremarkable at Sleaford. METHODIST, Northgate, 1848, yellow brick with two Tudor porches, but made more Gothic in 1909. – CONGREGATIONAL, Southgate, 1868, rock-faced Gothic. – BAPTIST, Eastgate, 1881. – METHODIST, Westgate, 1907.

CASTLE. Of a castle of Bishop Alexander (*c.*1130), who also built the castles of Newark and Banbury, no more remains than some mounds and some masonry of a tower. They are to be found NW of the station. J. C. Cox)

PERAMBULATION

We start W of the church in the MARKET PLACE. The combination of the two as visually one is more unusual than people may think. In the NE corner of the Market Place, i.e. N of the church, is the VICARAGE. C15 with an oversailing upper floor with close timber-framing and a gable. The bargeboarding is C19, as is the red-brick wing added by *Charles Kirk* in 1861. To the l. of the old part small gateway with a four-centred head. Inside a chimneypiece dated 1568. In the Market Place a FOUNTAIN, dated 1874, Gothic with pyramid roof on polished granite columns. The SESSIONS HOUSE marks the NW corner of the Market Place. It is in *H. E. Kendall*'s Tudor Gothic, dated 1831. Open arcades on the S and W fronts. Kendall was a local architect. Now the S side. The former BRISTOL ARMS HOTEL has a five-bay, three-storey Late Georgian stone front with a one-bay pediment, but crenellation. E of this is *Charles Kirk*'s Gothic CORN EXCHANGE of 1857. E again the SAVINGS BANK, by a builder, *Maxey*, of 1879. Then straight on into EASTGATE with CARRE'S HOSPITAL at the start, i.e. S of the church. *Kendall* was again responsible here. A nine-bay E range of 1830 and a seven-bay S range of 1841–6. Castellations and porches. In the centre of the S range the CHAPEL with a large Perp window and a pointed bell-gable. It looks as if a W wing had been intended. The turfed forecourt with contemporary fitments: sundial, lamp, and water-pump. Next door is OLD HOUSE of the early

c17. L-shaped, with three-light windows and Georgian bi
In the garden are fragments from Sleaford Castle, notably
c15 escutcheon of kneeling angels. Then along Eastgate No
with a c17 gable-end, Nos 4 and 21 with blocked four-lig
c17 windows, and No. 23 dated 1788. Then comes LAFFO
TERRACE by *Kirk & Parry*, 1856 (now COUNTY OFFICE
a Palladian theme of pavilions: a tall centre, links, and low
wings, but with Louis XIV motifs. This faces the commc
as does Mr *Bennison*'s KINGSTON TERRACE of 1857. Y
further out is SLEAVIEW, the old WORKHOUSE of 18
monumental Tudor, with a gatehouse-like centre, and certai
by *Kendall*, and *Kendall* must also have done the entrances
the GAS WORKS still further E.

Back to the Market Place and into SOUTHGATE. s of the Wh
Hart Hotel an inn-sign, a stone tablet of a horse dated 16
then opposite in a back yard a high TOWER MILL deprived
its gear. Nearly opposite the entry to JERMYN STREET, wh
No. 15 has an archway with two medieval lion corbels from
castle. Then another stone tablet of an inn, the Black B
dated 1689. Then the GIRLS' HIGH SCHOOL, a steep thr
bay front in the Jacobean style, built by *Charles Kirk*
himself before 1850. Built into a wall are two pre-Conqu
fragments of interlace, probably c11. The sequence ends
the HANDLEY MEMORIAL, a belated child of the Elea
Crosses, erected in 1850 to designs by *Boyle*; the standi
figure of Henry Handley, M.P. for South Lincolnshire, e
by *John Thomas*.

Back to the Market Place again and into WESTGATE. No. 20
plain brick, in early c19 Gothic, and No. 23 plain to the str
but with a grander Regency façade to the garden. Five ba
three storeys, and a ground-floor projection with two gen
curved bows and a Tuscan portico *in antis*. LIVERPO
COTTAGES and REPTON'S COURT are both Georgian. N
56 is the stone front to the old THEATRE.

Again from the Market Place into NORTHGATE. No. 2, the m
remarkable house in the town, is yet unknown to literatu
A late c17 stone front pushed between the Sessions House a
Lloyds Bank. A miniature of three bays, two storeys, quoi
and bolection-moulded window surrounds. All the keysto
are copied from c17 engravings of a Charmeton style, a
robustly carved. The tall door with segmental pediment
more carving. The pulvinated frieze is broken thrice
bas-relief, ciphers, and a medallion. No. 23 is brick, L

Georgian, with canted bays and a Doric doorcase. No. 18 is of
the same date. The arch of No. 29 might belong to the Manor
House adjacent (see below). Again to the N are ALMSHOUSES
rebuilt in 1857, and next door to these is the GRAMMAR
SCHOOL in familiar gabled Tudor, by *Charles Kirk*, 1834.
Additions of 1904, 1906 etc., and 1956 and 1958, the latter
part of a rebuilding programme (*J. W. H. Barnes*, County
Architect).

ʌNOR HOUSE. A jigsaw puzzle with multitudinous bits from
Sleaford Castle. A courtyard adjoins No. 29. The w side
mostly C19, the narrow centre tower with a C14 pointed doorway. Octagonal capitals and colonnettes, head corbels, and
the arch jambs with a frieze of angels beneath ogee gables.
On the N side of this is a straight-headed four-light window
with a square drip-mould. To the r. of this wing are many
medieval fragments, early bits in the chimneystacks (C14 head
of a king) and in the N gable (a two-light C14 window). On the
N side of the courtyard a date plaque 1637, and above this a
remarkable chimneystack. It looks all C14, polygonal, with
attached shafts, moulded capitals, and turreted pots. The
return of this front is C17: stepped gable and ball finials.
Medieval bits here also. Then there is a two-storey canted bay
with six-light windows and a date plaque 1619. Beyond this
front all is Victorian. From the rear the different building
phases are read more easily. A seven-bay part has projecting
two-bay wings and pointed gables. It could be of 1619 or 1637.
Further N the NW angle has been filled in, and this gabled part
incorporates medieval quatrefoil panels. A fine grotesque
panel is built into the entrance wall of the garden. Only one
early room, and that behind the 1619 wing. Good panelling
with Tudor Renaissance motifs.

ᴸD PLACE, Boston Road, ½ m. E. A seat of the Carre family.
L-shaped. Of the L the N front is C19. The s garden walls consist of about 100 feet of lumped-together medieval fragments.

ᴇSTHOLME HOUSE. c.1849. Messrs *Kirk & Parry* were the
builders and *Charles Kirk the younger* the architect. French
Gothic with high roofs, crockets, pinnacles, and sprawling
dragons.

ᴴᴇ MALTINGS. For sheer impressiveness little in English
industrial architecture can equal the scale of this building.
A massive four-storey square tower is in the centre of a line
of eight detached pavilions. The total frontage is nearly 1000
ft. Each pavilion is in brick, of five bays and six storeys with

a projecting timber-framed crane hood. Fronting each pavili
are low one-storeyed offices. By the entrance gates are t
domestic quarters. The architect was *H. A. Couchman*. A fi
bore of 180 ft was driven in 1892, and the group complet
by 1905.

SOMERBY *see* OLD SOMERBY

9050

SOMERTON CASTLE

Antony Bek, Bishop of Durham, received a licence to crenella
the castle in 1281. It belongs to the then most up-to-date typ
that of the Welsh castles, quadrangular with circular towe
at the angles. The size was 330 by 180 ft. Of this buildi
there remain the SE tower – three storeys with a conical roof
and the ground floors of the NE and SW towers. The SE an
SW towers have domical vaults and shallow niches along t
walls. The NE tower has instead a central polygonal pier an
twelve radiating, single-chamfered arches. They rest on corb
against the wall. To the S a small vaulted room. Attached
the SE tower is the S front, extended by an L-shaped Eliz
bethan wing before 1595. Part of this, adjoining the SE tow
may be the original curtain wall. More curtain wall attach
to the SW tower. Behind, a three-quarter circular projectio
like a stair-turret sliced in half, but quite plain inside. Ha
all traces of the steps been removed, or what was it used fo
Also attached to the SE tower, but to the W, an equally hi
building with lancet windows to the N. What was the fu
tion of this? Equally puzzling are the encircling earthwor
The long thin moat extending N is explainable. But beyo
this to the E and W and around three sides of a mound to t
S are larger moats *within* an encircling earthwork. The reas
may be connected with the confinement here in 1359–60
King John of France.*

9060

SOUTH HYKEHAM

ST MICHAEL. Unbuttressed W tower, the lower parts C13
C14, i.e. lancets below and an arch to the nave with keel
responds, but a niche with a nodding ogee arch higher up a
Dec bell-openings. Nave and chancel in one, apse and tow
top by *M. Drury & Mortimer*, 1869. – PLATE. Chalice a
Paten Cover, London, 1569.

* Mr Harvey records works at Somerton Castle in 1334 by *Robert Sl*

SOUTH KYME

SOUTH KYME TOWER. This ashlar-faced tower-house stands alone in a field near the C18 manor house. It is 77 ft high. The builder was Sir Gilbert de Umfraville; the date lies between 1338 and 1381. Nothing is known about additions to this tower, but marks on the s side show the existence of communicating links. The tower is of four storeys, battlemented, with a square stair-turret slightly projecting at the SE angle and rising higher than the tower. The fenestration is fairly regular, with slits in the basement and above one two-light window to each floor on each side. An octopartite vault to the ground floor. Single-chamfered ribs and a boss with the arms of Umfraville. The second floor was called the Chequer Chamber because of its patterned floor, but no floors or ceilings survive higher up. At the top of the stair the roof sprouts out into a prettily panelled vault on a central colonnette which is the top of the newel-post. To Leland this was a 'goodly house and park'. But the house was dismantled between 1720 and 1725, when chimneypieces were bought by Mr Chaplin for Blankney Hall (*see* p. 459).

CHURCH. The present church is a fragment of a grand priory of Augustinian Canons founded before 1169. All that remains is the W end of the S aisle and the bit of the S part of the nave corresponding to it. In 1890 *Hodgson Fowler* made the whole into a neat oblong by a new N wall and E wall with Perp windows. So the big three-light S windows with their Dec tracery are aisle windows and the S porch is *in situ*. It is plain but has a niche above the entrance in which a Coronation of the Virgin in small figures, once apparently very fine. But inside the porch is a big, ambitious Norman doorway with two orders of shafts with scalloped and volute capitals and an arch with lozenges broken round the angle of a moulding and a kind of crenellation. Hood-mould with rope on long-snouted beasts. A lion's head at the top of the hood-mould. Inside, the W respond of the S arcade is exposed, triple-shafted with one fillet and continuous hollows between the shafts, and to its N the jamb of the former very large W window. Outside one can see below it also a jamb of the W doorway. – FRAGMENTS. In the N wall at the E end some important pieces of Anglo-Saxon carving, perhaps parts of a low screen. The most interesting motifs are foliage-scrolls and trumpet-spirals, the latter a decidedly Celtic motif familiar from Irish

illuminated manuscripts. In conjunction with the plant
scrolls they indicate a date in the C7 or the C8 at the latest
Also a good Norman capital. Another in the NW corner.
STAINED GLASS. By *Kempe*, 1890, the E and a S window
PLATE. Chalice, 1770, altered into a Flagon in 1896 and bac
into a Chalice and Paten in 1960. – MONUMENTS. Marmaduk
Dickinson † 1712. Tablet with two elementary little figures c
life(?) and death. – Anthony Taylor Peacock † 1829. By *T
Tyley* of Bristol. Grecian, almost Egyptian, i.e. very heavy an
with strongly tapering columns. On them poppies grow.

SOUTH RAUCEBY

0040

An estate village created in the later C19. The BUSTARD IN:
is dated 1860, and cottages are dated 1884.

RAUCEBY HALL. By *William Burn*, 1842, for A. Peacock Wil:
son, who called his house 'Parandum'. The style is Tudor
Gothic with gables, and strapwork bits. As against Revesb
(Lindsey; *see* p. 342) and Stoke Rochford (*see* p. 643), th
Baroque element is largely absent. Burn's chimneypieces ar
as usual remarkable: in the drawing room one with termin:
and an acroterion frieze – in imitation of an Early Georgia:
manner. The park is lush, with lawns sloping down to a lake
RAUCEBY HOSPITAL, 2 m. SE. Main buildings and chapel b
G. T. Hine, 1897–1902.

SOUTH STOKE

9020

ST MARY AND ST ANDREW. Is the W tower C11 below? Th
hood-mould of the small S window would suggest it. Highe:
up E.E. Twin bell-openings with plate tracery of quatrefoi:
and trefoil. Corbel table with heads. Only the W window i
Perp. Perp also the N chapel (externally) of three bays wit]
battlements and pinnacles, and the S chapel of two bays, als‹
with battlements and pinnacles. It makes an odd E view wit]
the chancel E window, smaller, recent, and straight-headec
between. From inscriptions in the former stained glass w
know that the S chapel was built at the expense of Ralp]
Rochford in 1448, the N chapel probably at that of Henry
Rochford *c.*1460–70. The interior is sadly scraped. But the :
arcade is Norman and earlier probably than 1150, i.e. an addi
tion to the nave that would belong to the early W tower. Thre:
bays, fat circular piers, square abaci, multi-scalloped capitals

The arches with one step and one slight chamfer. Early C13 S arcade. Slimmer circular piers. Abaci square with nicked corners. The arches double-chamfered but still round. The capitals, if they can be trusted, have crockets, but the W respond flat leaves. Dec the N chapel arcade. Quatrefoil piers with fillets, or rather square with semicircular projections. Two wave mouldings. The same for the arch to the N aisle. Perp S arcade, the piers with polygonal projections, those to the nave without capitals. Circular W arch. – REREDOS. Designed by *Mrs G. F. Watts* and with foliage etc. typical of her (cf. Compton, Surrey). It was erected in 1911. – SCREEN. Bits of the tracery displayed in the S chapel. – SCULPTURE. Upper half of a good figure of a female Saint, c.1500, and probably English. – PAINTING. Small panel of the Virgin of Humility by *Agnolo Gaddi*, given by Berenson to C. H. Turnor. Set in a mid-C17 Portuguese triptych. – STAINED GLASS. Original bits in the S aisle W window. – PLATE (also at North Stoke). Chalice and Cover, by *B.*, 1670; Flagon, by *I.G.*, 1670. – MONUMENTS. In the N chapel effigies of a couple under a blanket from which their feet as well as their busts stick out. Early C14. – Sumptuous tomb-recess, the front of the tomb-chest simply with shields, but the canopy with fleurons along one moulding and an ogee arch. – Between N chapel and chancel tomb-chest with shields in quatrefoils. – Between S chapel and chancel raw tomb-chest with shields in ogee-headed fields. Big ogee canopy. – Brasses of Henry Rochford † 1470 and of Oliver St John and wife † 1503, the former 30 in., the latter 19 in. – Henry Cholmeley, 1641. Big standing monument. In the centre the kneeling couple flanked by columns. To the l. and r., a little recessed and flanked by smaller columns, the inner overlapping the columns of the centre, two kneeling children. Top with obelisks and a big achievement. – Sir Edmund Turnor † 1707. Large reredos composition of white and black marble. Big inscription flanked by columns. Open segmental pediment with urn. – Christopher Turnor † 1886 and wife. Complex marble composition below the N chapel E window. The portraits in profile in roundels. Designed by *Christopher Turnor*. – CROSS in the churchyard, W of the church. The shaft Anglo-Saxon with interlace patterns.

STOKE ROCHFORD HALL (Kesteven Training College). The site has an unusually long history of domesticity. There was a Roman VILLA here (now lost), and this was followed by a C14 de Nevile, a C15 Rochford, and a C16 Coney house.

About 1665 Sir Edmund Turnor erected a grand but conser
vative L-shaped building with rows of mullioned window
This stood near the lake by the present BRIDGE. The STABLE
were built in 1676, and their stone frontispieces have bee
re-erected in the park: one NW of the bridge is dated 167(
the other has the date 1704 as part of a later inscription. Bot
have pairs of Doric pilasters and a niche each side of the oper
ing and broad segmental pediments pierced with an oval ligh
In 1794 yet another and smaller house was built. Then i
1841 this was pulled down by Christopher Turnor, and i
emulation of de Ligne Gregory's efforts at near-by Harlaxto
he called in *William Burn** to build a new house on anoth
site. It was well chosen. The approach crosses the bridge wit
views to the r. across the lower lake, then it ascends the hi
straight to Burn's sixty-foot OBELISK in honour of Newto
Then, at a right angle, it swings in full view of the hous
splendidly situated on a terrace of the valley. The forecou
SCREEN and GATES have magnificent ironwork and tall pier
Rochford is an after-effect of Harlaxton (*see* p. 561), and it
Burn without Salvin. There is nothing here of Salvin's lov
of abstract geometry. Burn employs a Jacobethan style
gables and gablets, varying and skilfully placed groups (
chimneystacks, and finial-capped turrets. The compositio
follows his rule, with a main block balanced on one side by
large office wing, on the other side by a low Orangery. Th
office block is as high as the house and projects boldly, th
Orangery continues the main façade. The closest Rochfor
gets to Harlaxton is in the centre of the W front: a big porc
bay, oriel, and fussily composed gable of obelisks, inturne
scrolls, and a Carolean-style pediment. To the r. and l. slightl
projecting wings, strapwork-crested. The office wing has strap
work details and urns in a Germanic style on the parapet. Th
E front should be viewed from across the valley. It has slightl
projecting wings and between them five regular bays of mu
lioned windows with gables above.

The INTERIOR surprises. The central HALL has a ceilin
divided into square panels with strapwork cartouches. Th
chimneypiece, carved in grey stone in a full-blooded Dietter
linesque manner, is splendid and entirely convincing. Th
mantel is supported by bearded termini. To the l. an arcad
(a reminder of past screens passages). Beyond it a vaulte

* A contract was drawn up on 24 April 1841. The total cost was abo
£60,000.

piece linked to the STAIRCASE with its unusual ceiling of
interlocking beams (cf. Harlaxton and Revesby, Lindsey). In
the MUSIC ROOM in the NE corner is an enormous chimneypiece of black and white marble. Winged caryatids with claw
feet, scrolled and feathered bosoms, and lovely winged heads,
support an entablature of massive proportions. This has a
white frieze of foliage with embracing putto heads in the centre.
Can this be by Burn? Is it not more likely that it is an original
Flemish later C17 piece? If so, it is the most spectacular of
its type in England. The LIBRARY fills the whole s front and
has the richest ceiling, a strapwork design dated 1845 and
similar to the dining room at Harlaxton. Also by Burn are
the Louis-Quinze rooms between Library and Music Room,
among the best and most elegant of C19 interpretations. They
have Italian townscape panels by *J. Kerr Lawson*, early C20
probably. (He did the decoration of the Senate House at
Ottawa.) In the gardens much statuary, notably a Diana Bor-
ghese in *J. H. Blashfield*'s artificial stone, and a Venus and
Cupid, and a Bacchus, by *J. B. de Bloeck*. The SOUTH LODGE
is dated 1834 and was built by *Cornelius Sherborne*. Of the
modern college building little need be said. Few parkscapes
can have received such brutal treatment.

ASTON PARK, *see* p. 521.

'he VILLAGE was laid out in the Tudor style by *William Burn*
between 1840 and 1845 – a picturesque grouping of grey stone
cottages.

SOUTH WITHAM

9010

T JOHN BAPTIST. Later C12 N arcade of three bays. Round
piers, square abaci, one crocket, one waterleaf capital. Early
C13 s arcade. Octagonal piers, semicircular responds. Of the
two octagonal piers only one has an original capital. The other
must be later. The E respond has a stiff-leaf capital, the w
respond some nailhead. Double-chamfered arches. E.E. bellcote, of the type more frequent across the border in Rutland.
It is a gabled piece with two round arches. They are separated
by a shafted pier standing on a middle buttress up the W front.
Pointed blank arcading on the sides of the bellcote. The s
transept of the church seems Dec, the N transept and the s
doorway (with heads and big fleurons in one moulding) are
Perp. The chancel was rebuilt in 1930. – FONT. Octagonal,
with sunk fleurs-de-lis etc. Is this C17? – STAINED GLASS.
Original bits in the N transept window. – PLATE. Chalice and

Paten Cover, Elizabethan. – MONUMENT. Mrs Stone † 167
Inscription flanked by a broad band of simple ornament, sti
almost strapwork in character.

The village is predominantly of stone. No. 7 HIGH STREET an
TANYARD FARM are both vernacular types, the latter I
shaped with moulded chimneys and mullioned windows. Th
house is probably Georgian.

SPALDING

The town grew out of the Benedictine priory which had bee
founded in 1052 but was renewed as a dependency of St Nichol
at Angers in 1074. It grew to have thirty or more monks and
be one of the richest religious houses of Lincolnshire. It lay
the S of the present market place and on E of Sheepmarket, b
nothing certain remains of it (however, *see* the Prior's Ove
p. 654). Spalding also possessed a castle. It stood on the E side
Pinchbeck Road and has disappeared too. The wealth of the tow
itself depended on the river Welland, which was the main trad
route for the import of coal, timber, and groceries and the expo
of corn and cole-seed. But the principal fame of Spalding (apa
from tulips) is the Spalding Gentlemen's Society, a society
antiquaries, founded in 1710, seventeen years before *the* Socie
of Antiquaries. Its founder, Maurice Johnson, a lawyer, was als
a founder member of the London society. Early members
the Spalding society were Newton, Stukeley (*see* Stamfor
p. 668), George Vertue, the engraver and chronicler of art an
artists, and also Pope, Addison, and Thomas Gray.

CHURCHES

ST MARY AND ST NICHOLAS. The church was built as a paris
church by the priory under Prior William de Littleport abo
1284. The agreement between prior and parishioners surviv
and is an interesting, detailed document (B.M., Cole MSS.
The site was that of the Norman cemetery chapel of St Thom
Becket of which certain details remain, and their extent ha
been ascertained. To start historically at the beginning o
ought to start at the E end. This also has the advantage th
the church here reveals its chief visual characteristic. It is
wide and varied building, not unified like Boston or Lout
Basically, to get one's bearings, one ought to keep in min
that the building of the late C13 was cruciform. All the rest
C14 and C15 accretions. At the E end there appear flat Norma
buttresses below the C19 group of three stepped lancets, an

these are assigned to a late C12 lengthening of the cemetery chapel. There are also such buttress stumps on the s side of the chancel. But the one lancet on the N side is (one only because *Sir G. G. Scott*'s N chapel of 1865-7 interferes), and the three on the s side must be, of *c.*1284. To the w, the cemetery chapel extended into the present crossing. From where we stand one gets the first glance at the Perp clerestory, its big five-light E window. The present chancel roof cuts into this, so the Perp roof must have had a lower pitch. On the clerestory gable pinnacles and a Sanctus-bell turret. The clerestory has to the N and s seven windows, not too close together. They are of three lights with panel tracery. The clerestory is embattled. Next appear the Perp s transept E window and, projecting E from the transept, St Mary's Chapel with interesting, unusual Perp tracery. The s transept s window has three ogee lights under one arch. This is said to be a replacement of the separate lancets of *c.*1284. The outer s aisle windows have Y-tracery, and this certainly harmonizes with the transept s window and would suggest a date early in the C14. The s porch is a Perp addition. It has a higher NE stair-turret and an inner doorway with typically Perp mouldings. The tower is in full view now. It stands to the s of the w bay of the s aisle and must have been started earlier than this, for the ground stages are still E. E. This seems to imply that the tower was begun at the same time as the E end, i.e. *c.*1284, but as a detached structure. The interior will yield more results in favour of or against this hypothesis. The bell-openings (Y-tracery cusped) reach well beyond 1300. The buttresses at this level have fine blank Y-tracery too. Then the battlements, the crocketed pinnacles, the thin, elegant flying buttresses, and the crocketed spire. Lucarnes in two tiers in alternating directions and with details already Perp. The total height is 160 ft. Round to the w front. The w window above the small doorway is of seven lights. It is of the time of Scott's restoration (1865-7; cost, £9000*). But the s aisle w window has reticulated tracery, i.e. it is a Dec contribution or alteration, and the N aisle has a Perp window. Then the exterior indeed continues Perp. The first window with shafted mullions seems Early Perp and so should be the N porch, more prominent than the s porch. Its entrance has large pierced tracery above the arch, in forms still Dec, and the N doorway is boldly trefoil-pointed, also a form one

---

* I owe this figure to Mr Spain.

would not expect in mature Perp. However, the wavy thi
shafts and mouldings do not allow for a Dec date, and insic
the porch is a fan-vault which is a fairly safe sign of a Lat
Perp date. Then the Perp windows of the outer N aisle an
the flower frieze above them, and the N transept front, wher
nothing tells now of its E.E. date. The window is in fa
Latest Perp. After that Scott's additions to the chancel.

So externally the earliest period of the church appears on
at the E end, in the S transept front, and in the tower. A clo
examination of the INTERIOR is needed to fill in the gaps. Th
interior also has nothing of the unity of Boston or Louth c
Sleaford. The arcades are of c.1284 etc., but they are only fo
bays long, and they are not quite in their original state. Th
piers are quatrefoil, the arches double-chamfered. The cler
story of course, as we have seen, is Perp, and the hammerbea
roof is Perp also. Angels against the hammerbeams and ange
against the principals not supported by hammerbeams. Mo
of the detail is Scott's. The aisles were originally narrow
than they are now. In the W wall of the N aisle appears th
lowest part of the splays of a lancet window, close to t
arcade respond. So that is why the tower must have bee
detached. It was linked up to the church early in the C14
when the aisle W wall was altered and the Dec window set i
At the same time probably the outer S aisle was added. Th
arcade between inner and outer S aisle also has quatrefoil pier
but they are Dec, no longer E.E. The difference is very tellin
The foils in the E.E. form are set off from one another crispl
in the Dec form they flow into each other with a deep hollo
undulation. The bases of the Dec piers are spoiled. The arch
are again double-chamfered. The W doorway into the tow
is of 1688.

The E.E. transepts must have had W and E aisles (like tho
of Patrington in Yorkshire and St Mary Redcliffe Bristol); f
the quatrefoil piers of the aisle arcade type repeat here, wit
one difference: they are much shorter. However, returning
the nave and checking, one can easily recognize that the na
piers were in fact at some date lengthened by five feet. Abo
the transept W and E arcades the original clerestory windo
survive, of oval shape. One can also, inside the S transept
aisle, recognize the line of the former aisle roof, much low
than now. The crossing is marked in an oddly inarticulate wa
There are just square chunks of wall. The transept arche
higher than the arcade arches, die into them, and it can b

seen that originally they went up higher, no doubt with a view to a crossing tower. The chancel interior needs little comment. The nice canted ceiling with its recent decoration is by *Stephen Dykes-Bower*. The chancel arch is E.E., but was raised when the nave arcades were raised. The N chapel arcade is due to Scott. So now to the N side of transept and aisle to note differences against the S side. In the N wall of the transept E aisle is a low tomb recess. The outer N aisle or chapel has a slender pier with typically Perp section. Shafts and hollows, both thin, and the shafts with small polygonal capitals. The diagonal arch in the N aisle helps the thin Perp pier to do its job.

FURNISHINGS. SCREEN. By *J. Oldrid Scott*, 1875. – DOORS. The W and N doors are traceried and Perp. – BENCH ENDS. Just three, with poppy-heads, NE of the pulpit. – STAINED GLASS. Much by *Clayton & Bell*, and easily recognized by the small figures and the prevalent brown and dark red. – BRASS CHANDELIER. Of three tiers; dated 1766. – PLATE. Chalice, by *R.S.*, 1562; Flagon, by *W.C.*, 1635; Almsdish, London, 1639; gilt Almsdish, by *A.M.*, 1668; Plate, by *S.R.*, 1674; Flagon, C17; silver-gilt Chalice, by *Gabriel Sleath*, 1721; Chalice, London, 1736; Wine Strainer, London, 1799. – MONUMENTS. C. M. Dinham Green † 1837. Large Gothic tablet by *Hopper* (S aisle). – Elizabeth Johnson † 1843. White statue on base. By *L. Francis* of London.

MMACULATE CONCEPTION AND ST NORBERT (R.C.), Henrietta Street. 1875–8 by *M. E. Hadfield & Son*. Red brick, with lancet windows and bellcote. Not in a detached position.

T JOHN BAPTIST, Hawthorne Bank. 1875 by *R. J. Withers*. Stone, E.E., the W portal set in a broad projection which is taken back gradually to receive the bell-turret. Wide, featureless nave interior. Lancet chancel.

T PAUL, Fulney. 1880, to the design of *Sir G. G. Scott*, who had died in 1878. Large, and externally all that prevents one from appreciating so much Victorian church design. The church is too townish for its setting. It is assertive and it is terribly mechanical in its execution. Hotly red, very even bricks, joyless stone carving. The church has a steeple 135 ft high set in a detached position W of the church and only connected to it by an arcade. Long nave and chancel. The forms Early E.E. The interior is more personal, with the arcades grouped in two under round arches – the composition of Boxgrove Priory.

ST PETER, Priory Road. 1875–6 by *Sir G. G. Scott*. Now decor
secrated and at the time of writing for sale. Of brick, larg
with lancet windows, circular clerestory windows, and r
tower. In the w front the w portal carries on its arch the mic
buttress which carries the bell-turret.

WYKEHAM CHAPEL (St Nicholas), 3 m. NE. This noble chap
was built in 1311 by Prior Hatfield of Spalding as the priva
chapel of his country house. It is 43 by 22 ft in size, beautiful
ashlar-built, and has tall windows, three to N and S, one to
and E. The w window and the NW and SW windows are bricke
up, and the tracery of the E window is broken out. But of th
other windows three have entirely uncusped intersectir
tracery, the fourth daintily cusped reticulated tracery. So i
1311 the Dec type was used side by side with the type of the la
C13. Small niches l. and r. of the E window inside. – PLAT
Chalice, by *William Fawdery*, 1708.

NONCONFORMIST CHAPELS *see* Perambulation.

PUBLIC BUILDINGS *see* PERAMBULATION

PERAMBULATION

The specific character of Spalding is determined by the riv
Welland, which bisects the town and of which the best use
made – a rare thing in England. Tree-lined streets run alor
both banks, and Georgian houses look at each other. There a
warehouses too, and plenty of Georgian houses in other par
of the town – nothing as swagger as say Fydell House at Bostor
but plenty to keep one happy.

Our perambulation starts in the MARKET PLACE. The dignifie
WHITE HART, seven bays long, was built shortly after 171
and has an early C19 porch on Tuscan columns across th
pavement. Much else is Neo-Georgian, but BARCLAYS BAN
by *William Eaves* is of 1862, and the old CORN EXCHANG
by *Bellamy & Hardy* is of 1854–6. The Corn Exchange
Jacobean, three bays, brick, with a shaped gable. In BRIDG
STREET the upper parts of C18 façades. Then, by the rive
turn r. into LONDON ROAD. This is one of the streets facir
the river. Soon we get the view of the parish church across th
river. Then we come to the part of London Road calle
WELLAND PLACE, where there are nice Georgian façade
especially No. 12, and after that to another part of Londo
Road called WELLAND TERRACE, a ten-house group thre

storeys high. The porches mostly have fluted Doric columns
and pediments. They may be those designed by *John Cunning-
ton* in 1813 (Colvin). Next, the intrusion of the ODEON
CINEMA of 1938 (by *H. W. Weedon*), an unforgivable insult.
Its accent is not even central, as is the unbreakable rule of the
Georgian neighbours. It is at one corner, and there brick gives
way to white and black faience. After this London Road continues, always with the river and the houses opposite in full
view. No. 34 is mid-Georgian, one-bay pediment, hipped roof,
central stack, and nice details. The cast-iron fretwork porch
and Adamesque gatepiers are pretty. The OLD HIGH
SCHOOL (Welland Hall) is much grander than anything
so far, a detached Georgian block of five by five bays and three
storeys standing in its garden. It is well proportioned and has
a parapet, a small pediment, and a fluted Ionic porch with
richly carved doorcase. Good ceilings inside. Crossing the
bridge we return on the other bank of the river along COWBIT
ROAD. WESTBOURNE LODGE is by *William Sands Jun.*,
*c.*1760–70, a hodge-podge of Palladian forms. Bow windows
to the ground floor, a thin Tuscan porch, and first-floor windows with rusticated surrounds. Pediment on top. Low side
wings originally built as mere screen walls. Rusticated doorways with blank circular lights above. Standing a little back is
TOWER HOUSE, a loony Victorian piece with crenellated and
machicolated parapets, turreted tower at one angle, finials,
pseudo-Romanesque as much as pseudo-Vanbrugh. Then No.
4 Cowbit Road, LANGTON HOUSE, looking like *William
Sands Jun.* A segmental bow and a Doric porch. No. 3 is also
by *Sands*, with a pair of canted bay windows, an Ionic porch,
and balustraded parapets. The wings are later. In the garden
wall a curious brick doorway, round-arched with zigzag
mouldings, said to have come from various sources but most
likely from Ayscoughfee Hall,* the grandest house in town,
which is now not far away and which is reached by continuing
along the river. The street is now called CHURCH GATE. One
has first to walk along a long irregular garden wall and then the
house appears, lying back from the street.

*See
p.
768*

YSCOUGHFEE HALL is a mixture of dates and styles. It is said
to have been built originally by Sir Richard Aldwyn in 1429.
Of a pre-Reformation brick house a certain amount no doubt
survives, namely the asymmetrically placed tower, the adjacent

---

* Has anyone suggested it is Revival rather than Survival?

wing to the N, and the adjacent wing to the W. In the latter
window with hood-mould, all brick. As one looks at the hous
one does not at once take in these early details; for to the rive
there is a straightforward Late Elizabethan front of the H-type
The wings are of single-bay width, the centre of five bay.
It originally had a hall bay window such as we shall find on th
E front. This has disappeared, as have other Elizabethan fea
tures. The front was gothicized c.1792 with simple pointe
lights, plain triangular gables, and a flattish pediment over th
centre. Then, in 1845, the house was given a Tudoresqu
face-lift, perhaps by *William Todd*,★ of bay windows, crene
lations, and shaped gables. The screen between the wings
also of this date. The S elevation is mostly C19, but the E ele
vation is a mixture never quite analysed. In the centre is
two-storeyed porch, broad and obtrusive. As it stands, it mu
be Victorian. It squeezes in the hall bay window of shortl
before the Reformation, with glazing in two tiers, with finel
spliced shafts and thin horizontal rolls crossing them. Th
upper lights are round-arched. In the S wing is a one-ligh
window with a trefoiled ogee head and a small circular C1
relief. The ogee-headed E doorway hidden by the porch is a
present behind a door marked Gents. Behind this doorwa
is the hall, remodelled in 1792 with a gallery on tall columns
The GARDENS have high walls and stone gatepiers. They wer
laid out c.1730, probably by *William Sands*. An unfortuna
WAR MEMORIAL replaces a castellated tower. Adjacent
Ayscoughfee was Holyrood House, also by *William Sand*
This, in true corporation manner, has been demolished. I
place is taken by the new MUNICIPAL OFFICES, 1960-2 b
W. E. Norman Webster, modern thank heavens and not im
tation Georgian, and indeed in a nice, modest, and friendl
Modern, light brick, asymmetrically composed, and set bac
to beyond the front of Ayscoughfee Hall. To its l. the san

★ Cf. the similar style of his Gamlyns's Almshouses of 1843-4.

‡ There is some interesting STAINED GLASS in the house. The upper ha
of the bay window has a patchwork of fragments from the C13 to C1
English and foreign. Near the top on the l., e.g., a French C16 Coronation
the Virgin. The bottom is a jumble of bits and pieces, including parts of
series of the Seven Sacraments, French, C16; in the middle light e.g. th
heads of the Virgin and St John from a large Crucifixion, perhaps Engli
C13; a Christ from a Coronation of the Virgin, C14, and two humble c.
figures; in the r. light a Christ risen, French, C16. Also in the gallery on th
opposite side of the bay window two later C16 Flemish roundels. Muc
heraldic glass too.

corporation that destroyed Holyrood House destroyed the character of this important part of the town much more disastrously by running an asphalted road dead on towards the church, with a ridiculous little roundabout right in front of its façade. Well meant? Probably, but certainly, and appallingly, ill-advised. After that some irregular property, and we are back to the TOWN BRIDGE (of 1838). But we don't cross it. We turn r. instead into CHURCH STREET. GAMLYNS'S ALMSHOUSES, 1843–4, are by *William Todd*. Red brick, Tudoresque. WISTINA LODGE, of brick, five bays and three storeys, is dated 1792, and beyond this follows No. 4 of 1721, with a small semicircular porch. Nos 5–8 are grouped towards the church, nice and irregular, including Ionic porches similar to those of Welland Terrace. Back to the bridge, again without crossing, and now along HIGH STREET, following the river in the opposite direction, with picturesque views across towards warehouses and house backs. No. 4 is Early Georgian and No. 5, the WHITE LION, is later, with a rusticated central archway. No. 9 is again Early Georgian, and No. 12 is dated 1746. It is by *William Sands* and not distinctive. The SOUTH HOLLAND MILLS of shortly before 1807 present a twelve-bay, four-storey front of rusticated cement rendering. Quite modern and not unpleasant. No. 15 has stone surrounds to the windows and may be the house built for John Richards by *George Sharpe* and *George Andrews*, in 1768. This is the date of HOLLAND HOUSE, the best architecturally in the town. It is by *William Sands Jun*. Reading up the centre, a pedimented doorway with narrow arched windows each side, a Venetian window, a square window with arched ones each side, and then a pediment. The wings have canted bays and balustraded parapets. Round the corner, in HOLLAND ROAD, is a new GOVERNMENT OFFICE BUILDING, 1960 by *E. Farrow*, a straightforward piece of modern frame construction with much glass, transparent and opaque. YEW LODGE is early C19 and has a nice doorway with attached, fluted Ionic columns, and CLEY HALL is dated on water pipes 1764, but the front with its Adamish porch looks later. Then, by the river, a weatherboarded shed, and beyond this WELLAND HOUSE, Early Victorian, cement-rendered, with Soanian giant pilasters and a heavy Ionic porch. Crossing the footbridge and turning r. into ALBION STREET one should at once go as far as WILLESBY, early C17, on a flattened H-plan with straight gables and two-, three-, and four-light windows. Then back the same way

and now to notice another rusticated cement WAREHOUSE an
then the Georgian LANGTOFT HOUSE of five bays. No
straight on into DOUBLE STREET to the FRIENDS' MEET
ING HOUSE, dated 1805. This is a simple, honest three-ba
job with its original fitments. Yew trees in front. Further o
No. 27 has nice details round the ground-floor windows an
doorway. Then, facing a stretch with trees along the rive
THE SYCAMORES, large, early C19, brick, of five bays an
three storeys with lower one-bay wings, and THE LIME
early C18, lower, also of five bays and with a parapet.* The
off to the r., by Herring Lane to BROAD STREET wit
HARRINGTON HOUSE on the r. Here an early C18 build
in the 'Stamford' style has gone to town with Palladia
details. In only three bays and two storeys, you get a doorwa
with pilasters set against a rusticated surround and a heav
segmental pediment, Gibbsian windows on the ground floo
and lugged windows with oversized keystones on the fir
floor, a pedimented centre window, and as a finish to the fro
a wilful shell-cum-acroterion ornament. The MANOR HOUS
nearly next door is of the same date but much plainer. Seve
bays with a three-bay pediment. Then the SPALDIN
GENTLEMEN'S SOCIETY MUSEUM, 1910 by *J. B. Corby*
Sons with detail in tile and brick, brings one to PINCHBEC
STREET and the INDEPENDENT CHAPEL of 1821 (three bay
red brick, arched windows, top balustrade), to its l. th
SUNDAY SCHOOL of 1856 and nearly opposite No. 72, la
C18 with a plain Venetian window over an Ionic porch. Bac
and now by New Road, long and wide like a market place, ar
on l. to the SHEEPMARKET. At once on the l. the PRIOR
OVEN, said to be medieval. The principal room is octagona
with eight radial chamfered wooden ribs. The date is n
easily determined. At the far end of Sheepmarket and dom
nating it the mock-heroic SESSIONS HOUSE of 1842, wit
battlements, angle towers, and Tudoresque bay window
As with the Boston Sessions House (*see* p. 471), the archite
was *Charles Kirk*. From the l. corner of the Sessions Hou
along The Crescent (don't think of Bath and Buxton) and
PRIORY ROAD. Here, on the l. ABBEY BUILDINGS,
brick range traditionally connected with the priory, who
buildings were in this part of the town. The range has to th
s six buttresses and two upper two-light windows with tra

* In the garden the traceried head of a Perp five-light window. Whe
does it come from?

soms and ogee-headed lights. To the N is one more such window, but with pointed lights, and the head of yet another. A doorway with two-centred arch on this side near the w end. Then the JOHNSON HOSPITAL of 1879 by *Weatherly & Jones*. So finally to the stock brick RAILWAY STATION by *J. Taylor*, 1848. Italianate and completely asymmetrical, one-to two-storeyed with a short three-storeyed tower, and, along the BOURNE ROAD, much further out, on the edge of the town, to MONK'S HALL FARM, L-shaped, with gables and mullioned windows. In the short arm is an Elizabethan or Jacobean six-light window, but in the long arm, under the gable, two windows have arched lights, i.e. an Early Tudor characteristic.

Yet further out is the PODE HOLE PUMPING STATION, with a date 1825 on a rainwater head and the original *Boulton & Watt* beam engines with thin Doric columns. MHLG)

PINCHBECK ROAD HOSPITAL. The former workhouse, built in 1836. Brick.

LOW FULNEY, 1⅜ m. E. The office of the Manager of the Land Settlement is supposed to have been the DAIRY of Spalding Priory. It is a rib-vaulted room, but all is boarded up now.

SPANBY

1¼ m. NNE of Threekingham

ST NICHOLAS. 1882. Very red brick. Nave and lower apse. Bell-turret of wood, projecting on a bracket beyond the w wall. The doorway is a genuine Dec piece with two continuous chamfers. – PLATE. Paten, by *R.K.*, 1641; Caudle Cup, by *G.S.*, 1664.

STAINBY

ST PETER. 1865 by *R. Coad*, a pupil of Scott. E.E. in style. w tower with broach spire. Nave and aisles, the N aisle apparently built with old materials. – WOODWORK. By the *Rev. W. E. Thorold*, after 1877. – STAINED GLASS. By *Clayton & Bell*.

RECTORY. An earlier building was done up in 1804 to plans that had been prepared by *William Lumby* in 1789 (windows with moulded surrounds and keystones). In 1888 it was again re-fronted.

CASTLE. At the SE end of the village, behind a farmyard, are the remains of a badly mutilated castle-earthwork, apparently

a small motte. It has been dug for gravel, and only enough
remains to indicate that it was of some degree of strength.

oooo STAMFORD

INTRODUCTION

2a Many will agree with Celia Fiennes (1697) that Stamford is 'a
fine a built town all of stone as maybe seen'. Moreover, it is fine
to look at throughout; there are no spoiled parts in the centre
and now that the opening of the by-pass has restored traffic
through the town to manageable proportions, it can once more
be enjoyed even on weekdays.

The importance of Stamford goes back a long way. It was
one of the five boroughs of the Danish Settlement, it is called a
market in Domesday Book, it had a university in the late C13 and
early C14,* it had several monastic halls, partly in connexion
with the university, it had up to seventeen churches in the Middle
Ages of which five and bits of two more remain. One medieval
hospital and a bit also survive, but of the five friars' houses only
one fragment of the Whitefriars is preserved.‡ Medieval Stamford otherwise has to be found in undercrofts below houses. The
town was sacked and burnt by the Lancastrian army in 1461
but even of the time of rebuilding after that disaster only ecclesiastical work bears witness. The architectural character of Stamford
is minor C17 to major C18. The C17 houses are characterized
by gables, mullioned windows, and canted bay windows, the
C18 houses by an engaging faith in the pattern book. For each
door and window a source can be found in such publications as
Batty Langley's, William Halfpenny's, and William Salmon's.
Morton in 1712 wrote that most of the noticeable houses were
'built by innkeepers and tradesmen and a few Gentlemen's
houses'. That stands to reason, considering the position of the
town on the Great North Road. For stone, Stamford is ideally
placed: within three and a half miles of Barnack in Northamptonshire to the E, Collyweston in Northamptonshire to the SW,
and Ketton in Rutland to the W. By rights Stamford should
belong to either of these two, or rather to both anyway. St Martin

---

* Alas, we can no longer believe that the university was established by
Prince Bladud in 863.
‡ At the E end of St Paul's Street. The Blackfriars were S of St Leonard's
Street, the Greyfriars W of the Whitefriars, the Austin Friars S of the W
bastion of the town walls.

s indeed in Northamptonshire, but the rest, i.e. Stamford w of
he river, ought to be Rutland and not Lincolnshire, of which it
orms no more than a greedy tongue.

CHURCHES

ALL SAINTS. The hub of Stamford. Facing down All Saints'
Place the church has the unusual feature of an even E.E.
blank arcading all along and even turning E as well. The
windows, owing to the falling ground, are above it. The
capitals are alternatingly moulded and stiff-leaf. On the W
wall the blank arcading carries on, though the arches are Perp
replacement. On the E wall, the S chapel and the chancel have
thin chamfered E.E. buttresses (one below the Perp E
window). Inside more is E.E., notably the sumptuous S
arcade. Three bays with the richest stiff-leaf capitals. The
piers are octofoil in two varieties, one with the main shafts
keeled and detached shafts in the diagonals, the other with the
keeled shafts between two spurs in the diagonals. Shaft-
rings all round. Many-moulded arches. Only the W bay is
Perp, but in the SW corner of the church is an E.E. respond,
and to it corresponds a shafted E.E. buttress outside. What
one has surmised from this is that the church originally had
a SW tower and that this was replaced by the present Perp
NW steeple (perhaps after the church had been damaged in
1461). In fact the Perp arch is the same as the arch from the
nave into the tower. Both have castellated capitals. But first
the N arcade, also E.E., but plain (circular piers, double-
chamfered arches) and perhaps partly rebuilt when the tower
was built. No chancel arch, but a two-bay arcade to the S
chapel. Round pier, stiff-leaf capitals. The pier capital has
heads as well. The arches have one chamfer and one fine
moulding. A little nailhead in the soffit of the E arch. The stiff-
leaf looks definitely earlier than that of the S arcade. So to the
Perp work, undertaken largely by William and John Browne
(see Browne's Hospital, p. 664), merchants of the Staple of
Calais. They were responsible for the steeple and the N chapel.
The tower stands out beyond the N aisle. Quatrefoil frieze at
the foot. N entry by a small projecting porch with pairs of
stepped buttress-shafts. Castellation between and a stone
decorative lean-to roof. To the W four-light window surrounded by three niches. Then a stage with windows and tall
blank panelling. At its foot a quatrefoil frieze. Bell-openings

in twins, each of two lights, with a transom. They stand
under one arch and the middle mullion reaches up into the
apex. Quatrefoil frieze. Polygonal turret pinnacles connected
by heavy horizontal chunks instead of flying buttresses with
the recessed spire. Three tiers of lucarnes in alternating
directions. Large Perp aisle windows. Perp clerestory. On the
s side battlements and shafts for former pinnacles. The
shallow s porch has again pairs of stepped buttress-shafts,
a panelled arch inside, and a crocketed ogee gable. The N
chapel has buttresses with pinnacles set on them low down. The
w front has a six-light w window, and the buttress to its r. a
niche corresponding to those in the tower. Inside, the tower
has a Perp vault of eight radial ribs. The diagonal ones are
treated as broad bands with arched niches. So are the four
wall ribs. In the N aisle a tall Perp niche. Perp panelled
doorway to the vestry. The nave and chancel have diagonal
roof braces, and the N chapel has a good panelled ceiling with
St Andrew's crosses and foliage in the panels. – FONT. Perp,
octagonal, with shields in cusped panels. – HOURGLASS
STAND, s arcade, E respond. – STAINED GLASS. The E
window is by *Heaton, Butler & Bayne,* 1874. – PLATE.
Paten, London, 1706; Paten, by *Seth Lofthouse,* 1706; Flagon,
by *Charles Williams*(?), 1709; gilt Chalice and Paten, by
Francis Nelme, 1729; Wine Strainer, by *Samuel Godbehere,
Edward Wigan,* and *J. Bult.* – BRASSES. N aisle E wall. John
Browne † 1442 and wife, 37 in. figures, his feet on two woolpacks. – John Browne the Younger † 1475 and wife, 44 in. –
Christopher Browne and wife(?), 24 in. – Then in the s
chapel William Browne † 1489, brother of John Jun. and
founder of Browne's Hospital, and wife, 4 ft 10 in. He stands
on two woolpacks and on the scroll above him it says 'X me
spede'. – Also Margaret Elmes † 1471 (20 in.) and on the s
wall Henry Wykys, vicar, † 1508 (headless, the figure was
*c.*24 in.).

ST AUGUSTINE (R.C.), Broad Street. By *G. Goldie,* 1864
(GR). E.E. with an unbelievable bell-turret, asymmetrically
placed and most crudely detailed. Steep hipped roof on its
top. All very asymmetrical, even inside. Short piers, some of
red granite. Apse at the (ritual) E end. – STAINED GLASS.
In the N aisle by *Wailes.*

ST GEORGE, St George's Square. E.E. three-bay arcades with
round piers, heightened in the C14 octagonally, a very queer
muddle. Octagonal C14 capitals. Double-chamfered arches.

The rest is all Perp except for the odd oblong w tower. Its
w window is Dec (intersecting ogees), but the bell-stage must
be early C18 or late C17.* Perp aisles, neo-Perp transeptal
widening of 1888, Perp narrow bays between arcade and
tower, on the N side with continuous mouldings, on the s side
different. Perp chancel arch. Late Perp windows. Embattled
aisles and clerestory. Nave roof with angels, moulded beams,
and bosses. The chancel and clerestory were built at the
expense of William de Bruges, first Garter King of Arms,
who made his will in 1449. In it he refers specifically to the
'aungel' in the roof who should bear the 'Signs of the Passion'.
– STAINED GLASS. In the chancel in a s window two
original figures of c.1450. – In a N window about 200 mottos
of the founder members of the Garter, from the windows
willed by William of Bruges which were to be dedicated to
these founder members. A glazier called *Exton* assembled the
mottos in 1732. – E window (Ascension) by *Wailes* and *Clayton
& Bell*, 1869. – PLATE. Paten, by *Francis Garthorne*, 1706;
Chalice and two Flagons, by *Michael Boult*, 1715. – MONU-
MENTS. Sir Richard Cust † 1734 and others. By *John Bacon*, 57a
1797. Large white standing monument. Over-life-size allegorical female figure by a tall pedestal with bust. Obelisk
background. – Savile Cockayne Cust † 1772. By *W. Tyler*.
Large slim urn in multi-coloured marble in front of white
drapery.

ST JOHN BAPTIST. Mostly Perp. The lower part of the NW
tower comes first. The arches to s and E are still between
Dec and Perp. The tower has clasping buttresses, three niches
round the w window, a small doorway to the N, bell-openings
of twins of two lights with the middle mullion going up into
the apex of the super-arch, a lozenge frieze, and battlements
and pinnacles. The w front of the nave has above a doorway
a five-light window with panel tracery and niches to r. and l.
The aisles have big three-light windows and battlements. s
porch shallow with an ogee gable. Decorated battlements and
pinnacles. The arcades have typical Perp piers with capitals
only on the demi-shafts to the arch openings and projections
to the nave flat in front and with waves in the diagonals.
Arches of two wave mouldings. The chancel arch of the same
type. The N and S chapel arches with castellated capitals.

* An engraving dedicated to Le Neve, i.e. probably of the 1720s or a little
later, shows the tower as it is now.

Nave roof and aisle roofs with many horizontal angels. In the chancel the angels are against the arched braces. – FONT. Octagonal, Perp, simple. – FONT COVER. Jacobean. – REREDOS. Victorian Gothic by *E. Browning*, 1878. – SCREENS. The finest on the W of the N chapel. One-light divisions. Ogee arches. Specially ornate doorway. Fine top friezes. Set into the r. part of this the doorway panels of the former rood screen, with two-light divisions. – In the chapel to the w two-light, to the N one-light divisions. – STAINED GLASS. Original fragments in the chancel s window. – Whole figures in the tracery of a N aisle and a S aisle window. – More fragments in the S aisle E window. – Chancel E window, Adoration of the Magi, by *Oliphant*, 1878. – PLATE. Paten, by *I.D.*, 1691. – MONUMENTS. Brasses to Nicholas Byldyson † 1489 and family (2 ft figures; nave floor). – Brass to Henry Sargeant † 1497 (2 ft; S chapel). – John Booth † 1799, by Messrs *Coade*, i.e. in Coade stone. Very small, with mourning female by an urn.

ST MARTIN, St Martin's. Rebuilt, according to heraldic evidence, at the time of Bishop Russell of Lincoln and perhaps his successor, Bishop Scott – i.e. c.1480, no doubt after damage done in 1461. So the church is Perp throughout. The w tower faces the street. Clasping buttresses, w doorway with two niches in the buttresses. Three-light w window. Then very closed walls. Bell-openings twin two-light windows under one arch, the middle mullion running up into the apex. Lozenge frieze, openwork quatrefoiled battlements, the middle ones on each side with a concave-sided gable. Pinnacles. Aisles with three-light windows with castellated transoms; four-centred heads. Battlements. N rood-stair turret with a spire with remarkable entasis. Two-storeyed s porch. Tierceron-star vault inside with an angel boss. The chancel projects one bay beyond the chapels. The window details all carry on. Only the chancel E window is of five lights. Three-light windows in the clerestory. This has battlements too. The only Victorian alteration is the enlargement of the Cecil family chapel so as to make it two bays wide instead of one. This was done in 1865. Inside, the tower has a tierceron-star vault. The aisles embrace the tower. Arcades of four bays. Piers slim with four shafts and four diagonal hollows. Arches with two wave mouldings. Chancel arch and chapel arches are all the same. – FONT. A tall early C14 bowl with flatly carved blank window patterns, none yet with ogees.

28a

STAINED GLASS. Much of the glass of the C15 is preserved, though very little that belonged originally to the church. Most of the glass came from Tattershall. More from Snape and also, it is said, from Warwickshire. It was set up by *Peckitt* of York *c.*1758 and does him much credit. His arrangement and his ornamental panels of purely geometrical forms are better than most that has been done with old glass in the century and a half after him. – PLATE. Cup, *c.*1570; Paten, 1630; two Plates, 1682; Paten, *c.*1688; Cup, two Flagons, and Arms of Walsburge, 1722. – MONUMENTS. William Cecil, Lord Burghley, † 1598. Queen Elizabeth's adviser and confidant. Alabaster. A six-poster. The columns are transversely connected by entablatures, and on these stand two coffered transverse tunnel-vaults. Also between the W and between the E columns smaller arches are set in. Recumbent effigy on a half-rolled-up mat. Top with coats of arms. – Richard Cecill and his wife who died in 1587. Alabaster. The two kneeling figures face one another across a prayer desk. Columns l. and r. and obelisks on them. Three daughters kneel below. – John, fifth Earl of Exeter, † 1700. By *Monnot*, Rome, 1703. Large, competent, and confident. White marble. Only the back obelisk light brown. Large sarcophagus, and on it the semi-reclining effigies, comfortable and at ease. On the floor to the l. and r. of the sarcophagus Wisdom and Art, i.e. a female figure holding a small gilt Pallas Athene and another holding a hammer and nails; at her feet L-square, compasses, palette and brushes. – William Wissing, the painter, † 1687. Small tablet with scrolly surround (N aisle, near the W end). – Edward Henry and Henry Poyntz Cecil † 1862 and 1858. By *G. M. Benzoni*, Rome, 1864. White marble. Large frontal angel in relief with a trumpet, in a shallow arched niche. L. and r. of the inscription below portrait medallions.

ST MARY. The W tower is E.E. Set-back buttresses, thin and chamfered. The W doorway is very strange. The actual opening is round-headed and perfectly plain. Is it Norman or a later reduction? Above it another round arch carried on imposts with stiff-leaf capitals. Then taller, richer shafts with richer stiff-leaf capitals carry a pointed arch. Its tympanum above the upper round arch has two plain circles and a lozenge as its only decoration. Were they meant to receive figure carving and never did? In the pointed arch dog-tooth in two mouldings. Then three roundels, two with quatrefoils,

the third with a delightful knot pattern. Above that thre
blank arches with stiff-leaf capitals. Then three more suc
arches with pointed-trefoiled heads, and set in them tw
roundels and a window. To the s and N plainer blank arcading
Three tiers of four arches below the trefoiled tier. Then th
bell-stage. The buttresses stop here and there are only angle
shafts. Three lancet bell-openings with shafts with shaf
rings and dog-tooth. Broach spire, the broaches not hig
Immediately on them small tabernacles with statues. The
three tiers of lucarnes in alternating directions. They hav
ogee arches and crocketed gables, i.e. take us forward in
the c14. The spire reaches a height of 162 ft. Inside, th
responds of the tower arch have simple stiff-leaf crocket
The arch has two chamfers and a keeled roll. Above, tw
trefoil-headed doorways and the original roof-line. The vau
in the tower is of course Perp: eight radiating ribs formin
cells which are arched towards the centre ring. But E.E
again the w and E responds, semicircular except for the N
respond, which shows that the arcade was like that at A
Saints. Detached shafts in the main directions. Attache
shafts between the spurs in the diagonals. E.E. the chanc
arch too, the one-bay s chapel arch, the w bay arch of the
chapel, and, outside the E wall, the chamfered thin buttresse
In the s vestry is in addition a small late c13 window of tw
lights with a stiff-leaf shaft and a trefoil in plate tracery
The rest is Perp, probably rebuilt after the damage of 146
All embattled, all with large windows. The s buttresses hav
gablets and little niches below them. Three-light clerestor
windows. s porch, small N doorway with fleurons up on
moulding. The N chapel, which was the Chapel of th
Corpus Christi Guild, is singled out externally by a five-ligh
E window. It is singled out internally too. But first the Per
replacement of the E.E. arcades. Piers with four fillete
shafts and small hollows in the diagonals. Castellated capital
Double-chamfered arches. Between N chapel and chanc
Phillips Monument – see below. The chapel has a panelle
27b ceiling with many bosses. It was given by William Hikha
and his wife. The E window of the chancel is a Victoria
replacement of 1860 (Browning). – FONT. Octagonal, Per
very plain. – ALTAR FRONTAL. 1890 by J.D. Sedding. Gi
busts of the twelve Apostles in two tiers round a medallio
of Christ. Cinquecento style. – ROOD SCREEN. Also b
Sedding. The rood was added in 1920. – SCULPTURE. Ou

standingly good female figure of *c.*1330 (N chapel). – STAINED
GLASS. Chancel E by *Wailes,* 1860. – N chapel E by *Whall,*
1891. In a belated Pre-Raphaelite style, the source of much
that was and is evil in English C20 stained glass. – PLATE.
Chalice, Paten, and Flagon, by *Emes & Barnard,* 1825. –
MONUMENTS. Between chancel and N chapel, Sir David
Phillips † 1506 and wife. Effigies recumbent on a tomb-chest 32b
with in niches the twelve Apostles and between them in the
middle of the two long sides an angel with a shield. Canopy
with four-centred head, all panelled and decorated with
flowers. Splendid top frieze. To the l. small doorway with
four-centred head. Quatrefoil bands up the jambs and the
arch. – In the chapel alabaster effigy of a Knight, *c.*1360;
mutilated. On a simpler tomb-chest. The high ogee-gabled
canopy, later by a hundred years, takes a three-light window
in. – Also two identical ogee-headed tomb recesses.

ST MICHAEL, High Street. (Of the medieval church there is
no more than a Norman arch in an undercroft below the W
tower.) The present church was built in 1835–6 by *John
Brown* of Norwich. It is in the E.E. style and with many
features typical of the date, e.g. the even paired lancet windows
and the even shallow buttresses between them, also the square
W tower with grouped lancets as bell-openings. Flat E end
with, in the aisle end walls, doorways. The chancel has
remained as short as it was built. Also the three galleries on
thin iron columns have never been removed. Slightly canted
ceiling. – FONT. Octagonal, Perp, with quatrefoil panels in
lozenges. – SCULPTURE. An oak statuette of Charity, probably Belgian and probably C17. – PLATE. Two Flagons, 1693,
and Paten, 1694, by *James Chadwick*; Paten, by *Richard
Bayley,* 1717; Chalice, by *Ambrose Stevenson,* 1719; four
Plates, by *Thomas Tearle,* 1725.

NONCONFORMIST CHAPELS, *see* Perambulation.

PUBLIC BUILDINGS

CASTLE. In the SW corner of the walled town, at the foot of
Castle Street and Castle Dyke. Once with motte and tri-
angular bailey. In the SE angle are three blank C13 arches.
(The MHLG adds that inside there are three corresponding
finely moulded C14 arches with damaged moulded columns.)
Part of C13 walling on the St Peter's Vale side (*see* p. 674).
The mound was levelled in 1935 to make a car park and the
base of a round tower was removed. O tempora, o mores!

WALLS. The walls went all round the town, only leaving ou
St Martin's. From the surrounding w bastion (*see* p. 672)
they went s by Austin Friars Lane, then E by Bath Row and
the Castle (in Bath Row a postern-gate, *see* p. 674), then
Wharf Road (with the base of another postern-gate, *see* p. 678)
Brazenose Lane, East Street, North Street, West Street
and so back to the bastion.

TOWN HALL, St Mary's Hill and St Mary's Place. Built i
1777 and said on dubious grounds to be by *Lovell*, an other
wise undocumented gent. Is it perhaps by *W. Legg*? A squar
of seven by seven bays, three floors, cornice and low parapet
On both fronts the three central bays slightly project. Th
details an odd perpetuation of the Stamford tradition: rusti
cated windows, channelling, etc., but all expressed in pape
thinness. The first- and second-floor windows have grace
fully decorated surrounds. To St Mary's Hill a judiciousl
placed terrace with stairs, railings, and cast-iron lamps,
perfect podium for the St Martin's vista. Low vestibule wit
Doric columns opening to a higher staircase beyond.

REGALIA. Silver Wand, said to have been given by Edwar
IV. – Cup, presented in 1650. – Loving Cup, presented i
1658. – Small Mace renewed in 1660. – Large silver-gi
Mace, given in 1678. – Punch Bowl and Ladle, given in 168§
– Waits' Badges, 1705.

MUNICIPAL OFFICES, St Mary's Hill. Mid-Georgian, bui
probably as a private house. In all nine bays. Above an arche
carriageway a Venetian window and a lunette.

PUBLIC LIBRARY, High Street. Once the Shambles. The bi
Tuscan portico evidently influenced by Inigo Jones's Cover
Garden church. When built by *W. Legg* in 1804, it was ope
between the columns.

RAILWAY STATIONS. STAMFORD EAST by *William Hurs*
1856, and one of the best in the county. Tudor with gable
and an asymmetrically placed square tower. – STAMFOR
TOWN, Gothic, and built a little earlier, in 1848. Als
delightfully asymmetrical and picturesque.

BROWNE'S HOSPITAL, Broad Street. This is one of the be
medieval hospitals in England. It was built in the 1480s an
the chapel was consecrated in 1494. William Browne ha
died in 1489. Leland calls him 'a merchant of very wonderfu
richnesse'. The main building is one range along the stree
It consists of the porch and passage behind, the low dormi
tory and altogether living-space of the ten poor men on th

r., with the taller audit room over and the chapel at the E end. The chapel has two tall three-light windows, the audit room five transomed windows, the hall sparser windows. The porch has two big polygonal, castellated buttress posts and a doorway with four-centred head and is panelled inside. Beyond it a SW turret rising higher than the rest. Behind are the premises of 1870, nicely picturesque, especially the W cloister. By *J. Fowler*. Inside, hall and audit room have fireplaces in the middle of their N walls. In the chapel SCREEN for the old men to look through into the chapel. Good, with two-light divisions and ogee arches. – STALLS. With angels on the arm-rests and MISERICORDS of angels, birds, a mermaid, etc. – PLATE. Chalice, given 1635; Paten, by *Robert Jones*(?), 1781.

LORD BURGHLEY'S HOSPITAL, St Martin's. Founded in 1597 on the site of the medieval hospital of St John Baptist and St Thomas Martyr. Of this witness is the E corner of the river-front. Here the arch of a backwater and the flat buttress with some minimum zigzag are Norman. The chronology of the building of 1597 is a little confusing. The building consists of a principal range facing the river and clearly in two parts, a return range on the E side along St Martin's and a detached W range. The W part of the main range has five steep dormers to the river and six high chimneys. The windows are of two lights with straight entablature. To the S there are three gables and four-light windows. The E part of this range and the E range are nondescript in their details, but their masonry, especially to the W, looks older, and in any case they are on top of the Norman remains.* Of the W range also not much can be said.

FRYER'S CALLIS, Kettering Road. By *George Basevi*, 1832. A small-scale essay in the Tudor style.

HOPKIN'S HOSPITAL, St Peter's Street. Gothic of *c.*1770. Attributed to *William Legg* on the basis of a comparison with Casewick Hall (*see* p. 491). The crenellations, pinnacles, and wayward details very jolly. The windows have Y-tracery.

ST PETER'S (or ALL SAINTS) CALLIS, All Saints Street. 1863. Small, one-storeyed, asymmetrical and Gothic. On a corner site.

SNOWDEN'S HOSPITAL, Scotgate. Tudor-Gothic, 1822. By *Thomas Pierce*, the mason, and *R. Goodwin*.

* In the street wall of the E range a small Norman capital is re-set.

TRUESDALE'S HOSPITAL, Scotgate. Also Tudor Gothic an
by *George Basevi*, 1832. A nice interplay of gables, pinnacle
and octagonal chimneyshafts. Ornate barbed quatrefoils i
the gables. The almshouses around a court at the rear.

STAMFORD SCHOOL, St Paul's Street. Little of 1833 and muc
of 1874 (by *Hay & Oliver*). The CHAPEL is what remains o
the parish CHURCH OF ST PAUL. Externally the corbel tabl
the flat E buttress, and the frieze at sill level of the window
show this S wall at once to be Norman, in spite of the extensiv
restorations carried out for the school in 1929–30. Inside, E. I
N arcade of four bays. Round piers, double-chamfered arche
The capitals and E respond have stiff-leaf. – SCULPTURI
Remains of two good C14 figures. – MONUMENTS. Two tom
recesses, one finely moulded, probably of *c.*1300, the othe
coarse. In this a coffin-lid with a black-letter inscriptio
arranged crosswise. It commemorates Henry de Elynsto
jadis parson de sa glyse (cette église).

STAMFORD HIGH SCHOOL FOR GIRLS, St Martin's. B
Edward Browning, 1876. An original design, treating th
stylistic materials freely, especially in the row of even, tal
one-light windows on the first floor – a functionally soun
motif.

BLUECOAT SCHOOL, All Saints Street. A C15 stone arch wit
four-centred head and polygonal turrets and part of an arcad
has been re-set here. It comes from some arcading in front o
Browne's Hospital (cf. also Star Lane, p. 670).

STAMFORD AND RUTLAND HOSPITAL, Deeping Road. Th
earlier range with Gothic centrepiece by *J. P. Gandy*, 182
The linked wings to the E are by *E. Browning*, 1879. To th
W is the WHITEFRIARS' GATE, the only remains of the hous
of the Whitefriars founded in 1260. The front of *c.*135
survives. Four-centred arch with hollow chamfers, steppe
buttresses and canopied niches in them. Also a niche above th
arch. We are told that William Cecil entertained Quee
Elizabeth on the former premises of the Whitefriars, which
credible, as Burghley House was then only in the initial stag
of his great building activity.

ALBERT BRIDGE, Water Street. 1881, in cast iron wit
Romanesque piers. The bridge replaces one of 1836 b
A. Salvin.

TOWN BRIDGE, St Martin's. By *Edward Browning*, 1849. Th
two Tudor houses on the N bank forming part of the com
position are dated 1849.

PERAMBULATION

\) *All Saints' Place – Barn Hill – Broad Street*

ᴸᴸ SAINTS' PLACE can be regarded as the visual hub of
Stamford. From here radiate the main arteries of the town,
and here All Saints church is placed like an axle. On the N
side No. 16 with two nice, gently curving c18 bows. The best
houses are on the E side. No. 1 late c18 and of clean lines.
No. 2 mid c18, three bays, moulded window surrounds, and
projecting eaves cornice. The ground-floor window treatment is unusual: one square window, one thin and pushed-up,
and then a tall thin doorway. No. 3 has a front of c.1730 added
to a house said to be dated 1683. This is the first of the
grander fronts of the town. Five bays, 2–1–2, two floors,
hipped roof, and three segment-headed dormers. The windows have moulded surrounds, the doorway a Gibbsian
surround, borrowed from Batty Langley's *A Sure Guide to
Builders* (1729). From here a view of the length of BARN HILL
can be gained. A vista with nice greenery and undisturbed
by any post-Georgian intrusion. Taking the hill on the l.
first, No. 3 is mid c18, a narrow front with a two-storey bay
and a Chinese fret porch. No. 4 has an early c18 front to a
c17 house. The s end of three bays, and a tall three storeys.
Arched windows to the ground floor set in an arcade. The N
end with wide windows and a pedimented doorcase. Nos 5–6
are c17 and c18, the latter punctuated by a c17 canted bay

with Georgian Gothic lights. Next comes BARN HIL
HOUSE, originally medieval, but rebuilt in the late C17 an
fitted-out in the C18, and then provided with a neo-classica
front about 1843 (date on a rainwater head). One would lik
to know the architect of the front. Five bays pushed to th
middle, two storeys, and a finely proportioned cornice. Abov
this is a low attic storey with windows punctuated by pseudo
pilasters and at the ends simulated Roman altars wit
bucrania swagged with fruit and drapery. Of the single-store
Doric tetrastyle porch the back wall is strangely reactionar
with its rusticated entrance. Beautifully crisp acanthus scroll
to the base of the windows. In the garden a mid-C18 GAZEBO
and in the NW corner a rusticated entrance beneath the ol
town wall. STUKELEY HOUSE opposite is on the site of th
house of William Stukeley, the antiquary. It is of three bay
with tripartite windows gently arched over the middle par
On the ground floor they have rusticated surrounds, on th
upper floor 'Batty Langley' Gothic shafts. Early C19 Gree
Doric porch. Later Georgian 'Batty Langley' Goth
windows. *George Portwood*'s design of 1741 for this house ha
the characteristics of the 'Stamford Style' and suggests tha
he was the leading architect in the town. Nothing remains o
Stukeley's enchanting garden. Returning down the hill, o
the l. No. 10, dated 1807, yet still with rusticated windo
surrounds and rusticated quoins. Just behind this is the BAR
HILL CHAPEL, dated 1810. Again of remarkable conser
vatism. Central doorway set between big pilasters and wit
heavy flat architrave. Arched windows to r. and l. and
Venetian window above. Inset plaques of Faith, Hope, an
Charity. Then the regrettable METHODIST CHURCH of 188
by *J. T. Ward*, Gothic, recessed and asymmetrical. No. 12
late C17, five bays, two floors, dormers with triangula
pediments and panelled ashlar chimneystacks. Entrance i
one end bay with big double-curved pediment on beauti
fully carved brackets. Then No. 13, one of the best houses i
town; dated on a rainwater head 1740. Perhaps it is a litt
too good to be by Portwood; for the details are first-class an
the window spacing is very subtle. Five bays, two floor
rusticated quoins, moulded modillion cornice, and ped
mented dormers. The ground-floor windows have Gibbsia
surrounds and keystoned heads, those on the first floo
moulded lugged surrounds and triangular pediments. Al
pedimented the doorway with flattish pilasters. The elevatio

50b

is repeated at Leasingham Manor (*see* p. 592). The interior is of the highest provincial quality. Carved chimneypieces and an upper room with delicately carved dados, overdoors, and window reveals. Next, No. 14, is a severe early C19 front, and No. 15 varies the same theme. Then No. 16, the earliest house on Barn Hill, late C16 or early C17, with two ranges of upright (lengthened?) two-light windows. Doorway with four-centred arch and a later stone dated 1695. No. 17 is late C18; a broad expanse of wall between two shallow bows.

rom All Saints' Place, Crown Street and Red Lion Street are like two legs. Go down Crown Street. At its end is BROAD STREET, the widest thoroughfare in the town and nearly perfect visually. On the N side Browne's Hospital dominates, on the S side the unsympathetic Central Cinema. Taking the N side, that is l., first, No. 1 is a mid-C18 refronting of a C17 house. Three bays, lower floors with later C18 canted bays, Gothic glazing bars, and a Tuscan porch. Raised terrace in front with railings and urn-topped piers. No. 2 is dated 1830. Big canted bays through both storeys, firmly locked at the angles by giant fluted pilasters banded with rustication. It is this type of giant pilasters – French Henri II rather than classical – where the late date betrays itself. C17 bits at the rear and one chimneystack that suggests a late C17 version of Artisan-Mannerism (cf. 19 St George's Square). No. 3 is late C17 with a plain four-bay, late C18 front. Then past Browne's Hospital to Nos 5–8 of the early C19. After that, No. 9 is later C18, eight bays, cornice and hipped roof, No. 14 of the 1740s. Five closely fenestrated bays with a heavy cornice. The upper windows with Gibbs rustication, the lower ones moulded with a five-part keystone. No. 15 also of five bays but a little later. No. 19 has a well proportioned mid-C18 front. Two bays, stone cornice and blocking course. On to Star Lane (*see* p. 670). Returning back along the S side, first Nos 25, 28, 30, a low C18 group, each of three bays and two storeys with variations in the doorways. In No. 25 it is to the r. of bay three, in No. 28 in bay one, in No. 30 in bay two. Then No. 32, which is early C17 with gables over two-storey canted bays and with four lights to their fronts. To the l. another, but a timber-framed gable. No. 33 is dated 1704, but the front is probably later. Flat raised window surrounds; triple keystones. No. 34 is a tall late C18 house with projecting, almost square bays and a mansard roof. Then a stretch of mediocrity; but note the former CORN EXCHANGE, 1839 by the *Rev. Henry*

De Foe Baker. Flat front, basically classical, but with Goth
details. And also note the endearing silhouette of Nos 50–5
The mansard roof is faintly ogee in outline. It looks Restoratio
but is probably Georgian. So on to All Saints' Place again.

(B) *All Saints' Place – High Street – St Paul's Street*

Along HIGH STREET. On the N side, that is l., Nos 6–7 a
late C17 with C18 upper floors. No. 7 has an undulatin
bowed front. No. 8 is of the 1760s, only the upper floor pr
served. Red brick – a rarity at Stamford – and three bays
tall balconied windows. Lunette window above, and bri
trim. A good staircase. Next are Nos 11–12 of the late C1
with half-hipped gables, nicely crooked, and Nos 14–17, a
unusual terrace group, in all twelve bays and three floors. T
bolection surrounds of the windows are continuous with t
strings, an 'Artisan' trait (cf. No. 19 St George's Square
Then Nos 18–19 with the two-floor upper part mid C1
Moulded surrounds and a panelled parapet. Six bays. C1
Corinthian shop-front below. No. 21 is dated 1732. To t
High Street only two bays, but with giant fluted angle pilaste
and over-heavy alternating rustication to the window su
rounds. The treatment goes on round the corner, in IRO1
MONGER STREET. Five bays divided by pilasters 2–1–2,
curiously jazzy Palladian effect. In Ironmonger Street litt
needs notice. Nos 9–10 are Georgian, seven bays and thr
storeys. No. 9 has a nice early C19 shop front. Nos 12–14 a
one composition, random rubble, early C19, very plain, fo
times three bays and the return into Broad Street. Back
High Street to No. 24, a modern shop but with a C13 cry
below. It has a quadripartite rib-vault. One oddly dividi
rib on the door bay. No. 26 has a shop-front with Tusc
columns. Then past the Public Library to No. 30, one bay on
It must be by the same hand as the Scotgate Inn (*see* p. 67
probably with the use of *Blashfield*'s terracotta. No. 41, on t
other side, faces down the High Street and is fully conscio
of it. It is mid Georgian with quoins of alternating siz
and over the middle a pediment raised out of the centre
the parapet. Then in ST PAUL'S STREET, continuing on t
same side, first for a moment into STAR LANE to sample t
CONGREGATIONAL CHURCH of 1819. Brick, four by thr
bays, with all windows arched, but on the r. a Tudorish gat
way. (From here one can go on to the end of Broad Stre
see p. 669.) Then, in St Paul's Street Nos 7–9, mainly C1

stone and timber-framing and much altered. Early fronts
continue to No. 12. The roofs an almost continuous stretch
of Collyweston slating. No. 11 is early C16 with five-light
windows on the ground floor and the arms of the Bakers'
Company. Dated 1715. No. 12 looks later C16, two gables,
moulded brackets, canted bays. A gable is dated 1663. Past
the School to No. 24, a C17 gabled front marked by a delicate
pink-brick façade of three bays. Three storeys, parapet and
stone enrichments. If one continues to the fork at the end of
the street, one comes to the Whitefriars' Gateway, *see* p. 676
Instead we cross over to the s side of St Paul's Street to the
C13 BRASENOSE GATE, rebuilt here in 1688 from the site of
Brasenose College near by. It is much mutilated. Richly
shafted jambs with stiff-leaf capitals. Very elaborate, deep
mouldings. Then, walking back to St Paul's Street, on the s
side, we come to BRAZENOSE HOUSE, a house of *c.*1688,
rebuilt in 1723. The front of six bays and two storeys, with
hipped roof and dormers. Windows with fluted keystones.
Inside is a competently detailed staircase with twisted
balusters. Then No. 31, early C18, of three bays and three
storeys. Nos 32–33 have canted bays and mullioned windows
and are similar to No. 12 opposite. Next to No. 35 is the old
CONDUIT. Two arched openings and rocky-rusticated face.
Nos 41–42 are early C18, of seven bays, with moulded cornice,
hipped roof, and quoins. No. 44 is of the same date. Don't
turn into St George's Street; for this *see* p. 676. Instead now
along the s side of the HIGH STREET to Nos 46–50, a mid-
C18 front to a once large C14 house. The doorway has continuous mouldings and head stops. The inside is mostly C18
with a large hall and chimneypiece of this date. No. 51 with
an early C18 doorway but a C17 straight-sided bay window
with mullioned windows. After that St Michael's church.
Then No. 53, C17; a gabled roof and massive projecting
stacks. Nos 54–55 are mid C18; rusticated quoins, moulded
window surrounds, and a parapet. No. 57 is an early C18
three-bay front with an eaves cornice on carved brackets.
No. 59 of the same date. Then LLOYDS BANK in the palazzo
style, far from pure; 1880, by *W. Talbot Brown.*

*All Saints' Place – Scotgate – Rutland Terrace – St Peter's
Street – All Saints' Street*

Along SCOTGATE, first, after a while, on the l., a Victorian
pub with a brick and terracotta façade. The detail of a robust

gaiety and probably made of *Blashfield*'s terracotta. Pa
Truesdale's and Snowden's Hospitals to the site of S
CLEMENT'S GATE, marked by a pier dated 1780. This is
the corner of North Street. Yet further along ROCK TERRAC
an ambitious row of 1841, really the stables of ROCK HOUS
opposite (now a garage). This sumptuous villa was built
1842 for Richard Newcombe. The architect is unknown.
is an unusually vigorous example of late (and free) classicisr
On the hill to the N is an C18 GATEWAY, the remains
a noted picturesque villa garden. Opposite is FOUNDR
ROAD, to be recommended for a view of Stamford's spire
Then back as far as St Clement's pier and now s into WES
STREET, where remains a round WALL TOWER and a t
of the town walls. Turn round it and go into St Peter's Stree
But here first turn r. to see RUTLAND TERRACE, a stucce
fronted speculative job of the 1820s, facing the gentle Wellar
meadows. Thirty bays with arched entrances, cast-ire
balconies, incised pilasters, and crisp anthemion ornament
Then, turning E on the S side of ST PETER'S STREET
Hopkin's Hospital (*see* p. 665), and s of this MELANCHOL
VALE with the picturesquely placed FREEMAN'S COTTAGE
They are dated 1838, an example of late Vernacular wi
mansard roofs. Back to St Peter's Street. On the s side, No.
is dated 1663. It has a gabled canted bay window with a thre
light front. No. 26 opposite is EXETER COURT, a small ear
C18 range of dwellings. Nos 8–9 are dated 1804. Then No.
or WILLIAMSON'S CALLIS;‡ C17. Inside, robustly cru
plasterwork with animals, fruit, and also Susanna and t
Elders. On the N side, Nos 31–32 are on the site of Sem
ringham Hall.§ They are now a garage. In a store-shed is
pair of pointed C15 doorways, in a position as if they h
been the entries to kitchen and offices from a screens passag
No. 33 is dated 1660, but has a Georgian front. No. 35 al
C17, with a canted bay window (four-light front) and a gab
No. 36 is late C16, and No. 38 probably of the same da
behind a later front. Then the street debouches into S
PETER'S HILL, once surrounding St Peter's church. T
church was demolished in 1560. St Peter's Hill boasts

* In fact replacing an earlier group of terraced houses, if Nattes's view
to be believed.

‡ Callis means an Almshouse. Williamson's Callis no longer has t
function.

§ That is the Stamford hostel of Sempringham Abbey.

delightful range of Stamfordian bay windows of all shapes and sizes. From the SW corner, No. 3 is early C17 with the deep canted bay intact on the ground floor only. No. 5 also C17 with canted bay and gable. No. 6 is later, with a bay to the l. It has four lights in the front. The side to St Peter's Street has timber-framing. Then on the N side the old STAMFORD INSTITUTION or the CAMERA OBSCURA HOUSE, built in 1842 in a Graeco-Egyptian by *Edward Browning*, before he turned Goth. Three bays, two storeys, emphatic string, emphatic cornice, and balustrade. The lower windows arched in square recesses with an oddly placed row of modillions. Doorway with tapered frame and triangular pediment projecting above the string. Tall upper-storey windows and formerly a cupola. Into ALL SAINTS' STREET. Here, most of what is interesting is on the N side. The WHEATSHEAF INN and No. 15 are early C17. Two gables to the r., one over a canted bay. To the l. a square bay shorn of the gable and done up with C18 quoins. No. 21, at the end, is late C16, but has to the E a tall thin early C19 bow providing the perfect vertical counterpart to the tower and spire of All Saints.

) *All Saints' Place – Sheepmarket – Austin Street – St Peter's Vale – Bath Row.*

From All Saints' Square down Horseshoe Lane to the SHEEP-MARKET, or else this perambulation can be a direct continuation from St Peter's Hill, at the end of Perambulation C. On the l. a C14 gateway with pointed arch, perhaps a POSTERN of the castle. The bus WAITING ROOM has a front re-erected from the High Street. Square bay to the r., canted bay to the l. with gables, one of them dated 1661. Two-, five-, and six-light windows. On through St Peter's Hill, where we have been before, and, from its SW angle, into AUSTIN STREET, with some of the best undisturbed Vernacular in town. The surprise is AUSTIN HOUSE. A bleak sophisticated front to the street. A bracketed bow window over the entrance right up to and beyond the roof-line. In contrast the garden front is the prettiest of Stamford. Pairs of elegant bows through both floors and Gothic glazing bars. In the centre an arched window topped with a pediment like a Chinese hat. Beneath it a porch with fluted columns at first-floor level reached by T-shaped dividing steps. Now to the l. into KINGS MILL LANE for more visual delights. First VALE HOUSE, C17 and C18, and then KINGS MILL HOUSE, with early bits

and a C19 front perhaps by *Browning*. Round the corner is the
lovely ST PETER'S VALE, a triangular Green with early C19
cottages. To the meadow side the KING'S MILL of c.1700.
Then along BATH ROW with attractive cottages, past a C18
POSTERN of the castle (after No. 13) to BATH HOUSE, C18
Gothick, perhaps by *Legg*, and in the spirit of Hopkin's
Hospital (e.g. with the same Y-tracery) and then to the corner
of Castle Dyke, where the castle wall with its blank arches
appears (*see* p. 663). Yet further to the E is BROOKS COURT,
an early C19 cul-de-sac. From here alleys wind to Castle
Street and to St Mary's Hill and so back to All Saints' Place.

(E) *All Saints' Place – Red Lion Square – St Mary's Street – St*
George's Square

Straight into RED LION SQUARE. The building on the S side
has an early C19 Ionic shop-front and a Tuscan shop-front
whose columns look as if they might be re-used. Above, the
curious octagonal cupola must be noticed and the proportions which suggest a rebuilt medieval hall. Inside indeed
the much-disguised remains of a timber-framed space, early
C18 door surrounds, and medieval fragments. Down to St
John's Street round the church and into ST MARY'S STREET.
On the r. is No. 44, dated 1656. Canted bay window and
gable. Further on No. 40, a timber-framed house with overhanging upper floor, dating probably from c.1500. Then come
two long early C19 speculative builders' façades in coursed
rubble. On the N side No. 4 has a charming early C19 shop-
front. Two shallow bows and a nicely undulating cornice
(No. 5 has another bow, and No. 6 a medieval buttress,
MHLG) No. 10 also has a shop with two bows. Nos 13 and 14
again shops, but these are Early Victorian and statelier, with
Ionic columns. They are identical and quite impressively
flank the entry to a cul-de-sac. No. 15 is early C18. Next the
STAMFORD HOTEL, a lavish job by *J. L. Bond*, begun in 1810
and not finished until 1829. It is one of the grandest of
Regency hotels. Nine bays and three storeys with a noble
range of giant Corinthian columns set *in antis* to seven bays
of the first and second floors. Above the fine entablature is a
figure of Justice by *J. Rossi*. Both architect and sculptor were
London men. The interior retains a good oval staircase with
a circular lantern. No. 20 is mid C18, No. 21 early C19 with
Gothic windows and doors, Nos 22–24 a first-rate group of
c.1740, perhaps by *Portwood*. No. 22 of five bays and two

storeys with lugged upper-floor windows and hipped roof.
The Gibbsian doorway identical with No. 3 All Saints' Place.
An oddity is the string dropping below the base of the
windows. No. 23 is of five bays but with shallower details and
a pedimented door on fluted Ionic pilasters. Finally No. 24
repeats the ground-floor windows of No. 22, completing a
triumvirate of varied façades by the same builder. On the s
side No. 27 is a Georgian coursed rubble range like No. 12
St Mary's Hill. Next to it the old THEATRE, dated 1768.
Broad doorways and broken pediment. Above this an arched
and alternatingly rusticated window. To the l. and r. on the
ground floor a doorway and square window, and above these
a pair of lugged windows. (Inside one fine Ionic doorcase
with broken pediment. MHLG) No. 28, ST MARY'S REC-
TORY, has a much altered C17 core. On the exterior a blocked
early C13 twin window with round sub-arches and a round
super-arch and C13 masonry fragments. Then No. 29
(supposed to have a medieval undercroft). Then turn back and
now have a look at the three houses facing down St Mary's
Street. They are treated as one. From l. to r. two bays, then
two bays with a canted bay window, then three bays with
a doorway in the centre. Common to the three units the parapet with urns and the curious doorways with open triangular
pediments. Making a diversion N to MAIDEN LANE, No. 9
is C16 (see the remains of mullioned and transomed windows),
but has an earlier oriel with a C15 oak shield of the Digby
family. Nos 4–6 are late C16 with three canted bays and gables.
eturn to St Mary's Street and turn SE into ST GEORGE'S
SQUARE, grouped, like many of the Stamford squares,
around its church, a composition rural rather than urban.
On the w side the return elevation of No. 27 St Mary's Street,
and next door to this in the SW angle the ASSEMBLY ROOMS
of 1725. Plain pilasters at the ends, tall entrance with pilasters
alternately blocked, and blank recessed moulded arches in
the bays between. A grand room behind, but evidently the
work of a builder unable to handle large spaces. Coved ceiling,
bracketed cornice, and big chimneypiece with crusty decoration. The upper part of the doorways with curious half-
pilasters scrolled at the base, a C17 rather than C18 form.
No. 21 is of c.1740. Four bays, keystoned windows, and a
later Greek Doric doorcase. (At the back a good balcony on
cast-iron pillars. MHLG) No. 20 has a mid-C18 front and five
chaste bays. Unmoulded window surrounds, doorway on

Doric pilasters. (At the back mullioned and transomed wir
dows. MHLG) Then No. 19 of the Artisan-Mannerist typ
the type that occurs in the surrounding district, particular
at Thorney Abbey by John Lovin, the Peterborough builde
and at Lyndon Hall Rutland by John Sturgis (1671). No. 1
is said to be dated 1675. The silhouette follows a Lo
Countries pattern with two rows of dormer windows, a
uncommon type in England. To accommodate this the roof
unusually high in relation to the front below. This is of on
six bays and two storeys. To one side the door with broke
scrolled pediment. As on Nos 14–17 High Street, the strin
continue around the windows as a moulding. The chimne
stacks are the *leitmotif* of this Artisan style. Groups of four
six, rusticated with simulated pilasters and blank arche
The rear elevation with timber divisions and infilling. T
fenestration is wilful. The rooms with much C17 joinery a
three robust chimneypieces, all in stone and all with f
Ionic pilasters, a pulvinated frieze and wide shelf. No. 18
mid C18 of five bays and just a little more sophisticated tha
was usual at Stamford. Inside a hall with excellent joiner
(No. 17 has a medieval buttress and half an arch. MHLG) N
14–15 are grouped around a courtyard open to the N. Th
are said to be the remains of the WHITEFRIARS COLLEG
E wing with two gables, one rebuilt. Dormers to the s win
The w wing looks C16 and has remains of blocked window
in its E face. On the N side of the E wing a tiny oriel, a kind
spy-window, triangular in plan. On the N side of the Squar
starting w again, that is with the return front from No.
St Mary's Lane. A small court forms an L to the main win
The front has blank arcades to the ground floor, architrav
windows, and a big Venetian window with a pediment.
may be by *George Portwood*, as it resembles his Stukel
design of 1741.* Next door, No. 1, is a grand essay in little a
said to be dated 1730. Three bays of ground-floor window
with rusticated heads, and the upper windows with lugg
architraves – all from Batty Langley. Above these a bro
fascia board with carved brackets and carved rosettes on t
eaves cornice. Above this again, a steep hipped roof with to
heavy dormers. Then Nos 2–4, cottages of the same da
but plainer. Round the corner, that is in ST GEORGE
STREET, Nos 17–18 which are mid C18. No. 17 has an aps
door-hood. To the E, in ST LEONARD'S STREET, No.

* But cf. also the similar theatre.

has a gable and a canted bay, No. 61 a date 1685. Opposite the
OLIVE BRANCH inn, dated 1666. Tall three-storey canted
bay and gable. Here this even walk must be interrupted and
a trip interpolated which is more convenient if done by car.
bout ½ m. out, in PRIORY ROAD, past some nicely placed and
grouped housing of 1911 by *J. H. Bowman*, are the impressive
remains of ST LEONARD'S PRIORY, a Benedictine cell
founded in 1082. What survives is part of the w front of the
church and the N arcade. It does not belong to 1082, though
partly to the early C12. The w front is later, but of the N
arcade piers three and four and their arches are heavy and
sturdy and have the characteristic capitals with few scallops.
Round piers, square abaci with nicked corners, arches of one
step and one half-roll. To the w an extension took place
towards the end of the C12, and to this belong piers one and
two (undetailed moulded capitals and on the w respond
stiff-leaf; more mouldings in the arches) and the w front
with a portal and blank single arches l. and r. which have
shafts with stiff-leaf crockets, but still round arches with the
most exuberant geometrical forms of Late Norman decoration.
Above an arcade of seven narrow blank arches with zigzag
and three windows set in it, and then in the gable an almond-
shaped window. One clerestory window is preserved in the
earlier part. The s side never had an aisle. It is blank with
shallow buttresses. Back after this to the w end of St Leonard's
Street and up N in St George's Street. No. 24 is C17, with a
canted bay, and so we are back in the High Street.

) *St Mary's Place – St Mary's Hill – Belton Street – St Martin's
– Burghley Lane – Barnack Road*

T MARY'S PLACE is of a dog-leg shape, s and E of St Mary's
church. The ensemble is a perfect expression of Georgian
elegance. No. 1 is plain C18. No. 2 of *c.*1740 strikes a grander
note. Five bays, two storeys, pitched roof and dormers. The
ground floor with treatment of blank arcading. Two arched
windows, then a pedimented door, then one arched window
and one arched doorway. Another bay to the l. of later
addition. Banded giant pilasters to the angles. Upper windows
with Gibbsian surrounds (cf. Nos 66–67 St Martin's). No. 3
is of the same date but has a taller elevation and is less
sophisticated. Two bays and two storeys divided by superimposed Doric pilasters. The lugged and keystoned windows
similar to those on No. 38 St Martin's. Round the corner,

No. 4 is late C18 and adjoins the return front of the town hall.
Below are the remains of an ambitious rib-vaulted area. One
bay sexpartite and probably C14.

Into ST MARY'S HILL with the curvaceous view up and along
St Martin's, the terrace of the town hall as its podium. This
is perhaps one of the best examples of Georgian townscape in
England. On the E side first the Municipal Offices. On the W
side, SCOTNEY'S shop (No. 13) has a quadripartite vault on
angle brackets with faces and a central pillar. The date is
c.1220. Exits on the street side show the early levels. No. 12 is
mid C18 in the style of the municipal offices. Then No. 1
incorporates the remains of a Norman house – the misnamed
Packhorse Arch. This arch of c.1150 with its zigzag at r.
angles to the wall surface leads to ST MARY'S PASSAGE
(exit from Bath Row, see Perambulation D) and is really the
doorway of the house. Behind it part of a shallow arch and a
long dividing wall running N–S. Nos 8–9 are early C17 with
timber-framed overhangs. To the E of the bridge and fronting
the river is a row of C17 WAREHOUSES. Their W termination
is the Tudor lodge of 1849 by the bridge (see p. 666). Along
WHARF ROAD, for a diversion to the remains of a wall BAS-
TION. Then the monumental archway to Messrs C. Gray &
Co, once BLASHFIELD'S TERRACOTTA WORKS. It is late
classical and looks c.1840–5. Further along in BELTON
STREET are the remains of a C17 house in the vernacular
style with mullioned windows. Then, returning back to the
bridge and crossing it, into ST MARTIN'S. First the E side.
Nos 8–10 are minor early C18. No. 11 is C17 with a canted
bay under a gable. This appears to be the house shown by
John Buckler as having had a Norman zigzag doorway. Nos
13–14 are minor early C18, and No. 18 plain late C18. Beyond
the church, No. 20 again early C18. Two bays to the l. with
arched windows on the ground floor, three bays to the r.
with a doorway framed by Tuscan columns. In an upstairs
room fragments of C17 floral decoration. Then, Nos 21–2
are early C17 with canted bays. Next a GARAGE with bits
that might be by *William Legg*,* and then No. 24, early C18,
a well proportioned house of three bays with an arched rusticated doorway. Beneath, a C13 quadripartite vault on corbels
with faces. No. 25 is mid C18. Then comes the turn to Burghley House (see *The Buildings of England: Northamptonshire*)
and then the C17 BULL AND SWAN inn. A pair of canted bays

* A C13 pier has been encased during internal alterations; MHLG.

windows, tall gables, and a third larger timber-framed gable over the arch to the N. The windows of four lights to the front below and five with a transom above. Beyond the school, No. 30 is mid C18 with a later balcony supported on the r. by a single Greek Doric column and on the l. by such a Doric porch. No. 31 is Neo-Georgian, No. 32, of the mid C18, has three irregular bays. Its acanthus keystones are duplicated next door (No. 33). This is a spread-out house of five-bays, 2–1–2, with a pitched roof, dormers, and rusticated stacks. The treatment of the angles is odd. First quoins, then superimposed Corinthian and Ionic orders of pilasters in an Artisan Mannerism, all in blatant incomprehension of correct ways to emphasize angles. Also odd is the upper quoining to the l., where an ogee scroll drops down to the level of the adjacent house. No. 34 is C18 now, but the front has earlier masonry and traces of earlier windows. No. 35 of c.1740. Five bays, two storeys, rusticated windows, a carved cornice, and a Gibbs-type doorway. No. 36 of the same date and proportions. Nos 37–38 are really four houses converted into one and mostly mid C18. Two bays, two bays, then a balanced five bays with moulded window surrounds, quoins, and parapet, then a high two-storey front with superimposed pilasters (cf. No. 3 St Mary's Place), finally a timber-framed porch added in 1884. In BURGHLEY LANE is one early C18 house with a hooded porch on carved foliage brackets. If one follows St Martin's out of the town, one gets to *Legg*'s monumental w gate lodges of Burghley House.

ck to the w side of St Martin's, returning down the hill. Nos 39–40 are early C17 with three canted bays rising and breaking above the roof. Four-light mullioned windows; the doorway with apsed hood on carved brackets a later C17 addition. No. 40 is the same date and visually part of the same composition. Its single canted bay with ten lights (one–two–four–two–one). Then first a C19 Tudor porch, and then a mid C18 front, before No. 42, of three bays, with tripartite windows and a doorway with pediment on pilasters.

he Kettering Road here turns w and leads to Wothorpe (*see The Buildings of England: Northamptonshire*). On the way, ⅝ m. out, up a lane (or drift) to the r. CLARE LODGE, c.1850 by *E. Browning*, built for himself. A large asymmetrical Tudor villa, with wooden, overhanging gables *à la française* rather than in the vernacular of England. Stone balustrade with a very big fleur-de-lis pattern. (Re-used ecclesiastical fragments.)

If we now continue our examination of St Martin's, No. 4
is of the mid C18, and No. 46 of the late C18. No. 47 agai
early C18, with three widely spaced bays, arched doorway
in between, and the ground-floor windows with unusual fla
leathery surrounds. The windows have excessively larg
keystones. No. 51 has an early C18 front, but pre-C17 wor
at the rear. No. 52 is C17 but converted to C19 Gothi
although the canted bays and gables and windows of the uppe
part look faithful restorations. It carries a date 1854. No. 5
is mid C18, rendered, No. 54 is dated 1882 and overlook
the railway, which crosses here below St Martin's and i
exemplarily hidden. No. 55 is dated 1868 and is probably b
the same hand as No. 56. Both have shaped gables. Fror
this point is the best vista in St Martin's, curving down an
terminating with the tower of St Mary's church. Progressin
along to Nos 59-60, late C18, then to Nos 61-63, the Burghle
Estate Office and an intrusion in the Tudoresque style b
J. B. Corby, 1879. Symmetrical r. part with two gable
asymmetrical l. part where the canted bay window is not eve
in line with the gable. Beyond this the Stamfordian theme
continue. Nos 64-65 are C17 and are followed by the ambitiou
fronts of Nos 66-67, a pair of houses each of four bays wit
alternately rusticated pilasters at the angles, a dividing one i
the centre, blocking course and parapet. On the ground floc
the order of windows and doors is window-door-five
windows-door-window. The windows have alternating rust
cation. On the upper floor they have moulded surrounds an
lugged corners. Next comes the complex GEORGE HOTE
The street front to the l. is irregular C18 with a C16 doorwa
(leaf in the spandrels) and a bulging, probably C19, ba
window squashed in one angle. Adjoining this is a three
storey, five-bay front with a rainwater head dated 1728. O
the N side and at the rear are C17 bits, and the court at th
back is mid C18 of three storeys with two canted bay window
The interior is now a maze of alterations. There is one amb
tious C18 stone chimneypiece and, in the gentlemen
lavatory, part of a wooden screen that might be C14. Tw
doors lead through it. To its N a large fireplace. Close to th
site, a little to the S, were the House of the Holy Sepulchr
(Augustinian Canons) and the Chapel of Mary Magdalen
A date of *c.*1592 has been suggested for the first main hot
(or hostelry) building. From this point a last diversion, N b
the bridge, to WATER STREET, where WELLAND HOUSE

five bays is mid C18 and No. 12 has three bays, moulded
windows, and pedimented pilastered door. Behind these are
late C18 and early C19 MALTINGS, one big building behind
No. 14 dated 1793 and another 1865. N of these maltings is
LUMLEY'S TERRACE, once belonging to them and probably
early C19 maltsters' dwellings. Two tall blocks flank an
entrance opening to a narrow court of single-storey cottages.*
Back across the bridge and to our start.

ROMAN ROAD. A section of ERMINE STREET runs s of
Quarry Farm. It is a clearly traceable stretch from its diver-
gence from the Great North Road, whence it goes s for over
1000 yds until it disappears beneath the modern spread of
the town. The N portion is represented by a broad bank, 30 ft
wide and 4 ft high, but over much of its length the bank has
been considerably reduced by cultivation.

STAPLEFORD

ALL SAINTS. Built in 1770 (Cox), but the w tower is older in
its masonry and has worked into it fragments such as small
E.E. polygonal shafts, two heads of two-light Dec windows,
and some small heads from label-stops. The date of the tower
is given by the arch towards the nave, which, with its keeled
responds and nailhead, is late C13. Tiled pyramid roof,
probably from the restoration of 1903–4. Inside two more
architectural survivals, a scalloped Norman capital and a
Norman pillar piscina with horizontally zigzagged shaft.
The building of 1770 is of red brick. The nave windows are
pointed; the chancel windows have round, keyed-in arches. –
BENCHES. With simple poppy-heads; C16 or C17. – COM-
MUNION RAIL. Simple, C18. – Also a HELM in the chancel.
– PLATE. Chalice and Cover, by *R.H.*, 1689.

STOKE ROCHFORD see SOUTH STOKE

STRAGGLETHORPE

ST MICHAEL. The church has an Anglo-Saxon w wall, see the
triangle-headed doorway and the round-headed opening
over. All the rest may be one Transitional job, mixing up
round and pointed arches and Norman and E.E. motifs.
To try for any chronological sequence makes no sense. The

* These are now demolished.

church is small, of nave and chancel in one with a double
bellcote, E.E. and altered Dec when the w buttress wa
erected and provided with its delightful little niche. The tw
chancel E windows are lancet-shaped but round-arched,* th
fragment of a pillar piscina is purely Norman. Round-heade
also the N aisle E window, the slightly chamfered N doorway
and the N arcade of two bays with round piers carryin
elementary E.E. capitals. The arches however, though round
are double-chamfered. The S doorway is pointed, but stil
has a billet frieze. The church has a happily unchange
interior, crowded and alive. – FONT. Drum-shaped, Norman
with blank arches on colonnettes. – BENCH ENDS. Minor, a
the w end. – BOX PEWS and two-decker PULPIT. – PAINTING
Adoration of the Magi, demi-figures, Veneto, early C16, in
fine Baroque acanthus frame. – PLATE. Chalice and Cove
by *Edward Holaday*, 1716. – MONUMENT. Richard Earl
† 1697. By *Green* of Camberwell. Tablet, black and whit
marble. Two busts in front of pilasters. Drapes pulled up t
reveal the following poem:

> Stay, Reader and observe Death's partial doom
> A spreading virtue in a narrow Tomb,
> A generous Mind mingled with common Dust,
> Like Burnish'd Steel cover'd and left in Rust
> Darke in the Earth he lies, in whom did Shine
> All the Divided Merits of his Line,
> The Lustre of his Name seems faded here,
> No fairer Star in all that fruitful Sphere
> In Piety and Parts extremely Bright;
> Clear was his Youth and filled with Growing light;
> A morn that promised much, Yet saw no Noon
> None ever Rose so fast, and Set so soon
> All lines of Worth were center'd here in One.
> But see, he lies in Shades, whose Life had none
> But while the Mother this sad Structure rears
> A double Dissolution there Appears
> He into Dust dissolves, She into Tears.

STRAGGLETHORPE HALL. What is modern and what is old
now difficult to decide. In any case the C20 restorations hav
produced a wholly successful effect. The plan is basically
late Elizabethan H with a symmetrical front. Old wor
includes the chimney-flank on the N front, the screens passag
and a good late C17 staircase with thick twisted balusters an
big globular finials.

* An oblong low-side window in the S wall.

STROXTON

9030

LL SAINTS. *Charles Kirk* in 1874–5 rebuilt the chancel and
made it a very handsome composition. E.E. with a saddleback roof to the w tower. Nave and aisles whose lean-to
roofs are almost one with the nave roof. Lower chancel. All
covered with Collyweston stone slates. Inside, the Norman
chancel arch re-used as the tower arch. The responds have
scallop capitals, the arch has one step, one slight chamfer,
and a bold half-roll. The N arcade of two bays is E.E. Round
pier, double-chamfered round arches. The capitals were left
unworked. A few more original bits re-used, e.g. parts of a
lancet and a blank quatrefoil from a two-light window. –
PLATE. Chalice and Paten Cover, by *John Morley* of Lincoln,
1569. – MONUMENT. William Blyth † 1648. Altar-like base
and back panel with achievement. No figure.

.ANOR HOUSE, some distance SE of the church. Mid C17,
with a two-storey front and chimneystacks growing from the
end elevations. On the upper floor four regularly-set two-
light windows. In grey stone, constrasting happily with the
brick of the outbuildings.

STUBTON

8040

T MARTIN. 1799, with an unfortunate chancel of 1869 and
equally unfortunate windows made correct at that time. The
Georgian church stands s of the Hall and visible from it and
is decently ashlar-faced. It was rock-facing for the Victorian
gothicist. The Georgian building has a w tower and a low w
porch, both with a pierced quatrefoil parapet and pinnacles.
The interior has lost its Georgian character entirely. – PLATE.
Chalice and Paten Cover, by *S.H.*, 1683; Paten, by *John
Fawdery*, 1699.

ᴛUBTON HALL. A sketch of 1805 shows a gabled C17 house
with C18 offices. The present Hall carries a plaque: 'This
house was erected by Robert and Amelia Heron in the years
1813–14, *Jeffry Wyatt* Architect', i.e. Sir Jeffry Wyatville.
The house is a simple five- by three-bay block of grey
brick with, on the s front, a shallow bow and, r. and l., tripartite windows under blank segmental arches – a typical
Wyatt motif. The elegant porch, a semicircle of delicate
Tuscan columns paired against the wall, is said to be an
addition from another house, perhaps Fenton Hall or Beckingham Park. From the latter came the heavy Tuscan early C19

portico on the N front. There are now modern additions
adapt the house to a school, including the conversion of th
C18 offices. The enclosure to the S was the MENAGERIE. I
doorway came from Fenton Hall. Tuscan pilasters and duck
billed pediment with a rustic bouquet of carving. Perhaps
the early C17.

HOME FARM. Gables crazily decorated in black and whi
pattern. Dated 1697.

RECTORY. 1857 by *David Brandon*.

SUDBROOKE HALL *and* VILLAGE *see* ANCASTER

2020

SURFLEET

ST LAURENCE. Ashlar-faced, not big, and externally most
Perp. The W tower however, which leans considerably,
probably Dec. Recessed spire with one tier of lucarnes. Tw
light bell-openings. W doorway with fine continuous moul
ings. The aisle windows are all Perp, but again, below th
battlements and pinnacles, at least on the S side, runs a ba
flower frieze which must be Dec. This frieze continues on th
S porch. The entrance of this anyway has a re-used piece
C13 dog-tooth. The S doorway is Dec too. Continuo
mouldings. Perp chancel E window.* Remodelled domesti
looking N and S windows. Perp clerestory. Now for the arcad
inside. Four bays. Piers quatrefoil with slim filleted shafts
the diagonals, i.e. Dec rather than Perp. Dec also the sun
quadrant mouldings of the arches, and Dec – please note
the shafting of the Perp S aisle windows inside. So much
what seemed Perp is indeed Dec. The church is very mu
older, however. Several of the pier bases are E.E., and belc
them are square Norman bases. The arcade must have be
leaning too; for it has been propped up with heavy buttress
Perhaps in connexion with such trouble one pair of pie
was renewed with Perp capitals, and one of the pair with
Perp base too. The chancel arch could be E.E. Pretty quat
foil window from the tower stair into the nave. C15 chan
roof cut down from a bigger roof (nave?) to fit the chancel
FONT. Octagonal, Perp. Prettily decorated stem (cf. Pinc
beck). Bowl with quatrefoils and close leaf decoration insi

* The existing contract for rebuilding the chancel is dated 1418. T
chancel has been shortened by one bay – see the position of the pries
doorway.

and outside the quatrefoils. – PULPIT. Minor; C17. –
STAINED GLASS. In the chancel on the S side fragments. –
PLATE. Paten, by *Thomas Chapman*, 1810. – MONUMENTS.
Effigy of a young Knight, later C14, but still cross-legged. –
Henry Heron † 1730. Nice tablet in grey, white, and brown
marble, with a putto head.

ΜERMAID INN. A comfortable, tubby five-bay house of two
storeys with a broad doorway flanked by Tuscan columns;
Early Victorian presumably.

SUTTERTON

2030

ΣΤ MARY. Ashlar-faced and cruciform with a recessed, crocketed
spire. Dec bell-openings. Lucarnes in three tiers in alternating
directions. The spire was rebuilt in 1787 and tower and spire
again, together with the walls of the aisles and the S transept,
in 1861–3 (by *Browning*). Of the exterior of the church otherwise the earliest item is the aisle doorways, round-arched,
Late Norman. The S doorway has three orders of colonnettes,
the upright leaf capitals pre-E.E. On the arch the still Norman
motif of a chain overlaid over a roll. Also many fine mouldings. The S porch has side walls with very decayed arcading.
The entrance is of 1861–3. The N doorway has only one order.
One capital has two birds, the other a head. In the arch zigzag
at r. angles to the wall. At the apex a head. Hood-mould with
a plait-motif. The chancel is or was E.E. – see the buttressing
of the E wall. The E window and much else is again of 1861–3.
The N windows (two pairs of shafted lancets) look more con-
fidence-inspiring. The N transept E aisle is late C13, see the
bar tracery with unfoiled circles. The N transept N window
big and Perp. The transept clerestory E.E. In the S transept
the E.E. S window is of 1861–3. The nave and aisles externally
Dec. The large nave w window is an uncommonly wilful
design. No-one can call it beautiful. Above it the date 1602,
but the design might well be Dec. The aisle w windows have
intersecting tracery, the N and S windows simple Dec tracery.
The clerestory also could be Dec but need not be. Inside the
church the five-bay arcades belong to the doorways. Round
piers, square abaci with nicked corners. Bases with angle-
spurs. Double-chamfered pointed arches. But the w responds
still have scalloped capitals. The other capitals with small
upright leaves and also small heads. The last arch to the E a
little lower. Ornate w crossing arch with zigzag, but pointed.
Scalloped capitals. Such capitals also on the w respond of the

N transept arch. The other responds belong to the E.E.
campaign. Moulded capitals. The N transept w and E clere
story windows are shafted inside. Off the transepts to the
one-bay E.E. chapels open also to the chancel. Moulde
capitals, double-chamfered pointed arches. Apparently th
chancel floor originally lay considerably lower than the nav
floor. The chancel rebuilt, also in 1861–3. Can the E.E
windows, pairs of lancets, shafted inside, be trusted? Sedili
under a wide segmental arch. Double piscina. – TILING
In the chancel. High Victorian, in strong colours, yellow, red
dark green, also white and light blue. – PLATE. Chalice an
Paten Cover, by *F.R.*, 1568; Almsbasin, by *Joseph Hardy*
1814. – MONUMENTS (S transept). Civilian and wife, Pries
Three stone effigies all belonging together: John Bonewort
† 1372, his wife † 1380, and their son † 1400.

BAPTIST CHAPEL, ⅜ m. NNE. 1826. Three bays, brick, tw
storeys, pyramid roof. The doorway like that of a house.

ROUND HOUSE, S of the church.

KIRBY'S FARM, ¼ m. N. The house has a two-storeyed porc
dated 1609.

4020

SUTTON BRIDGE

ST MATTHEW. 1843. A sizeable church. Knapped flint wit
stone dressings. w tower with a funny square top on the stair
case turret. Tall slim diagonal arcade piers. Short chancel.

A long, dreary street, owing its C19 prosperous look to the rail
way and the bridge across the Nene. In the HIGH STREE
Nos 44–48 are an early C19 terrace. By the river C19 wharve
a storehouse, and contemporary housing. To the N som
admirable examples of C20 thatched cottages erected by th
Ministry of Agriculture and Fisheries.

SWING BRIDGE. 1894–7, replacing *Robert Stephenson*'s bridg
of 1850.

LIGHTHOUSES, at GUY'S HEAD, 3 m. N. A disused pair (on
in Norfolk) on the mouth of the Nene.

3010

SUTTON ST EDMUND

ST EDMUND. 1795, but a rebuilding, see the old stone wallin
inside the w and s walls. Brick. Nave and polygonal chance
rounded apsidally inside. Large arched windows, altered ala
on the s side of the nave, when also the Transitional-Gothi
s porch was added. Nice w tower with square, recessed bel

stage and lead cupola. Unaltered interior with BOX PEWS, WEST GALLERY, and Gothic ORGAN CASE. – PLATE. Chalice and Paten Cover, London, 1577; Paten, London, 1819.

WANOCK HOUSE. L-shaped, brick, early C18, yet conservative in feeling. There is a nice BARN near by.

SUTTON ST JAMES 3010

ST JAMES. The nave disappeared during the Commonwealth. The tower and the chancel remain, the latter much re-done in 1879 and again in 1894. From that time the N aisle and the polygonal apse. The chancel is Perp, tall, with tall three-light windows. The priest's doorway alone seems not interfered with. The tower is of ashlar below, of brick (rendered) above. To the W a four-light window with a quatrefoil frieze below. But the door-head with traceried spandrels must be re-set. It is much too low. Was it a nave doorway? Parts of the chancel arch inside are genuine Perp. – FONT. Octagonal, probably Perp, with simple tracery and cusped fields. – PULPIT. Re-used parts of c.1700, a foliage frieze and an inlay panel. – PLATE. Chalice, c.1630.

ST IVES' CROSS. ½ m. W. Base and part of a shaft supported by three flying buttresses. So this was a little more than the customary crosses.

SUTTON ST NICHOLAS see LUTTON

SWARBY 0040

ST MARY AND ALL SAINTS. Broad ashlar-faced Perp W tower. Fancy-shaped battlements. Small recessed pyramid roof. The bell-openings are very strange. Two twins under an arch broken at the top, and this part replaced by a horizontal piece. Early C13 chancel, see the small S lancet, round-headed inside.* Dec N arcade. Low, with octagonal piers and double-chamfered arches. Perp S arcade. The piers are thin and have a complex section with four shafts and eight diagonal hollows. Capitals only to the shafts. They have nobbly leaves. Perp niche l. of the chancel E window. S aisle 1886, ornate. Original only the jambs of the doorway (with heads and also, it appears, beasts). – SCULPTURE. Beautiful small figure of a seated Christ, the legs parallel, the drapery good. Unfortunately

* The N aisle E lancets are Victorian.

the head has been knocked off. It is C13 work (N aisle E).
PLATE. Chalice and Paten Cover, London, 1581.

SWATON

1030

ST MICHAEL. Cruciform and ashlar-faced. Externally the story
is as follows. E.E. crossing tower with twin bell-opening
having an almond-shape in plate tracery. The tower was later
heightened, but never received a spire. The masonry of the
E.E. part is coursed rubble. The same in the transepts and
the chancel. The latter is indeed very patently E.E. Separate
lancet windows. Hood-moulds on heads or stiff-leaf. To the E
no more than a two-light window. This has bar tracery, a
foiled circle, i.e. is later than the crossing tower. But the
shafts still have stiff-leaf capitals. Dec nave and aisles with
reticulated tracery, very consistent. The aisles are embattled.
The S doorway is in the same style, much as at Helpringham
near by. The N doorway minor but contemporary. The N
transept N window also reticulated tracery. The S transept
seems C17. Now the interior. The E wall of the chancel has
shafts with rings to the windows. Pretty details. Damaged
piscina. The N and S lancets have hood-moulds even inside.
The crossing piers ought to be E.E. (see the tower outside)
but were re-done Dec. Shafts with fillets, polygonal abaci,
double-chamfered arches. In the N transept the pre-Dec roof-
line is showing. Dec piscina in this transept. Dec arches from
the aisles to the transepts. The nave and aisles are the most
impressive part of the church, too much so almost for the
crossing. The E.E. roof-line appears below the present one.
Three bays, but as high and as wide as if they belonged to a
cathedral. Quatrefoil piers with the foils more than semicircular and small hollows in the diagonals. – FONT. Octagonal, with diapering all over. Ballflower on the underside,
i.e. Dec too. – SCREEN. To the S transept; Perp. – BENCH
ENDS. With poppy-heads and tracery. – PAINTING. Remains
of a wheel (of Fortune?) on the S aisle E wall. – PLATE.
Chalice and Paten Cover, by *John Morley* of Lincoln, 1569.
MONUMENT. Early C14 effigy of a Lady.

SWAYFIELD

9020

ST NICHOLAS. E.E. tower, unbuttressed and ashlar-faced.
Twin bell-openings with blank foiled shapes in the tympanum

W and s. The twin openings below of 1875-8, when *F. Goddard* rebuilt the rest of the church. He used the E.E. style. – PLATE. Chalice, by *William Gamble*, 1697.

A house to the W of the church has mullioned windows in its gable-end.

SWINDERBY

8060

ALL SAINTS. Late Norman N arcade. Round piers, scalloped capitals, round abaci, unmoulded arches. The arcade is continued beyond the chancel arch by two more bays, i.e. now a two-bay chapel. This also has an unmoulded round arch. In the chancel moreover a Norman pillar piscina with polygonal pillar. The apse is of course not Norman but Victorian (1879 by *J. T. Lee*), as becomes at once clear inside by the effective lantern lighting. More that is E.E., namely the unbuttressed W tower with twin bell-openings separated by shafts and triple-chamfered arch towards the nave, partly on corbels. E.E. also the chancel arch (re-done?) and the second bay of the N chapel (keeled responds). – FONT. Octagonal, Perp, with plain shields. – STAINED GLASS. W window by *Kempe*. Date of death commemorated 1879. – RAILINGS to the N chapel. Wrought iron; C18. – PLATE. Chalice and Paten Cover, by *F.R.*, 1573. – MONUMENTS. John Drake † 1766. Inscription with pediment over. Urn on this before obelisk. Coloured marbles. – John Disney † 1771. Another pretty tablet.

SWINESHEAD

2040

ST MARY. A big church, with a high tower and a curious shortish spire. The tower is ashlar-faced and Dec to Perp. The aisles embrace it. W doorway with several groups of fine mouldings. W window of two lights Dec. Arches to the N and S of typical five-shafted Dec moulding. The arch to the nave is the same but higher. Vault with eight ribs and ring. A change of plan in the vault is at once noticeable. Three-light bell-openings with transoms. Battlements and pinnacles, and the recessed spire, which starts inside a very prettily decorated transparent octagon, as though a Boston effect had been intended and then discarded. The spire has two tiers of discreet lucarnes. It is 160 ft high. Dec the arcades. They are tall and of six bays. Slim square piers with semi-circular projections. Triple-chamfered arches. Good head-stops. The chancel arch is of the same type. Dec s aisle windows (reticulated tracery). Dec s porch inside with fine blank arches each side with ogee detail, crockets, buttress-shafts, and finials. Dec also the clerestory. Six two-light windows each side and two to the E. Frieze of heads etc.; battlements. Oddly rough, barn-like roof with tie-beams on arched braces and queenposts. Nice stair-turret at the SE corner. Is the top storey of it genuine? for the adjoining Perp chancel is not. It was rebuilt in 1848 by *Stephen Lewin* (GS). But the Perp N aisle is original. Formerly there must have been a tomb recess in the E bay which projected a little N. – SCREEN. Good, of two-light divisions. Ogee arch embracing the arches of the two lights. – DOORS. The s door has intersecting tracery, the N door reticulated tracery, i.e. both are the original doors for their doorways. – STAINED GLASS. E window by *Clayton & Bell*, c.1875. – (Other glass by *E. Baillie*, 1853.) – PLATE. Flagon, by *William Elliot*, 1823; Chalice, 1824, and Paten and Almsbasin, 1828, by *John Bridge*. – MONUMENTS. In the N aisle defaced incised slab to Richard Bennett † 1520 and wife. – In the chancel frieze of kneeling children for the monument to Sir John Lockton, 1628.

STENNINGS, 1m. WSW of the church. Brick, L-shaped, with stone quoins and gabled ends.

WESTHOLME, 400 yds W of the church. The house possesses a Georgian malthouse. Blank arches to the ground floor and lucarnes above.

VICARAGE. Part C18 and part C19. What is puzzling and somewhat startling is the sculptured stone keystones. They look C17 and of Arcimboldesque derivation.

SWINESHEAD ABBEY, 1 m. NE. The date given for the house is 1607. It was built for Sir John Lockton from remains of a Cistercian Abbey (founded in 1135). The date 1607 fits the L-shape and the leathery armorial cartouche. W front refaced in the C18, but with a juicy Victorian cast-iron porch. In the NE return a later C13 EFFIGY of a knight. STABLES C18. GATEPIERS Gothic and C19.

CASTLE. At BAYTHORPE, out on the edge of the Fen country, about ½ m. NE of the church, is a rather unusual motte-and-bailey castle. The bailey forms a counterscarp bank of great width all round the motte. Motte and bank are both very low, and their scarps have a poor slope. Plainly this castle depended on the wetness of its site, and its deep, undrainable ditches. It is mentioned in the reign of John.

ST MARY. The N arcade of three bays is of *c*.1200. Round piers, undetailed capitals, round abaci, double-chamfered round arches. Then follows the w tower, E.E., with Y-tracery in the bell-openings. Also E.E. the chancel arch and the S chapel arch. A little nailhead in the responds. Dec S arcade (octagonal piers, double-chamfered arches). Dec N aisle. The w window just a quatrefoil. Dec chancel, the E window of four lights with unusual, if moderate, flowing tracery. In the N windows a circle with mouchette wheel. Dec S aisle, the w window with reticulated tracery, on the S a four-light window with reticulation units under a low-pitched, four-centred arch – the same type of arch as those of the N aisle windows. The sedilia are mostly not original, but the two little carrier figures are. One has the defiant gesture usually called the toothache. – PAINTING. Heraldic painting on one of the N piers, early C14, i.e. a time when painted heraldry is rare. – PLATE. Silver-gilt Chalice, by *S.T.I.*, 1676; silver-gilt Paten, by *Robert Garrard*, 1830. – MONUMENTS. Fifth (last) Duke of Ancaster † 1809. By *Westmacott*. A pure Grecian relief in white marble. Two dead children on a couch, placed on a half-rolled-up mat. In front the disconsolate father. To the r. an angel with a leaf branch, to the l. Charity, a fine, typical Westmacott figure.* – Priscilla Barbara Elizabeth Bertie Baroness Willoughby de Eresby, sister of the fourth Duke, † 1828. By *Forsyth*, 1883. Gothic, of stone, but with small white marble statuettes on short red marble shafts.

SWINSTEAD HALL. Dull, unpretentious, and built in 1889. The architect was *J. J. Newman*.

SWINSTEAD OLD HALL. Evidence suggests that *Sir John Vanbrugh* built a big house here for the first Duke of Ancaster before 1720. It was in the Kings Weston style. Fragments on the site are built into a wall, and the mighty doorway of a cottage on the Green with the kind of rustication as at Grimsthorpe, though done in the flat, must also come from the house, though it has the date 1783 engraved in. The SCHOOL to the NE is said to have been the laundry or some other outbuilding. It has in its N wall a huge fireplace with arched niches l. and r., the rude square capitals-cum-abaci just as at Grimsthorpe. Im-

* Also occurring, as Dr Whinney kindly tells me, at St John Barbados, ʸinder Monument († 1799), and at Crowcombe Somerset, Barnard Monu-ᵐent († 1805).

mediately E of the school were cellars with brick vaults. Parts of
them have recently collapsed. The imprint of the same heavy
hand is discernible on cottages flanking the road. E of the terrace
the hill ascends steeply to a SUMMER HOUSE, an unmistakable
Vanbrugh pavilion, and a visual link between Swinstead and
Grimsthorpe. It has three bays and two storeys, but bay
one and three rise by one more storey into square towers.
The principal windows are arched. On the first floor is a
polygonal room from which to enjoy the magnificent views.
The additions at the back are probably due to *J. B. Papworth*,
and the infilling between the towers is modern.

SYSTON

9040

ST MARY. Of ironstone. Over-restored by *Charles Kirk*, 1861–2.
Norman W tower. Twin bell-openings. The colonnettes of
two sides of the Saxon mid-wall type. One capital has crockets.
Nailhead and zigzag in the arches. Perp top with eight pinnacles. The arch towards the nave all renewed. Also Norman
the S doorway. On the lintel figures in arcading, most of them
completely re-cut. Tympanum with diagonal trellis pattern.
Arch with chip-carved St Andrew's crosses. Late Norman
the low N arcade. Two bays. Circular pier, square abacus.
Multi-scalloped capitals. Round arch with one step and one
chamfer. The responds have crocket capitals. In the nave
side one tall Norman window. Finally Norman too the narrow
chancel arch, though the upper parts of the capitals are clearly
Victorian. The lower part has fluted upright leaves. In the
arch only the big demi-roll is original. Two-light mullioned
windows l. and r. of the arch to give a better view of the altar.
In the chancel two Norman windows. An inscription outside
the chancel records the year 1702. Perp clerestory with partly
decorated battlements and with pinnacles. – STAINED GLASS.
E window by *Ward & Hughes*. – S side nave by *Kempe* † 1894,
also 1901, also chancel S 1904. – PLATE. Paten, by *Edward
Holaday*(?), 1717. – MONUMENT. Sir John Thorold † 1718.
With two amply draped standing figures. Open scrolly pediment at the top. Ascribed by Mr Gunnis to *William Kidwell*
(cf. Mortlake, Surrey).

SYSTON HALL. The great house of the Thorold family, with
its splendid library designed by *L. Vulliamy* in 1824, has gone.
Only the park remains, and two octagonal lodges. The lake
was made in 1821.

SYSTON OLD HALL. Rebuilt in 1830, but retaining a late C

porch with the arms of the De Ligne family. It has an arched entrance with heavy strapwork. Inscribed on a garden wall is '*John North* his hand 1702' (cf. the inscription on the church chancel).

TALLINGTON

ST LAWRENCE. A problem church as bad as the worst in Northamptonshire. But first the straightforward parts. E. E. N arcade of two bays, round piers, round abaci, double-chamfered arches. One wider S arch, also E.E. The responds triple. Dec arches E of these connected with the transepts. The S transept indeed has a Dec S window (reticulated tracery), though a small E lancet (re-set, as we shall see). The N transept N window is Perp. The W tower is Dec. Tower arch with continuous chamfers (one hollow chamfer). Two-light bell-openings with transom. The spire was destroyed in 1762. But now, why is that tower inside not centred on the two E.E. arcades? And why does the S arcade start so much further E than the N arcade? In this piece of blank S wall is a Norman doorway in a later porch. The doorway has one order of shafts with block capitals and bases decorated with zigzag. The tympanum is entirely plain. Arch with zigzag. Hood-mould with St Andrew's crosses. If this doorway is *in situ*, can there perhaps have been a SW tower originally which was then replaced by the Dec tower? That is at least an answer, but there is no answer to the problem of the transept E walls. In the N transept is a straight jamb down, and Cox called its details long-and-short. Even if it is not that, what is it? And in the S transept are two straight joints isolating what seems to have been a Norman square pier. Can they have been connected with chapels, with *porticus*? – FONT. Octagonal, plain, on five short E.E. supports. – FONT COVER. Simple, Perp. – SCREEN. Perp, with one-light divisions. – PLATE. Chalice, by *I.M.*, 1638.

MANOR HOUSE. Georgian. Brick. Six bays and two storeys, with moulded stone window surrounds, a high hipped roof, and dormers.

The OLD RECTORY. 1862 by *C. E. Davis* of Bath.

DOVECOTE. C18 with gables.

TEMPLE BRUER

Temple Bruer was a preceptory of the Templars founded late in the reign of Henry II. The church, as Buck's engraving shows and as excavations have proved, had the round nave with round ambulatory favoured by the Templars, and in addition a chancel with apse and a w porch. The apse must almost at once have been replaced by a very strange E end consisting of a straight-headed bay flanked by two large square towers. That on the s of the chancel survives, and looks more like a keep than a church tower. It is 54 ft high and has the typical flat buttresses of the Norman style, though it must date from the very end of the C12. On its N side is a doorway with double-chamfered round arch which led into the chancel and a triple respond with two additional thin shafts in the diagonals. On this stands a double-chamfered springer. The respond belongs to the transverse arch which once separated the old from the lengthened part of the chancel. The chancel was vaulted, as the corbel above the doorway shows. The flat buttresses on this side could only begin above the chancel roof. Their brackets have curious bobbin shapes. On the w side of the tower are a double-chamfered lancet and above it a round-headed window. A roof-line cuts across this. The roof belonged to a C14 chapel added to the chancel on its s side. Buck shows the round piers and arches by which it opened to the chancel and the Norman nave ambulatory. On the E the tower has also a lancet and a round-headed window over, on the s instead of the former a Perp two-light window. Inside the tower, the ground floor has a quadripartite vault on corbels. The ribs are single-chamfered. Against the E and w walls is closely-set blank arcading. Big capitals with leaf, many-moulded arches. In the E wall a shallow recess for reredos, in the NW corner the interference of a spiral staircase. – ARCHITECTURAL FRAGMENTS of intersecting Norman arcading. – MONUMENT. Effigy in a sunk pointed trefoil. Defaced. – The first floor was vaulted too, with single chamfered ribs. Only the springers are preserved. In the gable of the Farmhouse the head of a two-light Dec window.

ST JOHN, ¾ m. N. By *Fowler*, 1874. Rock-faced, with lancet windows. Nave and chancel in one. Wooden bell-turret with spire.

THORPE LATIMER HOUSE *see* HELPRINGHAM

THORPE-ON-THE-HILL

ST MICHAEL. The tower is the puzzle of this church. It was built apparently in 1722, but has in its w face, re-set no doubt

a blocked Norman window and in its N face a simple blocked
E.E. doorway, also evidently re-set. The semicircular moulding above the W doorway could be of 1722, and the blocked
round window above this obviously is. And inside the tower
there is the most curious arcading, two bays with brick pier
to N and S and a group with the middle one wider to the
E. They are possible as a Vanbrughian conceit, even if unexpected. The rest of the church was rebuilt by *C. G. Hare*
(GR) in 1912. Nice N arcade with continuous mouldings. But
the W respond is genuine E.E. and keeled. – PLATE. Chalice
and Paten Cover, by *I.C.*, given 1663.

THORPE TILNEY
⅝ m. SW of Timberland

1050

THORPE TILNEY HALL. Georgian. Red brick, of five bays
and two storeys. The builder has made a showpiece of the
centre, emphasizing it by a tripartite doorway with a pediment oddly interfered with by a fanlight, then by a Venetian
and then by a lunette window, and finally by an open pediment.
Curving-down walls l. and r. of the façade. At the back the
house is irregular but has also two Venetian windows. Who
allowed the malicious extension to the front? In addition,
to the N, nice symmetrical STABLES with a lunette window in
the gable and a cupola, and, in the kitchen garden, a SUMMER
HOUSE with a gable crowned by a pineapple finial.

THREEKINGHAM

0030

ST PETER. Norman the chancel E wall with three tall, even
windows. Also one N window and part of the corbel table.
This chancel had a two-bay N chapel added soon after. Its E
parts were demolished later, and so much of the arcade
appears only outside now. Wide round arches, round pier,
stiff-leaf capitals (*see* more about this inside). The rest of the
arcade is hidden by the Dec N aisle. At the W end of this the
quoin of the original aisleless, no doubt Norman, nave is
visible and also a small lancet window whose position
shows that it belonged to the E.E., not the Dec aisle (*see* below).
On the S side the history must have been similar, for the doorway is E.E. (much renewed) and so is the blank arcading of the
S porch, but the aisle windows are Dec (cusped intersecting
ogee arches; only the last window straight-headed).* C13 W

* The Dec parts of the church may be connected with two wills to establish
chantries, one of 1310, the other of 1325. One chantry was consecrated in 1333.

tower with a spire whose big steep broaches are no doub
no later than the bell-openings with their bar tracery (trefoiled circles). Total height c.145 ft. Below the bell-openings
the masonry is not ashlar but rubble. So that must be earlier
than the mid C13. The spire has three tiers of lucarnes in
alternating directions. Inside the church, the tower arch
(triple responds with shafts more than semicircular) is now
earlier than the bell-openings. The arcades continue the
story recognized outside. The N arcade is of five bays, the last
two being the round-arched ones we have already met. Stiff-
leaf also the NW respond, and here specially lively. But the
rest just circular piers and circular abaci. Arches with one
chamfer and fine rolls. The fourth pier is quatrefoil with
fillets, the foils being more than semicircular. The s arcade is
similar but much plainer and probably later. The w pier and
w respond are octagonal, and the capitals have a little nailhead. A confirmation of the exterior also the chancel interior.
The E wall is richly shafted. Strange capitals, tall, plain, and
concave-sided. Slender N window, wider s window (now Dec
outside). Remains of an E.E. piscina. – FONT. Tub-shaped
E.E. Pointed-trefoiled blank arches on shafts.* – SCREEN
A fragment of tracery in the N aisle. – BENCH ENDS. With
tracery patterns, much renovated. – PLATE. Chalice, Paten
and Flagon, by *W.S.*, 1676. – MONUMENTS. Lambert de
Threekingham and wife, c.1310. Stone effigies, of enormous
size (he c.7 ft 6 in.). Two lions at his feet, two puppies at hers.
Very good quality. – Edward Dawson † 1787. Beautifully
lettered slate slab. – CURIOSUM. In the N aisle at the w end
the village STOCKS.

Against the wall of a house, c.150 yds w of the church, a STON
inscribed 'Vorax: Pestis Threk[ac]: Saevire Mese Maio 164(
Robert Gaton'.

THURLBY

ST FIRMIN. The tower is Anglo-Saxon, as appears from the
sw quoin (long and short work, though not consistently used
and from the triangle-headed doorway above the arch inside
This arch also was Anglo-Saxon, but it was later narrowed
The narrowing belongs to about 1200. The arch has one step
and one chamfer, the s respond a shaft-ring. The top of the
tower is Dec. Recessed spire with two tiers of lucarnes in the
same direction, sticking out more than is good for the outline

* On the foot the inscription: Ave Maria Gratia P.D.T.

of the steeple. Then, to continue the chronology, the piece of
zigzag in the chancel sedilia, but this surely must be re-used.
So to the arcades. They are of four bays, and the first two
pairs of piers are round with square abaci. The N arches have
two slight chamfers and a half-roll, the S arches one step and
one chamfer. All this is C12. The simple S doorway belongs
to this campaign, and so does the S aisle W window, if it is
original.* Then, immediately, the arcades were lengthened
to the E. The abaci are now octagonal, there is a little nailhead,
and the last arch is double-chamfered, though still round.
The arcade ends in quatrefoil piers instead with, in the
diagonals, pairs of thin shafts. Their purpose was evidently to
carry the chancel arch across. At the same time as this
transepts were built. The S transept has blank E.E. arcading
on the W wall, the N transept blank arcading with pointed-
trefoiled arches on the W and N walls. Both transepts have in
the E wall a shallow but wide reredos niche. Next to that in the
N transept is the rood-loft staircase, and as its remaining
shaft is E.E. as well, this is proof of a very early rood-loft
stair (but cf. Colsterworth). The chancel also belongs to the
same build, see the side lancets (the E window is Perp, of five
lights), the pointed-trefoiled piscina on shafts doubled in
depth, and the blocked doorway between this and the sedilia.
Moreover, the chancel received at once one-bay chapels. Their
arches are still round. The small lancet in the S chapel, though,
may not be *in situ*. The fenestration of the N chapel is Dec
(intersecting ogee arches). The clerestory could be Dec or
Perp. It has no battlements, while the aisles have. – FONT.
Circular, E.E., very crude. – COMMUNION RAIL. With
strong, vertically symmetrical balusters, i.e. latish C17. –
LADDER. A primeval ladder in the tower serving as a staircase. – CROSS. Set in the Anglo-Saxon upper doorway is a
cross, probably a gable-cross, and probably Norman. Each
arm ends in three parallel loops. The cross comes from Edenham. – STAINED GLASS. Some original bits in the S transept
S window. – A window by *Baillie*. This is most probably the
one in the N transept N window, and it dates presumably
from the time of the restoration, i.e. 1856. – The chancel E
window is also, it appears, from that time. – PLATE. Chalice
and Paten Cover, by *R.P.*, 1616; Paten, by *Thomas Parr*, 1712;
Paten, London, 1765; Flagon, by *I.M.*, 1769.

* And is the quatrefoil opening above it original? If so, is it later C13?

Several C17 houses in the village, notably PRIORY FARM, NORTHORPE HOUSE, and a farm at OBTHORPE near by.

THURLBY MANOR, on the main road, SW of the church. A fire in 1878 accounts for the W wing. The lower central part looks early C17, and the E wing is Early Georgian with moulded and keystoned windows and a comfortable-looking Restoration type of roof.* On the S front of this wing is a tall arched stair-light, and on the E front a protruding chimneybreast. The N front is symmetrical: two bays, two storeys, and quoins. The entrance in the centre wing suggests a normal C17 plan. In the garden a nice vernacular BARN with steps growing up to the loft.

9060   THURLBY
                    1¼ m. N of Bassingham

ST GERMAIN. The church looks ancient generally, see the very large quoins of tower, nave, and chancel. But the only early features are the S doorway, which is of before 1200, and a chancel S lancet. The low N arcade with its octagonal piers and double-chamfered arches may be of c.1300. The chancel arch is mostly destroyed. – FONT. The normal octagonal Perp type, but treated extremely lavishly. Against the bowl three bold diagonal leaves, three equally bold flowers, one different leaf, and a small figure with outstretched arms growing Daphne-like into a tree. – SCREEN. One-light divisions with ogee arches and panel tracery. – SCULPTURE. In the N aisle at the W end a length of Saxon interlace, next to some architectural pieces. – The CHANDELIER in the chancel is a domestic crystal piece. – PLATE. Chalice and Cover, inscribed 1713. – MONUMENT (N aisle, E end). Coffin-lid with the bust of a Lady praying, in sunk relief in a quatrefoil framing.

THURLBY HALL. Considering the antiquity of the Bromhead family, it is curious that they have never built grand. The present house is a comfortable but completely traditional brick block of c.1703, with a pair of chimneystacks treated as blank arches.

1050   TIMBERLAND

ST ANDREW. The W tower is Transitional to E.E. with a Perp top. Big, flat buttresses. The rest externally the work of the restoration of 1887 (Goddard). The details Geometrical to Dec

* Designs for a new house for Mr Denshire were made by Robert Wright in 1719.

Inside, the wide tower arch Transitional, i.e. round and si
chamfered. Put into it to make it safer a smaller, steep
crude E. E. arch. Blocked round-headed tower W window. T
arcades later C13 and early C14. Two bays, double-chamfere
arches. The N pier with square core and four demi-shafts, the
S pier quatrefoil with deep continuous hollows between the
foils, fillets, and a little nailhead. In the chancel a Norman
PILLAR PISCINA on four clustered shafts with decorated
scallop capitals. Nice Georgian nave ceiling with two rosettes.
– MONUMENTS. Quite a number of slate tablets and headstones, some of about 1800 signed by *W. Barnes*.

Hereabouts are several early C19 houses with simple screen walls,
each with a single recessed arch – obviously a local builder's
motif.

TYDD ST MARY

ST MARY. Perp brick W tower on a stone base. Recessed stone
spire. Two tiers of lucarnes in alternating directions. Brick
also the clerestory, very repaired. The rest stone-faced. Good
chancel of the same type as Gedney, though not so grand.
Windows with cusped Y- and intersecting tracery, but already
ogee-headed lights – i.e. *c.*1320 or so. The five-light E window
is Victorian (restoration 1869). Inside, much earlier evidence.
Norman zigzag bits in the chancel N wall, Norman heads from
a corbel table re-used as hood-mould stops, Norman volute
capital re-used as a corbel in the S aisle E wall. The arcades of
five narrow bays are Transitional. Circular piers, octagonal
capitals, some with faint starts of leaf carving not continued.
Octagonal bases with coarse spurs. The simple sedilia and
piscina in the chancel belong to the date of the chancel, the
nave roof belongs to the brick clerestory. The tie-beams are so
heavy and elementary that they look as though they were put
in later, because the Perp roof with its moulded beams and
purlins was endangering the walls. – FONT. Octagonal. Perp,
with busts of angels holding shields. – TILES. Some old ones
in the chancel. – STAINED GLASS. E window by *H. Hughes*,
1871, with nothing to recommend it. – PLATE. Chalice and
Paten, by *John East*, 1717; Almsbasin and Flagon, by *Robert
Brown*, 1736. – MONUMENTS. Incised slab of William de
Tidde, late C14. – Piece of a Perp tomb-chest with shields in
foiled fields (built into the N aisle N wall). – John Trafford
† 1719. Tablet with cherubs l. and r. Signed *Walton* Wisbech.
– Sigismond Trafford † 1741. By *Rysbrack* (Mrs Webb).

Tablet, and on its cornice portrait medallion with drapery
The cornice is supported by two corbels with beautifully
carved flowers and turned-down torches. Fine lettering.
RECTORY. Mostly 1855 by *J. H. Hakewill*.

UFFINGTON

St MICHAEL. We must start with the interior. The three-bay
arcades are early C13, i.e. round piers, round abaci, round
double-chamfered arches. The capitals of the N arcade have a
little more detailed mouldings and a little nailhead. There is in
addition a N chapel to the chancel with details of the same kind
The puzzling thing is that in the W wall of this same chapel a
formerly free-standing pier appears, again of the same kind
and that this is connected with the chancel arch – southward -
by a pointed arch but extends to the N half a round arch. The
only reasonable answer seems to be a former N transept with
E aisle, although the arcade has neither a wider nor a higher
arch to correspond with such a transept. The chancel has Dec
windows, but a Victorian E window, the S aisle a Dec E window, and the other windows Perp. The N aisle windows are
Dec again, though they are now Victorian. They are said to be
faithful copies. Perp N chapel, tall and embattled. Four-light
E, three-light N windows. Gables and shields on the buttresses
The W tower also is Perp. A shield on the S side dates it *c.*1490.
W doorway with ogee gable. Big helms in the spandrels. Niches
with high pedestals for statues in the clasping buttresses. Two-
light bell-openings with transom. Lozenge frieze, thin pinnacles, thin flying buttresses to the recessed crocketed spire.
Two tiers of lucarnes in the same directions. The vault inside
has a tierceron star with a large middle circle and some figured
bosses. Rich Victorian corbels for the nave roof representing
whole scenes. Rich naturalistic floral carving on the responds
of the chancel arch. A rich nodding ogee canopy of stone over
part of the pulpit. All this is by *E. Browning*, who restored the
church in 1864. – CHANDELIER. Of brass, two tiers of arms
and a winged cherub head at the top. A lovely piece, dated
1685. – STAINED GLASS. In the N chapel E window four large
figures by *Wailes*, 1851. – In the E window by *Clayton & Bell*,
1874. – PLATE (all but the tray silver-gilt). Cover, by *Benjamin Pyne*, 1689; Chalice, by *John Spackman*, 1690; Almsdish, by *Anthony Nelme*, 1690; Flagon, by *F.S.*, 1690; Chalice
and Cover, by *Anthony Nelme*, 1693; Flagon, by *Anthony*

Nelme, 1694; Tray, by *Abraham Buteux*, 1723; Spoon, by *Edward Hall*, 1724. – MONUMENTS. Knight on a tomb-chest, *c*.1400. Panelled ogee canopy with fleurons in a moulding. Between chancel and N chapel. – In the chancel Roger Manneres † 1587 and Olyver Manneres. The date perhaps that of the death of another Roger: 1607. Two kneeling Knights facing one another. Columns l. and r. Alabaster. – Dean Staunton † 1612. Also two kneeling figures facing one another. Also columns l. and r. Also alabaster. Both these monuments are signed by *Green* of Denton and are amongst the earliest signed monuments in England. – Two tablets with drapery round the inscription, one † 1679, the other † 1710, quite an instructive comparison.

FFINGTON HOUSE. The seat of the Earls of Lindsey and 'a good house of the King William cut'. But Lord Torrington, who wrote this, did not know his styles; for Uffington was begun *c*.1681. It was burnt down in 1904. The outbuildings and offices remain, and these are mostly of 1845 and by *Samuel Gray*. At the time of writing, despite the passing of two world wars, the confusion and litter of the fire is still evident. Uffington was the *belle-au-bois-dormant* house *par excellence*. The magnificent GATEPIERS, facing the churchyard, quite the best in the county. They may be by *John Lumley*, if he designed the identical ones at Burley-on-the-Hill, Rutland. The date must be about 1700. Tall rusticated brick piers faced with fluted stone pilasters and topped by urns with coronets. Reversed scrolled brackets garlanded with fruit swags link to lower walls. Opposite, as the entrance to the churchyard, is another set in miniature. One-bay LODGES, looking Georgian, on the E side of the estate.

WADDINGTON

9060

T MICHAEL. The church was destroyed in the Second World War and rebuilt in 1952–4 by *R. Corless* (Skipper & Corless of Lowestoft). Of the old church a big stiff-leaf capital in front of the new one. – PLATE. Cover, by *G.R.*, 1569; Flagon (damaged), 1646.

WALCOT
2 m. NW of Billinghay

1050

T OSWALD. 1852. Of stock brick with lancets and a bellcote. Outside some fragments from Catley Abbey, a Gilbertine house W of Walcot. The METHODIST CHAPEL a little

further s, also of stock brick and dated 1869, is with its st
classical forms a more convincing piece of architecture tha
the church.

WALCOT

0030

1½ m. NE of Pickworth

ST NICHOLAS. Ashlar-faced. Externally all Dec, but interna
earlier. Various Norman bits re-set in the porch. Late Norm
multi-scallop and leaf capitals re-used as bases in the N arcac
Late Norman chancel arch with one leaf capital. The N arca
otherwise E.E. Three bays, one pier round, one octofoil. T
capitals and much else maltreated in the C19. It makes t
interior rather depressing. Dec w tower with an unusual spi
Tall broaches; crockets up the edge of the spire start where t
broaches end. Three tiers of lucarnes in alternating positio
all with crocketed gables. Dec chancel, with a good five-lig
window with flowing tracery. Dec s aisle. The doorway has o
order of colonnettes with bossy leaf capitals and fine moul
ings in the arch. The small doorway further E was original
it seems, a window. But why then would it be so ornat
Fleurons up the jambs inside ending at the top in two lit
angels. The s aisle piscina has a crocketed gable too. Dec wi
dows with ogee lights, straight-headed in the s aisle, under
low-pitch head in the N aisle. Perp clerestory. – FONT. Tu
shaped. Arch heads with leaf motifs, also upside down, a
also heads. All badly re-cut, perhaps in the C18. – SOUT
DOOR. C17. Panelled; with a round-arched wicket. – BEN(
ENDS. With straight tops. Tracery motifs and also a tree.
PLATE. Paten, by *William Fountain*, 1809.

WASHINGBOROUGH

0070

ST JOHN EVANGELIST. Much of the church is E.E., and t
tower comes first and might even be called Transitional, s
the spacious w doorway with one order of shafts and a doubl
chamfered arch. But the tower arch is full E.E., and the tow
top with its eight pinnacles is of course Perp. Then the arcad
They are of four bays and have broadly-speaking round pi
and round capitals and double-chamfered arches. In fa
details differ to an amazing degree. The sw respond has in t
capitals a kind of frill which can only be described as vestig
scalloping, that is, belongs to the Transitional and the tow
Then the first two s piers and the first N pier have stiff-le
capitals, and finally the last arch is moulded, not simply cha

fered. To this period belongs the chancel arch too, with triple detached shafts in the responds and in the chancel the sedilia and piscina, plain but unmistakable. The N chapel appears to be Dec, see especially the s arch. Externally, matching is almost impossible, as the restoration of 1859–62 by *Sir G. G. Scott* and *Goddard* conceals everything. Their clerestory is to be regretted. The chancel has a Dec low-side window which seems original, a doorway, Dec too, but perhaps a little earlier, and the E window with at least its original hood-mould. – FONT. Drum-shaped, Norman, but much re-tooled. Blank arches on colonnettes and bits of leaf in the spandrels. – COMMUNION RAIL. C17. – Fine Perp CHEST with four quatrefoils cusped and given roses as their centres. – CHANDELIER. Very ornate, Georgian, and said to come from Brighton, via Eastgate House Lincoln. – MONUMENTS. Effigy of a Lady, demi-figure praying. Two angels at her pillow. She appears in sunk relief in a cusped framing. The rest of the slab is unworked, except for a foliated cross and her shoes, which come out at the bottom. It is interesting for the degree of reality aimed at that her sleeves lie on the unworked part of the slab. – A similar monument to a Lady, but her head in a simply trefoiled recess survives outside the chancel (s). – Eure Monument, chancel s, date of death 1664. Enjoyable tablet with convex inscription oval, punched drapes to its l. and r., bulgy, baluster-like pilasters (an odd idea) l. and r. of them, and an open pediment. At the foot an incised still-life of death.

WASHINGBOROUGH HALL. The house has canted bays, a Doric porch, and a semicircular window above. All Late Georgian.

WELBOURN

9050

CHAD. The unbuttressed tower is E.E. to the twin bellopenings with pointed lights under a round arch. But the doorway is Late Dec or Perp and the tower arch of the quatrefoil type with deep continuous hollows in the diagonals and a little nailhead, i.e. Early Dec rather than E.E. On the tower a Dec spire, crocketed and with an entasis perhaps exaggerated and often compared to the shape of the sugarloaf. Pinnacles and thin flying buttresses. Three tiers of lucarnes in alternating directions. Of the rest of the church, the s doorway with its thin shafts looks late C13 rather than Dec, but all the rest is Dec. Four-bay arcades of octagonal piers and double-chamfered arches, abaci with ballflower here, nailhead there. The responds triple shafts instead of semi-octagons. The roof-line

which belongs to these arcades appears against the tower an
the chancel, and there includes a circular window. Dec aisl
windows with flowing tracery, of three lights except for the
aisle E window, which has four. This building activity has bee
connected with the foundation of a chantry in the S aisle b
John of Welbourn, treasurer of Lincoln Cathedral. He died i
1380. So once again Dec with flowing tracery kept alive lon
certainly to after 1350. Dec also the S porch with a Trinity ov
the entrance. The porch as well as the aisle buttresses an
decorated. Finally Dec also the chancel arch, triple, with fille
The chancel itself was rebuilt in 1854. Perp only the clerestor
with uncommonly tall and prominent three-light window
with steep two-centred arches and panel tracery. Inside, tw
broad and high niches between each two clerestory window
On the E gable an enjoyable Sanctus-bell turret. – PLAT
Chalice, c.1570; Paten, by *Humphrey Payne*, 1714.

CASTLE HILL, in the middle of the northern part of the villag
S of the church. This is the remains of a large ringwork
moderate strength, which probably had wet ditches. Its exis
ence is only recorded once, close to the middle of the C1
when stone defences were being ordered.

THE MANOR. The present house is C17, H-shaped and muc
restored. C13 fragments remain, e.g. two head corbels, prol
ably transferred at the time of some church restoration.

9030

WELBY

ST BARTHOLOMEW. The chancel was rebuilt by *J. H. Hakewi*
in 1873. In the S wall re-used Norman stones. In the N wa
a lancet window which might be original and would da
the chancel. Hakewill anyway chose the E.E. style. The u
commonly thin unbuttressed W tower is also E.E., though t
bell-openings are Dec. Broach-spire with two tiers of lucarne
The W respond of the N arcade is E.E., the rest of the fou
bay arcade Perp. Perp also the ornate S porch with oversize
pinnacles and a parapet decorated with cusped lozenges, ar
Perp the clerestory. Six windows. Parapet with shields. –
SCREEN. One-light divisions, ogee arches and tracery over. –
BENCH ENDS. With minor poppy-heads. – SOUTH DOO
Traceried. – MONUMENT. Bust of a Lady in a quatrefo
The rest of the figure disappears in the slab, except for t
feet. Where the legs must be presumed lies a baby. C14.

BEDEHOUSES. Probably Georgian. One-storeyed, with a rais

two-storeyed pedimented centre. A panel of crisp foliage above the door.

RECTORY. Tudor style. 1834 by *Cornelius Sherborne* of Grantham (GA).

WELLINGORE

ALL SAINTS. The oldest feature in the church is the sedilia. Its slightly chamfered round arches and waterleaf capitals belong to the late C12. The chancel shows nothing else of this date. The arch as well as the E window with its flowing tracery prove a Dec date at once. Next in order of time the arcades and the tower. The arcades are of three bays. The S side has one round and one octagonal pier, the N side octagonal piers only. Very elementary capitals. Double-chamfered arches. The arch into the N chapel is of the same time. The unbuttressed W tower has a W lancet, three nobbly Dec corbels over, and Dec bell-openings. Plain, small, recessed spire. Perp the N aisle w window with a fleuron surround, and the clerestory of tallish two-light windows with panel tracery. – BENCH ENDS with plain poppy-heads. – PLATE. Bowl-shaped Paten, by *G.B.*, 1669. – MONUMENTS. Sir Richard de Buslingthorpe(?). Of about 1430–40. Alabaster effigies. Tomb-chest with three shields in quatrefoils and panelling between.

WELLINGORE HALL. A drawn-out pile of two main periods: the centre part of *c.*1780, with stone fronts, a pediment, and pedimented windows. Two-storey canted bays added not much later. Then in 1876 *J. MacVicar Anderson* (i.e. *Burn*'s office) came along and extended the front still further. Attached to the W portion is the CHAPEL, in a quasi-Romanesque style. Apse and circular tower at one angle. Inside, fairly lavish marble treatment. Six windows by *Burlison & Grylls* were put in after a fire of 1884.

MANOR HOUSE. Georgian and facing the Green. Near by a cottage dated 1670 with the usual mullioned windows and straight hoods, and opposite the church a BARN with blocked two-light windows and a blocked entrance with a moulded frame.

VILLAGE CROSS, at the N exit. Only the base and part of the shaft remain.

WEST ALLINGTON

HOLY TRINITY. Medieval nave of ironstone. The big double bellcote, probably of the early C13, is said to come from the demolished church of East Allington. So are the bits of Norman

corbel table, by the bellcote.* Holy Trinity was lengthened in
brick. To the s, half the nave is brick, and the whole chancel.
When was that done, and what does the one upright oval
window signify? It must be c17. The windows in the brick
parts are re-used medieval pieces – two lights with a lozenge
above, reticulated, etc. Norman s doorway with two orders of
shafts, scallop capitals, and roll mouldings in the arch. Four-
bay N arcade of c.1200. Round piers with round abaci. Double-
chamfered round arches. Hood-moulds with nailhead. – FONT.
Octagonal, Perp. Stem with leaf motifs. On the bowl lozenge-
shaped fields with flowers, heads, and a shield. – PULPIT.
Jacobean, with the typical short, broad blank arches. –
SCREEN. One tracery unit re-used in the reading desk. – WEST
GALLERY. Jacobean. – SHIELD. The large heraldic shield is
of *Coade* stone (Gunnis). – PLATE (also of East Allington).
Chalice, by *W.G.*, 1672.

ALLINGTON HALL. Some time after 1727 the house was given
a new E front of stone, two bays deep, six bays long, with three
floors and parapet. Entrances and tall windows in bays one and
six, provided with rusticated surrounds and broken segmental
pediments with cartouche. According to *White's Directory* there
were 'improvements' in 1874. At the time of writing ruinous.

OLD MANOR HOUSE. Of a rich golden ironstone dressed with a
lighter grey stone. Seven bays of windows with mullions and
transoms on the entrance front, a broad string, and a full cornice.
The doorway c18. The side fronts with pairs of Dutch (i.e. pedimented) gables and scrolly foliage volutes. An odd arrangement
of windows from the ground up, 2–1–2–1–2, all of two and three
lights. A dog-leg staircase possesses wonderfully round finials.
A date of c.1660 has been suggested, and this is not far from the
1653 of the similar Denton Almshouses (*see* p. 513).

WESTBOROUGH

8040

ALL SAINTS. Are the two small circular windows in the N aisle
re-set Anglo-Saxon pieces? The nave is the best part of the
church. Late c12, of three wide and high bays, with quatrefoil piers and double-chamfered arches. Very plain capitals,
probably left undetailed. On the responds shaft-rings, and
also waterleaf capitals, the latter an unmistakable sign of the
later c12. The E responds stand only to a certain height. There
were perhaps stone screens here. To these arcades belong the

---

* But Nattes drew the church of West Allington with the bellcote and the
church of East Allington as well.

N and S doorways with two and one orders of shafts respectively, and also the blocked N aisle W lancet. Then the chancel.
It is also E.E. and has single lancets to N (four of them) and S,
and to the N also the priest's doorway with an order of shafts
carrying stiff-leaf capitals. Of the large E window the shafts
with shaft-rings are preserved, but the window itself is a transomed domestic five-light piece. Two plain oblong low-side
windows. Inside, rather raw, and also damaged, double piscina and sedilia, the sedilia with pointed-trefoiled arches, i.e.
a later C13 motif. The N transept is in fact late C13, see the
two E windows with intersecting tracery. The great N window
is a sad C17 replacement, but the jamb shafts survive. Inside
the transept an odd arrangement. Immediately N of the arcade
pier marking the W start of the transept an octagonal pier was
put up, probably as a strengthening. The corresponding pier
for the S transept is dubious in its detail and belongs perhaps
to 1750, when the S transept collapsed and the rather C17-
looking five-light S window was put up. The W tower is entirely
of 1752 and has no features worth commenting on. Of features
not yet mentioned the finest is the big straight-headed four-
light Dec window in the chancel. The castellated clerestory
is Perp. On the N aisle also Perp battlements. The S aisle is
Perp altogether. – FONT. Octagonal, Norman, each side an
arch on angle-shafts. In each of these fields six long thin
intersecting arches and, in the tympanum, two affronted flat,
stylized leaves. – PULPIT. C17, simple. – SCREEN. With
straight-topped two-light divisions. – BENCH ENDS. In the
chancel. With decoration all of the same simple pattern of
tiers of panels and poppy-heads. – PAINTING. On the W wall
in arched panels Time and Death, C18, defaced. – PLATE.
Chalice and Cover, by *John Morley* of Lincoln(?), inscribed
1573; Chalice and Paten, by *I.S.*, 1673. – MONUMENTS.
Tablets of the Hall family, later C18 to early C19. – CHURCH-
YARD CROSS. Complete with the top knob.

RECTORY. Brick, C17 and C18. The S front is early C18. Five
bays and two storeys with a pedimented one-bay projection.
Staircase in an open well. Three slim balusters to the tread,
one columnar, two twisted. Carved tread-ends.

WEST DEEPING

ST ANDREW. E.E. three-bay arcades, both of round piers,
moulded capitals, round abaci, and double-chamfered arches,
but the N piers a little slenderer. The chancel arch E.E. too.

Of the late C13 the windows in the W bays of the aisles. Simp
Geometrical tracery (an unfoiled circle). Early C14 chance
The windows with tracery of a cusped intersecting variet
Ballflower frieze below the eaves. Sedilia and piscina in keep
ing, but not so the chancel decoration of 1876. Tiling in a
available colours. Stone SCREEN and REREDOS with mosai
The *Building News* of 1877 reports that *Butterfield* restore
the church but probably not the chancel (PF). Then the De
W tower. Clasping buttresses. Arch to the nave triple-chan
fered. Perp bell-openings with transoms. Recessed crockete
spire with two tiers of lucarnes in the same directions. – FON
Octagonal, C13(?). With panels with shields. – CHANDELIE
Brass, two tiers of arms; 1770. – STAINED GLASS. The gla
in the chancel all by *Gibbs*, c.1878.

To the SW of the church picturesque WATER MILL. To the
the OLD RECTORY, red brick with black brick bands, l
E. P. Loftus Brock, 1869. To the E of the church a cottage wi
a sundial dated 1700. Opposite this IVY HOUSE, Georgia
and nice, and to its S the MANOR HOUSE. In style this belon,
rather to Northants across the river. It is H-shaped and dat
1634. The W front is the only one that has escaped hea
restoration. It has the usual gables over the projecting win,
and mullioned windows. There is a central two-storey porc
also gabled, and a doorway with a flattened head. At the re
of the house a tall three-storey store or DOVECOTE.

The village is uncommonly charming, mostly of stone cottag
along the main street, which runs N. The RED LION INN
dated 1795, and two houses opposite 1790.

2020

WESTON

ST MARY. The church betrays its age at once by the clerestor
which looks Norman, but is, as it will turn out, rather E.
Small round-headed windows with a continuous roll on th
N side, but with sumptuous (if a little clumsily applie
double shafting on the S side. Here the capitals have stiff-lea
Contemporary corbel table. Then the S porch, clearly E. I
and with the cluster of detached shafts of the entrance pr
paring for the Lincoln style of the interior. The porch h
blank arcading inside, and the capitals of this and the entran
shafts display more stiff-leaf. Noble E.E. chancel, with widel
spaced single lancets in the beautiful masonry of the wal
Frieze of crockets below the wall. The E wall has four closel
set buttresses, the middle ones chamfered, and three lance

of equal height between. Above them an elongated quatrefoil. The priest's doorway still has a round head. The low-side window is later (see the interior). The aisle windows are Dec, the transept windows Victorian (*Scott*, 1858–67).* Perp w tower without spire. Bits of decoration on the gables of the buttresses. Now the magnificent interior. Five-bay arcades. The N piers circular with four detached shafts (cf. for similar 9b forms the Lincoln parish churches and Skirbeck), the s piers octagonal, set so that angles point in the main directions and also with four detached shafts. Round abaci embracing the whole, stiff-leaf capitals of the early C13, arches with one roll and one slight chamfer. The fifth, i.e. transept, bay is wider. So there was no doubt a crossing tower there before the w tower. The clerestory windows are above the spandrels, not the apexes of the arches. The chancel arch has an odd square projection in the responds and again detached shafts, stiff-leaf capitals, semicircular abaci, and rolls in the arch mouldings. In the chancel all the windows are placed inside giant blank arcading. Thin shafts, capitals with a little nailhead. The E windows are also shafted inside. Tall Perp tower arch and springers for a vault. – FONT. A large and stately E.E. piece. Circular, with eight shafts, and in each field a stiff-leaf 'tree 19a of life'. Unusual arrangement of the steps. – PANELLING. Bits and pieces, C17; also two small Flemish religious scenes, C16. – STAINED GLASS. In the chancel by *Clayton & Bell*. – PLATE. Chalice and Paten, London, 1611; Flagon, by *Thomas Parr*, 1720. – MONUMENT. Big incised slab in the N transept. Only an early C14 head of a lady remains recognizable. – CHURCHYARD CROSS, to the sw. Base and shaft remain.

CHOOL. Brick and stone; Tudoresque, by *J. Billing* of Reading, 1852.

IMBERLEY HALL, ¼ m. NE. A small early C17 manor house built of brown brick. Two short gabled wings of three floors project with four-, three-, and two-light windows. The doorway asymmetrically placed. Inside, the original oak stairs with fat balusters. The staircase rises through the centre of the house.

WESTON HILLS   2020
1½ m. NE of Cowbit

T JOHN EVANGELIST. 1888, tower 1896 (PB). Red brick. Nave and chancel. Funny N tower with recessed octagonal top piece. Red and yellow brick inside.

* Further restoration by *Pearson*, 1886. Are the fine lead roofs his?

2020

WEST PINCHBECK

ST BARTHOLOMEW. 1850 by *Butterfield*. Restored 1897 b
J. C. Traylen (GR). Not an interesting church. Coursed rubble
Nave and chancel; bellcote on a mid-buttress – the only note
worthy motif. Dec windows. In the chancel one windo
which is only an arch-head, in the S aisle one which is an oge
quatrefoil. – STAINED GLASS. That in the E window must b
of Butterfield's time.

VICARAGE. Basically probably by *Butterfield*, see the plat
tracery of the ground-floor windows.

3020

WHAPLODE

ST MARY. Neglected until very recently, but also unrestore
The former I felt strongly in the churchyard, and in look
ing at the windows of the church, the majority of which are i
a roughly restored late C17(?) state, but the latter even mor
strongly inside the church. As one tries to find one's wa
among the trees around the building, one notices the tow
first. It is almost detached now, was perhaps begun detache
but at once connected with the church (see the roof-line o
the N side); for the tower stands in lieu of a S transeptal pro
jection. It is E.E. Three stages of blank E.E. arcading, th
bottom one with arches still decorated by zigzag at r. angle
to the wall, i.e. still C12. Bell-stage with much-shafted twi
openings, shaft-rings, dog-tooth, but Dec tracery later set i
Later parapet and puny pinnacles. The doorway into th
tower is on the E side. It is shafted inside. The opening to the
transepts has triple responds with keeling. As for the body
the church, the salient evidence is the clerestory (cf. Moulton
It is all Norman or Transitional at the latest, but divided in
two parts. The W part has blank arcading of single-chamfere
round arches on shafts, the E part on the S side a triparti
rhythm of small round–wide segmental–small round. Th
windows are in the wider bays. On the N side it is instead a
small round, but windows are in every third bay and ar
shafted. In the E gable one shafted Norman window. All th
is promising for the interior, and the promise will be kep
But first on with the exterior. The W doorway is late C12
see the capitals of the three orders of shafts (cf. Moulton). Ver
many mouldings. Gable. Blank bays l. and r. The very large
window is of course later and now in the typical Whaploc

state of the late C17(?). The S doorway is also late C12 and extremely fine. Clustered shafts, characteristic late C12 capitals.
Beautiful arch mouldings. C14 S porch, tunnel-vaulted; entrance with continuous mouldings.

The interior bears out all that the outside suggested. The
arcades of seven bays clearly consist of two groups, the four E
bays first, the three W bays later. The E bays are fully Norman,
and not late. One pair of piers sturdy octagonal, one sturdy
round, one a sturdy cluster of eight round shafts on a square
plan. The first two pairs have heavy scallop capitals and square
abaci, the third has capitals also scalloped, but a little later. The
arches have a half-roll and two slight chamfers. In the spandrels
a blank roundel. In the clerestory, on the N side only, are windows with shafts carrying block capitals. The chancel arch is
Norman also, with zigzag at r. angles to the wall surface. This
motif repeats in the tower; so these two may be roughly contemporary. Zigzag used in this way is usually Later Norman,
but it appears at Peterborough about 1130, and that might well
be the date of the first phase of Whaplode. Then, say about
1180 or 1190, the decision must have been taken to lengthen
the nave to the W. The piers here are quatrefoils, the foils more
than semicircular. The capitals are early stiff-leaf. Only the 9a
NE respond still has scallops, and they are now of the trumpet
variety. Round arches with two slight chamfers. In the spandrels, on the S side only, blank quatrefoils. In the clerestory,
on the N side only, shafts of the windows with round moulded
capitals. Building proceeded apparently N before S. Finally
the chancel N chapel, full C13. Round piers, elementary
double-chamfered arches. Handsome nave roof of high pitch.
Thin hammerbeams and arched braces up to collar-beams.
Traceried braces. Is this Perp or later?

FURNISHINGS. FONT. Octagonal. Tall bowl with fluted
panels, perhaps C17. – PULPIT. Jacobean, with tester. –
PANELLING. In the chancel, of c.1700. – SCULPTURE. Out-
side the church, among architectural fragments, some Anglo-
Saxon stones with interlace. – PLATE. Chalice, rim early C18;
Paten, by *William Bennett*, 1805. – MONUMENTS. C13 coffin-
lid with elaborately foliated cross (S aisle W end). – Effigy of a
Lady, C14, only head and bust in a trefoil. Fragment (nave W).
– Sir Anthony Irby † 1610 and wife † 1625. Ten-poster with
ogee roof crowned by an achievement. Recumbent effigies.
Kneeling children against the the tomb-chest. Original railing
round.

VICARAGE. In style C17, and there is indeed a date 1683. Ye the details of the brickwork confirm that *H. J. Underwoo* rebuilt the house (sympathetically) in 1842 (GA).

WHAPLODE DROVE

3010

ST JOHN. 1821 by *J. Pacey & Swansborough* (Colvin). Brick classical. Nave and later chancel. The nave has a w pedimen and a square, lead-faced bell-turret with cupola. Arched win dows. Chancel and w porch 1907–8. – SCULPTURE. In th porch a Roman ALTAR, found c.1935. – PLATE. Chalice, in scribed WHAPLOTE DROVE, c.1569; Chalice with Elizabethan features, given 1717; Flagon, by *Charles Martin*, given 1733.

WHITE LOAF HALL see FREISTON

WIGTOFT

2030

ST PETER AND ST PAUL. The lower part of the w tower i mysterious. The small w doorway is Norman; so is the elabor ately-framed small window above it. This has shafts with si rings and in the arch zigzag at r. angles to the wall. But ca these two be *in situ*? For in the E wall of the tower, to the and r. of the E.E. tower arch, are signs of blocked Norma windows, two of a triplet. If that represents a Norman w wal before there was a tower, the Norman features of the towe w wall must be shifted. The tower above is Perp and carrie a short spire. Norman also a re-set piece of corbel table in th s porch (w side). Re-set probably the porch entrance too. is E.E. and has bold stiff-leaf. The aisle windows Dec. Th chancel has a pretty Perp s window and a priest's doorway in position which would indicate that the chancel was shortene The E window is indeed Victorian. Perp clerestory of eigl closely-set windows. Battlements, but on the E gable parape with a leaf trail. Dec four-bay arcades. The piers quatrefoi or rather square with semicircular projections. Moulde arches. Perp chancel arch. – PULPIT. Jacobean. – PLAT Chalice and Paten Cover, by *Matthew West*(?), 1702. MONUMENT. Recess below the SE aisle window, Dec, with very pretty frieze of small heads.

HOUSE, E of the Swan Inn. Early C18, with an apsed hood.

CASTERTON HOUSE. Late Georgian. Early C19 BARN wi Gothic windows.

WILLOUGHBY HALL see ANCASTER

WILSFORD

0040

т MARY. The nave is initially Anglo-Saxon; see the long-and-short SE quoins and also, inside the church and less clearly, the NE quoins. Next in order of time the arch from the chancel to the N chapel. This is obviously Norman. Scalloped capitals. It is probably not *in situ*, and may have been the chancel arch. The hood-mould with dog-tooth does not belong to it. The present chancel arch is of the restoration of 1860–1 (*Kirk & Parry*). The chancel is E.E., see the two S lancet windows. The exuberant four-light E window is of course Dec. The E.E. contribution continues with the N arcade, certainly no later than the early C13. Two bays, round pier, odd abacus, square with nicks and chamfers, double-chamfered round arches. Then the mysterious S aisle. This also is E.E. It has a W lancet, and beyond its E end, i.e. in the Anglo-Saxon wall, is another, taller lancet. Then the wall was pierced by two bays, one wide, the other narrow, but above the narrow one is a large blocked window cut into by the arcade arch. What was the sequence then, and what reasons were there for these changes of mind, all in the same short building period? Dec N chapel and N aisle windows. Perp S aisle windows. Short, embattled Perp clerestory of three pairs of two-light windows. On the N side nice canopied niches in addition. Perp W tower with recessed spire and two tiers of lucarnes in alternating directions. – FONT. A concave-sided octagon; Perp. Quatrefoils on the stem, pointed quatrefoils with flowers on the bowl. – BENCH ENDS. In the chancel. With poppy-heads, e.g. a bishop, a St Catherine, a St George, two dogs, two affronted eagles, a lion, a pelican. – SCULPTURE. Romano-British Votive Stone, a small standing male figure in relief, very weathered. He wears a kilt (cf. Ancaster).

WILSTHORPE

0010

т FAITH. Why did *James Fowler* ill-treat so cruelly such a perfect Early Georgian church? It has a façade dated 1715, and there is a touch of Vanbrugh in this oblong block with giant angle pilasters, a big broad doorway with broken segmental pediment on large paired brackets, an arched balustrade, and a square turret, its pilasters with the Gibbs motif exaggerated by three instead of one vertical connecting the blocks of rustication. The lowish chancel has alternatingly raised quoins. Fowler in 1863 put the ridiculous shingled

broach spire on, made the bell-openings Gothic, and altered
all other windows. – FONT. Square baluster set diagonally and
fluted bowl (cf. Langtoft). – COMMUNION RAIL and RAIL of
the tower gallery. Twisted balusters. – PLATE. Chalice
London, 1569. – MONUMENT. This effigy must be a C17 fake.
It has the arms of the Wake family. The crossing of the legs
is improbably done, and the surcoat and its carved pattern is
also improbable. The way the hand lies instead of holding the
shield has no parallel. Finally, although this tends to convey
a date about 1300, the lavish belt and the moustache would
spell 1375 or so.

WIMBERLEY HALL see WESTON

WITHAM-ON-THE-HILL

ST ANDREW. A strange, alas over-restored, church. The
strangeness is the S tower, an essay in medievalism of 1737–
(by *George Portwood*). Below, the date is unmistakable, see e.g.
the S window with its Gibbs surround, the cruciform shape
round the clock, and the urns instead of pinnacles. But the
bell-openings have round openings and Y-tracery, and there
is a recessed spire with two tiers of lucarnes which is certainly
more serious than the date would suggest. Is there a touch here
of the Vanbrugh–Hawksmoor medievalism – via Grimsthorpe? The church has a S doorway of the late C12 with
waterleaf capitals. Above the arch a piece of SCULPTURE, a
very fine small seated C12 figure. Of the date of the doorway
also the S arcade. Four bays, circular piers, octagonal abaci,
coarse waterleaf capitals. Double-chamfered round arches.
In the W wall of the aisle is a small round-headed window,
Norman perhaps also the N transept, see its clasping buttresses.
Then the chancel. It seems to have received a chapel in the
C13. Or what can the semi-octagonal respond in the E wall
with its defaced stiff-leaf capital mean?* The N arcade has
octagonal piers and double-chamfered arches taking in the
transept. Cox calls it E.E., though the N windows are De-
Ogee intersecting tracery. Perp W window in the nave. Five
lights. Perp chancel windows. Tall three-light clerestory
windows, also Perp. – FONT. Octagonal, with flatly carved
leaf, zigzag, etc. motifs, also a patriarchal cross. Is this C17
– SCREEN. No more remains than two grotesquely incompetent
painted figures from the dado – an East Anglian rather than

* It could of course be re-set.

Lincolnshire tradition. The source is early woodcuts. – PLATE. Chalice, by *Seth Lofthouse*, 1706; Flagon, by *Richard Bayley*, 1730.

STOCKS. Under a canopy, NE of the church.

SCHOOL. 1847. Inscribed 'Train up a child the way he should go and when he is old he will not part from it'.

MANOR FARM. Looks C17 but is more likely to be Georgian. In a field a stone DOVECOTE with a slightly ogee roof.

WITHAM HALL. The core of the house, just five bays to E and W, dates from 1752–6, though it looks, with its moulded window surrounds, early C18. Nothing Georgian remains inside, and the exterior was much added to by *A. N. Prentice* in 1903–5. He gave the house an H-plan and added a range on the E side. Along the W side of the house to the entrance, i.e. along the drive, a vista of pseudo-Jacobethan arches, dated in order 1876, 1830, and 1906.

WOODLANDS FARM *see* GOSBERTON

WOOLSTHORPE-BY-BELVOIR 8030

ST JAMES. By *G. G. Place*, 1847. Of ironstone, rock-faced, quite big. W tower, nave and aisles, chancel. Dec detail. – PLATE. Chalice and Paten, London, 1623.

The village street runs along the side of a hill immediately opposite the higher hill on which towers Belvoir Castle, and so it is a Leicestershire village rather than Lincolnshire. The SCHOOL of 1871 takes up the style of Place's church. In the centre of the village is a thatched cottage and one judiciously placed tree.

On the CANAL are charming lock cottages and a WHARF where the stone was unloaded for building Belvoir and Harlaxton. ½m. E is a LODGE of Belvoir Castle, heavily bargeboarded.

WOOLSTHORPE MANOR *see* COLSTERWORTH

WRANGLE 4050

ST MARY AND ST NICHOLAS. A marshland church, i.e. predominantly Perp. But there are older parts as well. What first of all does the billet frieze in the chancel wall, S and E, mean? Is it Norman? Is it re-set? The tower arch towards the nave is a serious Transitional piece with scalloped as well as stiff-leaf capitals, a pointed arch, and a hood-mould, where stylized

leaves play the part of beakhead. Then the s doorway, ¿
exciting E.E. job. Trefoiled entrance with dog-tooth and le
cusps. Two orders of shafts with dog-tooth accompanyi
them and nailhead in the capitals. To this moment in th
history of the building, arcades or at least a N arcade mu
have belonged, see the NW respond and its unmistakable bas
Otherwise the arcades are Dec, and so is the chancel. T
arcades are tall and of as many as six bays. Octagonal pie
arches moulded with one hollow chamfer and one keeled ro
Only the NE respond differs. The chancel has windows wi
cusped intersecting as well as reticulated tracery (the E wi
dow of five lights). This being so, it is important that we c
at least approximately date it. In the glass of the E window w
once an inscription: 'Thomas de Wyversty, abbas de Waltha
me fieri fecit', and the dates of his abbacy of Waltham a
1345–71. But the chancel arch with its concave-sided sen
octagonal responds and leaves and heads in the capitals loo
Perp rather than Dec. Perp the aisle windows, the tw
storeyed s porch (battlements), the clerestory of two-lig
upright windows (also battlements), and of course the
tower. It is embraced by the aisles. Between it and the
aisle a low stair-turret with spire. In the s aisle a low ton
recess. – PULPIT. Jacobean, with the usual short blank arche
also arabesque, and complex Ionic colonnettes at the angles.
STAINED GLASS. Unusually much is preserved of, as has be
said, c.1350–70. It is in the NE and N windows. Plenty of who
small figures in the tracery heads and an assembly of pa
lower down in the E window, including a nearly comple
Resurrection. – PLATE. Plate, London, 1694(?); Chalice,
Robert Peake, 1701, a refashioned Elizabethan Cup; Flag
by *William Pitts*, 1809; Chalice and Paten, by *Joshua Guest*(
1812. – MONUMENT. Brasses of John Reade † 1503, w
and children (chancel floor); 3 ft figures. – Sir John Rea
† 1626 and family. Two recumbent effigies, he lying behi
her and a little higher. The children against the tomb-che
The effigies are of stone, but the rest is of alabaster, includi
the children, as they are in relief. Good back wall with pe
ments etc.

OLD VICARAGE. Early C18, in brown brick with long tw
storey, seven-bay front, high hipped roof, and four gab
dormers.

CASTLE, c.1½ m. NW. On the low ground running out in
East Fen is a large area of moated works, centred on a ve

wide and very low motte and bailey, now known as KING'S
HILL. This castle is typical of those in the low country of
Lincolnshire.

WYBERTON

3040

ST LEODEGAR. Externally all Perp, except for the short, polygonal brick chancel, which is of course Georgian, but internally all is E.E. and very impressive, thanks also to the recent
blocking of the chancel windows. What could a good, really
modern altar do for this focal point! The arcades are of five
bays. The s arcade has plain octagonal piers and double-
chamfered arches. But the N arcade has piers of four major and
four minor shafts, one capital with nailhead and double-
chamfered arches. Only the last pier is thinner, quatrefoil, not
octofoil, and the last two arches are different too, one chamfer
and one keeled roll.* Why these anomalies? A look at the E
end of the arcade provides the answer. There was a crossing.
And a look at the bases of all the arcade piers provides the
second answer. The w crossing piers stood where the third
piers now stand. The crossing piers consisted of triple shafts
to each side and a detached shaft in each hollowed-out diagonal. Then, s of the SE crossing pier, there is another anomaly,
a respond which must have been supplied with a view to a
chapel or an aisle off the transept and parallel with the chancel.
So what has happened is that the church was designed to be
cruciform and grand, but that, before the w crossing piers were
erected, the plan was changed, the s arcade carried on, the N
arcade built, and the transept and aisle left off. The w tower,
being Perp, was built so that it cuts into the E.E. arcades.
The Perp aisle and clerestory windows date from 1881. The
tower can perhaps be dated from the contract with *Roger
Denys* to rebuild church and tower, a contract dated 1419.
Nave roof with tie-beams on arched braces alternating with
angels against principals. – FONT. Octagonal, Dec or Perp,
with some shields under shallow, thinly crocketed ogee arches.
– PLATE. Chalice, by *R.S.*, 1631; Flagon and Paten, by *John
Penfold*, 1727. – MONUMENT. Incised slab to Adam de Framp-
ton † 1325 and wife.

WYBERTON HALL. The s front is in the style of *William Sands
Jun.* of Spalding. It was built in 1761 for T. Burton Shaw and
Edward Shaw, whose names are inscribed on the angle stones.
Seven bays, two storeys, stone quoins, and a pediment in the

* The same pattern repeats in the NW and SW arches.

middle breaking up from the parapet with scrolled ends, concave sides, and a central finial. The windows have stone surrounds, but those on the ground floor have been lowered at a later date. Full Tuscan columns with a triangular pediment to the entrance door. The interior preserves fine plaster and woodwork, particularly the Rococo library ceiling and the panelling of the drawing room. The stairs are similar to those at Frampton Hall (*see* p. 531), but lit from the side by a spacious window.

(WOAD MILL. A red brick shed, C18, with some of the machinery still *in situ*. MHLG)

WYBERT'S CASTLE, *c.*½ m. E of the church. A large, irregular banked and ditched site. Elsewhere in England it would hardly pass as a castle, but in this low and fenny site it is likely to be what its name suggests.

WYKEHAM CHAPEL *see* SPALDING, p. 650

WYVILLE

8020

ST CATHERINE. Built in 1857. The chancel of 1868. Yellow brick and stone trim. Nave and chancel; bellcote. Style *c.*1300, but minimum.

HUNGERTON HALL, 1 m. NW. Built in 1785 for the de Ligne Gregory family. Stone, five-by-four-bay block of three storeys. Once flanked by pavilions, of which one remains. Seven later Tuscan porch to the S front. Bathos compared with Harlaxton.

GLOSSARY

ABACUS: flat slab on the top of a capital (q.v.).

ABUTMENT: solid masonry placed to resist the lateral pressure of a vault.

ACANTHUS: plant with thick fleshy and scalloped leaves used as part of the decoration of a Corinthian capital (q.v.) and in some types of leaf carving.

ACHIEVEMENT OF ARMS: in heraldry, a complete display of armorial bearings.

ACROTERION: foliage-carved block on the end or top of a classical pediment.

ADORSED: two human figures, animals, or birds, etc., placed symmetrically so that they turn their backs to each other.

AEDICULE, AEDICULA: framing of a window or door by columns and a pediment (q.v.).

AFFRONTED: two human figures, animals, or birds, etc., placed symmetrically so that they face each other.

AGGER: Latin term for the built-up foundations of Roman roads; also sometimes applied to the banks of hill-forts or other earthworks.

AMBULATORY: semicircular or polygonal aisle enclosing an apse (q.v.).

ANNULET: see Shaft-ring.

ANSE DE PANIER: see Arch, Basket.

ANTEPENDIUM: covering of the front of an altar, usually by textiles or metalwork.

ANTIS, IN: see Portico.

APSE: vaulted semicircular or polygonal end of a chancel or a chapel.

ARABESQUE: light and fanciful surface decoration using combinations of flowing lines, tendrils, etc., interspersed with vases, animals, etc.

ARCADE: range of arches supported on piers or columns, free-standing; or, BLIND ARCADE, the same attached to a wall.

ARCH: round-headed, i.e. semicircular; pointed, i.e. consisting of two curves, each drawn from one centre, and meeting in a point at the top; segmental, i.e. in the form of a segment; pointed; four-centred (a Late Medieval form), see Fig. 1(a); Tudor (also a Late Medieval form), see Fig. 1(b); Ogee (introduced c. 1300 and specially popular in the C14), see Fig.

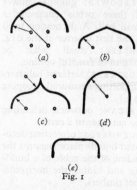

(a)   (b)

(c)   (d)

(e)
Fig. 1

1(*c*); Stilted, *see* Fig. 1(*d*); Basket, with lintel connected to the jambs by concave quadrant curves, *see* Fig. 1(*e*).

ARCHITRAVE: lowest of the three main parts of the entablature (q.v.) of an order (q.v.) (*see* Fig. 12).

ARCHIVOLT: under-surface of an arch (also called Soffit).

ARRIS: sharp edge at the meeting of two surfaces.

ASHLAR: masonry of large blocks wrought to even faces and square edges.

ATRIUM: inner court of a Roman house, also open court in front of a church.

ATTACHED: *see* Engaged.

ATTIC: topmost storey of a house, if distance from floor to ceiling is less than in the others.

AUMBRY: recess or cupboard to hold sacred vessels for Mass and Communion.

BAILEY: open space or court of a stone-built castle; *see* also Motte-and-Bailey.

BALDACCHINO: canopy supported on columns.

BALLFLOWER: globular flower of three petals enclosing a small ball. A decoration used in the first quarter of the C14.

BALUSTER: small pillar or column of fanciful outline.

BALUSTRADE: series of balusters supporting a handrail or coping (q.v.).

BARBICAN: outwork defending the entrance to a castle.

BARGEBOARDS: projecting decorated boards placed against the incline of the gable of a building and hiding the horizontal roof timbers.

BARROW: *see* Bell, Bowl, Disc, Long, *and* Pond Barrow.

BASILICA: in medieval architecture an aisled church with a clerestory.

BASKET ARCH: *see* Arch (Fig. 1e).

BASTION: projection at the angle of a fortification.

BATTER: inclined face of a wall.

BATTLEMENT: parapet with a series of indentations or embrasures with raised portions or merlons between (also called Crenellation).

BAYS: internal compartments of a building; each divided from the other not by solid walls but by divisions only marked in the side walls (columns, pilasters etc.) or the ceiling (beams etc.). Also external divisions of a building by fenestration.

BAY-WINDOW: angular or curved projection of a house front with ample fenestration. If curved, also called bow window; if on an upper floor only, also called oriel or oriel window.

BEAKER FOLK: Late New Stone Age warrior invaders from the Continent who buried their dead in round barrows and introduced the first metal tools and weapons to Britain.

BEAKHEAD: Norman ornamental motif consisting of a row of bird or beast heads with beaks biting usually into a roll moulding.

BELFRY: turret on a roof to hang bells in.

BELGAE: Aristocratic warrior bands who settled in Britain in two main waves in the C1 B.C. In Britain their culture is termed Iron Age C.

BELL BARROW: Early Bronze

Age round barrow in which the mound is separated from its encircling ditch by a flat platform or berm (q.v.).

BELLCOTE: framework on a roof to hang bells from.

BERM: level area separating ditch from bank on a hill-fort or barrow.

BILLET FRIEZE: Norman ornamental motif made up of short raised rectangles placed at regular intervals.

BIVALLATE: Of a hill-fort: defended by two concentric banks and ditches.

BLOCK CAPITAL: Romanesque capital cut from a cube by having the lower angles rounded off to the circular shaft below (also called Cushion Capital) (Fig. 2).

Fig. 2

BOND, ENGLISH or FLEMISH: see Brickwork.

BOSS: knob or projection usually placed to cover the intersection of ribs in a vault.

BOW-WINDOW: see Bay-Window.

BOX: A small country house, e.g. a shooting box. A convenient term to describe a compact minor dwelling, e.g. a rectory.

BOX PEW: pew with a high wooden enclosure.

BOWL BARROW: round barrow surrounded by a quarry ditch. Introduced in Late Neolithic times, the form continued until the Saxon period.

BRACES: see Roof.

BRACKET: small supporting piece of stone, etc., to carry a projecting horizontal.

BRESSUMER: beam in a timber-framed building to support the, usually projecting, superstructure.

BRICKWORK: *Header:* brick laid so that the end only appears on the face of the wall. *Stretcher:* brick laid so that the side only appears on the face of the wall. *English Bond:* method of laying bricks so that alternate courses or layers on the face of the wall are composed of headers or stretchers only (Fig. 3a). *Flemish Bond:* method of laying bricks so that alternate headers and stretchers appear in each course on the face of the wall (Fig. 3b).

(a)

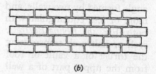

(b)

Fig. 3

BROACH: see Spire.

BROKEN PEDIMENT: see Pediment.

BRONZE AGE: In Britain, the period from *c.*1600 to 600 B.C.

BUCRANIUM: ox skull.

BUTTRESS: mass of brickwork or masonry projecting from or built against a wall to give additional strength. *Angle Buttresses:* two meeting at an angle

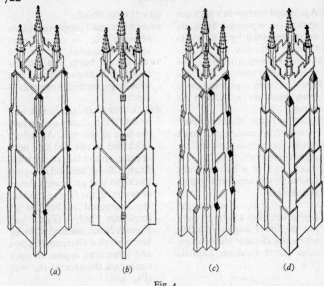

| (a) | (b) | (c) | (d) |

Fig. 4

of 90° at the angle of a building (Fig. 4a). *Clasping Buttress:* one which encases the angle (Fig. 4d). *Diagonal Buttress:* one placed against the right angle formed by two walls, and more or less equiangular with both (Fig. 4b). *Flying Buttress:* arch or half arch transmitting the thrust of a vault or roof from the upper part of a wall to an outer support or buttress. *Setback Buttress:* angle buttres set slightly back from the angle (Fig. 4c).

CABLE MOULDING: Norman moulding imitating a twisted cord.

CAIRN: a mound of stones usually covering a burial.

CAMBER: slight rise or upward curve of an otherwise horizontal structure.

CAMPANILE: isolated bell tower.

CANOPY: projection or hood over an altar, pulpit, niche, statue, etc.

CAP: in a windmill the crowning feature.

CAPITAL: head or top part of a column (q.v.).

CARTOUCHE: tablet with an ornate frame, usually enclosing an inscription.

CARYATID: whole figure supporting an entablature or other similar member. *Termini Caryatids:* busts or demi-figures or three-quarter figures supporting an entablature or other similar member and placed at the top of termini pilasters (q.v.).

CASTELLATED: decorated with battlements.

CELURE: panelled and adorned part of a wagon-roof above the rood or the altar.

CENSER: vessel for the burning of incense.

CENTERING: wooden framework used in arch and vault construction and removed when the mortar has set.

CHALICE: cup used in the Communion service or at Mass.

CHAMBERED TOMB: burial mound of the New Stone Age having a stone-built chamber and entrance passage covered by an earthen barrow or stone cairn. The form was introduced to Britain from the Mediterranean.

CHAMFER: surface made by cutting across the square angle of a stone block, piece of wood, etc., at an angle of 45° to the other two surfaces.

CHANCEL: that part of the E end of a church in which the altar is placed, usually applied to the whole continuation of the nave E of the crossing.

CHANCEL ARCH: arch at the W end of the chancel.

CHANTRY CHAPEL: chapel attached to, or inside, a church, endowed for the saying of Masses for the soul of the founder or some other individual.

CHEVET: French term for the E end of a church (chancel, ambulatory, and radiating chapels).

CHEVRON: Norman moulding forming a zigzag.

CHOIR: that part of the church where divine service is sung.

CIBORIUM: a baldacchino.

CINQUEFOIL: see Foil.

CIST: stone-lined or slab-built grave. First appears in Late Neolithic times. It continued to be used in the Early Christian period.

CLAPPER BRIDGE: bridge made of large slabs of stone, some built up to make rough piers and other longer ones laid on top to make the roadway.

CLASSIC: here used to mean the moment of highest achievement of a style.

CLASSICAL: here used as the term for Greek and Roman architecture and any subsequent styles inspired by it.

CLERESTORY: upper storey of the nave walls of a church, pierced by windows.

COADE STONE: artificial (cast) stone made in the late C18 and the early C19 by Coade and Sealy in London.

COB: walling material made of mixed clay and straw.

COFFERING: decorating a ceiling with sunk square or polygonal ornamental panels.

COLLAR-BEAM: see Roof.

COLONNADE: range of columns.

COLONNETTE: small column.

COLUMNA ROSTRATA: column decorated with carved prows of ships to celebrate a naval victory.

COMPOSITE: see Order.

CONSOLE: bracket (q.v.) with a compound curved outline.

COPING: capping or covering to a wall.

CORBEL: block of stone projecting from a wall, supporting some horizontal feature.

CORBEL TABLE: series of corbels, occurring just below the roof eaves externally or internally, often seen in Norman buildings.

CORINTHIAN: see Orders.

CORNICE: in classical architecture the top section of the entablature (q.v.). Also for a projecting decorative feature along the top of a wall, arch, etc.

CORRIDOR VILLA: see Villa.

COUNTERSCARP BANK: small bank on the down-hill or outer side of a hill-fort ditch.

COURTYARD VILLA: see Villa.

COVE, COVING: concave undersurface in the nature of a hollow moulding but on a larger scale.

COVER PATEN: cover to a Communion cup, suitable for use as a paten or plate for the consecrated bread.

CRADLE ROOF: see Wagon-roof.

CRENELLATION: see Battlement.

CREST, CRESTING: ornamental finish along the top of a screen, etc.

CROCKET, CROCKETING: decorative features placed on the sloping sides of spires, pinnacles, gables, etc., in Gothic architecture, carved in various leaf shapes and placed at regular intervals.

CROCKET CAPITAL: see Fig. 5. An Early Gothic form.

Fig. 5

CROMLECH: word of Celtic origin still occasionally used of single free-standing stones ascribed to the Neolithic or Bronze Age periods.

CROSSING: space at the inter-

section of nave, chancel, and transepts.

CROSS-WINDOWS: window with one mullion and one transom.

CRUCK: big curved beam supporting both walls and roof of a cottage.

CRYPT: underground room usually below the E end of a church.

CUPOLA: small polygonal or circular domed turret crowning a roof.

CURTAIN WALL: connecting wall between the towers of a castle.

CUSHION CAPITAL: see Block Capital.

CUSP: projecting point between the foils in a foiled Gothic arch.

DADO: decorative covering of the lower part of a wall.

DAGGER: tracery motif of the Dec style. It is a lancet shape, rounded or pointed at the head, pointed at the foot, and cusped inside (see Fig. 6).

Fig. 6

DAIS: raised platform at one end of a room.

DEC ('DECORATED'): historical division of English Gothic architecture covering the period from c.1290 to c.1350.

DEMI-COLUMNS: columns half sunk into a wall.

DIAPER WORK: surface decoration composed of square or lozenge shapes.

DISC BARROW: Bronze Age round barrow with inconspicuous central mound surrounded by bank and ditch.

DOG-TOOTH: typical E.E. ornament consisting of a series of four-cornered stars placed diagonally and raised pyramidally (Fig. 7).

Fig. 7

DOMICAL VAULT: see Vault.

DONJON: see Keep.

DORIC: see Order.

DORMER (WINDOW): window placed vertically in the sloping plane of a roof.

DRIPSTONE: see Hood-mould.

DRUM: circular or polygonal vertical wall of a dome or cupola.

E.E. ('EARLY ENGLISH'): historical division of English Gothic architecture roughly covering the C13.

EASTER SEPULCHRE: recess with tomb-chest usually in the wall of a chancel, the tomb-chest to receive an effigy of Christ for Easter celebrations.

EAVES: underpart of a sloping roof overhanging a wall.

EAVES CORNICE: cornice below the eaves of a roof.

ECHINUS: convex or projecting moulding supporting the abacus of a Greek Doric capital, sometimes bearing an egg and dart pattern.

EMBATTLED: see Battlement.

EMBRASURE: small opening in the wall or parapet of a fortified building, usually splayed on the inside.

ENCAUSTIC TILES: earthenware glazed and decorated tiles used for paving.

ENGAGED COLUMNS: columns attached to, or partly sunk into, a wall.

ENGLISH BOND: see Brickwork.

ENTABLATURE: in classical architecture the whole of the horizontal members above a column (that is architrave, frieze, and cornice) (see Fig. 12).

ENTASIS: very slight convex deviation from a straight line; used on Greek columns and sometimes on spires to prevent an optical illusion of concavity.

ENTRESOL: see Mezzanine.

EPITAPH: hanging wall monument.

ESCUTCHEON: shield for armorial bearings.

EXEDRA: the apsidal end of a room. See Apse.

FAN-VAULT: see Vault.

FERETORY: place behind the High Altar where the chief shrine of a church is kept.

FESTOON: carved garland of flowers and fruit suspended at both ends.

FILLET: narrow flat band running down a shaft or along a roll moulding.

FINIAL: top of a canopy, gable, pinnacle.

FLAGON: vessel for the wine used in the Communion service.

FLAMBOYANT: properly the latest phase of French Gothic architecture where the window tracery takes on wavy undulating lines.

FLÈCHE: slender wooden spire on the centre of a roof (also called Spirelet).

FLEMISH BOND: see Brickwork.

FLEURON: decorative carved flower or leaf.

FLUSHWORK: decorative use of flint in conjunction with dressed stone so as to form patterns: tracery, initials, etc.

FLUTING: vertical channelling in the shaft of a column.

FLYING BUTTRESS: see Buttress.

FOIL: lobe formed by the cusping (q.v.) of a circle or an arch. Trefoil, quatrefoil, cinquefoil, multifoil, express the number of leaf shapes to be seen.

FOLIATED: carved with leaf shapes.

FOSSE: ditch.

FOUR-CENTRED ARCH: see Arch.

FRATER: refectory or dining hall of a monastery.

FRESCO: wall painting on wet plaster.

FRIEZE: middle division of a classical entablature (q.v.) (see Fig. 12).

FRONTAL: covering for the front of an altar.

GABLE: *Dutch gable:* A gable with curved sides crowned by a

Fig. 8(a)

pediment, characteristic of c. 1630–50 (Fig. 8a).

Shaped gable: A gable with multi-curved sides characteristic of c.1600–50 (Fig. 8b).

Fig. 8(b)

GADROONED: enriched with a series of convex ridges, the opposite of fluting.

GALILEE: chapel or vestibule usually at the W end of a church enclosing the porch. Also called Narthex (q.v.).

GALLERY: in church architecture upper storey above an aisle, opened in arches to the nave. Also called Tribune (q.v.) and often erroneously Triforium (q.v.).

GALLERY GRAVE: chambered tomb (q.v.) in which there is little or no differentiation between the entrance passage and the actual burial chamber(s).

GARDEROBE: lavatory or privy in a medieval building.

GARGOYLE: water spout projecting from the parapet of a wall or tower; carved into a human or animal shape.

GAZEBO: lookout tower or raised summer house in a picturesque garden.

'GEOMETRICAL': see Tracery.

'GIBBS SURROUND': of a doorway or window. An C18 motif consisting of a surround with alternating larger and smaller blocks of stone, quoin-wise, or intermittent large blocks, sometimes with a narrow raised band connecting them up the

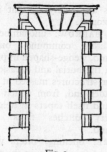

Fig. 9

verticals and along the face of the arch (Fig. 9).

GROIN: sharp edge at the meeting of two cells of a cross-vault.

GROIN-VAULT: see Vault.

GROTESQUE: fanciful ornamental decoration: see also Arabesque.

HAGIOSCOPE: see Squint.

HALF-TIMBERING: see Timber-Framing.

HALL CHURCH: church in which nave and aisles are of equal height or approximately so.

HAMMERBEAM: see Roof.

HANAP: large metal cup, generally made for domestic use, standing on an elaborate base and stem; with a very ornate cover frequently crowned with a little steeple.

HEADERS: see Brickwork.

HERRINGBONE WORK: brick, stone, or tile construction where the component blocks are laid diagonally instead of flat. Alternate courses lie in opposing directions to make a zigzag pattern up the face of the wall.

HEXASTYLE: having six detached columns.

HILL-FORT: Iron Age earthwork enclosed by a ditch and bank system; in the later part of the period the defences multiplied in size and complexity. They vary from about an acre to over 30 acres in area, and are usually built with careful regard to natural elevations or promontories.

HIPPED ROOF: see Roof.

HOOD-MOULD: projecting moulding above an arch or a lintel to throw off water (also called Dripstone or Label).

ICONOGRAPHY: the science of the subject matter of works of the visual arts.

IMPOST: bracket in a wall, usually formed of mouldings, on which the end of an arch rests.

INDENT: shape chiselled out in a stone slab to receive a brass.

INGLENOOK: bench or seat built in beside a fireplace, sometimes covered by the chimney breast, occasionally lit by small windows on each side of the fire.

INTERCOLUMNIATION: the space between columns.

IONIC: see Orders (Fig. 12).

IRON AGE: in Britain the period from c. 600 B.C. to the coming of the Romans. The term is also used for those un-Romanized native communities which survived until the Saxon incursions.

JAMB: straight side of an archway, doorway, or window.

KEEL MOULDING: moulding whose outline is in section like that of the keel of a ship.

KEEP: massive tower of a Norman castle.

KEYSTONE: middle stone in an arch or a rib-vault.

KING-POST: see Roof (Fig. 14).

LABEL: see Hood-mould.

LABEL STOP: ornamental boss at the end of a hood-mould (q.v.).

LANCET WINDOW: slender pointed-arched window.

LANTERN: in architecture, a small circular or polygonal turret with windows all round crowning a roof (see Cupola) or a dome.

LANTERN CROSS: churchyard cross with lantern-shaped top usually with sculptured representations on the sides of the top.

LEAN-TO ROOF: roof with one slope only, built against a higher wall.

LESENE or PILASTER STRIP: pilaster without base or capital.

LIERNE: see Vault (Fig. 21).

LINENFOLD: Tudor panelling ornamented with a conventional representation of a piece of linen laid in vertical folds. The piece is repeated in each panel.

LINTEL: horizontal beam or stone bridging an opening.

LOGGIA: recessed colonnade (q.v.).

LONG AND SHORT WORK: Saxon quoins (q.v.) consisting of stones placed with the long

sides alternately upright and horizontal.

LONG BARROW: unchambered Neolithic communal burial mound, wedge-shaped in plan, with the burial and occasional other structures massed at the broader end, from which the mound itself tapers in height; quarry ditches flank the mound.

LOUVRE: opening, often with lantern (q.v.) over, in the roof of a room to let the smoke from a central hearth escape.

LOWER PALAEOLITHIC: see Palaeolithic.

LOZENGE: diamond shape.

LUCARNE: small opening to let light in.

LUNETTE: tympanum (q.v.) or semicircular opening.

LYCH GATE: wooden gate structure with a roof and open sides placed at the entrance to a churchyard to provide space for the reception of a coffin. The word *lych* is Saxon and means a corpse.

LYNCHET: long terraced strip of soil accumulating on the downward side of prehistoric and medieval fields due to soil creep from continuous ploughing along the contours.

MACHICOLATION: projecting gallery on brackets constructed on the outside of castle towers or walls. The gallery has holes in the floor to drop missiles through.

MAJOLICA: ornamented glazed earthenware.

MANSARD: see Roof.

MATHEMATICAL TILES: small facing tiles the size of brick

headers, applied to timber-framed walls to make them appear brick-built.

MEGALITHIC TOMB: stone-built burial chamber of the New Stone Age covered by an earth or stone mound. The form was introduced to Britain from the Mediterranean area.

MERLON: see Battlement.

MESOLITHIC: 'Middle Stone' Age; the post-glacial period of hunting and fishing communities dating in Britain from c. 8000 B.C. to the arrival of Neolithic communities, with which they must have considerably overlapped.

METOPE: in classical architecture of the Doric order (q.v.) the space in the frieze between the triglyphs (Fig. 12).

MEZZANINE: low storey placed between two higher ones.

MISERERE: see Misericord.

MISERICORD: bracket placed on the underside of a hinged choir stall seat which, when turned up, provided the occupant of the seat with a support during long periods of standing (also called Miserere).

MODILLION: small bracket of which large numbers (modillion frieze) are often placed below a cornice (q.v.) in classical architecture.

MOTTE: steep mound forming the main feature of C11 and C12 castles.

MOTTE-AND-BAILEY: post-Roman and Norman defence system consisting of an earthen mound (the motte) topped with a wooden tower eccentrically placed within a bailey (q.v.), with enclosure ditch and palisade, and with the rare addition of an internal bank.

MOUCHETTE: tracery motif in curvilinear tracery, a curved dagger (q.v.), specially popular in the early C14 (Fig. 10).

Fig. 10

MULLION: vertical post or upright dividing a window into two or more 'lights'.

MULTIVALLATE: Of a hill-fort: defended by three or more concentric banks and ditches.

MUNTIN: post as a rule moulded and part of a screen.

NAIL-HEAD: E.E. ornamental motif, consisting of small pyramids regularly repeated (Fig. 11).

Fig. 11

NARTHEX: enclosed vestibule or covered porch at the main entrance to a church (see Galilee).

NEOLITHIC: 'New Stone' Age, dating in Britain from the appearance from the Continent of the first settled farming communities c. 3500 B.C. until the introduction of the Bronze Age.

NEWEL: central post in a circular or winding staircase; also the principal post when a flight of stairs meets a landing.

NOOK-SHAFT: shaft set in the

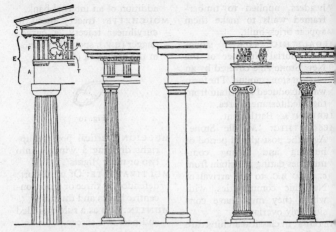

Fig. 12 – Orders of Columns (Greek Doric, Roman Doric, Tuscan Doric, Ionic, Corinthian) E, Entablature; C, Cornice; F, Frieze; A, Architrave; M, Metope; T, Triglyph

angle of a pier or respond or wall, or the angle of the jamb of a window or doorway.

OBELISK: lofty pillar of square section tapering at the top and ending pyramidally.

OGEE: see Arch (Fig. 1c).

ORATORY: small private chapel in a house.

ORDER: (1) *of a doorway or window:* series of concentric steps receding towards the opening; (2) *in classical architecture:* column with base, shaft, capital, and entablature (q.v.) according to one of the following styles: Greek Doric, Roman Doric, Tuscan Doric, Ionic, Corinthian, Composite. The established details are very elaborate, and some specialist architectural work should be consulted for further guidance (see Fig. 12).

ORIEL: see Bay-Window.

OVERHANG: projection of the upper storey of a house.

OVERSAILING COURSES: series of stone or brick courses, each one projecting beyond the one below it.

PALAEOLITHIC: 'Old Stone Age'; the first period of human culture, commencing in the Ice Age and immediately prior to the Mesolithic; the Lower Palaeolithic is the older phase, the Upper Palaeolithic the later.

PALIMPSEST: (1) *of a brass:* where a metal plate has been re-used by turning over and engraving on the back; (2) *of a wall painting:* where one overlaps and partly obscures an earlier one.

PALLADIAN: architecture following the ideas and principles of Andrea Palladio, 1518–80.

ANTILE: tile of curved S-shaped section.

ARAPET: low wall placed to protect any spot where there is a sudden drop, for example on a bridge, quay, hillside, housetop, etc.

ARGETTING: plaster work with patterns and ornaments either in relief or engraved on it.

ARVIS: term wrongly applied to a room over a church porch. These rooms were often used as a schoolroom or as a store room.

ATEN: plate to hold the bread at Communion or Mass.

ATERA: small flat circular or oval ornament in classical architecture.

EDIMENT: low-pitched gable used in classical, Renaissance, and neo-classical architecture above a portico and above doors, windows, etc. It may be straight-sided or curved segmentally. *Broken Pediment:* one where the centre portion of the base is left open. *Open Pediment:* one where the centre portion of the sloping sides is left out.

ENDANT: boss (q.v.) elongated so that it seems to hang down.

ENDENTIF: concave triangular spandrel used to lead from the angle of two walls to the base of a circular dome. It is constructed as part of the hemisphere over a diameter the size of the diagonal of the basic square (Fig. 13).

ERP (PERPENDICULAR): historical division of English Gothic architecture covering the period from *c*.1335–50 to *c*.1530.

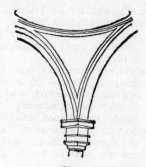

Fig. 13

PIANO NOBILE: principal storey of a house with the reception rooms; usually the first floor.

PIAZZA: open space surrounded by buildings; in C17 and C18 England sometimes used to mean a long colonnade or loggia.

PIER: strong, solid support, frequently square in section or of composite section (compound pier).

PIETRA DURA: ornamental or scenic inlay by means of thin slabs of stone.

PILASTER: shallow pier attached to a wall. *Termini Pilasters:* pilasters with sides tapering downwards.

PILLAR PISCINA: free-standing piscina on a pillar.

PINNACLE: ornamental form crowning a spire, tower, buttress, etc., usually of steep pyramidal, conical, or some similar shape.

PISCINA: basin for washing the Communion or Mass vessels, provided with a drain. Generally set in or against the wall to the S of an altar.

PLAISANCE: summer-house, pleasure house near a mansion.

PLATE TRACERY: *see* Tracery.

PLINTH: projecting base of a wall or column, generally chamfered (q.v.) or moulded at the top.

POND BARROW: rare type of Bronze Age barrow consisting of a circular depression, usually paved, and containing a number of cremation burials.

POPPYHEAD: ornament of leaf and flower type used to decorate the tops of bench- or stall-ends.

PORTCULLIS: gate constructed to rise and fall in vertical grooves; used in gateways of castles.

PORTE COCHÈRE: porch large enough to admit wheeled vehicles.

PORTICO: centre-piece of a house or a church with classical detached or attached columns and a pediment. A portico is called *prostyle* or *in antis* according to whether it projects from or recedes into a building. In a portico *in antis* the columns range with the side walls.

POSTERN: small gateway at the back of a building.

PREDELLA: in an altar-piece th horizontal strip below th main representation, often use for a number of subsidiar representations in a row.

PRESBYTERY: the part of th church lying E of the choir. I is the part where the altar i placed.

PRINCIPAL: *see* Roof (Fig. 14

PRIORY: monastic house whos head is a prior or prioress, n an abbot or abbess.

PROSTYLE: with free-standin columns in a row.

PULPITUM: stone screen in major church provided to sh off the choir from the nave an also as a backing for the retur choir stalls.

PULVINATED FRIEZE: friez with a bold convex mouldin

PURLIN: *see* Roof (Figs. 14, 15

PUTTO: small naked boy.

QUADRANGLE: inner cour yard in a large building.

QUARRY: in stained-glass wor a small diamond or squar shaped piece of glass s diagonally.

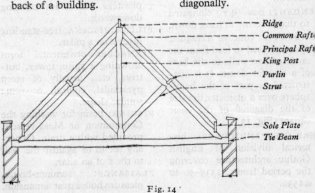

Ridge
Common Raft
Principal Raf
King Post
Purlin
Strut
Sole Plate
Tie Beam

Fig. 14

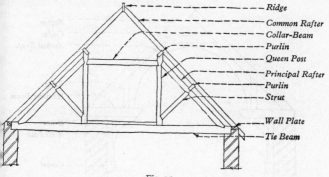

- Ridge
- Common Rafter
- Collar-Beam
- Purlin
- Queen Post
- Principal Rafter
- Purlin
- Strut
- Wall Plate
- Tie Beam

Fig. 15

QUATREFOIL: see Foil.

QUEEN-POSTS: see Roof (Fig. 15).

QUOINS: dressed stones at the angles of a building. Sometimes all the stones are of the same size; more often they are alternately large and small.

RADIATING CHAPELS: chapels projecting radially from an ambulatory or an apse.

RAFTER: see Roof.

RAMPART: stone wall or wall of earth surrounding a castle, fortress, or fortified city.

RAMPART-WALK: path along the inner face of a rampart.

REBATE: continuous rectangular notch cut on an edge.

REBUS: pun, a play on words. The literal translation and illustration of a name for artistic and heraldic purposes (Belton = bell, tun).

REEDING: decoration with parallel convex mouldings touching one another.

REFECTORY: dining hall; see Frater.

RENDERING: plastering of an outer wall.

REPOUSSÉ: decoration of metal work by relief designs, formed by beating the metal from the back.

REREDOS: structure behind and above an altar.

RESPOND: half-pier bonded into a wall and carrying one end of an arch.

RETABLE: altar-piece, a picture or piece of carving, standing behind and attached to an altar.

RETICULATION: see Tracery (Fig. 20).

REVEAL: that part of a jamb (q.v.) which lies between the glass or door and the outer surface of the wall.

RIB-VAULT: see Vault.

ROCOCO: latest phase of the Baroque style, current in most Continental countries between c.1720 and c. 1760.

ROLL MOULDING: moulding of semicircular or more than semicircular section.

ROMANESQUE: that style in architecture which was current in the C11 and C12 and pre-

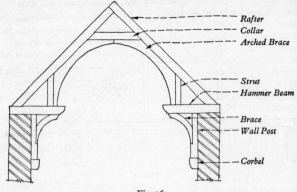

Fig. 16

ceded the Gothic style (in England often called Norman). (Some scholars extend the use of the term Romanesque back to the C10 or C9.)

ROMANO-BRITISH: A somewhat vague term applied to the period and cultural features of Britain affected by the Roman occupation of the C1–5 A.D.

ROOD: cross or crucifix.

ROOD LOFT: singing gallery on the top of the rood screen, often supported by a coving.

ROOD SCREEN: see Screen.

ROOD STAIRS: stairs to give access to the rood loft.

ROOF: *Single-framed:* if consisting entirely of transverse members (such as rafters with or without braces, collars, tie-beams, king-posts or queen-posts, etc.) not tied together longitudinally. *Double-framed:* if longitudinal members (such as a ridge beam and purlins) are employed. As a rule in such cases the rafters are divided into stronger principals and weaker subsidiary rafters.

Hipped: roof with sloped in stead of vertical ends. *Mansar* roof with a double slope, th lower slope being larger an steeper than the upper. *Saddl back:* tower roof shaped like a ordinary gabled timber roo The following members hav special names: *Rafter:* roo timber sloping up from th wall plate to the ridge. *Pri cipal:* principal rafter, usual corresponding to the main ba divisions of the nave or chanc below. *Wall Plate:* timber la longitudinally on the top of wall. *Purlin:* longitudin member laid parallel with wa plate and ridge beam son way up the slope of the roo *Tie-beam:* beam connecting th two slopes of a roof across at i foot, usually at the height the wall plate, to prevent th roof from spreading. *Colla beam:* tie-beam applied high up the slope of the roof. *Stru* upright timber connecting t tie-beam with the rafter abo it. *King-post:* upright timb connecting a tie-beam and collar-beam with the ridge beam. *Queen-posts:* two struts placed symmetrically on a tie-beam or collar-beam. *Braces:* inclined timbers inserted to strengthen others. Usually braces connect a collar-beam with the rafters below or a tie-beam with the wall below. Braces can be straight or curved (also called arched). *Hammerbeam:* beam projecting at right angles, usually from the top of a wall, to carry arched braces or struts and arched braces (*see* Figs. 14, 15, 16).

SE WINDOW (or WHEEL WINDOW): circular window with patterned tracery arranged to radiate from the centre.

TUNDA: building circular in plan.

BBLE: building stones, not square or hewn, nor laid in regular courses.

STICATION: *rock-faced* if the surfaces of large blocks of ashlar stone are left rough like rock; *smooth* if the ashlar blocks are smooth and separated by V-joints; *banded* if the separation by V-joints applies only to the horizontals.

DDLEBACK: *see* Roof.

TIRE CROSS: equal-limbed cross placed diagonally.

NCTUARY: (1) area around the main altar of a church (*see* Presbytery); (2) sacred site consisting of wood or stone uprights enclosed by a circular bank and ditch. Beginning in the Neolithic, they were elaborated in the succeeding

Bronze Age. The best known examples are Stonehenge and Avebury.

SARCOPHAGUS: elaborately carved coffin.

SCAGLIOLA: material composed of cement and colouring matter to imitate marble.

SCALLOPED CAPITAL: development of the block capital (q.v.) in which the single semi-circular surface is elaborated into a series of truncated cones (Fig. 17).

Fig. 17

SCARP: artificial cutting away of the ground to form a steep slope.

SCREEN: *Parclose screen:* screen separating a chapel from the rest of a church. *Rood screen:* screen below the rood (q.v.), usually at the W end of a chancel.

SCREENS PASSAGE: passage between the entrances to kitchen, buttery, etc., and the screen behind which lies the hall of a medieval house.

SEDILIA: seats for the priests (usually three) on the S side of the chancel of a church.

SEGMENTAL ARCH: *see* Arch.

SET-OFF: *see* Weathering.

SEXPARTITE: *see* Vaulting.

SGRAFFITO: pattern incised into plaster so as to expose a dark surface underneath.

SHAFT-RING: motif of the C12 and C13 consisting of a ring

round a circular pier or a shaft attached to a pier.

SHEILA-NA-GIG: fertility figure, usually with legs wide open.

SILL: lower horizontal part of the frame of a window.

SLATEHANGING: the covering of walls by overlapping rows of slates, on a timber substructure.

SOFFIT: underside of an arch, lintel, etc.

SOLAR: upper living-room of a medieval house.

SOPRAPORTE: painting above the door of a room, usual in the C17 and C18.

SOUNDING BOARD: horizontal board or canopy over a pulpit. Also called Tester.

SPANDREL: triangular surface between one side of an arch, the horizontal drawn from its apex, and the vertical drawn from its springer; also the surface between two arches.

SPERE-TRUSS: roof truss on two free-standing posts to mask the division between screens passage and hall. The screen itself, where a spere-truss exists, was originally movable.

SPIRE: tall pyramidal or conical pointed erection often built on top of a tower, turret, etc. *Broach Spire:* spire which is generally octagonal in plan rising from the top or parapet of a square tower. A small inclined piece of masonry covers the vacant triangular space at each of the four angles of the square and is carried up to a point along the diagonal sides of the octagon. *Needle Spire:* thin spire rising from the centre of a tower roof, well inside the parapet.

SPIRELET: *see* Flèche.

SPLAY: chamfer, usually of th[e] jamb of a window.

SPRINGING: level at which a[n] arch rises from its supports.

SQUINCH: arch or system of con centric arches thrown acros[s] the angle between two walls t[o] support a superstructure, fo[r] example a dome (Fig. 18).

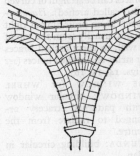

Fig. 18

SQUINT: hole cut in a wall [or] through a pier to allow a vie[w] of the main altar of a churc[h] from places whence it cou[ld] not otherwise be seen (al[so] called Hagioscope).

STALL: carved seat, one of a ro[w,] made of wood or stone.

STAUNCHION: upright iron [or] steel member.

STEEPLE: the tower of a churc[h] together with a spire, cupol[a,] etc.

STIFF-LEAF: E.E. type of folia[ge] of many-lobed shapes (Fig. 1[9]).

Fig. 19

STILTED: *see* Arch.

STOREY-POSTS: the principal posts of a timber-framed wall.

STOUP: vessel for the reception of holy water, usually placed near a door.

STRAINER ARCH: arch inserted across a room to prevent the walls from leaning.

STRAPWORK: C16 decoration consisting of interlaced bands, and forms similar to fretwork or cut and bent leather.

STRETCHER: *see* Brickwork.

STRING COURSE: projecting horizontal band or moulding set in the surface of a wall.

STRUT: *see* Roof.

STUCCO: plaster work.

STUDS: the subsidiary vertical timber members of a timber-framed wall.

SWAG: festoon formed by a carved piece of cloth suspended from both ends.

TABERNACLE: richly ornamented niche (q.v.) or free-standing canopy. Usually contains the Holy Sacrament.

TARSIA: inlay in various woods.

TAZZA: shallow bowl on a foot.

TERMINAL FIGURES (TERMS, TERMINI): upper part of a human figure growing out of a pier, pilaster, etc., which tapers towards the base. *See also* Caryatids, Pilasters.

TERRACOTTA: burnt clay, unglazed.

TESSELLATED PAVEMENT: mosaic flooring, particularly Roman, consisting of small 'tesserae' or cubes of glass, stone, or brick.

TESSERAE: *see* Tessellated Pavement.

TESTER: *see* Sounding Board.

TETRASTYLE: having four detached columns.

THREE-DECKER PULPIT: pulpit with Clerk's Stall below and Reading Desk below the Clerk's Stall.

TIE-BEAM: *see* Roof (Figs. 14, 15).

TIERCERON: *see* Vault (Fig. 21).

TILEHANGING: *see* Slatehanging.

TIMBER-FRAMING: method of construction where walls are built of timber framework with the spaces filled in by plaster or brickwork. Sometimes the timber is covered over with plaster or boarding laid horizontally.

TOMB-CHEST: chest-shaped stone coffin, the most usual medieval form of funeral monument.

TOUCH: soft black marble quarried near Tournai.

TOURELLE: turret corbelled out from the wall.

TRACERY: intersecting ribwork in the upper part of a window,

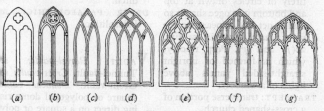

(a)   (b)   (c)   (d)   (e)   (f)   (g)

Fig. 21

or used decoratively in blank arches, on vaults, etc. *Plate tracery: see* Fig. 20(*a*). Early form of tracery where decoratively shaped openings are cut through the solid stone infilling in a window head. *Bar tracery:* a form introduced into England *c.*1250. Intersecting ribwork made up of slender shafts, continuing the lines of the mullions of windows up to a decorative mesh in the head of the window. *Geometrical tracery: see* Fig. 20(*b*). Tracery characteristic of *c.*1250–1310 consisting chiefly of circles or foiled circles. *Y-tracery: see* Fig. 20(*c*). Tracery consisting of a mullion which branches into two forming a Y shape; typical of *c.* 1300. *Intersected tracery: see* Fig. 20(*d*). Tracery in which each mullion of a window branches out into two curved bars in such a way that every one of them is drawn with the same radius from a different centre. The result is that every light of the window is a lancet and every two, three, four, etc., lights together form a pointed arch. This treatment also is typical of *c.*1300. *Reticulated tracery: see* Fig. 20(*e*). Tracery typical of the early C14 consisting entirely of circles drawn at top and bottom into ogee shapes so that a net-like appearance results. *Panel tracery: see* Fig. 20(*f*) and (*g*). Perp tracery, which is formed of upright straight-sided panels above lights of a window.

TRANSEPT: transverse portion of a cross-shaped church.

TRANSOM: horizontal bar across the openings of a window.

TRANSVERSE ARCH: *see* Vault.

TRIBUNE: *see* Gallery.

TRICIPUT, SIGNUM TRICIPUT sign of the Trinity expressed by three faces belonging to one head.

TRIFORIUM: arcaded wall passage or blank arcading facing the nave at the height of the aisle roof and below the clerestory (q.v.) windows. (*See* Gallery.)

TRIGLYPHS: blocks with vertical grooves separating the metopes (q.v.) in the Doric frieze (Fig. 12).

TROPHY: sculptured group of arms or armour, used as a memorial of victory.

TRUMEAU: stone mullion (q.v. supporting the tympanum (q.v.) of a wide doorway.

TUMULUS: *see* Barrow.

TURRET: very small tower, round or polygonal in plan.

TUSCAN: *see* Order.

TYMPANUM: space between the lintel of a doorway and the arch above it.

UNDERCROFT: vaulted room sometimes underground, below a church or chapel.

UNIVALLATE: of a hill-fort defended by a single bank and ditch.

UPPER PALAEOLITHIC: *see* Palaeolithic.

VAULT: *Barrel-vault: see* Tunnel-vault. *Cross-vault: see* Groin-vault. *Domical vault* square or polygonal dome rising direct on a square or poly

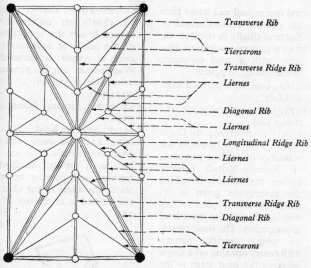

Transverse Rib

Tiercerons

Transverse Ridge Rib

Liernes

Diagonal Rib

Liernes

Longitudinal Ridge Rib

Liernes

Liernes

Transverse Ridge Rib

Diagonal Rib

Tiercerons

Fig. 21

gonal bay, the curved surfaces separated by groins (q.v.). *Fanvault:* Late Medieval vault where all ribs springing from one springer are of the same length, the same distance from the next, and the same curvature. *Groin-vault* or *Crossvault:* vault of two tunnel-vaults of identical shape intersecting each other at r. angles. Chiefly Norman and Renaissance. *Lierne:* tertiary rib, that is, rib which does not spring either from one of the main springers or from the central boss. Introduced in the C14, continues to the C16. *Quadripartite vault:* one wherein one bay of vaulting is divided into four parts. *Rib-vault:* vault with diagonal ribs projecting along the groins. *Ridgerib:* rib along the longitudinal or transverse ridge of a vault. Introduced in the early C13. *Sexpartite vault:* one wherein one bay of quadripartite vaulting is divided into two parts transversely so that each bay of vaulting has six parts. *Tierceron:* secondary rib, that is, rib which issues from one of the main springers or the central boss and leads to a place on a ridge-rib. Introduced in the early C13. *Transverse arch:* arch separating one bay of a vault from the next. *Tunnelvault* or *Barrel-vault:* vault of semicircular or pointed section. Chiefly Norman and Renaissance. (*See* Fig. 21.)

VAULTING SHAFT: vertical member leading to the springer of a vault.

VENETIAN WINDOW: window with three openings, the central one arched and wider than the outside ones. Current in England chiefly in the C17–18.

VERANDA: open gallery or balcony with a roof on light, usually metal, supports.

VESICA: oval with pointed head and foot.

VESTIBULE: ante-room or entrance hall.

VILLA: (1) according to Gwilt (1842) 'a country house for the residence of opulent persons'; (2) Romano-British country houses cum farms, to which the description given in (1) more or less applies. They developed with the growth of urbanization. The basic type is the simple corridor pattern with rooms opening off a single passage; the next stage is the addition of wings, while the courtyard villa fills a square plan with subsidiary buildings and an enclosure wall with a gate facing the main corridor block.

VITRIFIED: made similar to glass.

VITRUVIAN OPENING: A door or window which diminishes towards the top, as advocated by Vitruvius, book IV, chapter VI.

VOLUTE: spiral scroll, one of the component parts of an Ionic column (see Order).

VOUSSOIR: wedge-shaped stone used in arch construction.

WAGON-ROOF: roof in which by closely set rafters with arched braces the appearance of the inside of a canvas tilt over a wagon is achieved. Wagon-roofs can be panelled or plastered (ceiled) or left uncovered.

WAINSCOT: timber lining to walls.

WALL PLATE: see Roof.

WATERLEAF: leaf shape used in later C12 capitals. The water-leaf is a broad, unribbed tapering leaf curving up towards the angle of the abacus and turned in at the top (Fig. 22).

Fig. 22

WEATHERBOARDING: overlapping horizontal boards, covering a timber-framed wall.

WEATHERING: sloped horizontal surface on sills, buttresses, etc., to throw off water.

WEEPERS: small figures placed in niches along the sides of some medieval tombs (also called Mourners).

WHEEL WINDOW: see Rose Window.

INDEX OF ARTISTS

INDEX OF PLACES

ADDENDA

(MARCH 1964)

141 [Lincoln, Roman Lincoln] Since the section on Roman Lincoln was written, the report on the excavations conducted by the Lincoln Archaeological Research Committee has been published. Work in the N part of the grounds of the Old Bishop's Palace enabled the position of the southern defences of the legionary fortress, on the escarpment overlooking the river crossing, to be determined. With the planning of this fourth side of the legionary fortress, it is now known to have occupied an area of 41½ acres, considerably less than other legionary fortresses in Britain, and perhaps implying a garrison below normal strength. The excavations further demonstrated that the stone defences of the *colonia* are to be ascribed to the Severan period and not to Domitian, as had hitherto been supposed.

143 [Lincoln.] ST JOHN, Sudbrooke Drive, Ermine Estate East. By *H. S. Scorer*, 1962–3. With a hyperbolic paraboloid roof, rising from two points right on the ground.

168 [Alkborough, Walcot Old Hall.] Also known as Walcot Manor Farm House.

180 [Barrow-on-Humber, Barrow Hall.] Excellent ceilings and chimneypieces (MHLG).

204 [Broughton.] YARBOROUGH PLACE. Red brick, early C19, three bays, doorway with fluted Doric columns (MHLG).

235 [Fillingham, Fillingham Castle.] Mr Alastair Rowan convincingly suggests that the second courtyard is a later link.

257 [Great Grimsby.] In HUMBER ROAD a new headquarters building for the ROSS GROUP, eleven storeys, concrete frame, and glass and slate infillings. Designed by *Howard Lobb & Partners*; 1963–4.

263 [Hainton, St Mary.] Mr Gunnis suggests that the choice of an Italian sculptor may be due to George Heneage having married in 1728 a daughter of a Fieschi, count of Lavagna.

274 [HOLME, 6m. W of Brigg.] HOLME HALL. Built of rubble. Early C18 five-bay E front (MHLG).

290 [Kirton-in-Lindsey.] BECKINGHAM HOUSE, Ings Road. C18 and early C19. Red brick, four bays with pilasters (MHLG).

298 [Little Carlton, St Edith.] Head of a CHURCHYARD CROSS. C15, with Crucifix on one side, a standing saint on the other. (Information kindly provided by the Rev. Hugh Casson.)

340 [Redbourne.] MANOR HOUSE. C17; heightened *c.* 1800. Original staircase with carved tread-ends and wrought-iron balustrade (MHLG).

p. 358 [Scunthorpe, Civic Centre.] The building consists of an offic
block of four storeys on a basement. This faces w. To the
projecting from the s end of this block, the shorter wing wit
the Council Chamber, a livelier composition, with the tran
parent main entrance hall, the completely closed staircase en
of the office block on the l., and the Council Chamber referre
to in the text appearing behind the slate-faced piers on the
It is an excellent, entirely unmannered design.

p. 396 [Thealby.] THEALBY HALL. Grey brick, late C18, three bay
doorway with demi-columns (MHLG).

p. 405 [Thornton Curtis, Thornton Hall.] Good staircase with turne
balusters (MHLG).

p. 419 [West Halton.] COLEBY HALL. Of c. 1600, altered c. 170
Two storeys, rubble and brick, irregular plan. The centr
ground-floor room of c. 1700. Good chimneypiece. An ou
building to the sw with a large hipped roof makes a fine grou
with the Hall (MHLG).

p. 424 [Winteringham.] WINTERINGHAM GRANGE. Early C1
three bays, whitewashed brick, original staircase. Also C1
Gothick BARNS. – OUTBUILDINGS with blank oval pane
(MHLG).

p. 426 [Winterton.] THE ELMS, King Street. C18, rubble, five bay
doorway with pilasters and open pediment. – BLANKNI
HOUSE, Low Street. Late C18, rubble, three bays, pedimen
Good wrought-iron railings and gates (MHLG).

p. 430 [Wootton.] OLD VICARAGE. Early C18, with later C18 w wir
and early C19 E wing (MHLG).

p. 483 [Branston, All Saints.] The church was badly damaged by fi
in 1962. The chancel was destroyed. (Mr Gunnis kindly to
me this.)

p. 522 [Edenham, St Michael.] Dr H. M. Taylor drew my attention
the fact that part of the s wall of the nave, above the C13 arca
is Anglo-Saxon. There is a string-course of rectangular secti
visible from the aisle, and part of this are two roundels of 2
diameter. One has a swastika arrangement of leaves, the other
basically cross-shaped with four circles at the ends of the arn
A date later than the C8 is proposed.

p. 651 [Spalding.] Mr W. A. James draws our attention to the WHI
HORSE INN, at the corner of Church Gate and CHUR
STREET. It is one of the oldest buildings in Spalding, sto
built and thatched, and used to be known as Burguery Hou
It belonged to the Willesby family.